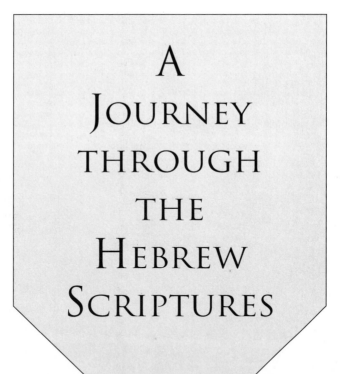

A
JOURNEY
THROUGH
THE
HEBREW
SCRIPTURES

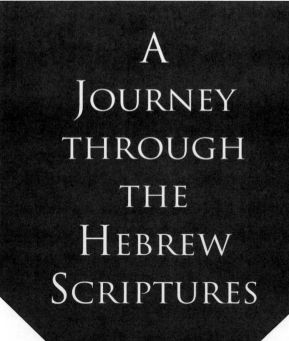

A JOURNEY THROUGH THE HEBREW SCRIPTURES

FRANK S. FRICK
ALBION COLLEGE

HARCOURT BRACE COLLEGE PUBLISHERS

Fort Worth   Philadelphia   San Diego   New York   Orlando   Austin   San Antonio

Toronto   Montreal   London   Sydney   Tokyo

Publisher	TED BUCHHOLZ
Senior Acquisitions Editor	DAVID TATOM
Developmental Editor	LAURIE RUNION
Project Editor	SARAH E. HUGHBANKS
Production Manager	JANE TYNDALL PONCETI
Art Director	BURL SLOAN
Cover Design	EDIE ROBERSON
Photo Editor	CHERYL THROOP

Cover photo © Erich Lessing/PhotoEdit.

ISBN: 0-15-501297-5

Library of Congress Catalog Card Number: 94-78468

Address editorial correspondence to:
Harcourt Brace College Publishers
301 Commerce Street, Suite 3700
Fort Worth, TX 76102

Address orders to
Harcourt Brace & Company
6277 Sea Harbor Drive
Orlando, FL 32887-6777
1-800-782-4479 or 1-800-433-0001 (in Florida)

Printed in the United States of America

4 5 6 7 8 9 0 1 2 3 090 9 8 7 6 5 4 3 2 1

To Bonnie, Kimberly, and Rachel. They know why.

To the People of Central Methodist Mission, Cape Town,
in celebration of their liberation.

PREFACE

A Journey through the Hebrew Scriptures is a guidebook for a trip through the body of literature known as the Old Testament or the Hebrew Scriptures. It is intended for use by a teacher-guide and student-travelers setting out together on what is for the student a first-time trip through unfamiliar territory. Other than assuming that the Hebrew Bible is an unfamiliar region for most of those who have signed up for such a course, this journey does not presuppose any preparation for the academic study of religion nor any particular personal religious perspective as a starting point.

This guidebook is one that can be used by anyone who believes the journey to be worth taking. While the Hebrew Scriptures have obvious, enduring significance for those who identify themselves as Jews or Christians, any students studying the humanities soon discover the need to be acquainted with this literature because of its considerable cultural and historical importance. Western literature and art are filled with themes, metaphors, and images drawn from the Hebrew Bible. They range from the frequent painting of Old Testament scenes in the Middle Ages to metaphors in modern novels, such as John Steinbeck's *East of Eden* and Toni Morrison's *Song of Solomon*. Familiarity with the Hebrew Scriptures leads to a deeper understanding of and appreciation for these cultural applications.

The term "scripture" defines the classical nature of this literature as providing a religious constitution or "canon" for Judaism and Christianity. For Jews the Hebrew Bible consists of twenty-four books, beginning with Genesis and ending with Chronicles. For Protestant Christians, the same books (some of which are arranged in a different sequence or subdivided) comprise the thirty-nine books of the Old Testament, the first part of their Bible, which also includes the New Testament. Roman Catholic Christians also include in their Old Testament some "deuterocanonical" books, in effect, a second set of canonical Old Testament books, some of which we shall encounter in our journey.

While the relevance and authority of the Hebrew Bible for these religious traditions are well established, a question with which the student will be confronted at many places along this journey is the contemporary "relevance" of the Hebrew Scriptures as literature. An important assumption is that the Hebrew Bible can still communicate important moral and social truths to those who are willing to give it a fair hearing—even if they approach it as humanists. There is, in fact, no word in the Hebrew Scriptures for "religion." The Hebrew Bible is a humanistic as well as a religious work, and it often communicates "religious" truth in surprisingly humanistic terms.

When talking about the starting point of the journey and this kind of guidebook, one cannot separate the issues of audience and genre. Anyone embarking on this journey, whether for the first time or for the nth time, needs to have reasonable expectations about what can be seen in a journey of limited length. One must also expect to be surprised. This means that one needs, as much as possible, to bracket out personal preconceptions and approach the journey with flexibility and a willingness to let things happen. Both students and teachers need to come to the biblical texts with flexibility, being prepared to investigate them for what they are, human literary products, with all that is involved with respect to honoring human imagination and creativity, as well as human limitations. While the Hebrew Scriptures, viewed as scripture, contain the words of God, those words are in human language.

Another important consideration at the beginning of the journey is the relationship between the territory being traversed and the traveler—the relationship between texts as literary products of human beings who lived long ago and their modern readers. To what degree and how do biblical texts determine and regulate the way in which we read and understand them? To what extent and how are the meanings attributed to those texts the result of what we as individual human beings bring to them as people who live in a particular place and time? Or, to put it in another way: Do texts *have* meaning on their own, or do we *give* texts meanings through our reading and interpretation? To raise such questions also raises critical concerns about the nature of biblical studies in an academic setting.

Scholarly biblical study, which began in Europe as a child of the Renaissance, has been undergoing significant changes in the past several decades. Before the last twenty years or so, the changes in scholarly biblical studies were incremental. In recent years, however, this incremental change has been replaced by what can be called "paradigm shifts" that call earlier methods into question, especially concerning the relationship between text and reader.

The paradigm of scholarly biblical studies that prevailed until the last several decades, and has recently been repeatedly challenged on several fronts, included several methods that can be grouped together under the name "historical criticism." In its beginnings and development, historical criticism was seen as an alternative to an uncritical or "confessional" reading of the Bible, which is still represented today by "fundamentalism." Fundamentalism is usually characterized by the attitude that the Bible (or Qur'an, or other sacred text) has only one "correct" meaning, which is usually taken to be the literal, physical, overt denotation of the passage in question. Historical criticism, which developed as a "scientific" way of interpreting the Bible, treats biblical literature like other ancient literature, asking questions about authorship, sources, historical context, and the like. Answers to these questions, it is believed, can provide the reader with "objective" interpretations, interpretations determined by the circumstances under which the texts were produced, meanings that belong to the text itself.

Historical criticism has developed a variety of tools to be used in the scholarly study of the Hebrew Bible. After these tools are introduced in the first chapter, they will be encountered at various points along the journey. None of these tools can be used in isolation from the others, nor does any one tool provide the key that unlocks meanings in the text. Neither can any one student of the Bible claim to be expert, nor even competent, in the use of all these tools. To be an "expert" in the historical criticism of the Hebrew Bible, one would ideally have to know half a dozen ancient languages, be familiar with developments in archaeology, and have a thorough grasp of the changing historical and cultural conditions of the ancient Near East from Paleolithic times until the first century C.E. This journey will use the various tools of biblical criticism selectively. Not every tool will be applied at every point. Nevertheless, by the end of this journey through the Hebrew Bible the student should have a basic understanding of the kinds of tools that have been used in the study of the Bible, how they have been used, and what some results of their use have been.

Chapter 3 will introduce a cognate discipline of biblical studies—archaeology—and discuss its role and limitations in biblical interpretation. Some interpreters of the Bible have tended to be quite selective in the use of archaeological data, using only those data that seem to be immediately relevant, instead of being concerned with the broader archaeological context of those data. The error of this selectivity will be seen in Chapter 8, where an overview of the range of available archaeological evidence for Israel's "conquest" of Palestine will be presented.

In recent years, some limits of historical criticism have been exposed as scholars have become aware of its inability to provide answers to important questions. While historical criticism could answer some historical questions, it could not produce satisfactory answers to questions about the literary shape of the Bible and the social environment of ancient Israel. Two of the more important developments in the study of the Hebrew Bible explore these areas. The past twenty years have seen an increased application of methods and theories from the social sciences to the study of social structures and processes that lay behind the biblical texts, the social world of ancient Israel. There has also been an interest in looking at biblical literature *as literature,* rather than as theology or history. Seen from one angle, these two new approaches may seem to be at odds with one another. Social scientific criticism, with its concern for the social world *behind* the text, is often allied with a historical criticism that sees meanings in the text that are determined by the circumstances of its production. On the other hand, the newer literary methods, with their focus on the world *in* the text, seem to be in agreement with those who say that the historical circumstances of a text's production are unimportant and that we can interpret literature in any way we like. Our perspective here is that these two methods work best when used with one another, with one serving to check and correct the other. Common to both is a concern with structure—the structure of the literature in the Hebrew Bible and the structure of the society that produced and preserved that literature.

Because of the broad scope of the Hebrew Bible with respect to the time span it covers (about 1,000 years), the variety of types of literature it includes, and its sheer size (from 750 to more than 1,200 pages in different English translations, not including the apocryphal/deuterocanonical books), it is impossible to cover all of it in a one-semester introductory course. So this journey, like any journey, is necessarily selective, treating representative selections in the Hebrew Bible, with some brief explorations of apocryphal/deuterocanonical literature. Instructors can choose which selections of the Hebrew Bible they wish their students to read beyond those selections treated in this textbook. This guidebook should serve to navigate the student through selected portions of the Hebrew Scriptures, pointing out key passages and themes, providing sufficient background to students to enable them to read the biblical text critically and perceptively. The study questions for each chapter ask students to formulate answers to a variety of questions about selected portions of the biblical text, encouraging them to interact with the biblical text. In the early chapters, the questions are more objective and are designed to help students become familiar with the shape of the Bible and biblical geography. In subsequent chapters, questions become more subjective and open ended, asking students to do their own interpretive work.

Excerpts from Matthews and Benjamin *Old Testament Parallels: Laws and Stories from the Ancient Near East* are quoted at numerous places. Their book should be used as a supplementary textbook. Beginning with Chapter 6, portraits of biblical personalities taken from Frederick Buechner's *Peculiar Treasures: A Biblical Who's Who* are set in text boxes. The assumption should not be made that the author necessarily believes that Buechner captures the essence of these biblical characters as they are represented in the biblical texts. His portraits are included, rather, as bases for discussion. It might be helpful to compare Buechner's portraits with one's own impression of these personalities, gained from one's own reading of the biblical texts. One of Buechner's sketches concerns the rape of Dinah (in Chapter 8) and is particularly provocative; some may consider it offensive. However, I present it here, in the context of an approach that seeks to be sensitive to gender issues, for purposes of discussion and reflection, not to trivialize the issue of sexual violence. Because this is a journey, maps that assist location in space are used in many chapters. The students should consult these maps in the context of the discussion of the land and its natural regions in Chapter 2.

There is much to discover on a journey through the Hebrew Bible. Because no single perspective provides a comprehensive view, this guidebook adopts an eclectic method that will attempt to successfully provide the advantage of multiple perspectives. It is hoped that these perspectives, represented by the work of many individuals, have been honestly and fairly represented. If they have, those using this guidebook will have the advantage of having not just one "expert," but several as guides along the way. *Bon voyage!*

Acknowledgements

Every book is the end product of a journey for the author. I would like to acknowledge the contributions of some of those who have been my companions at some stage of this journey. First, I thank my students at Albion College who read and commented on early drafts of some chapters, and those students whose questions and comments in class helped to instruct and enrich this book. I am also in debt to my colleagues at Albion, especially those on the Faculty Development Committee, who have supported me in various ways, enabling me to sustain this project. Sharon Hostetler, secretary of the Departments of Religious Studies and Philosophy at Albion, has been a valuable helper from the earliest stages to the project's completion. Kimberly Frick Arndts carefully read first drafts and provided solid critical comments that helped "clean up" inelegancies of style. Colleagues in the Society of Biblical Literature groups of which I have been a part have provided a high level of professional support. The study questions at the end of each chapter come from many sources, but I am especially indebted to the work of Michael Dick and Celia Marshall, whose similar questions, designed to help students engage the biblical text, guided the formulation of mine. The people at Harcourt Brace have been a most understanding and encouraging team, especially Laurie Runion, developmental editor, who guided the book through its various stages and Sarah E. Hughbanks, the project editor. The comments and suggestions provided by those who reviewed early drafts of the book have made this a more reliable guide for those students who will use it for their journey through the Hebrew Bible: Daniel Breslauer, University of Kansas; Donna Dykes, Wimberly School of Religion; Frederick Greenspahn, University of Denver; Desmond Kilkeary, Glendale Community College; Jeffrey Rogers, Furman University; Carol Selkin, Claremont Graduate School; Pauline Viviano, Loyola University; and Donald Wimmer, Seton Hall University. A special thank you to Ruben R. Richards, a "fellow traveler" in the final stages of the journey at the University of Cape Town.

Frank S. Frick
Cape Town, The Republic of South Africa
April 27, 1994—The First Day of the New South Africa

CONTENTS

PART III ♦ THE FORMER AND LATTER PROPHETS IN THE HEBREW CANON

PART

I

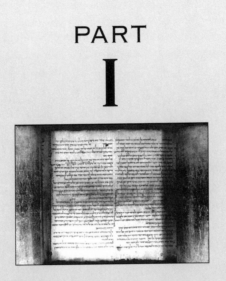

THE LAND, LITERATURE, AND PEOPLE OF THE HEBREW BIBLE

Chapter 1

THE LITERATURE
OF THE HEBREW BIBLE AND
TOOLS FOR UNDERSTANDING IT

Before beginning a journey through new and unfamiliar territory, it is a good idea to prepare for the trip by learning something of what we might expect to encounter and what signposts can be used to guide us on our way. For our journey through the Hebrew Scriptures, we need to know something about what kind of literature we may expect to encounter, some features of the physical landscape in which this literature is set, and some characteristics of the people we will encounter—the people who produced this literature, about whom it is written, and to whom it was initially addressed. These introductory concerns will be addressed in this chapter and the one to follow on "The Land and People of the Hebrew Bible."

THE LITERATURE OF THE HEBREW BIBLE

Biblical References

Persons who write about or speak of a particular passage in biblical literature have developed a fairly standard way of referring to where it can be found in the Bible. Because every printed edition of the Bible has different page numbers, it is obviously unsatisfactory to say that a certain passage can be found on a specific page. The conventional system of referring to biblical passages works as follows:

1. The name of the book is given first, usually abbreviated.

2. Following the name of the book, the number of a chapter is given. Thus Genesis 1 (or Gen 1) means the entire first chapter of the book of Genesis. If the reference is to more than one chapter, it is written as Genesis 1; 2, which means the first and second chapters of Genesis (sometimes written as Genesis 1-2 or Genesis 1, 2). Genesis 1-11 means chapters one *through* eleven of Genesis.

3. Chapters in the Bible are subdivided into verses. Verses do not necessarily include only one sentence, nor are verses always units of meaning. Verse numbers, when used with chapter numbers, do provide a standardized way of referring to a biblical passage. For specific verses within a chapter, a colon (:) is used to separate the chapter and verse number. Thus, Gen 1:1 means the first verse of the first chapter of Genesis. A dash (-) means to read through from one chapter to another. For example, Gen 1:1-2:4 refers to a passage that runs from verse one of the first chapter through verse four of the second chapter. A semicolon (;) indicates a chapter break. Thus, Gen 1:6; 3:1 means the sixth verse of the first chapter and the first verse of the third chapter.

4. Because verses do not necessarily constitute units of meaning, sometimes a verse is subdivided. When this is done, the first part of the verse is denoted by the letter *a* following a verse number, the second part with *b,* etc. Gen 2:4*a* thus refers to the first half of the fourth verse of the second chapter of Genesis.

5. If a reference is made to more than one verse following a chapter and verse notation, the symbol ff. is sometimes used. For example, Gen 7:6 ff. refers to a passage beginning with the sixth verse of the seventh chapter of Genesis and continuing through the next several verses.

6. A fairly standard set of abbreviations is commonly employed, which will be used in this book. For the books of the Hebrew Bible (understood here as the equivalent of the Jewish canon) and the apocryphal/deuterocanonical books, these abbreviations are (in the order in which these books appear in Protestant Bibles) shown in Tables 1.1 and 1.2.

The chapter and verse numbers that appear in printed English Bibles did not exist in early Hebrew biblical manuscripts. They were inserted later as a

TABLE 1.1 Abbreviations of Books in the Hebrew Bible (in the order in which they appear in Protestant Bibles)

Gen = Genesis	2 Chr = 2 Chronicles	Dan = Daniel
Ex = Exodus	Ezra = Ezra	Hos = Hosea
Lev = Leviticus	Neh = Nehemiah	Joel = Joel
Num = Numbers	Esth = Esther	Am = Amos
Deut = Deuteronomy	Job = Job	Ob = Obadiah
Josh = Joshua	Ps = Psalms	Jon = Jonah
Judg = Judges	Prov = Proverbs	Mic = Micah
Ruth = Ruth	Eccl = Ecclesisastes	Nah = Nahum
1 Sam = 1 Samuel	Song = Song of Solomon	Hab = Habakkuk
2 Sam = 2 Samuel	Isa = Isaiah	Zeph = Zephaniah
1 Kings = 1 Kings	Jer = Jeremiah	Hag = Haggai
2 Kings = 2 Kings	Lam = Lamentations	Zech = Zechariah
1 Chr = 1 Chronicles	Ezek = Ezekiel	Mal = Malachi

TABLE 1.2 Abbreviations of Apocryphal/Deuterocanonical Books

Tob = Tobit	Song of Thr = Prayer of Azariah & the Song of the Three Jews
Jdt = Judith	
Add Esth = Additions to Esther	Sus = Susanna
Wis = Wisdom	Bel = Bel and the Dragon
Sir = Sircah (Ecclesiasticus)	1 Macc = 1 Maccabees
Bar = Baruch	2 Macc = 2 Maccabees
1 Esd = 1 Esdras	3 Macc = 3 Maccabees
2 Esd = 2 Esdras	4 Macc = 4 Maccabees
Let Jer = Letter of Jeremiah	Pr Man = Prayer of Manasseh

way of indicating where units and subunits of meaning might be in the text, also providing a convenient, standardized way of referring to where in the Bible a certain passage can be found. We will discover, however, that sometimes these chapter and verse notations do not, in fact, fall at natural divisions in the text, but rather split up such units. In Chapter 4, we will look at one such instance where the standard chapter and verse notations might be misleading—the two creation stories found in Genesis, one in Gen 1:1–2:4a and another in Gen 2:4b–25.

Biblical Dates

In the Hebrew scriptures, dates are not referred to with the system of absolute numbers that we commonly use. Rather, dates are characteristically noted with reference to some important event. The book of Amos, for example, says in the very first verse that the activity of Amos can be dated as follows: "The words of Amos . . . which he saw . . . *in the days of Uzziah king of Judah and in the days of Jeroboam . . .* , king of Israel, *two years before the earthquake*" (Am 1:1, emphasis mine). Another common way of indicating dates is by the regnal year: "In *the fourth year of Solomon's reign* over Israel, in the month of Ziv, which is the second month, he began to build the house of the LORD" (1 Kings 6:1*b*, emphasis mine).

When modern authors write about biblical events, however, they convert these relative notations into the kind of dates with which we are more familiar, a system of absolute numbers with the notations B.C. and A.D. or B.C.E. and C.E. In the Gregorian calendar, dates after the birth of Jesus of Nazareth are noted as A.D. (an abbreviation for the Latin phrase *Anno Domini,* "In the year of our Lord"). In this system, one then counts backwards from the time of Jesus to indicate dates "before Christ," or B.C. Another method, widely used by scholars and adopted in this book refers to dates after Jesus using the notation C.E., which is an abbreviation for "Common Era." This kind of notation is religiously neutral in that it does not presuppose the Christian belief that Jesus of Nazareth was the Christ or Messiah. Dates before the time of Jesus of Nazareth are referred to as B.C.E., "before the Common Era." When you encounter B.C. or B.C.E. dates, you should remember that dates get *smaller* as they get nearer to the time of Jesus' birth, because in B.C.E. dates one is counting backwards. For example, Isaiah is said to have begun his work as a prophet in 742 B.C.E. He worked for about fifty-three years until 687 B.C.E. (742 - 53 = 687).

When speaking of centuries and millennia (a millennium = one thousand years), the convention is less obvious. The dates for the first century C.E. include the years 1 - 100; the second century C.E. from 101 - 200; and the twentieth century C.E. from 1901 - 2000. The same system applies to millennia. The first millennium C.E. runs 1 - 1000. The second millennium C.E. will end in 2000. Thus, the year 2000 will mark both the last year of the twentieth century and the last year of the second millennium.

In working with B.C. (or B.C.E.) dates, the system is reversed. The first century B.C.E. lasted from 99 to the beginning of 1 B.C.E.; the second from 199 to 100 B.C.E.; etc. Similarly, the first millennium B.C.E. went from 999 to 1 B.C.E. Because we are counting backwards, the higher numbers are *earlier* in B.C./B.C.E. dates. Thus, when we speak of the eighth century prophets in the Hebrew scriptures, we are referring to individuals who worked in the 700s B.C./B.C.E. The phrase "early eighth century B.C.E." means closer to the year 799 than to the year 700.

We will discover in the course of our journey that, due to the nature of biblical literature, many dates in the Hebrew Bible cannot be established with certainty. To indicate approximate dates we will sometimes use the abbreviation *ca.,* from the Latin word *circa* meaning "around." Thus one might say that the XIX Dynasty in Egypt (a probable historical setting of the Exodus of the Hebrews from Egypt) ruled in Egypt *ca.* 1350 - 1200 B.C.E.

The Canon

Those books that make up the Hebrew Bible, or the Old Testament as it is called by Christians who believe it to be part of a Bible including the New Testament, are often called the **canon** of scripture. The English term "canon" comes from the Greek word *kanon.* This term was used to refer to a straight reed that was used as a standard or measure for straightness, much as a bricklayer might use a plumb line as a measure of verticality. When we speak of the Jewish canon or the Hebrew Scriptures, we are referring to a specific collection of writings that came to be viewed as a written source of authority, or scriptures, for a religious community, first for the Jewish community and then for Christians (who renamed them the Old Testament). A canon, or scripture, becomes the standard against which the beliefs and practices of persons belonging to a given religious community are measured. A canon provides a religious community with an important way of defining what makes it unique, much like a constitution defines a country.

The formation of the Jewish canon—a process also called canonization—is a complex process about which we know some things, but certainly not everything. Actually, there was no formal process that could be called canonization but the publication of a list of books regarded as authoritative by the Jewish community at the point when it was felt that a canon was needed. For Judaism, the need for a canon that would form a kind of constitution of faith became particularly acute in the first century C.E. with the rise of Christianity, which in its early years saw itself as a movement *within* Judaism. With the production of Christian literature, and especially in view of the theological statements that Christians made regarding Jesus as the Messiah, Judaism needed to redefine itself against the emerging Christian movement. An important question was "Just how inclusive could Judaism be?" A canon could provide a written standard by which any changes in belief and practice might be evaluated. The beginnings of the idea of a canon are discernible in the Hebrew Bible itself. There are "canonical" formulas in Deut 4:2; 12:32; Jer 26:2; Prov 30:6; and Eccl 3:14.

Deliberation over a canon was a part of the reformation of Judaism near the end of the first century C.E. Jewish tradition says that Rabbi Yohanan ben Zakkai, after being smuggled out of Jerusalem when it was under siege by the Romans in the first Jewish Revolt (66–73 C.E.), set up a rabbinic academy in the coastal city of Jamnia. By the time the rabbinical discussions got underway at Jamnia, however, there was already a broad consensus in the Jewish community about which books should be included in the canon. The deliberations at Jamnia were apparently confined to particular controversial matters regarding the canon. Three books that were seen as "problematic" for one reason or another were the Song of Songs (or Song of Solomon as it is called in English Bibles), because of its explicit erotic imagery; Ecclesiastes, due to its pessimistic philosophy of life; and Esther, because of the fact that it nowhere mentions God. Thus a canon *in fact* existed in the Jewish community even before Jamnia, and the deliberations of the rabbis at Jamnia did little more than give formal recognition to an authority that was already acknowledged in the Jewish community.

PARTS OF THE CANON

The canon of the Hebrew Scriptures can be divided into three parts: the *Torah* (or Law = the first five books), the *Prophets* (or *Nevi'im* in Hebrew = Joshua through the Book of the Twelve), and the *Writings* (or *Ketuvim* in Hebrew = Psalms through Chronicles). The first letters of *Torah, Nevi'im,* and *Ketuvim* (TNK) are used in a common acronym for the Hebrew scriptures, the *Tanak.* The list below indicates the order in which the books appear in the Hebrew Bible.

The Torah.   The *Torah* includes the first five books in the Hebrew Bible (sometimes called the *Pentateuch,* with reference to the fact that there are five books):

1. Genesis
2. Exodus
3. Leviticus
4. Numbers
5. Deuteronomy

The Prophets and the Writings.   The collection of the *Prophets* (which is subdivided into the *Former Prophets* and the *Latter Prophets*) is second in the Hebrew Bible. The *Latter Prophets* is also divided into what are sometimes called the Major Prophets (because the books are relatively long) and the Minor Prophets (because the books are relatively short). The Minor Prophets are combined in one book called the Book of the Twelve in the Jewish canon. The entire section of the *Prophets* includes the following books:

THE FORMER PROPHETS

Joshua	Judges	1 and 2 Samuel	1 and 2 Kings

THE LATTER PROPHETS

Isaiah	Jeremiah	Ezekiel

Book of the Twelve

Hosea	Joel	Amos	Obadiah
Jonah	Micah	Nahum	Habakkuk
Zephaniah	Haggai	Zechariah	Malachi

THE WRITINGS (A MISCELLANEOUS COLLECTION)

Psalms	Proverbs	Job	Song of Songs
Ruth	Lamentations	Ecclesiastes	Esther
Daniel	Ezra-Nehemiah	1 and 2 Chronicles	

The Jewish canon is usually spoken of as evolving in three broad phases.

1. The first step in the creation of Scripture began with the *Torah.* The authority of the Torah did not derive from any concept of "canon" but simply because it was in fact the law, and thus the source of authority for the administration of the Jewish community. The Torah is generally regarded as having been fixed as a collection by the fourth century B.C.E.

2. The addition of the *Prophets* to the canon is an intriguing process. The Former Prophets attained their status because they were seen as narrating defining events in the life of a people. Those books in the Latter Prophets became revered when the community saw that the prophets, whose activity is talked about in the books that bear their names, had indeed discerned the currents of history correctly and had warned Israel of the catastrophe that had in fact occurred. The Prophets were probably fixed as a collection by the beginning of the second century B.C.E.

3. With the third canonical collection, the *Writings,* we have to reckon with books that at first individually enjoyed some independent authority, again for different reasons. The Psalms had long existed as a collection of poetry and hymns that was used both publicly and privately in the devotional life of ancient Israel. Other books in this collection came to be traditionally attributed to an important historical figure—Solomon in the case of Proverbs, Ecclesiastes, and the Song of Songs, or Jeremiah in the case of Lamentations. The decision to make these a formal collection and declare them canonical, together with the Law and the Prophets, occurred only at Jamnia, at the end of the first century C.E. It is interesting to note that in several places in the New Testament, when Jesus and others quote "Scripture," they often refer to it as "The Law and the Prophets" (Matt 7:12; 22:40; Luke 16:16; Acts 13:15; Romans 3:21). In one instance the reference is to "The law of Moses, the prophets and the psalms . . ." (Luke 24:44). This suggests that in the first century C.E., the books in these two collections already enjoyed authoritative status in the Jewish community. It also implies that the *Writings* were not yet viewed in the same way.

THE CANONICAL PROCESS

We might legitimately raise the question, "Why these books and not others?" Certainly we know of the existence of other religious writings from the same period that were not included in the canon. There were three important tests that were used to determine a book's canonicity: date of authorship, language, and usage. No books were included that the rabbis thought were written after Malachi, a prophet whose book appears last in the Book of the Twelve (or after *ca.* 400 B.C.E.), because the rabbis believed that with the death of the postexilic prophets (prophets who were active in the period following the Jews' return from exile in Babylonia), "the Holy Spirit departed from Israel." The test of language refers to the language in which the book was written (Hebrew except for portions in Aramaic, see following section on "The Text of the Hebrew Scriptures"). The test of usage reflects the fact that, for the most part, the rabbis at Jamnia recognized a list of books that *already* had been agreed upon as authoritative by the Jewish community. These books had survived the test of time and continued to speak to the needs of Jewish life and thought. To use a contemporary analogy, what happened at Jamnia was not an election of candidates to office so much as an installation ceremony for persons who had already been elected.

What the rabbis effectively did at Jamnia was to "close" the canon, to set, once and for all, the limits on what books could be considered authoritative. As inferred above, one reason for the closure of the canon was the rise of Christianity in the first century C.E. It was important for the rabbis to define which books were sacred, so Jews would not be misled by similar Christian writings. Another reason for canonization was that with the destruction of the temple by the Romans in 70 C.E. and the dispersion of Jews from Palestine into the Diaspora (a term from the Greek referring to Jews living outside of Palestine), the center of Judaism had shifted away from temple and ritual to "portable" sacred writings that could be the focus of Jewish life wherever Jews lived.

The canon of Hebrew Scriptures as it was defined at Jamnia in 90 C.E. also was, and is, Holy Scripture for Christians. Protestant Bibles order the books differently, and subdivide some of them so as to come up with a total of thirty-nine books instead of the twenty-four books of the Jewish canon. This set of books is also sometimes called the Hebrew or Palestinian canon.

THE SEPTUAGINT

A more inclusive list of books developed among the Jewish community living in Alexandria, Egypt, in the third century B.C.E. These books were included in the Septuagint, the first translation (into Greek) of the Hebrew Scriptures. In addition to all of the books in the Jewish canon, the Septuagint includes the following books or sections added to certain biblical works in the Greek version:

1 and 2 Esdras	Tobit	Judith
Wisdom of Solomon	Ecclesiasticus	Prayer of Azariah
Song of the Three Young Men	Susanna	Bel and the Dragon
1 and 2 Maccabees	The Prayer of Manasseh	Additions to Esther
The Letter of Jeremiah	Baruch	

The books in this list are separated from the Jewish canon by Jews and Protestants. When they are included in published Bibles, they are grouped together and called, by Protestants, the *Apocrypha,* from a Greek term meaning "hidden things or writings," referring to these books having been "hidden" from the public because it was believed that their content was "dangerous"or "heretical." These books were written between *ca.* 200 B.C.E. and 100 C.E. Although used by Greek-speaking Jews living outside Palestine, they did not become a part of the accepted Jewish canon. These books were also admired by early Christians and became a part of the canon of Catholic Christianity and Eastern Orthodoxy, as eventually confirmed by the Council of Trent in 1546, at which Roman Catholicism's doctrinal response to sixteenth-century Protestantism was formulated. They were called "deuterocanonical" (that is, the "second" set of canonical Old Testament books) in the face of objections to them from Protestant Christians. In Roman Catholic and Eastern Orthodox Bibles these deuterocanonical books are not separated out as the apocrypha, but are interspersed among the other canonical books. The listing of books (in the order in which they appear) in the four canons is shown in Table 1.3.

Why were the books in this expanded list not accepted as part of the Jewish canon by the Council of Jamnia? For one thing, as mentioned above, the rabbis considered these books as having been written too late to be considered as inspired by the Spirit of God. Also, some of these books were written in Greek rather than in Hebrew, which was the language of the prophets. Ultimately, however, the reason these books were not recognized was because they were not widely used by the Palestinian Jewish community.

Hebrew fell into disuse as a spoken language among Jews of the Diaspora and was replaced by Greek, which became a universal language, or *lingua franca,* in those countries included in the area conquered by Alexander the Great in the fourth century B.C.E. As a result, the Bible used by Jews living outside Palestine was not the Hebrew Bible, but the first translation of the Hebrew scriptures (into Greek), which was called the *Septuagint* (abbreviated with the Roman numeral LXX), from the Greek word for "seventy." This translation of the Hebrew scriptures took its name from the tradition that seventy (or seventy-two in another version of the tradition) Jewish scholars, one from every known nation, were brought to Alexandria at the order of Ptolemy II (*ca.* 285–247 B.C.E.) to work on a translation of the Torah. The Septuagint became the favored translation of the Old Testament among early Christians.

THE VULGATE

With the rise of Latin as the common language of the Roman Empire, the Hebrew scriptures were translated once again. Most of the translation was done by Jerome, who translated the Hebrew scriptures into Latin in the late fourth century C.E. at the behest of Pope Damascus (382 C.E.) The Pope did this in order to bring to an end the proliferation of inferior Latin versions. Jerome's translation, completed in 405, is known as the *Vulgate* (from the Latin word meaning "common, popular"). Jerome's translation of the books of the Hebrew Bible circulated separately until they were bound in one volume in the mid sixth century. These bound editions also included translations of some books that were not done by Jerome. All of the books in the Jewish Bible/Old Testament were translated by Jerome, but of the apocryphal/deuterocanonical books only Tobit and Judith can be attributed to him. Jerome based his translation on the Hebrew but used the Septuagint as well. He chose to follow the Jewish canon rather than the Septuagint, separating those books not included in the Jewish canon into a collection he called "apocrypha." Jerome's translation became the official Bible of the Roman Catholic Church. Jerome was the first to translate the Hebrew Bible into a Christian language. The older Latin versions that existed in Jerome's time had been translated from the Greek, not Hebrew. Because Jerome used the Hebrew original for his translation, he noted the distinction between the Jewish and Christian canons and spoke of the higher sanctity of the Hebrew original.

TABLE 1.3 **The Books of the Jewish Bible, Greek Septuagint, Protestant, Catholic and Orthodox Canons of Scripture**

JEWISH BIBLE	GREEK SEPTUAGINT	PROTESTANT BIBLE	ROMAN CATHOLIC AND ORTHODOX BIBLE (italics = deuterocanonical)
1. Genesis	1. Genesis	1. Genesis	1. Genesis
2. Exodus	2. Exodus	2. Exodus	2. Exodus
3. Leviticus	3. Leviticus	3. Leviticus	3. Leviticus
4. Numbers	4. Numbers	4. Numbers	4. Numbers
5. Deuteronomy	5. Deuteronomy	5. Deuteronomy	5. Deuteronomy
6. Joshua	6. Joshua	6. Joshua	6. Joshua
7. Judges	7. Judges	7. Judges	7. Judges
8. 1–2 Samuel	8. Ruth	8. Ruth	8. Ruth
9. 1–2 Kings	9–10. 1–2 Kings (=1–2 Samuel)	9–10. 1–2 Samuel	9–10. 1–2 Kings (=1–2 Samuel)
10. Isaiah	11–12. 3–4 Kings (=1–2 Kings)	11–12. 1–2 Kings	11–12. 3–4 Kings (=1–2 Kings)
11. Jeremiah	13. 1 Esdras	13–14. 1–2 Chronicles	13–14. 1–2 Chronicles
12. Ezekiel	14. 2 Esdras (=Ezra–Nehemiah)	15. Ezra	15–16. 1–2 Esdras (=Ezra–Nehemiah)
13. Book of the Twelve	15. Esther	16. Nehemiah	17. *Tobias* (=Tobit)
14. Psalms	16. Judith	17. Esther	18. *Judith*
15. Proverbs	17. Tobit	18. Job	19. Esther (includes Additions to Esther)
16. Job	18–21. 1–4 Maccabees	19. Psalms	20. Job
17. Song of Songs	22. Psalms	20. Proverbs	21. Psalms
18. Ruth	23. Odes	21. Ecclesiastes	22. Proverbs
19. Lamentations	24. Proverbs	22. Song of Solomon (= Song of Songs)	23. Ecclesiastes
20. Ecclesiastes	25. Ecclesiastes	23. Isaiah	24. Song of Songs
21. Esther	26. Song of Songs	24. Jeremiah	25. *Wisdom of Solomon*
22. Daniel	27. Job	25. Lamentations	26. *Ecclesiasticus* (=Sirach)
23. Ezra–Nehemiah	28. Wisdom of Solomon	26. Ezekiel	27. Isaiah
24. Chronicles	29. Sirach (=Ecclesiasticus)	27. Daniel	28. Jeremiah
	30. Psalms of Solomon	28. Hosea	29. Lamentations
	31. Hosea	29. Joel	30. *Baruch* (includes The Epistle of Jeremiah— R.C. only)

JEWISH BIBLE	GREEK SEPTUAGINT	PROTESTANT BIBLE	ROMAN CATHOLIC AND ORTHODOX BIBLE (italics = deuterocanonical)
	32. Amos	31. Ezekiel	
	33. Micah	31. Obadiah	32. Daniel (includes Additions to Daniel—Susanna, Song of the Three Young Men, Bel and the Dragon)
	34. Joel	32. Jonah	33. Hosea
	35. Obadiah	33. Micah	34. Joel
	36. Jonah	34. Nahum	35. Amos
	37. Nahum	35. Habakkuk	36. Obadiah
	38. Habakkuk	36. Zephaniah	37. Jonah
	39. Zephaniah	37. Haggai	38. Micah
	40. Haggai	38. Zechariah	39. Nahum
	41. Zechariah	39. Malachi	40. Habakkuk
	42. Malachi		41. Zephaniah
	43. Isaiah		42. Haggai
	44. Jeremiah		43. Zechariah
	45. Baruch		44. Malachi
	46. Lamentations		45–46. 1 and 2 Maccabees
	47. Epistle of Jeremiah		
	48. Ezekiel		
	49. Susanna		
	50. Daniel		
	51. Bel and the Dragon		

Jerome's evaluation of the importance of the Hebrew text was taken up by the Protestant reformers.

When Martin Luther translated the Hebrew Bible into German in 1534, he noticed the absence of the extra books of the Greek Bible, called them "secret" or apocryphal, and set them apart in a section by themselves in his Bible translation. Thus with the Protestant Reformation, the Apocrypha as a separate non-canonical entity was born, and the existence of two different canons of scripture was officially recognized.

THE TEXT OF THE HEBREW SCRIPTURES

The language in which almost all of the Hebrew Bible was written was Hebrew, a language belonging to the family of Semitic languages. A small portion of the Hebrew Bible (Gen 31:47; Jer 10:11; Ezra 4:8-6:18; 7:12-26; Dan 2:4-7:28) was written in a closely-related Semitic language, Aramaic, which was the successor to Hebrew as a spoken language in Palestine, and was the language spoken by Jesus in the first century c.e. Both Hebrew and Aramaic are written from right to left, and the oldest manuscripts were written using only the consonants that make up the Hebrew alphabet (which contained no vowels), without punctuation, and without any separation between words. Hebrew written without vowels is sometimes called "unpointed." This situation can create some interesting dilemmas for the student of the text of the Hebrew scriptures in their original language. To use an analogy from English, the group of letters "GDSNWHR" could be supplied with vowels, divided into words, and read either as "God is now here" or "God is nowhere." Obviously, possibilities for confusion existed that could be replicated in the process of making handwritten copies of manuscripts.

Before the invention of movable type by Johannes Gutenberg in 1456, copies of the Hebrew Bible, like every other book, had to be made by hand. This manuscript duplication was done either by a scribe who copied a manuscript that was before him, or by one scribe reading a manuscript aloud in front of several scribes, who would write down what they heard. The latter method could produce copies more quickly, but was also more vulnerable to errors than the work of a single scribe copying by sight. For example, upon hearing the word "*lo*" in Hebrew, the scribe might write one of two words that are both pronounced "*lo.*" One of these words, however, means "not," while the other means "to him" or "his."

Realizing that errors could creep into biblical manuscripts while they were being copied, Jewish scribes began at an early point to develop elaborate schemes to preserve and transmit the biblical text in as error-free a state as possible. The importance of this literature to the community and the concern for accuracy in preserving the received text lent considerable status to the profession of those who worked with biblical manuscripts.

Jewish scholars instrumental in copying and safeguarding the biblical manuscripts were called *Sopherim,* "scribes" (from the same root as the word *sepher,* "book" in Hebrew). The Sopherim had their origins as a class or occupational group sometime in the fourth century b.c.e. and were still active in the early Christian era. They not only copied manuscripts, but also marked questionable passages, added marginal notes with suggestions as to readings they thought were more accurate than those in the body of the text, and divided the manuscripts into sections for use in public reading of the Bible in the synagogue.

These Sopherim were succeeded by another group called the *Masoretes,* who collected and catalogued errors found in the text, noted every unique form, and even counted the letters of individual books—all as means of preserving the accuracy of the text. They put their notes in the margins of the biblical manuscripts, thus surrounding the sacred text with a kind of protective hedge of "tradition" which they called the *Masora,* thus their name, the Masoretes.

In the seventh to ninth centuries C.E., these families of Masoretes added vowels and accents to the consonantal text. By doing so they made it possible for modern scholars to be able to understand better the grammatical structure of the Hebrew language, which by the seventh century was no longer a spoken language but principally the language of the holy book, the Bible. The Masoretes, like other Jews, no longer spoke Hebrew, but they knew the sound and structure of the language from memory, and because of their invention of a system of vowel points (the symbols used with the consonants of the Hebrew alphabet to indicate vowel sounds), they passed on the written text in a form that could be pronounced by worshiping communities that no longer spoke Hebrew. The work of the Masoretes also preserved the text in a form that could be analyzed more fully by future scholars.

By the tenth century C.E., two main families of Masoretes were active in Palestine: the ben Asher and the ben Naphtali family. For a period the two versions of the biblical texts produced by these families were seen as rivals, but in the twelfth century C.E. the ben Asher version came to be accepted as the standard.

Textual Criticism

Modern English translations, such as the New Revised Standard Version (NRSV), are the result of a long process of transmission of the biblical text. Since no original manuscript of any biblical book has survived, even the oldest Hebrew manuscripts in our possession are copies of copies. One branch of biblical scholarship has as its intent, the restoration, as nearly as possible, of the original form of the biblical text. This branch of biblical study is called *textual criticism,* and it seeks to uncover "textual corruptions" or places where errors have crept into the original text, intentionally or accidentally, during its transmission.

Some of these textual corruptions can be spotted easily, even in modern English translations of the Hebrew text. When there is some question about what the original Hebrew reading was, and there are different readings in different Hebrew manuscripts, the NRSV, as well as some other modern translations, often inserts a footnote to alert the reader both to where there is a textual problem and how the translator has resolved it. For example, 1 Sam 13:1 reads as follows in the NRSV:

> Saul was . . .[c] years old when he began to reign; and he reigned . . . and two[d] years over Israel.
>
> [c] The number is lacking in the Heb text.
>
> [d] *Two* is not the entire number. Something has dropped out.

The NRSV literally translates the Hebrew text with its missing material, that is, Saul's age upon taking the throne and the actual length of his reign.

Errors.   Some textual errors are results of unintentional human errors of the same kind that we often make when we are copying material by hand. One of these kinds of errors is known as *dittography,* in which we write something twice that should have been written only once. A comparison of Lev 20:10 in the King James Version (KJV) and the NRSV preserves an interesting example of dittography:

KJV
And the man that committeth adultery with *another* man's wife, *even he* that committeth adultery with his neighbor's wife, the adulterer and the adulteress shall surely be put to death.

NRSV
If a man commits adultery with the wife of[f] his neighbor, both the adulterer and the adulteress shall be put to death.

> [f] Heb repeats *if a man commits adultery with the wife of.*

The KJV here preserves the dittography of four words in the Hebrew manuscript from which it was translating. The NRSV, using older Hebrew manuscripts that were not yet known when the KJV translation was made (1611), deletes the dittography as a textual corruption.

While dittography expands the text, another copying error known as *haplography* shortens the text. In haplography a syllable, word, or line is omitted because a repeated sequence of a letter, word, or phrase was copied only once when it should have been written twice. In the Babylonian Talmud (Nedarim 37b-38a) there is a list of haplographies that rabbis had identified in the Hebrew Bible. This list is given under the heading "these [words] are to be read [i.e., supplied by the reader] though they are not written [in the biblical text]." Haplographies were a kind of copying error that occurred frequently. An example of this type of error can be seen in Judg 20:13. The Hebrew text here reads: "And . . . Benjamin were not willing" (where . . . represents a word that has been missed in the copying). The plural verb does not agree with the singular subject. The plural verb shows that the original text probably read "And the sons of Benjamin were not willing." It is easy to see how the copyist made the error when we restore the missing consonants of the Hebrew text, which would have been *bny bnymyn,* "the sons of Benjamin." It is clear that the copyist copied the letters *bny* once instead of twice. The same accident has afflicted the Hebrew text of many passages, including 2 Sam 2:15, 31; 4:2; 1 Chr 7:6; 11:31.

Another copying error is called *homoioteleuton,* which comes from a Greek word meaning "having similar endings." This error involves the omission of material that appears between two words that are the same or that have similar endings. An example of this error can be found in the NRSV of 1 Sam 14:41:

> Then Saul said, "O Lord God of Israel, why have you not answered your servant today? If this guilt is in me or in my son Jonathan, O Lord God of Israel, give Urim; but if this guilt is in your people Israel,[v] give Thummim."

> [v] Vg Compare Gk: Heb *Saul said to the* Lord, *the God of Israel.*

The Hebrew manuscripts at this point omit that part of Saul's speech that is found between the two occurrences of the word "Israel." When a scribe was copying this verse, he must have looked up from the page at the first occurrence of the word "Israel" to write down a phrase, and then when he looked back at the page he resumed at the second occurrence of the same word. This error was then duplicated in subsequently hand-copied Hebrew manuscripts but was revealed as an error in both the Vulgate (Vg in the NRSV footnote), and Septuagint, (Gk in the NRSV footnote), which preserved the full reading of the text at this point.

Since scribes often copied from oral dictation, homonyms (words with the same sound but different meanings) could be a problem. Again, an example of this kind of error can be seen by comparing the KJV and the NRSV translations of Psalms 100:3:

KJV
Know ye that the LORD he *is* God: *it is* he *that* hath made us, and *not* we ourselves; *we are* his people, and the sheep of his pasture.

NRSV
Know that the LORD is God!
  It is he that made us, and we are *his*[q];
we are his people, and the sheep of his pasture.

[q] Another reading is *and not we ourselves.*

The word that has been underlined in the two translations is a homonym in Hebrew that is pronounced like the English word "low," but can be spelled in two different ways in Hebrew. The KJV translates the Hebrew word *lo'*, which means "not," while the NRSV translates the Hebrew word *lo*, which although pronounced the same, means "for him" or "his."

Although most scribal errors were of this unintentional kind, there were some occasions when a copyist would intentionally alter a reading to correct what he thought was a theological error, or at least something that might lead to some misunderstanding. One example of this can be seen in Gen 18:22. The Hebrew manuscript translated by the NRSV reads: "So the men turned from there, and went toward Sodom; while Abraham remained standing before the LORD." Another manuscript, noted in the NRSV footnote, probably copied by a scribe who thought it pretentious to say that Abraham stood *before* the LORD, changes the reading to "while the LORD remained standing before Abraham."

Versions.   Most Hebrew Bible text critics begin their work using the "received" or standard form of the Hebrew text known as the *Masoretic tradition* (MT), which was punctuated and furnished with vowel points by the Masoretes, the authoritative teachers of scriptural tradition. The text critic next compares readings in the MT with ancient manuscripts and versions that reflect a form of the Hebrew text that is older than the MT. Until the Dead Sea Scrolls were found, beginning in 1947, the oldest existing Hebrew manuscripts of the Hebrew Bible,

Figure 1.1 Egyptian Scribes

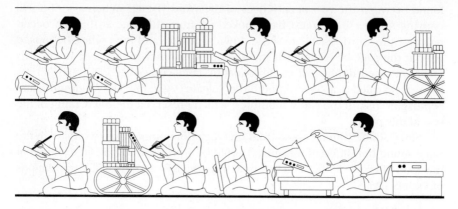

and thus those from which the KJV translation was made, dated only to the ninth century C.E. The scrolls, found at Qumran on the northwest shore of the Dead Sea (known as the Dead Sea Scrolls), included manuscripts of at least part of every Hebrew Bible book, excepting Esther and Nehemiah (suggesting perhaps that the particular Jewish community whose scrolls these were, did not hold these books in high regard). We know that there were heated debates about Esther's inclusion in the Jewish canon. These manuscripts from Qumran date to the second and first centuries B.C.E. and the first century C.E. Having studied Hebrew manuscripts, the text critic next considers the ancient versions, early translations of the Hebrew scriptures into other languages. The most important of these versions is the Greek *Septuagint* (LXX), discussed earlier.

Another of these ancient versions, the Aramaic *Targums,* developed as Hebrew waned as the spoken language of Palestinian Jewry, and oral paraphrases in Aramaic were needed to follow the reading of the scriptures in Hebrew in the synagogues. These oral paraphrases were then committed to writing in the Targums. The two most important Targums are the *Targum of Onkelos,* for the Torah, and the *Targum of Jonathan,* for the Prophets.

The most important early Christian translations of the Hebrew scriptures are the two ancient versions known as the *Peshitta* and the *Vulgate.* The Peshitta is a translation into Syriac, the dialectical form of Aramaic that was common among Christians in Syria and Mesopotamia durng the Byzantine and later eras. It was completed in the late first or early second century C.E. Until the English translation of William Tyndale in 1529, all English translations were based on the Vulgate.

The tasks of textual criticism today are unfinished; there remain unresolved textual problems. Modern scholars, however, have been amazingly successful in recovering a reliable text of the Hebrew Bible, and contemporary translations benefit from their work. When using a modern English translation of the Bible, one should be aware that behind the translation are hundreds of decisions regarding the reconstruction of the biblical text in the original language.

English Versions of the Hebrew Bible

Why are there so many English translations of the Bible? Which ones are the best? For the student of the Hebrew Bible who does not know Hebrew, it is especially important to know what principles guided a translation. One should know what the "ground rules" and biases of the translator/s were, something that is usually stated in the preface of a Bible. It is also helpful to know whether the translation is the work of a single individual or a group of scholars.

The entire Bible was not translated into English until the fourteenth century (*ca.* 1384) by the followers of John Wyclif, who has been called the "Father of English prose," the "Morning star of the Reformation," and the "Flower of Oxford scholarship." The translation of the Bible into the vernacular languages of Europe was one of the aims of Renaissance humanism, and it gained support from the Reformation, from the invention of movable type, and from the development of the English language. In England, William Tyndale undertook the task of translating the Bible into English in the early sixteenth century, but faced difficulties because of England's hostility toward Luther. He carried out his work, however, and his translation, which was the first English translation to be made directly from the Hebrew, was printed in Worms, Germany, in 1526. Tyndale's work set off a flurry of translations that climaxed in the King James Version (KJV) in 1611. Preceding the KJV were the Great Bible (1539), the Geneva Bible (1560), and the Bishop's Bible (1568). The Geneva Bible remained in use long after the KJV appeared on the scene and was the Bible used by the Pilgrims when they came to America in 1620. The Pilgrims disliked the KJV and called it a "fond thing vainly invented." They considered their old version to be the better one. The Geneva Bible was also the favored version of the Elizabethan age and was the Bible of William Shakespeare.

The King James Version is also known as the Authorized Version (AV), since it was commissioned by King James I of England, the head of the Anglican Church, to be the official or authorized version to be used in the worship services of the Church of England. Forty-seven scholars, divided into six panels, made the translation using existing versions, but also paying attention to the original text. Although it did not receive instant acceptance, this translation became a landmark in the religious history of English-speaking peoples. Its enduring use derives in part from two reasons: the absence of any controversial sectarian annotation gives it a broad, ecumenical appeal, and its literary quality makes it useful for public reading. Much of the credit for this literary quality should be given to Tyndale, however, for much of the KJV comes directly from his work.

Although the KJV is a classic of English literature, for three reasons it should *not* be used by itself for scholarly biblical study today. First, the KJV is based on late and comparatively poor Hebrew manuscripts. Since the seventeenth century, many older and better manuscripts of the Hebrew scriptures have been discovered. Secondly, the KJV was based on a limited understanding of Hebrew grammar and syntax. Thirdly, English language usage also has changed markedly since the seventeenth century, so that while some phrases of the KJV have a classic quality, others are virtually unintelligible to the contemporary reader. An example of this can be seen in Ps 88:13, which in the KJV reads: "But unto thee have I cried, O Lord, and in the morning shall my prayer prevent thee." The meaning of the verb "prevent" has changed since the seventeenth century. Based on our understanding of the verb "prevent" in contemporary English, one might suppose that the function of prayer in this verse is to keep God from doing something. The KJV "prevent," however, translates the Latin *prae-*, "before," and *venire*, "to come," i.e., "to come before." The NRSV translation of this verse: "But I, O Lord, cry out to you; in the morning my prayer comes before you" better expresses in modern English, what both the Hebrew meant *and* the KJV says!

Because of the shortcomings of the KJV, several revisions of it have been undertaken in the twentieth century. *The English Revised Version* (ERV) and the *American Standard Version* (ASV, 1901) are predecessors of the best-known and most widely used of these revisions, *The Revised Standard Version* (RSV). As a revision of the KJV, the RSV comes closest to fulfilling the broad purpose once filled by the KJV. It is stylistically superior to both the ERV and the ASV and is based on the earliest and best manuscripts as reconstructed by modern textual criticism. Like the KJV and other revised versions, the RSV stays as close as possible to the exact words and phrasings of the original language, although the RSV has sought to be more intelligible to its modern English readers. Thus, while it follows the theory of translation called formal equivalence or formal correspondence (which means that one attempts a direct correlation of words in the original language and in the translation language), it is a less literal translation than its predecessors.

MODERN ENGLISH TRANSLATIONS

There have been a large number of other English translations that have appeared since 1952. A complete discussion of these can be found in *The Anchor Bible Dictionary,* Volume 6, in a series of articles that fall under the heading "Versions, English." Some of these are not revisions, but constitute breaks with the KJV tradition. Among these are the *New English Bible, The Good News Bible/Today's English Version, The Jerusalem Bible, The New American Bible,* and *Tanakh: A New Translation of* THE HOLY SCRIPTURES *According to the Traditional Hebrew Text.*

Many Bible translators of the modern era have not worked alone but have had behind them organizations that provide support. These organizations include Bible societies, denominations, and interdenominational groups. One Protestant interdenominational effort, *The New English Bible,* marked a genuine departure in the history of British translations when it appeared in its complete form in 1970. It was done by a team of Protestant British scholars.

The break with the KJV in America came from the American Bible Society and their "common language" translation *The Good News Bible/Today's English Version* (TEV), the Hebrew Bible portion of which appeared in 1976. It uses idiomatic American English and has been published in inexpensive paperback editions.

One of the most significant of the denominational translations is the *Jerusalem Bible* (JB) and now the *New Jerusalem Bible* (NJB). This fresh, Roman Catholic translation departs from the tradition of Catholic translations based on the Latin Vulgate. From 1948 to 1954, this translation appeared in French by the Jerusalem Dominicans and was subsequently translated into English. It had a twofold objective: to translate the Bible into the language we use today and to provide notes that are neither sectarian nor superficial. In 1985, the *New Jerusalem Bible* was completed. It is a complete revision and updating of the original, based on new insights from the last twenty years of biblical scholarship.

The *New American Bible* (NAB) is an American counterpart of the *Jerusalem Bible.* When the complete New American Bible was published in 1970, it was the first American Catholic translation of the entire Bible from the original languages. The NAB often includes colloquial forms of American English, but it seeks to render faithfully words and phrases of the original language.

A major translation produced by an international group of Protestant Evangelicals is the *New International Version* (NIV), 1978. This translation reflects a conservative theological outlook. Its preface states that all translators were committed to "the full authority and complete trustworthiness of the Scriptures which they believe is God's Word in written form." Beyond reflecting a particular theological perspective, the translators were primarily concerned with the accuracy of the translation and its fidelity to the thought of the original authors.

A new Jewish version, sponsored by the Jewish Publication Society, appeared in its complete form in 1985 (5745 in the Jewish calendar) under the title *Tanakh: A New Translation of* THE HOLY SCRIPTURES *According to the Traditional Hebrew Text* (NJPS). Not only does its language reflect current literary usage, its philosophy of translation is idiom for idiom instead of word for word.

Since the publication of the RSV Old Testament in 1952, important advances have been made in the discovery and interpretation of documents related to Hebrew. Other early copies of books of the Hebrew Scriptures have also been found. To take these discoveries into account, a revision of the RSV translation was undertaken, producing the New Revised Standard Version (NRSV) in 1989. The NRSV remains essentially a literal translation. The NRSV, however, attempts to use gender-inclusive language without altering those passages that reflect the historical situation of ancient patriarchal cultures. It also eliminates the use of the archaic pronouns "Thee" and "Thou" when referring to the deity. The NRSV is the version that will be quoted throughout this book, unless otherwise indicated.

Translation Philosophies. Modern English translations, whether they are revisions of earlier translations or new translations, tend to follow one of two basic philosophies of translation. "Formal correspondence" translations render the technical vocabulary, sentence structure, and imagery of the original Hebrew as closely as possible, even when the result is a rather stilted English style. The other type of translation is one called "dynamic equivalence," in which the meaning of the original is rendered into natural, fluent English. Both kinds of translations ought to be used by any serious student of the Bible

Some widely used post-1952 English translations can be classified according to their style of translation as follows:

Formal Correspondence

Revised Standard Version (RSV)

New American Bible (NAB)

New International Version (NIV)

New King James Version (NKJV)

Tanakh: A New Translation of THE HOLY SCRIPTURES *According to the Traditional Hebrew Text* (NJPS)

New Revised Standard Version (NRSV)

Dynamic Equivalence

Jerusalem Bible (JB)

New English Bible (NEB)

The Good News Bible/Today's English Version (TEV)

New Jerusalem Bible (NJB)

(adapted from Gottwald 1985:127–129)

READING THE BIBLE: THE CRITICAL TOOLS

Exegesis vs. Eisegesis

The process by which one reads in order to draw meaning or meanings *from* a text is called *exegesis.* The opposite of exegesis is *eisegesis,* in which one simply forces pre-existing meanings *onto* a text, discovering in the text only what one, guided by one's presuppositions, expected to find there. Most modern biblical exegesis also can be called "historical biblical criticism." This kind of biblical criticism was born in Europe during the Enlightenment and is a general umbrella under which can be found most modern scholarly biblical study. In this journey we will be using various tools to navigate our way through the Hebrew Bible, to help us understand more clearly and appreciate more fully what we encounter there. No single tool will suffice. Just as a photographer uses different lenses and filters to capture different images, so the tool box of the biblical scholar includes various tools that are used selectively. Some of these tools are described here, and their use will be suggested at different points along our itinerary—a literary approach at some points, a gendered reading in another, a classical "historical critical" approach in still another. To do justice to the Hebrew Bible, one ought to use as many of the tools as possible as often as possible.

Space limitations prevent our doing so here, however, so we can only give illustrations of how different tools "work" on selected texts.

Classical *historical criticism* rests on the basic principle that the process of exegesis involves discovering as much as possible about the author of the text, the circumstances under which the author wrote, and the primary audience for whom the text was intended. In other words, the Bible ought to be studied in ways similar to those that we use to study other ancient literature. When we study the Bible in this way, we are interested in discovering as much as we can about such questions as the authorship of a text or the process by which it was composed, its historical, social and religious settings, the sources (oral and written) used by its author or authors in its composition, and the purpose(s) for which it was written. In short, by means of the process of exegesis using the various tools of historical criticism, we are concerned with establishing lines of communication between the ancient text and ourselves as modern readers—we want to understand what the text has to say to us.

Language Usage and Communication Theory

Communication, understood by those who study the sociology of language, refers to a social transaction involving a sender, a receiver, and a message. In this transaction, a sender transmits a message along a channel to a receiver in a particular situation to achieve some specific effect or effects. This general understanding of communication can be useful for us in approaching the Hebrew Bible as scripture—that is, as literature regarded by both the Jewish and the Christian traditions as containing communications from God to human beings—and in our role as interpreters or receivers. Let us consider the main elements of this definition of communication.

Because the Hebrew Bible is a form of communication, it has a sender or senders. One of those senders is the human author (or authors) who wrote in Hebrew or Aramaic. These human authors were considered by persons reading what they wrote at some later point in time, to have been "inspired," or in some way spiritually influenced by something or someone. From the perspectives of Judaism and Christianity, however, this literature also has another sender—God. The Bible is thus seen as the *simultaneous* work of God and the human author. To disregard either, to make the Bible only a human product or only divine in its origin, would misrepresent the way the Bible is regarded in much of Jewish and Christian thought—even though some believe that what the Bible says can be precisely equated with what God says. The mainstream of Jewish and Christian thinking concerning the Bible, however, is that it *contains* the word of God, not that it is, equally and in every part, the very word of God.

LANGUAGE OF BIBLICAL COMMUNICATION

The channel along which the biblical message comes to us is the language of the author, often translated into the language of the reader—a written text which commonly had an oral tradition behind it. A text can be defined as a unit of meaning intended to express a message, for example, a complete biblical book. For some theologians, the whole Bible as a single volume, both Old and New Testaments, is the text. Their belief is that every passage in the Bible ought to be understood, as far as possible, in the context of the entire Bible. The important thing to notice is that a phrase, a verse, or even a chapter from the Hebrew Bible is not *necessarily* a text, a unit of meaning, from this perspective. A single phrase, verse, or passage is better understood as a *text segment,* a piece of a whole. Like a piece of a jigsaw puzzle, text segments have little or no meaning by themselves, but achieve clarity when they become part of a larger picture. We do not communicate clearly with one another using text segments, but in texts. Similarly, it is difficult to discern what an ancient author is saying by studying only text segments. The substitution of text segments for a text is what is meant when someone refers to "quoting out of context."

The main thing to notice is that isolated phrases and single sentences are abstractions that have some basis in reality, but do not really exist as such in the world of human communication except as partial units of analysis. Even nonliterate people, who do not use written texts, manage to express themselves quite effectively, especially through stories that, for them, are units of meaning.

While words and sentences might make some kind of sense in and of themselves, they cannot necessarily be interpreted. Take a sentence like: "She did so." Anyone who knows English can understand this simple sentence at a certain level, for according to the rules of English grammar it is a complete sentence with a subject, verb, and object. But how can one interpret it, discover what it means, since there is no larger framework into which to set it? Part of the larger framework that we need to be able to extract meaning from texts is the social system out of which they come. *All* communication takes place in a particular social setting. We communicate within a given social framework that includes a shared language together with the idea that certain speech patterns are appropriate to particular social situations. No one can communicate meaningfully with someone else using his or her own private language; the speaker must use a language shared by both speaker and listener. Language is a social construction. Moreover, the kind of speech we use depends on the social context in which we find ourselves. Language (grammar, vocabulary, style, etc.) that is appropriate with friends at a party, might well be inappropriate in the college classroom or during a job interview. This remains true even if the topic of conversation is the same in both instances; for example, the state of the economy.

RECEPTION OF BIBLICAL COMMUNICATION

The receivers of biblical communication are, of course, a varied lot. At the first level, there are the initial receivers, the people to whom the biblical message was first addressed. It is these people to and for whom the original authors wrote, not for some imagined audience in the far-distant future. This group was part of the same social system as the biblical author. To understand what an author said and meant to say *socially* is to understand that author primarily and essentially as a member of a given social group, addressing other members of that same group. This first group of receivers is the one that we, as Bible readers today must keep in mind and must empathize with to comprehend the meaning or meanings a biblical text may have had for its primary audience. We must also bear in mind that *any* understanding of a biblical text apart from the time and context of the original receivers is a derived meaning, not necessarily a wrong one, but certainly secondary. Fair and appropriate use of a biblical text by persons encountering that text hundreds and even thousands of years after it was written requires some awareness of the fact that they are like persons reading mail addressed to someone else, or like eavesdroppers on a conversation that is not really meant to include them. It is important that we come to terms with this truth at the beginning of our journey through the Hebrew Bible. Any use of biblical literature by persons like us, who are removed by centuries from its origins, is unintended, indirect, or "eavesdropping" usage. The history of biblical interpretation bears this truth out repeatedly, as we shall see throughout the course of our journey.

By selecting certain writings and "canonizing" them, declaring them to be Scripture, the Jewish and Christian communities made these biblical texts normative, that is, they saw them as telling us about how life should be lived. They provide moral norms. These norms can be expressed both negatively and positively— "Thou shalt not!" or "Thou shalt!" Certainly some negative norms expressed in biblical texts have served as guidelines for persons living in subsequent generations, offering "Thou shalt nots" and informing them when they were morally out-of-bounds. Significantly, for example, most of the Ten Commandments (Ex 20:1–17), which many believe express valid moral norms for today, are stated as prohibitions: you shall not steal, you shall not commit adultery, etc.

The relationship between norms in the biblical text and contemporary ones is a complex one that raises many questions for us. What about ancient texts and positive norms? Can ancient texts, coming as they do from very different social situations, positively express meaning in subsequent history and differing cultural contexts? Can a moral precept from the Hebrew Bible inform those living at the turn of the second millennium C.E. about appropriate social roles for men and women in the world today, what position one ought to take on issues like gender roles, prayer in public schools, on abortion and other issues in biomedical ethics, on economic policies in a world economy? Can any time- and space-conditioned instance of human language be that elastic? These are questions that will confront anyone who undertakes a thoughtful study of the Bible.

Once again the problem of being a receiver of biblical communication raises the question of what it means to be an informed reader. One common "religious" objection to the perspective being outlined here is that God can make the Bible mean anything God wants it to mean. While this might sound piously perfect and religiously correct, it requires a peculiar notion of both God and language. It requires a God who does not understand that human language is finite, tied to time and culture. It also requires a language that is infinitely and eternally stretchable, a language that can mean anything at all, and consequently nothing at all.

RESULTS OF BIBLICAL COMMUNICATION

Finally, biblical communication consists of messages sent to have a specific result or effect. What sort of effect? The effects sought by biblical authors, like the results we seek in our communication with others, can be quite varied. The desired outcome might be to communicate instructions for obtaining some goods or services. Or it might be to get people to behave in a certain way. It might be to maintain or enhance emotional ties with others. It might serve to identify oneself to others, or to explore the world of others. Sometimes the effect sought might be to create a particular kind of social environment with others. Obviously a text may deal with several of these effects at once, or just one of them. Again, the problem is whether the effects sought by the biblical authors are limited to effects in the past or can be extended to effects for the present. This leads us to consider the situation in which communication takes place.

CONTEXT OF BIBLICAL COMMUNICATION

People always direct their communications to others in a certain situation within a larger social framework. (Awareness of the situation-specific quality of any use of written language for communication, including the Bible, began with the Renaissance and the development of a sense of history in the West.) Even anti-historical, anti-intellectual Americans who manage to finish elementary school are burdened with a sense of history, an awareness that things need not be as they are, nor were they always the way they are. This sense of history is lacking in a society that lacks writing or in a traditional society that changes extremely slowly. With a sense of history, parents can laugh at a child who tells how Joshua, in the story of Israel's conquests in the book of Joshua, drove around the country in a jeep, or the child who understands the biblical maxim "Man does not live by bread alone," to mean one needs peanut butter and jelly as well. Yet these same parents may suspend their sense of history by imagining the values and meanings of the Bible in twentieth century contexts.

Some modern Bible readers get around the problems raised by a sense of history in the Bible by simply claiming that the Bible is full of mystery. They maintain that there are things in the Bible that are beyond our ability to understand. They might claim that these mysteries are things that were obvious to the original receivers of the communication, but make little sense to us in our different situation. Many who seek meaning in a twentieth-century context from a collection of texts dating from the second-century B.C.E. and earlier, make a distinction, often unconsciously, between what the biblical language refers to in its own cultural world and what it might mean to us as modern readers.

When cursed or blessed with a sense of history, people cannot just make the biblical text mean everything, much less anything they might want it to. Neither capitalism nor communism can be found in any real sense in the Bible because both economic systems emerged in human history some 2,000 years after the last book in the Hebrew Bible was written. Historical sense makes us realize that there is no specific historical event after the second century B.C.E. that is mentioned specifically in the Bible.

A sense of history makes the Bible reader aware of differences between the biblical world and one's own, aware of what Thomas Aquinas, the famous thirteenth-century theologian, labeled "literal meaning." To take the Bible *literally* is to take it *historically*. To take any message in the context intended by a sender is always to take it historically or literally. Meanings in history will always be perceived in terms of some social system. Depending upon the social sensitivity of the interpreter, those meanings will be either the meanings of the present day interpreter, reflecting his or her own social system (therefore ethnocentric) or that of the people she or he interprets (hence based on some sort of comparative social approach).

In sum, contemporary communication theory seems to point to the central, crucial position of social systems for an understanding of meaning in texts. Sociolinguistics, sociology, anthropology, and the study of history that is informed by the social sciences all ask more or less the same question: How does human group structure and group behavior circumscribe what and how human beings can perceive, interact, and mean? The modern reader might ask: How does belonging to certain groups make me perceive reality as I do, interpret as I do, and behave as I do? This is not meant to suggest that one's individuality is unimportant. Rather, it is to affirm that there is a "we" dimension to human existence, a social belonging dimension that is as natural as the individualistic aspect. It is on this "we" level that communication takes place. Because of the fundamental social nature of communication, in this guide for the study of the Hebrew Bible, we will often ask about the social location of both the writer and the reader.

We turn now to a consideration of some of the tools that have been developed to facilitate the understanding of the literature in the Hebrew scriptures. We will look at them in the order in which they were developed.

Source Criticism

Besides textual criticism, which seeks to determine the original text as closely as possible, and has thus sometimes been called "lower criticism," historical criticism of the Bible since the Renaissance has developed an array of tools for interpreting the text established. These tools together are sometimes grouped under the label of "higher criticism."

The oldest of these tools is *source criticism*, which attempts to discover the written sources behind the text in the form in which it now exists and to suggest how these sources became part of larger units. Source criticism dominated the historical biblical criticism of the nineteenth and early twentieth centuries and established the framework for much of the subsequent discussion of the literary development of the Hebrew Bible.

It should be noted that none of the sources that source criticism seeks to discover exist as actual written documents (or at least none has yet been found) but exist only in theory. Source criticism began with the study of the Torah, observing the existence of such things as repetition, doublets (twin passages dealing with the same subject), different perspectives or theologies, and contradictions in the text. Based on such observations, the next step was to infer that these phenomena pointed to the existence of multiple sources behind a composite finished product. We will examine some results of source criticism and its current status in Chapter 4.

Form Criticism

While source criticism concentrates on the literary origins of the Hebrew Bible, *form criticism* focuses on the smaller units that make up the larger texts, especially in the oral or preliterary stage of a text. Form critics analyze a text based on its constituent *genres* or peculiar forms. They seek to clarify the form, function, and social setting of such specific small units. The form critic compares all biblical passages that have a similar vocabulary and format and then tries to theorize about the social context within which such speech was at home: Was it the language of the law court, of religious ritual, of the marketplace, and so on?

Form criticism is a tool that can be used to detect the literary types or genres used in the Bible. A literary genre is a category of written composition characterized by a particular style, form, or content. A limerick, for example, is an example of a genre we know, characterized by both a particular form, style, and content—a humorous verse of five lines, in which the first, second, and fifth lines rhyme while the shorter third and fourth lines also rhyme. Limericks originated in a particular *Sitz im Leben* (a German expression meaning "setting in life"), in that they are said to go back to social gatherings where the group sang, "Will you come up to Limerick?" (a town in Ireland) after each set of verses, which were then extemporized in turn by the members of the party.

Form criticism, however, has more to say about human communication than merely pointing out its literary genres. Form criticism is also sensitive to the fact that the type of communication we choose is related to our social circumstances. Society dictates that we adopt one letter form for business correspondence and a different one for a personal letter to a friend. Consequently, when you open your mail and find a business letter, you immediately recognize this genre by the form and style of writing, and you expect a certain kind of content from this letter, content that you would not expect to find in a thank-you note or a postcard from a friend.

The Hebrew Bible is written as the story of the encounter of the people of Israel with their God. We would make a serious error, however, if we were to read every word of that account as if it belonged to a genre we might call documentary history. History is but one of many genres found in the Bible. One cannot read very far into the Hebrew Bible without being struck by its uneven character. Not only does one discover abrupt transitions between poetry and prose, but one becomes aware of subtypes of both poetry and prose. Not only does the Bible consist of a variety of books with different purposes that have been brought together, but within individual books there are a variety of genres that need to be recognized and properly understood. From the perspective of literary forms, the Bible is clearly a composite, although that important fact is constantly forgotten by some biblical interpreters, who operate as if it were of a single genre.

There is a close link between form and content, and once one understands the "rules" of genre, one is better prepared to understand what a text is saying. One should also recognize, however, that Israelite writers, like contemporary ones, sometimes do not play by these rules, but *imitate* genres for particular effect. For example, obviously one must, when reading something like Jonathan Swift's "A Modest Proposal," recognize the fact that Swift is writing satire. Otherwise, his meaning would be missed. Noteworthy as well, Swift duplicates the genre of an economic treatise with all his pretentious style, complete with "facts" and economic figures. So Swift's satirical proposal also imitates the scholarly economic genre—in fact, it is this imitation that makes the satire work, for Swift satirizes those whose style is based on cold, inhuman calculations. We do much the same thing in our everyday language when we borrow genres from a particular sphere of our activity and use them in another way. For example, a person who has been involved in baseball, either as a participant or a fan, might use figures of speech from that game to describe another aspect of life. Thus, when one fails to achieve a goal, he or she might say, "I struck out!" When one is quite successful, the expression might be "She really hit that one out of the park, didn't she!"

Form criticism also deals with how traditional, stereotypical forms are used. A passage might indeed be a genre stemming from a courtroom setting, but it might be used ironically and thus not indicate a primary legal context. When we say something we wish we had not said, we might implore our hearer, in the style of the judge in a courtroom, to "Strike that from the record!" In many ancient Israelite towns, the equivalent of our municipal court was held in the city gate or a public square next to the gate (Amos 5:10; Ruth 4:1). Since many people would be familiar with court procedures and language, when a prophet used the language of the courts, the prophet's hearers obviously understood the seriousness of the accusations being made.

Redaction Criticism

Redaction criticism carries the processes begun by source and form criticism one step further. Redaction criticism focuses on the final stage in the formation of a biblical unit or book, and is concerned with the perspectives and intentions of the redactor/editor as perceived in the way in which that redactor/editor arranged, edited, and expanded upon the sources that were available to him or her. Once the source critic has "excavated" a text and discovered what he or she believes to be the various layers beneath the text's surface, the text consists only of an assortment of disconnected parts. The important question remains, however, about why and how these parts or sources came to be assembled into the whole text. While the Hebrew Bible includes an extraordinary variety of literary units, a significant part of the fascination with the biblical text is that it *is* a single text. What is most significant about the biblical text from a literary point of view is what Robert Alter has called "the composite artistry" of the biblical redactors in making a single unified text out of the many pieces (1981: 131–33, 154). (For example, a loose literary unit such as an anthology is put together based on some editorial criterion, as in an anthology of short stories by women.) Redaction critics ask questions like: According to what editorial viewpoint were source A and source B brought together, even though they seemingly contradict one another? Why were they arranged in a particular order, and so on? Redactors are seen not just as cut-and-paste editors, but as interpreters of the materials out of which they construct a text. Thus, new meaning is given to a variety of materials of differing points of view. The book of Judges, for example, is a kind of anthology of stories about early Israelite tribal heroes, upon which a redactor has imposed an editorial framework to make these originally disconnected stories serve the book's theme.

Sociological Criticism

Sociological criticism is a recent extension of historical criticism that seeks to place texts (and sometimes readers as well) in their appropriate social context. It uses methods and theories from the social sciences to help bridge the gap between our society and the social world of ancient Israel. As persons living in a highly industrialized, technological society, our perspectives on the world have been shaped by sociological factors quite different from those that shaped the worldviews of the people of ancient Israel.

One of the ways that sociological criticism can help us to bridge this gap is by studying, by way of the results of anthropological fieldwork, recent nonindustrialized societies whose patterns of life and social organization are similar to those of the ancient biblical world. The study of these societies can provide useful analogies for understanding social structures and processes in the biblical world.

The contributions of sociological criticism relate to the work of form criticism. As form critics tell us, behind written sources there is sometimes a complex oral tradition that grew up in particular social settings. The more we know, for example, about recent nonliterate societies and the way oral tradition functions there, the better we can understand the functions of the various literary genres in the Hebrew Bible.

Sociological criticism also studies parallels between social institutions and practices in ancient Israel and those of other cultures. Such analysis of the social structures of early, premonarchical Israel has been particularly helpful in enriching our understanding of the history of Israel's settlement in Canaan. It has done this by delineating the interaction of social, political, and religious forces that led to the sociopolitical evolution of Israel from a group of autonomous tribes, through tribal confederacies, to a paramount chiefdom, and finally to a state under a king. We will examine this development in Chapter 9. Beyond shedding light on this early period in Israel's story, sociological criticism has broadened perspectives on the social role of Israel's religious literature and institutions, and has aided in the reconstruction of Israel's history—not just political history as the story of prominent individuals, but also Israel's social history as it was formed from the everyday acts of ordinary men and women.

Tradition Criticism

Modern biblical scholarship recognizes that much of the literature of the Bible came into existence through a process in which oral and written materials were handed down from one generation to another, with successive generations making their own contributions. *Tradition criticism* or tradition history, studies the entire process of change and adaptation of a tradition from its earliest oral stage, through the compilation of written sources, to the final redaction into books as we now have them, and even further through its later use and readaptation by subsequent generations. It is, in some ways, the most comprehensive critical tool, covering as it does the entire "history" of the tradition. As a tool, it is one of the steps of exegesis, attempting to recover the meaning that the handed-down tradition had at each stage in its growth. It follows on source and form criticism, making use of their results. Tradition history has assumed a widely accepted role in biblical exegesis. Its significance lies in the effort to understand the creative process the result of which is the biblical literature. It is very democratic in that it recognizes that many people and groups, not just single authors, made contributions to the process, adapting and applying the traditions they received to make them relevant to their situations.

Literary/Rhetorical Criticism

Literary or *rhetorical criticism* is not interested in how narratives were put together nor in the social or historical context out of which they arose. Literary critics are concerned rather with the literary features of texts. They expose the literary structures and techniques used in fashioning a biblical text through a study of a particular author's use of literary devices. As contrasted with form criticism, which stresses the use of typical forms, rhetorical criticism focuses instead on the distinctive and unique style of a given author.

The literary critic takes a text as it stands, analyzes its characters and the roles they play in the narrative, and looks for the tensions and resolutions of the plot. The literary critic is concerned with literary features such as the following (Holman 1980):

1. *Theme* — the central dominating idea in a text; sometimes explicitly stated but often an abstract concept that is made concrete through its representation in plot structure, character, action, and images. The theme is the central idea of a literary work; it enables readers to relate the work to their own world by providing a point of contact between the text and the life of the reader.

2. *Plot* — the formulation about the relationships existing among the incidents of a narrative; a guiding principle for the author and an ordering control for the reader. Plot focuses life by selecting a few emotions, conflicts, characters, and episodes out of many, and representing them in an orderly way. Plot is the plan of the narrative that makes it interesting.

3. *Climax*—the point of highest interest, the point at which readers make their greatest emotional response, often a turning point in the action.

4. *Denouement* — the unraveling of the plot, the solution of the mystery, the explanation or outcome.

5. *Interlude* — episodes that interrupt the continuity of the main narrative, but often relate to and further the theme of the main narrative.

6. *Characterization* — the revelation of character by exposition—that is, identification, definition, classification, illustration, analysis; by presentation of the character in action and by dialogue.

7. *Symbol* — something that suggests universal meaning; an image that goes beyond the reality it images to suggest other levels of meaning.

A literary critical reading of the Hebrew scriptures discovers a skilled use of language to clarify theme and develop plot. Thematic and symbolic words serve to focus the historical, social, psychological, and religious meanings of the narratives. Such literary features are not, of course, present in all texts. Plot and characterization are common in prose narrative, but missing in proverbs, psalms, and most prophetic oracles, which are expressed in poetic form. Theme, image, and metaphor are more widely present. Everywhere, except perhaps in lists of laws and in genealogies, literary art is present, helping the author to express meaning. Thus the Hebrew scriptures can be viewed as a work of art, or better yet, as an entire art gallery. The Hebrew narratives we will encounter in the pages of the Hebrew Bible are more than a coldly objective chronicling of events; they are the skilled use of literary devices to image an intimate, but at the same time transcendent encounter between a people and their God. This literary art is certainly one of the reasons, in addition to its religious import, that Hebrew Bible literature has had lasting appeal to persons living in all ages.

STUDY QUESTIONS

LITERATURE

Exercise in Determining Dates

1. Give the century, then the millennium, for each of the following dates:

	century	millennium
a. 27 B.C.E.		
b. C.E. 14		
c. C.E. 1492		
d. your birthday		
e. 1290 B.C.E.		
f. 3100 B.C.E.		
g. C.E. 2000		

2. David began his rule as king over Israel ca. 1000 b.c.e. and ruled until his death thirty-nine years later. In what year did his reign end? In what century would you place David's rule? In what millennium?

3. The Northern Kingdom of Israel was conquered by Assyria in 721 B.C.E. The Southern Kingdom of Judah outlasted its sister kingdom by 135 years, when it fell to the Babylonians. In what year was Judah conquered by the Babylonians? In what century was this? Did the fall of Judah occur early or late in that century?

4. If a person was born in the year 40 B.C.E. and lived to be eighty-two years old, what would be the date of her death?

LITERARY GENRES

Part One

1. Write a discription of your home in ways appropriate to the following circumstances:
    A. Describe your home as you would in a real estate advertisement in the classified section of a newspaper.
    B. Describe your home as you would in response to any inquiry from your tax assessor, who is trying to determine your annual property tax.
    C. Describe your home as you would in a letter to a close friend whom you haven't seen in several years.
    D. Describe your home to an architect.

Part Two

2. Now work backwards in determining literary genres. In the left column below, you will find a phrase or sentence that illustrates a common literary genre in use today. In the columns to the right, briefly describe what specifically is being talked about (content) and the specific *social circumstances* in which that genre would be used (context).

	content	context
1. . . . so help me God.	_____	_____
2. Dear Ms. Petersen:	_____	_____
3. . . . and they lived happily ever after.	_____	_____
4. There was a young maid from St. Paul, Who went to a newspaper ball . . .	_____	_____
5. Dear Occupant:	_____	_____
6. four out of five doctors recommend Brand X	_____	_____

7. Read my lips, No New Taxes!   _____   _____
8. Gene Kelly presents three
   new reasons to buy an RCA.   _____   _____
9. He is survived by his wife,
   Sally, two sons, and a brother
   in Tulsa.   _____   _____
10. What has four wheels and
    flies?   _____   _____
11. Dlx, beautiful room, laundry,
    cable, etc. 629-3839 eves.   _____   _____
12. Her dress was trimmed with
    French lace and caught at the
    waist with a satin bow. She
    carried a bouquet of yellow
    roses.   _____   _____

Part Three

In preparing your responses to these questions use a good dictionary or English textbook to define each genre. Then decide whether you think the genre will be written in poetic form or in prose. Finally, turn to the biblical example(s) cited for the genre and determine to what degree it meets the requirements of the genre defined.

1. Allegory: _____ poetry, or _____ prose
   definition:
   Prov 9:1-6; Isa 5:1-7
2. Aphorism: _____ poetry, or _____ prose
   definition:
   Skim the book of proverbs
3. Ancient songs: _____ poetry, or _____ prose
   definition:
   Exod 15:21; Judg 5
4. Autobiography: _____ poetry, or _____ prose
   definition:
   Skim Neh 1-7
5. Biography: _____ poetry, or _____ prose
   definition:
   Jer 26
6. Creed: _____ poetry, or _____ prose
   definition:
   Deut 26:5-10
7. Elegy: _____ poetry, or _____ prose
   definition:
   2 Sam 1:19-27

8. Epic: _____ poetry, or _____ prose
   definition:
   Skim the first two chapters and the last chapter of Job

9. Etiology: _____ poetry, or _____ prose
   definition:
   Gen 32:22-32

10. Didactic narrative: _____ poetry, or _____ prose
    definition:
    Skim the book of Jonah

11. Fable: _____ poetry, or _____ prose
    definition:
    Judg 9:7-15

12. History: _____ poetry, or _____ prose
    definition:
    Skim 1 Kings 1-2

13. Hymn: _____ poetry, or _____ prose
    definition:
    Ps 100; 149; 150

14. Lament: _____ poetry, or _____ prose
    definition:
    Ps 22; 51

15. Law: _____ poetry, or _____ prose
    definition:
    Exod 20:1-17; Lev 19

16. Liturgy: _____ poetry, or _____ prose
    definition:
    Lev 16

17. Prophetic oracle: _____ poetry, or _____ prose
    definition:
    Amos 1-2

18. Parable: _____ poetry, or _____ prose
    definition:
    2 Sam 12:1-4

19. Short story: _____ poetry, or _____ prose
    definition:
    Skim the book of Ruth

THE TOOLS FOR CRITICAL BIBLICAL STUDY

When we interrogate a biblical passage and ask how it functions as a literary piece and what literary devices it uses in order to get across meaning, we are using what scholars call *literary* or *rhetorical criticism.* In this course, we are not just interested in what we think, i.e., intuit, a passage means. Rather, we are interested in learning ways or skills by which we can see *how* meaning is effected.

Literature is in many ways like painting, or sculpture or architecture. Because both artist and writer have the disadvantage (or maybe sometimes the advantage!) of not being present when their works are viewed or read, they build into their work aids to guide their readers or viewers in their appreciation and understanding of what the artist or writer intended. Study a reproduction of Pablo Picasso's painting *Guernica*. Picasso painted *Guernica* to depict his outrage at the suffering inflicted on the inhabitants of the Basque village of Guernica following a saturation bombing raid on the town during the Spanish Civil War. Answer the following questions about the painting.

1. Where does Picasso direct your eye?
2. Now look at the painting's structure. What shape(s) dominate the picture? Trace them with your finger on the picture. Relate this to what you think Picasso is communicating.
3. On the lower left there is a mother and child. How does the position of the two figures relate to the overall meaning of the work? Notice the position of the child in relation to its mother's body.
4. Now list some concrete ways in which a painter can use organization and structure in a work to manipulate your attention and convey meaning.
5. Now think of ways (at least five) a *writer* can guide your attention as a reader. (These are the devices that tell us how a writing functions, how it is to be understood.) The show how each of these five techniques might be used to express a meaning.

writing techniques	meaning
A. _____	_____
B. _____	_____
C. _____	_____
D. _____	_____
E. _____	_____

When we attempt to discern the patterns or structure in a biblical passage, when we analyze how its parts have been put together, and when we relate all of this to the meaning of the passage, then we are practicing rhetorical or literary criticism.

BIBLIOGRAPHY

Alter, Robert. 1981. *The Art of Biblical Narrative*. New York: Basic Books.

Bruce, F. F. 1978. *History of the Bible in English: From the Earliest Version*, 3rd ed. New York: Oxford.

Childs, Brevard. 1985. *An Introduction to the Old Testament as Scripture*. Philadelphia: Fortress.

Gottwald, Norman K. 1985. *The Hebrew Bible: A Socio-Literary Introduction*. Philadelphia: Fortress.

Holman, C. 1980. *A Handbook to Literature*, 4th ed. Indianapolis: Bobbs-Merrill.

Rogerson, John and Philip Davies. 1989. *The Old Testament World*. Englewood Cliffs, NJ: Prentice-Hall.

Chapter 2

THE LAND AND PEOPLE OF THE HEBREW BIBLE

THE GEOGRAPHY AND ECOLOGY OF THE LAND

"Keep, then, this entire commandment that I am commanding you today, so that you may have strength to go in and occupy the land that you are crossing over to occupy, and so that you may live long in the land that the Lord swore to your ancestors to give them and to their descendants, a land flowing with milk and honey. For the land that you are about to enter to occupy is not like the land of Egypt, from which you have come, where you sow your seed and irrigate by foot, like a vegetable garden. But the land that you are crossing over to occupy is a land of hills and valleys, watered by rain from the sky, a land that the Lord your God looks after." (Deut 11:8-12)

The connection between a land and a people is a vital one, as has been evidenced throughout history and is still evident today in contemporary struggles for national liberation and ethnic identity in our world. In this speech by Moses to the twelve tribes of Israel, he describes the longed-for land that they were about to enter, a land that is first of all seen as the land that was promised to their ancestors centuries earlier.

The land is then described as one "flowing with milk and honey," a description of the land in terms of what would be its economic base throughout all of the biblical period: milk, representing the products of the herder of sheep and goats, and honey representing one of the by-products of the farmer, who cultivated fruit and olive trees and thereby attracted the honeybee with the trees' blossoms. This land of promise is then contrasted with Egypt, the land of bondage, again in a way that is related to an agriculturally-based economy. Egyptian agriculture was irrigation-based, dependent upon the Nile River as an unfailing source of water for crops—thus the reference to a land "irrigated by foot," an allusion to the foot-operated irrigation devices that lifted water out of the Nile into irrigation canals. In contrast to Egypt, the land of promise is one that is almost totally dependent upon rainfall agriculture, a compelling symbol of the people's dependence upon God for rain and, therefore, basic sustenance.

This land of God's promise, this Holy Land, was to be known by various names as its political status underwent profound changes during ancient Near Eastern history. These names are surveyed below, roughly in the order in which they came into use.

1. One of the earliest names of the region was *Canaan*, after the name of its principal inhabitants, the Canaanites, who were a people made up of several subgroups.

2. *Israel* was the name given to this area after it was settled by a people bearing that name, a people who called themselves Israel because they saw themselves as descended from Jacob (whose name was changed to Israel according to Gen 32:27–28) and his twelve sons, who were the "fathers" of the twelve tribes of Israel. Later, this same name, Israel, was used as the name of a separate kingdom in the northern part of the land, a kingdom that existed for two hundred years, from the time of Solomon's death (922 B.C.E.) until the Assyrian conquest in 722/21 B.C.E., which had its capital at Samaria.

3. *Judah* was the name of the southern part of this region (Judah being the name of one of Jacob/Israel's sons and of the largest tribe in the south). It was also the name of the southern kingdom ruled by the descendants of David in a hereditary monarchy, which existed from 922 to 586 B.C.E., when it fell to the Babylonians. Jerusalem, the capital of the kingdom, was the major city in this region.

4. The region was called *Palestine* in the Hellenistic era (beginning with the conquests of Alexander the Great in the fourth century B.C.E., because the Philistines (in Greek, *Palaistino*), one of a group of peoples, collectively

known as the Sea Peoples, who emigrated from the Aegean area and settled in the southern coastal plain in the thirteenth century B.C.E., were known to the Greeks before the interior Jewish communities were known to them. The ancient Greek historian Herodotus was the first to use *Palaistene,* the Hellenistic form of Philistia, in the inclusive sense.

5. *Judea* is a geographical name that is initially attested in Ezra, Nehemiah, and Maccabees, denoting the postexilic Jewish state. After Persian rule had given way to Macedonian in the fourth century B.C.E., Judea strove for independence. Maccabean rulers won extensive territorial holdings, including Samaria and Galilee, Idumea to the south, much of the coastal plain, and Perea to the east. Judea is related to the term *Yehudi,* or Jews, residents of Judea.

Physical Structure of the Land

The topography of this land is characterized by six strips, placed side by side and running from north to south, as shown in Figure 2.1. On the west is the *coastal plain,* broad in the south and quite narrow in the north (area 1 in figure 2.1). The Mediterranean coast south of Mount Carmel has no natural harbors; thus neither the Israelites nor their predecessors were seafaring peoples, and most of the images relating to the sea in the Hebrew Bible are ones that evoke terror or awe.

The next one of these longitudinal strips (area 2 in Figure 2.1) is only a partial one, and separates part of the coastal plain from the hill country of Judah. This region is called the *Shephelah,* a term referring to the foothills leading up to the central hill country. As the name implies, this is a transitional area between the coastal plain and the central hill country.

The third strip (area 3 in Figure 2.1) is the *central hill country,* which runs like a backbone through the middle of the land. It consists of rugged mountains in the northern part of the area and a high plateau in the south, an area called the Negev. It is, in many ways, the most important of the six strips in the narratives of the Hebrew Bible (in that it sees the most action), and is also the most varied. The central hill country can be subdivided into three main areas: (a) the Galilee in the north; (b) the Samaria and Bethel hills in the center; and (c) the Hebron hills in the south. This central hill country is broken from east to west in a major way at only one spot, the valley of Jezreel (or Esdraelon), which is really a large triangular plain about 20 x 50 miles in size. This valley constitutes the only major clear passageway from the coastal plain to the Jordan valley.

The fourth strip (area 4 in Figure 2.1) is the *rift valley,* through which the Jordan River flows. This valley, called the Arabah in its southern extension below the Dead Sea, is part of the great Syro-African rift, a geological fault in the earth's surface that extends from Syria in the north to Tanzania in Africa in the south. It includes the lowest place on the earth's surface, the surface of the Dead Sea, which is some 1,300 feet (400 meters) below sea level, with the bottom of the

Figure 2.1   Regions in Palestine

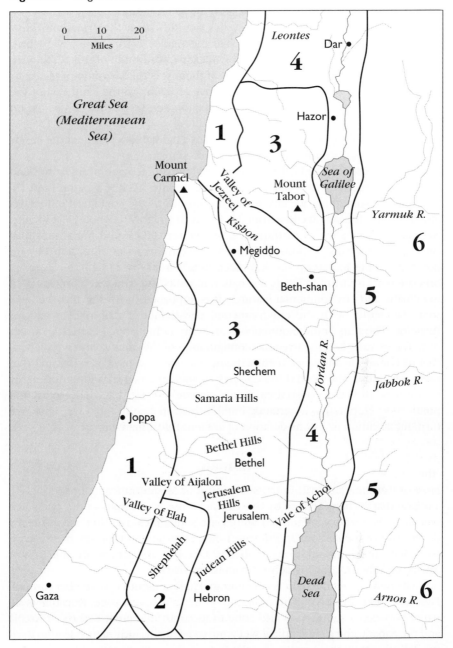

Dead Sea, in its northern end, being another 1,300 feet deep. Even the Sea of Galilee, which is also in the rift valley, is about 700 feet below sea level.

On the east side of the rift valley lies the fifth strip, the *Transjordanian plateau,* (area 5 in Figure 2.1). Opposite the Galilee is the region of Bashan. South of the Yarmuk River is the area of Gilead. To the south of this is the territory of the Ammonites, and to the south of them was the kingdom of Moab. At the southern end of this strip is the territory of Edom, to the southeast of the Dead Sea (on the Ammonites, Moabites and Edomites, see the section below on "The People of the Hebrew Bible").

The sixth strip (area 6 in Figure 2.1) is not a habitable region, but the *desert* that extends eastward into what is now Saudi Arabia.

Within these longitudinal zones exists a variety of geographical features and microenvironments with their own climatic regimes. While weather and climate may be something we talk about, for most of us the ecological milieu has little effect on the way we live from day to day in a highly technological society. Natural disasters such as earthquakes, floods, tornadoes, and hurricanes may cause temporary dislocations and considerable human suffering, but they do not threaten our long-term survival. Accordingly, it may be difficult for us to appreciate what it meant to live in a situation in which survival was closely related to climatic and environmental features. It is important, however, that we have some familiarity with the environmental constraints of daily life in ancient Palestine. The soils in the mountainous areas are rather poor, perennial sources of water are rare, and the irregular configuration of hills and valleys were obstacles to communication between settlements. The system of dry farming that predominated in the central hill country of ancient Israel developed primarily in response to water constraints. While climate did not determine social and political developments, it certainly limited them in significant ways. Thus, we turn our attention to a consideration of ancient Palestinian climate.

Climate

Most of Palestine falls within the subtropical or Mediterranean climatic region, a region that is characterized by two distinct seasons per year—a dry one and a wet one (the terms summer and winter are sometimes used but are not really descriptive of the seasons in Palestine). The rainy season typically begins with some light precipitation in September or October, and tapers off in March or April (see Table 2.1, The Israelite Agricultural Year).

The bulk of precipitation is concentrated in four months, November through February. Being on the northern margin of the subtropical zone, Palestine is situated between a subtropical arid zone to its south, the great deserts of Arabia and the Sahara, and a subtropical wet zone to its north. Although Palestine itself is relatively small, this location results in some marked climatic differences between the northern and southern regions of the area, with considerable variations in weather from one year to the next.

TABLE 2.1   The Israelite Agricultural Year

HEBREW MONTHS (LUNAR)	OUR MONTHS (SOLAR)	HARVESTS	FESTIVALS/ AGRICULTURAL ACTIVITIES
Nisan	March–April	Barley	Festival of Passover & Unleavened Bread
Iyyar	April–May		Vine tending
Sivan	May–June	Wheat	Festival of Weeks/Pentecost (50 days after Passover)
Tammuz	June–July		
Av	July–August		
Elul	August–September	Grapes and Figs	
Tishri	September–October		Festival of Booths/Tabernacles Sowing of cereals
Marchesvan	October–November	Olives	Plowing and grain sowing
Kislev	November–December		
Tevet	December–January		
Shevat	January–February		
Adar	February–March		

One of the principal meteorological factors influencing the uncertainty of the Palestinian climate is the shifting global system of high- and low-pressure areas (Figure 2.2). During the dry season, Palestine sits on the western edge of an extensive low pressure area that is centered over India (the cause of the Indian monsoons) and extends over the Persian Gulf and Mesopotamia. There is also a secondary low centered over Cyprus. As the air circulates in a counter-clockwise direction around the Indian low, and is in turn deflected by the Cyprus low, the resulting air flow over Palestine is from northwest to southeast, bringing what was known to the ancient Greeks as the "etesian winds," which were filled with moisture.

The wet season commences when this entire system of low pressure areas is displaced southward by a shift in the path of the jet stream, which brings Palestine into the zone of the westerlies of the temperate zone, with its cy-clonic storms—units of low barometric pressure with circular, counterclock-wise air flow. These cyclonic storm systems move eastward toward Palestine following the path of a low-pressure trough in the Mediterranean, which is situ-ated between one high pressure area in Central Asia and another in the Sahara. As these cyclones (there are about twenty-five in an average year) travel across the Mediterranean (usually in four to six days), they are reinforced by the

Figure 2.2   Lows in the Eastern Mediterranean

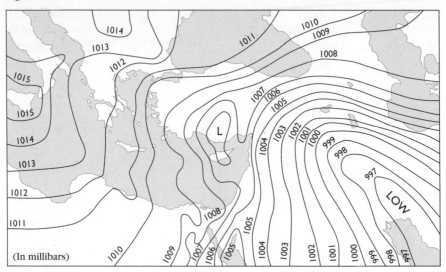

confluence of warm African air with cooler European air, producing unstable conditions in the atmosphere, commonly resulting in rainfall.

A second factor affecting Palestinian climate, especially with respect to sunlight intensity and temperature, is its distance from the equator, which determines both the amount of heat from the sun and the moderate seasonal variations in the length of daylight hours. Palestine lies between 31 degrees 15 minutes and 33 degrees 15 minutes north latitude, approximately equivalent to southern California.

With the stable conditions of the dry (summer) season (typically, April through September), Palestine is typically sunny and warm. There are *no* completely overcast days in the summer, and only a fourth of the summer days are partly cloudy, with fair-weather clouds. Summer sunshine hours may approach close to 98 percent of the possible. Even in the winter season this figure remains at 50 percent, which is higher than either Western Europe or eastern North America. The latitude also means that the sun strikes the ground at a high angle, as high as 80 degrees during the dry season.

Palestine's general temperature patterns are also products of its latitude. While temperatures vary within the area from north to south and depend upon regional topography and distance from the sea as well, they are generally comparatively high. Highest temperatures normally occur in August and the lowest are in January in all the longitudinal strips.

Palestine's geographic position at the southeastern corner of the Mediterranean, where the sea is in close proximity to the desert, and between the Sahara and Arabian Deserts on the one hand and the Russo-Siberian plains on the other, greatly influences its climate. Local winds are generated by differ-

Figure 2.3   Rainfall Map

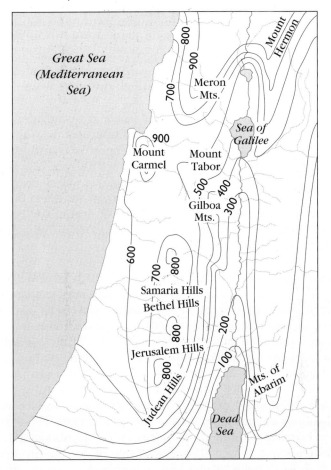

ences in temperature at the border of water and land masses. Land warms more quickly than the sea during the day and cools more rapidly at night. Therefore, there are ordinarily offshore winds at night and onshore winds during the day. The onshore breeze is stronger and more persistent than the offshore breeze in the summer, due to the low over the Persian Gulf. Rainfall tends to decrease and the temperature range tends to increase with distance from the sea (Figure 2.3).

REGIONAL VARIATIONS

While climatic contrasts between the southern and northern parts of the area are largely explained by Palestine's global position, other differences in weather within the area are due to the differences in the regions mentioned above, whose lines of relief run in a north-south direction, at right angles to the movement of

the cyclonic storms. Rainfall distribution is decisively influenced by landscape relief because air ascending a slope cools, while its relative humidity increases.
Descending air warms and decreases in humidity. While the general rule is that
rainfall decreases with distance from the sea, an increase in elevation changes
this. While there is a general decrease in precipitation in the area from north to
south and there are other variations within each region from north to south, the
general climatic patterns of the regions can be described as follows:

The Coastal Plain.   Including the central section of the valley of Jezreel, this
area is naturally greatly influenced by the sea. Throughout the year, the relative
humidity is high and the twenty-four hour temperature range (about 13 degrees) is considerably less than it is in the Central Highlands. Because the average temperature in January is 55 degrees, both snow and frost are quite rare in
this region. The sirocco (see Transitional Seasons, p. 48) is less frequent here
than in other parts of the country. Rainfall is both heavier and begins earlier
than inland. Rainfall also increases from an average of ten inches annually in the
south to 32 inches in the north of this region.

The Central Highlands.   Including Mount Carmel, this region has lower relative humidity than the coast and both the daily and annual temperature ranges
are greater. Its level of precipitation is the highest west of the Jordan, though
the onset of the rainy season occurs later than on the coast. Due to considerable
variations in topography, however, the rainfall map in the highlands shows
significant variability within the region. Both frost and snowfall are common in
the higher elevations.

The Jordan Rift Valley.   Both in the rain shadow on the lee side of the
Central Highlands and below sea level in most of its length, this valley endures
sharply decreased precipitation from that in the highlands and markedly
warmer temperatures as well. The general rule of decrease in precipitation
from north to south holds for this region, but there are other differences as
well. The northern part of this region has a large annual temperature range,
with frost common in the winter and long, hot summers. To the south around
the Dead Sea, the lowest spot on earth is surrounded by mountains on the east
and west, and thus has unique climatic conditions. The relative humidity stays
quite low but is modified somewhat by the extremely high evaporation rate of
water from the Dead Sea, which results from the high temperatures. The annual
mean temperature at the southern end of the Dead Sea is 78 degrees, and falls to
only 62.5 degrees in January. The highest temperature ever recorded in Palestine, 124 degrees, was recorded here. Precipitation amounts are the lowest in
Palestine, less than five inches annually.

The Transjordanian Plateau.   The climate of this region generally resembles that of the central highlands. There are, however, differences caused by its
higher elevation and greater distance from the sea. The seaward slopes of these

higher elevations see more rainfall than do the central highlands. The annual and daily temperature ranges are also greater. Frost and snow are more common.

WET AND DRY SEASONS

While the terms summer and winter are used to describe the seasons in the temperate zone, they are not as descriptive of the seasons in Palestine as are the terms dry season and wet season. As an indicator of seasonality, temperature variation is not as marked as is the sharp shift in rainfall. In the Bible the season called *horef* is one of rainy, stormy weather (Lev 26:4; Deut 11:14; Isa 4:6; 25:4; Job 37:9; Ezra 10:9, 13; Song 2:11). The word *setav,* another meteorological term in Hebrew (which occurs only once in the Bible, Song 2:11), is the same as the Arabic, *sita,* which in the dialect of Arabic spoken in Jerusalem is the common word for rain as well as winter.

The rainy season begins first in the northern part of the area, usually mid-October, and ends there last in the spring, usually March. About 70 percent of the rainfall in Palestine falls from November to February, with January being both the wettest and the coldest month. There are significant differences in rainfall patterns as well as amounts in the different regions. The Coastal Plain receives 50 percent of its annual rainfall by early January, the Central Highlands attain that figure about the end of January, and the Transjordanian plateau only in February. At the beginning and end of the rainy season come what the Bible speaks of as "the early rain" and "the later rain" (Deut 11:11, 14; Ps 84:6; Joel 2:23. Jer 5:24 speaks of the "autumn rain and the spring rain"). Especially important for farming is the date of the initial rainfall that marks the end of the dry season and the date of the last rain. The former is needed to prepare the soil for plowing and the latter influences the maturation of crops. Rain at the end of the season, if the timing is right and not too late, serves to bring cereal crops to successful maturation, especially wheat. But such rains, if too late, can easily devastate barley, which is particularly susceptible to rain during harvest. Such rain during the harvest season is a rare occurrence. In 1 Sam 12:17, Samuel says: "Is it not wheat harvest today? I will call to YHWH [the Israelite personal name for God, often spelled out as Yahweh. See Chapter 7 for a discussion of the meaning of this name] and he will give thunder and rain . . ." When the prophet successfully called for rain in a normally dry period, his prophetic credentials were confirmed.

To such variations in the temporal distribution of rainfall in a season must be added significant variations from one year to the next. A dry year in a series of more or less normal years or of wet ones rarely has serious consequences for the farming economy. But while the farmer can weather a single dry year, a series of such years can be disastrous. A three-year figure is used to describe the disastrous drought in the time of Elijah (1 Kings 18:1): "After many days the word of the LORD came to Elijah, in the third year of the drought, saying, 'Go, present yourself to Ahab; I will send rain on the earth.'"

While the annual amount of rainfall in farming areas in Palestine roughly approximates that of some agricultural areas in temperate zones, the difference between the two lies not in the annual amount of rain, but in the number of rainy days and in the intensity of rainfall in a given hour or day. A rain day, in international terminology, is one in which there is at least 0.1 mm of rainfall. Thus, while Jerusalem and London have about the same average annual rainfall (22 inches), London has over 300 rain days while Jerusalem has only 50. The number of rain days per season (like the amount of annual rainfall) decreases from north to south and from west to east. Rain also tends to be concentrated within a few hours of the day, with sunny intervals between showers. The heaviest showers tend to occur at the beginning and toward the end of the season when there are clashing air masses that differ considerably in temperature and moisture. The net result of these patterns is high intensity rainfall, resulting in increased runoff and, consequently, frequent flash flooding.

The dry season typically begins in May or June and lasts until September, with three to four *completely* rainless months. Although the air moving into Palestine from the Mediterranean is moisture-laden, during this season rain cloud formation is inhibited by the presence of high pressure in the upper atmosphere.

Although rainfall is not triggered during the dry season, the steady, moist westerly winds do bring dew, the formation and amount of which are dependent on both relative humidity and nighttime cooling, as well as on the properties of the cooling surfaces of soil and vegetation upon which the dew falls. Dew falls on nights when the soil becomes cooler than the air with which it comes into contact. The number of such nights increases as one travels southward in the coastal plain where the moisture-laden air from the sea is coupled with the cool nights caused by the nearby desert. Dewfall is important for agriculture, especially in the southern Coastal Plain, where melons can be grown as a typical dry season crop. The presence and value of dew are frequently mentioned in the Bible (Gen 27:28; Deut 33:28; Judg 6:38; 2 Sam 1:21; 1 Kings 17:1; Isa 18:4; Hos 14:5; Mic 5:7; Zech 8:12; Hag 1:10; Job 29:19).

TRANSITIONAL SEASONS

Palestine does not have a spring and fall in the sense of seasons as they are known in the temperate zones, but two short, irregular transitional periods that fall between the dry and rainy seasons and are characterized by their own weather patterns. These periods typically last about six weeks, with one occurring from early April to mid-June, the second from mid-September to the end of October. These transitional periods are clearly demarcated from the dry season and merge into the wet season, there being some overlap with the end of the rainy season in April–May and with its beginning in September–October.

Two distinctive meteorological phenomena characterize these transitional seasons, the sirocco and desert storms. The name sirocco is derived from the Arabic term *sharqiyyeh,* meaning an east wind, and is known in Egypt by the name *khamsin* and in modern Israel as a *sharav,* although these terms do not always refer to precisely the same conditions and thus are not strictly interchangeable.

The sirocco proper (or true *khamsin*) which occurs sporadically during the transitional seasons, is characterized by dry, hot, stagnant air, and strong dust-carrying east winds blowing across Palestine from the Arabian desert (cf. Ezek 12:10; 19:12). During a sirocco, which may last from two or three days to three weeks, temperatures may rise rapidly by as much as 16–22 degrees, with a corresponding lessening of the difference in temperatures during the day and at night. Relative humidity can drop by as much as 40 percent, and the air becomes filled with very fine dust. Although the average maximum daily temperature typically occurs in August, the record high temperatures for the area have been recorded in May and June during a sirocco. In such conditions, people with heart conditions, nervous complaints, or sinus trouble are particularly affected, but even the mildest-tempered person may become irritable. Biblical references to the sirocco and its affects on people are frequent (Isa 27:8; 40:6–8; Ezek 17:10; Hos 12:1; 13:15; Ps 103:16; Job 37:16–17).

LANDS AND PEOPLES OF THE ANCIENT NEAR EAST

Geographical Setting

While most of the Hebrew Bible is set on the stage of Palestine, one must also view Palestine in its larger geographical setting in the ancient Near East. The nations and peoples with whom Israel shared the ancient Near East helped to shape Israel's history and culture. Israel simply cannot be understood in isolation. Due to its position between the two early centers of civilization in the ancient world—Mesopotamia (from a Greek term meaning "between the rivers"), the area between the Tigris and Euphrates rivers, and Egypt, which was based on the Nile River, and its location south of the states that flourished in Asia Minor—Palestine served as a land bridge.

Palestine, with Mesopotamia and Egypt, made up what has been called the "Fertile Crescent." [see Figure 2.4, The Fertile Crescent] This name for the area was first used by James H. Breasted, a renowned Egyptologist. The population of the ancient Middle East was concentrated in this relatively fertile area, and the two areas on either end of the fertile crescent gave rise to the powerful empires of the ancient world—Assyria and Babylonia in Mesopotamia and Egypt in the Nile valley. A striking feature of the land area of ancient Babylonia, Assyria, Syria, Israel, and the kingdoms east of the Jordan Valley is the distinction between fertile land and desert. In Babylonia and Assyria fertility was mainly dependent on the Euphrates and Tigris rivers and their tributaries. Egypt was known as "the gift of the Nile." In Israel, as we have seen above, fertility depended upon rainfall and springs. Because patterns of human settlement were dependent upon cultivable land, Israel functioned as a land bridge because travel across the desert, especially before the domestication of the camel, was next to impossible.

Figure 2.4   The Ancient Near East with the Fertile Crescent

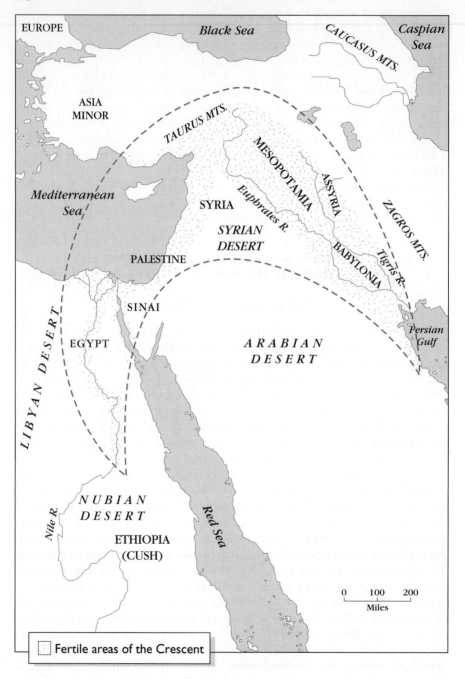

Surrounding Nations

The area surrounding Israel in the ancient Near East included those nations that bordered on Israel, as well as those empires, mentioned in the previous paragraph, whose imperialistic expansion extended into Israel's territory in the period of the Hebrew Bible. Israel's near neighbors included states east of the Jordan River: Aram, or Syria, to the northeast, and Ammon, Moab, and Edom to the east and southeast. The people who lived in these areas were Semites, like the Israelites, so the Bible traces their ancestry back to Abraham. In Genesis, Aram (Syria) is traced back to a grandson of Nahor, Abraham's brother (Gen 22). Both Ammon's and Moab's origins stem from Lot's sons, born of an incestuous sexual liaison with one of his daughters (Gen 19); Edom is identified with Esau, Jacob's twin brother (Gen 36).

Powerful Nations

The empires of which Israel became a part during its history as narrated in the Hebrew Bible are (in the order in which they appear in history) the Assyrian, Babylonian, and Persian. In the fourth century B.C.E., the Macedonian Empire (with its successors, the Ptolemaic and Seleucid) extended into Palestine (as narrated in the apocryphal book of 1 Maccabees). In the first century B.C.E., the Roman Empire included Palestine. Throughout much of the second millennium B.C.E., Palestine was under Egypt's influence. Assyrian imperialistic expansion began early in the first millennium B.C.E., followed by the Babylonian empire. The northern kingdom of Israel fell to the Assyrians in the eighth century B.C.E. and the southern kingdom of Judah fell to the Babylonians at the beginning of the sixth century B.C.E. The Persian empire controlled the ancient Near East from the sixth to the fourth centuries B.C.E., near the end of the period of history covered by the Hebrew Bible. By the end of the second century B.C.E., when the Persian empire had been replaced by the Macedonian, all of the books of the Hebrew Bible had been written.

THE PEOPLE OF THE HEBREW BIBLE

As we make our way through the Hebrew Bible, we shall encounter several peoples with whom Israel had relationships, friendly and unfriendly. For now, we can introduce some of those who play a significant role. This list is not exhaustive, but includes most of the "major players."

Canaanites

Canaanites were a group of peoples who together made up the non-Israelite population of the land of Canaan. The term Canaan derives from an East Semitic (Akkadian) term *kinahhu,* meaning purple dye, which was extracted from the Mediterranean murex shell. The Canaanites were not one racial or ethnic group, but were made up of an uncertain number of subgroups, which are listed in several places in the Hebrew Bible (Gen 10:15; 15:19; Deut 7:1; Josh 3:10). As we shall discover in Chapter 3, the distinction between "Israelite" and "Canaanite" based on material culture, is a difficult one for archaeologists to make. Canaanites were in the land before the formation of the Israelite state, and were still there after it. The Canaanites themselves never formed a unified political state. The term Amorites is sometimes used, in special ways, to designate these peoples in the Bible. Lying behind the term Amorite is the Akkadian word *Amurru,* which is used in Mesopotamian texts as a reference to "Westerners." The *Amurru* were found in most of the fertile crescent at the end of the third millennium B.C.E.

Phoenicians

The Phoenicians were Israel's neighbors to the north. Undoubtedly the Phoenicians of the biblical period were a part of the Canaanites culturally and ethnically. The Hebrew Bible makes no distinction between the people who lived on the northern coastal strip and those who occupied inland Canaan or Palestine—they are all Canaanites (see Gen 10:15–18; Josh 5:1; 2 Sam 24:6–7; Isa 23:11). At the beginning of the second millennium they were trading out of Palestinian harbors. The coastal city of Tyre, in what today is Lebanon, became their most important center at about the same time that the Israelites established themselves in Palestine. From this center in Tyre, the Phoenicians spread southward into Palestine, whose culture bore the stamp of the Phoenicians. They are mentioned in the Hebrew Bible as making political alliances with David and Solomon, and Solomon is said to have hired a Phoenician architect to design the temple in Jerusalem (2 Sam 5:11; 1 Kgs 5:1 ff.; 7:13 ff.).

Philistines

A third major population element in Canaan was the Philistines, one of the "Sea Peoples" who migrated to the southwest coastal plain of Palestine from their home in Crete or Asia Minor after failing in their attempt to settle in Egypt. This migration occurred *ca.* 1200 B.C.E., at about the same time the Israelites were establishing themselves in the country. They lived in five major cities: Ashkelon, Ashdod, Ekron, Gath, and Gaza. From these cities in the coastal plain, they expanded into the highlands where they came into conflict with the Israelites. They also expanded northward up the coastal plain, through the Jezreel valley, and established a presence at Beth-shean. The Philistine expansion has often been cited as a reason for the formation of the Israelite state. We shall return to this question in Chapter 9. The Philistine threat was not dealt with decisively until the time of David.

Amorites

For a long time scholars thought that Amorites, Canaanites, and others were many different peoples who inhabited pre-Israelite Palestine. The diversity of these peoples was attributed either to their speech, deriving from different linguistic sources, or to their having come into Palestine at different times. Recently it has become clear that linguistically, "Canaanite" is a local derivation of "Amorite" and that cultural elements known from archaeology and associated with the Canaanites are a local development of elements that can be traced back to the Amorites. Thus, most scholars now maintain that the Amorites and Canaanites should not be separated into two peoples, whether by origin, culture, or date of arrival.

When the word "Amorite" is encountered in the Hebrew Bible, it may be interchangeable with "Canaanite." The use of one term rather than the other is due to the preference of an author or the tradition on which he depends. Source criticism of the Pentateuch (see Chapter 4) has generally assumed that the use of "Amorite" was preferred by the Elohist tradition (E) and the word "Canaanite" by the Yahwist tradition (J). All Hebrew Bible references to the Amorites have one characteristic in common—the reference is always to a people living in the past. The present knows Philistines, Arameans, Moabites, Edomites, Assyrians, and Egyptians. It does not know Amorites, who did not correspond to any historical reality at the time when the Hebrew Bible was composed.

Moabites and Edomites

Israel's near neighbors to the south and east were the Moabites and Edomites. Biblical evidence for the early Moabites and Edomites is sparse and debatable. The Israelites thought of the Moabites as closely connected with the Ammonites (see Gen 19:30 ff.; Deut 23:3; Neh 13:1). Edom, however, is always thought of apart from Moab and Ammon, and is described as a "brother" to Israel through Esau, the brother of Jacob (see Gen 25:30). Traditionally, Edom had kings before Israel had them. According to Num 20:14, "Moses sent messengers from Kadesh to the king of Edom . . ." Edom and Moab were problems for Israel until they were reduced to vassaldom by David (2 Sam 8:2, 12 ff).

Little is known about the religious and cultural life of Moab and Edom. In the Hebrew Bible the Moabites are called the "people of (the god) Chemosh" (Num 21:29). The inscription on the Mesha Stele (see Chapter 10) tells of the building of a "high place" (that is, a worship place) for Chemosh and says that booty and prisoners could be devoted to Chemosh. Solomon is said to have made a high place for Chemosh outside Jerusalem (1 Kgs 11:7, 33). The Edomite religion is barely mentioned in the Hebrew Bible. Edom was known for its "wisdom" (cf. Jer 49:7; Obad 8), presumably the same kind that was known elsewhere in the ancient Near East. Any religious insights peculiar to Edom and Moab have only survived through the medium of the biblical tradition and are not clearly discernible there.

Arameans

The Bible notes a kinship of Arameans with the Hebrew patriarchs: "A wandering Aramean was my ancestor; he went down into Egypt and lived there as an alien . . ." (Deut 26:5). It also records a checkered history of relationships between the two peoples in later times. The Aramaic language is used in parts of the biblical books of Ezra and Daniel and remained in everyday use among Jews for over a thousand years.

In Egyptian sources, Aram is mentioned as a place name in Syria, to Israel's north. An obscure reference in Amos 9:7 traces the origins of the Arameans to a place called Kir (cf. also Amos 1:5). In the "Table of Nations" (Gen 10:22-23), Aram is viewed as descending directly from Shem, as does Israel. By *ca.* 1100 B.C.E. Arameans were present not only in Syria, but in the northern Transjordan (the area east of the Jordan River). It was only with the rise of the monarchy in Israel, however—late in the eleventh century B.C.E.—that conflict broke out between the Arameans and the Israelites.

The kingdom of Aram, which was centered in Damascus, became the foremost Aramean state in Syria in the ninth-eighth centuries B.C.E. This state is sometimes simply referred to in the Bible as Damascus. The rise of this powerful Aramean state was facilitated by the power vacuum caused by the division of the united Israelite monarchy into two rival states. Aramean pressure on northern Israel increased to the point of threatening its very existence.

Of the few traces of Aramean culture that have survived, the Aramaic language and its script are the outstanding ones. The spread of Aramaic in the ancient Near East was due in part to the simplicity of the script in which it was written, especially in contrast to the complex non-alphabetic cuneiform (from a term meaning "wedge-shaped") scripts of the Assyrians and Babylonians. Aramaic played an important role in facilitating international diplomacy and commerce. The spread of the language was furthered by large-scale population movements: mass deportations of Arameans by the Assyrians, their service in the Assyrian army and administration, and their widespread commercial activities.

Assyrians

In Gen 10:10-12 the origins of the Assyrians is connected to the cultural influence of "Shinar," a term representing what is today southern Iraq. The primary strength of Assyria derived from the strength of its agricultural economy. From their base in Mesopotamia the Assyrians began expanding westward, beginning with the reign of their king Adan-nirari II (911-891 B.C.E.) Under their king Shalmaneser III (858-824 B.C.E.) Assyria's contacts with the eastern Mediterranean region were intensified. The threat of Assyrian expansion affected all states of Syria and Palestine and induced them to forge a coalition to halt the aggressor, bringing about the first direct contact between Assyria and Israel. In 853 B.C.E. there was, according to Shalmaneser's annals, a major battle at Qarqar on the Orontes River in which Ahab the king of Israel was involved (see Chapter 10). Under Shalmaneser V (727-722 B.C.E.) the Israelite capital, Samaria, fell to the Assyrians in 722-721 B.C.E.

The surviving southern kingdom of Judah came under intense Assyrian pressure in the time of Sennacherib, who laid siege to Jerusalem at the end of the eighth century B.C.E. (see Chapter 12). The Assyrian menace for Israel was only relieved when the Assyrians were defeated by the Babylonians at Carchemish in 605 B.C.E.

The significance of the Assyrians for the Hebrew Bible does not stem solely from their having been the predominant military and political power during the crucial centuries of the Israelite monarchy. The Assyrians also had considerable cultural influence. A good deal is known about Assyrian religion. As in Israel, so in Assyria the form of gods and goddesses was conceived in an anthropomorphic way, although some were symbolized by heavenly bodies. Ishtar, for example, was represented by the planet Venus and is referred to as the "Queen of Heaven" in Jeremiah (44:17, 25). In the religion of Assyria there were various means of gaining access to the will of the gods. Some of these are comparable to techniques known from the Hebrew Bible. Divination was one of these (see Chapter 15). Some evidence suggests that the Assyrians also knew of a phenomenon corresponding to the function of the prophets in the Hebrew Bible.

Babylonians

Babylonia is a flat, alluvial plain between the Tigris and Euphrates Rivers, about 300 miles long. Human occupation of this region was almost totally dependent on irrigation agriculture because its rainfall is insufficient for dry agriculture. There are three points at which the stories of the Babylonians and those of Israel meet. The first is Abraham's origin in "Ur of the Chaldees" (Gen 11:27–31, see Chapter 5). The second contact point was much later. Merodach-Baladan, King of Babylon, sent a diplomatic mission to king Hezekiah of Judah in the closing years of the eighth century B.C.E. (2 Kgs 20:12 ff.; Isa 39:1 ff.). The third point of contact is the Babylonian exile under Nebuchadnezzar II. Nebuchadnezzar dates the fall of Jerusalem in his chronicles to the second day of the month of Adar in his seventh year, which in our calendar corresponds to March 16, 597 B.C.E.

Culturally, the Babylonians contributed much to the ancient Near East. Many Babylonian documents are known to us. Babylonian literature in the strict sense is represented by myths, legends, and epics concerning historical events. The most famous Babylonian text is the *Enuma Elish*, their epic of creation (see Chapter 4). This poem celebrates the rise of Marduk, the city god of Babylon, to his position as head of the Babylonian pantheon. Marduk became known as Bel, "the lord," and is mentioned three times in the Hebrew prophets by this name: Isa 46:1; Jer 50:2; 51:44). Babylonian religion had nothing that corresponded to sacrifice among the Hebrews and Canaanites. Their cultic buildings were of two kinds: temples (a rectangular structure with the entrance on the long side and the statue of the deity on a platform at one end) and ziggurats (a kind of stepped pyramid with a shrine on top).

Egyptians

All of the peoples that we have discussed so far were Semites, meaning they used a language belonging to the Semitic family of languages. The language of the ancient Egyptians, however, belongs to the Hamito-Semitic family. Their language is of special interest linguistically because it provides us with written records spanning a period of some four and a half thousand years. In its early phases the language was written with hieroglyphs, a form of picture-writing. Hieroglyphs were later supplemented by a cursive writing known as hieratic. Hieratic was further simplified to a more cursive script called demotic. In the latest stage of the Egyptian language, the Greek alphabet was adopted and was called Coptic.

In the course of our journey through the Hebrew scriptures we will encounter the Egyptians at points too numerous to detail here. Only a few outstanding points of contact will be mentioned. Beginning in the eighteenth century B.C.E. for a period of more than half a century there was a continuous infiltration of Asiatics into the eastern delta of the Nile. By about 1720 B.C.E. some of these invaders, known as the Hyksos, established themselves as rulers over the Egyptians. During the era of Hyksos domination Semitic tribes continued to move into Egypt. The story of Joseph in Genesis has been placed by some scholars during the Hyksos era, although many features of the Joseph story reflect a later date.

The Amarna period in Egypt saw the accession to the throne of the Pharaoh Akhenaton (*ca.* 1379 B.C.E.). The "Hymn to Aton" from this period bears striking similarities to Psalm 104 (see Chapter 13). Under one of Egypt's strongest Pharaohs, Rameses II in the thirteenth century B.C.E., many scholars place the oppression of the Hebrews in Egypt (see Chapter 7). Merneptah, one of the many sons of Rameses II, came to the throne *ca.* 1236 B.C.E. In a famous inscription he celebrates a victory over Israel, the first occurrence of the word Israel in Egyptian texts. It is suggested by many scholars that Merneptah's monumental inscription would be contemporary with the campaigns of Joshua in the biblical book of Joshua. Sheshonk I (whose name in the Bible is Shishak) seized the throne of Egypt *ca.* 945 B.C.E. Jeroboam fled to his court for refuge from Solomon (1 Kgs 11:40). This same Sheshonk later invaded Palestine and sacked the Jerusalem temple (1 Kgs 14:25 f.) The Pharaoh Neco marched into Palestine at the end of the seventh century B.C.E. (see Chapter 12). Josiah, King of Judah, was killed in an ill-considered attempt to stop the Egyptian army at Megiddo.

Israel inherited much from Egyptian culture. A biblical reference to "all the wisdom of Egypt" (1 Kings 4:30) testifies to the deep impression made by Egyptian culture throughout the ancient Near Eastern world. Throughout its history, however, ancient Egypt gave more to other cultures than it absorbed. Because of its geographical isolation, cut off by deserts to the south and the west, buffered from Palestine by the Sinai wilderness, and with the Mediterranean to the north, Egyptians were culturally isolated from the outside world to a remarkable degree, resisting foreign influences.

FAMILY AND KINSHIP IN ANCIENT ISRAEL

Most of us, unless we are genealogical buffs, do not know very much about our family backgrounds any farther back than our grandparents. Furthermore, we are not convinced that knowing more about our ancestry would make much difference in our lives. If we are to imaginatively enter the social world of the Hebrew Bible, however, we must be prepared to conceive of a situation in which individuals see their identity as members of a family, a lineage. While we may identify persons by a first name and surname, knowing that a person's surname is a family name, family names basically serve as labels, not to convey any substantive information about a person to others. The origins of some of our family names, like Carpenter or Baker, may have originally been given to an ancestor because of his occupation, but now have no particular meaning.

In ancient Israel, persons did not have surnames, but were known in terms of family relationships. For them the innermost circle of one's social environment consisted of the immediate family—one's spouse, children, parents, and grandparents. Even beyond this inner circle, relationships with other persons are described in kinship terms, and relationships are determined, to a large degree, by kinship connections. In other words, people depended on the kinship system for information on how they stood in relationship to other persons and how they should relate to others.

Lineage

In the Hebrew Bible, this relational system is expressed in several ways. In 1 Sam 9:1, in a narrative telling how Saul came to be the first king of Israel, he is introduced in this way: "There was a man of Benjamin whose name was Kish, the son of Abiel, son of Zeror, son of Becorath, son of Aphiah." Saul is here described in terms of his kinship group or, in anthropological terms, his *lineage* (Rogerson and Davies: 1989, 46). Lineages were made up of families that were interrelated by marriage. One's immediate family was part of a large lineage. What we have in 1 Sam 9:1 is what anthropologists call a *maximal lineage,* in which Saul is linked back to a person we would call his great-great-grandfather, Aphiah, whom we also can take to be the person after whom the maximal lineage is named. The farther back one's maximal lineage is traced, the greater the number of relatives. In Saul's case, one can assume that his father had brothers, who as Saul's uncles would be a part of his maximal lineage. We know from 1 Sam 14 that Saul's grandfather Abiel had at least one other son, Ner, (in our terms Saul's great-uncle), who was also a member of Saul's maximal lineage. Abiel probably had brothers, as did Zeror, as did Aphiah, and so on. Saul's maximal lineage can be represented in terms of a kinship tree (in which N = the names of unknown, hypothetical kinsmen) as represented in Table 2.2.

Maximal lineages served a very important function of social control in early Israelite society, where there was no state with its police power. With no centralized agency charged with maintaining law and order and restraining lawbreakers, a person's security and safety were dependent, to a large degree, upon one's kinship group. In conditions of plenty, peace, and tranquility, one's larger kinship group, those members of one's maximal lineage, played a small role. On the other hand, when problems arose it became critical to know who the members of one's lineage were. Problems like boundary disputes, for example, could

TABLE 2.2   Saul's Lineage

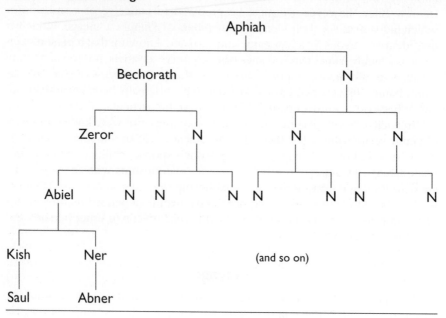

lead to confrontations between different lineages. Given the microenvironments of which Palestine was constituted, one part of a lineage might well have a bountiful harvest one year, while another branch of that lineage might have a bad harvest. Lineages dictated the ways to deal with such problems. Problems within a lineage, such as a bad harvest, were dealt with internally, with one branch of the lineage coming to the aid of the other. Conflicts between or among lineages were resolved through negotiations or feuds.

An example of how the kinship system functioned in this way can be seen in an incident narrated in Judges 20, which describes conflict between lineages, here between Saul's tribe (see the section below on "Social Groupings"), Benjamin, and other tribes. The town of Gibeah (which may be the equivalent of a clan) in the tribal territory of Benjamin had been party to the rape of a traveler's concubine (Judg 19), for which the other tribes wanted to punish the Benjaminite (tribal) town of Gibeah (clan). Out of a sense of solidarity *within* a kinship group, when threatened by another kinship group, the members of the tribe of Benjamin banded together to defend Gibeah, even at the cost of going to war against the other tribes. In the end the Benjaminites were defeated, and the other tribes imposed the additional punishment of prohibiting the marriage of any of their daughters to Benjaminite men. When, however, this measure led to the threat of extinction for Benjamin, the other tribes, reaching farther back into the maximal lineage and drawing on the resulting sense of solidarity with Benjamin based on their common ancestor Israel/Jacob, took measures to find wives for the remaining men of Benjamin.

GENEALOGIES

In the Hebrew Bible the relational system is often expressed through genealogies. Genealogies were composed for different purposes and function at several levels, but they helped provide individuals with a way of locating themselves within a meaningful social framework. Genealogies are encountered early in the Hebrew Bible story, by the fourth chapter of Genesis. The genealogies in Genesis begin with the supposed first couple, Adam and Eve, the mythical progenitors of all human beings. Genesis 10 then maps the known human family in terms of three branches or lines, stemming from the three sons of Noah. One of the sons of Noah, Shem (from whose name comes the term "Semites") heads the branch from which comes Abraham (Gen 11:10-31). The resulting genealogical map not only locates Abraham in relation to the rest of humanity, it expresses the affinities and distances in relations to other peoples that were felt by the Hebrew Bible writers (Rogerson and Davies: 52). The Israelites regarded themselves as having a closer relationship to Assyrians, for example, because they also were Semites, whereas they were not so close to the Egyptians, whom they saw as descended from another of Noah's sons, Ham. In terms of Israel's later history, it is also interesting to note that peoples such as the Jebusites (a subgroup of the Canaanites who held Jerusalem until the time of David) and the Philistines, with whom Israel competed for land, are also seen in these Genesis genealogies as belonging to the Hamitic rather than Semitic branch of the human family.

Beyond these early chapters of Genesis, genealogies are used to express perceived relationships, some of which are real and others of which may be fictional. Their intent is to create links between peoples based on common ancestry. In the end, Israel is regarded as a single large kinship group, and all Israelites trace their ancestry back to a single ancestor whose name they bear, Jacob, whose name is changed to Israel, according to Gen 32:28: "Then the man said, 'You shall no longer be called Jacob, but Israel, for you have striven with God and with humans, and have prevailed.'" In actuality, "Israel" may well have been a confederation of groups of diverse origins, around whose ancestors various traditions collected, who thus "created" their identity as a people stemming from a common ancestor.

One of the purposes of Genesis, according to Rogerson and Davies (55) was to link Israel's ancestors together, using genealogies and story. This unified story is then incorporated into a larger genealogical canvas. These genealogies may be "fictional," but to call them that is not to dismiss them as deceitful or fraudulent. In the ancient Near East, genealogies were not regarded as a type of historical record, but were the expression of a people's need to plot existing local social realities onto a chart that explained them in terms of a comprehensive scheme of things. Thus every Israelite was able, at least in theory, by being able to describe his or her ancestry, to demonstrate that he or she belonged to this people called Israel. He or she also was able to know how he or she was related to another Israelite and what the implications of this relationship were for patterns of social interrelationships.

Social Groupings in Israel

There are three sociological terms used in Hebrew to describe Israelite social organization in kinship terms. At the primary level there is the *bêt 'āv*, which means literally "father's house." The closest counterpart of this in English is the nuclear family. In several places in the Hebrew Bible there appears a related term, *bêt 'ēm* which means "mother's house" (Gen 24:28; Ruth 1:8; Song 3:24; 8:2), thus *bêt 'āv* and *bêt 'ēm*, might be translated as "family household." This translation suggests that this was a group which shared a common residence. In actuality, this primary term in the Israelite social lexicon is used to refer to a variety of social groupings that range from a family who lived together under the same roof, up to and including the lineage. The *bêt 'āv*, understood not as a residential unit but as a descent group, is clearly intended in references like the one in Gen 24:38. There, Abraham's servant is sent from Palestine to Mesopotamia to find a wife for Abraham's son, Isaac, from Abraham's *bêt 'āv*, which here represents members of Abraham's family line from which Abraham is separated geographically.

When the *bêt 'āv/bêt 'ēm* is understood as a residential unit, does it refer to an "extended" or "nuclear" family? By "extended family" scholars have usually understood several generations living together, and until recently, it was assumed that this was the norm in ancient Israel. Gottwald, for example, has said that the *bêt 'āv* comprised up to five generations, and he considers that a thriving *bêt 'āv* might easily comprise from fifty to one hundred persons, depending upon the economic support base and the freedom of the community from external threats (1979: 285). More recent scholarship, however, maintains that nuclear families were more frequent in ancient Israel than extended families. Lemche (1985: 231–2, 250–9) believes that in view of the short life-span that was prevalent, it is unlikely that an "extended family" would include any more than three generations (grandparent, parent, child) at the most. He also observes, based on archaeological evidence, that no domestic structures in ancient Israel were large enough to house a group of people of the size envisaged by Gottwald.

THE CLAN

At the next level is the *mišpāchâ*, which is usually translated "clan" in modern English Bibles. This translation is somewhat misleading, however, since in anthropological literature the term "clan" has a multiplicity of meanings. On the basis of Josh 7:16–17, the *mišpāchâ* was the intermediate level between the *bêt 'āv* and "tribe": "So Joshua rose early in the morning, and brought Israel near tribe by tribe, and the tribe of Judah was taken; and he brought near the families (*mišpāchôt*, the plural of *mišpāchâ*) of Judah, and the family (*mišpāchâ*) of the Zerahites was taken." Lemche reaches the following conclusions about the *mišpāchâ* (1985: 260–74). It was possible to refer to any of several levels within Israelite social structure as a *mišpāchâ*, but most probably what is intended is the lineage, which, as we have seen, is a level for which the term *bêt 'āv* is also used, and the "maximal lineage," the level that comes between the lineage and the tribe. The terms *mišpāchâ* and *bêt 'āv* overlap somewhat, and the boundaries between them are not fixed. Lemche also argues that the *mišpāchâ*, as a distinct social unit, did not play an important social or political role in ancient Israel. A *mišpāchâ* ought to be regarded primarily as a maximal lineage—that is, a descent group that established ties of kinship between families through a common ancestor, real or imagined, who was no longer living.

THE TRIBE

In the outermost circle of Israelite social groupings is the *šēvet*. The word *šēvet* is usually translated as "tribe." "Tribe" is difficult to define, both anthropologically and biblically. What was an Israelite *šēvet* or "tribe?" While little can be said with any certainty, it appears that there is a strong correlation between geographical references and tribal designations in the Hebrew Bible. The membership of a tribe seems to consist of the membership of those lineages and clans who lived in the geographical region with which the name of the tribe in question was associated, and were thus bound by common residence *and* descent. Although there is much that we do not know about Israelite tribes, Rogerson and Davies (1989: 58) offer the following minimal definition of *šēvet:* "The largest social unit for mutual defence against other Israelite social units."

Tribal association was expressed in ancient Israel in terms of kinship. Thus, in the narratives about the birth of Jacob's sons (Gen 29 – 30) we are told of the tribal ancestor for each tribe in a narrative that is organized in a way that makes clear the hierarchical relationship they have to one another.

This understanding of "tribe" differs from earlier descriptions that typically said members of the same tribe were related to one another through ties of blood. The older understanding of what a tribe was rested on a lack of awareness that tribal designations actually were ways of describing what were really political and social relations, not kinship relations. Today most sociologists and historians of the Hebrew Bible have given up the notion that actual genetic ties link together the individuals in a tribe or nation. Instead they point out that an individual's social affiliation is always the result of choices made by that individual. These choices are made on the basis of a number of factors, of which the blood ties is but one. Others factors can include such things as a common history, common destiny, common economic interests, common external enemies, and so on. Affiliation with a tribe, like one's relationship to a nation, is basically an expression of where one feels that one belongs (Lemche 1988: 98 – 9).

THE HEBREW BIBLE AND YOU

The survey in these first two chapters of the literature of the Hebrew Bible, the critical tools used in its interpretation, and of the land in which it is set and the people of whom it speaks, suggest that the Hebrew Bible has come to us as by a complex process. It took shape among and was preserved by a people that saw themselves as having a special relationship with God—what has been called a covenant relationship in which they saw themselves as being called to special responsibility, to be a "light," a witness to other peoples. Certainly behind this body of literature is the consciousness on the part of the people, Israel, that something unique was going on in the story they were telling. They believed that their God was directly involved in working out definite purposes in the events being reported and the words being preserved. Such was the self-consciousness of those who produced this literature, and sensitive interpretation of it on our part must take this awareness into account.

Anyone who would discover the meanings of the Hebrew Bible must be prepared to encounter the text on its own terms, realizing that every reader brings to the process of interpretation his or her own sense of personhood, his or her unique set of experiences. The historical and social matrix of the religious communities that produced the literature, with one of which we as individuals may or may not be associated, is only one of the contexts of interpretation. The other context is supplied by the psychosocial world of the interpreter. None of us comes to the Bible as an empty vessel or a blank slate. Being what we are as unique individuals, each one of us brings our own set of questions to the scriptures. In taking our questions to the scriptures, however, we need to be prepared for a dialogue in which our contemporary ways of thinking and expressing ourselves (conditioned as they are by our particular social location) interact with those of the biblical authors and redactors in an ongoing process of rethinking, rephrasing, and readjusting our questions, as the text itself begins to mirror new questions back to us. The result of this questioning and being questioned is what has been called "the hermeneutical circle," in which the object (the text) and the subject (the interpreter) interact with one another in a cyclical fashion, generating new questions in the process.

One of the most significant things that we bring to the interpretation of the Bible is a view of the *authority of scripture*. The theological term most often used this way, which we have mentioned before, is the word *inspiration.* How we view the inspiration of scripture is certainly an important part of our interpretive stance. On one end of the spectrum, some individuals believe that the scriptures speak with absolute authority, or inerrancy, in all matters—science, politics, religion, morals, and so on. This perspective is sometimes called a fundamentalist one—The Bible (all of it) is God's word to human beings. On the other end of the spectrum there are those who see the Bible as yet another piece of literature, not qualitatively different from other literature, humanly devised and reflecting only human experience, not supernatural ideas. For these people the Bible is a reflection on human experience, written by humans. These extreme positions make clear that the question of biblical authority is inextricably linked with the question of inspiration. It is not enough simply to ask whether one believes in the inspiration of scripture; one must ask about the specifics of one's belief in inspiration. There is an intermediate position that says that the Bible contains the words of God in human words *and* the words of human beings. For this position, it is important that one learns to make judgments about which words are which.

Crucial to the question of inspiration is the issue of authority and its source. To say, as fundamentalists do, that the original Hebrew manuscripts of biblical books were inspired so as to contain no errors of any kind, does not really solve the problem of authority because no original manuscripts exist. On the other hand, to call "inspired" only the present canonical form of the Bible does an injustice to those faithful figures who were involved in the process long before canonical status came to be granted to a particular collection of books. Can we assume, for example, that the prophet Jeremiah was inspired, but not those later editors and compilers who brought the present book of Jeremiah to the form in which we have it? Or should authority be given to the later redactors to the exclusion of the original "authors"? And what about the "inspiration" of biblical readers through the years who have interpreted the scriptures on a variety of levels and have given meaning, help, and direction to others through their interpretation? Churches in the Reformed tradition have often used a revealing prayer before the public reading of scripture: "May the same Spirit that inspired the writing of these words inspire our understanding of them."

These kinds of questions suggest that it might be helpful to think of inspiration more as a process than as an ephemeral happening. The people of the Hebrew Bible believed that God was at work in the processes of history, not just in the initial act of the creation of the world. Just so, the contemporary reader of the Hebrew Bible may be able to affirm that God is at work in the ongoing interplay between narrators who tell, authors who write, editors who rework, religious communities that canonize, and contemporary readers who find an authoritative word for their situation.

STUDY QUESTIONS

THE LAND OF THE OLD TESTAMENT

1. Palestine has a wide variety of climates within a small area. How does its geography contribute to this characteristic?
2. Refer to a map showing rainfall distribution in Palestine (See the article on Palestine, Climate in the *Anchor Bible Dictionary*). What areas of the region get the highest amounts of rainfall? What areas get the least annual precipitation?

THE PEOPLE OF THE OLD TESTAMENT

1. Using the series of three concentric circles, map your social relationships. In the innermost circle list those with whom you have the closest social relationships (particular family members, sorority sisters, friends, members of the same athletic team, etc.). In the next circle out list those with whom you have social relationships on a regular basis, but who are not so close to

you. In the third circle, list those with whom you have occasional social relationships and whom you know by name. How do you think your social map would differ from that of a person your age in ancient Israel?

2. Reconstruct as much as you can of your family tree *from memory*.

BIBLIOGRAPHY

Baly, Denis. 1974. *The Geography of the Bible*. Rev. ed. New York: Harper & Row.

Gottwald, Norman K. 1979. *The Tribes of Yahweh: A Sociology of the Religion of Liberated Israel, 1250–1050 B.C.* Maryknoll, NY: Orbis.

Hopkins, David C. 1985. *The Highlands of Canaan. Agricultural Life in the Early Iron Age*. Social World of Biblical Israel, 3. Sheffield: Almond/JSOT Press.

Lemche, Niels Peter. 1985. *Early Israel. Anthropological and Historical Studies on the Israelite Society before the Monarchy*. Leiden: E. J. Brill.

—. 1988. *Ancient Israel. A New History of Israelite Society*. Sheffield: JSOT Press.

Martin, J. D. 1989. "Israel as a Tribal Society," pp. 95–117 in R. E. Clements, ed. *The World of Ancient Israel: Sociological, Anthropological and Political Perspectives*. Cambridge: Cambridge University Press.

Rogerson, John, and Philip Davies. 1989. *The Old Testament World*. Englewood Cliffs, NJ: Prentice-Hall.

Wiseman, D. J., ed. 1973. *Peoples of Old Testament Times*. London: Oxford University Press.

Chapter 3

AN ILLUMINATING SIDE TRIP: ARCHAEOLOGY AND THE HEBREW BIBLE

*B*efore we enter into the book of Genesis, our itinerary at this point calls for an illuminating side trip into the archaeology of the biblical world. We call this a side trip not as a comment on its significance, but because it is not concerned, as is the rest of this book, with the study of written materials. While it is true that ancient written, or epigraphic, materials may be recovered by archaeologists, the study and interpretation of such materials is not the principal task of archaeologists, though some archaeologists have the skills to do so. Epigraphic materials that are found in the course of archaeological excavations are studied by epigraphers, specialists in the languages in which ancient texts were written. Archaeology, as we are using the term here, is concerned primarily with the recovery of aneipgraphic, or nonwritten artifacts from the past. An artifact is anything that has been created by humans. Archaeology as the study of artifacts is an important tool that, if scientifically conducted and honestly interpreted, can help illuminate the biblical text. It is therefore useful for any serious student of the Bible to understand something about how archaeologists work and how that which they find can be interpreted.

While archaeology has been, for many years, an important source of data for understanding the material culture behind the biblical text, the physical settings in which biblical peoples lived, it has also been terribly misused. It is clearly not, as some have proposed, a scientific panacea for solving all the problems encountered in the interpretation of the biblical text. In fact, archaeology as a scientific discipline can neither prove nor disprove the Bible; it can only illuminate some things about the material culture of those who produced the biblical text.

HOW ARCHAEOLOGISTS WORK

Tales Told by Tells

Archaeology is an enterprize whose goal is the recovery and interpretation of artifacts from the past. It is partly the meticulous work of the scientist and partly the exercise of the creative imagination. It includes both the physical work of excavation and the intellectual labor of analyzing findings in the study and laboratory. The nature of archaeology as detective work has made it the vehicle for several authors of fiction and modern filmmakers, as represented by James Michener's novel *The Source* and Steven Spielberg's trilogy of films about Indiana Jones. While most, if not all, *real* archaeologists would dismiss such portrayals of archaeology as overly romantic, they would also admit that they do capture the reality that archaeology is a truly exciting quest—the quest for knowledge about ourselves and our human past.

Paul Lapp has described archaeology as "a love affair between an archaeologist and an ancient ruin" (1975: 1). With respect to the archaeology of the biblical world, Palestinian or Syro-Palestinian archaeology as it is called by many current practitioners, most of the major ruins in the eastern Mediterranean region are what are known as tells. *Tell* is a word in Hebrew and Arabic that refers to an uninhabited mound whose formation is the result of repeated human occupation in the past. In the past each succeeding occupation was built on top of the remains of earlier occupation with only minimum ground-clearing operations before the commencement of new building. The Hebrew Bible talks about a town standing on its tell (that is, of a city situated on top of a mound of ancient ruins—Josh 11:13; Jer 30:18) and of turning a town into a desolate tell (that is, ending its history of occupation by total destruction—Jer 49:2).

What goes into the formation of a tell? Most tells in Palestine began when a settlement was established on a naturally elevated spot that had a suitable location. The desirability of the location was determined by such things as its access to trade routes, the availability of a water supply, defensibility, and exposure to cooling breezes. When the first settlers either moved away from the site or it was destroyed, the site could remain deserted for a long period. Eventually, however, the same reasons that had attracted the initial settlers to the site would attract new occupants. Lacking heavy earthmoving equipment, these newcomers simply leveled off the remains of the earlier occupation, adding fill where necessary, and built on top of them, causing the tell to grow higher. The earlier settlement, even after centuries of abandonment, also provided building materials for the new town. As the new settlers discovered the stumps of the foundations and walls of earlier structures beneath the surface, they frequently dug out the stones to use in their own structures. This digging left behind what are known as "robber trenches" in the archaeological record. Often structures would be built following the same lines as previous structures, re-using old foundations. A tell is formed when this process of abandonment and resettlement is repeated again and again. This has been going on at sites in the Near East for millennia. This process creates *strata* or layers of human occupation. The physical record of these strata is called stratigraphy. Each tell has a unique occupational history that can be understood from its stratigraphic deposits (see Figure 3.1). Some smaller tells represent only a few periods of occupation and have only a few strata; larger tells that were settled over centuries may have as many as two dozen.

The excavation of a tell occurs when an archaeologist, for one reason or another, is attracted to a particular tell. Before excavation begins, however, there is a good deal of pre-dig investigation. The area in which the tell is located is investigated, alternate sites are considered for excavation, and careful attention is given to the goals of excavation at this particular site. What can be known about a tell before excavation? Many distinctive features of a tell are accessible before excavation—environment, relation to trade routes, water supply, geography,

Figure 3.1   Cross-section of a tell showing its strata

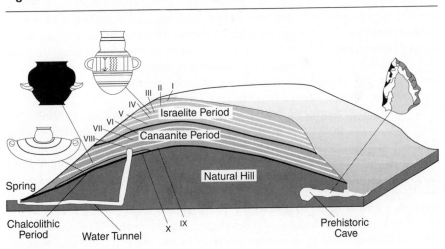

size. Aerial photographs, both ordinary and false-color infrared, can reveal architectural features that are not visible from the surface. Surveys of surface remains, especially of *potsherds,* that is, pieces of broken pottery, can give a rough indication of the site's occupational history.

Some Fundamentals of Method in Archaeology—Excavating a Tell

Once the archaeological team has learned as much as possible through the pre-dig investigation, the excavation proper can begin. How does one approach a tell? The site is first mapped by a surveyor and a grid is superimposed on the tell. This grid divides the surface of the site into basic units of digging, which are often called *squares.* These commonly measure five meters on a side, but their size and the number of squares to be excavated can be adjusted to fit the characteristics of the site and the scope of the excavations. Several squares in a given area of the site together make up a *field.* As one digs downward in these squares, the unexcavated soil remaining between each square forms a one-meter thick balk (or baulk). The balk not only functions as a path between squares, but because care is taken to dig straight down, the sides of the balks serve as vertical surfaces in which the tell's stratigraphy can be seen and recorded, both by drawing and photography.

Figure 3.2 depicts a tell divided into squares with balks. At a greatly over-simplified level, a tell might be compared to a giant layer cake. When one "cuts the cake," layers, or strata, of human occupational remains can be seen, interspersed with intervening layers representing destruction and/or abandonment of the tell. In the process of excavation, the archaeologist begins at the top of the "cake" and slowly excavates down through the successive strata. However, in reality human occupation almost never deposits strata that are as uniform as those of a layer cake. Deciphering the variations in the stratigraphy of a multi-layered tell is not an easy task. Two troublesome things that disturb the straightforward stratigraphy of a tell are robber trenches and foundation trenches. Robber trenches, which were mentioned above, were dug in the attempt to recover building materials from earlier occupation of the site, cutting through and disturbing strata. The digging of foundation trenches for new walls, refuse and storage pits, graves, cisterns, and the like, also resulted in breaks in the uniform pattern of occupational deposits (see Figure 3.3).

Two basic strategies of excavation have been developed in Palestinian archaeology in the period since World War II. In one of these, sometimes called the architectural approach, the aim is to expose complete architectural units on as wide a scale as possible. Those following this approach think that a site's stratigraphy can be seen in the area between such architectural features as walls and floors. The second excavation strategy was developed by Dame Kathleen Kenyon, a British archaeologist who is perhaps best known for her work at the site of Jericho. The techniques she developed, known as the "Wheeler-Kenyon" method (named for Kenyon and her teacher), or the "balk-layer-debris" method,

Figure 3.2   A tell divided into squares

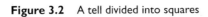

Figure 3.3   Stratigraphy of a tell, showing "robber trenches"

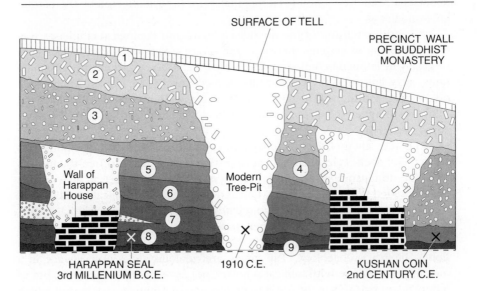

aim at consistent verification of strata and careful analysis of their contents. This method is described in simple form in the preceding paragraph. Current field work in Palestinian archaeology combines features of both the "architectural" and the "balk-layer-debris" approaches. As much as possible of the site's area is exposed to get the "big picture." Cross-examination of the occupational history is then achieved by excavating squares in detail at strategic points on the site. The integration of the two methods has led to a balanced method of digging whose results can be analyzed and verified even by those who were not involved in the excavation.

Theory in Archaeology

In addition to refinements in archaeological methods, there have also been significant developments in archaeological theory, meaning the way the discipline of archaeology sees its task. The first significant post-World War II development in theory was the impact of the "New Archaeology" on the archaeology of the biblical world. Pioneered by New World archaeologists beginning in the late 1960s, the theoretical assumptions of the "New Archaeology" became increasingly evident in Palestinian archaeology.

One contribution of the "New Archaeology" was the idea that archaeology ought to be multidisciplinary. Its aim ought to be the recovery and analysis of *all* data on material culture that has been preserved in the archaeological record, not just structures and stratigraphy. With a multidisciplinary approach came an increasing concern with ecological matters, questions concerning a site's relation to its environment. This ecological orientation slowly began to replace an earlier one that sought explanations for cultural change in "major" historical events. The newer approach understood cultural change as coming about as a result of economic factors that were in turn affected by the natural environment.

A logical extension of the multidisciplinary and ecological emphases was the application of systems theory to archaeology. *Systems theory,* which was originally developed in biology, talks about systems and their relation to subsystems, including such things as feedback mechanisms. As applied to archaeology, human cultures were viewed as systems with means of receiving vital information about the state of things from subsystems and making necessary adjustments.

Theoretically, archaeology today is not a branch of any other discipline. It is a discipline itself. Palestinian archaeologists have struggled to free themselves from the dominance of a "biblical archaeology" (see the section later in this chapter called "What Archaeology Can and Cannot Do for Biblical Studies") that sought to use (and sometimes manipulate) archaeology to "prove" that events narrated in the Bible occurred when and in the manner in which the biblical narratives say they did. Having freed themselves from domination by the traditional "biblical archaeology," Palestinian archaeologists can now engage in a meaningful dialogue with biblical scholars, not as servants to the latter, but as independent partners in the quest to understand our human past, part of which is represented in the Bible. What is it that archaeology can contribute to the dialogue? We will provide some answers for this question in the section later in this chapter, "What Archaeology Can and Cannot Do for Biblical Studies."

Analyzing and Dating the Finds

What one finds obviously varies from one site to the next. Besides the architectural remains of a site's defensive walls, public and domestic structures are usually excavated. Palestinian excavators characteristically encounter a wide range of artifacts. These include such things as potsherds (typically the most abundant find), artifacts made of metal and stone, as well as occasional inscriptions, art objects of various kinds (seals, figurines, jewelry, ivory carvings, etc.), bones, and other organic remains such as pollen, carbonized grain, and so forth. Sometimes, in the very arid regions of Palestine, wooden, leather, textile, and other organic artifacts may be found. In most of the region, however, such organic remains are not preserved. The analysis of these artifacts in modern archaeology is carried out by an interdisciplinary team that includes, but is not necessarily limited to:

- architects (who can interpret building techniques and suggest how a structure might have looked based on its remains)
- physicists (who help in the analysis of things like water systems and know what is involved in preparing samples for dating tests)
- chemists (who analyze findings for their chemical makeup)
- physical and social anthropologists (who can make inferences on such things as family size, population, and the like)
- osteologists (who analyze burial remains)
- paleobotanists (who analyze plant remains)
- geologists (who interpret the ways in which different kinds of strata are deposited and assist in understanding environmental factors)
- ceramicists (who know pottery forms from the different periods of the site's occupation and the technology of their manufacture)
- art historians (who assist in the interpretation of architectural forms and art objects)
- historians (who know ancient Near Eastern history)
- paleographers (who interpret epigraphic finds in their stratigraphical context)
- statisticians (who set up computerized methods of storing and analyzing data).

When all these specialists work together effectively, archaeology can help provide answers to many questions about the variety of human experience that underlies the biblical text.

Through the interdisciplinary analysis of artifacts, archaeology can provide clues about how biblical societies were organized. It can help us understand the biblical environment, including the relationships among plants, animals, and humans. Archaeology can provide us with information about subsistence strategies, diet, disease, deformity, and causes of death in ancient human populations. Artifactual evidence is also a very valuable source of information about the manufacture and use of tools in antiquity. Analysis of artifacts can provide information about trade and exchange patterns. At its best, archaeology can provide us with information about the way people thought about their symbolic world.

Pottery Analysis

As mentioned above, the most abundant type of artifact found on a Palestinian excavation is potsherds. The abundance of potsherds is not difficult to explain. Pottery made its appearance in parts of Palestine as early as the seventh millennium B.C.E. and was generally present by *ca.* 5000 B.C.E. Until the advent of glass and the mass production and availability of metal utensils, pottery vessels were used as everyday utensils by all classes of people in a society, not just by the elite. Pottery was thus a part of ancient daily life. Furthermore, although the pottery found by archaeologists is usually broken (whole pots are typically found only in sealed burials), potsherds themselves are virtually indestructible. They survive in the archaeological record, unaffected by environmental factors that destroy other kinds of artifacts over time.

Pottery is a sensitive indicator of cultural change, and thus it is a primary tool for analyzing aspects of daily life in biblical antiquity. The study of pottery has many different facets: pottery experts study the technical aspects of pottery manufacture; *petrography* (the microscopic examination of thin sawn sections of pottery) provides knowledge of the physical composition of the clay; *neutron activation* provides a fingerprint of trace elements in clay, making possible the pinpointing of clay sources. In addition, the study of the changing forms of discrete pottery types provides a most important tool for the dating of strata and their artifacts.

Pottery has many variables. Few clays can be formed into vessels in their naturally-occurring state. Most must be cleaned and prepared for use. Impurities in clay can be removed by combining the clay with water to form a suspension in which the coarse particles sink to the bottom while the fine-grained clay particles remain on top. An elaboration of this technique is known as *levigation,* which involves passing the suspension through a series of traps or channels. Preparation of clay for the manufacture of pottery also includes adding non-clay particles called inclusions or temper. *Inclusions* are added to clay to improve its workability, lessen shrinkage, and prevent cracking when the vessel is fired. Commonly used tempering materials include sand, organic materials (chaff, seeds, ashes), lime or shell, and so forth. Small fragments of ground up fired pots can also be used as temper. Materials used as temper are pulverized to an appropriate size and mixed with the clay, usually constituting about 20 to 50 percent of the total volume of the mixture.

Ceramic vessels can be made completely by hand, by using a slow or fast wheel, by using a mold, or by some combination of these methods. The finished pot can then be decorated in many ways before firing. Firing can be done at either a relatively high or low temperature and in an environment that leads to either chemical reduction or oxidization. Further decoration can be added after firing. All these variables can be discerned in the finished product, and nearly all of them are of at least potential chronological significance. Some variables are more sensitive chronological indicators than others. The same clay beds, potter's wheels, and kilns may have been used for a very long period. But one feature of ceramic vessels undergoes a continuous evolutionary process of change that can be observed at intervals of even a quarter- or half-century: shape. Important for precise dating is the change that takes place in the shape of a particular vessel type, which is reflected in many potsherds. The observation of these changes in a particular pot type leads to the formation of a typological sequence in which the shape of a particular type of vessel can be seen to evolve with the passage of time. (See Figure 3.4, which shows a typological sequence of oil lamps that ranges from late fourth millennium B.C.E. at the bottom to the fourth century C.E. at the top). Such changes in pottery shapes have their closest counterparts in the modern phenomenon of model changes for cars and appliances. An expert in ancient Palestinian pottery is thus an indispensable member of any excavation team dealing with a Palestinian site whose history postdates 5000 B.C.E.

The form and decorative details of a ceramic vessel are the end-products of a complicated process. The process begins with the selection and preparation of the clay and temper and continues through various shaping techniques, surface finishing, and firing. Standard analysis of the ceramic types of an archaeological corpus has usually assumed that a potter tried to produce a particular form in clay corresponding to a conscious or unconscious cultural tradition: a mental template. From this limited perspective, particular pieces of pottery served specific functions in a society, whether as utilitarian or prestige items, and changes in ceramic styles reflected corresponding changes in that society as it interacted with its environment and other societies over a period of time.

More recent typological analysis of pottery, however, maintains that the emergence and subsequent development of a stylistic tradition was influenced by and could be dependent on technology. For example, the unavailability of suitable raw materials or of necessary expertise in their preparation could affect the development of ceramic styles. The form of a piece of pottery can also be a function of the decoration that is envisioned for it. A further consequence of an appreciation for the significance of the technology of pottery production is that the same finished form or type of decoration might have been accomplished in several different ways, even within the same culture. While two vessels might look identical, they can be distinguished by closer examination that analyzes the way in which they were made. Sometimes these techniques aimed at understanding the technology behind the pottery can be more valuable than visible criteria in explaining the socio-economic development and foreign contacts of a society.

Once a relative chronology has been established by constructing a typological sequence of pottery and confirmed by comparative study of stratified pottery assemblages from other Palestinian sites, other means of determining

Figure 3.4   A typological sequence of Palestinian pottery lamps

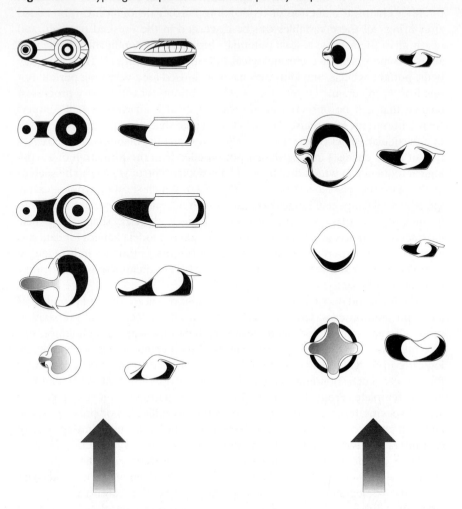

absolute dates can be employed. While a full discussion of methods of absolute dating is beyond the scope of this chapter, there follows a brief description of some principal dating methods that are currently used.

Radiocarbon Dating

Radiocarbon dating is one of the best-known and most useful methods of dating organic artifacts employed by archaeologists. It does, however, have its limitations, both in terms of accuracy and for the time range for which it is useful. Geologists and paleontologists have long been able to measure the dates of fossils and rocks through the measurement of the radioactive decay of elements such as uranium-238. In 1931, scientists at the University of Chicago discovered carbon-14, a previously unknown radioactive isotope of ordinary carbon.

Figure 3.5   Carbon-14 formation

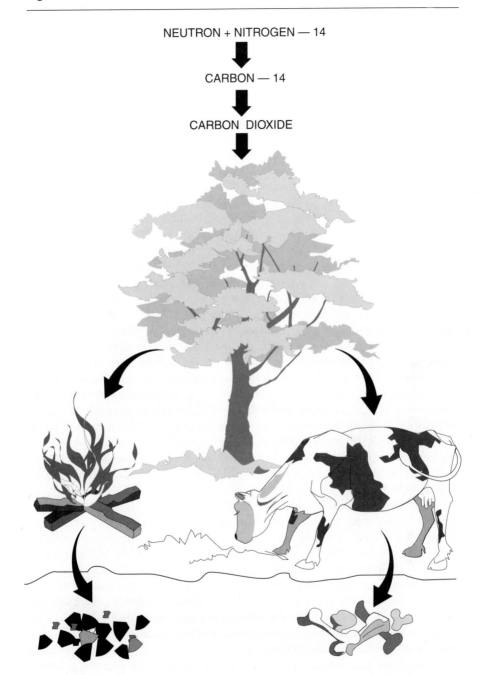

Carbon-14 is produced in the atmosphere, where cosmic rays bombard nitrogen-14 with neutrons. These neutrons then react with the nitrogen atoms to produce atoms of carbon-14 (^{14}C), or radiocarbon, which, unlike ordinary carbon atoms, are unstable because they have eight neutrons instead of the usual six in ordinary carbon (^{12}C). The radioactive carbon-14 combines with oxygen, as does ordinary carbon (see Figure 3.5). All living plants absorb this radioactive carbon as carbon dioxide and animals in turn take it in by eating plants. Once the plant or animal dies and intake ceases, the carbon-14, now no longer being replenished, begins to disintegrate or decay at a known rate, a half-life rate of 5,730 (± 40) years. The half-life figure means that if there is a total of one unit of carbon-14 in the organism at the time of death, 5,730 years later there would be only one-half unit left, the rest of the original carbon-14 having decayed to nitrogen-14. After another 5,730 years there would be a quarter-unit of carbon-14 remaining, after another 5,730 years an eighth-unit, and so on. Because of this continuing decay, the amount of residual carbon-14 eventually becomes so infinitesimal that it is impossible to measure accurately. Therefore radiocarbon dating can only be pushed back 50,000 years, or perhaps as much as 80,000 years with newer methods.

Radiocarbon dates are published in a specific way. In 1949, an American chemist, Willard Libby, published the first radiocarbon dates, using a half life of 5,568 years, which was later revised to 5,730 years. Laboratories that determine radiocarbon dates provide an estimate of the age of a sample based on the amount of radiocarbon activity in it. The level of activity is converted to an age expressed in the number of years that have elapsed between the death of an organism and the present. To avoid confusion caused by the fact that the present is a "moving target," laboratories have adopted c.e. 1950 as the "present" for the purposes of publishing radiocarbon dates. All radiocarbon dates are thus stated in years b.p., before the present, in the following manner: 3700 ± 100 b.p., where the first figure is the year b.p. (that is, before c.e. 1950) and the second is the associated probable error known as the standard deviation. For 3700 ± 100 b.p. there is a 95 percent chance that the radiocarbon age of the sample lies between 3900 and 3500 b.p.

A problem with earlier methods of radiocarbon dating is that they required a rather large sample that had to be destroyed in the process of carrying out the dating procedures. A significant decrease in the size of the sample required came with the introduction of special gas counters in the late 1970s and early 1980s. In the conventional method one needed five grams of pure carbon after purification, which meant an original sample of some 10 – 20 grams of wood or charcoal, or 100 – 200 grams of bone. The gas counter requires only a few hundred milligrams of charcoal. Some laboratories have recently adopted an even more advanced method called accelerator mass spectrometry, which requires even smaller samples. This method counts the atoms of carbon-14 directly, disregarding their radioactivity. The minimum sample size is reduced to as little as 5 – 10 milligrams, thus enabling the dating of irreplaceable objects without their destruction. In 1988, for example, the application of accelerator mass spectrometry made possible the dating of the Shroud of Turin, a piece of linen with the image of a man's body on it. Some believed that this imprint was that of the body of Jesus of Nazareth and that he had been buried in the shroud. Three laboratories, using double-blind procedures and working independently, all dated the shroud to the fourteenth century c.e., thus eliminating the possibility that it could have been Jesus' burial shroud.

A basic assumption of the radiocarbon method, as it was originally proposed by Libby, has turned out to be incorrect. Libby's assumption was that the amount of carbon-14 in the earth's atmosphere has remained constant through time. It is now known that the amount has varied over the centuries due to several factors. The method that showed this variation—tree-ring dating, or *dendrochronology*—has also provided the means of correcting or calibrating radiocarbon dates to compensate for this variation. Radiocarbon dates obtained from tree-rings show that before *ca.* 1000 b.c.e. radiocarbon dates are increasingly too young in relation to true calendar years. In other words, before 1000 b.c.e. trees (and all other living things) were exposed to greater concentrations of carbon-14 in the atmosphere than exist today. By obtaining radiocarbon dates from tree-ring sequences (see below), scientists can plot radiocarbon ages against tree-ring ages to produce calibration curves back to *ca.* 7000 b.c.e. When using published radiocarbon dates, it is important to note whether they have been calibrated.

Although radiocarbon dates have certain unavoidable levels of error built into the process of their determination, one of the serious limitations of radiocarbon dating stems from the possibilities of sample contamination. Contamination can occur for several reasons. One of the more common causes comes from contact with other sources of carbon, such as having been exposed to water that has flowed over other organic remains. Thus, samples for radiocarbon dating should be obtained, wherever possible, from contexts where the material to be dated has been sealed in a non-contaminating, inert matrix. Examples of such a matrix would be grain that is embedded in mud brick or charcoal that is encased in burnt clay.

Tree-Ring Dating (Dendrochronology)

Tree-ring dating (dendrochronology) has two distinct archaeological uses: (1) for calibrating radiocarbon dates, as mentioned above; and (2) as an independent method of absolute dating. Dendrochronology is based on the fact that most trees produce a ring of new growth every year. These growth rings are not, however, of uniform thickness, but vary with climatic fluctuations and with the age of the tree (with older trees producing narrower growth rings). In tree-ring dating these rings are measured and plotted to produce a diagram showing the pattern of growth rings in an individual tree. Trees of the same species growing in the same general area will show the same pattern of rings. Thus, the growth sequence in individual wood samples can be matched with that of successively older trees to build up a chronology for an area. By matching sequences of rings from living trees as well as from old timber, dendrochronologists can produce a continuous sequence going back thousands of years

Figure 3.6 Dendrochronological sequencing

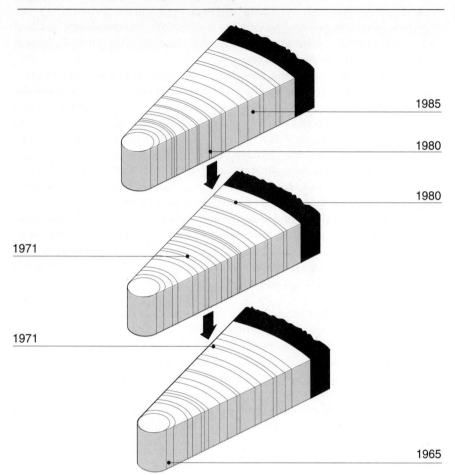

1985

1980

1980

1971

1971

1965

(see Figure 3.6). The tree-ring date that is determined in this way is the time when the tree was cut down. The radiocarbon date also marks the time the tree was cut down. In drier parts of the world such as Palestine, where wood was often hard to find, a wooden beam might have been preserved and reused many times. Thus the date of the log, as determined by radiocarbon or tree-ring dating, might well be older than the architectural context in which it was found by the archaeologist.

Thermoluminescence Dating

Of all the methods of absolute dating developed in recent years, thermoluminescence (TL) dating of ceramics is one of the most interesting and promising.

It has a distinct advantage over radiocarbon dating: it can be used to confirm dates of pottery, the most abundant inorganic material on most Palestinian archaeological sites. This dating method rests on the fact that all natural clays contain small amounts of radioactive elements, notably uranium, thorium, and radioactive potassium. These elements, like radiocarbon, decay at a known rate, emitting alpha, beta, and gamma radiation that displaces the electrons of other materials, which become trapped at points of imperfection in the crystal lattice structure of the clay. When a pot is fired in a kiln, the intense heat causes these trapped electrons to escape. The process then starts over, resetting the TL clock to zero. As the trapped electrons escape, they also emit a tiny quantity of light known as thermoluminescence. By flash-heating a sample of ground up pottery to 500 degrees Celsius and measuring the amount of TL emitted, scientists can calculate how many years have elapsed since the original firing of the pot. The dates provided by TL dating have a reliability of ±300 years, which is considerably less precise than dates discernible for most ceramic samples through pottery typology. TL dating does, however, provide an important external check on typology and on dates where a pottery typology has not been clearly established. There is also a special application of TL dating in the identification of fake pottery and terracotta objects.

WHAT ARCHAEOLOGY CAN AND CANNOT DO FOR BIBLICAL STUDIES

Archaeology and Biblical Illumination

In 1865, the Palestine Exploration Fund was inaugurated in Great Britain. Its statement of purpose was to investigate the archaeology, topography, geology, geography, manners, and customs of Palestine "for the illustration of the Bible." Five years later, a similar society emerged in the United States called the American Palestine Exploration Society. It modeled its statement of purpose after that of the British society but added one significant word: "for the illustration and *defense* of the Bible" (emphasis mine). This statement of purpose was to guide the development of what could be called "biblical archaeology" in the United States for nearly a century. This development is associated above all with two American academics, William Foxwell Albright and George Ernest Wright. Albright was a highly productive scholar, who published more than 1,200 items. For a generation he was the unquestioned leader in the study of archaeology and the Old Testament/Hebrew Bible in the United States. He first served as director of the American School of Oriental Research in Jerusalem (which has since been renamed the Albright Institute of Archaeological Research in his honor) in the 1920s and 1930s. Then, until 1958, he was a professor at the Johns Hopkins University in Baltimore, where he was the mentor for more than fifty doctoral students, many of whom became active as field archaeologists. Together they constitute what has been called the "Albright school" of biblical archaeology.

The "Albright school" saw archaeology in the biblical world principally as an adjunct of biblical studies. The excavations sponsored by the Albright-directed American School of Oriental Research in Jerusalem in the 1920s and 1930s were carried out at sites whose names and/or locations were known from the Hebrew Bible. These digs were directed by biblical scholars, and funded, to a large extent, by theological seminaries and church-related colleges and universities. To Albright's credit, clearly he transformed what was a very amateurish brand of archaeology in Palestine into an emerging, scientifically-based discipline.

Following in Albright's footsteps in the 1950s to 1970s was George Ernest Wright, who was associated with McCormick Theological Seminary in Chicago until 1958. In 1958, he became Parkman Professor of Divinity at Harvard. Like Albright, he produced a large number of Ph.D.s who became active in Palestinian archaeology. Wright's views on biblical archaeology are especially significant because he, more than anyone else, stressed the combination of biblical theology and Palestinian archaeology, whereas Albright had basically limited archaeology's role to one that illuminated biblical history.

William Dever, a student of Wright who has become a leader in current American involvement in Palestinian archaeology, has described the biblical-archaeology movement that dominated the American scene until about 1970 (1990: 19–20). Dever characterizes the biblical archaeology movement as a subsidiary of biblical and theological studies that drew its agenda not from archaeology but from problems of biblical research. Its method stressed academic training in biblical languages (Hebrew, Aramaic, Greek) and biblical history, combined with practical field experience. It did not emphasize graduate professional work in archaeology, anthropology, and science. The principal strategies employed in excavation by biblical archaeology—stratigraphy and ceramic chronology—focused primarily on recovering political history of pivotal individuals and public events, not economic or social history. Fortification systems, public buildings, pottery sequences, and destruction layers received special attention because it was believed that they could be related directly to Biblical chronology and the supposedly historical accounts of the Biblical literature.

So, why did this approach to archaeology fade from the scene? The biggest problem encountered by "biblical archaeology," which proved to be its undoing, was its inability to solve the very problems in biblical history to which it had directed itself under Albright's encouragement. In particular the questions of the historicity of the patriarchs as pictured in Genesis, of the Mosaic era, and of Israel's "conquest" of Canaan were ones whose solutions were thought to be most amenable to archaeological investigation. While archaeology did not disprove the historicity of the patriarchs, neither did it provide significant illumination of the patriarchs beyond what could be known from the literary traditions about them in Genesis. Of the Exodus from Egypt and the wandering in the Sinai wilderness, biblical archaeology has provided no evidence at all. The settlement of the Israelites in Palestine, which we shall discuss in Chapter 8, has proven to be a most perplexing problem for archaeology. Dozens of sites from this period have been excavated, and surface surveys have been done on hundreds more. Yet here again the evidence is largely negative. Certainly, the picture of a rapid, coordinated, total military conquest of the country, which was derived principally from the book of Joshua, has been largely discredited. David Noel Freedman, himself one of the more prominent supporters of the "Albright school" has described the decline, if not the demise, of "biblical archaeology." He admits that the combination of the Bible and archaeology is somewhat artificial and that the two have not really matched up very well. The biblical scholar and the archaeologist deal with different kinds of material. Sometimes there has been significant contact, and both disciplines have gained from the exchange of data and ideas. More often than not, however, there has been no point of contact. Freedman thinks that, on the whole, the results of such interchange that has taken place between archaeology and the Bible have been somewhat disappointing. While Palestinian archaeology has had some success in discovering monumental remains and inscriptional materials, there has been nothing like the quantity of these discovered in Mesopotamia and Egypt. Unwritten materials are extensive in Palestine, to be sure, but not always easy to interpret, and the biblical connections have been difficult to make. Freedman concludes that Albright's great plan and expectation to set the Bible firmly on the foundation of archaeology, buttressed by verifiable data, seems to have foundered or at least floundered. Archaeology has not proved decisive or even especially helpful in answering frequently-asked questions and has failed to prove the historicity of Biblical persons and events, especially in the early periods (Freedman 1985: 6).

Freedman's pessimistic reading of the results of biblical archaeology for biblical illumination is fortunately, however, not the last word on the subject of the relationship of archaeology and the Bible. As we indicated above, in the last several decades archaeology in the biblical world has been undergoing a transformation. Although the transformation is not yet complete, its contours are by now clear enough that we can reflect on how it might illuminate the biblical texts in ways quite different from those proposed by earlier biblical archaeology. The changes most evident in the newer Palestinian archaeology are those we discussed above in the section on theory. The newer Palestinian archaeology, in short, asks new and more inclusive questions of its data, questions that broaden the more narrowly historically focused questions of the older "biblical archaeology." These questions, moreover, are not generated only, or even primarily, by the Bible nor by the interests of biblical scholars. A by-product of archaeology's independence from biblical studies is a healthy, potentially very productive relationship to biblical studies, a relationship formulated by archaeology *on its own terms.* Dever, one of the foremost proponents of an independent Syro-Palestinian archaeology, has outlined ways in which it can contribute to biblical studies (1990: 32–35):

1. *Archaeology has restored the Bible to its original, material environment.* This makes it possible to see the Bible as a book produced by real people in a particular time and place. These people were in contact with neighboring cultures which have been remarkably "fleshed out" by archaeological data. Archaeology is at its best in providing information about the larger context in which particular events took place instead of the individual events themselves. Through archaeology we now have extensive knowledge of ancient Israel's environmental setting—topography, climate, land and water resources, subsistence systems, exchange networks, settlement patterns, demography, and so forth. Archaeology can also help biblical scholars move beyond the "great person" way of doing history. Instead of focusing solely on the "great" persons of ancient Israel, archaeology can now give us a window on the lives of ordinary people and how they, as well as the so-called "movers and shakers," were significant players on the stage of cultural history. In other words, we can see ancient Israel holistically as a complete society. This society was one in which religion, to be sure, played an important role. Religion itself, however, was part of a system, affecting and being affected by other subsystems.

2. *Archaeology can play a significant role in the illumination of specific cultural references* in the biblical text. Many previously opaque references to unknown cultural artifacts have become transparent, thanks to archaeology. Only one example will be cited here, but we shall have occasion to refer to other illustrative clues from archaeology in the following chapters. The Hebrew term *pîm* occurs only once in all of the Hebrew Bible—in 1 Sam 13:19-21— in the following context:

> Now there was no smith to be found throughout all the land of Israel;
> for the Philistines said, "The Hebrews must not make swords or spears for
> themselves"; so all the Israelites went down to the Philistines to sharpen
> their plowshares, mattocks, axes, or sickles; the charge was two-thirds of
> a shekel (*pîm* in Hebrew) for the plowshares and for the mattocks, and
> one-third of a shekel for sharpening the axes and for setting the goads.

Until archaeologists excavated small, stone balance weights inscribed in Hebrew with the word *pîm*, the correct translation of this Hebrew term was anybody's guess (the KJV translates 1 Sam 13:20: "They had a file for the mattocks, and for the coulters, and for the forks, and for the axes, and to sharpen the goads"). We now know that a *pîm* was a fraction weight of the shekel. The average weight of the known examples of *pîm* weights is 7.8 grams, or a little over three-fifths of the "heavy" shekel, therefore the translation of *pîm* in the New Revised Standard Version and the New American Standard Bible is "two thirds of a shekel" (see Figure 3.7).

3. While archaeology cannot meaningfully comment specifically on many, if not most, particular biblical texts, it can often *supply missing elements of a narrative, and sometimes even an alternate version.* It can fill in textual gaps by adding information that was simply not of interest to the biblical authors, or of which they were not aware. Again, one example will suffice here, but we will refer to a number of such supplementary pieces of information supplied by archaeology in the following chapters. Archaeology has led to the recovery of

Figure 3.7   A stone *pîm* weight

two extra-biblical sources that confirm a severe destruction of the city of Lachish at the very end of the eighth century B.C.E. The Assyrian siege of Lachish is hinted at in 2 Kings 18:14–17. One of the important archaeological finds related to the Assyrian campaign in which Lachish fell is a relief carved in stone that was found in the Assyrian palace at Nimrud, which gives a pictorial representation of the siege of Lachish, mentioning it by name (see Figure 3.8). This find is important not only because it lends support to what has been uncovered in recent excavations at Lachish, but because it gives a vivid picture of the military tactics employed by the Assyrians in laying siege to a city.

The second piece of evidence is the compelling stratigraphical evidence of destruction at the very end of the eighth century B.C.E. at the site of Lachish. Although the destruction of Lachish must have been important in the life of ancient Judah, opening as it did a path for Assyria's advance on Jerusalem itself, the fall of Lachish is not explicitly mentioned in that part of the book of 2 Kings dealing with this period nor in its parallel in 2 Chronicles. The closest the biblical narrative comes to telling of the fall of Lachish is the reference in 2 Chr 32:9: "King Sennacherib of Assyria, was at Lachish with all his forces." The parallel passage in 2 Kings 18:14 only mentions the fact that the king of Assyria was at Lachish. It is not surprising that the biblical authors did not write about the fall of Lachish. It was, after all, a crushing defeat, and its narration would detract from what they considered the miraculous deliverance of Jerusalem from its siege by the Assyrians that followed shortly after the fall of Lachish. Yet, were it

Figure 3.8   Bas-relief of the Assyrian siege of Lachish

not for archaeology, we would know nothing about the fall of Lachish as an event preparing the way for the Assyrian siege of Jerusalem.

4. Although archaeology cannot necessarily illuminate many aspects of ancient religious belief and practice, much less compel modern readers to accept biblical faith statements, it can and does *provide abundant evidence regarding the material culture of ancient Israel,* the stuff of everyday life that constitutes the raw material and concerns with which religion deals.

What Archaeology Cannot Do

For all that archaeology can legitimately contribute to biblical studies, there are things it cannot do. Archaeology cannot answer "Why" questions—certainly not in terms of the ultimate or transcendent causes of human events. If one thinks of religion only in terms of the supernatural or of pure spiritual abstraction, then one might say that archaeology has nothing to do with religion. While archaeology cannot excavate God, it can and does excavate images of gods. Archaeology does not dig up Spirit, though it does recover physical manifestations of spiritual encounters.

What, then, is the relevance of the science of Syro-Palestinian archaeology for the study of biblical religion? At its most fundamental level, relevance is a matter of application. Physics becomes relevant to biology when a radioactive isotope is used to trace the circulation of the blood. Archaeology becomes relevant to biblical studies when the data it supplies is applied to the life and times of people and events in the Bible. Archaeology can neither prove nor disprove biblical statements, but it can illuminate the Bible. Archaeology cannot confirm realities behind the religious convictions of people in the past, nor can it compel faith for those of us living today. Suppose, for example, that the results of the radiocarbon dating of the Shroud of Turin had supported a first century C.E. date rather than one in the fourteenth century. Obviously, this by itself would not have proved that the shroud was the piece of linen in which the body of Jesus was wrapped for burial. Still less would it compel belief in Jesus' resurrection for those living today. Similarly, archaeology cannot prove that today there is or is not an afterlife, any more than a history of the development of psychology proves that today there is, or is not, a valid academic discipline called psychology. A knowledge of the history of psychology does, however, "prove" there is such a discipline; it shows how the discipline has developed. Without it, we might not know what it is we are trying to prove or why we are bothering with it at all.

Clearly, our world and the world of the Bible are separated from one another by centuries. Archaeology helps us span that gap by providing us with windows on the past. Another way of looking at the concern with proof is to note that religious studies as an academic discipline, and biblical studies as a subdiscipline, try to understand the religious thought and practices of the Bible and to give as accurate a description of them as possible. As a biblical scholar and as a professor of religious studies, I do not try to decide for myself and then "prove" to my students whether what the ancient Israelites believed is true or not. Rather, I seek to help my students understand, as clearly as possible, what the ancient Israelites believed and how they expressed their beliefs in word and deed.

The question, for example, of whether Moses was or was not a monotheist is a theological idea that archaeology can neither prove nor disprove. Archaeology, together with the study of other ancient Near Eastern texts, can show that it was possible in Moses' world to have such abstract ideas. Archaeology is concerned with contexts in which our ancient brothers and sisters expressed their belief in God or the gods. In the end, it is true that archaeology can neither prove nor disprove the existence of God. Ultimately the belief that God exists, or the belief that God does not exist, is a matter of faith and not subject to proof of any kind, archaeological or otherwise. William Foxwell Albright, with whom we began this discussion of archaeology and the Bible, also supplies us with a fitting conclusion: "The profoundest intuitions of faith are not subject to logical proof—but neither are the axioms on which all science and technology are erected" (1964: 322).

STUDY QUESTIONS

The late Father Roland de Vaux, who was both an archaeologist and a biblical scholar, said the following in an essay titled "On Right and Wrong Uses of Archaeology":

One will always have to reconstruct biblical history by starting with the texts, and the texts must be interpreted by the methods of literary criticism, tradition criticism and historical criticism. Archaeology does not confirm the text, which is what it is; it can only confirm the interpretation which we give it.

Write a brief essay on de Vaux's statement in light of what you have read in this chapter about the development of archaeology. Conclude your essay with your assessment of right and wrong uses of archaeology as related to the study of the Bible.

BIBLIOGRAPHY

Albright, William F. 1964. *History, Archaeology, and Christian Humanism.* New York: McGraw Hill.

Dever, William G. 1990. *Recent Archaeological Discoveries and Biblical Research.* Seattle: University of Washington Press.

—. 1991. "Unresolved Issues in the Early History of Israel: Toward a Synthesis of Archaeological and Textual Reconstructions," in *The Bible and the Politics of Exegesis: Essays in Honor of Norman K. Gottwald on His Sixty-Fifth Birthday,* 195–208. Edited by David Jobling, Peggy L. Day, and Gerald T. Sheppard. Cleveland: Pilgrim.

Freedman, David Noel. 1985. "The Relationship of Archaeology to the Bible." *Biblical Archaeology Review,* Vol. 11, no. 1: 6.

Lapp, Paul. 1975. *The Tale of the Tell: Archaeological Studies.* Edited by Nancy Lapp. Pittsburgh: Pickwick.

Mazar, Amihai. 1990. *Archaeology of the Land of the Bible: 10,000 – 586 B.C.E.* New York: Bantam Doubleday Dell.

Renfrew, Colin and Paul Bahn. 1991. *Archaeology: Theories, Methods, and Practice.* New York: Thames and Hudson.

Thompson, Henry O. 1987. *Biblical Archaeology: The World, the Mediterranean, the Bible.* New York: Paragon House.

Wright, George Ernest. 1957. *Biblical Archaeology.* Philadelphia: Westminster.

PART
II

THE TORAH
OR PENTATEUCH
IN THE HEBREW CANON

Chapter 4

THE STRUCTURE AND COMPOSITION OF THE PENTATEUCH

SOURCES OF THE PENTATEUCH: THE HISTORY OF AN IDEA

One cannot read very far in Genesis before encountering literary phenomena that present difficulties for the idea that what one is reading was written as the single creative act of one author. Some of these phenomena are:

1. *Duplicate Stories.* There are, for example, three different stories dealing with one of the patriarchs attempting to pass off his wife as his sister (Gen 12:10-20; 20:1-18; 26:1-11).

2. *Inconsistencies.* The Genesis flood story, for example, says in 6:19-20 that Noah was to take one pair of all animals onto the ark. In 7:2-3, however, Noah is instructed to take seven pairs of "clean" animals (that is, animals that could be sacrificed) and only one pair of "unclean" animals.

3. *Anachronisms.* Gen 36:31, narrating events that happened long before the monarchy was established, mentions a king in Israel. This takes us forward to a period not earlier than Saul, in the last decades of the second millennium B.C.E. There are also anachronisms in geographical designations. Gen 14:14 mentions the city Dan, which has this name (replacing the earlier Laish) only from Judg 18:29 on.

4. *God's name.* Some passages simply use "God" as the name for God (translating the Hebrew word *'elohim*), while others use "LORD" (translating the Hebrew word *Yahweh*). According to Ex 6:2–3, Moses was the first person to know God's personal name, Yahweh. Gen 4:26, however, says that this name had been used from the earliest times.

5. *Digressions and sudden stylistic changes.* There are instances where material appears to have been inserted, interrupting the structural integrity of a passage. (For example, in Gen 5:29 material closely related to chapters 2 and 3 interrupts a genealogy, yet chapter 5 begins with a clear reference to 1:26–30.)

These kinds of phenomena, in the cultural and intellectual contexts of the seventeenth and eighteenth centuries, are what led to the development of source criticism, which was introduced in Chapter 1. Source criticism of the Hebrew Bible did not come into being because some skeptical scholars who had no appreciation for the Hebrew scriptures got together one day and said, "Here is a beautifully unified and coherent work; how can we chop it up into little pieces?" It began as the natural outgrowth of the questions individuals raised about difficulties they experienced when they read the first books in the Bible. It began in particular with questions about the first five books of the Hebrew scriptures, the Pentateuch or Torah. Early Jewish and Christian tradition had come to label these books the Five Books of Moses, believing that Moses himself wrote them. But this supposition of Mosaic authorship ran into difficulty as people observed contradictions within the Pentateuch, contradictions that seemed to be inconsistent with the idea that these five books were the product of a single author. People also noticed that the Torah included things that Moses, without presuming some kind of special supernatural knowledge on his part, could not have known about or was not likely to have written about, things that were unknown in Moses' time. The text, after all, as these early readers observed, told of Moses' death and burial.

This process of questioning the Mosaic authorship and unity of the Pentateuch went through three stages, as outlined by Friedman (1987:18–21). In the first stage of such questioning, people still hung onto the belief in the Mosaic authorship of *almost all* of the Torah. They simply suggested that a few additions had been made here and there by others at some later time. This could provide an explanation for those passages that referred to Moses in the third person, such as the account of Moses' death and burial. It could also explain references to places that Moses had never been, as well as for terms or language that Moses would not have known, because they did not exist in his time.

In the second stage of the process, scholars still maintained that Moses indeed wrote the Five Books. Later, however, trying to update them for readers in their time, editors went over the books, adding words or phrases of their own. A clue to this type of editorial activity was found in the phrase "to this day," which recurs throughout the Pentateuch (especially in Genesis and in that part of Deuteronomy outside the Deuteronomic Code—Gen 19:37, 38; 22:14; 26:33; 32:32; 35:20; 47:26; 48:15; Ex 19:6; Num 22:30; Deut 2:22; 3:14; 10:8; 11:4; 29:4; 34:6).

In the third stage of this process, beginning in the seventeenth century, scholars asserted outright for the first time that Moses *did not* write most of the Pentateuch. The first person that we know of who said this was the British philosopher Thomas Hobbes. One of the most famous of these seventeenth century scholars was Richard Simon, a Frenchman who converted from Protestantism and became a Catholic priest. Simon said that the nucleus of the Pentateuch (that is, the laws) was the work of Moses. There were, however, additions to Moses' work that stemmed from scribes who collected, organized, and elaborated upon the Mosaic core of legal material. Simon believed that these scribes were guided by the Holy Spirit in their work, and so he did not see his work as attacking, but as defending the authority and sanctity of the biblical text. Simon's contemporaries, however, were not persuaded by Simon's proposal. Because of his work on the Pentateuch, Simon was vigorously attacked by other Catholic clergy and subsequently expelled from his religious order. Protestants showed similar distaste for Simon's work as well, and forty refutations of his work were written by Protestants. Of the 1,300 copies that were printed of Simon's book, all but six of them were burned.

Sources

OLD DOCUMENTARY HYPOTHESIS

Simon's idea that the Pentateuch was the result of the combination of multiple sources by several authors prepared the way for what was to follow in the eighteenth century. The observations made by Simon and others were put into even sharper focus during the first half of the eighteenth century by a German pastor, Henning Bernhard Witter, and a French Catholic physician at the court of Louis XV, Jean Astruc. The occurrence of different divine names as a means of identifying parallel sources was first developed by Witter in a book published in 1711. Astruc, interestingly enough, was the son of a Protestant minister who had converted to Catholicism in the period of the dragonnades, a time of persecution directed by Louis XIV. As an amateur biblical scholar, Astruc published his findings in 1753. Both Witter and Astruc, independently of one another, observed the phenomenon of different divine names coupled with differences in style. They observed that usually one of the two versions of a duplicate story would refer to the deity by the divine name Yahweh (which the KJV translators translated as Jehovah), while the other version of the story would refer to the deity simply as "God," which translates the Hebrew word *'elohim*. An example of this can be seen in two stories about Hagar—one in Gen 16:4-14 that uses Yahweh throughout (translated as Lord in the NRSV) and another in Gen 21:8-21 that uses *'elohim* (translated as God in the NRSV). Added to this correlation of two stories with two different divine names was the discovery that it was not only the names of the deity that lined up in this way. Several other terms and characteristics were noted that appeared consistently in one group of narratives or the other. Astruc named the source that uses "God" when referring to God the "Elohist" source and termed that which called him by the name Yahweh the "Jahwist" source. Neither Witter nor Astruc, however, took on the question of Mosaic authorship. Witter, in fact, spoke of sources used by Moses in composing the Pentateuch. Astruc was simply interested in explaining how there could be duplications and discrepancies in what was supposed to be the work of a single author. His explanation, like Witter's, was that Moses used "notes" in writing the Pentateuch; in other words, he used preexisting sources. The work of Witter and Astruc has been called the Old Documentary Hypothesis in order to distinguish it from the Newer Documentary Hypothesis of Graf and Wellhausen (see below).

NEW DOCUMENTARY HYPOTHESIS

The intellectual climate at the beginning of the nineteenth century brought about considerable development in the study of the documentary hypothesis, culminating in its classical statement in 1878 with the publication of Wellhausen's *Prolegomena to the History of Israel* (a second, and perhaps better-known edition of which was published in 1883). Throughout the nineteenth century much of the scholarship dealing with the Hebrew Bible focused on identifying, dating, and describing sources, with much less attention given to the processes by which these sources became part of a larger piece of literature. With benefit of hindsight, we can now see the intellectual currents of the day that affected the direction taken by the work of these nineteenth-century scholars. What inspired their work was the goal of reconstructing the historical development of religious ideas and institutions in ancient Israel, and for this, the placing of sources in chronological sequence was an important first step. Their scholarship was dominated by the concept of development, especially the development of ideas. Ideas of cultural primitivism, prevalent in the Romantic movement of the late eighteenth and early nineteenth centuries, were brought to bear on the religion of early Israel as reflected in sources identified as coming from that time (Blenkinsopp 1992:8).

The attempts to explain the composition of the Pentateuch at the beginning of the nineteenth century began with the work of Wilhelm Martin Leberecht de Wette. De Wette, a young German scholar, in his doctoral dissertation in 1805 identified the law book discovered in the temple during the reign of Josiah, king of Judah in the second half of the seventh century B.C.E., with an early version of the present book of Deuteronomy. He concluded that in its final form Deuteronomy was the latest of the literary strands in the Pentateuch. He postulated two other strands that preceded Deuteronomy and a later prophetic source. These hypothetical strands of De Wette correspond roughly to J, P, and E in the Graf-Wellhausen statement of the documentary hypothesis (see below), though in a different order.

Then followed what might be called the supplementary hypothesis. This hypothesis suggested that there was only a single source, which was gradually supplemented by the addition of other texts. The best-known proponent of this idea was the German, Heinrich Ewald. Ewald argued that an Elohistic source was filled out with excerpts from a Jehovistic source by an editor active in the late Judean monarchy. The final form of the first six books of the Bible (a Hexateuch, not a Pentateuch) was arrived at by a process of editorial amplification over several centuries.

In the latter part of the nineteenth century, two German scholars, Karl Heinrich Graf and Julius Wellhausen, pulled together these earlier findings and came up with what became the classic statement of what has been called the documentary hypothesis, also referred to as the Newer Documentary Hypothesis or the Graf-Wellhausen hypothesis. This hypothesis prevailed in biblical scholarship until it met serious challenges in the last third of the twentieth century. Still today, however, it forms a starting point, even for those who reject the documentary hypothesis in the form proposed by Wellhausen.

Four Sources.   In its classic statement the hypothesis says the following: The Pentateuch is composed of four documents or sources. These four sources (in the order in which they came into being) can be designated by symbols as follows:

J, the "Yahwist" (for Yahweh, *Jahweh* in German) can be dated in the tenth-ninth centuries B.C.E.

E, the "Elohist" (for *'Elohim*) is somewhat, but not very much, later than J.

D, the "Deuteronomist" is largely identical with the book of Deuteronomy and was first produced in the late seventh century B.C.E.

P, the "Priestly" source was composed at the end of the Babylonian exile or a little later (550–450 B.C.E.).

Wellhausen's system was powerful in the simplicity of its structure and persuasive in the way in which it provided explanation. As clearly stated and revolutionary as it was, Wellhausen's historical reconstruction was very much a product of the intellectual milieu of the late nineteenth century (Blenkinsopp 1992: 11–12). It is dominated by the kind of generalization characteristic of the Hegelian philosophy of history, which proceeds from thesis to antithesis to synthesis. This philosophy of history was an evolutionary one and sought to account for the ascent of human thought from its "primitive" beginnings to its "enlightened" state in Christianity. In the attempt to explain historical process in an evolutionary manner, history was divided into periods, following a common tendency in nineteenth-century religious scholarship. This periodization begins with "nature religion," which develops into "prophetic religion," and then into Judaism. In Wellhausen's work, J and E, the earlier sources, correspond to the period of nature religion, characterized by spontaneity and religious festivals that were closely connected to the agricultural calendar. With the Deuteronomist, this spontaneity was suppressed in favor of a written law. As Wellhausen himself said:

> With the appearance of the law came to an end the old freedom, not only in the spheres of worship, now restricted to Jerusalem, but in the sphere of the religious spirit as well. There was now in existence an authority as objective as could be; and this was the end of prophecy.
>
> as quoted by Blenkinsopp: 11

By the time of the latest of the sources, the Priestly Code, the spontaneity of nature religion had disappeared completely. Religion had been transformed from the spontaneous responses of people to their world into a structured ecclesiastical community. While there is no doubt that Wellhausen had a genuine aversion to Judaism and worked at a time and place where antisemitism was prevalent, his censure was aimed at the church as well as Judaism. According to Wellhausen, both Judaism and Christianity had abandoned their origins as vital religious movements and changed themselves into religious institutions, stifling the free and spontaneous expressions of the human spirit.

Wellhausen isolated the four sources by relying on what came to be called "the five pillars of documentary criticism":

1. the use of divine names,
2. language and style,
3. contradictions and divergences within the text,
4. duplication and repetition of material, and
5. the evidence that different accounts have been combined.

The Graf-Wellhausen hypothesis maintained that these four documents underwent three broad stages of *redaction* or editing. First, D worked with a combined form of J and E; thus Wellhausen proposed that the redaction JE had to have been created sometime before 650 B.C.E. Then, Deuteronomy was added by a D redactor about 550 B.C.E., forming JED. Finally, the Priestly document was added in *ca.* 400 B.C.E., resulting in JEDP, or the Pentateuch as we know it. While there has never been unanimous agreement among scholars about what parts of the Pentateuch belong to which source, there has been a general agreement on the broad locations of the four sources. This consensus is represented graphically in Figure 4.1.

Source Analysis in the Early Twentieth Century.   Although the full complexity of Pentateuchal composition has been recognized only in the last century, difficulties with the traditional view of Mosaic authorship have long been apparent. Wellhausen's hypothesis was accepted, at least in its broad outlines, by the majority of biblical scholars for about a century. Since its initial formula-

Figure 4.1   General locations of sources in the Pentateuch

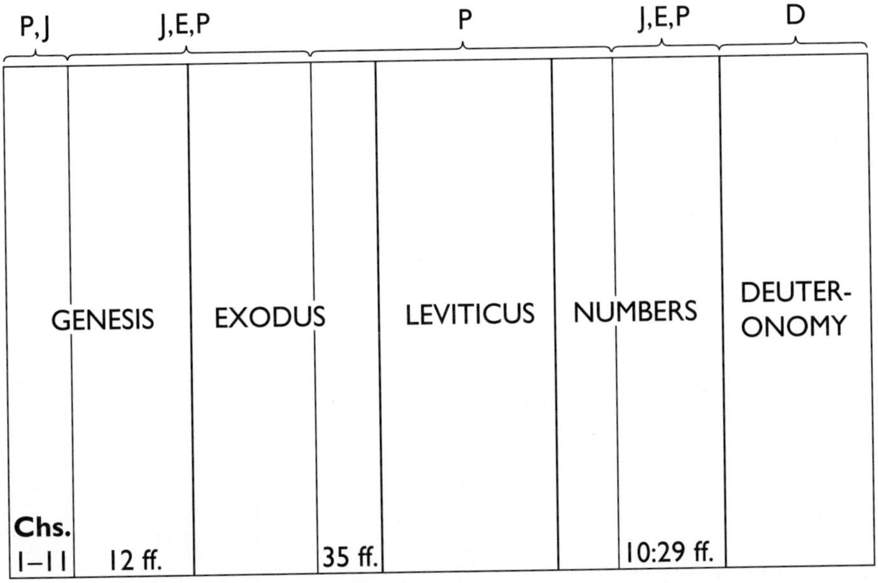

P,J	J,E,P		P		J,E,P	D
GENESIS	EXODUS		LEVITICUS	NUMBERS		DEUTER-ONOMY
Chs. 1–11	12 ff.		35 ff.		10:29 ff.	

tion, however, it has been considerably modified. Thus, for example, the assumption that J, E, D, and P existed as four discrete, parallel written source documents, such as one might use in writing a research paper, has been abandoned. In its place is the idea that there were living clusters of traditions, originally oral, which developed in parallel streams and in a close relationship with the religious life of the communities they represented. Each of the four "sources," understood in this way, includes some very old oral traditions with expansions and reinterpretations. Therefore, some parts of D and P are as old as or older than parts of J or E. When viewed in this way, the dates that Wellhausen proposed become only the end points by which these traditions had achieved their fixed, written forms. While there were many who pointed out the limitations of Wellhausen's work and suggested refinements of it, those who rejected it entirely were few.

A high point in the exposition of the documentary hypothesis was reached in the 1930s and 1940s in the work of two German scholars, Gerhard von Rad and Martin Noth. Both these scholars produced their own accounts of the way in which the Pentateuch developed from its beginnings to its final form (von Rad 1966; Noth 1972 [the dates given here are those of the English translations]). Noth suggested that five broad themes, originally independent from one another, had already been brought together in a continuous history before either J or E wrote. Noth saw P only as a final editor, not as a source document at all. For von Rad, J, working in Solomon's time (the mid-10th century B.C.E.), was the author of the earliest version of the Pentateuch. This version of the

Figure 4.2 The development of the Pentateuch

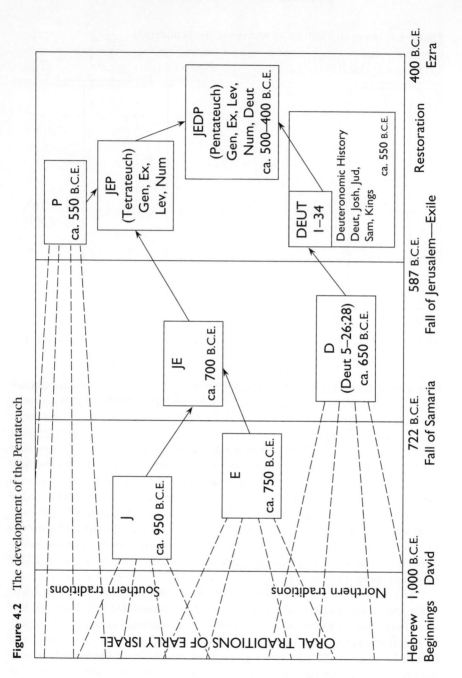

Pentateuch narrated the story of Israel's origins and history, up to the occupation of Palestine following the Exodus. It had an added "prehistorical" preface which dealt with the origins of the world and humankind in general (Gen 1 – 11). A graphic version of the fully developed documentary hypothesis is represented in Figure 4.2.

Neither Noth nor von Rad, however, ever questioned the fundamental proposition of the documentary hypothesis, which until the last twenty years has been the hypothesis of choice among German, English, and American biblical scholars. This excludes, of course, a small minority of scholars that has held onto the Mosaic authorship of the Pentateuch.

Those scholars who operate within the playing field established by the documentary hypothesis continue to discuss the dating of the sources, their theological profiles, and whether a particular verse or verses can be assigned to a particular source. They express varying degrees of satisfaction with the usefulness of the hypothesis for literary or historical purposes. The hypothesis itself, however, has continued to be an important starting point for study of and research on the Pentateuch for many students of the Hebrew Bible. A working knowledge of the four-source hypothesis, of the traditions or strata and their characteristics, and their general locations in the biblical text are indispensable for an intelligent reading and analysis of the Pentateuch. This knowledge becomes especially important in recognition of the fact that no other explanation of the evidence before us in the text has yet established itself as a completely satisfactory alternative. The following brief summaries of the principal characteristics of the four sources should be useful in reading the Pentateuch.

THE YAHWISTIC (J) TRADITION

The Yahwistic tradition (J) takes its name from the fact that the divine name "Yahweh" is predominant in this stratum as God's personal name. The symbol J is used to designate this source, rather than Y, because the first analysis of the source was done in Germany, where Yahweh is spelled *Jahve*. In the NRSV Yahweh is translated Lord, using an upper-case "L" and small upper case letters for the "ord." J alone among the sources preserves a tradition that the name Yahweh was used for God before the time of Moses: "To Seth also a son was born, and he named him Enosh. At that time people began to invoke the name of the Lord" (Gen 4:26), instead of being revealed for the first time to Moses. The anonymous "author" of this source is accordingly called the Yahwist. J is also appropriate as a symbol for this source, because Judah, the southern kingdom, is prominent in it.

Around the middle of the tenth century B.C.E. a skilled narrator shaped existing traditions about Israel's origins into a continuous narrative, apparently for the first time. The J author composed these narratives about Israel's forebears with an eye to explaining *and* justifying the political and social realities of the contemporary world, the unified Israelite monarchy in the days of David and

Solomon. J's purpose, however, was not fundamentally a political one, but theological. The Yahwist believed that God's plans for Israel, begun with the creation of the ancestors of all humankind, were presently being realized in the reigns of David and his son Solomon. Just as God began by choosing Abraham and his descendants as the particular line of the human family through whom *all* humanity would be blessed (Gen 12), so now a strong, unified Israelite state had been chosen as the political instrument through which God would work to achieve his purposes for all nations.

J has about it the distinct flavor of folklore. The actions of God are described in a very human and personal, or *anthropomorphic* manner. J pictures a God who can, like his human creations, regret having done things (Gen 6:6, 7), who personally closes the door to the ark (Gen 7:16), and smells the pleasant aroma of Noah's sacrifice after the flood (8:21). This God, acting like a potter, molds the first human from the dust, breathes life into its nostrils, like a person doing CPR (2:7), and takes a stroll around the Garden of Eden in the cool of the day (3:8).

The human characters in J's narrative, similarly, are "real" people, not idealized saints. Israel's patriarchs and matriarchs are described as persons with obvious moral flaws. J, for example, tells of Abraham's misrepresentation of his wife Sarah as his sister in order to save himself from the hand of the Egyptian Pharaoh, who might have killed Abraham to get access to Sarah (Gen 12). J tells this story without offering any explicit ethical judgments, allowing the vivid description of the event to speak for itself.

J is a source that emphasizes locales and personalities from the southern part of the Palestinian region. Not only does the tribe of Judah play a prominent role in this source, but special attention is directed toward southern personalities, localities, and shrines. For example, in those stories in Genesis where God is called Yahweh, Abraham is said to reside in Hebron, a principal city in the southern highlands of Judah. According to another J story, Moses sends a group of scouts from the Sinai wilderness into the promised land to reconnoiter. All but one of these scouts report that the land cannot be entered because of the size and ferocity of its inhabitants. The one spy, however, who challenges this negative report and encourages the people to have faith is Caleb, a southerner (Num 13:30). In the story, the scouts travel through the Negev (the southern extension of the central hill country), the central hill country, as far north as Hebron, then to the Wadi Eshkol. All these places are in Judah's territory, so that in J's report, the scouts actually saw only the region of Judah.

J constitutes the basic narrative core of the books of Genesis, Exodus, and Numbers. Although it has been added to and redacted by others, the essential shape of the Yahwistic narrative can still be discerned, and it is this shape that gives to the Pentateuch much of its epic, dramatic character. Using a pattern of promise and fulfillment, J relates one incident to another, giving continuity to what were originally unrelated, disconnected units. The theme of J's work is one of repeated human trial and failure—the human attempt to play God and the inevitable failures that result. It is also the story of God's intervention for judgment and renewal of flawed creatures, who keep getting themselves into trouble by forgetting the all-important distinction between Creator and creature. This implicit chain of promise, guidance, and renewal first becomes explicit in the promises made to the patriarchs. It moves in J toward its fulfillment in the Exodus with the movement into the land of the promise.

J also has a distinctive vocabulary, some of which is more accessible in the original Hebrew than in English translation. J uses the term "Canaanites" for the indigenous people of Palestine, whereas E refers to them as "Amorites." J uses "Sinai" to refer to the mountain where Moses received the law; E calls it "Horeb." In referring to a female servant, J uses the Hebrew term *shiphchah,* while E prefers the term *'amah.* J calls Moses' father-in-law "Hobab" or "Reuel"; E says his name was "Jethro."

Certainly J's basic message can be discerned readily: Yahweh's will to salvation overcomes human faithlessness. Not just once, but repeatedly, J's story shows that human lack of trust is compensated for by Yahweh's trustworthiness.

THE ELOHISTIC (E) TRADITION

The Elohistic tradition, like J, takes its designation from the word it uses when referring to God, here, the Hebrew word *'elohim,* which is translated into English as "gods" or "God." (The word is actually a plural noun in Hebrew, and its translation as "God" or "gods" depends upon the way it is used in Hebrew. If the verb or adjective used with *'elohim* is singular then it is taken as "God." If it is used with a plural verb or adjective it is translated "gods.") The "author" of this source, who is called the Elohist, in his account of Moses' call (Ex 3:9–14), maintains that the personal name "Yahweh" was unknown until it was first disclosed to Moses, in preparation for his leading his people out of slavery in Egypt.

E is also a useful symbol for this source because it can stand also for Ephraim, the most important of the northern tribes. E is thus a northern Palestinian source. Because the two tribes pictured as descended from Joseph—Ephraim and Manasseh—together with Reuben, are northern tribes, understandably, much of the cycle of stories about Joseph comes from this source. Reuben is portrayed as the protector of Joseph. Northern locales such as Bethel and Shechem are prominent. In a story that refers to God as *'elohim* (Gen 32:25–31), Jacob has a face-to-face wrestling match with a mysterious someone who, in the end, turns out to be God (or an angel). As a result, the place where it happened is named Peni-el ("The face of God," *'el* in Hebrew being another name for God). We know from the history of the two kingdoms, found in the book of 1 Kings, that Peni-el was, in fact, a city built by King Jeroboam, the first king of Israel's northern kingdom, ruling from 922–901 B.C.E. (1 Kings 12:25).

The Elohist's work is frequently so closely interwoven with J that it is difficult to separate the two. E has been distinguished, nevertheless, on the basis of the way in which it pictures both humans and God. Unlike J, E sometimes offers rationalistic explanations for the questionable behavior of the patriarchs and matriarchs, seeking to defend their moral character. For example, in the story concerning the Egyptian Pharaoh's attraction to Sarah and the potential threat posed to Abraham, E explains that Abraham did not lie in representing Sarah as his sister. He merely told a half-truth, because Sarah was in fact his half-sister. E is also careful to point out that Abimelech did not sexually violate Sarah (Gen 20:2-6). According to J, Joseph's brothers sold him into slavery to the Ishmaelites (Gen 37:27, 28b). E, however, says that he was abducted from the well by Midianite travelers (Gen 37:22-24, 28, 29).

A similar attention to detail can be seen in the way in which E avoids the type of anthropomorphic description of God that J sometimes uses. E does this by using angels and dreams as the media through which God reveals his will to humans. A major exception to this, however, shows in E's treatment of Moses. E has God speak directly to Moses (Ex 31:18) and God writes the Ten Commandments on the tablets of stone with his own finger. E's avoidance of anthropomorphisms in his portrayal of God may thus be less an expression of belief in God's transcendence, as some have supposed, and more of a device for setting Moses apart from all other human beings, as the one human being who could communicate with God in this direct, face-to-face manner.

Elohistic material does not appear at all in the first eleven chapters of Genesis, but alternates with J in the patriarchal accounts and in portions of the books of Exodus and Numbers. The partial preservation of E in the Torah has been explained by the fact that after the northern kingdom fell to the Assyrian onslaught in 722 B.C.E., the narrative was reshaped by southern editors in Judah. These editors gave preference to their own Yahwistic or Judean form of the stories of national origins.

For the Elohist, God's purpose for his people transcended the royal structures of the Davidic dynastic monarchy. This, of course, is a natural position for a northerner to take, because it was the northern tribes who pulled away from the Davidic dynastic monarchy after the death of Solomon and never entirely endorsed the idea of a hereditary monarchy. From the perspective of these tribes, however, this division of the united monarchy was nothing more than a political act initiated in response to the oppressive policies of Solomon. It was not a religious act of rebellion from the authority of Yahweh, as other southern theologians subsequently would interpret it.

A date that is commonly proposed for E is the mid-ninth century B.C.E., when the northern kingdom was the stronger of the two states. About half a century later, after the fall of the northern kingdom, the Elohistic traditions were combined with J to form JE in a way that resulted in the accommodation of E to J.

THE DEUTERONOMIC (D) TRADITION

The Deuteronomist is the name given the tradition or school that produced the Deuteronomic Code (the central section of the book of Deuteronomy, chapters 12-26). The book of Deuteronomy, to which this source is almost, if not exclusively, limited was appended to the JE epic sometime after the seventh century B.C.E.

The literary style of Deuteronomy is very different from that of the JE epic. It consists largely of laws couched in sermonic form rather than narrative and is marked by phrases that are exhortations to ethical living. Examples of such phrases are: "Hear, O Israel," "remember," "take heed to yourselves," "with all your heart and soul," "that you may live," "keep all the commandments," and so on. Although Deuteronomy now stands as part of the Torah, removing it would have little effect on the continuity of the narrative that begins from Genesis and continues through Numbers, except to remove the description of the death and burial of Moses and Joshua's succession to leadership.

Deuteronomy is structured around three "sermons" of Moses in which he exhorts Israel to be faithful to God's law, which is the only thing that can guarantee their corporate survival and well-being. Moses, in the third of these "sermons," assures the people: "And if you will only obey the Lord your God, by diligently observing all his commandments that I am commanding you today, the Lord your God will set you high above all the nations of the earth" (Deut 28:1). Israel's disobedience, however, will bring the opposite results: "But if you will not obey the Lord your God by diligently observing all his commandments and his decrees, which I am commanding you today, then all these curses shall come upon you and overtake you" (Deut 28:15).

This theological formula: obedience to God's law brings blessing and disobedience brings curse is a consistent hallmark of the Deuteronomist. This formula of D's also is reminiscent of the language used by prophets. Perhaps at periodic ceremonies of covenant renewal, prophets would encourage fidelity to Yahweh and social justice, obedience to the covenant law, not merely political loyalty to the king. The present book of Deuteronomy probably began to take shape in such a context at about the same time that the Elohist was working on his narrative of Israel's origins. In a sense, then, Deuteronomy is a prophetic encouragement to faithfulness, intended as a supplement to the Elohist's story of beginnings.

THE PRIESTLY (P) TRADITION

The Priestly document or tradition is still the clearest one to discern in the face of alterations and refinements in source criticism, and there is a fair degree of consensus on its date, theological profile, and intention. This tradition, as its name suggests, is marked by the unmistakable interests of the priesthood and ceremonial sanctity, and by the kind of precise attention to detail that is associated with a priestly way of thinking and acting. A concern with ritual origins and laws, as well as with the chronological details of Israel's past is evident. Because the priesthood was a hereditary office in Israel, there is also an interest in genealogies. The detailed attention given to cultic institutions in the latter part of Exodus, the prescriptions governing sacrifices, festival days, and ritual purity that make up all of Leviticus, and the assorted ritual laws and traditions in Numbers are all from this source.

The Torah was apparently completed during the latter part of the Babylonian exile by a priestly narrator and redactor. The priestly community, partially because they were part of Israel's small literate minority, was one of the groups that took on the job of the conservation of Israel's religious heritage during the time of the Babylonian exile and in the period of the restoration in Palestine following the exile. The priests believed that Israel as a people could preserve their identity only by strict separation from other peoples. The numerous priestly institutions and laws were thus meant to assure the survival of the people. The goal of the Priestly writers was to help believing Israelites deal with the experience of exile, separation, and the loss of liberty, and to offer some certainty among the insecurities of exile. This they tried to do by emphasizing that God himself upholds the cosmic order, ensures the survival of the world, and averts the threat of chaos. This divine order, in their view, is particularly evident in the rituals over which they presided.

The priestly narrator supplemented the JE narrative with his own materials. The creation account in Genesis 1 comes from the priestly narrator, as do most of the genealogical lists and chronological notations. A comparison with the J creation account, which begins in Genesis 2:4b, reveals P's detached reserve in describing the acts of God. This is achieved not just by avoiding J's anthropomorphisms, but by using simple speech forms in which human encounters with the deity are cited without any elaboration at all. In P, it is said quite simply that "God called," "God said," and so on—leaving any superfluous details to the human imagination and in that way protecting God's holiness.

P was clearly written as a theological alternative to JE. The JE stories often say: "And Yahweh said to Moses . . ." The author of P, however, often makes this phrase read "And Yahweh said to Moses *and to Aaron*," thereby giving more prominence to Aaron as the progenitor of Israel's priestly class (Friedman: 190-1). In P there are no sacrifices until the very last chapter of Exodus. There, the first sacrifice in P is the story of the sacrifice performed on the day that Aaron is consecrated as High Priest. Any sacrifice performed before or apart from this properly consecrated priesthood would be illegitimate (or nonexistent) from P's perspective. All sacrifices in P are performed by Aaron or his sons. The J version says that Noah took seven pairs of clean animals (that is, ones fit for sacrifice) onto the ark (Gen 7:2-3). P, however, says that there was only one pair of every kind of animal (Gen 6:19-20). Why the difference? Because, in J, at the end of the flood, Noah offers an animal sacrifice. If only one pair of a species had been saved on the ark, Noah would have, by this act of sacrifice, doomed that species to extinction. From P's perspective, however, one pair was obviously sufficient since there could not have been any sacrifice before the time of Aaron.

The issue here is not just the mechanics or chronology of sacrifice. For P, it is the larger principle that properly consecrated priests with appropriate credentials and a correct genealogy are the *only* admissible intermediaries between humans and the divine. In the P versions of the stories in Genesis, there are no angels, no talking animals, no dreams. Even the word "prophet," meaning a spokesperson for God, occurs only once in P, referring, of course, not to Moses, but to Aaron (Friedman: 191).

Throughout P we read about a God whose creation is neatly structured. If human beings wish to communicate with such a God, the only reliable channel is through formally constituted, well-ordered structures. Such communication cannot be trusted to talking serpents or other animals, nor can it come through angels or dreams, nor even by means of prophets. It can only take place through prescribed sacrifices, offered in a stipulated manner, at a determined time, performed by a proper priesthood (Friedman: 192).

THE SOURCES IN THE PENTATEUCH (GENESIS THROUGH NUMBERS)

Where are the four sources found in the Pentateuch? The following list (adapted from Friedman: 246–55) presents a general idea of their locations, although scholars might not agree on details. In this list R = Redactor.

GENESIS

NARRATIVE UNIT	J	E	P	R
Creation	2:4b–25		1:1–2:3	
Generations of heaven and earth				2:4a
Garden of Eden	3:1–24			
Cain and Abel	4:1–16			
Cain genealogy	4:17–26			
Generations of humans	5:29			5:1–28, 30–32
Sons of gods and human women	6:1–4			
The flood	6:5–8, 7:1–5 7, 10, 12, 16b–20, 22 –23; 8:2b–3a, 6, 8–12, 13b, 20–22		7:8–10, 11, 13–16a, 21, 24; 8:1–2a, 3b–5, 7, 13a, 14–19; 9:1–17	
Noah's drunkenness	9:18–27			
Noah's age				7:6; 9:28–29
Generations of Noah's sons	10:8–19, 21, 24–30		10:1b–7, 20, 22–23, 31–32	
The tower of Babel	11:1–9			

NARRATIVE UNIT	J	E	P	R
Generations of Shem				11:10a, 10b–26
Generations of Terah				11:27a, 32
Abraham's migration	12:1–4a		11:27b–31	12:4b–5
Promise to Abraham	12:6–9			
Wife/sister	12:10–20			
Abraham and Lot	13:1–5, 7–11a, 12b–18		13:6, 11b–12a	
Abraham's covenant	15:1–21		17:1–27	
Hagar and Ishmael	16:1–2, 4–14		16:3, 15–16	
The three visitors	18:1–33			
Sodom and Gomorrah	19:1–28, 30–38		19:29	
Wife/sister		20:1–18		
Birth of Isaac	21:1, 2a, 7	21:6	21:1b, 2b–5	
Hagar and Ishmael		21:8–21		
Abraham and Abimelek	21:22–34			
The binding of Isaac		22:1–10, 16b–19		22:11–16a
Abraham's kin	22:20–24			
The cave of Machpelah			23:1–20	
Rebekkah	24:1–67		25:20	
The sons of Keturah	25:5–6	25:1–4		
Death of Abraham			25:7–11a	
Generations of Ishmael			25:13–18	25:12
Generations of Isaac				25:19
Jacob and Esau	25:11b, 21–34; 27:1–45		26:34–35; 27:46; 28:1–9	
Wife/sister	26:1–11			
Isaac and Abimelek	26:12–33			
Jacob at Beth-el	28:10–11a, 13–16, 19	28:11b–12, 17–18, 20–22		
Jacob, Leah, and Rachel	29:1–30			
Jacob's children	29:31–35; 30:24b	30:1–24a	35:23–26	
Jacob and Laban	30:25–43	31:1–2, 4–16, 19–54; 32:1–3		
Jacob's return	31:3, 17, 18a; 32:14–24	32:4–13; 33:1–17		31:18b; 35:27
Jacob becomes Israel	32:25–33	35:9–15		
Shechem	34:1–31	33:18–20		33:18
Return to Beth-el		35:1–8		
Rachel dies		35:16–20		

NARRATIVE UNIT	J	E	P	R
Reuben takes Jacob's concubine	35:21–22			
Death of Isaac			35:28–29	
Generations of Esau	36:31–43		36:2–30	36:1
Joseph and his brothers	37:2b, 3b, 5–11, 19–20, 23, 25b–27, 28b, 31–35	37:3a, 4, 12–18, 21–22, 24, 25a, 28a, 29, 36	37:1	37:2a
Judah and Tamar	38:1–30			
Joseph and Potiphar's wife	39:1–23			
The butler and the baker		40:1–23		
Joseph and the Pharaoh		41:2–45a, 46b–57	41:45b–46a	
Jacob's sons in Egypt	42:1–4, 8–20, 26–34, 38; 43:1–13, 15–34; 44:1–34; 45:1–2, 4–28	42:5–7, 21–25, 35–37; 43:14; 45:3		
Jacob in Egypt	46:5b–28, 34; 47:1–27a, 29–31; 49:1–27; 50:1–11, 14–23	46:1–5a; 48:1, 8–22; 50:12–13, 23–26	46:6–27; 47:27b, 28; 48:3–6; 49:29–33	48:7; 49:28

EXODUS

	J	E	P	R
Those coming to Egypt				1:1–5
The new generation			1:6–7	
The enslavement		1:8–12	1:13–14	
Killing the male infants	1:22	1:15–21		
Moses' birth and youth	2:1–23a			
God hears Israel's cry			2:23b–25	
Yahweh summons Moses	3:2–4a, 5, 7–8; 16–22; 4:1–17	3:1, 4b, 6, 9–15; 4:18, 20b	6:2–12, 14–25; 7:1–9	4:2b; 6:13, 26–30; 11:9–10
Moses and Pharaoh	5:1–6:1; 7:14–18, 20b–21a, 23–29; 8:3b–11a, 16–28; 9:1–7, 13–34; 21–26, 28–29; 11:1–9		7:10–13, 19–20a, 22b; 8:1–3a, 12–15; 9:8–12	8:11b; 9:35; 27; 10:20

NARRATIVE UNIT	J	E	P	R
The Exodus	12:21–23	12:24–27, 29–36, 37b–39; 13:1–16	12:1–20, 28, 40–49	12:37a, 50–51
The Sea of Reeds	14:5–7, 10b, 13–14, 19b, 20b, 21b, 24, 27b, 30–31; 15:1–18	13:17–19; 14:11–12, 19a, 20a, 25a; 15:20–21	13:21–22; 14:1–4, 8, 9b, 10a, 10c, 15–18, 21a, 21c, 22–23, 26–27a, 28–29	
Water in the wilderness	15:22b–25a			15:22a, 27
Commandments			15:25b–26	
Food in the wilderness		16:4–5, 35b	16:2–3, 6	16:1, 35a, 36; 17:1
Water in the wilderness		17:2–7		17:1
Amalete		17:8–16		
Jethro		18:1–27		
Horeb/Sinai	19:10–16a, 18, 20–25	19:2b–9, 16b–17, 19; 20:18–26	19:1	19:2a
Ten Commandments			20:1–17	
Covenant Code		21:1–27; 22:1–30; 23:1–33		
Horeb/Sinai (continued)		24:1–15a, 18b	24:15b–18a	
Tabernacle instructions			25:1–31:11	
Sabbath			31:12–17	
Tablets			31:18	
Golden calf		32:1–33:11		
Theophany to Moses	34:1a, 2–13	33:12–23		34:1b
Ten Commandments	34:14–28			
Skin of Moses' face			34:29–35	
Tabernacle construction			35–40	

LEVITICUS

Entire book			1–27	
Except: booths or Sukkot and restoration from exile				23:39–43; 26:39–45

NUMBERS

Last days at Mt. Sinai			1:1–2:34; 3:2–9:14; 10:1–10	3:1; 9:15–23

NARRATIVE UNIT	J	E	P	R
Departure from Mt. Sinai			10:11–12, 14–27	10:13, 20
Taberah			11:1–3	
Food in the wilderness			11:4–35	
Moses' Cushite wife		12:1–16		
Scouts	13:17–20, 22–24, 27–31, 33; 14:1b, 4, 11–25, 39–45	13:1–16, 21, 25–26, 32; 14:1a, 2–3, 5–10, 26–39		
Additional sacrificial law				15:1–31
A Sabbath violation			15:32–36	
Fringes on clothing			15:37–41	
Korah, Dathan, and Abiram	16:1b–2a, 12–14, 25–26, 27b–32a, 33–34			16:1a, 2b–11, 15–24, 27a, 32b, 35
Aaronids and Levites			17:1–18:32	
Red heifer			19:1–22	
Water in the wilderness			20:1b–13	20:1a
Israel and Edom	20:14–21			21:4a
Death of Aaron			20:23–29	20:22
Israel and Arad	21:1–3			
Bronze serpent		21:4b–9		
Sihon and Og	21:21–35			
Balaam		22:2–24:25		22:1
Heresy of Peor	25:1–5		25:6–19	
Census			26:1–8, 12–65	26:9–11
Daughters of Zelophehad			27:1–11	
The appointment of Joshua			27:12–23	
Additional sacrificial laws				28:1–31; 29:1–39
Laws on annulling women's vows			30:1–17	
Defeat of Midianites			31:1–54	
Tribal portions			32:1–42; 33:50–56; 34:1–29; 35:1–34; 36:1–13	
Stations list				33:1–49

THE SOURCES IN THE PENTATEUCH: A CONTEMPORARY ASSESSMENT

In the last twenty years or so, Pentateuchal criticism has taken some new directions, some tentative, but some with considerable promise for the future. Many of the conclusions that we have outlined above are being vigorously questioned. The whole edifice of Wellhausen's hypothesis is coming under heavy bombardment and may not stand much longer. The existence of the four sources as written sources, for example, has been totally abandoned by some. Of the four, the only one that is not seen as hypothetical is D, seen as the Deuteronomic law code (Deut 12–26). Of the three other sources postulated, the E source is considered, in a best case scenario, to be represented only intermittently and, in a worst case scenario, never to have existed. The Priestly writer has come to be seen less as a source and more of an author/reviser of the Pentateuch in its final form. Schmitt, for example, combines the source, fragment, and supplement hypotheses according to the nature of the individual texts, thereby correcting an excessive emphasis on the source hypothesis (1985: 177–8). The advantage is that he can agree with the theological profiles of J and E presented by classical Pentateuchal criticism yet also give a more satisfactory account of the redaction process.

There are several reasons that stand behind current challenges to the documentary hypothesis. For one thing, it is now emphasized that Wellhausen was a child of his age and thus worked in the context of a certain set of presuppositions. The dominant philosophy in German universities in Wellhausen's time (the late nineteenth and early twentieth centuries), as we have noted, was Hegelian. Both Graf's and Wellhausen's mentors were Hegelians. Some contemporary scholars who have rejected the documentary hypothesis have done so by arguing that Graf and Wellhausen simply applied to the study of the Pentateuch a scheme drawn from the Hegelian philosophy of history. Recent ethnological fieldwork has raised serious questions about the existence of the kind of spontaneity and freedom from ritual restraints that Wellhausen and his nineteenth-century colleagues assumed existed in so-called "primitive" societies, let alone whether early Israel could be classified as a "primitive" society. One might respond in Wellhausen's defense, however, that to recognize a scholar as part of the intellectual currents of his or her time is not a sufficient argument, by itself, against the validity of any particular theory he or she might propose. The "discovery" that Wellhausen's theory might have Hegelian foundations not only fails to falsify the theory, it is also interesting to observe that this kind of objection was made only with the benefit of hindsight, from the 1930s on. Before then it did not seem to have occurred to anyone!

Current Literary Approaches

A much more serious kind of challenge, not just to the documentary hypothesis as applied to the Pentateuch but to the method of historical criticism of which it is the child, is connected with the interest in newer kinds of literary study of the Pentateuch. It is observed that Wellhausen worked with a rather limited view of how ancient literature was produced—a kind of "scissors-and-paste" method. The assumption is that an editor or redactor took four documents, separated them into pieces, put a piece from one here and a piece from another there, and finally put forth this composite piece as a new document. This method may make good sense to some modern students, for this is precisely the way that they approach the task of writing a research paper. It may not, however, represent the way in which literature was produced in antiquity.

Concentrating on source criticism, the approach to "understanding" the Hebrew Bible has often been limited to reversing the process envisioned by Wellhausen, operating out of the assumption that the way to "understand" a document is to explain its source or sources. This "excavative" approach to understanding biblical literature provides the basis for many Old Testament/Hebrew Bible introductions that are preoccupied with questions of origin, date, and authorship. Current literary approaches, however, rest on the assumption that the quest for understanding literature must begin with focusing on the text as it stands, without reference to the circumstances of its production, the intentions of the author/s, and other historical information. Such approaches, represented by the formalist, structuralist, and deconstructionist schools of literary theory, maintain that no matter what literary strata may lie beneath the surface, no matter how many sources and redactions, the meaning of a text must be sought in its existence as a text, in the form in which we find it. On this basis, some scholars today argue that some of the literary features upon which Wellhausen based his theory that posited different sources can just as convincingly be explained as intentional stylistic and literary devices used self-consciously by an author.

Areas of Uncertainty

Much of the current debate about the Pentateuch centers on J. Among scholars who still accept the existence of a Yahwist, however, there is considerable debate about when J wrote, with several dating J to the exilic period. John Van Seters (1975), for example, sees the Abraham narratives in Genesis as having been produced by a J who wrote during the Babylonian exile (587–538 B.C.E.). J is indeed an author, not a compiler of oral tradition. Van Seters understands Abraham not as a historical figure, but as one who was created by J for theological purposes. Nevertheless, Van Seters continues to endorse the kind of literary and source criticism employed by those operating out of the documentary hypothesis. While the state of research on J is currently in a rather puzzling state, the majority of scholars still follow Wellhausen and von Rad. They assign to J a date and ideological intention belonging to the period of the early monarchy, to the time of Solomon or his son Rehoboam.

The greatest variance of views on J, however, centers on the issues of J's origin and intentions. One of the most provocative recent assessments of J appeared in 1990 in a popular work by Bloom and Rosenberg, *The Book of J.* David Rosenberg gives a new and very free translation of J and Harold Bloom, who is not a professional biblical scholar, comments on the J source. Bloom maintains that J lived at or nearby the court of Solomon's son and successor, King Rehoboam. J was not a professional scribe but a highly placed member of the Solomonic elite. Bloom's provocative idea, picking up on a suggestion of Richard Friedman, is his contention that J was a woman, and that she wrote for her contemporaries as a woman, in competition with her only strong rival, the male author of the court history narrative in 2 Samuel. In putting forth such an idea Bloom admits that he was aware that this idea about the identity of J would be condemned as a fantasy or fiction. In defending himself, Bloom begins by pointing out that *all* our accounts of the Bible (even the most scholarly ones) are scholarly fictions or religious fantasies that often serve rather tendentious purposes. He says that in proposing that J was a woman, at least he cannot be accused of furthering the interests of any religious or ideological group. He maintains: "Rather, I will be attempting to account, through my years of reading experience, for my increasing sense of the astonishing differences between J and every other biblical writer" (Bloom and Rosenberg 1990: 9 – 10).

Assessing the status of the documentary hypothesis, Blenkinsopp has listed five main areas of uncertainty that characterize scholarship in the last two decades (1992: 25 – 26):

1. There is no longer a consensus about the existence of discernible, continuous narrative sources from the pre-exilic period that cover the entire range of the Pentateuch.

2. Much of the criticism of the classic sequence of J, E, D, and P has concentrated on the J source.

3. The prevalent tendency in recent scholarship to date the sources later is not without its problems because it often rests on arguments from silence and leaves a large vacuum in the pre-exilic period.

4. Excepting J, there has been little attention paid to the other sources.

5. The legal material in the Pentateuch, in spite of its size and significance, has not received much attention throughout the development of the documentary hypothesis, leaving the relation between law and narrative unclear.

Some of the ferment regarding the composition of the Pentateuch arises out of a general dissatisfaction with biblical criticism primarily concerned with a detailed analysis of the components of the Torah, rather than with an assessment and evaluation of its contents. Current scholarship often finds the older "excavative" approach to the study of the Pentateuch to be very limiting if pursued in isolation. It can result in a detailed study of Pentateuchal "trees," but miss the Pentateuchal "forest."

The Approach in this Text

We recognize that there are some serious problems with the kind of source criticism epitomized in Wellhausen's work. At the same time, we also acknowledge that even a century after Wellhausen's work, there is no consensus about what should take its place. Therefore, in the chapters that follow in this textbook, we will present different interpretive systems with different, but not necessarily incompatible, agendas. On one hand, we believe that there are aspects of the religious experience of ancient Israel and levels of meaning in the Hebrew Bible that are accessible only by using the tools of historical criticism, source criticism among them. A considerable cultural and temporal gap separates us from the world of the Hebrew Bible. The Hebrew scriptures were written in a language with which we are not familiar, using literary conventions that differ from what we are accustomed to in English literature. The tools of historical criticism can help us bridge these gaps.

On the other hand, we shall pay heed to the work of those who have challenged the historical-critical method out of a concern for the literary character of the scriptures. We will, for example, present some interesting new readings of individual texts that come from those pursuing some newer theories of literary criticism. In particular, we will look at the work of those who offer a structuralist approach to texts, a literary approach that can help us to appreciate the purely literary and aesthetic qualities of the Hebrew Bible and especially its narrative component.

On the assumption that new theories do not necessarily totally invalidate their predecessors, we will use both the tools of historical criticism *and* newer literary methods. The former will help us understand Pentateuchal texts in their historical and cultural setting. The latter will help us get at the Pentateuch's structure and internal organization and those of its major components and individual texts. In all of this, we will insist on a plurality of meanings that can be extracted from the biblical text, some that emanate from the text itself, and others that stem from the reader and the background that he or she brings to the text.

STUDY QUESTIONS

SOURCE CRITICISM OF GENESIS 1:1–3:24

In our examination of the Creation stories in Gen 1:1–3:24 we start with source criticism so that we can discern the different traditions that underlie this section. Next we shall use redaction criticism to see how these different accounts of creation were brought together, despite some tension between them.

A. As you read Gen 1:1–3:24, notice that there are really two stories about the Creation. Where exactly do the two accounts separate? (Note: The chapter and verse numbers were *not* included in the original Hebrew text, but were added to the text at a later point. They do not always, therefore, represent reliable indicators of breaks or transitions in the text).

B. List some of the differences in literary style, attitudes toward God, and different attitudes about the roles of male and female. Illustrate your answers from the biblical text.

C. List factual contradictions between the two accounts. (Note: A contradiction is not just something left out in one account that is mentioned in another; contradictions are elements that are present in both accounts but seem to be at odds with one another, for example, the order in which things are created.)

REDACTION CRITICISM OF GENESIS 1:1–3:24

A.   Gen 2:4a reads (in the NRSV): "These are the generations of the heavens and the earth when they were created." The phrase "These are the generations . . ." occurs elsewhere in Gen 6:9, 10:1, and in Num 3:1. The language of the phrase in all four instances is similar, but the *function* is not. In 2:4a does the phrase function as a *summary* of Gen 1:1–2:3 or as an *introduction* to 2:4b–3:24? Is the expression in 2:4a a *summary* of what precedes or an *introduction* to what follows? First of all, how is this phrase handled in Gen 6:9, 10:1, and in Num 3:1? Does it introduce or summarize? Secondly, how does this broader usage of the phrase help answer the question about its role in Gen 2:4a?

B.   There is another clue that can help in determining the function of Gen 2:4a. Hebrew literature likes to use *inclusion* as a device for setting off discrete segments (beginning and ending a literary unit using the same word, phrase, or sentence). The Hebrew Bible uses this device in a way similar to the way that we use paragraph indentation. Now if there were an inclusion in either Gen 1:1–2:3 or 2:4b–3:24, then this would determine the actual beginning or ending of that particular account. Look at Gen 2:3b, which in Hebrew says literally: ". . . and he sanctified it because on it he ceased from all his work which God created to do." What role does this phrase play in the first Creation account? Do you see any way in which this phrase could serve as one element in an inclusion? Therefore, according to the literary structure of the first story of Creation, where exactly would it end? How does this evidence help in determining the function of Gen 2:4a? If 2:3b serves as an inclusion, then what possibilities would that exclude for the function of 2:4a? Explain the significance of your conclusion for how the two Creation accounts have been edited and *by whom?*

You should now have sufficient evidence to decide who the editor was who combined these two Creation stories. Why do the contradictions between the two accounts make your findings about the role of Gen 2:4a more of a problem? Could the editor/redactor whom you have uncovered have done anything about these contradictions or tensions?

BIBLIOGRAPHY

Blenkinsopp, Joseph. 1992. *The Pentateuch: An Introduction to the First Five Books of the Bible.* The Anchor Bible Reference Library. New York: Doubleday.

Bloom, Harold, and David Rosenberg. 1990. *The Book of J.* New York: Grove Weidenfeld.

Friedman, Richard Elliott. 1987. *Who Wrote the Bible?* Englewood Cliffs, NJ: Prentice-Hall.

Knight, Douglas A. 1985. "The Pentateuch" in *The Hebrew Bible and Its Modern Interpreters,* Douglas A. Knight and Gene M. Tucker , eds.. Philadelphia: Fortress.

Noth, Martin. 1972. *A History of Pentateuchal Traditions,* tr. by B. W. Anderson. Englewood Cliffs, NJ: Prentice-Hall.

Rad, Gerhard von. 1966. *The Problem of the Hexateuch and Other Essays.* Edinburgh: Oliver & Boyd.

Rogerson, John W., and Philip R. Davies. 1989. *The Old Testament World.* Englewood Cliffs, NJ: Prentice-Hall.

Schmitt, H. C. 1985. "Die Hintergründe der 'neuesten Pentateuchkritik' und der literarische Befund der Josefgeschichte Gen 37-50." *ZAW 97:* 161–79.

Van Seters, John. 1975. *Abraham in History and Tradition.* New Haven: Yale University Press.

West, James King. 1981. *Introduction to the Old Testament.* 2nd ed. New York: Macmillan.

STORIES OF BEGINNINGS—NATURAL AND HUMAN: GENESIS 1–11

Suggested Bible Reading
Genesis 1 - 11

MYTH AND HISTORY IN GENESIS 1–11

The book of Genesis can be divided into two main parts: chapters 1 - 11, which has been called the "Primeval History" or "Prehistory," and chapters 12 - 50, which has been referred to as the "Patriarchal History." With this division, there has also been the recognition that Gen 1 - 11 is basically myth, while Gen 12 - 50 approximates something between legend and history. It is hardly possible to do even a quick reading of the first eleven chapters of Genesis without recognizing that they are very different in character from what one encounters beginning with chapter 12. The material in Genesis 1 - 11 has few if any of the characteristics a modern historian would require in order to label it "history." Only the presupposition that everything in the Bible is necessarily factually accurate would lead one to call this material "history." Is it then myth?

The Meaning of Myth

Any treatment of myth that is to avoid crippling ambiguity must begin with an assessment of the many senses in which this very slippery word is used. Unfortunately in the popular mind the word "myth" has come to mean a story with no foundation in fact, a sheer fiction, falsehood, or fantasy. We often call something a "myth" and mean that it is obviously not considered truthful in any sense. At the other extreme myth may cover the whole range of theological language; any "god-talk," any sentence containing the word "God," is myth. These misconceptions of myth are unfortunate because, as we shall see, it is difficult to avoid the term myth in describing the kind of material that we encounter in Genesis 1–11. Scholars do not use the term "myth" in its popular sense, but there has been a great deal of debate among them concerning its definition and its role in ancient society and literature.

Myth is a narrative literary genre that appears in one form or another in nearly every religious tradition. On one level myth describes a story about the actions of gods and goddesses, talked about as if they were human beings. The Greek word *muthos,* from which our word "myth" stems, originally meant simply "something said" or "something told," in essence, a story. Much of the modern study of folklore has used the definition of myth made popular by the brothers Grimm. Jakob (1785–1863) and Wilhelm Grimm (1786–1859) collected popular tales in Germany and studied Germanic mythology. Their work made a major contribution to the serious study of folk tales and comparative mythology. In their studies of folklore and fairy tales, a myth is basically a story about the gods. Much of Greek and Roman mythology fits this meaning of myth, but it has proved to be inadequate.

In the continuing discussion of myth, while scholars may not agree on its precise definition, a consensus has emerged regarding elements that myths have in common. To qualify as a myth scholars suggest that the material must:

1.   be a story,

2.   be traditional — that is, passed down, usually orally, within a communal setting,

3.   deal with a character or characters who are more than ordinary humans, and

4.   treat events in remote antiquity (Oden 1992: 949).

At another level, however, "myth" makes reference to a story that narrates profound truth in story form, the kind of truth that escapes scientific or historical documentation. In this sense then, myth provides one of the most penetrating ways of talking about the meaning of life, about the relationships between human beings, and about the relationships between God and persons. Myth is a specialized kind of metaphor, a story about the past that embodies and expresses truths about a people's traditional culture.

MYTH AND THE HEBREW BIBLE

The narratives in Genesis 1–11 fall under the final category of myth, as they contain myths and are mythic in scope. In addition to Genesis 1–11, many other stories in the Hebrew Bible fit this definition of myth. One clear example is found in Isa 14:12–15:

> How you are fallen from heaven, O Day Star, son of Dawn! How you are cut down to the ground, you who laid the nations low! You said in your heart, "I will ascend to heaven; I will raise my throne above the stars of God; I will sit on the mount of assembly on the heights of Zaphon; I will ascend to the tops of the clouds, I will make myself like the Most High." But you are brought down to Sheol, to the depths of the Pit.

The prophet here is using a story about the planet known to us as Venus, but to the Hebrews as "Day Star," which is called "son of Dawn," the morning star. According to the myth "Day Star" planned to become king by climbing the walls of the heavenly city, only to be vanquished by the all-conquering sun. The biblical text, however, makes it clear that the prophet is not speaking about a mythical creature but about the king of Babylon and his aspirations to world dominion. By looking at a contemporary tyrant through the perspective of myth, the prophet is grouping him with all other rebels against the authority of God, and forcefully communicating his conviction that Babylon will soon fall.

In a similar way Ezekiel draws upon the myth of paradise lost to talk about the imminent fall of Tyre (28:13–16):

> You were in Eden, the garden of God; every precious stone was your covering . . . and worked in gold were your settings and your engravings. On the day that you were created they were prepared. With an anointed cherub as guardian I placed you; you were on the holy mountain of God; you walked among the stones of fire. You were blameless in your ways from the day that you were created, until iniquity was found in you. In the abundance of your trade you were filled with violence, and you sinned; so I cast you as a profane thing from the mountain of God, and the guardian cherub drove you out from among the stones of fire.

There are echoes here of the Garden of Eden myth that appears in Gen 2–3, and for Ezekiel the myth owed its power to the fact that the story of Adam and Eve was the story of Everyone, constantly being replayed in the subsequent history of people and nations.

In several areas of biblical scholarship, the modern encounter between biblical studies and myth began in the eighteenth and early nineteenth centuries, in this case following the work of the brothers Grimm. At first, the work of the Grimms was used by those who insisted that there was no myth in the Hebrew Bible. Using the Grimms' definition that a myth is "a story about the gods," scholars insisted that since the Hebrew Bible talked of monotheism, or belief in one God, there could, by definition, be no talk of gods in the Bible, thus no myth.

The Grimm brothers' definition continued to play an important role in the discussions of biblical scholars who denied the presence of myth in the Bible well into the twentieth century, even though scholars outside biblical studies rejected that understanding of myth as inadequate. Most introductions to the Old Testament/Hebrew Bible, however, up until about 1960, continued to insist on a practice of "demythologization" in connection with myth. They say, in one way or another, there is no myth in the Hebrew Bible. Their argument characteristically follows the line that since myth demands multiple gods and/or goddesses, those stories in the Hebrew Bible that look "mythical" are, at best, broken myths, the decaying remnants of myths that exist elsewhere. They argue that mythical themes of the ancient Near Eastern environment were taken over and inserted into historical contexts, losing the distinctive ahistorical character of myth in the process. For example, the myth telling of marriages between gods, which in the Canaanite world was echoed in the cult through ritual prostitution so as to guarantee the fertility of the family, flocks, and fields, in Israel was represented as the marriage between God and his people Israel. While this might be regarded as a mythical theme, it is a "broken" myth in that Israel went on to historicize this relationship by speaking of God's action *in history* to institute, protect, and sustain this marriage.

In the last several decades, however, the issue of myth and the Hebrew Bible has become an important one in biblical scholarship (Oden 1992: 959–60). The discovery of ancient Near Eastern myths with obvious similarities to Hebrew Bible stories, especially the Canaanite myths from Ras Shamra (the ancient city of Ugarit) near the Mediterranean coast in present-day Syria, made it difficult to continue insisting that there was not myth in the Bible.

These new discoveries were coupled with a demise of older understandings of myths and their functions. Around the middle of this century, anthropologists began to take myths more seriously as a source of information about the societies that produced them. In particular, the French anthropologist Claude Lévi-Strauss led the way. The work of anthropologists on myth influenced biblical scholars, and some openly began to question the old definition of myths as stories about gods. While a number of scholars prepared the way, a groundbreaking work was that of Brevard Childs, *Myth and Reality in the Old Testament* (1960). Childs shows how the use of the Grimm brothers' definition blocked the investigation of myth in the Hebrew Bible. To Childs' groundbreaking work can be added the work of Frank Cross in his *Canaanite Myth and Hebrew Epic* (1973). Using the evidence from Ugarit, Cross breaks down the artificial barrier that has been erected between the religion of ancient Israel and that of neighboring peoples. Cross argues that much of the literature of the Hebrew Bible is based on myth, and that in the Bible myth can be found both in its pure form (for example, Ps 29; 89; 93) and in what might be described as a hybridization of myth and history: "In Israel, myth and history always stood in strong tension, myth serving primarily to give a cosmic dimension and transcendent meaning to the historical, rarely functioning to dissolve history" (Cross 1973: 90).

GENESIS: HISTORY OR MYTH?

No single section of the Hebrew Bible has been more thoroughly and heatedly debated than the first eleven chapters of Genesis, largely because of the attempt to label them as *either* "history" or "myth." Related to the history-myth debate, the Genesis creation stories have fueled many debates about the proper domains of science and religion, especially since, but even long before, Charles Darwin published his *Origin of the Species* in 1859, with its thesis about human evolution. Those who regard the scientific method as a threat to faith and want to defend the religious claims of the biblical material, while casting doubts on modern science, prefer to call it "history." In doing so, they understand "history" to mean a report of something that "actually happened," something that could have been videotaped had the technology been available.

To regard Genesis 1–11 as "history," however, puts one on a collision course with modern science, as seen in some of the recent controversy about the teaching of evolution and/or "creationism" in the public schools. A particular kind of belief in the inspiration of the Bible, coupled with a belief that there are no errors of any kind in the Bible, has led some to assume that these chapters contain accurate, factual information about science, history, and geography. Others, however, have been aware of difficulties with this assumption for centuries, certainly long before Darwin.

For example, the fact that Genesis speaks of the creation of light in 1:3 *before* the sun was created in 1:16 (where it is called "the greater light") bothered some interpreters as early as the fifteenth century. Calling the moon "the lesser light" (1:16) was a problem for the Swiss Protestant Reformer Jean Calvin in the sixteenth century, because he accepted the fact that the moon does not give off light, but only reflects it. Calvin was asked by some literalists of his day how he could explain Gen 1:6–7, which talks about the "firmament" ("dome" in the NRSV, understood as an upside-down bowl) dividing the water underneath it from the water above it. Even scientists in the sixteenth century, with their limited understanding of astronomy, had difficulty in believing that the blueness of the sky was due to the fact that one was seeing water through a crystal-clear dome. In his *Commentary on Genesis,* Calvin agreed with these scientists and said that this idea was "opposed to common sense, and quite incredible" and went on to say: "To my mind, this is a certain principle, that nothing is here [i.e., in Genesis] treated of but the visible form of the world. He who would learn astronomy, and other recondite arts, let him go elsewhere . . ." (1965: 79–80). Calvin also acknowledged—in contradiction to Gen 1:16, where the moon is identified as one of the "two great lights"—that there were in fact planets much larger than the moon. His ingenious solution was that Genesis 1 described the world as it would have been seen with the naked eye by Moses and his contemporaries, not as it was seen through the telescopes of his own time. Calvin was thus quite clear in asserting that the Bible was never intended to serve as a scientific textbook, and that reading it as if it were could only lead to confusion and a distortion of its intended message. In spite of what Calvin said, however, many people continued to regard Genesis 1–11 as *the* scientific authority on the origins of the world and humankind until the end of the eighteenth century, and many fundamentalists still regard it in that way today.

At the beginning of the nineteenth century, in the 1820s, biblical interpreters were confronted with the discovery of fossils by geologists, who declared that the world was thousands (*sic*) of years older than the date of creation implied by biblical chronology (which at that time, based on calculations made by an Irish priest, James Ussher, was believed to have occurred in 4004 B.C.E.) The response of orthodox interpreters to the findings of the geologists was to disparage their scientific method by asserting that the great flood described in Genesis had destroyed and distorted the earth's original geological strata, and therefore the geologists, whose work was based on the assumption of an orderly deposition of strata, had been misled. Some fundamentalists today, who do not accept the theory of evolution, discount scientific dating methods such as radiocarbon dating in a similar way by maintaining that some catastrophe in the past has rendered the results of these methods unreliable.

The next challenge came about three decades later, with the publication of Darwin's *Origin of the Species.* Darwin's work was a challenge to Genesis 2–3, for if it was true that human beings had evolved from lower forms of life, what was one to do with the biblical story that told of how a once perfect human couple had "fallen"?

The most formidable challenge to the understanding of Genesis 1–11, however, came toward the end of the nineteenth century when ancient Babylonian and Assyrian texts were discovered containing material resembling the narratives in Genesis. In 1872, a young scholar on the staff of the British Museum, George Robertson Smith, gave a lecture entitled "The Chaldean Account of the Deluge." It dealt with what is now known to be part of Tablet XI of the Babylonian *Epic of Gilgamesh.* Three years later Smith announced the discovery of a Babylonian creation account, part of a text now known as the *Enuma Elish.* These discoveries aroused a great deal of interest, and within a few years some biblical scholars were arguing that Genesis was dependent upon the Babylonian material as a source.

OTHER NEAR EASTERN MYTHS

A powerful salvo in what developed into a raging academic war was fired by a German professor, Franz Delitzsch, who between January 1902, and October 1904, delivered a series of lectures entitled in German "*Babel und Bibel,*" or "Babylonia and the Bible." In the course of his lectures, Delitzsch concentrated upon the derogation of the Old Testament and a corresponding elevation of the religion of the Babylonians. He alternated between emphasizing parallels between Babylonia and Israel ("How very much alike everything is in Babylon and Bible!") and stressing the contrasts between them ("In the case of the Babylonians all this was managed differently and better," with reference to the status of women). Defending the ancient Babylonians against the claims made by Old Testament scholars, Delitzsch tried to show that Israelite religion, far from being superior to the supposed crude paganism of the Babylonians, had actually *evolved* from Babylonian culture and religion. He attempted to demonstrate that certain texts from the Hebrew Bible were nothing more than revisions of Babylonian myths. For many years after Delitzsch's lectures, biblical scholars were involved in attempts to respond to Delitzsch. Delitzsch, like all scholars, was a child of a certain time and place. It should not be surprising to note then, that his writing, as well as his famous lectures, were infused with German nationalism. For example, he recommended replacing the Old Testament with Wilhelm Schwaner's *Germanen-Bibel,* which includes the thoughts of German heroes concerning God, eternity, and immortality. This is much better, says Delitzsch, than the "barbaric" qualities of the Ten Commandments! Delitzsch, in his last work of serious scholarship published in 1920, became an outspoken opponent of Judaism in words that have a most ominous ring in light of the Holocaust engineered by Nazi Germany in the 1930s and 1940s, directing a program of genocide at Jews. Delitzsch said that Jews "as a homeless or international people, present a great danger for all the other people on the earth." He saw "the Jewish question" as the most decisive issue for the German people of his day. In Delitzsch's final work he no longer championed Babylonia as the key to the interpretation of the Bible. He does not even argue for Babylonia versus the Bible. Instead, he ends his diatribe with the assertion that Jesus was not born a Jew, but he had converted to Judaism. Being from Galilee, Jesus was actually a Babylonian and therefore not even a pure Semite. Delitzsch even goes on to assert that Jesus was probably in part an Aryan (Huffmon 1987: 135).

As more literature from Mesopotamia was discovered, the debate became more intense as scholars sought a method for assessing Old Testament literature in this newly emerging literary context. An important contribution to this debate was one made in 1958 by an eminent Assyriologist, Jacob J. Finkelstein in an article titled "Bible and Babel," an obvious inversion of Delitzsch's title. Finkelstein summarized Delitzsch's lectures and then presented a balanced survey of the positive results of comparing the Bible with the literature of Mesopotamia.

In light of the intensity of the scholarly debate concerning myth and its place in the Bible and in the ancient Near East, it is obviously an important category for consideration. In our discussion of the narratives in Genesis 1–11 we will present some of the similarities and differences between the biblical and ancient Near Eastern material, attempting to assess the "mythic" quality of the biblical literature in comparison with and in contrast to Babylonian myths, as they are understood by contemporary scholarship.

An example of a more recently discovered Mesopotamian mythic text is the Babylonian *Atrahasis* myth, the earliest surviving copies of which are from the seventeenth century B.C.E. This myth, like the early chapters of Genesis, tells of the beginnings of humanity. It is a kind of "primeval history" that relates events associated with the creation of humanity, the problems arising after creation, the near-destruction of humanity by a flood, and its re-creation after the flood. Atrahasis plays a role corresponding to that of Noah in the biblical flood story. In a discussion that is typical of the newer understanding of myth and its relation to biblical literature, Isaac Kikawada and Arthur Quinn have made the suggestion that the structure of Genesis 1–11 has a pattern that is also found in Atrahasis (Kikawada and Quinn 1985: 47–8). In both Atrahasis and Genesis there are five major movements:

I. CREATION

ATRAHASIS (I.1–351)	*GENESIS* (1:1–2:3)
Summary of work of gods	Summary of work of God
Creation of humanity	Creation of humanity

II. FIRST THREAT

ATRAHASIS (I.352–415)	*GENESIS* (2:4–3:24)
Humanity's numerical increase	Genealogy of heaven and earth
Plague, Enki's help [Enki was one of the four great cosmic gods in Mesopotamian culture. He is the god of wisdom, incantation, and of fresh waters on the earth and under the earth].	Adam and Eve

III. SECOND THREAT

ATRAHASIS (II.i.1–v.21)	*GENESIS* (4:1–26)
Humanity's numerical increase	Cain and Abel
Drought, numerical increase	Cain and Abel genealogy
Intensified drought, Enki's help	Lamech's threat

IV. FINAL THREAT

ATRAHASIS (II.v.22–III.vi.4)	*GENESIS* (5:1–9:29)
Numerical increase	Genealogy
Atrahasis' flood, salvation in boat	Noah's flood, salvation in ark

V. RESOLUTION

ATRAHASIS (III.vi.5–viii.18)	*GENESIS* (10:1–11:32)
Numerical increase	Genealogy
Compromise between Enlil and Enki [Enlil was also one of the principal Mesopotamian deities. He was god of the atmosphere and the earth. As the most powerful of the gods he was the possessor of the "tablets of destiny," by means of which the fates of humans and gods were decreed.]	Tower of Babel and Dispersion genealogy
	Abram leaves Ur
"Birth Control"	

TWO KINDS OF HISTORY:
HISTORIE AND *GESCHICHTE*

"History" is a term that is, like myth, a remarkably slippery one in English. The biblical-theology movement of the 1950s and 1960s observed that in German there are two different words that can be translated as "history" in English. *Historie* refers to what we might call something presented as a "factual" account or story of past events—the who, what, where, and when of things—an "objective" description of events (even though it is recognized that even so-called "factual" accounts include some kind of interpretation). *Geschichte,* on the other hand, represents the past as event plus interpretation or meaning—marked by a concern with the causes and effects of historical happenings, their interpretations and significance.

If, for example, you were to attempt to write a biography of some well-known person as *Historie,* you would give the name of the person's parents, the place and date of the person's birth, places the person lived, schools attended, places traveled, and so on. Such a story would be "true" in the sense that the data in it could be cross-checked and verified by anyone reading the story. But this kind of biography would not help the reader know what kind of person the subject of the biography was, what people had an influence in shaping that person's life, what kind of impact that person had on others, or what was that person's self-understanding and philosophy of life. A biography written as *Geschichte,* on the other hand, would include the author's interpretation of the biographee's story: the ways in which the person was influenced by family and friends, things that affected the development of personal values, and so on. One might choose to tell of only selected events in the person's life and reflect on the ways in which those particular events are especially significant for the person's story.

The material in the first eleven chapters of Genesis contains five narratives that can be understood as both *Geschichte* and myth. They constitute the biblical "history" of human and natural beginnings, expressed in mythical terms. The five stories we shall examine are:

1. The Priestly Creation Story (1:1–2:4a)
2. The Yahwistic Creation Story (2:4b–3)
3. A Tale of Two Brothers: Cain and Abel (4)
4. The Great Flood (5–9)
5. A City and a Tower (11:1–9)

These stories do not attempt to give us data in the way a chronological time line or a scientific treatise gives us factual information. Rather, they serve as the vehicles by which the people of ancient Israel explained how they saw the nature of human beings as the creatures of one Creator. By telling these stories of human beginnings, they express their understanding of the world, of themselves, and of God.

The first eleven chapters of Genesis have sometimes been called "primeval history" or "prehistory." This kind of "history" is concerned with etiology — the origins of things and with the explanation of how things got to be the way they are. Behind this lies the assumption that if one knows how something came into being, one can explain a good deal about its current state. While we might begin by approaching these stories on the level of *Historie* — asking such questions as "Who is involved? What happened?" — we must soon move on to explore them on the level of *Geschichte* and myth, asking a completely different set of questions. Now the questions are from the narrator's perspective: "Why did these things happen the way they did? What do these stories tell us about the social location and faith orientation of the people who told them?"

If we try to extract "factual" historical information from these chapters, we will be very disappointed (unless of course we read it *into* them). If, for example, we look for "real" historical individuals or specific geographical locations or dates, we will discover that such information was apparently irrelevant to the purpose of the author(s). If we look for objective "facts" that could be used, for example, to construct a proof of the existence of God, we will notice once again that this is not a concern shared by the author(s) of Genesis 1 - 11, for whom the existence of God was simply built into the nature of things and not debatable. The concerns of Genesis 1 - 11, then, are not philosophical (at least as we understand philosophy), not scientific (at least as we understand science), and not historical (at least not in the *Historie* sense of history). These first stories in the Bible are concerned instead with theology (understood as reflection on the way God acts) and anthropology (understood as reflection on the way human beings act). The major themes in these narratives are creation, sin, and judgment. These themes are expressed in relational terms — relationships between Creator and creatures, between humans and animals, between humans of different sex, between parents and children, between siblings, and so forth.

As well, in our journey we must note the larger literary context of Genesis 1 - 11, for example, its relationship to chapters 12 - 50 in Genesis and to the rest of the Torah. This context is especially important because many scholars hold that these first eleven chapters of Genesis function not only as an introduction to the book of Genesis but as an introduction to the entire Torah. The Torah, in turn, is an introduction to the rest of the Hebrew scriptures. The Torah serves as an introduction in the sense that it sets the tone for the work it introduces and presents the major themes and motifs that are developed in the larger unit. Because the Torah traditionally constitutes the core of scripture (recall the fact that the Torah was the first of the three sections of the Hebrew Bible to be regarded as scripture), we must detect, beginning in Genesis 1 - 11, those themes that carry through the Hebrew Bible.

How an introduction is to be read depends, to some degree, on how the unit it introduces ends (remember how much an ending can affect your reading of a mystery novel). Four of the five books of the Pentateuch (Exodus through Deuteronomy) focus on the generation of the Exodus. Genesis serves as a prologue to the liberation from bondage in Egypt and the giving of the Law at Sinai that dominates Exodus, Leviticus, and Numbers. Deuteronomy serves as an epilogue to Genesis' prologue. The Pentateuch itself does not include the story of God's establishing Israel in the land promised to them but contains only the story of God's promise to do so.

Thus, the first book in the Old Testament is appropriately named Genesis, "beginning." In Hebrew, the book's name is *bereshith,* which is the first word in the Hebrew Bible, and means "in beginning." In the Septuagint translation of the Hebrew scriptures, the Greek word *genesis* was used as the title for the book. This name was carried over into the Vulgate and into English.

This story of beginnings looks back from things as they are in the author's day to things as they were in the mythic past. We must be careful to distinguish between the sociopolitical context of the recorders of these stories and the settings of the stories themselves. The theologians who speak here of "creation and fall" are not reporters on the scene. The setting of the primeval traditions is the time before Abraham, the ancestor of the various peoples who, after the Exodus and settlement in Palestine, composed the community of Israel.

THE CREATION MYTHS IN GENESIS 1–3 AND IN *ENUMA ELISH*

The Priestly Creation Story (Gen 1:1–2:4a)

The first textual unit in Genesis is the well-known story of the creation of the world in six days, after which God rests on the seventh day, the Sabbath. There is general agreement among scholars that the two creation stories in Genesis 1–3 come from two different contexts, and each has its own distinctive ways of referring to the creation of human beings. For the first story, generally regarded as the P or Priestly story, the key words are *order* and *balance.* The acts of creation are presented in a repetitive, ordered pattern. The pattern contains five elements, not all of which are present for each act of creation (for example, element five is not present at the conclusion of the creation of the earth, nor after the creation of the land animals; element four is missing after the creation of the "dome"):

1. an announcement of what God said;
2. the command by which God created;
3. the assertion that what God commanded did happen;
4. God's assessment that what had been created was good; and
5. a statement about when the creative act concluded.

The overall effect is a picture of the creation as unfolding rationally and in order from the mind of God. In this story, the order in which things are created is clearly important. Human beings are the last to be created, in what is a lower-to-higher sequence. This makes humanity the pinnacle of creation, to which all the other acts of creation were a prelude.

In 1:26 "humankind" ('*adam*) is differentiated from all other created beings through the assertion that here is a creature made in the image of God. Here, even before we get beyond the first chapter of the first book of the Hebrew Bible, we encounter an issue relating to gender. Most translations of the Hebrew Bible, other than the NRSV, translate Gen 1:26 something like "Then God said, 'Let us make man in our image.'" It is important to note, however, that the word translated "man" ('*adam* in Hebrew) here stands for all human beings, not just the male gender, as is accurately reflected in the NRSV translation "humankind." This is made clear in 1:27, where it is specified that "humankind" includes both male and female:

> So God created humankind in his image,
> in the image of God he created them
> male and female he created them.

Obviously difficulties arise from the ambiguity of the English word "his" in this verse, which seems to refer to God as masculine, even though "his" image includes both male and female. The NRSV tries to use gender inclusive language wherever possible, but problems obviously remain, because neither Hebrew nor English has a gender neutral or gender inclusive third person singular personal pronoun. We will return to gender questions at a number of points below.

For the Priestly writer to say that the world is created means that it is ordered, classified into three sectors, each with its own appropriate life forms:

SECTOR	LIFE FORMS
Heavens	Greater and lesser lights; birds
Waters	Fishes and sea creatures
Earth	Plants
	Animals
	Human beings

This three-sector classification is reinforced with a chronological pattern of creation as follows, in which the second three days balance and complete the first three days. In the first three days God created the places for which inhabitants were created on days four to six respectively:

SECTOR	DAY
Heavens	1 Creation of light, separating light from darkness
	4 Creation of greater and lesser lights; separating day and night
Waters	2 Creation of the dome, separating the waters
	5 Creation of the sea creatures and birds
Earth	3 Creation of dry land and plants
	6 Creation of land animals and humans

The priestly account is written in prose, but in intention and character it is poetical. The account moves from an initially chaotic situation at its beginning to a well-ordered one at its conclusion. The beginning and the end of the poem are marked by the rhetorical device of inclusion, indicated here by the phrase "the heavens and the earth," which occurs in 1:1 at the beginning of the narrative, and again in 2:4a, at its conclusion. While creative acts fill six days, the seventh day is distinctive and an important part of the ordered structure of this narrative. The seventh day, the Sabbath, the major religious holy day in the Jewish calendar, has its origins in the very structure of the created order. By working a six-day week and then observing the Sabbath day of rest, Israelites were imitating the actions of God and doing that which was built into the very structure of the world.

Although the acts of creation are structured in a way that makes the first three days balance the last three days, the most attention is directed to the sixth day. On this day both land animals and human beings are created, supplementing the work of the third day, which saw the creation of the land and the vegetation that would provide sustenance for land animals and humans. While the description of the creation of the land animals (1:24–25) follows a literary pattern established early on (1:11–12), the account of the creation of humans (1:26–30) has several features that set it off from all the other creative acts of God:

1. Its description is longer than that of any other creative act.

2. It begins in a different way, with the phrase "Let us make humankind in our image"—in contrast to the literary pattern at the beginning of the other creative acts in 1:3, 6, 9, 14, 20, 24).

3. Only humans are said to have been made "in the image of God."

4. Humans are made without reference to any natural context or substance, unlike the other creatures.

5. Sea, land, and air animals are differentiated by species, "of every kind." There is no such differentiation for humans—there is only *one* human species.

6. Only human beings are designated sexually as male and female (1:27).

7. Only to humans does God give the right and power to "have dominion over all . . . the earth" (1:26, 28).

8. Only to human beings does God speak directly in the first person (1:29–30).

"Clearly, in form, content, and context, this report of the creation of male and female is unique . . . Of primary concern for us is the uniqueness of the narrated discourse. This text gives the first clue in scripture for studying God and the rhetoric of sexuality" (Trible 1978: 15).

The Cosmologies of Creation Myths

In addition to those structural features we have observed, this story also organizes itself around its *cosmology,* a picture of the way in which the creation is structured. Creation myths in the ancient world typically reflected the cosmology behind them. Ancient Near Eastern cosmologies all conceived of a three-tiered universe, with a flat, circular earth occupying the middle tier, water above the earth as the upper tier, and water beneath the earth as the lower tier. This was probably a view that grew out of experience: the existence of wells and springs

Figure 5.1   Graphic representation of Egyptian cosmology

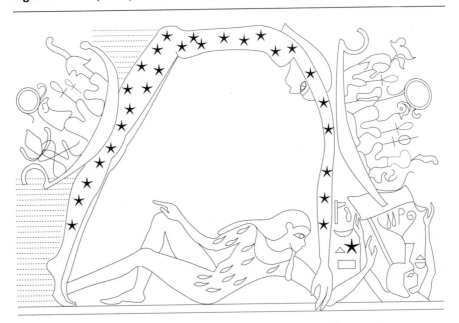

testified to the fact that the earth sat above a great pool of fresh water; rainfall confirmed the existence of water above the dome of the sky.

EGYPTIAN COSMOLOGY

Figure 5.1 is based on an Egyptian New-Kingdom (1570–1085 B.C.E.) papyrus and illustrates a tripartite universe similar to that which lies behind the creation account in Genesis 1. The Egyptians viewed the earth as a flat platter with a corrugated rim. The bottom of the platter was the alluvial plain of Egypt, the area created by the annual overflowing of the Nile. The rim was mountainous foreign lands. The platter of existence floated on the fresh water of a great abyss, out of which life first issued. These primordial fresh waters were also the source of the Nile. Above the earth was the sky, an inverted bowl defining the outer limits of the universe.

For the Egyptians, the creation resembled the annual flooding of the Nile, which renewed the land with the deposition of the fertile silt after the waters of the Nile receded. Because they saw new land created in this way, reason suggested that what they saw each year was a re-enactment of the way that the earth was created in the beginning. In Figure 5.1 the sky goddess Nut, whose body is covered with stars, stands on Geb, the earth god, whose body is covered with reeds. A boat (shown twice) bearing the sun is traveling from east to west on the waters above Nut's body. The sun is represented as a disk on top of the head of the falcon-headed god Horus, who holds in his hand the hieroglyph *ankh,* the sign for "life." The boat is shown twice in the picture, representing the two stages in the sun's journey: the boat on the left represents the sun in its rising, the eastern part of the trip; the boat on the right is being received by Osiris, the god of the underworld, as the sun sets in the west. It will then travel through the underworld back to the east, where it will begin its journey again on the following day.

BABYLONIAN COSMOLOGY

The best-known extrabiblical ancient Near-Eastern myth of creation is the Babylonian *Enuma Elish.* This creation myth was recited annually as part of the great Babylonian New Year festival. It tells of the birth of the gods and of the creation of humankind in a well-ordered universe. Beginning with the picture of earliest primordial time, only the first pair of gods, Apsu (a male deity representing the fresh water) and Tiamat (a female deity representing the salt water) existed:

When on high . . .
No heaven had been named,
No earth called,
No Anunnaki . . .[gods]
There was nothing . . . ,
    nothing but . . .
Old Father Apsu and Mummu-Tiamat, Mother of All Living,
Two bodies of water becoming one. (Matthews and Benjamin 1991: 8)

This mythic description of the beginning of things is appropriate to the geographical setting from which it came. The Babylonians could observe the "creation" of new land at the mouth of the Tigris and Euphrates Rivers, where they emptied into the Persian Gulf, "creating" land in the form of the delta. So, this "creation" at the point where fresh and salt water came together, is reflected in the myth.

Many other gods were the offspring of the original pair of Apsu and Tiamat, and eventually these younger, more active gods rebelled against the authority of their older, inactive parents. Apsu was killed by the younger gods, and Tiamat sought revenge against them. In preparation for combat, the younger gods chose Marduk, the principal god of the city of Babylon as their champion for one-on-one combat with Tiamat. After a fierce struggle, Marduk won the battle, killed Tiamat, and from her body made the heavens and the earth.

Thus, in *Enuma Elish,* order was established out of chaos. The victorious younger gods then wished to rest, so Marduk decided to create human beings as servants for the gods. The "Savages" or "Aborigines" were formed from the blood of one of the vanquished gods who had aided Tiamat. Marduk declares:

I will knead blood and bone into a Savage,
    Aborigine will be its name.
The Aborigines will do The Gods' work,
    The Savages will set the Gods free. (Matthews and Benjamin: 14)

Figure 5.2   A representation of Babylonian cosmology

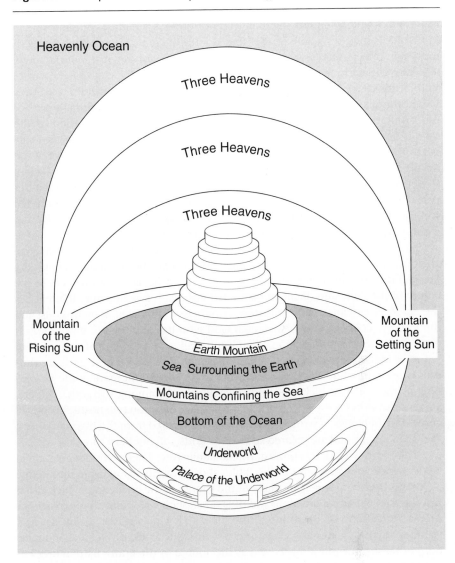

The Babylonian conception of the universe, reflecting the story told in *Enuma Elish,* is pictured in Figure 5.2.

ISRAELITE COSMOLOGY (ACCORDING TO P)

To a considerable extent, the Egyptian, Babylonian, and Israelite creation accounts are based on a similar understanding of cosmology. This cosmology reflects the way things appeared as a person looked up and out at the sky and the world. One should not expect such a view to correspond to modern scientific conceptions of the nature of the universe that depend on the scientific observations of astronomy, made using an array of technological instruments.

The cosmology underlying the P creation story is the most complete one in the Bible. It pictures a solid bowl (the "dome" of Gen 1, from a Hebrew verb meaning "to beat out," as one might beat out a copper bowl in a mold) stretching over the earth, resting on the mountains around the edge of the earth. Within this dome the sun, moon, and stars move in regular courses, as if they were on tracks. Above the dome were the waters that were originally part of the primeval fresh-water ocean before it was divided at the creation of the world. These waters were normally restrained by the dome, but occasionally fall to the earth as rain, snow, and hail when God opened the "windows of the heavens" (Gen 7:11; 8:2). Above these upper waters was the dwelling place of God. Underneath the earth was another great reservoir of fresh water, the other part of the primeval ocean. This great "deep" (Gen 7:11; 8:2) was the source of wells and springs. The earth rested securely on great pillars (1 Sam 2:8) that were sunk deep in the subterranean waters, as shown in Figure 5.3.

Sharing equal importance with the features which Genesis and other ancient cosmological views share, striking contrasts exist between the Genesis stories and the ancient Near-Eastern creation myths, especially with respect to the nature of the deity and divine-human relationships. A fundamental difference is the one between ancient Near-Eastern *polytheism,* the belief in many gods, and the Hebrew concept of one sovereign God who has a purposive will. *Enuma Elish* describes the procreation of multiple deities by the original pair, each of whom is identified with some feature of the natural world. These gods are thus not *above* nature but are constituent parts of it. A dominant motif of the *Enuma Elish* is the constant bickering and struggle of wills among the gods. The creation of the world is the final battle in the warfare between two hostile groups of gods. Human beings, a virtual afterthought, are formed from the blood of one of the fallen enemy and are created so that the gods will not have to work.

The Hebrew God, by contrast, has no family tree. There is no speculation in Genesis, nor anywhere else in the Bible, about how this God came into being. Neither is there any speculation about the source of the great deep which exists prior to the first act of creation, and thus no explicit statement about *creatio ex nihilo* ("creation out of nothing," the view that God creates "from scratch," without any raw materials). Nevertheless, this God is clearly seen as independent of the matter put in order and as the source of the entire natural order as humankind knows it. Interestingly, in this connection the Hebrew verb *bara',* the second word in the Hebrew text of Genesis, translated "create," is used in the Hebrew Bible *only* with God as its subject, the inference being that only God can create; humans can only procreate.

In Gen 1:1–2:4a, God brings order out of chaos by pushing back the primordial "deep," forming dry earth. The account speaks of darkness and the primeval waters prior to God's first creative work. The sequence of the works of creation in the Priestly creation account follows essentially the same sequence as the Babylonian *Enuma Elish.*

Figure 5.3   An Israelite cosmology

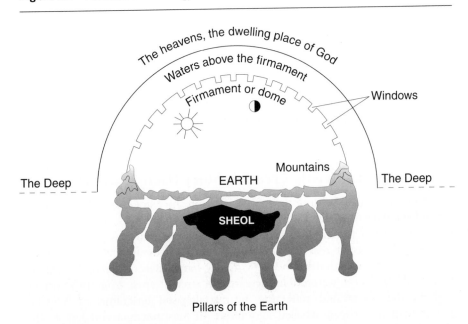

Enuma Elish

1. *Primordial water chaos—Apsu and Tiamat enveloped in darkness.*
2. *Appearance of Marduk, "Sun of the heavens"*
3. *Chaos overcome by Marduk in titanic battle with Tiamat; the sky fashioned from half of her body*
4. *Earth formed*
5. *Constellations established*
6. *Humankind made (as an afterthought) to serve the gods*
7. *A banquet held by the gods*

Genesis 1

1. *Earth formless and void; the chaotic deep* (tehom, *which closely resembles the name of Tiamat) enveloped in darkness*
2. *The creation of light*
3. *The dome of the heavens created*
4. *Waters gathered together; dry land appears*
5. *Bodies of light created*
6. *Humankind created in God's image to have dominion over all creation*
7. *Seventh day, God rests*

Both Genesis 1 and *Enuma Elish* arose in similar political circumstances. The Babylonian creation story was written *ca.* 1100 B.C.E., during the reign of King Nebuchadrezzar I, whose namesake presided over the destruction of

Jerusalem some 500 years later. In 1200 the Assyrians had conquered Babylon and removed the statue of Babylon's chief deity, Marduk, to Assyria. This political and religious catastrophe was not avenged until the reign of Nebuchadrezzar, a century later, when Babylon defeated Assyria and recovered the statue. The writing of *Enuma Elish* celebrated Babylon's victory, attempting to explain how Marduk, considered throughout Mesopotamia to be a rather insignificant god, could have risen to his high status. And so, like the Priestly creation story, the *Enuma Elish* was a work of political propaganda composed after a religious calamity, the P account having been written after the destruction of Jerusalem at the beginning of the sixth century B.C.E..

The Yahwistic Creation Story (Gen 2:4b–3)

The cosmology lying behind the second creation story in Genesis 2:4b–25, differs substantially from that in the first, assuming the perennial shortage of water of a Palestinian setting rather than the abundance of water, as presupposed in the Genesis 1 account, that reflects a Mesopotamian geographical setting. In Gen 2:4b–25, God is pictured as working with dry, barren desert. Out of this arid setting, God creates the watered, fertile earth. "A stream" arose from the earth and watered the dry ground, reflecting the rainfall-based agriculture of Palestine, rather than the irrigation-based agriculture of Mesopotamia and Egypt. God planted a garden in Eden, out of which four rivers are said to flow: the Pishon, Gihon, Tigris, and Euphrates (2:10–14). While the Tigris and Euphrates are known major rivers, neither the Pishon nor Gihon can be identified with any certainty (Gihon is known elsewhere in the Hebrew Bible as a spring in Jerusalem: 1 Kings 1:33, 38, 45; 2 Chr 32:30; 33:14). Because the Tigris and Euphrates do not have a common source, the mention of these four rivers may simply be an attempt to locate the Garden of Eden at the "center of the earth," the mythical source of the rivers.

Jerome Walsh has demonstrated how the action of Gen 2:4b–3:24 unfolds in a series of **seven scenes** that are distinguished from one another principally by shifts in *dramatis personae* (characters in a drama) and changes in literary form (1977: 161, 169–70, 173). The seven scenes are listed below:

1. **2:4b–17**: a predominantly narrative section whose only active figure is Yahweh. The human creature is present in a completely passive role.

2. **2:18–25**: a second predominantly narrative section in which the active role of Yahweh is supplemented by subordinate activity on the human's part.

3. **3:1–5**: a dialogue section, with dialogue between the snake and the woman.

4. **3:6–8**: a narrative section with two characters, the woman and the man.

5. **3:9–13**: a dialogue section involving Yahweh, the man, and the woman.

6. **3:14–19**: a monologue section featuring Yahweh—the snake, the woman, and the man are present as passive figures.

7. **3:22–24**: a predominantly narrative section whose only active figure is Yahweh. Humans are present in a completely passive role.

According to Walsh, the basic structural principle of the Yahwist's creation story is the concentric arrangement of these seven scenes. The overall pattern involves *dramatis personae,* themes, and in some cases, internal structural elements of each scene, with the fourth scene being the climax and turning point.

Scene 1 (2:4b–17)

type: narrative
dramatis personae: YHWH & the human
theme: from *'adamah* (soil) to garden
structure: vocabulary

Scene 2 (2:18–25)

type: narrative
dramatis personae: Yahweh, man,
   woman, and the animals
theme: relationships among the creatures
structure: 2:24-5 [etiology]

Scene 3 (3:1–5)

type: dialogue
dramatis personae: the serpent
   and the woman
theme: eating from the tree
structure: three statements

Scene 7 (3:22–24)

type: narrative
dramatis personae: YHWH & the humans
theme: from garden to *'adamah*
structure: vocabulary

Scene 6 (3:14–19)

type: monologue
dramatis personae: Yahweh, man,
   woman, and the serpent
theme: relationships among the creatures
structure: 3:20-21 [etiology]

Scene 5 (3:9–13)

type: dialogue
dramatis personae: Yahweh, the man,
   and the woman
theme: eating from the tree
structure: three questions-and-answers

Scene 4 (3:6–8)

type: narrative
dramatis personae: the woman and her husband
theme: eating from the tree
structure: concentric structure of the scene

The fourth scene includes the climax and turning point of the story. At the center of the narrative stands the account of the humans' sin. More precisely, the concentric structure of scene four reveals that the man's sin—the single phrase "and he ate"—serves as the turning point of the entire Eden account:

> So when the woman saw that the tree was good for food, and that it was a delight to the eyes, and that the tree was to be desired to make one wise, she took of its fruit and ate; and she also gave some to her husband, who was with her, and he ate. Then the eyes of both were opened, and they knew that they were naked; and they sewed fig leaves together and made loincloths for themselves. (3:6–8)

So, while this passage is narrative in form, its distinctive structure as well as its content help it deliver a threefold message:

1. *anthropological:* Humans, not God, hold responsibility for human sinfulness and its consequences. This reality is present from the first moment of human history.

2. *moral-theological:* Human sin has cosmic dimensions; no matter how petty or private the deed may seem, it violates the sacred at the heart of reality. It rejects the whole order of creation as instituted by God.

3. *instructional:* There is nothing exhilarating or exciting about sin; it is ultimately profitless.

TRADITIONAL INTERPRETATIONS AND THE ROLE OF WOMAN

If the Yahwistic creation story has its focus in the woman's action of giving the "forbidden fruit" to the man and his eating it, what does this say, in a fundamental way, about the role of women and their relationships with men? Much male-centered interpretation of this story holds the story to be about "Adam and Eve," (rarely, Eve and Adam), proclaiming male superiority and female inferiority as willed by God and portraying woman as "temptress" and troublemaker, eternally dependent upon and dominated by her husband. Having already decided what the text is about, an androcentric preunderstanding of the story then reads into the text specific sexist assumptions.

- A **male** God **first** creates man (2:7) and then creates woman **last** (2:22). *First* here means superior and *last* means inferior or subordinate.
- Woman is created **for the sake of** man: a helpmate to cure his loneliness (2:18–23).
- **Contrary to nature,** woman comes out of man; she is denied even her natural function of birthing and that function is given to man (2:21–22).
- Woman is the rib of man, **dependent** upon him for life (2:21–22).
- Taken **out of man** (2:23), woman has a **derivative,** not an autonomous existence.
- Man **names** woman (2:23) and thus has power over her.
- Man **leaves his father's family** in order to set up through his wife another **patriarchal** unit (2:24).
- Woman **tempted** man to disobey and thus **she is responsible** for sin in the world; she is **untrustworthy, gullible,** and **simpleminded.**
- Woman is **cursed** by pain in childbirth (3:16); pain in childbirth is a more severe punishment than man's struggles with the soil; it therefore signifies that **woman's sin is greater than man's.**
- Woman's **desire for man** (3:16) is God's way of keeping her faithful and **submissive** to her husband.
- God gives man the **right to rule over** woman.(3:16). (Trible 1978: 73)

In commenting on this list Trible notes that although such specifics continue to be cited as support for traditional interpretations of male superiority and female inferiority, none of them is completely accurate, and most of them are simply not based on the text itself. These ideas, supposedly drawn from the biblical text, fail to respect the integrity of the text as an interlocking structure of words and motifs with its own intrinsic value and meaning. In short they violate the rhetoric of the story (1978: 73). Popular tradition concerning "the Fall," "apples and snakes," and so forth has also interpreted this narrative as if its focus were on sex and the evil wrought by sex, again with the woman cast in the role of the "heavy." But to find in this story any prominent focus on sex or any linkage between sex and sin is not faithful to the narrative as we have it.

A MODERN INTERPRETATION OF THE ROLE OF WOMAN

Woman as "Helper."   While it is true that the woman has an important role to play in this narrative, it is not the negative one that popular perception has so often perpetuated. Yahweh, having created the first human and placed that being in the garden, concludes that it is not good for the human to be alone; the human needs "a helper as his partner" (2:18—cf. the KJV translation "an help meet for him" and the RSV translation "a helper fit for him"). The use of the term "helper" here has been misleading, implying a subordinate role—a boss supervises a helper. Significantly, however, the most common usage in the Hebrew Bible of the term here translated "helper" is in reference to God. Frequently in the book of Psalms, God is referred to as one who can be counted on to help in times of trouble. For example, Ps 70:5, which uses the same word for "help" as the word translated "helper" in Gen 2:18 (*'ezer* in Hebrew) reads:

> But I am poor and needy;
> hasten to me, O God!
> You are my help and my deliverer;
> O LORD, do not delay!

Clearly the term "help" or "helper" does not of itself imply any kind of subordination. The "helper" rescues people from themselves, which is true of the woman in the garden as well as in the assertion of the Psalmist.

Woman as Taken from Man.   Woman is thus created from the rib of the sleeping man (2:21-22). Scholars do not agree on what idea the creation-from-the-rib reflects. It is probably nothing more than etiological—it seeks to explain why women have a birth canal while men do not, or the existence of the navel, or why ribs cover the upper but not the lower half of the human torso. At any event, where the animals had failed, the woman succeeds: "This at last is bone of my bones and flesh of my flesh" (2:23). The man, using a play on words in Hebrew, calls his companion "Woman," *'ishshâ* in Hebrew, because she was taken out of "Man," *'îsh* in Hebrew. J concludes his account of creation with a statement relating marriage to creation: "Therefore a man leaves his father and mother and clings to his wife, and they become one flesh" (2:24), and with the comment that "The man and his wife were both naked, and were not ashamed" (2:25). Seen from the vantage point of the Israelite monarchy, where clothes were a status symbol of a growing elite, nudity without shame may very well refer to a world where relations among people are not troubled by fear, oppression, or suspicion.

With the coming into being of the woman, creation is complete—a fact that points to the remarkable significance of the woman, the capstone of creation in J. To be sure, the fact that she is named by man suggests some subordination. Yet this suggestion is more than offset by other features of the narrative. Whereas the creation of the man is described in one short verse (7), the woman's creation (22) and the man's response to it (23) is more extended, coming as the climax of 2:18–23. In the Priestly story the creation of humans came as the last act of creation, a case of "saving the best for last"; similarly in J's story, woman is the crown of creation. This account of the creation of woman as a separate act of creation is all the more extraordinary because it is the *only* one in all of ancient Near Eastern creation myths.

Woman as "Weaker."   The woman's position is equally remarkable in chapter 3, the second part of J's seven scene drama. The chapter begins with the serpent's approach to the woman. Why did the serpent confront the woman rather than the man? A common explanation, one that has been around at least since Augustine in the fourth century C.E., holds that the woman, the weaker of the two sexes, made an easier target for temptation. However, this explanation does not align with the view of woman that emerges from a careful reading of Gen 2. More accurately, the serpent approaches the woman as the more sensitive—and therefore the more human—of the two; she is more open to suggestion and therefore, more vulnerable. The centrality of the woman here contrasts sharply with the passivity of the man in relation to the woman, whom he seems to trust more than he does Yahweh. As a result of their joint act of mistrust of Yahweh, the man and the woman are punished, striken at a basic level—she in her function as wife and mother, he in his role as farmer. Because the woman's punishment involves her fertility and the man's punishment involves the land's fertility, at some point in the past interpretation of this passage, both the serpent and the fruit came to be regarded as sexual in nature. Nevertheless, a careful reading of the text rules out the central role of sex traditionally ascribed to the passage.

The common understanding of the severity of the woman's punishment rests on a questionable translation of Gen 3:16, which reads as follows in the NRSV:

> To the woman he [God] said,
> "I will greatly increase your pangs in childbearing;
> in pain you shall bring forth children,
> yet your desire shall be for your husband,
> and he shall rule over you."

Concerning this verse Carol Meyers has said: "Perhaps no single verse of scripture is more troublesome, from a feminist perspective" (Meyers 1988: 95). Meyers observes that the history of the translation of this verse, from the ancient versions to the most recent translations, has kept alive the belief that pain in childbirth served as women's punishment for disobedience, as is their subordination to men. Meyers, however, suggests that a more faithful rendering of the Hebrew here would be:

> I will greatly increase your toil and your pregnancies;
> (Along) with travail shall you beget children.
> For to your man is your desire,
> And he shall predominate over you. (118)

Meyers' translation reflects the biological and socioeconomic realities of early Israel. Women, as part of a social system that was struggling to survive, had to perform agricultural labor *and* bring forth many children who could, in the face of famines and a relatively low life expectancy, keep the population levels in early Israelite society at acceptable levels. The last two lines of the oracle tell us that female reluctance to conceive and give birth to numerous children is overcome by the passion they feel toward their men.

The Yahwist's account closes with the man and the woman being expelled from the garden and barred from ever re-entering it, suggesting that humans "can never go home again," cannot return to Eden. Rather, they are convicted rebels who cannot be reformed and cannot be trusted to take good care of God's garden. The supposition is that having eaten of the fruit of the one tree, "the tree of the knowledge of good and evil," they will, if given the opportunity, eat from the other tree, "the tree of life." They would do so in spite of their punishment because they do not know as much as they think they know, they do not recognize the limitations of their knowledge. Having superior knowledge, if they were to gain immortality as well, any distinctions between Creator and creature would become hopelessly blurred for them, with disastrous consequences.

The Two Stories Compared

The most obvious structural difference between the Priestly and Yahwist creation stories is in their ordering of events. The Priestly version begins with things in a watery chaos (appropriate to the alluvial plain between the Tigris and Euphrates rivers in time of flood); the Yahwist's beginning is a dry setting (fitting for a Palestinian setting). The Priestly narrative, as we have seen, carefully orders God's creative acts into six days, sanctifying the seventh as the first Sabbath; the Yahwist makes no mention of a time frame for the acts of creation. In the two accounts, the order of creative acts proceeds as follows:

PRIESTLY	YAHWIST
1. light (but not the sun)	1. a human (*'adam*) from the soil (*'adamah*)
2. dome of the sky, with water above and below	2. the garden
3. land and earth separated, plants	3. trees
4. greater and lesser lights in the sky (sun and moon), stars	4. animals
5. birds and aquatic creatures	5. woman (*'ishshâ*) made from man (*'ish*)
6. animals and humans, male and female	

In addition to the structural differences, the two accounts also describe God in very different ways. In the Priestly version, God is pictured as distant, removed from the creation. This God creates by speaking, not through any direct, "hands on" contact with matter. The Priestly God is one who works out of a carefully-conceived master plan that unfolds without a hitch in a properly-ordered sequence. Here a sovereign God builds order into his creation by royal edict. Not the least hint of any folkloric element exists in this account, no trial-and-error in the unfolding of creation. Even though there are clear echoes of the *Enuma Elish* myth, there is also an attempt to prevent any polytheistic confusion. The words "sun" and "moon," cognates in the Babylonian language for the names of deities, are not used here, but are replaced with the phrases "the greater light" and "the lesser light" (Gen 1:16).

The Yahwist's God, by contrast, has intimate contact with his creation. Like a potter, God molded the first human and then "breathed into his nostrils the breath of life" (2:7b). Experimentally it seems, God first created the animals, hoping that they would provide appropriate companionship for the man. When this did not work out, like a surgeon God anesthetized the man and removed one of his ribs, out of which he made the woman. God is pictured as strolling about the garden and carrying on conversations with the man and the woman. This kind of representation of God is sometimes called anthropomorphic, meaning that God is described *as if* God were a human being—hearing, walking, talking, and so forth. The Yahwist's God is thus not so much transcendent, or "at a distance," but immanent, intimately involved with creation.

Taken together, the two accounts emphasize two aspects of God central to all biblical reflection about the nature of God—transcendence and immanence. Theologians have always insisted that these seemingly contradictory aspects of God's nature should be held in tension; to stress one to the exclusion of the other is risky. To emphasize God's transcendence at the expense of God's immanence creates a situation in which God becomes distant, almost out of touch, and even unconcerned. An overly transcendent God creates the universe as a kind of self-regulating mechanism and then ceases any further involvement, so as not to "dirty his hands." On the other hand, to stress God's immanence is perilous as well. By doing so, God can become a "warm and fuzzy" deity, an indulgent parent, "on call" at the whim of his creatures, a kind of "heavenly bellhop." The redactor who placed the Priestly and Yahwist accounts back-to-back was a wise theologian, indeed!

A TALE OF TWO BROTHERS: GENESIS 4

Gen 4 should be read with Gen 3, not just because of the textual order, but because these two chapters belong together thematically. As we progress through Genesis 1 - 11, with the movement from the narrative of a "very good" orderly creation to the story of increasing human strife and disunity, we observe that the humanly initiated rupture in the relationship between God and humans (ch.3) has the immediate and inevitable consequence of a break in relationships on the human plane (ch. 4). That break is manifested in a violent fratricide. Gen 4 begins with family harmony (v. 1) and ends with a situation of unresolved estrangement within the family (v. 16). Having been expelled from the garden, with its promise of harmony among all of God's creatures, the issue now at hand is whether and how human beings can live together in peace and harmony.

In the story of Cain and Abel, the two brothers represent the two primary subsistence strategies of the Palestinian peasant—farming and herding—with Abel as "a keeper of sheep," and Cain "a tiller of the ground" (4:2). In the background of this story may be the perennial conflict in Palestine between the farmer and the herder, as they competed with one another over the use of land (a problem that replayed itself in the early American West, as reflected in the song from the popular Rogers and Hammerstein musical *Oklahoma,* "The Farmer and the Cowman Should be Friends!").

Cain and Abel also represent the continuing biblical theme of what might be called "the brother problem," "brother" representing "sisters" as well in its theological implications. This story marks the first of numerous biblical stories concerning "the brother problem." In Genesis conflict erupts between the brothers Isaac and Ishmael, sons of Abraham (Gen 21), between Jacob and his twin brother Esau (Gen 25:29-34; 27:1-45), and between Joseph and his brothers (Gen 37). In David's story conflict is reported between two of his sons, Amnon and Absalom (2 Sam 13:22-33).

Like many biblical names, the names chosen by the Yahwist for the two protagonists, Cain and Abel, are significant, and they may well have provided significant clues to the Hebrew reader at the very beginning of the tale. By giving the first son the name Cain, who is the farmer, the author makes an association with the Hebrew verb *qanah.* When Eve gave birth to Cain she reportedly said: "I have produced (*qaniytiy*) a man with the help of the LORD." The association of the name Cain with the Hebrew verb meaning "to create" or "to acquire" leaves open two interpretations for what Eve said: either Eve acknowledges the work of God through her in "creation" or she recognizes God as the only Creator, the ultimate source of Cain. The name Cain actually has its etymology in a root *qyn,* which does not appear in the Hebrew Bible except in proper names. Cain, as the elder son of Adam and Eve, would in the normal course of human families likely dominate any younger brothers.

Abel, Cain's younger brother, is given a name suggesting his rather insignificant role in the continuing story of humanity. The name Abel, *hevel* in Hebrew, is the same word that recurs in the book of Ecclesiastes, ". . . all is vanity, (*hevel*)" and means "vapor" or "nothingness."

While Cain's name suggests that he, not his brother, is the character to reckon with in the story, Abel takes an early lead in the story when God accepts Abel's animal sacrifice. However, God rejects Cain's vegetable sacrifice. Note that the text provides not even the slightest hint as to why one brother's offering was accepted and the other's was rejected. While the value of animal sacrifice relative to vegetable sacrifice, like the farmer-shepherd conflict, may lie behind the story, the story does not dwell on such details, but quickly moves on to what is important to the narrator—the fracturing of the human community and its consequences.

Cain—whose name may be intended to suggest the creative capacity of humanity—becomes a destroyer and murders his brother because his pride is injured. Here is a powerful representation of the human predicament. Created by God and set in a well-ordered environment that can provide for all their needs, humans reject community under a God whom they find hard to understand and seek to prevail over rather than co-exist with their neighbors.

Cain the first-born, Cain the farmer, gains what he regards as his "rightful" place with the elimination of his brother. Or does he? Abel is murdered in verse 8. In verse 9, a God who is pictured by the Yahwist as less than all-knowing, asks Cain, "Where is your brother Abel?" to which Cain responds, "I do not know; am I my brother's keeper?" Walter Brueggemann describes the narrative from this point on (vv. 9–16) as being in the form of a lawsuit, in which Yahweh tries Cain for his life. Brueggemann observes that the narrative has close parallels to the lawsuit of Gen 3:9 ff. as it moves through investigation (vv. 9–10), sentence (vv. 11–12) and, finally, to banishment (v. 16). In the initial exchange, Cain's counterquestion (v. 9) resembles the rhetorical questions of Jacob (30:2) and Joseph (50:19). They intend to dismiss the point raised and limit the scope of responsibility (Brueggemann 1982:60). Cain refuses his responsibility as a brother. His sentence is to be a fugitive, but Cain pleads for mercy from the judge. The killer now fears that he will be killed (vv. 13–14). He is given a mark that indicates both guilt and grace. God's mark on Cain (v. 15) has evoked endless speculation. There is still no consensus about its meaning. While it may originally have referred to a visible mark such as a tattoo, we should understand it in terms of its function in the narrative. That function is two-edged. On the one hand, it proclaims the guilt of Cain. On the other, it marks Cain as under God's special protection (1982: 60).

As a footnote to the story of Cain and Abel, the Yahwist appends notes describing the origins of some of the institutions that constitute civilization. A veiled anti-civilization, anti-urban theme appears here when we are told that the first city was built by Cain (4:17). The Yahwist sees in Cain's city-building the human answer to God's curse on Cain, which condemned him to be a "fugitive and a wanderer on the earth" (4:12). The anti-urban element thus surfaces: the first city was built as a human attempt to provide security apart from God, and indeed "away from the presence of the LORD" (4:16). Cain builds his own "city of refuge" to escape from the social institution of blood-revenge. Also it is implicitly suggested that Cain's city could not be under the protection of Yahweh because, in the theology of early Israel at least, Yahweh's circle of power was sometimes conceived of as being limited to Canaan, leaving other gods sovereign in other lands. Cain's city is thus a foreign city. The motif of the city as a fortress, having its origins and reason for being in humans' attempts to provide their own security instead of placing final faith in Yahweh, recurs throughout the Hebrew scriptures.

THE ATRAHASIS MYTH, THE GILGAMESH EPIC, AND THE GREAT FLOOD IN GENESIS 5–9

While we might expect most cultures to have a creation myth of some kind, the presence of a story about a great flood is more unexpected because it is not a necessary ingredient in an account of how the world came to be. Given the Palestinian setting of the Hebrew Bible, the existence of a flood story is especially striking because anything more than a small-scale flash flood is difficult to imagine, given Palestinian geography. It is thus interesting to note that the story of a universal flood is well-attested in ancient Near Eastern literature, including the Bible. There are two Babylonian accounts of a great flood: The *Atrahasis Myth* and the *Epic of Gilgamesh.*

The Atrahasis Myth and the Epic of Gilgamesh

A major motif in *Atrahasis* is overpopulation. Humans become so numerous and so boisterous that the gods decide to eliminate them. The gods send a number of catastrophes—plague, drought, famine—all unsuccessfully. Finally, a flood is sent. Atrahasis is told of the coming destruction and builds a boat in which animals and birds are saved. It is assumed that other people were saved besides Atrahasis, but gaps in the text obscure the details.

In Tablet XI of the Babylonian *Epic of Gilgamesh* we find a close parallel to the biblical story. The parallels between the biblical account of the flood and the Gilgamesh epic are even more significant than the parallels found in the creation stories. More than in any other literary tradition, scholars have concluded that the Mesopotamian and biblical myths of a flood cannot be thought of as having been independently composed. Most scholars believe that the Mesopotamian myths are the ultimate source of the flood traditions reflected in Genesis. Either the Genesis account is based on the Mesopotamian myths, or both depend on the same general stock of ideas. The Sumerians, who preceded the Babylonians in the southern part of Mesopotamia, also had a flood story. The hero in this story, Ziasudra, survived by building a boat after being warned by one of the gods of an imminent deluge.

The *Epic of Gilgamesh* is perhaps the best-known myth of the ancient Near East. The world's oldest epic poem, it was written on clay tablets in the Akkadian language (an eastern Semitic language) *ca.* 1750 B.C.E. Copies of at least part of the epic have been found all over the Near East, from ancient Sumer (the southern part of modern Iraq) to the Hittite capital (in what is modern Turkey), to the Israelite city of Megiddo. The part of this epic containing the flood story can be found in Matthews and Benjamin's *Old Testament Parallels* (35–40). Tablet XI in the epic opens with Gilgamesh's visit to Utnapishtim, the Babylonian equivalent of Noah. Gilgamesh, the epic's hero and described as being half god and half human, sets out on a quest to achieve immortality after seeing his closest friend, Enkidu, die. Utnapishtim is himself immortal, but he looks like an ordinary human. This causes Gilgamesh to ask the question: How did Utnapishtim become one of the gods? Utnapishtim then tells Gilgamesh the story of the great flood, how the gods rewarded him and his wife with immortality for saving humans and animals from the flood. Sardonically, Utnapishtim ends his account by asking Gilgamesh to tell him and his wife how he, Gilgamesh, is going to become immortal.

The theme of relations between the gods and humans appears at the beginning of the Genesis story of the flood in one of the most thoroughly mythological text segments in all of the Hebrew Bible. Gen 6:1–4 tells how the "sons of God" (divine beings related to the plural "let us" in 1:26) mated with the "daughters of humans" and parented the "Nephilim," creatures of gigantic stature (compare Num 13:33; Deut 2:10–11). This story is inserted here to demonstrate the increase of wickedness on the earth. The mating of divine men and human women did not create a new race of semi-divine or immortal creatures. It rather symbolizes a moral perversion that so corrupts the natural order of things that God "was sorry that he had made humankind on the earth" (Gen 6:6)—hence the flood!

The Flood Story in Genesis

The Genesis flood story preserves two versions of a flood story, originally separate, but now interwoven. These two stories agree in essentials but differ in details. For example, the number of animals taken aboard the ark in Gen 6:19–21 is given as one pair of each species. In 7:1–3, however, it is stated that there were seven pairs of clean animals and one pair of unclean animals. Because the Priestly source did not accept the institution of sacrifice until there was a proper priesthood, it did not differentiate between clean and unclean animals in the flood story. Thus, one pair of animals of each species would be sufficient, because there would be no sacrifices. Gen 7:17 says "The flood continued forty days on the earth," but 7:24 reports that "the waters swelled on the earth for one hundred fifty days." Scholars who see multiple sources in the Pentateuch believe that 7:17 belongs to the Yahwistic stratum of materials, 7:24 to the priestly. Despite the discrepancies between the sources, the theme of the story as it stands is clear: the God who created the earth acts as both judge and redeemer of a rebellious creation.

In the analysis of Gordon T. Wenham (1978: 337–40), the flood narrative, in its literary structure, forms an extended *chiasm* or palistrophe, a structure that builds to a climax element-by-element and then unfolds those elements in reverse order. In a chiasm the first item matches the last item, the second item matches the next-to-the-last item, and so on. The second half thus reflects a mirror image of the first. While we will observe this literary structure elsewhere in the Hebrew Bible, this one is one of the more extended forms. Why the flood narrative extends so may be due, in part, to the fact that a flood story is particularly suited to such a form. It begins with dry land, the water rises, then the waters recede, and the story ends where it began—with dry land. Gen 6:10–9:19, according to Wenham is a chiasm containing 31 items. Particularly striking are the references to numbers of days in lines H, I, L, O and O', L', I', and H'. The turning point is line P (Gen 8:1):

GENESIS 6:10–9:19 AS A CHIASM

A   Noah (6:10a)

B   Shem, Ham, and Japheth (10b)

C   Ark to be built (14–16)

D   Flood announced (17)

E   Covenant with Noah (18–20)

F   Food in the ark (21)

G   Command to enter ark (7:1–3)

H   7 days waiting for flood (4–5)

I   7 days waiting for flood (7–10)

J   Entry into the ark (11–15)

K   Yahweh shuts Noah in (16)

L   40 days flood (17a)

M   Waters increase (17b–18)

N   Mountains covered (19–20)

O   150 days water prevail ([21]–24)

P   **GOD REMEMBERS NOAH** (8:1)

O'   150 days water abate (3)

N'   Mountain tops visible (4–5)

M'   Waters abate (5)

L'   40 days (end of) (6a)

K'   Noah opens window of ark (6b)

J'   Raven and dove leave ark (7–9)

I'   7 days waiting for waters to subside (10–11)

H'   7 days waiting for waters to subside (12–13)

G'   Command to leave ark (15–17[22])

F'   Food outside ark (9:1–4)

E'   Covenant with all flesh (8–10)

D'   No flood in future (11–17)

C'   Ark (18a)

B'   Shem, Ham, and Japheth (18b)

A'   Noah (19)

God's intervention was decisive in saving Noah, and the literary structure highlights this fact. Noah is saved and afterwards, in 9:11–17, God's bow is set in the heavens, *pointing away from the earth.* Any arrows shot from such a bow are no threat to human existence. The world will never again be destroyed because of the evil of humankind. The re-creation motif ends here with the re-capitulation (in 9:1–2, 6b) of the language of Gen 1:26 ff.:

> God blessed Noah and his sons, and said to them, "Be fruitful and multi-ply, and fill the earth. The fear and dread of you shall rest on every ani-mal of the earth, and on every bird of the air, on everything that creeps on the ground, and all the fish of the sea; into your hand they are deliv-ered . . . for in his own image God made humankind."

The Genesis Flood Story and the Epic of Gilgamesh Compared

The similarities between the Genesis account of the flood and the *Gilgamesh Epic* are striking, both in structure and content. Where they differ, they do so because the authors of the Old Testament story presuppose a different under-standing of the nature of God, which they attempt to communicate in the way they tell the story. In *Gilgamesh,* unlike *Atrahasis,* no explanation is given for why the flood happened. In Genesis, however, clearly the flood is sent by God as judgment on human disobedience. The intent is not to obliterate the human race, but to purge it and make possible a new beginning! The Genesis story does not portray a God angry because the creation has gotten out of control, but a concerned God who intends to re-form his creation—a God who "remembers Noah." Indeed, the phrase "God remembered Noah" stands structurally at the very center of the Genesis flood story (8:1). Just as the Garden of Eden story turned on the phrase "and he ate" (Gen 3:6), so the flood story turns on the phrase "God remembered Noah."

GENESIS 11:1–9: A CITY AND A TOWER

Immediately preceding the narrative in Genesis 11 is the table of nations (Gen 10). This table gives the genealogies of the three sons of Noah: Japheth, Ham, and Shem. The descendants of Japheth are centered in the area of Asia Minor (modern-day Turkey). They spread from there to the "coastlands," probably Greece and Europe. The descendants of Ham are connected with Egypt, north-ern Africa, and Palestine. The descendants of Shem are the Semitic peoples, among whom were the Hebrews, who were first located in Mesopotamia and later settled in Palestine. Semitic peoples founded nation-states in Syria, Moab, and Edom, as well as Israel.

The table of nations attempts to account for the diversity of languages and peoples in the ancient Near East (see 10:5, 20, 31). The table concludes with the line, "These are the families of the sons of Noah, according to their genealogies, in their nations; and from these the nations spread abroad on the earth after the flood" (10:32).

The tower of Babel story in 11:1-9 appears to be out of harmony with its immediate context in Genesis 10. Genesis 10 (from P) accepts the phenomenon of a multiplicity of nations without negative comment. But Genesis 11 (from J) opens with humankind still unified, and the dispersion that follows is viewed negatively. We will examine the tower of Babel story, not because it offers a scientific explanation of linguistic diversity, but for what it says about human aspirations and divine judgment.

In Gen 11:1-9 apparently a redactor (the Yahwist or someone else) has combined what may originally have been two independent stories, one dealing with a tower and the other dealing with a city. The part of the story concerning the city and the concept of the city that underlies it has been obscured by commentators' preoccupation with seeing in this story the "Tower of Babel," reflecting a Mesopotamian temple-tower or ziggurat. Ziggurats were temple-towers found in ancient Mesopotamia, which was a flat plain between the Tigris and Euphrates. Ziggurats were terraced towers that represented an artificial mountain, with a stairway leading to a temple at the top.

The anti-urban judgment implied in this story lies on a different level and is much more closely related to the concept of the city in Israelite thought than is assumed when the story is seen as condemning a kind of Babylonian temple. The expression "a city and a tower" (11:4) illustrates a literary phenomenon known as *hendiadys,* a figure in which two words linked by a conjunction express one compound idea. Taken in this sense then, "tower" is used in this story to mean "citadel," thus the phrase "a city and a tower" can be translated "a city with a citadel" (see Figure 5.4).

The phrase "and its top (was) in the heavens," (11:4) is part of typical urban terminology in the Old Testament, being employed as figurative language describing urban fortifications of monumental proportions. Such language is used, for example, in Deut 1:28, ". . . the cities are large and fortified up to heaven!" A rather striking example of such language, and perhaps even a reminiscence of the Genesis 11 story, can be seen in an oracle of the prophet Jeremiah that condemns Babylon:

> "Though Babylon should mount up to heaven,
> and though she should fortify her strong height,
> from me destroyers would come upon her,"
> says the LORD. (Jer 51:53)

Viewed in this way, the story popularly known as "The Tower of Babel" becomes another example of the futile human attempt to gain security apart from God through the human enterprize of city-building, even if the city purports to be a holy city, protected by a deity. Connected with this, a particular thrust seems to be directed against a city that represents an imperial center. This thrust is illustrated perhaps most clearly in the judgment of Yahweh, "from there

Figure 5.4   A city with a citadel (Lachish)

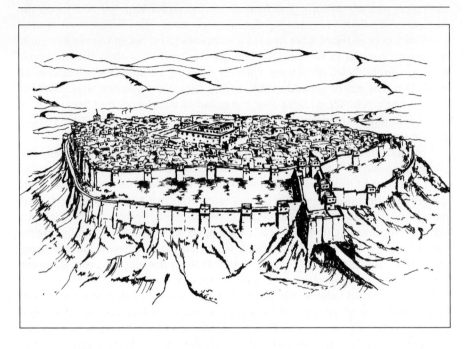

the LORD scattered them abroad over the face of all the earth" (11:9). This city represents the prototype of all cities that were the visible center of a centralized, acquisitive imperial authority. The monumental architecture of the city was important as a symbol of the city's power, particularly when the city was the center of an empire. This story demonstrates the recurring resistance in ancient Israel to the concentration of power in a central authority, where oppression of the people may result.

This interpretation does not imply that the story in Genesis 11 has nothing at all to do with Mesopotamian temple-towers, but rather this view suggests that the story as it now stands is more closely related to the more immediate surroundings and constant threats to the champions of faith in Yahweh. The human attempt to provide security apart from Yahweh presented the most potent threat to the faith, seen perhaps most clearly for the Israelite, not in Babylon, but in their own capital city of Jerusalem (and later, Samaria, which became the center of the northern kingdom). These bastions of monarchical power possessed a whole spectrum of socioreligious problems associated with urban centers.

The tower of Babel story also may have had an etiological element, to explain the origins of different languages and peoples living in different geographical regions. The theological impact of the story clearly overshadows any etiological element. What may once have been simply a story explaining a ruined city on the plains of Mesopotamia, with what may have looked like an unfinished ziggurat, now stands at the conclusion of the first eleven chapters of

Genesis and their account of human beginnings. It offers the final note on the spread of sin throughout the world and its effects. Michael Fishbane has observed a striking parallelism between this story about the aggressive motivations that underlie culture and the earlier descriptions of Cain's descendants, who developed cities and art. This parallelism highlights that in both cases the achievements of culture are portrayed with sarcasm. Through their small deeds, brick by brick, humans build a tower so as to "make a name for ourselves" (1979: 38).

THE UNITY AND MESSAGE OF GENESIS 1–11

Throughout the first eleven chapters of Genesis, the author (or authors) deals with universals. Just as myths have no firm chronological or geographical ties but deal with "everywhen" and "everywhere," so these stories are about "everyone," not just the ancestors of one particular ethnic group. Creation is treated as a unity. Where individuals like Cain and Abel are mentioned, they represent humanity.

The central theme of these chapters is the distinction between Creator and creature. This crucial distinction raises the core questions in this section of scripture. How does the Creator relate to his creatures and vice versa? What legitimates human power and what are its limits? The answers to these questions that are offered in these chapters are summarized in two points made by Brueggemann: First, the Creator has a purpose and a will for creation. The Creator continues to address the creation, calling it to faithful response and glad obedience. The creation has not been abandoned and turned loose on its own. Neither has it been given free rein for its own inclinations. The purposes of the Creator are not implemented in a coercive or tyrannical way. The Creator loves and respects the creation. The freedom of creation is taken seriously by the Creator. Second, the creation, which exists only because of the Creator's purpose, has freedom to respond in various ways. As the texts in the early chapters of Genesis indicate, the response of creation to Creator is a mixture of obedience and self-assertion. Both are present, though the negative, self-assertive response tends to dominate the narrative (1982: 13).

The "primeval history" of Genesis 1–11 ends in 11:10–26 with a genealogy of Abraham (Abram is a variant of the same name and Sarai is a variant of Sarah). His story and that of his descendants provide the focus for the rest of Genesis. Whereas Genesis 1–11 was concerned with universals, the interest of the rest of Genesis becomes increasingly focused, dealing with the origins of a peculiar people, Israel. While the myths of Genesis 1–11 tend toward a negative evaluation of the human condition, the story that begins with Abraham concerns the attempt of God to redeem humanity by working through one particular branch of the human family. The next-to-the-last verse of chapter 11 begins the movement of Abraham's family to a particular land, Canaan, pointing us to the next stop in our journey through the Hebrew Bible: "Terah took his son Abram and his grandson Lot son of Haran, and his daughter-in-law Sarai, his son Abram's wife, and they went out together from Ur of the Chaldeans to go into the land of Canaan; but when they came to Haran, they settled there."

STUDY QUESTIONS

GENESIS 1–3

Draw a line in your Bible after Gen 2:4a. Answer the questions below for Gen 1:1–2:4a, making sure that you use *only* the information in the portion of the text above the line you have drawn. Then answer the same questions using Gen 2:4b-25, again limiting yourself to the material found below the line you have drawn.

1. What is the name of the Creator in the NRSV translation of this account? (Gen 1:1–2:4a ; Hebrew = *'Elohim*); Gen 2:4b–25; Hebrew = *Yahweh*)
2. How long did it take to complete the task of creation?
3. From what original "stuff" was the world made?
4. How is the creation of humans described?
5. For what purpose are humans created?
6. The Hebrew word *ruach* means "breath," "wind," or "spirit." Where and how is "breath," "wind," or "spirit" used in 1:1–2:4a? in 2:4b–25?
7. The Hebrew word *'adam* means "humankind" or "humanity." How is *'adam* used in 1:27? How is *'adam* used in 2:7–8?

    You should notice that 1:1–2:4a is a carefully structured account. The following questions should provide clues for the structures in Gen 1:1–2:4a. After you have thought about these clues, you will then be asked to sketch the patterns that appear. Numbers in this story are obviously important to the overall literary structure. During a span of *seven* days there are *six* days of creating and *eight* creative acts. There are numerical patterns according to which days and activities have been arranged. The beginning verses (1–2) are misleading and may cause problems in your structure, so treat these verses as an introduction to the account which sets the stage for the first creative act in verse 3. In addition to the structural use of numbers, the story also organizes itself around its cosmology, which divides everything into three locations: (1) earth, (2) waters around and beneath the earth, (3) waters above the earth.

8. Construct a table below to show how the first creation account is structured.

TABLE OF THE LITERARY STRUCTURE OF THE CREATION STORY IN GEN 1:1–2:4a

Day	Creative Activity	Cosmic Location
first	_____	_____
second	_____	_____
third	_____	_____
fourth	_____	_____
fifth	_____	_____
sixth	_____	_____
seventh	_____	_____

9. Once you have filled out the table, try to see an overall pattern. Draw arrows or use whatever other visual devices you need to show the relationships between these parts. For example, is there a pattern in the arrangement of locations? On what days does God perform more than one activity?   Do these days appear in any order?

10. The strange phrase "Let us make humankind in our image" where God speaks in the first person plural, is also echoed in Gen 3:22 and 11:7. Is there any element common to all three passages? How do all three treat the relationship between humans and God? How is Gen 1:26 different in this respect? What does a comparison of these three passages say about the ideal relationship with God?

11. Look at the phrase "in our image, according to our likeness" in vv. 26–27. The use of this phrase here is unusual because Israelite law prohibited the making of images of God, and so the phrase "image of God" would most likely appear quite shocking to the ancient Israelite reader. If it is so outrageous, then the author here must want to make an important point, for he appears to be willing to risk the reader's misunderstanding, and maybe even hostility by using it. In what sense do you think this phrase is meant here?

12. Now we are interested in finding out what this ancient author understood by *human sexuality* ("male and female"). Keep in mind that our inquiry here is a *social* and *literary* one, not *biological!* We are not trying to determine what the ancient biological knowledge about sexuality was; we seek to uncover clues *from the text alone* about the function of human sexuality in this creation myth. Does sexuality here deal primarily with reproduction?

13. How does the author of 1:1–2:4a understand the male and female sexual roles in human society? Does the author relegate certain distinct role expectations to each sex?

14. In 1:27–29 ("You" in v. 29 is plural in Hebrew) the author continuously alternates between the singular and plural ("him/them, human/male and female"). Take this into account in your assessment of how Gen 1:1–2:4a understands male and female. Does this section also fluctuate between singular and plural in talking about God?

The second creation story, as we have seen, has been attributed to the Yahwist, because it calls the deity by the proper Hebrew name, Yahweh, which the NRSV translates with LORD. (Because of the sacredness of God's name, Jews prefer to read the word "LORD" wherever "Yahweh" occurs in the Hebrew Bible. The translation in the NRSV, as an ecumenical translation, follows this practice).

15. Locale plays an important role in the organization of the Yahwist's narrative. Is there motion from one location to another? Where is the center?

16. The Yahwist is also concerned with relationships. Almost every scene has something to say about the relationship between the various component elements in the created cosmos. Describe the relationship between the actors in each of the scenes and how it changes. Does this help you understand the meaning of the overall story?

17. How are the punishments (3:14–19) of each of the guilty parties related to their transgression? Do the punishments relate to changing character relationships noticed above? Try to illustrate your answer in terms of humankind's (*'adam*) relationship throughout the story to the soil/ground (*'adamah*) in Gen 2:7, 9; 3:17–19.

18. What does the second creation story say about the relationship between male and female? (Be sure to justify your response from the text and compare it with the account in 1:1–2:4a.) Throughout history many have argued that this account considered woman to be inferior for the following reasons: (1) the male was created first, and woman was only created to meet man's needs; (2) to call something by name (Gen 2:19) is to exercise control over it, and because the male seems to name the woman (2:23), he would have dominion over her; (3) woman was created from the male's side; therefore woman is "derived" from man and thus secondary. Test these three arguments against the text: Does a careful reading of the text support these arguments? (*Clues:* (1) Remember that *'adam* beginning in Gen 2:7 generally means "humankind," not "male," and does not denote a proper name (Adam); (2) The proper words for "male" and "female" occur for the first time in Gen 2:23).

Genesis 4

It is tempting to ask questions of this text that are purely factual in nature. Why did God prefer Abel's sacrifice instead of Cain's? What was the purpose of sacrifices at this time? If Adam, Eve, and Cain were the only people in the world, why was Cain concerned that someone might kill him? From where did Cain's wife come? This story is obviously problematic if we just want to know "Who did what to whom and when?" We should remember, however, that we are looking here for literary-theological understanding in these chapters in Genesis, not for factual historical data. The individual stories are pieces of a larger whole. Each story of Genesis 1–11 is, in turn, part of a larger picture, and that picture is a theological one. The primeval history points out that sin as alienation from God, from other humans, and even from the rest of creation, came into the world with the "fall" in the Garden of Eden, and the effects of this alienation grow more disturbing with each generation. Here, in just the second generation of humanity, that alienation is expressed in its ultimate form: the taking of human life by another human. Even worse, it happens within a family—the first homicide is a fratricide. The horror of fratricide is the focus of the story.

1. What picture of sin do you get from Gen 4:7?
2. Why did Cain kill Abel? If you were on a jury, would you call this killing impulsive manslaughter or premeditated (that is, "first degree") murder? Why?
3. Why did Cain ask God, "Am I my brother's keeper?"
4. What was Cain's punishment? Why did Cain say that his punishment was greater than he could bear?

5. Describe the rupture in the relationships between humans in 4:8, 14b.
6. Describe the rupture in the relationship between humans and the created order in 4:10-12.
7. Describe the rupture in the relationship between a human and God in 4:9, 14a, 16.
8. How did God show mercy on Cain before sending him away? What might the specific nature of this "mark" have been?

Gilgamesh and the Genesis Flood Story

1. In what ways is the spread of sin throughout the earth described in 6:5 and in 6:11, 12 and why does God decide to destroy the earth?
2. How is the flood described in 7:11 and 7:18-22?
3. How does the chaos of the deluge compare with the creation account of Gen 1:6-10?
4. How is the end of the flood described in 8:1-3?
5. How does the work of the wind (*ruach*) in 8:1 compare with the Spirit (*ruach*) in Gen 1:2?
6. What was Noah's first act after he disembarked from the ark? What was God's response to this act?
7. After the flood (Gen 9), how does God renew the blessing first given in 1:28?
8. What does God promise Noah, his descendants, and the whole earth?
9. Read 9:12-17. What is the sign of God's covenant with Noah and all humanity? What is the significance of this particular sign?
10. Is the covenant with Noah conditional (that is, does it depend on a particular human response), or is it unconditional?

The Tower and the City (Gen 11:1–9)

1. As the story opens, how is the "whole earth" described?
2. What motivates the people to build the tower? If urged by the ambition to achieve unity, as some interpreters suggest, what might the results of this unity be?
3. How is God characterized in this story? What is God's judgment, and *why* does God propose to carry out this judgment?
4. *Babel* (which in the Semitic languages was the name for Babylon, and means "Gate of god") is similar to the Hebrew word for "to confuse," *balal* (compare the English *babble*). How does the story end?

BIBLIOGRAPHY

Brueggemann, Walter. 1982. *Genesis. Interpretation: A Bible Commentary for Teaching and Preaching.* Atlanta: John Knox.
Calvin, Jean. 1965. *A Commentary on Genesis.* Reprint of the Calvin Translation Society. New York: Banner of Truth.
Childs, Brevard S. 1960. *Myth and Reality in the Old Testament.* Naperville, IL: Allenson.

Cross, Frank M. 1973. *Canaanite Myth and Hebrew Epic.* Cambridge, MA: Harvard University Press.

Finkelstein, J. J. 1958. "Bible and Babel: A Comparative Study of the Hebrew and Babylonian Religious Spirit." *Commentary* 26: 431–44.

Fishbane, Michael. 1979. *Text and Texture.* New York: Schocken.

Frick, Frank S. 1977. *The City in Ancient Israel.* SBL Dissertation Series 36. Missoula, MT: Scholars.

Huffmon, Herbert B. 1987. *"Babel und Bibel:* The Encounter between Babylon and the Bible" pp. 125–36 in *Backgrounds for the Bible,* Michael Patrick O'Connor and David Noel Freedman, eds. Winonna Lake, IN: Eisenbrauns.

Kikawada, Isaac, and Arthur Quinn. 1985. *Before Abraham Was.* Nashville: Abingdon.

Matthews, Victor H., and Don C. Benjamin. 1991. *Old Testament Parallels: Laws and Stories from the Ancient Near East.* New York: Paulist Press.

Meyers, Carol. 1988. *Discovering Eve: Ancient Israelite Women in Context.* New York: Oxford University Press.

Oden, Robert A., Jr. 1992. "Myth and Mythology." *Anchor Bible Dictionary.* Vol. 4. New York: Doubleday, 946–56.

Pritchard, James B. 1969. *Ancient Near Eastern Texts Relating to the Old Testament.* 3rd ed. Princeton: Princeton University Press.

Trible, Phyllis. 1978. *God and the Rhetoric of Sexuality.* Philadelphia: Fortress.

Walsh, Jerome T. 1977. "Genesis 2:4b–3:24: A Synchronic Approach." *Journal of Biblical Literature 96/2,* 161–77.

Wenham, Gordon T. 1978. "Coherence of the Flood Narrative." *Vetus Testamentum 28:* 336–48.

Chapter 6

THE FATHERS AND MOTHERS OF ISRAEL: GENESIS 12–50

Suggested Bible Reading
Genesis 12-50

ANCESTRAL TRADITIONS

As we begin our exploration of the stories of the fathers and mothers of Israel in Genesis 12-50, we encounter a new sociohistorical context and a fresh theological purpose behind these chapters. We shift from the overarching view of the stories of human beginnings in Genesis 1-11 to a focus on one human being and his descendants: a Mesopotamian named Abraham. A noted biblical scholar, E. A. Speiser has said: "The break between Primeval History and the Story of the Patriarchs is sharper than is immediately apparent" (1964: liii). We should also keep in mind that these narratives derive their deepest religious significance from their relation to the Exodus theme. As we shall see in the next chapter, from the very beginning of the book of Exodus connections are made with the ancestral traditions in Genesis. When reading Genesis 12–50, one should keep in mind that although the heroes are spoken of as though they were individuals, they actually are representative figures in two senses. First, these individuals are not portrayed as solitary figures. They are pictured at the head of large family units. The stories, which on the surface might seem to concern them as individuals, at a deeper level describe groups of people, who are seen as the forerunners of Israel and her neighbors. All these ancestors are traced back to Abraham, a representative of the line of Shem, the son of Noah, who is regarded as the patriarch of all the Semites in the ancient Near East, a group of people related to one another by similar languages. In Israelite thought, individuals gained their significance, to a large degree, as members of the larger groups of which they were members. One's individual identity was secondary to one's group identity. An individual saw him- or herself as a member of a family, a clan, a tribe, or a people, as we saw in our discussion of kinship in Chapter 2. Therefore, narratives that on the surface appear simply to be describing the actions of individuals also often see those individuals as representatives of a larger group.

The patriarchs and matriarchs of Israel also represent the narrator's understanding of the character of Israel's faith. The narrator does not describe some "golden age of faith," nor call for "that old-time religion." The author intends the readers of the text, who see themselves as the descendants of the characters in the narratives, to see themselves mirrored in the life and faith of their forerunners. Thus, the fathers and mothers of Israel are pictured as "real people," *not* as idealized human beings or picture-perfect "saints" who had an unfaltering faith. The "faith-doubt" relationship with God, prominent throughout these chapters, represents the ambiguous relationship with God so typical of later Israel. An ever-present tension pervades these stories, a tension produced by the reader's concern about whether the figures in the narratives will be faithful or will, on the contrary, doubt God's ability to make good on his promise and act precipitously and even foolishly.

The family relationships of the matriarchs and patriarchs in the text closely parallel those of its readers. The "love-hate" relationships between members of the same family—husbands and wives, brothers and brothers, brothers and sisters, uncles and nephews, fathers and sons—are narrated in a way that calls forth from the readers, both ancient and modern, a confirming nod of the head. The spiritual pilgrimage of the characters in Genesis reveals an uncertainty about the future, based on the kind of human decisions and actions represented throughout Israel's faith journey. Thus, to attempt to read these stories simply as narrating "the good old days" misses the cardinal point they are trying to make, for the reader to identify with the characters in the drama that develops.

The narrators of Genesis 12–50 tell fascinating and theologically important stories about Abraham and Sarah, Isaac and Rebekah, Jacob and his wives, and Joseph and his brothers—characters who are remembered as the founding mothers and fathers of Israel. In a real sense, these stories are part of the history of Israel, a history that begins in earnest with the Exodus from Egypt and the settlement in Palestine. These events mark the "historical" origins of an entity called "Israel." In terms of the Exodus and settlement traditions, the patriarchal and matriarchal stories are prehistory. The question that then arises is, "Where do the stories of the fathers and mothers of Israel belong in the larger context of ancient Near Eastern history?"

THE ERA OF THE PATRIARCHS AND MATRIARCHS

The Era as History

Many scholars today are deeply skeptical regarding the possibility of treating the Genesis narratives as historical in any modern sense of the term, or of regarding the patriarchs and matriarchs as historical individuals. Even among those scholars who assert that there is a historical nucleus within the legendary overlay of these stories, none come to any consensus as to the precise historical context of the stories or even their appropriate cultural setting.

Efforts to situate the patriarchs and matriarchs historically and culturally have proceeded primarily by attempting to establish correlations between textual data in Genesis and Near Eastern sources, especially texts from the Mesopotamian sites of Mari, a city located on the Euphrates River in Mesopotamia, and Nuzi, a city situated on the Tigris River. Based on chronological calculations made from biblical references alone, Abraham could have lived anywhere from the twenty-first to the nineteenth century B.C.E. Attempts to calculate the beginning of the patriarchal period using biblical chronological references usually begin with the base date of *ca.* 960 B.C.E., a date that can be confirmed with some confidence as the year in which Solomon began construction of the temple in Jerusalem. According to a reference in 1 Kings 6:1, 960 B.C.E. was the 480th year after the Exodus from Egypt. Working backwards from this date, Abraham's era has been calculated in three different ways, as shown in Table 6.1.

Obviously from these calculations, biblical chronological references for these early events do not produce consistent results. For one reason, the Bible often uses "round numbers" in its chronology. For example, "40 days" represents "a relatively long period." In Gen 7:12, the rain of the great flood fell for forty days; Moses was on Mt. Sinai for forty days (Ex 24:18); the spies sent by Moses to reconnoiter Canaan were there for forty days (Num 13:25); Goliath challenged the Israelites to fight him for forty days (1 Sam 17:16); Elijah's trip to Mt. Sinai took forty days (1 Kings 19:8); and Jonah was told that Nineveh would fall in forty days (Jonah 3:4). Similarly, forty years represents an approximation for one generation. Israel spent forty years in the wilderness (so that those entering the Promised Land would be of a different generation than those having known slavery in Egypt); periods of peace in the book of Judges are described with the phrase "and the land had rest for forty years" (Judg 3:11; 5:31); Eli is said to have "judged" Israel for forty years (1 Sam 4:18); and Egypt is to be desolated for forty years in Ezekiel's prophecy (Ezek 29:11).

TABLE 6.1 CHRONOLOGICAL CALCULATIONS OF ABRAHAM'S ERA

CALCULATION 1	CALCULATION 2	CALCULATION 3
960 B.C.E. = the date of the 4th year of Solomon's reign	960 B.C.E.	960 B.C.E.
+ 480 years (1 Kings 6:1)	+ 480 years	+ 480 years
= 1440 B.C.E. = the date for the Exodus from Egypt	= 1440 B.C.E.	= 1440 B.C.E.
+ 430 years = the number of years the "sons of Israel" were in Egypt (Ex 12:40)	+ 400 years = the number of years spent in Egypt (Gen 15:13)	+ 430 years = the number of years in Egypt *and* Canaan (Ex 12:40; Septuagint)
= 1870 B.C.E. = the date for the arrival of Jacob's family in Egypt	= 1840 B.C.E. = the date for the arrival of Jacob's family in Egypt	= **1870 B.C.E.** = the date for Abraham's journey to Canaan
+ 215 years = the number of years spent by patriarchs and matriarchs in Canaan (based on biblical references in Genesis)	+ 215 years	
= **2085 B.C.E.** = the date for Abraham's journey to Canaan	= **2055 B.C.E.** = the date for Abraham's journey to Canaan	

The 480-year interval between the construction of Solomon's temple and the Exodus mentioned in 1 Kings 6:1, used in the calculations above, is probably *not* actually 480 years but apparently represents twelve generations ($12 \times 40 = 480$). If twenty five years for a generation is substituted, twelve generations equals 300 instead of 480 years. As a result, the Exodus from Egypt dates in the thirteenth rather than the fifteenth century, a period that fits what we know of Egypt far better, as we shall see in the next chapter. If the Exodus is dated to the thirteenth century and the other chronological notes referred to above are used, Abraham's entrance into Canaan would fall in either the nineteenth or seventeenth century.

In assessing this or any biblical chronology, one should remember that most of the historical sources in the Old Testament were collected at a time much later than the events they describe. The biblical chronology for the patriarchal period represents one of the most obvious examples of this phenomenon. As we have seen, using biblical data, the patriarchs can be dated to *ca.* 2000–1700 B.C.E., whereas the oldest collection of literary traditions concerning that era was made at least eleven hundred to fifteen hundred years later. This time lag obviously has serious implications for the question of the historicity of narratives concerning the matriarchs and patriarchs. The questions may be posed as follows: About what do the narratives concerning the patriarchs tell us? Do they tell us about a patriarchal era in the distant past or about a later society's understanding of its past?

Scholars concerned with establishing a historical and/or cultural context for the patriarchal narratives have considered data from extrabiblical ancient Near Eastern sources. Earlier scholars maintained that the migration of Abraham from Ur to Canaan was part of a large-scale migration of Amorites around the beginning of the second millennium B.C.E. Today, however, there is a tendency to abandon this association because the notion of large-scale population migrations has been discredited by historical research. Historians—including biblical scholars—previously were inclined to use such hypothetical shifts of large population groups in their attempts to explain cultural change. If a significant cultural change occurred in a given area, it was explained by positing the influx of some new population group, which carried a distinctive culture with them. Today, in contrast, we have learned that many social changes take place *within* the population already present in a given region, since that population follows the social, economic, and political developments of the society. Cultural change is only secondarily the result of external causes (Lemche 1988: 76).

PATRIARCHAL NARRATIVES AND OTHER NEAR EASTERN DOCUMENTS

Those scholars who seek to assert the historicity of the patriarchal narratives have often sought to achieve a "fit" between the Genesis narratives and data from other ancient Near Eastern documents. Such efforts generally have focused on either the eighteenth century B.C.E. archives from Mari or on parallels between social and legal customs in Genesis and in the fifteenth century B.C.E. texts from Nuzi. Even if such correlations were unproblematic, obviously they still would not help us to locate the patriarchs and matriarchs very precisely in history because the Mari and Nuzi materials cover a span of three centuries.

The Nuzi Archives.   Soon after the discovery of the Nuzi archives, scholars enthusiastically began to postulate the existence of many parallels between the Nuzi documents and the patriarchal narratives in Genesis. As time passed, however, and the Nuzi materials were examined more carefully, this initial enthusiasm was tempered. Many supposed parallels that had been identified in the initial stages of the investigation evaporated under the scrutiny of scholars like Thompson (1974) and Van Seters (1975). The conjectured parallels between the Nuzi texts and the Genesis narratives can be divided into three categories: (1) parallels giving additional examples; (2) parallels providing supplementary details; and (3) parallels aiding reconstructions (Walton 1989: 52–58).

The *first category of parallel* is illustrated in a proposed "match" between Gen 25:33 and the Nuzi text JEN 204. In Genesis 25:33, Esau surrendered his rights of inheritance as the elder son to his younger brother Jacob in exchange for food. The example cited from the Nuzi texts describes Tupkitilla, who exchanged a grove that he inherited for three sheep traded by his brother, Kurpazah. Thompson observes many problems with this parallel. For one, no birthright, a promised future inheritance, is sold, but already inherited property is traded instead. Also, no indication in the text shows which of the brothers was the elder or younger. Thompson cites other difficulties and suggests that this transaction is not a sale at all but merely the division of inheritance. Thus, the Nuzi material offers us no parallel to the transfer of inheritance rights that took place between Jacob and Esau (Thompson 1974: 284–285).

An example of the *second category of parallel* attempts to "fit" Gen 16:2 with Nuzi text HSS V 67:19–21. Both concern the provision of a second wife to a husband in case of the first wife's supposed inability to have a child. Some scholars suggest that Sarah's insistence that Abraham father a child with Hagar could be compared with clauses found in Nuzi marriage contracts, which gave a husband the right to take a second wife if his first wife could not conceive. In some cases, the first wife even had the responsibility to provide the "substitute" in such a situation. A son born to the second wife would then be considered a full heir of the husband. Thompson cites several discrepancies between the biblical case and the supposed Nuzi parallels. He concludes that Genesis reflects a situation that was known throughout the Near East concerning the role of concubines. Genesis does not directly parallel the Nuzi material, largely because there is no indication in Genesis that husbands were restricted by marriage contracts from taking a second wife, which becomes obvious in the cases of both Abraham and Jacob (1974: 256–258). Walton, however, suggests that this parallel at least provides some background about a practice that would otherwise be unclear to the Western reader. Even if cases cannot be cited where Abraham's situation is matched precisely, and even if we are unaware of the contract stipulations between Abraham and Sarah, Walton maintains that the parallel confirms that their solution was not an unusual one in the ancient Near-Eastern context (1989: 55).

The *third category of parallel* can be seen in a parallel proposed between Gen 15:4 and the Nuzi texts HSS IX 22 and V 60. Because he lacks a son, Abraham adopts a male slave, Eliezer, as his heir. It was customary in the Nuzi society for childless individuals to adopt an heir. The rights of this adopted heir, however, would be nullified, or at least secondary, if a true heir were born later. It was proposed that the Nuzi material provided an example of the practice reflected in Genesis. Thompson, however, undertook a thorough study of adoption texts from Nuzi and concluded that no situation there describes a man adopting his slave. The terminology used in Nuzi adoption texts could only refer to a freeborn citizen. As a result, he sees no possibility of correlating Eliezer's situation with anything found at Nuzi (1974: 203–230).

Despite the negation of direct parallels, the Nuzi archives still can provide us with helpful insights into the patriarchal narratives as "realistic" literature. The patriarchs and matriarchs appear to have been a part of the material culture of the ancient Near East. Even if we cannot identify specific one-for-one parallels, the Nuzi materials still provide useful evidence for common social, economic, and legal practices in the ancient Near East.

The Mari Archives.   The attempt to utilize the Mari archives in the study of the patriarchal narratives has proceeded on a somewhat different course. French excavations since 1933 at Tell el-Hariri on the middle Euphrates, the ancient city-state of Mari, have produced more than twenty-five thousand documents dating from *ca.* 1765–1694 B.C.E. The materials from Mari are especially important because Mari was situated on the borders of the settled and the vast unsettled area of the steppe. This border situation reflected social and political relations between urban populations and nomadic (or more correctly, semi-nomadic) groups. The Mari materials are important for biblical studies not only for providing general historical background, but also because Israel's ancestors most likely originated from semi-nomadic tribal groups like those described in the Mari texts.

The Genesis narratives place Abraham and his extended family in Haran in upper Mesopotamia before their move to Canaan. Part of the family, with whom the Canaanite branch that moved on to Canaan maintained contact, remained in the Haran region. The Haran region has a prominent place in the Mari texts as an area into which tribal groups migrated. The Mari texts have thus provided scholars with a far better analogy for our understanding of the tribal society of the patriarchs and of later premonarchic Israel than the earlier model based on analogies from bedouin camel nomads of classical Arabic sources. The tribal groups at Mari were not nomadic groups locked in a cultural conflict between "the desert and the sown." Similar to the way in which the patriarchs are pictured in Genesis, they lived in a constant symbiotic relationship with the settled agricultural towns and villages. There was movement back and forth between the two sides of this society, sometimes called a dimorphic society, meaning that it had two groups, settled agricultural towns and groups of semi-nomadic herders, in relationship with one another. William Dever's assessment of the Mari material is a sensible one: The Mari material provides the best available data, and the concept of a dimorphic society provides the best analytical model, for research on patriarchal backgrounds. He does not believe that we can locate a patriarchal era precisely. He does, however, maintain that the more we know of the historical and cultural framework of the early West-Semitic peoples, the more suitably the *nucleus* of the patriarchal traditions may fit into the second millennium B.C.E. As an archaeologist he concludes that it may even be possible to narrow the time-span somewhat. The MB I period (Middle Bronze I period, *ca.* 2200–2000 B.C.E.) can be ruled out simply because the urban sites in the background of the Genesis narratives were not yet occupied and the requisite urban element of the dimorphic society is missing (Dever 1977: 117–118).

The dimorphic nature of ancient Near-Eastern society is clearly echoed in the narratives of Genesis 12–50. At times, Abraham and Jacob are described moving from place to place with their flocks and herds, not as nomads but as herders who relocate with the change of seasons in search of adequate pasture for their animals (Gen 13:1–7; 37:12–17). In other passages, they are closely associated with particular settlements, especially with regard to religious practices (Gen 22:19; 35:27).

PATRIARCHAL NARRATIVES AS HISTORY

Most likely, in light of all the above, two realistic options exist regarding the historical nature of the narratives in Genesis 12–50. One option is to regard them as literary constructs of later Israel, stories that satisfied the need for an account of how the people of Israel came to be. The other option, perhaps a more plausible one, is to see these narratives as preserving ancient traditions. These traditions, like many biblical traditions, were rearranged and reshaped in the light of later needs and understandings, but were not products of literary imagination. Certainly, the antiquity of much of the material associated with Abraham and Sarah, Isaac and Rebekah, and Jacob and Rachel remains well established in spite of recent attempts by Thompson (1974) and van Seters (1975) to assign the bulk of Genesis 12–50 to the monarchical and exilic periods.

Our final word on the "historicity" of the patriarchal narratives, or lack of it, must be a note of caution. In areas where hard facts are scarce, as in any attempt to figure out a "patriarchal era," there have been, and probably always will be, temptations to plug the gaps in our knowledge by indulging in fanciful reconstructions or constructing arguments from silence. Students of the Bible should be especially watchful for "logical deductions" established by stringing together statements, which may have rather low levels of probability, and then drawing what appear to be "certain" conclusions. The elementary principles of logic suggest just the opposite. The combination of a string of low-probability hypotheses leads to a conclusion that is weaker than the individual statements, because every one of them must be true to validate the conclusion. As an example of how such cases have been constructed to "demonstrate" the "essential historicity" of the patriarchal narratives, read Gen 12:10–20 and then consider the following hypothetical arguments:

1. It is possible that camels were domesticated in the early second millennium B.C.E.

2. Abraham was a wealthy and influential nomadic leader, typical of those involved in the Amorite migration of *ca.* 2000 B.C.E.

3. The wife-sister combination is witnessed in legal documents from Nuzi, and may well have been known to Abraham.

4. The fact that Egyptian texts nowhere mention Abraham is not surprising because the incident would have been embarrassing for the Pharaoh.

5. During the Twelfth Dynasty, Egypt dominated Canaan with the help of Semitic mercenaries, and there was much traffic between the two regions.

   Therefore: Given the weight of such evidence, surely only a hardened skeptic would deny the historicity of Genesis 12:10–20.

We will leave it up to the individual reader to recognize the fallacies in this "proof." It is, of course, a totally fallacious argument, but it is not too much exaggerated from the kind often found in studies of the history of ancient Israel.

A LITERARY ANALYSIS OF THE PATRIARCHAL STORIES

The stories we encounter in Genesis 12–50 do not present a documentary history but are put together to reflect Israel's faith. They are, in our view, neither pure fiction nor pure history. Perhaps the most descriptive term for what we have in these chapters in Genesis is Robert Alter's term "historicized prose fiction." Speaking of the patriarchal narratives, Alter says:

> To cite the clearest example, the Patriarchal narratives may be composite fictions based on national traditions, but in the writers' refusal to make them conform to the symmetries of expectations, in their contradictions and anomalies, they suggest the unfathomability of life in history under an inscrutable God. (1981: 24)

The now-continuous account of Genesis 12–50 is composed of what were originally unrelated sagalike stories. A *saga* is a dramatic and traditional story of heroic adventures, especially concerning members of certain prominent families. Sagas often serve as expressions of the cultural identity of a people. An exciting aspect of the contemporary study of the materials in Gen 12–50 is the attempt to discover devices that were used to bind the individual stories into a continuous narrative.

Devices Used in the Narrative

One obvious device is the *use of familial relationships.* Abraham, Isaac, and Jacob are treated as though they followed upon one another as father, son, and grandson, although the stories about them probably originated among different groups of people, who later came to call themselves Israel. These individual stories were then clustered around the central figure of whom they told. Large cycles of traditions clustered around Abraham and Jacob, to which was added the Joseph novella, a form resembling a short novel. Within the larger cycles smaller units tell of the relationships between the dominant figure and one or more of his relatives who represent later Israel's near neighbors. There is, for example, a group of stories about Abraham and his brother's son Lot, who represents the patriarch of the Moabites and the Ammonites (19:37–38), Israel's two immediate neighbors to the east. Stories about Hagar and Ishmael tell of the origins of yet another group of peoples, the nomadic Arabs (as does the brief mention of Keturah in Gen 25:1–4 [cf. also 1 Chr 1:32–33], identified specifically with the Midianites). Within the Jacob cycle are stories about Jacob and his older twin, Esau, identified as the patriarch of Edom, Israel's neighbor to the southeast. Bracketed within the cluster of stories about Jacob and Esau is a set of stories about Jacob and his mother's brother, Laban, who represents the Arameans or Syrians to Israel's north. This inclusion of one literary complex within another assists plot development by explaining Jacob's visit to Laban as an escape from Esau and his return to Canaan as a reunion with him.

Another device used to connect independent traditions is the *geographical* one. As we have seen, individuals in the stories sometimes represent neighboring regions. Disparate geographical regions are also tied together by their being points on Abraham's itinerary from Ur to Haran to Canaan. As a hint of things to come later in the story, Abraham goes down into Egypt and returns to Canaan. Abraham sends a servant back to the region of Haran to find a wife for Isaac. Jacob also returns to relatives in the Haran region to find his wives, Leah and Rachel. Gen 12–50 ends with the Joseph novella, which puts Jacob and his family in Egypt and which sets the stage for the continuation of the story in the book of Exodus. While the mention of these movements and places serves a literary function, some of these movements, such as the movement of both Abraham and later of Jacob and his family into Egypt, are well documented.

As we observed in Chapter 2, Palestine suffers from occasional famines due to the lack of sufficient rainfall. In such cases, Egypt, with its irrigation-based agriculture drawing on the Nile, became a source of food. An Egyptian painting from the tomb of the provincial governor Khumhotep (*ca.* 1890 B.C.E.), reproduced in Figure 6.1, shows a caravan of (bearded) Semitic men, with their families and animals, presenting themselves before an Egyptian administrator and his officers. Another function of such geographical notes is to explain how places that had special significance for later Israel, such as Egypt, first figured in the lives of the matriarchs and patriarchs.

The last device used to help unify separate units is the *chronological* one supplied principally by the Priestly writer. Oral tradition—the way many of these stories first circulated—rarely supplies precise chronological indicators. As one of the latest layers of tradition, P, generally characterized by a concern with numbers and dates, supplied a comprehensive chronology, which provides a structure for the first four books of the Pentateuch.

FROM SEPARATE STORIES TO UNIFIED NARRATIVE

While the form in which we have them is thus a unified one, the Abraham cycle of stories probably first circulated as individual tales among the southern (Judean) tribes. This is suggested by the prominence given to southern Palestinian sites in these stories. The Jacob cycle and the Joseph novella, for similar reasons, probably originally represented a northern tradition. Yet these two clusters of stories, one originally southern and the other originally northern, belong together theologically. Each of these clusters has therefore been skillfully merged using theme and plot, and the individual cycles or chains have been combined thematically. The Genesis narratives in their final form present a unified narrative of Israel's origins, unified around the theme of God's covenant promise. No matter how diverse Israel's origins might have been, the literary unity of the Genesis narratives demonstrates that Yahweh is responsible for their being together.

Recent study of these Genesis narratives has gone beyond the insights supplied by form criticism regarding their oral stages and of source criticism with its atomistic concern for separating the text into separate documents or tradi-

Figure 6.1   Bearded Semites entering Egypt

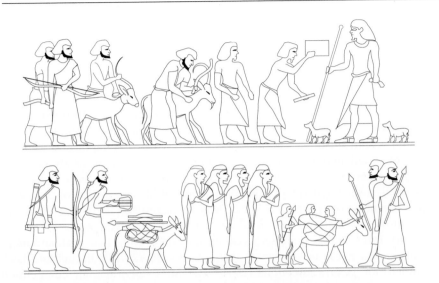

tions. Contemporary study seeks to understand the artistic skill of the biblical storyteller, which is revealed in a literary analysis of Genesis 12–50 as a unit. Like any good narrative that "works," the one in Genesis 12–50 does not seem to be a montage assembled out of assorted bits and pieces. It reads as a unit achieved by the kinds of devices mentioned above as well as through other literary devices such as *theme, plot, climax, dénouement, symbolism,* and *characterization.* We will explore some ways in which these devices are used in our discussion below. For now, the *theme* of these chapters can be stated very simply: God, for his part, will remain faithful to the covenant offered to Israel and humankind in spite of humans' often-misguided attempts to take matters into their own hands and play the role of God. A subtle tension here presents a problem for people of faith in all times and places. When, on the one hand, is it appropriate to exercise human initiative? When, on the other, should one "Be still and know that I am God" (Ps 46:10)?

Another theme of the patriarchal story shows that God acts in history through the actions of Abraham, Sarah, and their descendants in order to bring about the redemption of humanity. In the language of the biblical text itself, this theme, underscoring the covenant faithfulness of God, appears at the beginning of this section of Genesis in God's command to Abraham:

> Go from your country and your kindred and your father's house to the land that I will show you. I will make you a great nation, and I will bless you, and make your name great, so that you will be a blessing. I will bless those who bless you, and the one who curses you I will curse; and in you all the families of the earth shall be blessed. (12:1–3)

The essence of this promise is restated to Abraham at two different points (18:18; 22:17–18). The promise is also repeated to Isaac (26:3–4) and to Jacob (28:13–14). The theme of God's covenant promise is dramatically focused, enforced, and illustrated by the subordinate themes, plot structures, and characterizations that make up Genesis 12–50.

A subtheme in these chapters has to do with the role played by the matriarchs, given the overarching theme of covenant and faith. While Savina Teubal, as we shall see below, and others decry the *androcentrism* (male-centered perspective) of the Genesis narratives as we now have them, Gottwald maintains that a particularly intriguing aspect of the stories is the prominence of women within them. He sees Sarah as a strong-willed equal of Abraham, capable of expelling her handmaid in a jealous fit (16:1–6) and not above laughing at the promise of a son in her old age (18:9–15). Hagar, according to Gottwald, is sketched as a person able to risk her life and the life of her son in the wilderness (16:7–14; 21:15–21). Rebekah assertively addresses Abraham's servant at the well and agrees to go to Canaan as Isaac's wife (24:15–25, 55–58). Later, Rebekah assists Jacob in outmaneuvering her weak and inept husband and helps him escape Laban (27:5–17, 42–45). Rachel and Leah compete for Jacob's affections (29:15–35; 30:1–24); in their competition to have sons they know how to bargain with one another (30:14–16). Both wives are loyal to Jacob when he flees from Laban with his questionably acquired goods (31:14–16), including the household gods that Rachel stealthily conceals (31:33–35). Tamar, the daughter-in-law of Judah, cunningly adopts a prostitute's ruse to father a son by Judah since he has unjustly denied her one of his sons (38:1–26). Commenting on the roles played by women in these Genesis narratives, Gottwald observes that a common approach of earlier scholars to the initiatives taken by women and to the supposed signs of *matrilocality* (that is, a situation in which a man leaves his family to live with his wife's family) was to argue either that the "patriarchal" society of ancient Israel was really matriarchal or at least that it attested to survivals of an earlier Semitic matriarchal society. He says that the evidence for this hypothesis is extremely tenuous. Behind the Genesis stories, rather, lie the preservations of ancestral traditions, usually involving male leaders who were accompanied by very strong women, themselves forceful actors in the domestic sphere. He concludes that because the horizons of the stories, apart from the tensions with outside groups, were largely domestic, women have significant, often essential, parts in the unfolding of plots. "These women are as sharply etched characters as are the men" (1985: 175–176).

As you read Genesis 12–50, note your impressions about gender relationships and the role of women in these stories. As you note your impressions, consider the following questions: Where are women given voices? How are they referred to? Do they have an independent identity or are they simply called "the wife of . . . ," "the mother of . . . ," "the daughter of . . . ," or "the sister of . . ."? Do they have names, and what do those names mean? What responsibilities do they have?

The Abraham and Sarah Cycle: 11:27–25:18

Origins of Abraham and Sarah

The first cycle of stories in Genesis 12–50 tells of Abraham and Sarah, whose names also appear as Abram and Sarai at places in the cycle. The story of Israel's ancestors begins with the geographical notice that they came out of a place called Ur of the Chaldeans, which is at the southeastern end of the fertile crescent. Ur is consistently identified in the Hebrew text as "Ur of the Chaldeans" (Gen 11:28, 31; 15:7; Neh 9:7). Just as uniformly, however, the Septuagint *never* speaks of "Ur of the Chaldeans," but always just "the land of the Chaldeans." Some scholars prefer to follow the Septuagint reading and would place Abraham's home in Haran, in northwest Mesopotamia, a place that figures prominently in both the Abraham and Jacob cycles of stories. The Septuagint text obviously stands behind the speech of Stephen in the book of Acts in the New Testament, which does not mention Ur, but only the "land of the Chaldeans" and Haran:

> The God of glory appeared to our ancestor Abraham when he was in Mesopotamia, before he lived in Haran. . . . Then he left the country of the Chaldeans and settled in Haran. (Acts 7:2b, 4a)

The name Haran can be confusing to the English reader because it transliterates two different Hebrew words. In Gen 11:27–31, Haran (transliterating the Hebrew *haran*) is Abraham's brother, who died before Abraham and the family left Ur. Beginning in Gen 11:31 (and also in 11:32; 12:4, 5), Haran (transliterating the Hebrew word *charan*) is named as the place where the family settled, where Abraham's father, Terah, died, and from where Abraham set out for Canaan (after an indefinite stay in Haran). Haran, the place, also figures in the Jacob cycle as where Jacob goes (from Canaan) to find a wife from among his own people, specifically from the family of his mother's brother, Laban (Gen 27:43–28:5). A traditional patrilineal genealogy, that is, one that traces ancestry through the father's line only, of the principal *dramatis personae* in the stories of the patriarchs and matriarchs is presented in Figure 6.2, in which women's names, not usually included in a patrilineal genealogy, have been supplied in italics.

If one follows the Hebrew text, Abraham and Sarah went from Ur to Haran to Canaan. One difficulty, however, is that the city of Haran does not lie on the trade route from southeastern Mesopotamia to Canaan. If they left from Ur, that route should have taken Terah and his family north along the Euphrates to Terqa (near Mari), then southwesterly toward Damascus in Syria, and on into Canaan. Instead, the family group continued northward along the Euphrates to the city of Haran. So, we are left with the question of whether the family started out from Ur or from Haran. Savina Teubal has offered an ingenious solution, coming from the perspective that Genesis generally remains silent about women (1984: 20–21). She observes that various passages in Genesis point to Haran and an unidentified place called Nahor, towns in the north, as the home of Abraham. She

Figure 6.2   A patrilineal genealogy of Genesis 12–50

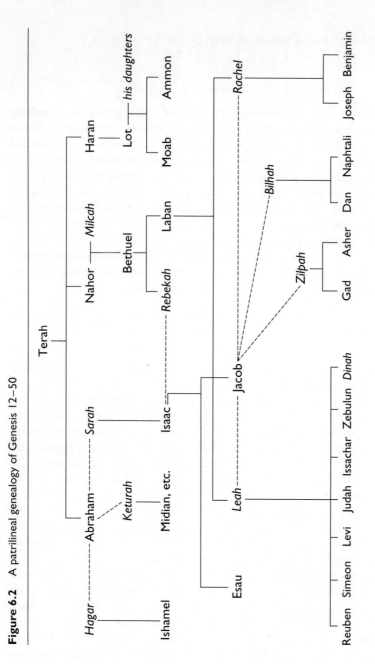

goes on to suggest that Abraham came from the north and that Ur of the Chaldeans may have been Sarah's birthplace. Patriarchal tradition assumed a connection between Abraham and Ur simply because Ur is mentioned in Genesis. Because of the patriarchal nature of ancient traditions, it was inconceivable, to both ancient as well as to later scholars, that the name of the city of Ur is in the text only because of Sarah. Teubal maintains that much of Sarah's story may have been lost as time went on but that occasional evidence remained, such as the mention of Ur of the Chaldeans in the texts. As Sarah's importance was diminished in the stories, an alternative explanation was needed for this evidence. Since Abraham had become the principal character, the city of Ur became accepted as his birthplace.

Teubal, in her imaginative and sometimes speculative book *Sarah the Priestess,* also argues that many other puzzling features of the patriarchal narratives can be explained by the assumption that the matriarchs were struggling to maintain family traditions and customs different from those of their husbands. She suggests that the apparent problem of incest, as Sarah and Abraham have the same father, presents a problem only in patrilineal descent systems because descent is traced only through the male line. In Sarah's society, however, Teubal suggests that this way of tracing descent was not the custom. Sarah is introduced to us as Terah's daughter-in-law, not as his daughter. In a matrilineal system, descent is traced through the mother, and because Abraham and Sarah had different mothers, they would not be considered siblings, or in any way blood relatives. For this reason, they could be married (1984: 14).

With this beginning the cycle of stories about Abraham develops into a model/example of the story-cycles in the Hebrew Bible. It forms one of the broadest and most inclusive cycles in the Bible. While it illuminates Abraham's character in many ways, it is not a complete biography because of the specific aims of the narrator. We learn nothing, for example, about Abraham's life before he received the command to make his way to a land that God would show him. Abraham is portrayed on two levels: he is the supposed historic ancestor of a people and also a model of the faithful life. The narrator casts Abraham this way because he is reaching far back into history. The narrator writes with much of a people's history in the foreground, and much of this history remains just under the surface, nuances in the Abraham material. Besides the story of the people of Israel, the narrator also knows that Israel's neighbors speak closely-related languages and have similar ceremonies. These similarities needed to be accounted for, and so Abraham is made the father of many peoples, including those born to him by Keturah, perhaps the least-known woman in the Hebrew scriptures (see Figure 6.2).

Later generations of Jews, Christians, and Muslims have seen Abraham as a model person of faith and obedience (or submission) to God. Certainly the story of Abraham sets forth some complex concepts of faithfulness. Abraham's faith is not an unquestioning obedience or human passivity in the face of hoped-for action initiated by God. The Abraham cycle develops a complicated relationship between a God with a plan and human beings who form part of that plan. Abraham seems to grow in his understanding of his part in God's plan—a role which calls for a curious mixture of dependence and independence. God's plan means a promise of descendants and land for Abraham, Sarah, and their descendants, but the story must continually deal with the gap between promise and probability.

God's Promise to Abraham

The story opens with a brief notice about the most obvious of those gaps in Genesis 11:30: "Now Sarai was barren; she had no child." This statement is not just fact but acts as a motif that shapes the whole Abraham cycle, lending profundity to God's promise to bless Abraham in 12:2–3. The promise is repeated near the end of the story (22:16–18) and includes the assurance of many descendants for Abraham. Without this motif two stories that stand at the very center of the Abraham cycle, structurally speaking, would make little sense, and the pathos of the near-sacrifice of Isaac in Genesis 22 would be considerably diluted. These two central stories concern the covenant God makes with Abraham.

ABRAHAM SEEKS TO FULFILL THE PROMISE

The first of these stories is in Genesis 15, a chapter distinct from the narrative context that surrounds it. The structure of this chapter emphasizes its isolation. The structure does not develop the stages of a tale; it reveals no plot of a story; it is not narrative. It is composed mostly of speeches. It reports that after having so despaired of having a son that he adopted a slave to be his heir, Abraham prepared for what was probably a common ritual of covenant-making in the ancient Near East, a ritual that, in this context, would be the confirmation of the promise of descendants. In this ritual an animal was slain and cut into pieces. The parties entering into the covenant then passed into the space between the parts of the animal, signaling that they were ready to take upon themselves the obligations of the covenant. The symbolism may be related to sanctions related to the breaking of a covenant, in that the parties making the covenant effectively say, "If I do not keep my covenant obligations, may I be as this animal" (that is, cut into pieces). In this instance, however, Abraham beholds an unusual spectacle in which "a smoking fire pot and a flaming torch passed between these pieces" (15:17). Yahweh, symbolized here by fire, replaces the other human with whom covenants were commonly made and renews the promise of a land and descendants for Abraham. Immediately following this rite of covenant renewal, Abraham responds with doubt. The ambiguity of faith and doubt characterizes Abraham. In sharp contrast, God is seen as always faithful and able to do what he intends. The entire Abraham cycle emphasizes this contrast.

Hagar and Ishmael.   In chapter 16 we are introduced to Hagar, the Egyptian maidservant of Sarah. Hagar's story is limited to two short segments of the Sarah and Abraham story—this one in chapter 16, usually associated with J, and one in Gen 21, from E. Source critics have generally regarded these two stories about Hagar as doublets. There is, to be sure, a similar pattern discernible in both stories. Hagar in Genesis 16 and Ishmael in Genesis 21 are the protagonists, not Abraham, as many commentators would have us believe.

While these are the only narratives concerning Hagar in the Hebrew Bible, there are, by contrast, many stories in the Islamic tradition concerning Hagar, who is regarded as Abraham's wife, not his concubine. Abraham and Hagar, according to Muslim tradition, are buried near the *Ka'aba* in the Grand Mosque in Mecca. Ishmael is Abraham's most prominent son and the one with whom he labors to construct the great Islamic sanctuary in Mecca, the *Ka'aba,* according to the *Qur'an* (2:125 ff.). In the New Testament, in Galatians 4:21-31, Paul interprets the Hagar narrative allegorically. Ishmael, as the son of a slave, and Isaac, the son of a free woman, respectively symbolize the old and new covenants.

In Genesis 16, because she is childless, Sarah proposes that Abraham have intercourse with Hagar to have a child by her. Abraham accepts and acts on Sarah's proposal without raising any questions: "And Abram listened to the voice of Sarai (16:2)." Hagar becomes pregnant, which causes the "inferior" Hagar (a servant) to feel superior to her mistress Sarah, and to constitute a threat to Sarah. What Hagar represented to Sarah is represented in the numerical proverbs of the book of Proverbs as one of four intolerable situations: "a maid when she succeeds her mistress" (Prov 30:23). Sarah mistreats Hagar, who flees into the desert where she meets Yahweh in earthly manifestation, a *theophany.* God tells her to call the child she will bear Ishmael ("God hears" in Hebrew), who will be regarded as the patriarch of the Ishmaelites, a nomadic people who, like later Israel, were organized into twelve tribes, each with a tribal prince (25:16). Chapter 16 ends with Ishmael's birth.

In another of her books in which she seeks to recover the lost tradition of the matriarchs, Savina Teubal suggests that Sarah's story is incomplete without an in-depth look at Hagar's role and the consequent relationship that existed between her and Sarah. Teubal says that the figure of Hagar, as portrayed in the biblical texts and in the history of their interpretation, contains all the elements necessary for a doctrine of the subordination of women (1990: xxi-xxii). Hagar, as Teubal sees her, more than any other of the biblical matriarchs, is the prototype of a human being made into an object, an "other." She maintains that no male figure in the Bible is so "objectified." The most striking fact about Hagar is that nothing reports that she said even one word. Her only personal characteristics include her Egyptian origin (that is, foreign), perhaps dark-skinned, and her insolence toward her mistress. Hagar has no voice to reject her role as a patriarch's concubine and substitute womb for the barren Sarah. She is depicted as having no control over her destiny. When she runs away from her mistress, an angel demands that she return. She is promised a child, but that child belongs to Abraham. After she is sent away her child almost dies of thirst, implying that a woman with offspring is not able to survive alone. God, however, comes to the rescue, and the boy lives to become the progenitor of a tribe.

Teubal goes on to claim that the biblical story of conflict between Sarah and Hagar largely results from the androcentric writing and editing of the biblical narratives, which interwove Hagar's text with the story of Sarah to focus the narrative on the patriarch Abraham. This merging of stories creates the impression of a lost soul, manipulated by God and mistress, with no destiny but that of her son's and the father who begot him. Teubal argues that when we get beneath the androcentric overlays, the main theme of the Hagar stories concerns neither sexual activity nor the birth of a son. Rather Genesis 16 (verses 1–5) and 21 (verses 6–12, 14, 17, 18, 20a, 21) describe Hagar and her association with Sarah. Teubal suggests that predicaments concerning the destinies of the matriarchs create a central theme, but the main theme of the story is derived from the appearance of God to Hagar in the wilderness. There she is designated, by divine election, the ancestor of a people: the Hagarites. In this way Hagar's story is much like Sarah's (1990: 195).

Certainly the Hagar stories make a point about the ways human beings, because of their status (real or perceived), attempt to manipulate the lives of others. This point is forcefully made here, illustrating power exercised over one of the most vulnerable people in society: she is female, slave, and foreign.

GOD FULFILLS THE PROMISE

In the second story about covenant (Gen 17), God renews the covenant with Abraham, this time ritually sealing it with the rite of circumcision. This covenant pledge is accompanied by the promise of a son and a blessing for Sarah (17:15–16). The plot structure supports the theme, centering on doubts raised by the inability of Abraham and Sarah to have children. Without children, how can God's promise be fulfilled? Besides the problem of childlessness, the giving of the promise is accompanied repeatedly by other events that threaten its fulfillment: famine in Canaan (12:10); Sarah's being taken into the Pharaoh's house (12:11–16); strife between Abraham and Lot (13:1–12). God's "abstract" promise is threatened repeatedly by "reality," so Abraham acts "in the real world" to try to "force" the promise. He *fights* for Lot against raids by foreign kings (14) and against the wickedness of Sodom (18:16–19:29). He *adopts* a servant as his heir (15:16) and *fathers* a son by Sarah's Egyptian maid (16). As it turns out, however, neither the adopted Eliezer nor Ishmael is the promised child, through whom God's promise to Abraham would be realized.

And so, throughout the story, the plot thickens as the suspense mounts. The two covenant chapters (15 and 17) focus the tensions sharply. In the first, God makes a pledge to covenant faithfulness. In the second, Abraham performs a ritual act as symbol of his acceptance of the proper human response to God's pledge, which is covenant faith and responsibility. The narrative reaches its climax in the story of the birth of Isaac (21:1–7). Isaac (whose name is related to the Hebrew "laughter"), the child of the promise, is circumcised, and the laughter of derision and doubt about God's ability to do as promised (in ch. 18), turns into the laughter of joy and thanksgiving. The reader knows that this child has been given to Sarah and Abraham in God's own mysterious way of and timetable for promise-keeping. But note how the narrator ties the story of Isaac's birth to what follows. Abraham's gain in the birth of Isaac leads to Abraham's loss of Ishmael. The choice of Isaac and his descendants does *not*, however, mean the rejection of the rest of humankind.

GOD TESTS ABRAHAM

The tension of the story of the promise of descendants and its fulfillment is heightened in the story that follows in chapter 22. This chapter has commonly been assigned to E. Climax builds on climax and merges with the dénouement. *Genesis 22 is both the climax and summary of the entire Abraham cycle.*

The narrator informs the reader at the very beginning of this story (22:1a) that what follows is a test, not the real thing. Of course, the participants in the story do not know that this is "just a test"—that would ruin the test. The whole of the Abraham cycle is held in suspense and called into question by God's command at the beginning of this story: "Take your son, your only son Isaac, whom you love, and go to the land of Moriah, and offer him there as a burnt offering on one of the mountains that I shall show you" (22:2). God's command here plays a striking counterpart to the command with which the Abraham cycle began, "Go from your country and your kindred and your father's house to the land that I will show you." It brings the story of Abraham's on-again-off-again journey of faith and doubt to resolution. The key to understanding the entire Abraham cycle must be here in this story.

Faith Versus Family.   The story of the near sacrifice of Isaac is not just one story among others. It is, according to Spiegel "Central to the nervous system of Judaism and Christianity" (1969: xvii). But we might ask: Why is the theme of child sacrifice the theme chosen by biblical writers to express devotion to God? Why is Abraham's willingness to kill Isaac seen as an expression of faith? Why is Sarah totally absent from this episode?

The literature on this story, which is known in Judaism as the *Aqeda*, from the Hebrew word for "bound" (22:9) is vast. Certainly one of the most penetrating analyses of it as literature was done by Erich Auerbach in his book *Mimesis: The Representation of Reality in Western Literature* (1953). In a chapter entitled "Odysseus' Scar," Auerbach compares and contrasts Genesis 22 with a scene in Homer's Odyssey. In this scene, the nurse Eurycleia, while washing the feet of a guest in Penelope's house, sees a distinctive scar on the guest's leg, and recognizes that the "guest" is none other than the long-lost Odysseus, Penelope's husband. The narrative is then interrupted at this point with a lengthy excursus about how Odysseus got the scar. Auerbach contrasts the "wordiness" of Homer with the extreme economy of language in the narrative about the near-sacrifice of Isaac. This use of language by the Hebrew narrator has the effect of drawing the reader into the story and of inviting the reader to provide the missing details. For example, as the story opens we are not told what its geographical setting is. Neither are we told from where Yahweh comes nor what Abraham was doing at the time. The story is stripped bare of its Homeric-type details. Auerbach maintains that it would be difficult to imagine styles more different than these two found in equally ancient and equally epic texts. In Homer, phenomena are externalized, uniformly illuminated, occur at a definite time and definite place, and are connected together without gaps. Thoughts and feelings are expressed completely and events take place in leisurely fashion, with very little suspense. In Genesis, by contrast, Auerbach observes that there is the externalization of only so much of the phenomena as necessary for the purpose of the narrative. Everything else is left in obscurity. Only the decisive points of the narrative are emphasized; time and place remain undefined and must be supplied by the interpreter. The characters do not express their thoughts and feelings but only suggest them with silence and fragmentary speeches. The whole episode is permeated with unrelieved suspense (Auerbach 1953: 12). What is the purpose of writing this way? Auerbach's answer is:

> If the text of the Biblical narrative . . . is so greatly in need of interpretation on the basis of its own content, its claim to absolute authority forces it still further in the same direction. Far from seeking, like Homer, merely to make us forget our own reality for a few hours, it seeks to overcome our reality: we are to fit our own life into its world, feel ourselves to be elements in its structure of universal history. (1953: 15)

Auerbach's analysis means that we must supply many of our own answers to the questions posed by this narrative, not only questions about narrative detail, but about why this story has the centrality it does in the Abraham and Sarah cycle of stories. The history of interpretation of this story has sometimes sought to provide answers for some of its questions, rather than leaving it up to the reader. The indefiniteness of place in the story, for example, has redefined "the land of Moriah" with Jerusalem, a tradition that began already in 2 Chr 3:1: "Solomon began to build the house of the LORD in Jerusalem on Mount Moriah. . . ." The location of Moriah, unspecified in Genesis 22, becomes the very site upon which the Jerusalem temple would be built, a tradition reflected also in the present-day Muslim shrine in Jerusalem, the Dome of the Rock.

Apart from questions and answers about details in the story, however, it raises larger religious questions. What the story seems to say is that love of God, or what we might call a "sense of duty," should come before love of people, even before concern for members of one's own family. This idea appears in the New Testament in the words of Jesus as reported in Luke 14:26: "Whoever comes to me and does not hate father and mother, wife and children, brothers and sisters, yes, and even life itself, cannot be my disciple." In the story in Gen 22, however, a general principle is sharpened to say that love for God and faithful obedience actually *opposes* love of family. While we recognize that specific instances might require one to temporarily suspend allegiance to one's own family in the name of a higher loyalty, does this story mean to suggest this suspension as *the* acid test of faith? One strain of Jewish tradition seems to suggest so, based on the last verse of the story (22:19), which if read literally suggests that Abraham returned from the mountain alone, implying that Isaac had been sacrificed. Other Jewish interpreters reflected on this story at length, concluding that Abraham offered up Isaac as a burnt sacrifice, and subsequently God transported Isaac's ashes to the Garden of Eden, where the dew "reconstituted" Isaac.

We need to remember to read this story in as wide a context as possible—certainly in the context of the rest of the Abraham and Sarah cycle. Filled with anxiety, fear, and pathos, the story's central thrust, and the core idea of the entire cycle, comes in its affirmation that "God will provide" (22:8, 14). This constitutes the bottom line of all the Abraham stories—confidence in God's faithfulness is what human faith is all about.

Kenneth Gros Louis offers this assessment of Genesis 22 as a summation of the Abraham cycle:

> How else, then, can we read Genesis 22 except as Abraham's testing of the Lord, as well as the Lord's testing of Abraham? What more can the narrative do to remind us of Abraham's past and to indicate to us the nature of the Lord in this narrative? Everything that the Lord has promised or done for Abraham is recalled for us before the Lord says, in Genesis 22: "Abraham!" Everything that Abraham has learned from his relationship with the Lord is recalled before Abraham answers, "Here am I." (Gros Louis 1982: 79)

The story of Abraham's near-sacrifice of Isaac should not shock us because, as Gros Louis suggests, we have been prepared for it all along. In the context of the Abraham cycle we should know that God makes good on his promises, and if what he has promised for Isaac is to happen, Isaac cannot die at this point in the story.

● ●

An Imaginative Portrait of Abraham

If a *schlemiel* is a person who goes through life spilling soup on people and a *schlemozzle* is the one it keeps getting spilled on, then Abraham was a *schlemozzle*. It all began when God told him to go to the land of Canaan where he promised to make him father of a great nation and he went.

The first thing that happened was that his nephew . . . Lot took over the rich bottom-land and Abraham was left with scrub country around Dead Man's Gulch. The second thing was that the prospective father of a great nation found out that his wife couldn't have babies. The third thing was that when, as a special present on his hundredth birthday, God arranged for his wife Sarah to have a son anyway, it wasn't long before he told Abraham to go up into the hills and sacrifice him. It's true that at the last minute God stepped in and said he'd only wanted to see if the old man's money was where his mouth was, but from that day forward Abraham had a habit of breaking into tears at odd moments, and his relationship with his son Isaac was never close.

In spite of everything, however, he never stopped having faith that God was going to keep his promise about making him the father of a great nation.

Continued

Night after night, it was the dream he rode to sleep on—the glittering cities, the up-to-date armies, the curly-bearded kings. There was a group photograph he had taken not long before he died. It was a bar mitzvah, and they were all there down to the last poor relation. They weren't a great nation yet by a long shot, but you'd never know it from the way Abraham sits enthroned there in his velvet yarmulke with several great-grandchildren on his lap and soup on his tie.

Even through his thick lenses, you can read the look of faith in his eye, and more than all the kosher meals, the Ethical Culture Societies, the shaved heads of the women, and the achievement of Maimonides, Einstein, Kissinger, it was that look that God loved him for and had chosen him for in the first place.

"They will all be winners, God willing. Even the losers will be winners. They'll all get their names up in lights," say the old *schlemozzle*'s eyes.

"Someday—who knows when?—I'll be talking about my son, the Light of the world."

Buechner (1979:3–4)

THE JACOB CYCLE: 25:19–37:1

Isaac and Rebekah: Bridge to the Jacob Narrative

The Jacob cycle begins as a parallel to a note about the descendants of Ishmael. In Genesis 25–37, however, Isaac and Jacob are front and center. Actually, the figure of Isaac, unlike his father, Abraham, and his son, Jacob, is not a powerful magnet around which a cycle of stories gathers. His character is not well fleshed-out, and he is essentially a bridge figure in the background, linking the Abraham cycle with the Jacob cycle. Only in the last chapter of the Abraham cycle (24) does he really come forward, and then one might say that Rebekah, Isaac's wife, stands more in the foreground than Isaac. Isaac's mother, Sarah, has died, his father is quite old, and Isaac, "the son of the promise" still has not married—yet another threat to the fulfillment of the promise of land and descendants made to Abraham. Not just any wife, however, will do for Isaac. In composing this story, the author must be looking back on years of contact between Israelite and Canaanite religion and culture, contact that led to religious compromise, which came to be viewed negatively by the champions of Yahwistic faith. Besides the threat of Isaac's childlessness, the added, more subtle threat of religious syncretism, stemming from intermarriage, appears here. If Isaac were to choose a Canaanite woman as his wife, distinctions between Abraham's line and the Canaanite line could become blurred, and any distinctiveness of a covenant people could be lost. Abraham's servant is sent to the patriarchal homeland in Haran (note that Isaac himself does *not* go), reversing the itinerary of Abraham, in search of a wife for Isaac from his own people. Still another threat crops up here: if Isaac himself went to Haran, he might like it there and remain, or his wife might be unwilling to leave her home, thus forfeiting the promise of a land. This last threat to the promise is dealt with specifically in Abraham's charge to the servant, which contains Abraham's last words as reported in Genesis:

> The servant said to him [i.e., Abraham], "Perhaps the woman may not be willing to follow me to this land; must I then take your son back to the land from which you came?" Abraham said to him, "See to it that you do not take my son back there. The Lord, the God of heaven, who took me from my father's and from the land of my birth, and who spoke to me and swore to me, 'To your offspring I will give this land,' he will send his angel before you, and you shall take a wife for my son from there. But if the woman is not willing to follow you, then you will be free from this oath of mine; only you must not take my son back there [and leave him]." (24:5–8)

Once Rebekah enters the scene (24:15), she dominates the story. She makes her own decision to return with Abraham's servant (24:58). She is no submissive female at the service of the men in her family. The close of Gen 24, and indeed the end of the Abraham cycle, unites Rebekah with Isaac in a way that emphasizes her importance: "Then Isaac brought her into his mother Sarah's tent. He took Rebekah, and she became his wife; and he loved her. So Isaac was comforted after his mother's death" (24:67).

Jacob and Esau

The legend of the struggles of Jacob and Esau in Rebekah's womb (25:22) serves as an effective introduction or prelude to the story of Jacob, whose name is a play on the Hebrew word for "heel," that is, "he takes by the heel" or "he supplants." Jacob is clever, deceptive, and strong. By most standards of human appeal he is not a very likable person. Yet, underneath the cycle of stories concerning him lies the theme that God works with and through such a person as Jacob, the trickster. In these stories, Jacob, whose name is changed to Israel in 32:28, represents the nation of Israel. In the Jacob cycle, the narrator expresses Israel's fundamental belief that, in spite of weaknesses and moral failures as a people, Israel was still "the people of the covenant," the people through whom God will bless all peoples.

Structure in the Jacob Cycle

BLESSING IN THE JACOB CYCLE

The Jacob cycle (Gen 25 - 36), like the Abraham cycle, had its origins and early development as several separate units of independent materials, which were only later worked into a coherent whole. Four kinds of materials appear in the Jacob cycle:

1. those concerning Jacob and his relations with his brother, Esau;
2. those concerning Jacob's dealings with his uncle, Laban;

3. those concerning Jacob and his sons; and

4. those dealing with theophanies (encounters with God who is temporarily visible in some way).

Note that three out of four of these blocks of material concern human relationships.

The Jacob cycle differs from the Abraham cycle in several ways. Geographically, it has a distinct preference for northern sites, in contrast to the southern orientation of the Abraham cycle. It also stands in contrast to the Abraham cycle in more fundamental ways, as suggested by Claus Westermann (1980: 74–78). First, the Abraham cycle is multigenerational—concerned with the transmission of the promise from one generation to the next. The central problem it addresses centers on securing an heir in the following generation. By contrast, the Jacob cycle is predominantly one-generational. Its concern is with family relationships and how those relationships endanger the promise. In other words, the Abraham cycle has a basically vertical viewpoint—it sees things as centered on the religious issue of God's promise and the human response of faith. The Jacob cycle, in contrast, takes a horizontal view of things—the issue is the social one of blessing, understood primarily in terms of prosperity and physical well-being. Jacob's desire for blessing is a driving force in the Jacob cycle. God blesses Isaac in Philistia (26:3); Jacob steals Isaac's blessing from Esau (27:27-29); Isaac blesses both brothers (27:38-40); Jacob is blessed by a divine messenger at Bethel (28:13-15); and God blesses Jacob at Peniel (32:26-29). The issue of blessing is of primary importance in Jacob's relations with Laban (30:27, 30) and Esau (33:17). The hope for a blessing and fear of a curse clearly charge the action of this cycle. Jacob seeks to wrest a blessing from all whom he encounters, beginning with his brother, Esau, and before his story ends, even from God. Because of this focus on Jacob's drive, the unconventional way that God works to keep the covenant alive comes across even stronger in the Jacob cycle and in the Joseph novella following it than it did in the Abraham cycle. The Jacob cycle makes it clearer than ever that God's purposes are continually threatened by "enlightened" human self-interest. Jacob's selfish drive to succeed and extract a blessing from all whom he encounters places him into conflict with God, with other persons, and even with himself.

CONCENTRIC STRUCTURE OF THE JACOB CYCLE

Recent study has revealed that the unity of the Jacob cycle has been achieved by the same kind of concentric structure in the Eden stories of the previous chapter. The structure unfolds a certain number of elements in order, up to a pivotal element, after which similar elements unfold in reverse order. This literary structure is sometimes called a *chiasm* for its shape similar to the Greek letter *chi,* which looks like an English X. Because the Priestly material in 35:6-7, 9-15 disrupts the chiastic pattern, apparently the person responsible for the chiastic arrangement, possibly the one who combined the work of the Yahwist with that of the Elohist, worked independently from the Priestly source (Gammie 1979).

CONCENTRIC STRUCTURE IN GEN 25-36

INTRODUCTION: GENEALOGICAL FRAMEWORK (25:1-11)

A   Death of Abraham; burial by two sons (Isaac, Ishmael); genealogy and death of Ishmael; birth and youth of Jacob (25:12-34)

B   Regional strife (in the South); Isaac vs. the Philistines: honorable covenant (26)

C   Beginnings of fraternal strife in Cisjordan (Jacob vs. Esau: settler-farmer vs. hunter); Isaac blesses Jacob, not Esau (27)

D   Departure of Jacob alone to the northeast with a theophany enroute at Bethel (28)

E   Arrival alone at the northeast (Haran in Upper Mesopotamia); marriage to Leah and Rachel; acquisition and naming of sons by Leah; commencement of strife with Laban (29)

F   Acquisition and naming of sons by handmaidens and of first son (Joseph) by Rachel (30:1-24)

F'   Preparation to leave the northeast; acquisition of herds (30:25-43)

E'   Departure from northeast with flocks, progeny, and two wives; conclusion of strife with Laban with a covenant in Gilead (31:1-32:2)

D'   Return from the northeast with a theophany enroute at Peniel; change of name to Israel (32:3-32)

C'   Conclusion of fraternal strife in Transjordan (Jacob vs. Esau: herder vs. herder); Jacob blesses Esau (33:1-17)

B'   Regional strife (in North); Jacob's sons vs. Shechemites; deceitful covenant; putting away of foreign gods (33:18-35:5); theophany at Bethel; change of name to Israel (35:6-7, 9-15); combines parts of E and E'

A'   Birth of second son of Rachel (Benjamin); death of Rachel; genealogy of Israel; death of Isaac; burial by two sons (Esau, Jacob) (35:8, 16-29)

CONCLUSION: GENEALOGICAL FRAMEWORK (36)

"TYPE SCENES" IN THE JACOB CYCLE

Within this chiastic structure the perceptive reader may hear echoes of the Abraham cycle. This *déjà vu* experience results from what have been called "type scenes" by Robert Alter (1981: 47-62). Alter introduces us to the "type scene" through the following analogy:

> Let us suppose that some centuries hence only a dozen films survive from the whole corpus of Hollywood westerns. As students of twentieth-century cinema screening the films on an ingeniously reconstructed archaic projector, we notice a recurrent peculiarity: in eleven of the films, the sheriff-hero has the same anomalous neurological trait of hyper-reflexivity—no matter what the situation in which his adversaries confront him, he is always able to pull his gun out of its holster and fire

before they, with their pistols poised, can pull the trigger. In the twelfth film, the sheriff has a withered arm and, instead of a six-shooter, he uses a rifle that he carries slung over his back. Now, eleven hyperreflexive sheriffs are utterly improbable by any realistic standards—though one scholar will no doubt propose that in the Old West the function of a sheriff was generally filled by members of a hereditary caste that in fact had this genetic trait. The scholars will then divide between a majority that posits an original source-western (designated Q) which has been imitated or imperfectly reproduced in a whole series of later versions (Q_1, Q_2, etc.—the films we have been screening) and a more speculative minority that proposes an old Indian myth concerning a sky-god with arms of lightning, of which all these films are scrambled and diluted secular adaptations. The twelfth film, in the view of both schools, must be ascribed to a different cinematic tradition. (48)

Alter points out in this analogy that conventions play an important role in our understanding of literature or movies. We readily recognize the convention represented by the typical sheriff in the standard western movie. Knowing this convention, unlike the scholars in Alter's story who do not know it, we see a point in the twelfth—unusual—western. We recognize that the convention of the quick-drawing hero is present in this movie through its deliberate suppression.

Alter recognizes conventions called "type scenes"in the Abraham and Jacob cycles. "Type scenes" are the stylized treatment of conventional situations, that is, typical episodes in the life of an ancestor made up of stock elements that a narrator can vary and elaborate upon. Here are some stock type scenes that are found in both the Abraham and Jacob cycles:

TYPE SCENE	*ABRAHAM CYCLE*	*JACOB CYCLE*
Birth of a hero to a childless mother	15:1-2, 4-14; 16:1b-2,7-14 (J); 18:1-21; 21:1-2, 21, 24 (J)	29:31-35; 30:4-5, 7-16 (J) 30:1-3, 6, 17-20, 22-23; 35:16-20 (E)
Encounter with future spouse at a well	24:1-67 (J);	29:1-30 (J)
Hero pretends that his wife is his sister	12:10-20; 13:1 (J); 20:1-18 (E)	26:1-11 (J)
Rivalry between childless, favored wife and a fertile wife or concubine	6:1b-2, 4-14 (J); 21:6, 8-21 (E)	29:31-35; 30:4-5, 7-16 (E), 24 (J); 30:1-3, 6, 22-23 (E)
Treaty between a hero and a local king	14:1-24 (J); 21:22-34 (E)	26:12-33 (J)

Type scenes like these do not occur in Genesis alone but are also found elsewhere in the Pentateuch and the Former Prophets. The recognition of type scenes offers an alternative explanation for the existence of doublets and triplets in the biblical narrative to the one proposed by source criticism. Instead of viewing them as indications of different authors who provide alternative readings of some hypothetical "original" version of a story, type scene analysis suggests that there never was an "original" full story. There was only a traditional episode with conventional elements. It was a challenge to each narrator or writer to fill out the episode and its conventions as his or her particular situation and audience dictated.

While type scenes describe relations between the hero and other individuals as well as contribute to the plot development when placed in a unifying structure, another kind of scene often repeated in the Hebrew scriptures, as one might anticipate, is theophany. While not exactly a type scene with conventional elements, theophanies often draw on traditional imagery. Two theophanies occur at key points in the Jacob cycle—elements D and D' in the chiastic structure outlined above. In these two chapters (Gen 28 and 32), Jacob, having done his best to get the best of other people, is left alone to encounter God. While the first encounter is rather inconclusive, it prepares the way for the second, the climax of the entire cycle.

Jacob's First Theophany

Jacob's first lonely encounter with the divine takes place after the onset of regional and family strife (elements B and C in the chiasm above). The second encounter preludes Jacob's reconciliation with Esau. In Gen 28, because of the conflict with Esau, Jacob has left his family and the land of promise when he has a dream. This happens where no religious experience was expected, a place identified at the beginning of the story simply as "a certain place" (28:11).

For the first time in the cycle, there is a respite from the ongoing human conflict that characterizes the cycle. Jacob is alone and apart. For a change, what happens does *not* result from Jacob's scheming but comes to him unexpectedly in a dream while he sleeps. In the dream, Jacob sees what was probably a staircase, rather than a "ladder" as English translations usually render the Hebrew word. The image here would be of the ramp of the Mesopotamian ziggurat or temple-tower, on which religious functionaries would ascend and descend. "A certain place" at the beginning of the story is transformed into the very "center of the earth," the *axis mundi,* the place where the "space" separating God and humans is spanned at the initiative of God. The angels in this story are messengers from God—in fact, the same Hebrew word means both angel and messenger. The message they bring to Jacob (in 28:13-14) renews the promise of land and descendants as made to Abraham and Isaac. An added dimension to the promise in 28:15, meant uniquely for Jacob and his risky lifestyle, points forward to the dénouement of the story: "Know that I am with you and will keep you wherever you go, and will bring you back to this land; for I will not leave you until I have done that of which I have spoken to you."

Theophanies often serve to establish the legitimacy in antiquity of what were for the writer, living at a later time, important cultic centers. At some stage of the transmission of this tradition, this narrative must have served that function for the site of Bethel. In the story, Jacob first responds to his dream by naming the place where the encounter took place "Bethel," which in Hebrew means "house of God." The mention of Luz in v. 19 suggests that a site with existing cultic associations was "claimed" by Israel and legitimized by means of this patriarchal tradition. After making a vow, Jacob resumes his journey. But does this encounter change Jacob's behavior in significant ways, or does that happen only after the second theophany?

Jacob and Laban

Between the two theophanies in the Jacob cycle an extended narrative describes Jacob's sojourn with Laban, his uncle, and includes a good deal of deception and conflict. Jacob comes into this section as an empty-handed fugitive and leaves as a prosperous man of power and authority, with two wives, two concubines, eleven sons, and at least one (named) daughter. But, as chapter 32 opens, clearly he is still estranged from his brother Esau, whom he must again face.

Jacob's Second Theophany

The theophany in Genesis 32:22–32 is preceded by Jacob's elaborate preparations for a meeting—with Esau, not God! Jacob sees to it that if worse comes to worst, and Esau's reception of him is something short of amicable (a fair assumption given the fact that messengers report to Jacob that Esau is coming to meet him with *four hundred* men), he will lose no more than one half his property. He also attempts to "buy off" Esau by sending ahead a substantial gift (32:13–21). But, after securing his family and his property, "Jacob was left alone" (32:24).

Most readers perceive that the theophany in 32:22–32 is narrated in a deliberately cryptic manner. A puzzling ambiguity exists concerning the identity of the actors in vv. 25–26, and again in 27–28. We might overlook such ambiguities except that they are accompanied by logical inconsistencies and nonsequiturs in the story's development. What is this story's meaning? Who was Jacob's opponent? What were his motives? Who won the struggle, Jacob or his rival? Was the latter a human being or a supernatural entity? As Elie Wiesel has observed, this is a strange adventure, mysterious from beginning to end. In a confused and confusing episode, the protagonists bear more than one name, words have multiple meanings, and one question raises another. The reader gets the feeling of being shut out, of watching an event through an almost opaque screen. Wiesel compares this chapter to a mystical poem that is barely coherent, barely intelligible, not only to the reader but even to the protagonists. He considers it one of the most enigmatic episodes in Jacob's life and even in Scripture (1976: 106, 109–110).

The idea of "rites of passage"—a translation of the French *rites de passage*—provides a clue to understanding this enigmatic story. This expression denotes those critical points in the life of an individual or community at which a fundamental change of status takes place. We mark some of these with secular and/or religious ceremonies—birth (baptism or circumcision), coming of age (bar/

bat mitzvah, confirmation), graduation (commencement ceremonies), marriage (weddings), and death (funerals or memorial services). Social anthropologists apply the concept to an even wider range of human experience.

Several elements in the story of Gen 32:22-32 belong to the language of a rite of passage. Jacob crosses the Jabbok River, which had to be forded to leave the old state of things with Laban behind and enter into a new state of things with Esau in the promised land. The human-divine encounter is symbolized by the wrestling match, for although Jacob's adversary is identified only as "a man," Jacob recognizes in him the presence of the divine: "For I have seen God face to face" (v. 30). The receiving of a new name also symbolizes leaving behind the old and taking on a changed identity. Jacob is told that his name no longer will be Jacob, "he who supplants," but Israel (v. 28). This both marks the fact that he has had a decisive encounter with God and makes him the ancestor whose name is adopted by the people of Israel.

In the light of such features in the story, the introductory comment that he was "left alone" is doubly important; Jacob is stripped of everything that connected him to his previous life as prerequisite preparation for his rite of passage. As we have seen, this was Jacob's second mysterious encounter with the divine. On his journey away from his parents and the land of promise, he had a dream that transformed a place—Luz became Bethel, the "house of God." This encounter takes place while he is returning to the land of promise, and it transforms him.

One might see in these two encounters the motifs of separation and rejoining, of division and unity that give a discernible structure to the whole cycle of stories, motifs that could be considerably elaborated. For now, however, just two points are relevant. First, the kind of approach we have taken to the Jacob cycle raises questions and offers insights quite different from those of more traditional historical inquiry or source criticism. Stories like these are not related to any identifiable historical period. Source critical analysis of these stories forms a part of many discussions of Genesis. Whatever earlier sources may have been used, however, the cycle in its present form has surely been drawn together to set forth the themes and motifs we have mentioned. Second, this kind of approach provides insights that are both literary, a tribute to the storyteller's art, and anthropological, illustrations of the customs of real human beings in realistic social groupings.

Following the second theophany, Jacob is clearly a changed person as he meets and is reconciled to Esau. The actual meeting with Esau (33:1-17) makes something of an anticlimax in the story. The tension has been resolved in chapter 32, so Jacob/Israel says to Esau, "To see your face is like seeing the face of God" (33:10). His days of being a fugitive are over, and he can now put down roots at Shechem in the land of promise.

Jacob and His Children

The remaining chapters of the cycle provide some miscellaneous information about Jacob, most of it from the Elohist and not centrally important to the tradition. Some of the information reprises what we have already seen. In Gen 34,

A Provocative Portrait of Dinah

Everybody agreed that Jacob's daughter Dinah had something special about her. She was off visiting friends in Canaan when young Shechem the Hivite was so dazzled that he couldn't control himself and took advantage of her. Considering the degree of temptation, you could hardly blame him in a way, but when Dinah's brothers got wind of it, they hit the roof.

Shechem by this time had fallen head over heels in love, but even when he wanted to make an honest woman of her and came to beg Jacob for her hand in marriage, the brothers were not mollified. On the contrary, they felt he was only adding insult to injury.

Shechem would not take no for an answer. He said that if Jacob would give his permission, he would make it worth his while by arranging some advantageous trade agreements between their two tribes with some personal gifts of cash and real estate thrown in for good measure. It was the kind of offer Jacob always found hard to refuse, but at the urging of his sons, he agreed to make one more condition.

If Shechem wanted to marry a nice Jewish girl like Dinah, he said, then he and all his fellow tribesmen would have to get themselves circumcised. It was the custom. Shechem didn't find it the easiest thing in the world to sell his fellow tribesmen, but somehow he managed it, and that was the break Dinah's brothers had been waiting for.

While the Hivites were still recovering from surgery, the brothers appeared out of nowhere and mowed them down to the last Hivite. When Jacob chided them about it afterwards, they seemed quite nonplussed. For Dinah's sake, who would have done less?

Dinah herself had done nothing except be who she was, which was the kind of person men naturally want to die or kill for, but that was enough. "Terrible as an army with banners" is the way Solomon describes beauty in his *Song*, and you picture her standing there with downcast eyes before her brothers' butchery, totally innocent of the knowledge that there were glittering battalions in her mildest smile and that if she wanted to take the world on single-handed, the world wouldn't stand a chance.

Buechner (1979: 27-8)

however, we find the story of the rape of Dinah, the only named daughter of Jacob and Leah. This story is one of two in the Hebrew Bible that tell of a brother or brothers avenging the rape of a sister. (The other is the story of Absalom's avenging the rape of his sister Tamar in 2 Sam 13.) Historical-critical scholarship has characteristically seen this story as an etiological legend that explains why the city is called Shechem, why there were hostile relations between Israelites and Shechemites, why Simeon and Levi are landless tribes (cf.

Gen 49:5-7), and why it was seen as bad form for Israelites to intermarry with foreigners (for the development of the last of these themes, see the discussion of the book of Ruth in our Chapter 14). To interpret this story as etiology makes Dinah, and what happens to her, rather peripheral. Feminist interpretation, however, sees such interpretation as an insult to women. On the pretext of defending a woman, hostility between peoples is justified. Dinah is given no voice in the story about her—she never says so much as one word. She is a victim, first of Shechem who rapes her, then of her brothers who both deceive her would-be spouse and then use her as a justification for further rapacious behavior, murder, and pillage. Dinah is never vindicated, and the sensitive reader is left to wonder about what happens to raped women who do not marry their rapists. While the author may not have had the intention of raising consciousness about sexual violence against women, he may well have been trying to tell us that while Jacob may have conquered the demon of deceitfulness, the underhandedness of the old Jacob lived on in his sons. Another unfortunate aspect of patriarchalism is its practice of passing "properties" as well as property from father to son. Sadly, at the end of the narrative (34:31), Jacob's sons seem to have learned nothing, and Jacob despairs of teaching them anything.

THE JOSEPH NOVELLA: GEN 37:2–50:26

The Joseph narrative differs noticeably from the episodic material that precedes it. At its heart is a well-crafted short story or novella, a short novel, primarily from J. It stands as a coherent unit and narrates a plot from a point of crisis to its conclusion. The plot line in the Joseph novella develops its narration in a series of scenes, structured as distinct movements toward the resolution of the story's basic crisis. Each scene unfolds with a limited number of *dramatis personae* and a specific arrangement of events. Joseph is sold into Egypt (Gen 37), is imprisoned (for false accusation of attempted rape—39), and interprets dreams (40-41). He is then "set . . . over all the land of Egypt" (41:43) and becomes a very successful administrator. Because of a famine in Palestine, Joseph's brothers, knowing that there was grain in Egypt, go there (except Benjamin) and meet Joseph, who negotiates with them without their recognizing him. Joseph accuses them of being spies. As a way of proving they are not spies, Joseph proposes that they must bring Benjamin to Egypt. Simeon stays behind as a hostage, and the other brothers return to Palestine with grain (42-44). They return to Egypt with Benjamin, and Joseph finally unmasks himself to his brothers (45), after which his father, Jacob, with the rest of his family, moves to Egypt. They are granted land in a region called Goshen and take on the status of welcome resident aliens. Joseph's considerable administrative skills strengthen Pharaoh's hand (46-47). Jacob adopts Joseph's two sons Ephraim and Manasseh (48), and after a farewell speech in which Jacob foretells the future of his sons (49), he dies and is taken back to Canaan for burial.

At the end of the novella (and at the end of Genesis) Joseph dies with a speech on his lips that both recalls the promise to Abraham and anticipates the Exodus from Egypt: "I am about to die; but God will surely come to you, and bring you up out of this land to the land that he swore to Abraham, to Isaac, and to Jacob" (50:24). No external historical evidence supports the historicity of events in the Joseph novella, although Egyptian texts and art, as we have observed, sometime speak of foreigners who came into Egypt to escape famine. Many Egyptian words, social customs, and practices in the novella testify to the craft of the narrator, but should not be used to make historical judgments about the narrative.

Unity and Structure

Anyone who reads the Joseph story can scarcely help being struck by the symmetry of its plot. The craft of the narrative makes an immediate impression. The sustained story is broken only by the following elements that appear to be intrusions in the novella:

1. Gen 38—A curious story about Judah and Tamar that is unrelated to its context.

2. Gen 46:1-7—A theophany concerning Jacob/Israel. In the Joseph novella, there are no other theophanies, but an emphasis on the mysterious ways of God's providence.

3. Gen 46:8-27—An inserted genealogy from P.

4. Gen 47:28-48:22; 49:28-33; 50:1-14—Miscellaneous materials about the death of Jacob.

5. Gen 49:1-27—A poem, possibly from the time of David, which portrays the character of the tribes in the person of the ancestor whose name they bear.

6. Gen 50:15-26—A report of the death of Joseph.

The story of Joseph is made up of six major structural elements:

 I. **Exposition:** introduction of *dramatis personae*—37:1-4
 II. **Complication:** Joseph's power is challenged, the family is broken—37:5-36
 III. **Digression:** Joseph rises to new power—39:1-41:57
 IV. **Complication:** Joseph challenges the power of his brothers—42:1-38
 V. **Dénouement:** by Joseph's power, reconciliation of the family—43:1-45:28
 VI. **Conclusion:** from Canaan to Egypt—46:28-47:27 (Coats 1983: 263-264)

The span of tension holding these six elements together as a single unit develops two contrasting themes—a *power* theme and a *reconciliation* theme. The power theme runs from an initial rupture in family relationships, apparent in the exposition, develops to a peak in the narration of the crisis (II above), and broadens by a reversal of roles in a repetition of the crisis (IV above), to a reconciliation of family members, established in the plot's dénouement and carried to its conclusion in the final element.

The second theme magnifies the alienation-reconciliation theme with a closely related point of tension, focused on Joseph's use of power. The power theme opens in the exposition, heightens by a challenge to Joseph's power in the narration of the crisis (IV above) and, in fact, functions as a means for effecting the reconciliation of the family in the final elements (Coats: 264).

THREE MOVEMENTS

The story has three movements, each of which deals with the themes of power and conflict outlined above, but, when taken together emphasize the theme of reconciliation.

Joseph and His Brothers Conflict.   In the *first* movement, we see a recapitulation of a motif in Genesis since its introduction in the story of Cain and Abel—the problem of fraternal conflict. Joseph, as the firstborn son of Jacob's favorite wife, Rachel, born to Jacob in his advanced years, is favored by his father, who gives him what the KJV calls "a coat of many colours" (37:3). (This translation serves as the traditional basis for the name of Andrew Lloyd Weber's musical, "Joseph and His Amazing Technicolor Dreamcoat.") The NRSV, however, translates the Hebrew at this point as "a long robe with sleeves." While the exact nature of the garment is unknown to us, it was clearly a special one that served, as clothes often do, as a status symbol that set Joseph apart from his brothers. This status symbol, coupled with Joseph's own behavior, understandably leads to resentment and revenge. The brothers sell Joseph into slavery— ironically enough to the descendants of Ishmael. Part of the genius of the story lies in the way God uses these hateful and deceptive actions, providentially and "behind the scenes," for constructive purposes.

Joseph Gains Favor in Egypt.   In the story's *second* movement, set in Egypt, Joseph regains a position of favor, this time in the house of the Egyptian Potiphar, for whom Joseph becomes estate manager. At this point, Joseph becomes involved in an incidence of sexual entrapment. Joseph spurns the advances of Potiphar's wife, who is sexually attracted to him. Marriages in the ancient Near East, and even today in traditional Arab societies, were not the result of romantic attraction leading to proposal but were arranged between the two families involved. Because the ownership and disposition of land and property were intimately connected to marriage and inheritance, it was believed that marriage was too important to be left to romantic feelings or sexual attraction. Marriage was (and is) arranged by parents, and the romantic interests of their sons and daughters were secondary considerations. Therefore, literature that speaks of romantic attraction in the ancient Near East describes something outside the social norm. The possibility that the attraction might not be mutually felt by the man or woman involved is thus a significant element in several ancient stories.

The wife of Joseph's master invites Joseph to have sex with her, and when he spurns her, she accuses him of attempted rape and has him imprisoned. The Genesis story of a spurned seductress has a parallel in an Egyptian story, "The Story of Anubis and Bata" (Matthews and Benjamin 41–45). In this story the elder brother is a married property owner. His younger brother, described as strong and handsome, does most of the work on the family estate. One day the younger brother is sent home by his brother to get some seed, and there the older brother's wife tries to seduce him, but without success. When her husband returns home she tells him the brother attempted to rape her, but when she refused him, he beat her. The story goes on to tell of the younger brother's escape from his infuriated brother and his further adventures.

Joseph again falls from a favored position, this time to prison. In prison, Joseph's dreams that had got him into trouble with his brothers in the first place now provide the way out. He interprets dreams with such skill that he eventually comes to the attention of the Pharaoh himself. The dreams in the Joseph novella serve the function of all dreams in tales, which is *to come true*. Dreams tell the reader of the future and shift the interest from *what* will happen to *how* it will happen. So we *know* from the beginning of Joseph's story that he will be the most eminent of Jacob's sons, though he is the next-to-youngest. The second movement of the story ends with Joseph again "on top" and again wearing clothes that indicate his elite status.

Joseph Reconciles with His Brothers.   The *third movement* of the story shifts back to Joseph's conflict with his brothers. The story of Joseph as a now-successful administrator leads him to meet his brothers when they come to Egypt to buy grain because of yet another famine in Canaan. Such a story about unexpected success is not very prominent in ancient Near-Eastern literature. The Bible, however, often lifts up the theme of "the success of the unpromising." The preference in other ancient Near-Eastern literature is for stories of gods and heroes who succeed predictably, following human expectations about what makes for success, in an ever-escalating scale of heroic exploits, what Sir Walter Scott called "the big bow-wow strain" of literature. Hebrew Bible authors were not nearly so interested in such manifest machismo, as Thompson and Irvin observe:

> In any case, although the Old Testament has its share of hero tales . . . it has also a large number of tales about women and men whose success astounds all the more because it could not reasonably have been looked for at the beginning of the story. And heroic literature yields a theology less suited to dealing with the world one ordinarily encounters than does the literature of the unpromising. The Old Testament authors understood this well. (Thompson and Irvin 1977: 190)

AN INTRUSION? THE JUDAH AND TAMAR NARRATIVE

Before concluding our investigation of the Joseph novella, we need to look at Gen 38, commonly seen as an "intrusion" in the novella. Careful analysis of this chapter serves to underscore the limitations of conventional historical-critical biblical study, even at its best. Nearly every commentator sees this chapter as an insertion into the Joseph story that interrupts the development of the plot and has little or nothing to do with the story. Almost the only positive comment that most commentators have concerning placement of this story is that it helps to build suspense by providing an interlude between the sale of Joseph into slavery and his appearance as a successful man in the house of Potiphar. But that is hardly a sufficient reason for the story's being placed here. Why is this story included in the Joseph novella? What meanings does it have in this context?

The story line is straightforward enough. Judah, the son of Jacob and Leah, while traveling in the area of Bethlehem, meets and marries an unnamed Canaanite woman, who bears him three sons: Er, Onan, and Shelah. Judah arranges a marriage between Er and a woman named Tamar (which means "date palm" in Hebrew), introduced at this point with no other identifying information. Er, however, dies before Tamar and he have any children. Relying on a practice known as *levirate marriage,* Judah then directs his next-oldest son Onan to marry Tamar, his brother's widow. The term "levirate" comes from the Latin word *levir,* meaning a husband's brother. According to the ancient widespread custom of levirate marriage (still practiced in some African societies), the legal details of which are spelled out in Deut 25:5-10, a brother was obligated to marry the widow of his *childless* deceased brother. The patriarchal purpose of the law was clear—to raise up a male descendant for the dead brother who would perpetuate his name and secure his inheritance. Onan, however, seeing what had happened to Er and realizing that the children of his union with Tamar would not be his, but his deceased brother's, practiced *coitus interruptus* and "spilled the semen on the ground" (38:9) during sexual intercourse with Tamar. (Curiously enough many nineteenth and early-twentieth century commentators cited this verse as a prooftext in their condemnation of masturbation—although it actually has nothing to do with masturbation!) Onan then dies, apparently creating the impression that Tamar somehow brought down a curse on her mates, a theme repeated in the short story of Tobit in the Apocrypha. Judah thus fears for the life of his remaining son, Shelah, should he marry Tamar, but he misleads Tamar into thinking that as soon as Shelah was old enough, she and Shelah would be married.

Some time later, Judah's own wife died, and after a period of mourning, he went off with a friend to shear sheep in Timnah. Suspecting that Judah's promise to her was insincere, Tamar devised a clever plan to trick Judah. She took off her widow's garments, dressed as a prostitute, and positioned herself at a point on the road to Timnah she knew Judah would be passing. Not recognizing her through her veil, and taking her for a prostitute, Judah propositioned her. She asked what he was willing to pay, and he agreed to send her a kid from his flock. Not taking Judah's word to be his bond, she thought for good reason, Tamar asked that he give her something in pledge, specifically requesting that he leave his signet, cord, and staff, the symbols of his legal person. With the transaction completed, Judah had intercourse with Tamar, and as a result she became pregnant. Having accomplished what she set out to do, she took off the prostitute's garb and put on her widow's garment.

Some time later, Judah sent a friend to deliver the promised kid to a certain prostitute at Enaim on the way to Timnah and to retrieve his collateral. When the friend asked about the whereabouts of the prostitute, the people in the neighborhood reported that no such person existed in their neighborhood. Judah kept the kid, and the woman, her identity still unknown to Judah, kept the signet, cord, and staff.

About three months later Judah was informed that his widowed daughter-in-law had been "sleeping around" and was pregnant. Judah ordered that she be burned, a punishment prescribed *only* for a daughter of a priest who acted as a prostitute in Lev 21:9 (the normal penalty being stoning). Tamar then exposes Judah by producing his signet, cord, and staff and saying that their owner was her child's father. Judah confesses: "She is more in the right than I, since I did not give her to my son Shelah" (38:26).

Tamar gives birth to twins who contended with one another in the womb, reminding us again of the Jacob and Esau story. This time the two boys represent what would become rival clans in the tribe of Judah. The older twin, Perez, is mentioned as one of David's ancestors in Ruth 4:12, and as an ancestor of Jesus in Matthew 1:3.

Connections with the Joseph Novella   Traditional interpretation of this episode, reflecting male interests, has emphasized either the levirate marriage law or the sons born to Tamar, neither of which help us to understand why this story exists *where* it does. Most commentators have failed to see this story's intimate connections through motif and themes with the Joseph story. From the very beginning of this "excursus," however, pointed connections are made with the Joseph novella. Robert Alter has pointed out that there is thematic justification for these connections, because the story about Judah and his offspring, like the Joseph story and the entire book of Genesis, is about the reversal of the usual supremacy of the eldest son (1981: 6).

Alter also establishes connections between the Judah–Tamar story and the Joseph novella by observing the recurrence at the climax of Tamar's story of the formula of recognition used before with Jacob and his sons. The verb *ykr* from the Hebrew root (*nkr*), "to recognize or acknowledge" occurs when Joseph's brothers present his coat to their father in 37:32–33: "'See now (*hakker*) whether it is your son's robe or not?' He *recognized* (*yakkiyrah*) it." In the Tamar–Judah story, this same formula, using the same verb, appears when Tamar presents Judah's signet and cord and staff in 38:25–26: "'Take note (*hakker*), please, whose these are . . .?' Judah *acknowledged* (*yakker*) them." The same verb also plays a crucial thematic role in the dénouement of the Joseph novella when he confronts his brothers in Egypt. "Although Joseph had *recognized* (*yakker*) his brothers, they did not *recognize* (*hikkiruha*) him" (Gen 42:8).

This recurrence of the same verb at the ends of Genesis 37 and 38 respectively most likely results from an artistic splicing of sources by a literary artist. The first use of the formula involved deception, the second an unmasking. Judah with Tamar, after Judah with his brothers is an instance of the deceiver being deceived. Because Judah was the one who proposed selling Joseph into slavery instead of killing him (Gen. 37:26-27), he can easily be thought of as the leader of the brothers in the deception of their father. Now he is subject to a bizarre but peculiarly fitting principle of retaliation, taken in by a piece of attire, just as his father was. He is exposed through the symbols of his legal self given in pledge, as Jacob had been tricked by the garment symbolizing his love for Joseph, which had been dipped in the blood of a goat (Alter 1981: 10).

The Joseph novella ends with two speeches of Joseph to his brothers, with whom he is now reconciled:

> "Do not be afraid! Am I in the place of God? Even though you intended to do harm to me, God intended it for good, in order to preserve a numerous people, as he is doing today. So have no fear; I myself will provide for you and your little ones." (50:19-21)
> "I am about to die; but God will surely come to you, and bring you up out of this land to the land that he swore to Abraham, to Isaac, and to Jacob. . . . When God comes to you, and you shall carry up my bones from here." (50:24-25)

These two speeches underline the intent of the entire Joseph novella, and indeed of all of the stories of the matriarchs and patriarchs—to show that God's ways of working with the creation are mysterious, especially when human beings are involved. On the one hand, God works *with* ambiguous, self-serving, or even malicious human behavior. On the other hand, God works to keep the covenant *in spite of* such behavior. At the conclusion of Genesis, the promised land seems out of sight, but Joseph's dying dream is of his bones finding their final resting place there. As we shall see in the next chapter, the "descent" of Jacob's people into Egypt will turn into a steep slide, but they will not fall from God's faithfulness to the covenant people.

THE HOW AND WHY OF GENESIS

How was Genesis written? It should by now be obvious that Genesis was not "written" in the same manner as we think of an author writing a "book" today. Even the relatively general analysis that we have done does not support the idea that a single author sat down and wrote the whole of Genesis. Many blocks of material from diverse authors and/or traditions have been brought together. For example, we have looked at the main units in Genesis—the primeval "history," the cycles centering on Abraham and Jacob, and the Joseph novella—some of which had their origins as oral traditions and were subsequently brought together in varying configurations before being assembled finally into a continuous narrative. Within each of these blocks there is also a variety of different types of materials—genealogies, etiological stories about origins of places, theophanies, type-scenes, and so forth.

Why was Genesis written? A conclusive, comprehensive answer to this question would have to include conjectures about why each unit in Genesis was written, as well as suggestions about what various redactors had in mind. Given this situation, a definitive answer simply cannot be given. A general answer, in such a context, is that at least some elements among the people of Israel were intensely interested in putting together the story of their origins and their past as a way of solidifying their identity as a people. No doubt many other peoples have been similarly interested, as the wealth of the world's traditional literature testifies.

However, some special aspects of this general human tendency to reconstruct the past should be kept in mind when we consider Israelite traditions. While most peoples at some point in their history show interest in their ethnic background and generate stories to help keep their background alive through the generations, the people of Israel believed that their past was uniquely significant. While other peoples, no doubt, have thought along similar lines, the Israelite traditions coupled the theme of distinctiveness as a people with the theme of a unique deity who covenanted with and providentially guided and protected this people—"I will take you as my people, and I will be your God" (Ex 6:7).

Part of the genius of the Hebrew scriptures lies in the fact that *both* the richness of human history *and* the sense of a God who guides that history are expressed in an unusual way, if not unique in world literature. Most religious literature that we might compare to the Bible (as well as some of the Bible itself, especially Gen 1–11) consists of myths in which the action occurs not within, but outside of, ordinary time and place. Biblical literature, for the most part, sets the action in human history and conceives of a God who works in that arena, often through quite ordinary events, and often in hidden or ambiguous ways. The so-called "mighty deeds of God" are such only when interpreted through the eyes of faith. Outside the sphere of faith it is possible to see them as coincidences, natural occurrences that are timed just right, or ordinary happenings. The God of Genesis does not work in a way that compels belief. We are thus justified in thinking that the authors and redactors of the biblical materials were motivated to compose books such as Genesis not simply to preserve ethnic memories and assist in the process of a people's self-definition, but also to portray in literature what to them was the unquestioned reality of the God that the traditions either presupposed or on reflection provoked.

Not long ago, most surveys of the Old Testament/Hebrew Bible characterized biblical literature as setting forth the first linear view of history, in contrast to the cyclical or mythical views dominating other literature in the world. The Bible, it was said, began with Creation and depicted human history as a series of unique, unrepeatable events that could be placed along a timeline leading to a goal-oriented end of history in some distant future. By contrast, other literatures reflected the view in which there was an annual cycle of natural events that were repeated year in and year out—a cycle that was built into the order of things and one which human beings ought to imitate in their religious life.

Further reflection has made it necessary to adjust this view, but it remains true that such stories as those of the Yahwist have few parallels in other people's literature. They so illumine human nature—motivation, humor, irony, passion, and so forth—that through them Western peoples took a major step toward the sense of reality that came to prevail in traditional Western culture, and which to this day deeply influences our basic thought patterns.

In other words, the story of God's promises to Abraham is not just a bit of ethnic tradition, belonging first to the ancient Israelites and then to the Jewish people. It also has a universal character that sets forth a philosophy, theology, or wisdom about how to live. When Abraham trusted God and acted out of faith, he not only gave assent to the process that made him a patriarch of the Israelite people, but he also made present in history, perhaps for the first time, a way of dealing with the mystery of life that was stunning in its depth of implication. Many questions still surround the question of just what God's revelations to Abraham might have been. But the result of Abraham's faith, whether we take it in its historical sense or in its literary sense was the very provocative claim: ***Do this and you will "live"!***

STUDY QUESTIONS

GENERAL

1. Does the fact that it is not possible (with any real historical probability) to associate the patriarchs and matriarchs with a definite period in history make the narratives about them more or less believable as stories and as theological statements? Why or why not?
2. In the Genesis stories, individuals (especially males) may represent groups. What people do each of the following individuals in the Abraham and Jacob cycles represent: Abram/Abraham, Lot, Ishmael, Laban, Esau, and Jacob?
3. The narratives of Genesis 12–50 report conflicts between a number of individuals. List as many of those conflicts as you can. Why are these conflicts a significant theme in Genesis? In your opinion, which of these conflicts is given the most emphasis? Why?

THE ABRAHAM AND SARAH CYCLE

1. At the beginning of this section of Genesis (12:1–3), God makes a covenant with Abraham, which consists of a three-part promise. What did God promise Abraham concerning each of the following: a) descendants; b) land; c) relationship to other people?
2. Now compare the covenant accounts in Gen 13:14–17; 15:17–21; and 17:1–21. How are they alike and how are they different? How is the information about the land promised in these passages significant in the contemporary Middle East?

3. Fill in the geographic sites in the blanks below, and follow them on a map of the Near East as you trace the route of Abraham's migration:

(11:31) from _____ to_____;

(12:5) from_____ to_____;

(12:10) from _____ to_____;

(13:1) from_____ to_____;

(13:11–12) from_____ to_____.

Why is there a problem with regard to the location of Ur? Why is Haran a particularly significant place?

4. Why is it significant, in light of what follows in Genesis and Exodus that Abraham's original home was *not* in Canaan, and that he spent some time in Egypt?

5. Scholars differ in their evaluations of the role played by the matriarchs (and women in general) in Genesis (cf., for example, the assessments of Gottwald and Teubal). What is your assessment of their role? Who is the most assertive? Who is given the biggest voice by the narrator? Which of the matriarchs most exemplifies the subordination of women in Israelite society?

6. Some interesting patriarchal stories are not discussed in the chapter. Among them is a story about Abraham's defeat of the four kings (14:1–24) and the story of the destruction of Sodom and Gomorrah (19:1–29). Choose one of these and make a literary analysis (theme, plot, climax, dénouement, symbolism) of it. How does this story fit into and contribute to Genesis 12–50 as a whole?

7. How do you account for the similarities between the stories about Sarah and the Pharaoh (12:14–20), Sarah and Abimelech (20:10–20), and Rebekah and Abimelech (Gen 26:6–11)?

8. The story of the binding of Isaac (Gen 22:1–14) is called "both the climax and summary of the entire Abraham cycle" (p. 171). Analyze this story by supplying answers to the following questions.

What do you imagine might have been going on in Abraham's mind during this episode? What do you think Isaac might have been thinking? Sarah is never mentioned in Genesis 22. What do you think her response might have been when she was told of what had happened? Is the narrator's placement of the note in 23:1–2 significant in this regard?

9. What does the narrative about the binding of Isaac suggest about the nature of faith in the patriarchal narratives?

THE JACOB CYCLE

1. On the way to Haran, Jacob had a dream (28:1–22). Where did the dream take place? What was the content and meaning of the dream? What effect did this dream have on Jacob's behavior?

2. In the story of Jacob's encounter at the ford in the Jabbok River (32:22–32), Jacob wrestles with someone or something that is not specified. In what sense is Jacob wrestling with himself? With Esau? With God? How are the three related? What effect, other than a change of name, does this experience have on Jacob?

3. What is your assessment of Frederick Buechner's provocative portrait of Dinah? Do you think it is demeaning to women? Why or why not? Is it an example of blaming the victim?

THE JOSEPH NOVELLA

1. One commentator has said, with reference to the story of Judah and Tamar (38:1–30): "The author is likely deliberate in exposing the double standard of sexual morality that held in ancestral times, and there is not doubt that Tamar is to be considered admirable." Do you agree with this interpretation? Why or why not?
2. How does the picture of God in the Joseph novella differ from that in the preceding patriarchal narratives?
3. *Joseph: A Contemporary Reading.* Using the Joseph novella, the material in this chapter, and your notes, write an essay on Joseph in the manner of Frederick Buechner's imaginative portraits. The title of your essay is to be: "Joseph: A Modern Hero." Choose a subsection of the Joseph novella and rewrite it in a modern setting of your choice. Choose: (a) a specific time and place for your story; (b) a narrator for the story (first person narration [e.g. you are Joseph, or Josephine, or one of the brothers, or the Pharaoh, etc.] or third person narration [you are an ideal observer, one who hears and sees everything that is going on, as well as knowing what the characters are thinking and feeling]; (c) a particular subsection of the novella that you will rewrite. Do *not* rewrite the entire Joseph novella. Some possible subsections of the narrative are: Joseph's boyhood in Canaan; Joseph as a slave and prisoner in Egypt; Joseph's interpretation of dreams and elevation to power; Joseph's meeting(s) with his brothers; or Joseph's reunion with his family in Egypt; (d) the kind of person Joseph is in this subsection. Do this same thing for the other characters you choose to include. Feel free to use dialogue as well as narration. Remember: this is a creative exercise. Use your imagination, but do not invent a totally different character for Joseph than that which you find in the Old Testament.
4. The last verse in Genesis reads: "And Joseph died, being one hundred ten years old; he was embalmed and placed in a coffin in Egypt" (50:26). What is significant about this as an ending for the book of Genesis?

BIBLIOGRAPHY

Alter, Robert. 1981. *The Art of Biblical Narrative.* New York: Basic Books.

Auerbach, Erich. 1953. *Mimesis: The Representation of Reality in Western Literature.* Tr. by Willard Trask. Princeton: Princeton University Press.

Buechner, Frederick. 1979. *Peculiar Treasures: A Biblical Who's Who.* New York: Harper & Row.

Coats, George W. 1976. *From Canaan to Egypt.* Washington, D.C.: Catholic Biblical Association.

———. 1983. *Genesis: With an Introduction to Narrative Literature.* The Forms of the Old Testament Literature, Vol. 1. Rolf Knierim and Gene M. Tucker, eds. Grand Rapids: Eerdmans.

Dever, William G. 1977. "The Patriarchal Traditions. Palestine in the Second Millennium B.C.E.: The Archaeological Picture." *Israelite and Judaean History,* John H. Hayes and J. Maxwell Miller, eds. Philadelphia: Westminster, 70-120.

Gammie, John G. 1979. "Theological Interpretation by Way of Literary and Tradition Analysis: Genesis 25–36." *Encounter with the Text,* Martin J. Buss, ed. Philadelphia: Fortress, 117-34.

Gottwald, Norman K. 1985. *The Hebrew Bible: A Socio-Literary Introduction.* Philadelphia: Fortress.

Gros Louis, Kenneth R. R. 1982. "Abraham: II." *Literary Interpretations of Biblical Narratives,* Vol. II. Kenneth R. R. Gros Louis, ed. Nashville: Abingdon.

Lemche, Neils Peter. 1988. *Ancient Israel: A New History of Israelite Society.* Sheffield, England: JSOT.

Matthews, Victor H., and Don C. Benjamin. 1991. *Old Testament Parallels: Laws and Stories from the Ancient Near East.* New York: Paulist.

Speiser, E. A. 1964. *Genesis.* Anchor Bible. Garden City, New York: Doubleday.

Spiegel, Shalom. 1969. *The Last Trial.* Tr. by Judah Goldin. New York: Schocken.

Teubal, Savina J. 1984. *Sarah the Priestess: The First Matriarch in Genesis.* Athens, Ohio: Swallow.

———. 1990. *Hagar the Egyptian: The Lost Tradition of the Matriarchs.* New York: Harper & Row.

Thompson, Thomas L. 1974. *Historicity of the Patriarchal Narratives: The Quest for the Historical Abraham.* BZAW 133. Berlin: Walter de Gruyter.

Thompson, Thomas L., and Dorothy Irvin. 1977. "The Joseph and Moses Narratives." *Israelite and Judaean History,* John H. Hayes and J. Maxwell Miller, eds. Philadelphia: Westminster, 149-212.

Van Seters, John. 1975. *Abraham in History and Tradition.* New Haven: Yale University Press.

Walton, John H. 1989. *Ancient Israelite Literature in its Cultural Context.* Grand Rapids: Zondervan.

Westermann, Claus. 1980. *The Promises to the Fathers: Studies on the Patriarchal Narratives.* Tr. by D. E. Green. Philadelphia: Fortress.

Wiesel, Elie. 1976. *Messengers of God.* New York: Random House.

Chapter 7

THE EXODUS AND THE SINAI COVENANT: EXODUS, LEVITICUS, NUMBERS, AND DEUTERONOMY

Suggested Bible Reading
Ex 1–31; Lev 17–26; Num 10:11–14:45; 21–24; 32–33; Deut 12–26

Although some of Israel's values and beliefs are reflected in the stories about the patriarchs and matriarchs, the birth of what can be called a distinctive Israelite community occurs in the context of the foundational event of the experience of liberation from oppression in Egypt—the Exodus. This liberating event was interpreted by the ancient Israelites as having been accomplished through the agency of Yahweh. The central event in Israel's recital of her history and, indeed, *the* point of departure for many scholarly studies of the history of ancient Israel, is the Exodus from Egypt. A basic understanding of God as the one who delivered a people from oppression in Egypt echoes throughout the pages of the Hebrew Bible—in the prophets and the Psalms as well as in the books of Exodus, Numbers, and Deuteronomy. Even those scholars who believe that only a small portion of the people who became Israel in Palestine actually experienced slavery in Egypt accept the decisive nature of the experience for Israelite self-understanding.

When it comes to relating the Egypt and Sinai wilderness traditions to a specific set of historical circumstances, however, there is no such scholarly unanimity. There has been a continuing scholarly interest in raising questions about the possible historicity of these events. Are these historical traditions? If so, when did the oppression in Egypt and the Exodus from Egypt occur? Because the Bible does not mention the names of any Pharaohs, who was the Pharaoh of the oppression? Who was the Pharaoh of the Exodus? What route did the Exodus take? These queries point to obvious historical issues, some of which we shall examine below. A note of caution, however, as we begin our study of Exodus: Though the narratives tell of an event that was clearly very important in the people's history, the nature of the data available cannot lead to firm historical conclusions.

At the same time we should observe, as we did when looking at the narratives concerning the patriarchs and matriarchs, that the theme of the first part of the book of Exodus—liberation from oppression in Egypt—is developed in an independent way from its historical moorings. We will follow an approach suggested by R. J. Coggins, who has said that it is of no real consequence who the particular Pharaoh may have been who was responsible for the oppression. There is even a positive, symbolic value in the fact that the Pharaoh is not identified. With no particular Pharaoh named, "the Pharaoh" can stand as a representative figure who symbolizes all unjust and oppressive rulers. We agree with Coggins who maintains that, for an understanding of the Exodus, whether the liberation took place in the fifteenth or the thirteenth century B.C.E. is not critical. The crucial point is the reality of the oppression (1990: 100–101).

In the early chapters of Exodus we encounter a process of consciousness-raising, a process in which a miscellany of persons with no particular ethnic or national character arrives at a recognition of their collective identity as a people. The second part of Exodus develops this idea of peoplehood by focusing on the obligations and possibilities of life as a particular people. Genesis, beginning with Cain and Abel, told its story by focusing on tensions in interpersonal relations within the family circle that threatened to break it apart. Would Abraham sacrifice Isaac? Would Sarah be reconciled with Hagar? Would Esau accept Jacob upon his return? In the early chapters of Exodus, however, the heart of the narrative concerns the coming together of a people, who first seek liberation from oppression. Interestingly enough, the first section of Exodus ends with a genealogy (Ex 6:14–25 = P) that functions to establish the identity of the people. Following the genealogy are the stories of plagues (Ex 7–10) that tell of the oppressors' persecution. This whole account reaches a climax with the account of the deliverance at the "Red Sea" and the hymn in praise of Yahweh as deliverer:

> Sing to the LORD, for he has triumphed gloriously;
> horse and his rider he has thrown into the sea. (15:21)

THE HISTORICAL BACKGROUND OF EXODUS

A Summary of the Exodus Narrative

Exodus begins with a brief but significant note of the Yahwist, "Now a new king arose over Egypt, who did not know Joseph" (Ex 1:8). This indicates a change of conditions in Egypt. This note suggests that as we turn from the last chapter of Genesis to the first chapter of Exodus, there has been a dramatic turn of affairs for Joseph's people in Egypt. They have grown from "all the persons of the house of Jacob who came into Egypt were seventy," (Gen 46:27) to a people undergoing rapid population growth. The advantageous position that they had enjoyed under the Pharaoh in Joseph's day has deteriorated and they now found themselves doing forced labor for the Egyptians. They worked on state construction projects, building the store-cities of Pithom and Rameses (Ex 1:11). Joseph had brought his family to Egypt during a famine in Palestine and set them up in the area of Egypt called Goshen. This area is now turned into a ghetto for Hebrew slaves.

This forced labor for the state, or *corvée,* was begun by the Pharaoh when he became concerned about the threat posed by a large and growing number of resident aliens in his country. When the *corvée* failed to curb Hebrew population growth, the Pharaoh initiated a program of genocide, ordering midwives to murder Hebrew males at birth. One Hebrew boy, however, was saved when his family put him in a basket and set it afloat in the Nile, where it was found by none other than a daughter of the Pharaoh. This baby, Moses, was raised in the Egyptian court, as if he were the son of Pharaoh's daughter, with his own mother serving as his nurse. The story further tells us that upon reaching adulthood, Moses witnessed an Egyptian beating a Hebrew slave; in retaliation, he killed the Egyptian. Because of this act, he was forced to become a fugitive from Egyptian law, and fled into the Sinai wilderness. In the Sinai, Moses married into a family of pastoralists and remained there until he had a vision of a burning bush on "the mountain of God" (3:1). In this experience, God called him, commanding him to return to Egypt to lead his people out of bondage and into a land of their own (Ex 2-6).

When Moses returned to Egypt, he found a new Pharaoh ruling, who refused to loosen his grip on the Hebrew slaves. The next four chapters of Exodus (7-10) tell of God's judgment against the Egyptians in a series of plagues—beginning with turning the water in the Nile, the very lifeline of Egypt, into blood (7:17), and ending with the death of the eldest child of every Egyptian family, including the Pharaoh's son (Ex 11:12-30).

Devastated by the last plague, the Pharaoh capitulated and told Moses that he and his people could leave Egypt. Soon after the Hebrews began their departure, however, the fickle Pharaoh changed his mind and pursued the fleeing people at the head of a chariot force. The Egyptian army caught up with the Hebrew people at a body of water called in Hebrew the *yam suf,* Sea of Reeds (13:18). (*Yam suf* was translated "Red Sea" in the Septuagint, and that translation was retained by the KJV and the NRSV). God pushed back the waters of the sea so that the escaping Hebrews could cross over. When the Egyptian chariots attempted to pursue them, the waters returned to their original position, drowning the Pharaoh and his army (12:31 - 15:21).

Moses led the people through the Sinai wilderness to "the mountain of God," where God made a covenant with them and gave them a code of laws (Ex 16 - 31, 33 - 35). From Sinai the people moved on to a site called Kadesh-Barnea, located on the southern borders of Canaan. When scouts sent by Moses brought back disturbing reports that Canaan was protected by strongly fortified cities manned by enormous warriors, the people gave up on the journey to the promised land and rebelled against Moses. God punished this rebellion by proclaiming that, except for Caleb and Joshua, none of the people who came out of Egypt with Moses would enter the land of promise (Num 10:11 - 14:45). The story pauses at this point, inserting a generation of life in the wilderness around Kadesh-Barnea. When movement resumes, Moses leads his people through the Transjordan to Mount Nebo on the eastern bank of the Jordan, where he dies without crossing into the promised land (Num 21-24; 32-33).

THE HISTORICAL LOCATION OF THE EXODUS

In discussions of the Exodus as a historical event, most biblical scholars advocate one of three positions. Most scholars argue for placing the Exodus in the thirteenth century B.C.E. A smaller group supports a date in the fifteenth century B.C.E. A third group, represented by N. P. Lemche, says that the data simply do not support any particular date. Lemche and others would argue that the traditions about Israel's time in Egypt and the Exodus are legendary in nature. The notion that one family could in the course of a few centuries develop into a whole people, a nation, consisting of hundreds of thousands of individuals, is the stuff of which legends are made. At the same time, these narratives are quite intelligible from the viewpoint of a society based on kinship. They express the self-understanding of Israelite society well, that they were are members of the same family. Following Lemche's argument, there is no real reason even to attempt to find a historical background for the events of the Exodus (Lemche 1988:109).

What kind of evidence can be called forth by those who *do* support a historical location of the Exodus and the Sinai wilderness experience? The evidence is of two kinds: chronological references in the Bible and extrabiblical evidence.

Biblical Chronology of the Exodus

As we mentioned in the previous chapter, the narrative in 1 Kings 6:1 concerning Solomon's building of the Jerusalem temple, includes a statement about the date of the Exodus relative to the dedication of the temple: "In the four hundred eightieth year after the Israelites came out of the land of Egypt." If one were to take this reference literally, it would appear to support a fifteenth-century B.C.E. date for the Exodus—960 (the date of the fourth year of Solomon's reign) + 480 = 1440

B.C.E. How do those who argue for a fifteenth-century date for the Exodus support their case, using what we know about Egypt and Palestine at the time?

The Case for a Fifteenth-Century B.C.E. Exodus

What is called the New Kingdom in the history of ancient Egypt began with the XVIIIth Dynasty, a dynasty that included some powerful and well-known Pharaohs (see Table 7.1). The New Kingdom was preceded by the Second Intermediate Period (Dynasties XIII-XVII), which included a period of about one hundred years (1665-1560) when Egypt was ruled by a group of Pharaohs known as the Hyksos. The XVIIIth Dynasty began when Ahmose expelled the Hyksos from Egypt in 1560 B.C.E. The Hyksos were a group of Asiatics, mostly Semites, who first consolidated their power in the area of the eastern Nile delta. Then in a period of Egyptian weakness they took control of the country, ruling from their capital at Avaris in the delta region.

Some scholars who support a fifteenth-century date for the Exodus, make a connection between Hyksos rule and the patriarchal migration into Egypt. Certainly the story of a Semite like Joseph rising to power in Egypt makes especially good sense if Asiatics or fellow Semites were ruling at the time. Some also would connect the reference in Ex 1:8, "Now a new king arose over Egypt, who did not know Joseph" to Ahmose's reassertion of Egyptian rule and the expulsion of the Hyksos. This event would have meant a loss of favor for the people of Israel, leading to their oppression and the movement for liberation under Moses some time later.

Thutmose III and Amenhotep II ruled Egypt in the fifteenth century. Both initiated major building operations, including some in the Nile delta region. Inscriptions and tomb paintings from the time of Thutmose I and Thutmose III depict Semites working as forced labor on state construction projects.

THE AMARNA LETTERS

Extrabiblical support for a fifteenth century Exodus has also been claimed for a collection of correspondence known as the Amarna Letters. This archive, found near the modern Egyptian village of el-Amarna, adjacent to the site of the Egyptian capital in the fifteenth century, contains letters from Egyptian vassals in Palestine to the Pharaohs Amenhotep III and Amenhotep IV (who, as part of a program of religious reform, changed his name to Akhenaton). This correspondence testifies to a very unstable situation in Palestine, with infighting among the Egyptian agents there and considerable unrest that was generated by a group called the Habiru. The similarity of this group's name to "Hebrew" ('ibri in Hebrew) has been observed by many scholars. If the Israelites had exited Egypt in the mid-fifteenth century, so the argument goes, they would have been coming into Canaan at the time when the conditions described in the Amarna correspondence prevailed.

Those supporting an early date for the Exodus sometimes point to an inscription from the time of Hatshepsut (1503-1483—Egypt's first woman

TABLE 7.1   Ancient Egyptian Chronology (Dynasties I–XX)

ARCHAIC PERIOD	**3100–2700 B.C.E.**
DYNASTIES I–II	
OLD KINGDOM	**2700–2200**
DYNASTIES III–VI	
FIRST INTERMEDIATE PERIOD	**2200–2060**
DYNASTIES VII–XII	
SECOND INTERMEDIATE PERIOD	**1800–1560**
DYNASTIES XIII–XVII	
HYKSOS RULE IN EGYPT	**1665–1560**
NEW KINGDOM	**1560–1070**
DYNASTY XVIII	**1570–1293**
Ahmose	1570–1546
Amenhotep I	1551–1524
Thutmose I	1524–1518
Thutmose II	1518–1504
Thutmose III	1504–1450
Hatshepsut (♀)	1503–1483
Amenhotep II	1453–1419
Amenhotep IV (Akhenaton)	1350–1334
Smenkhkare	1336–1334
Tutankhamun	1334–1325
Ay	1324–1321
Horemheb	1321–1293
DYNASTY XIX	**1293–1185**
Rameses I	1293–1291
Seti I	1291–1279
Rameses II	1279–1212
Merneptah	1212–1202
DYNASTY XX	**1184–1070**
Rameses III	1182–1151

ruler), as translated and interpreted by Hans Goedicke. According to Goedicke, this inscription tells that Hatshepsut annulled the former privileges that had been extended to Asiatics in Egypt, forcing them to work on state building projects. They refused to do their assigned work, which caused conflict (see Figure 7.1). Finally, Hatshepsut allowed them to leave Egypt, but the gods punished them— "the earth swallowed up their footsteps" through an unexpected upsurge of Nun (the Egyptian name for the primeval waters) (Shanks 1981:

Figure 7.1   Hatshepsut's Mortuary Temple

49–50). If the inscription analyzed by Goedicke was a description of the Exodus from an Egyptian viewpoint, then Hatshepsut, was both the Pharaoh of the oppression and the Pharaoh of the Exodus.

THE MERNEPTAH STELE

Another Egyptian text that has been used to support a fifteenth-century date for the Exodus is the Merneptah Stele (see Figure 7.2). This same text, interpreted in a different way, is also used in support of a thirteenth-century date for the Exodus. The inscription includes the first mention of Israel outside the Bible. It comes from the fifth year of the reign of Pharaoh Merneptah (*ca.* 1207). This victory inscription celebrates Merneptah's victories over peoples living in Libya and Palestine. The relevant part of the inscription reads as follows:

> The princes who have opposed me now bow before me, saying: "Peace!" Not one raises his head in revolt. I have desolated Tehenu and quieted the land of the Hittites. I have plundered Canaan in a fierce manner and carried off spoil from the city of Ashkelon and captured the city of Gezer. The town of Yanoam in northern Canaan I have utterly destroyed, leaving it as if it had never existed. The people of the tribes of Israel have been laid waste, their offspring destroyed. Hurru—Canaan has become a widow by Egypt's action! All of the lands there are now pacified: all those who were restless and rebellious have been bound into submission by

Figure 7.2   The Merneptah Stele

the Pharaoh of Upper and lower Egypt—Ba-en Ra Meri-Amon; the Son of Ra: Merneptah Hotep-hir-Maat, who is given life like Ra, the God of the Sun, every day. (Matthews and Benjamin 1991: 81)

As an Egyptian inscription, the Merneptah Stele was written in hieroglyphics, which makes use of special signs called determinatives. A *determinative* was placed before a proper noun to indicate what class of noun the following word was (that is, a place, a country, a god, a tribe, a female person, and so on). Several words in that portion of the Merneptah Stele quoted above would be preceded by the determinative for country or city—for example, Canaan, Ashkelon, Gezer. The proper noun "Israel," however, is preceded by the determinative for a people rather than a place, as reflected in the translation in Matthews and Benjamin. Those who support a thirteenth-century date for the Exodus commonly cite this as evidence in their favor. Because the Merneptah Stele seems to indicate that a people known as "Israel" was present in an area that did not yet bear their name as the name of the country, they must have only recently come into the area.

Those who favor a fifteenth-century date for the Exodus, however, interpret the Merneptah Stele differently. It has recently been argued that the structure of the inscription, read as a poem, dictates that Israel should be read as a synonym for Canaan (Ahlström and Edelman 1985). As we will see when we look at the structure of Hebrew poetry in Chapter 13, the text often uses a device called *parallelism*. Parallelism puts forth an idea in one line and then repeats the idea in slightly different words in a successive line. According to Ahlström and Edelman, the parallelism in the Merneptah Stele does not follow the pattern of successive lines, but the first line parallels the last line, the second line parallels the next-to-the-last line, and so on, forming a parallelism. Thus the line: "I have plundered Canaan . . ." parallels "the people of the tribes of Israel have been laid waste." The two lines that list Palestinian cities also parallel one another. If one follows this line of interpretation, the use of determinatives is not critical, and Israel becomes synonymous with Canaan, both simply designating geographical areas. Thus, by the time of Merneptah's reign in the thirteenth century, Israelites had given their name to at least a portion of Palestine and were in a position of prominence—a state of affairs consistent with a fifteenth-century Exodus.

TELL ES-SULTAN

The last piece of evidence used in support of a fifteenth-century Exodus is cited in most books about the Old Testament/Hebrew Bible written between 1931 and 1957. It comes from archaeological work done by John Garstang in the 1930s at Tell es-Sultan, the site of the ancient Israelite Jericho. Garstang found what he thought were a pair of parallel defensive walls that had been destroyed *ca.* 1400–1385 B.C.E. He then claimed that this proved that Jericho had fallen to Joshua *ca.* 1400 B.C.E., obviously requiring a fifteenth century date for the Exodus. We will return to a discussion of archaeological evidence pertaining to the narratives in Joshua concerning the "conquest" of Canaan in Chapter 8.

Problems with a Fifteenth-Century Date

While there thus appears to be some support for a fifteenth-century Exodus, in many cases the evidence does not stand up under scrutiny. We have already pointed out that the 1 Kings 6:1 reference cannot be used unquestioningly in support of a fifteenth-century date. The extrabiblical evidence is even less certain. Accepting the inscription of Hatshepsut as an Egyptian account of the oppression and Exodus rests on Goedicke's debatable translation of an admittedly difficult text. The "Asiatics" referred to in the text might well be the Hyksos who had ruled Egypt for about a century before Hatshepsut. Other Egyptologists, however, find no reference in this text to a repeal of the Asiatics' former privileges, nor to their disregard of their work, nor to a destruction by the waters of Nun. The "father of fathers" who has ordered the earth to carry off their footprints is probably Ra, not Nun. Only by adopting a very idiosyncratic translation and some unlikely interpretations can this text be seen as related to the Israelite Exodus.

The argument that Israel parallels Canaan in the Merneptah Stele is also problematic. The use of determinatives in Egyptian hieroglyphics, especially in the same context, should not be regarded as insignificant. The "people" determinative for Israel in the text seems to indicate a significant population group in the area, and not necessarily a term for all or part of Palestine. Ahlström and Edelman's analysis of poetic parallelism in the Merneptah Stele has also been criticized.

Garstang's interpretation of the archaeological data at Jericho has been called into question as well. Later excavations at Jericho, conducted by Kathleen Kenyon from 1952 to 1958, using greatly improved stratigraphical digging methods, showed clearly that Garstang had misinterpreted the evidence. Stratigraphically it was clear what Garstang interpreted as parallel defensive walls were actually two separate walls that were not contemporary with one another. One of them was part of the Early Bronze Age fortifications of Jericho that had been destroyed *ca.* 2300 B.C.E. Kenyon found no traces of any fifteenth-century (Late Bronze Age) walls. She held that Jericho had been destroyed in the Middle Bronze Age and was only sparsely settled in the fifteenth century. Certainly it was not the site of a significant city in that century.

The Amarna Letters have also been subjected to further study. As it turns out, Habiru is not an ethnic term in that correspondence, but a label applied to an ethnically diverse group of people who were united by the fact that they shared a similar social status—people without a country or property, mercenaries, migrant laborers, and so forth. They do not seem to have been organized in tribes nor is there any indication that they "invaded" Palestine.

The evidence favoring a fifteenth-century B.C.E. Exodus has been fairly evaluated by William Stiebing (1989: 52–53, 55), who does not find it to be compelling. He believes the main reason many scholars have rejected the fifteenth-century date for the Exodus is because of its poor "fit" with the historical and archaeological picture of the time. He observes that in the biblical story, Moses and Aaron make frequent trips back and forth between the Israelite camps and the Pharaoh's court, which implies that the residence of Pharaoh was in the delta area at the time. In the fifteenth century B.C.E., however, the capital of Egypt was not in the delta region, but at Thebes, more than four hundred miles up the Nile. The itinerary of the Exodus given in Exodus 12:37 and Numbers 33 also starts in the delta. This provides further support for the idea that all of the events narrated, from the beginning of the oppression to

Figure 7.3   Exodus locations in Egypt and the route of the Exodus

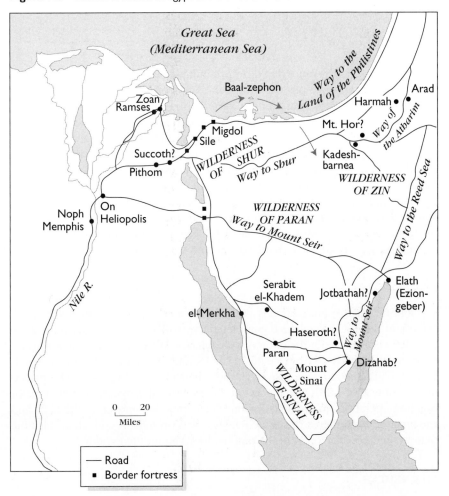

the Exodus, took place in the delta area. This delta location would make an XVIIIth Dynasty date for the Exodus very unlikely (see Figure 7.3).

The Case for A Thirteenth-Century Exodus

Within the biblical text, besides explicit chronological references, clues point to a thirteenth-century date for the Exodus. The single most important one is found in Exodus 1:11: "Therefore they set taskmasters over them to oppress them with forced labor. They built supply cities, Pithom and Rameses for Pharaoh." If this passage could be determined to be historically reliable, and if the two cities mentioned could be positively identified, archaeology probably could provide a chronological framework for the story of the oppression and

Exodus. Unfortunately, however, the remains of these two cities have not been positively identified.

PITHOM

Pithom is the Hebrew rendering of *Pr-itm* in Egyptian, which means "the house of Atum." The principal place at which the Egyptians worshiped the god Atum was in Heliopolis, near present-day Cairo. During the XIXth Dynasty, however, Atum was also worshiped in the eastern delta region, the site of Goshen where the Israelites lived. The eastern delta was neglected before Rameses II set up his capital there. Genesis 47:11, in an obviously anachronistic reference (that is, one that refers to Rameses at a time before Rameses ruled), locates the area of Israelite settlement in this area: "Joseph settled his father and his brothers, and granted them a holding in the land of Egypt, in the best part of the land, in the land of Rameses, as Pharaoh had instructed." Although the reference is anachronistic in Genesis, it shows that later biblical writers understood the term Goshen to refer to the area that later became known as the "land of Rameses."

RAMESES

The Rameses of the biblical text is a shortened version of the Egyptian *pr-r'mssw,* "House of Rameses." Rameses II completed the work on the city started by his father Seti I on the site of the old Hyksos capital of Avaris. The naming of the city as Rameses seems to rule out a date for the Exodus before the time of Rameses II. If the biblical accounts are historical, then the story should probably be placed in the context of XIXth Dynasty Egypt. Pharaohs of this dynasty initiated major building operations in the delta region. The capital was moved to the delta and the Pharaoh lived there. The name Rameses was prominent enough at this time that it could become a part of the oral traditions about the Exodus.

MERNEPTAH

The Merneptah Stele has also been used as an important piece of evidence for a thirteenth-century setting for the Exodus. Merneptah was the last noteworthy Pharaoh of the XIXth Dynasty. In the fifth year of his reign, Egypt was invaded by a coalition of Libyans from the west and "Sea Peoples," coming from the Mediterranean. The stele celebrates his victory over this coalition and a successful military expedition into Palestine. This document, which we discussed above as a piece of evidence for a fifteenth-century Exodus, is more commonly read using the determinative "people" before the mention of Israel and the determinatives for "city" or "land" for the other proper names. Those favoring a thirteenth-century Exodus assume that no Egyptian scribe would have mentioned such a politically insignificant entity as Israel, let alone placed it in Canaan, unless it reflected a reality. Israel is one of four names listed between the synonymous terms Canaan and Hurru. The other three names represent city-states. Ashkelon and Gezer are mentioned together as a pair of southern cities. Similarly paired are Yanoam and Israel. Yanoam is a northern city, so "Israel" should also be placed in the north, or at least in the central highlands. Reading the Merneptah Stele in this way, it is then suggested that at the end of the thirteenth century, Israel was in Canaan, but had not yet settled down to become a political entity with definable borders. Its presence there was of recent origin, so that the Exodus would have taken place in the thirteenth century.

THE EXODUS AS HISTORICAL EVENT

Having briefly surveyed the evidence for two different historical settings for the Exodus, what can we conclude about the Exodus as a historical event before moving on to other issues? Considering the mixed evidence, Terence Fretheim has set forth what seems to us to be a reasonable perspective (1991: 7-9). Maintaining that the book of Exodus is not historical narrative, at least in any modern sense of that phrase, he believes that we hear in this book the living voice of the community of faith that was Israel. In that sense the material has a purpose profoundly historical, yet the text of Exodus makes no such claims for itself. Nevertheless, the concern for "what really happened" has often occupied the attention of modern scholars. Much remains uncertain in their attempts to reconstruct the history of the Exodus. The result, without going into detail, is that Exodus contains a very mixed set of materials from a historiographical perspective. Fretheim maintains that while a nucleus of the Exodus account is probably rooted in events of the period represented, the narratives also reflect what thoughtful Israelites over the course of a millennium considered their meaning(s) to be. In such an ongoing reflective process, the writers used their imaginations freely. In doing so they believed they were doing justice to what they had inherited. Fretheim also concludes that it was likely that the celebration of these events in Israel's worship generated materials for these stories. The community's valuing of these materials means that they had a continuing place quite apart from the question of "happenedness." "Even where the historiographer's judgment may be quite negative, the material does not lose its potential value to speak a word of God across the centuries, in Israel's time or ours" (9).

THEMES IN THE BOOK OF EXODUS

The Book of Exodus is dominated by two interrelated themes: *liberation from oppression in Egypt* and *covenant at Sinai*. These themes are stated in the famous story of the burning bush:

> "I have observed the misery of my people who are in Egypt, I have heard their cry on account of their taskmasters. Indeed, I know their sufferings, and I have come down to deliver them from the Egyptians, and to bring them up out of that land to a good and broad land, a land flowing with milk and honey." (Ex 3:7-8a)

The two themes of liberation and covenant also provide the book of Exodus with its basic organization, consisting as it does of two main sections, chapters 1-15 and 16-40. The first section tells of what God has done for Israel (liberation); the second how Israel should respond to God's action (covenant). The first section begins with a prologue (chapter 1) that describes the situation of Israel's oppression. Chapter 2 tells of Moses' preparation for his role as God's agent in the liberation of Israel. The next two chapters (3-4) tell of Moses' commissioning by God and of his return to Egypt where he confronts the Pharaoh with God's call for liberation of Israel. Chapters 5 and 6 describe Pharaoh's response to this call with increased oppression. God's demand for liberation is then repeated. A confrontation follows that pits Moses and his brother Aaron (as agents of Yahweh) on the one side, against the Pharaoh (as a representative of the gods of Egypt) on the other. This encounter is described in a series of ten plagues that strike Egypt (chaps. 7-14). In the narrative about the plagues, an extravagant amount of space is allotted to the tenth and final plague, the killing of the first-born of Egypt, which occupies three chapters (11-13). The first section of the book of Exodus, all of which has been in prose, concludes with a poem in chapter 15. This poem is a song of praise celebrating the incomparability of Yahweh, who has shown himself as sovereign of both Egypt and Israel. This song of Moses, set beside the Sea of Reeds, celebrates the definitive liberation of Israel from slavery in Egypt.

The second section of the book of Exodus begins by telling of a series of crises that Israel confronted following her definitive separation from Egypt at the Sea of Reeds (chaps. 15:22-18). During these crises, Israel was moving toward Mount Sinai, which is the geographical focus of the second part of the book. Beginning with chapter 19, Mount Sinai is at the center of things, with Israel encamped at its foot for nearly fourteen months. Not until Numbers 10:11 does Israel move away from Sinai and on toward the Promised Land. The account of a theophany (ch. 19) and the offering of the covenant (ch. 24) bracket a section of legislative material, which includes the *Decalogue,* or Ten Commandments (20:1-17), and the Book of the Covenant (20:22-23:19). The second part of the book of Exodus continues with another legislative section (25-31). In it, God gives Moses instructions for constructing the wilderness sanctuary (the tabernacle) and its ritual objects, as well as rules about priestly vestments and ordination. The book then concludes with Moses and craftspersons carrying out God's instructions.

The Situation of Israel's Oppression (1:8–22)

The account of Israel's oppression in Egypt begins with allusions that remind us of the Joseph novella. The mention of supply cities in Ex 1:11 echoes Joseph's advice to the Pharaoh in Gen 41:33-36 concerning storage of grain. One function of the state in Egypt was to extract "surplus" grain from farmers by way of taxation and then to store it for people to have food in times of want. Ironically, what is intended to save the people, the construction of storehouses for grain, was also used to enslave them. In exchange for state-guaranteed security, the Egyptians handed over to the state their right to their own crops, herds, and even persons. And, according to Gen 47:25, apparently they acquiesced to such an arrangement: "They said, 'You have saved our lives; may it please my lord, we will be slaves to Pharaoh.'"

The social system under which Israel was oppressed in Egypt has been called the "Asian mode of production." The use of the word "slave" in the NRSV is misleading, because the rural poor in such a social system were not slaves in the sense of being the property of the wealthy landowners. They were, however, obligated to work for the state on demand. Legally, the state owned all land, and collected a portion of all produce as rent for the land. The peasants, however, lived on these state lands, leaving them only when called to work on some state project, such as the construction of "store cities." This system also presupposed a class society. The Pharaoh and his courtiers lived off the work of the peasants in their villages, a situation that called for the peasants agreeing to trade their grain, animals, and labor in return for state-guaranteed security.

The beginning of the book Exodus, however, speaks of a situation in which the dominant class suspects that a rebellion is at hand. The response has been repeated time and time again by repressive governments everywhere—a tightening of the screws placed in their hands by the system. By increasing the amount of state labor required of the Israelites, the Pharaoh hopes to minimize their ability to rebel against the system. Just how serious the Pharaoh was about keeping the Israelites in line is shown by his institution of a policy of genocide to tighten the screws even more. In doing so, he sets the stage for the life-and-death conflict that follows.

The Preparation of God's Agent for Liberation (Ex 2)

The central figure in all the traditions in the book of Exodus-Deuteronomy is Moses. Moses is introduced in Ex 2:1–10 with the story of his birth that has miraculous elements. Moses' birth is not the occasion for rejoicing, as the birth of a son usually is in the Hebrew Bible. In the context of the Pharaoh's program of genocide, the birth of a male child presents a problem, since only males were targeted for destruction. Not sons, however, but daughters, Moses' sister and the daughter of Pharaoh, save the future savior. The Nile, the source of life for Egypt, is also the instrument used to preserve Moses' life. The story of Moses' rescue employs a common legendary motif in which the life of a future leader is saved in association with water. Romulus and Remus were saved from the Tiber River to found Rome. A Babylonian text recounts that Sargon, king of Akkad (2371–2316 B.C.E.), was saved from the Tigris River:

> Because my mother was a priestess who would be expected to offer her children as sacrifices, she did not want anyone in the city of Asupiranu to know that she had conceived and given me birth. Therefore, she hid me along the bank of the Euphrates River in a basket woven from rushes and waterproofed with tar.

The river carried my basket down to an irrigation canal where Akki, the royal gardener, lifted me out of the water and reared me as his own. Akki trained me to become his assistant in the royal gardens. (Matthews and Benjamin 1991: 55)

In Exodus 2:10, Moses is named by Pharaoh's daughter. The Hebrew writer suggests that the name *Moshe* (the spelling of Moses in Hebrew) comes from the fact that Moses was "extracted" or "drawn from" (the verb *mashah* in Hebrew). More likely, however, the name is an Egyptian one, based on the word *mesu,* meaning "to beget a child." This word appears in the names of the Pharaohs Ahmose, Rameses, and Thutmose. These pharaonic names are *theophoric* (that is, they are names that include a divine element). They indicate that the god mentioned in the first part of the name gave birth to the person bearing his or her name. Omitting the name of the god, which is the case in Moses' name, the name becomes a kind of nickname, for which there is also evidence in Egyptian. Ironically, Moses' very name thus identifies him with the oppressor of his people.

But as Moses matured, clearly he felt no solidarity with the dominant Egyptian class. On the contrary, he recognized Egyptian oppression and acted against it. He recognized the Hebrews as "his people" (2:11). The struggle with the Egyptian overseer is the first act in the liberation struggle. The word translated "beating" in 2:11 and "strike" in 2:13 (both of which are translated "smite" in the KJV and have the same Hebrew term behind them), is the same word used for the ten plagues ("smitings") beginning in Ex 8. But Moses was not yet ready to be a "hero." Instead, he escaped into the desert area of Midian and took up the life of a shepherd. Here he tried on the role of hero by *delivering* seven daughters of a Midianite priest from mistreatment at the hand of some local shepherds (Ex 2:16-17). Moses married one of the daughters and settled down as a resident alien, a *ger* in Hebrew, living away from his own people as a person who lived in a place without being integrated into its society or holding real property. His son was symbolically named Gershom, *ger sham* in Hebrew, or "stranger there," indicating his status as an alien. Up to this point in Exodus, neither God nor religious motivation has been a part of the story. But in Ex 3 God comes onto the scene.

Commission and Return (Ex 3–4)

An essential requirement for a revolution is the recognition of a situation as intolerable, not due to some unfortunate turn of events, but because of an oppressive system. The problem for the Israelites was not simply the fact that an inconsiderate Pharaoh had chosen to increase their workload for the state. The system itself is the problem—a system that permitted the Pharaoh to use other people in this way. Who was it, at this point in Exodus, that realized that the Israelites must break free from this system? Certainly it was not the Pharaoh. Neither was it Moses. According to Exodus, God alone is aware of this necessity, and God initiates the liberation process by selecting Moses as the leader.

God's self-revelation to Moses (Ex 3:1-12) combines elements from both J and E, as evident from the alternation in the names for God, Moses' father-in-law, and the holy mountain. The narrative also follows the pattern of a prophetic call scene (even though Moses is never called a prophet in Exodus), a pattern repeated in the calls of Gideon (Judg 6:11-24), Jeremiah (Jer 1:4-9), and Isaiah (Isa 6:1-13). This call narrative, like others, includes six elements:

1. theophany (vv. 1-4a);
2. introductory word (vv. 4b-9);
3. God calls the prophet to perform some task (v. 10);
4. the prophet objects and resists the call (v. 11);
5. God responds to the objection, repeating the call and reassuring the prophet; and
6. a confirming sign is foretold (v. 12b).

The section of Exodus this passage introduces expands on the third and fourth elements, the prophet's resistance to God's call and God's response. Besides Moses' protestations of unworthiness in 3:11, he objects *seven times* in chapters 3-6 (3:13; 4:1; 4:10; 4:13; 5:22-23; 6:12; 6:30), each followed by a reassuring response from God.

YAHWEH

One of God's responses to Moses is particularly significant, as it reveals the name Yahweh to Moses. In response to Moses' objection to the call on the grounds of personal inadequacy, God tells Moses that the only necessary adequacy is that of God, who both calls Moses and will be present with him. God first identifies himself to Moses as the ancestral God: "I am the God of your father, the God of Abraham, the God of Isaac, and the God of Jacob" (3:6). The narrator tells us, however, that this identification did not satisfy Moses: "If I come to the Israelites and say to them, 'The God of your ancestors has sent me to you,' and they ask me, 'What is his name?' what shall I say to them?" (3:13). The proper name of God, Yahweh, is then given to Moses and explained etymologically, as related to the common verb *hyh,* "to be, to become."

According to the text, God answers Moses by saying: "I AM WHO I AM." And he said, "Thus you shall say this to the Israelites, 'I AM has sent me to you'" (3:14). This is the only place in the Hebrew Bible where the first-person form, *'ehyeh,* of the divine name is used. Everywhere else the name occurs in its third-person form, *Yahweh.* If the disclosure of God's name at the same time also represents a revelation of God's nature, what does this name say about God's character?

The original Hebrew phrase, *'ehyeh 'asher 'ehyeh,* can be translated in more than one way. One way of translating it, the simplest way and the way the KJV and NRSV do it, is simply "I AM WHO I AM!" This translation underscores the mystery of the divine nature. God does not really fully reveal his nature to Moses at this point. Another way of reading the name is "I am [the one] who is." This translation can be supported by the principles of Hebrew grammar. Hebrew, unlike European languages, has pronouns and verbs in a dependent clause agree with the subject of the main clause, not with the noun of the predicate. For example, Gen 15:7 translated literally says "I am Yahweh, who *have* brought you out of Ur" rather than the correct English expression "I am Yahweh, who has . . ." By saying "I am [the one] who is," the reality of God is stressed.

Yet another way of translating the phrase, which rests upon the fact that Hebrew does not have the same tense structure as Indo-European languages, is "I will be who I will be." This translation can be understood in one of two ways. One way is to see this as a promise of God's adequacy for any and all situations in the future. It is a way of saying that the nature of God will be revealed in God's actions in behalf of Israel. The question "Who is God?" would be answered in time through what happened in the liberation of God's people. What God is, will be seen in what God does, not in any immutable list of character traits. This translation also emphasizes the hiddenness of God's nature. God will be what God will be, not what humanly-devised religion expects or wants the deity to be. God does not give Moses a name that can be used like some magic charm to call God into action in support of any human venture. God will act when and how God sees fit.

God then informs Moses that he is about to act to liberate the Israelites from their Egyptian bondage and bring them into their own land (3:16–17). Moses is now ready to return to Egypt to play the role of God's agent in the liberation of Israel.

MOSES RETURNS

As Moses journeys back to Egypt, nothing in the text to this point has prepared the reader for the shocking assertion encountered in 4:24: "On the way, at a place where they spent the night, the LORD met him and tried to kill him." Absolutely nothing is said about God's motivation for doing this. What follows this startling statement (4:24–26) is one of the most enigmatic episodes in all of the Hebrew Bible, one that has baffled most commentators. While we have seen God's attacks on the hero before (for example, Jacob in Gen 32:22–32), this passage seems to reveal a particularly dark side of God. It is Moses' wife, Zipporah, who saves him from the divine attack, although her role often has been minimized by commentators. In the context of Exodus, however, she is another in a line of women whose actions save the hero—a line that includes the midwives, Moses' mother and sister, and Pharaoh's daughter. Moses owes his life so far to the action of women, two of whom are "foreigners." Of all these women, only Zipporah is called by her name. Her action here is not without personal risk. Fretheim cites the difference between Zipporah and the other women: while they saved Moses from Pharaoh, she saves him from God. She thus plays the role of mediator between God and Moses, anticipating the very role that Moses will play on Israel's behalf. However much Moses reached heroic stature in later activity, he is shown here to be vulnerable and in need of a mediator in his relationship with God. And it is a non-Israelite woman who provides that mediation, saving Moses from sure death (1991: 80–81).

But how does Zipporah save Moses? The Hebrew text says that Zipporah cut off the foreskin of her son's penis and touched "his feet" with it. The word "feet" is often used in the Hebrew Bible as a euphemism for genitals (Deut 28:57; 1 Kings 15:23; 2 Chr 16:12; Isa 6:2; 7:20; Ruth 3:4,7). But whose genitals did Zipporah touch? The NRSV removes all ambiguity with the translation "[she] touched Moses' feet with it," adding in a footnote that the Hebrew simply says "his." If it were their son Gershom who was being attacked, we might understand God's actions as motivated out of retribution against Moses for not circumcising their son, who is saved here by Zipporah's act. But this leaves unanswered the repeated phrase "bridegroom of blood" (4:25, 26), which suggests that Zipporah touched her son's foreskin to Moses' penis. The puzzling nature of this passage is attested to by the way in which it appears in the Septuagint. In the Septuagint version, Yahweh does not attack Moses, but an angel. Instead of touching Moses' penis with the bloody foreskin, Zipporah falls at the angel's "feet" and says: "Here is the blood of my child's circumcision."

So we cannot be certain whether Moses or his son was threatened in this incident. Nor do we know whether the "bridegroom of blood" refers to Moses or to Yahweh. One thing is clear from this passage: Yahweh has a menacing side. In this incident, Moses was certainly made aware of God's seriousness in commissioning him, together with the serious consequences of disobedience.

A Contest of Wills (Ex 5–14)

Upon returning to Egypt, Moses and his brother, Aaron (described as Moses' "prophet" in 7:1), confronted the Pharaoh with God's demands. The narrative at this point is filled with dramatic suspense. The contest is not just between Moses and the Pharaoh. The underlying struggle is between Yahweh as sovereign and the gods of Egypt, represented by the Pharaoh. In this contest, the Pharaoh displays the skills of an experienced oppressor. In response to Moses' request to allow the Israelite workers to worship Yahweh in the wilderness, the Pharaoh disparages Moses and seeks to teach the workers a lesson by increasing their workload. He also employs a divide-and-conquer strategy by using Israelites as supervisors. Moses wavers and has to be reassured (5:22–6:8) in a way that recalled the covenant with the ancestors and anticipated the plagues that were to come, the liberation from Egypt, and the possession of a land.

THE PLAGUES

At this point the stage is set for the "plagues," or "signs and wonders" as they are called in the text (7:3). There have been many attempts at discerning the structure of the plague narrative, but none have been very successful. It is common to talk of the plagues as ten in number. None of the traditions that make up the Torah, however, mention all ten. J tells of eight plagues (as does Psalm 78), to which P adds the plagues of gnats and boils. Psalm 105 also lists ten plagues, but in a different order than Exodus. The plagues increase in intensity, beginning with things that are more or less nuisances, and ending with death.

Two observations about the structure of the narrative concerning the plagues are significant. Assuming ten plagues, there are three groups of three plagues, each of which is introduced in a characteristic manner: set 1 = plagues 1, 4, 7; set 2 = plagues 2, 5, 8; set 3 = 3, 6, 9—see the chiasm below, noting that the first *sign*, Aaron's rod turning into a snake, is not a plague. The other observation is that the signs have a *chiastic* structure—that is, signs 1 and 10 are linked, 2 and 9 are linked, and so on. In any attempts to discern structure in the plague narrative, however, the tenth plague (or eleventh sign), the death of the Egyptian first-born falls outside the structure. As noted earlier, the tenth plague also receives an inordinate amount of attention. The unique nature of this most disastrous of plagues is also emphasized by interweaving two types of text in its narration. Narrative and legislative language alternate and interpenetrate as follows: 11 is narration; 12:1-28 is legislation; 12:29-42 is narrative; and 12:43-13:16 is legislation. Within this alternation, 11:10b; 12:28; 12:40-42; and 12:50-51 mark the conclusion of each section and can be read as a series of short reports that carry the story line forward (Fokkelman 1987: 56).

Whatever the structure of the plague narrative, the themes expressed are certainly clear. One theme is that of rivalry between Yahweh and the Pharaoh. At first, the Pharaoh's court magicians could duplicate Yahweh's "signs and wonders." In the end, however, their sleight-of-hand failed them. A second theme appears in these narratives: negotiation. Moses and the Pharaoh bargained with one another as opposing personalities. Yahweh's differentiation between the Egyptians and the Israelites as targets of the plagues, is part of the negotiation theme, as this undermined the Pharaoh's political foundation.

CHIASTIC STRUCTURE OF SIGNS AND PLAGUES IN EXODUS 7–12

1. Aaron's rod turns into a snake (set 1)
2.   Water in Nile changed to blood (set 2)
3.   Frogs (set 3)
4.   Gnats (set 1)
5.   Flies (set 2)
6.   Cattle disease (set 3)
7.   Boils (set 1)
8.   Hail (set 2)
9.   Locusts (set 3)
10. Darkness

What are these plagues? Most of them resemble natural occurrences in Egypt. Seven of them can be associated with the annual inundation of the Nile, the lifeblood of Egypt. Even though one might "explain" the plagues by reference to natural phenomena, such an attempt to view these "signs and wonders" *merely* as occurrences in the realm of nature is foreign to the intentions of the text. The environmental impact of the plagues is important, however, for the text makes it clear that not only human beings are affected, but that God's action can be seen in the created order itself. Threatened implicitly, God's judgment on human evil could cause the orderly created world to revert to its primeval chaos as in the story of the great flood.

Our modern distinction between "natural" and "supernatural" is foreign to the Hebrew scriptures. A "sign" is not necessarily a supernatural occurrence. Or, put in another way, "miracles" are not limited to those instances in which the laws of nature appear to be broken. "Signs" may be ordinary occurrences when viewed through the eyes of faith. When looked at in this way they become "signs" or evidence of Yahweh's continuing action on behalf of God's people. From this perspective, the plagues in Exodus are seen as the extraordinary acts of Yahweh in taking on the gods of Egypt and defeating them on their own turf.

The account of the final plague introduces Israel's observance of the Passover. At the moment of triumph over the tyrant, the text pauses to tell of the beginning of the annual celebration in which Israel will remember its victory and be reminded that the struggle against tyranny is a perpetual one. Originally, the festival of Passover and the festival of unleavened bread may have been separate holidays. They are already linked in the Bible, however, and by the first century c.e. the two had become combined into a single festival, commemorating the liberation from bondage in Egypt.

Excursus 1: The Passover in Jewish Tradition

The Passover is a major festival day in the Jewish calendar. It celebrates the breaking of the chains of human bondage, not just the ancient act of deliverance from slavery in Egypt, but freedom from oppression in all places, for all people, at all times. The Hebrew word for Passover is *Pesach,* which is associated with a Hebrew verb meaning "protect" (Isa 31:5).

Pesach is celebrated during the first month of spring (Nisan) in the Jewish calendar. The celebration of *Pesach* lasts for eight days (seven days for Reform Jews) and includes traditions that have developed within Judaism over the centuries, reflecting the history of the Jewish people and their appropriation of the biblical story. One of these traditions is eating only unleavened foods during the festival. Leavening causes food to "raise," and thus Jews abstain from eating not only ordinary bread but anything else that has yeast or a leavening agent in it. Any leavening agent is removed even from the home. The unleavened bread eaten during Passover is called *matzah.* The celebration of *Pesach* begins with the *Seder* (from the Hebrew word "order"). The *Seder,* a festive meal full of symbols and symbolic acts, is celebrated at home with members of one's family and guests. The *Seder* dramatizes the story of the Exodus from Egypt with special foods, songs, stories, games, and symbolic actions. The central idea is to *actualize* the Exodus, that is, not just to remember what happened in the past, but to *relive* the deliverance and be made aware of where liberation is needed in the world today. The *Haggadah* "narration" is the guide used for conducting the *Seder.* While many versions of the *Haggadah* exist, they all contain the same basic elements. They all declare that "in each generation, the Jew must feel as though she or he personally had been delivered from the hands of the Egyptians." For those who ask why?, the answer replies that they would still be slaves in Egypt if their ancestors had not been set free.

CELEBRATING THE SEDER

To make the event contemporary and involve even the youngest family members, one of the initial rituals of the *Seder* requires the youngest child present to ask four questions which focus on the uniqueness of the celebration:

1. Why on other nights do we eat ordinary bread, but on this night only *matzah*?
2. Why on other nights do we eat various herbs, but on this night only bitter herbs?
3. Why on other nights do we not dip out food even once, but twice on this night?
4. Why on other nights do we sit up to eat, but recline on this night?

The *Haggadah* then goes on to answer these questions by retelling the story of the Exodus.

The *Haggadah* has been in use for over 2,000 years. Its form is not fixed, however, and new material is always being added to emphasize contemporary forms of oppression. Customs associated with the *Seder* have been adapted over the years. In the first century B.C.E., for example, it was the custom to leave the door of the home open so that the master of ceremonies could call out into the street, "Let all who are hungry come and eat." The persecution of Jews in Medieval Europe made it unsafe to celebrate the *Seder* with the door open throughout the ceremony, so the ritual was modified; the family would first check to see if all was clear. This act has been retained in the *Seder* as a symbolic one, and today the door of the home is opened briefly during the *Seder.*

After the Middle Ages, another custom developed. An empty cup is now placed on the table and filled with wine for the prophet Elijah. According to tradition, Elijah did not die but was "translated" into heaven. Elijah is also the forerunner of the Messiah in the Jewish tradition. Elijah's cup in the *Seder* symbolizes both the humble wayfarer and the anticipation of the coming of the Messiah.

In the sixteenth century, still another ritual was added to the *Seder.* As the names of the ten plagues are recited, each person at the table deliberately "spills" wine into a saucer by dipping one's finger into the wine and "spilling" one drop of wine for each plague. In this way, the joy of drinking the wine is diminished with the recollection of the price of freedom: the lives of God's people were won with others' lives. This interesting ritual developed from a rabbinic story that said when the Hebrews crossed over the sea into safety and the pursuing Egyptians were

Figure 7.4 The Seder plate with its symbolic foods

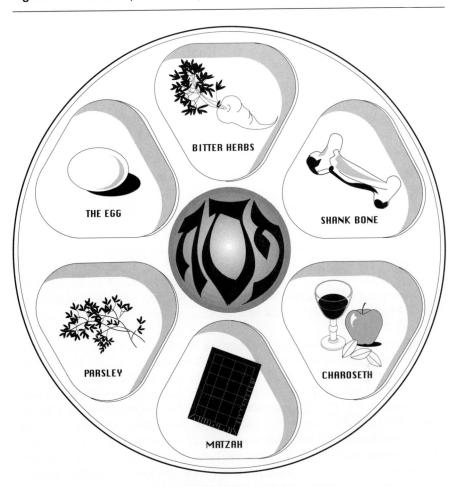

drowned, the angels wanted to sing. But God silenced them, saying, "What, human beings of my creation have drowned, and you want to sing?"

Six symbolic foods are placed on a special *Seder* plate in front of the leader (see Figure 7.4):

1. *matzah* (plural, *matzot*)—the unleavened "bread of affliction" that the Hebrews ate on the night they left Egypt. Tradition says that they left in such haste that there was no time to allow the bread to rise.

2. *charoseth*—a condiment made of apples or dates with nuts, cinnamon, and wine; resembling the mortar used by the Hebrew slaves in the Pharaoh's construction projects.

3. *maror*—bitter herbs, usually horseradish; symbolizes the bitter life of servitude.

4. *zeroah*—a roasted shank bone; symbolic of the Passover lamb.

5. *karpas*—a green, leafy vegetable such as celery, parsley, or watercress; a symbol of spring harvest. It is eaten after being dipped in salt water, which represents the tears shed by the Hebrew slaves.

6. *beitzah*—a roasted egg; symbolic of new life.

The fourteen steps enumerated in the *Haggadah* for performing the *Seder* include recital of blessings, washing of hands, eating the symbolic foods and the festive meal that follows, reciting psalms, and group singing. The leader ends the *Seder* by saying "Next Year in Jerusalem!" Since 1967, when all of Jerusalem came under Israeli administration, the leader often says instead, "Next year in rebuilt Jerusalem."

Victory at the Sea (Ex 13–15)

The Israelites leaving Egypt initially encountered the wilderness on Egypt's eastern border. This part of the book of Exodus includes stories concerning only the initial dangers faced in the wilderness. The later and more difficult perils of the wilderness sojourn are described in the book of Numbers. Inserted between this part of Exodus and Numbers are the legislative materials in the latter part of Exodus, the entire book of Leviticus, and the first part of Numbers (1:1–10:10).

Talking about the route that the escaping Israelites did *not* take poses fewer problems than plotting the course they did follow (see Figure 7.3). The text tells us that "God did not lead them by way of the land of the Philistines . . . [but] by the roundabout way of the wilderness toward the Red Sea" (or, as in the footnote, 'Sea of Reeds') (13:17–18). The "way of the land of the Philistines" is a known route from Egypt to Canaan, but the "way of the wilderness" cannot be pinpointed. Neither can we know for sure to what body of water the "Sea of Reeds" refers. Locating particular places becomes complicated by the sometimes fragmentary biblical data, most of the place names in the story cannot be identified today, and it is not certain that the biblical traditions are consistent. Some place names seem to have been invented in an *ad hoc* manner in response to an incident that occurred at a given site.

The most direct route from Egypt to Canaan runs parallel to the Mediterranean coastline. This route was taken by Egyptian Pharaohs on their military campaigns into Asia. The route called the "way of the land of the Philistines" (13:17) subsequently came to be called the "Way of the Sea" (Isa 9:1), and still later by its Latin name, *Via Maris.* Both routes are logically ruled out for the fleeing Israelites, as they would be guarded by the Egyptians. The only logical alternatives would be wilderness routes.

The phrase "Sea of Reeds" translates the Hebrew *yam suf.* This phrase has commonly been translated "Red Sea" in English translations. This translation goes back to the Vulgate's *Mare Rubrum* and *Mare Erythraeum,* which were derived from the Septuagint's *Erythra Thalassa,* "red sea." How the Red Sea got its name is unknown, nor is it clear why the Hebrew *yam suf* came to be connected with the Red Sea.

What is the "Sea of Reeds" if not the Red Sea? The name "Sea of Reeds" suggests a body of water with a growth of plants such as papyrus. The designation "Sea of Reeds" may refer to a whole network of marshy freshwater lakes that bordered the wilderness in the northeast delta region of Egypt. The *yam suf* that the Israelites crossed has been identified with no less than nine different bodies of water in various locations, and thirteen different sites have been suggested for Mount Sinai. (The locations shown in the map in Figure 7.3 are *traditional* locations).

While considerable doubt exists about what specific body of water is to be identified with the "Sea of Reeds," the narrator has no doubt at all about the tremendous significance of what happened there. Here the definitive victory of Yahweh over Egypt occurred. The "victory at the sea" is first described in prose in 13:17–14:30. In outline, what occurred was this: A strong east wind drove back the waters, allowing the Israelites to cross to the other side. The pursuing Egyptians tried to follow them, but their chariots became immobilized, and they drowned as the waters of the sea returned.

The prose account is followed by the poetic composition that marks the end of the first section of Exodus. In this poetic version, the victory at the sea is described with language influenced by an ancient Canaanite myth of a divine battle against *Yamm* (Sea). Yamm was the embodiment of the chaos that God overcame at the time of creation, which broke loose for a time during the great flood, and continued as a symbol of hostility to God's rule (cf. Ps 77:16–19; 114:3–6):

> "At the blast of your nostrils the waters piled up,
>> the floods stood up in a heap;
>> the deeps congealed in the heart of the sea,
> The enemy said, 'I will pursue, I will overtake,
>> I will divide the spoil, my desire shall have its fill of them.
>> I will draw my sword, my hand shall destroy them.'
> You blew with your wind, the sea covered them;
>> they sank like lead in the mighty waters." (Ex 15:8–10)

This "Song of Moses" (15:1–18) is the first celebration of a free people. In its present form it presupposes the later entrance into Canaan (15:13–15), and is probably a later cultic hymn. Later Israel celebrated her liberation in her worship with songs such as this. The first two lines of the "Song of Moses" are repeated in v. 21, where they are sung by Miriam, Moses' sister. Miriam is described as "the prophet, Aaron's sister" (15:20). There is an anti-Miriam tension that surfaces in Num 12, so that it is unlikely that the detail of Miriam's dance and song here was invented and probably represents the earliest tradition. Structurally, the important role given to women at the beginning of Exodus, including Miriam, surfaces again here and provides a device that brackets the beginning and end of the section Exodus 1–15. The importance of

An Imaginative Portrait of Moses

Whenever Hollywood cranks out a movie about him, they always give the part to somebody like Charlton Heston with some fake whiskers glued on. The truth of it is he probably looked a lot more like Tevye the milkman after ten rounds with Mohammed Ali.

Forty years of tramping around the wilderness with the Israelites was enough to take it out of anybody. When they weren't raising hell about running out of food, they were raising it about running out of water. They were always hankering after the fleshpots of Egypt and making bitter remarks about how they should have stayed home and let well enough alone. As soon as his back was turned, they started whooping it up around the Gold Calf, and when somebody stood up and said he ought to be thrown out, the motion was seconded by thousands. Any spare time he had left after taking care of things like that he spent trying to persuade God not to wipe them out altogether as they deserved.

And then, of course, there was the hardest blow of all. When he finally had it all but made and got them as far as the top of Mt. Pisgah, where the whole Promised Land stretched out before them as far as the eye could see, God spoke up and said this was the place all right, but for reasons which were never made entirely clear, Moses was not to enter it with them. So he died there in his one hundred and twentieth year, and after a month of hanging around and wishing they'd treated him better, the Israelites went on in without him.

Like Abraham before him and Noah before that, not to mention like a lot of others since, the figure of Moses breathing his last up there in the hills with his sore feet and aching back serves as a good example of the fact that when God puts the finger on people, their troubles have just begun.

And yet there's not a doubt in the world that in the last anaylsis Moses, like the rest of those tough old birds, wouldn't have had it any different. Hunkered down in the cleft of a rock once, with God's hand over him for added protection, he had been allowed to see the Glory itself passing by, and although all God let him see was the back part, it was something to hold on to for the rest of his life. And then there was one other thing that was even better than that.

Way back when he was just getting started and when out of the burning bush God had collared him for the first time, he had asked God what his name was, and God told him so that from then on he could get in touch with him any time he wanted. Nobody had ever known God's name before Moses did, and nobody would ever have known it afterwards except for his having passed it on; and with that thought in his heart up there on Pisgah, and with that name on his lips, and with the sunset in his whiskers, he became in the end a kind of burning bush himself.

Buechner (1991:110–12

women for the story is prominent at the beginning and the end of this section. The expansion of Miriam's song in the mouth of Moses is probably a later song in the same tradition, but both are acknowledged to be some of the oldest poetry in the Hebrew Bible. The "Song of Moses" is given special status in the traditional Jewish synagogue. When it is read in the synagogue, people stand, out of respect for its unique importance (a tradition also observed during the reading of the Ten Commandments).

Both songs celebrate what Yahweh has done. In the first half of the "Song of Moses" there is no mention of either Moses or Israel. Yahweh the warrior defeats the Pharaoh. But what God has done is not recounted apart from the specifics of the human situation. The second part of the song focuses on the people acquired as Yahweh's own because of the victory over Egypt.

Excursus 2: In What Sense Did Yahweh Bring Israel Out of Egypt?

In a recent commentary on the book of Exodus, written from the perspective of contemporary liberation theology in Latin America, George Pixley asks and seeks to answer the question, "In what sense did Yahweh bring Israel out of Egypt?" Pixley says that to the question "Who is God?" the Bible replies: "Yahweh, who brought us out of slavery in Egypt" (1987: 77). He goes on, however, to suggest that this profession of faith, the kernel of the faith of Israel, raises two serious questions, one historical and the other philosophical.

The historical question arises from the fact that Israel was a tribal alliance first formed in Canaan. The Levites (or whoever the group was that followed Moses) were incorporated into Israel only after they reached Palestine. Of course, this group that had come from bondage in Egypt was an important one in the formation of the identity of the young Israel. Strictly speaking, however, one cannot equate "Israel" with the group delivered from Egypt any more than one can equate "Americans" with passengers on the Mayflower and their descendants, even though we as Americans claim their story as part of the American experience, whether or not any of our own ancestors sailed on the Mayflower.

Pixley raises the philosophical question: "In what sense is it correct to speak of God as the agent of a historical event such as the liberation of the Hebrews?" In the account of the plagues, God is represented as the principal agent, attacking the Pharaoh and the Egyptians to make them let the Israelites leave. Pixley offers two extreme interpretations of the action of God in history. First there is the notion that God, external to the world, occasionally intervenes in the course of human affairs. God's action is distinct from human action; God is an exceptional cause to be contrasted with normal causes. Pixley says that this interpretation enjoys the advantage of permitting a more or less direct reading of any biblical passage that speaks of God's intervention in history. But it suffers from the fact that it rules out any criteria for recognizing divine activity other than that taking place in the absence of any other known cause. And it has the further, practical disadvantage of encouraging political passivity. Human political activity would imply a lack of faith in divine activity. Pixley believes that we should be able to develop an interpretation of divine initiative that will not detract from the value of active human involvement (77).

At the other extreme is the position that Israel only *believed* that God intervened. Exodus is only the expression of the faith of a primitive people, and such divine involvement has no objective reality. Again Pixley argues that if we deny the possibility of a genuine, objective divine participation, we postulate a humanity that will make history "by itself." The poor will be at the mercy of the mighty, and religion might serve to control the credulous masses, but not to instruct the elite. Pixley resists this view of history. He concludes: "Indeed, I believe that the history of philosophy can be of help to us in avoiding both the extremes here presented" (77-78). On the one hand, God does nothing, if by "do" we mean God is the exclusive agent. On the other hand, God does everything, if by "do" we mean that God is present in some way in every event, assisting it to realize its fullest and best potential. God is the co-creator of everything new that emerges in this historical world. So, Yahweh indeed delivered Israel from Egypt.

ISRAEL AT MOUNT SINAI (16–40)

In chapter 19 Israel finally arrives at Mount Sinai, the place where the nation will receive the Mosaic covenant. Once the issue of power has been settled and Yahweh's deliverance of Israel has established a bond between subjects and sovereign, appropriately, this people learn what their sovereign expects from them. After liberation comes covenant, an agreement made between God and God's people. Gottwald (1985: 202) has observed that "covenant" is an awkward and somewhat misleading term for the Hebrew word *berith* (as in the contemporary Jewish organization B'nai B'rith, which means "sons of the covenant"). The Hebrew term refers to a formal, solemn, and binding agreement between parties, an agreement that carries with it obligations to do or refrain from certain acts. Also involved are positive promises and negative threats of consequences that will follow on fulfillment or breach of the obligations. The English word "covenant" is now used in such specialized legal or sentimental contexts as to be very inadequate. Yet no other term fully grasps the meaning, although some aspects of *berith* may be better captured by terms such as "agreement," "arrangement," "compact," "contract," "commitment," "treaty," "alliance," "obligation," "bond," and "relationship."

God has made a commitment to Israel, and Israel accepts certain obligations in return. Yahweh, the liberator God, holds the place held by rulers in other nations. The first commandment given to the new Israel will be the prohibition of the worship of any God but Yahweh, the God of the Exodus, a commandment that has its political equivalent in a pledge of allegiance to a ruler. The remaining chapters of the book of Exodus are made up of legislative material that spells out the terms of the covenant. Here, then, is the constitutional basis of the new society of the people of Yahweh.

Suzerainty Treaty Form

The idea of a "covenant" between sovereign and people was not unique to Israel in the ancient world. The form of the Sinai covenant has been said to resemble the suzerainty treaties of the Hittites, a people who lived in what is now Turkey (Mendenhall 1955). The assumption is that Israel conceived of its relation to Yahweh as a subject people to a sovereign or suzerain. They therefore expressed the relationship in a form resembling the suzerainty treaty, a treaty between a sovereign and the people ruled.

It was once thought that this treaty form disappeared after the thirteenth century B.C.E. If so, then Moses, it was argued, devised the covenant form based on the treaty form before such treaties fell out of use. We now know that the suzerainty treaty form continued in use for centuries outside the Hittite Empire. The most that can be said is that Moses might have known about this treaty form. Also, possibly the treaty form only influenced Israel's views of the covenant at a later point. The important issue here concerns whether the suzerainty treaty form is mirrored in the biblical texts and whether the earliest covenant texts show dependence on it. Those who deny the treaty form in Exodus covenant traditions claim that the theophany replaces the historical prologue and that the curses and blessings are absent. Those who advocate treaty-form influence on the Mosaic covenant admit that the treaty schema in biblical texts has been altered. Instead of the formal text of a covenant, we have formulae taken from covenant rituals. These formulae, however, more closely correspond to the typical concepts and language of the suzerainty treaty form than they do to any other ancient Near Eastern forms of agreement (Gottwald 1985: 205, 207). The essential elements of the suzerainty treaty form, with biblical passages that have been claimed to correspond to these elements are as follows:

1. *Preamble* The treaty text frequently begins with the phrase "These are the words of . . ." Following this the suzerain gives his name and titles. The treaty is thus cast as a message from suzerain to subjects (cf. Ex 20:2a; Deut 5:6a; Josh 24:2a).

2. *Historical Prologue* In this section, the suzerain rehearses the past history between the treaty partners that forms the basis for making the treaty. The benevolent acts of the suzerain are emphasized, calling for gratitude in response (cf. Ex 20:2b; Deut 1–3, 5:6b; Josh 24:2b–13).

3. *Stipulations* This section contains the obligations imposed on the subordinate party to the treaty. First and foremost, the subject must not enter into any alliances with other suzerains. The subject must pledge to be a friend to the suzerain's friends and an enemy to the suzerain's enemies, coming to his aid in the time of war (cf. Ex 20:3–17; Deut 5:7–21; 12–26; Josh 24:14).

4. ***Deposit and Public Reading*** Typically there is a provision for depositing the treaty text in a temple, and for its periodic public reading (cf. Ex 25:21; 40:20; Deut 10:5; 27:2-3; 31:10-11).

5. ***List of Witnesses*** The gods of both parties to the treaty were listed as witnesses, with precedence given to the gods of the suzerain. In addition, natural features such as mountains, rivers, heaven and earth, wind, and clouds were cited as witnesses (cf. Josh 24:22, 27; Isa 1:2; Micah 6:1-2).

6. ***Blessings and Curses*** This part of the treaty consists of a list of good things that will result from obedience to the treaty and a list of evil things that will happen if the treaty stipulations are not obeyed (Deut 27-28).

The Ten Commandments (20:1–17)

In our journey through the Hebrew scriptures, we arrive here at what many would call the "center of the earth." If the Torah is the core of the Hebrew Bible, then the Ten Commandments, or the Decalogue, constitute the core of the Torah. Here is the essence of the covenant demands on Israel. Here is a classic within a classic. Solomon Goldman has artfully described the classic character of the Ten Commandments, which has made them one of the most familiar and valued parts of the Bible:

There is nothing ornate, circuitous, diffuse, or remote about them. The shortest of them, come upon us precipitately, like a rapid series of explosions. At first we barely distinguish them from one another. What re-echoes in our whole being is a resounding monosyllable, the Hebrew *lo* or the three English monosyllables "you shall not." The longest commandments are so phrased that the explanatory and completive matter can be peeled off without disturbing the essence or meaning, the intent or purpose of the law. . . .

The directness and familiarity of the language of the Decalogue [are striking]. From the first to the last commandment it is the singular "thine, thine, thou, thou." It is God speaking directly to every man [sic], pointing, as it were, His finger at him, impressing him with his worth, with his responsibility for action and that of his community. In the circumstances the individual is lifted out of the crowd, out of automatism, indifference, neutrality, and apathy. . . .

Age after age this miniature code, presented in the Bible much more as a thunderous overture to the rules and laws of the covenant between God and Israel than as a system of law in itself, has been acclaimed as the foundation-stone of civilization, the anchor of associative living, a comprehensive summation of the fundamental duties of a human being toward God and his neighbor, laying down the basic articles of religion—the sovereignty and spirituality of God, and asserting the claims of morality in the sphere of human relations—home, occupation, society, and though addressed to one people, far from national narrowness. Its very words, its Thou shalt and Thou shalt not, have come to symbolize faithfulness, virtue, uprightness, moral rectitude, scrupulousness, good behavior, and goodheartedness. They have come to be employed as synonyms for temperance, continence, self-restraint, and self-discipline. They have been accepted as directives to men how best to live among themselves and up to God. (1958: 613–15)

The phrase "The Ten Commandments" (in Hebrew, "the ten words," hence the name Decalogue or the Ten Words, as they are called in Judaism) occurs only in Ex 34:28. It occurs in connection with what is sometimes called "The Ritual Decalogue," because it concerns ritual and ceremony. The more familiar Ten Commandments are found in the list that appears in Ex 20:1–17. This familiar version of the Ten Commandments is paralleled by a very similar list in Deut 5:6–21. Although all three Decalogues are set at Sinai, the hand of late redactors has been discerned in all three.

THE FORM OF THE COMMANDMENTS

In form, the Decalogue in Ex 20:1–17 lists commandments addressed to the adult Israelite, worded in the second person singular masculine. They are expressed in categorical form, without any reference to mitigating circumstances. They do not specify any particular penalties that should be imposed on the lawbreaker. They represent a type of law that has been called apodictic. *Apodictic* law is stated absolutely, without any conditions. Apodictic law is characteristically Israelite, not common in other ancient Near Eastern law codes. The other type of law found in the Hebrew Bible, one that is common in the ancient Near East is called *casuistic* or case law. This law is typically stated in the form: if *x* occurs, then *y* will be the legal consequence. This type of law is found in the first part of the "Book of the Covenant" and in Deut 12–26. While case law in the Torah sometimes presupposes a later, agriculturally-based society, the apodictic form of the Ten Commandments is independent of any particular societal form.

Only two of the commandments, the one concerning the Sabbath and the one concerning parents, are expressed positively as "Thou shalts," whereas the other eight are prohibitions. The fact that most of the commandments are stated as prohibitions is significant in understanding the basic focus of the Decalogue. While in form they are addressed to individuals, their concern is not personal well-being but the health of the community. What these commandments state are minimal, not maximal requirements for community. They are expansive rather than restrictive; that is, they focus on outside limits on conduct rather than specific behaviors. The negative formulation suggests that the primary concern is not to create the human community but *to protect* it from behaviors that have the potential of destroying it.

Three of the prohibitions, those dealing with homicide, adultery, and theft, are stated in just two words in Hebrew, "No murder," "No adultery," and "No stealing." Four of the laws—those concerning the making of images, the Sabbath, parents, and coveting—have explanations or reasons appended, thus interfering with the rhythm of a series of briefly stated absolutes. These breaks in the rhythm have led scholars to suggest that the Decalogue was originally a unified list of short prohibitions or commands without any elaborations. The hypothetical "original" form of the Ten Commandments might look as follows:

1. You shall not have other gods before me.
2. You shall not make images for yourself.
3. You shall not misuse the name of Yahweh your God.
4. Remember the Sabbath day, to keep it holy.
5. Honor your father and your mother.
6. You shall not kill.
7. You shall not commit adultery.
8. You shall not steal.
9. You shall not bear false witness.
10. You shall not covet.

This listing represents the Protestant way of numbering the commandments. Jews read the statement in Ex 20:2, "I am the LORD your God, who brought you out of the land of Egypt, out of the house of slavery" (Ex 20:2) as the first commandment. To preserve a total of ten commandments, they combine commandments 1 and 2 in the above list. Roman Catholics, whose numbering of the Ten Commandments comes from Deut 5, combine commandments 1 and 2 above and divide the last of the commandments to form two commandments, one against covetousness of another's house and another against coveting his wife, servants, or animals.

THE LAW PRESENTED IN THE TEN COMMANDMENTS

Because the Ten Commandments are a basic statement of Mosaic law, we shall examine briefly each commandment.

1. *"You shall not have other gods before me"* (20:3). While there is some disagreement about how the phrase "before me" should be translated, there is no debate concerning the basic intent of this commandment. It demands exclusive loyalty to Yahweh on Israel's part. While it implicitly recognizes the existence of other deities, it says that Israel owes absolute allegiance to Yahweh, who makes the covenant with Israel. The existence of this commandment also suggests that idolatry, substituting something that is a human creation for the Creator, is a universal human problem, certainly one that causes Israel much grief in her history.

2. *"You shall not make images for yourself"* (20:4–6). This commandment is an extension of the first, and suggests the risks involved in any attempt to make an image of a deity, whether of Yahweh or of other gods. Given the first commandment, the reason for prohibiting images of other gods is obvious. But why the prohibition of images of Yahweh? It is, of course, impossible for the human mind to conceive of God in pure abstractions. Even words are symbols

that "image" God in one way or another. The feminist movement, for example, has pointed out the problems associated with using only masculine language in reference to God. To refer to God as "he" or "him," or to always call God "Father," may lead some to think that God is masculine. But the problem with imaging God goes deeper than this. The basic problem is that an image of God, any image, limits God by suggesting that God is this but not that. Images are static, not dynamic, and therefore fix God. Israel's God, by contrast, was to be seen as free from such human attempts to limit God. God's nature cannot faithfully be reflected in an image, but only in God's self-disclosure in nature, in history, and in the life of Israel itself. The ethical imperative is thus that Israel *be* an image of God rather than a maker of images.

3. *"You shall not misuse the name of Yahweh your God"* (20:7). One "image" of God in Hebraic thought was God's name because names were believed to represent the essence of one's nature. The familiar translation of this commandment (in the KJV and RSV) includes the phrase "in vain," which means "for nothing," "for a trivial purpose." This commandment is closely related to the one that precedes it because to use God's name cheaply makes the false assumption that knowing God's name gives human beings some kind of power over God, rather than letting God be God. This commandment prohibits using God's name as a kind of magic charm to achieve our own purposes instead of God's. It is a misuse of God's name, for example, to use the phrase "God damn you," to call down God's wrath on an enemy. Discussions of this commandment, however, have often trivialized it. It has commonly been associated with simple profanity. The simple thrust of the Hebrew phrase "for nothing," however, suggests that God's name can naively be associated with hollow phrases, or cheap religion, or the latest social or political trend.

Orthodox Jews "fence" this commandment by refusing even to say the name of God, thus insuring against its misuse. When an orthodox Jew encounters the name Yahweh in writing, the word *'adonay,* LORD, is substituted (thus the NRSV translation). Another substitution is simply *ha-shem,* "The Name." Out of respect for this Jewish tradition, God's name is sometimes written without the vowels as YHWH. The practice of substitution for the name of God is very old and was carried into the Christian Church. Both the Greek and the Latin Bible used the term "Lord" to translate YHWH. This practice also has a background in royal protocol in the ancient Near East. In the court, one never addressed the king (or his representative) by the first name nor did one use one's own first name. Rather one called oneself, "your servant" and the king "[my] Lord." In biblical narrative this is illustrated in the last meeting of Joseph and his brothers (Gen 44).

4. *"Remember the Sabbath day, to keep it holy"* (20:8-11). The basic meaning of "holy" in biblical Hebrew is "set apart" or "consecrated for a special purpose." The word "remember" seems to be a peculiar one at the beginning of a commandment. In the context of the book of Exodus as a whole, however, it recalls that Israel already observed the Sabbath, even in the wilderness (Ex 16). In the version of this commandment in Deut 5:12, it begins with the imperative

verb "Keep!" Another difference between the versions in Exodus and Deuteronomy is the rationale given for Sabbath observance. The rationale offered in the Deuteronomy version (5:15a), "Remember that you were a slave in the land of Egypt, and the LORD your God brought you out from there with a mighty hand and an outstretched arm," is what one might expect in Exodus. Instead, the Exodus version includes a reason based on God's resting after the creation, reflecting the P creation story in Genesis 1. Even in its earlier forms, this commandment must have stressed the need for a day of rest. But what can be said about the origins of the Sabbath as an Israelite institution? There have been attempts to link the Sabbath with the monthly Babylonian *sabbatu,* a day on which one ceased all ordinary activities because it was a day of ill omen. But the meaning of Israel's Sabbath is quite different. In Israel's legislation the Sabbath is a day of rest, and this makes a good deal of sense because Israel's law was spelling out principles for a people who worked as part of and for the sake of a community in rebellion against a state that demanded forced labor. In Israel, even the *ger,* the resident alien, as well as servants and animals would be guaranteed one day of rest a week. Curiously enough, the commandment makes no mention of worship on the Sabbath. Rather, the institution here seems to focus on human need. The human focus of the Sabbath is also reflected in the words of Jesus, "The Sabbath was made for man, not man for the Sabbath" (Mark 2:27). The humanitarian concerns associated with the Sabbath are emphasized in Ex 23:12; 34:21, and especially in Deut 5:14-15. Socially, the Sabbath is a fundamentally egalitarian institution. The Sabbath constantly reminds human beings that class divisions in human society are not built into God's creation. The Sabbath also gives a foretaste of a new world order, looking forward to the disappearance of social inequities. The humanitarian emphasis of this commandment serves as a bridge to the remaining commandments, all of which are concerned with human relationships.

5. *"Honor your father and your mother"* (20:12). The only other positive commandment concerns the institution of the family. At the center of human community is the relationship between children and parents. The survival of both the individual and the community rests upon this relationship. The positive formulation of this commandment, with the use of the rather open verb in English "honor," might suggest that this commandment does not dictate specific behaviors. In its ancient Near Eastern and Hebrew context, however, the verb "honor" is rooted in legal contracts that demanded that adopted children "honor" their parents. This meant they should provide for their material well-being when they were old and infirm. This understanding is also found in Jewish law in the Talmud, where "honor" means to care for. It is a commandment that asks children to behave in honorable ways toward their parents. Walter Harrelson has shown, however, that the commandment is more directed at adults rather than children (1981: 92-95). The formulation of this commandment covers the case where elderly parents are ignored or mistreated after they are no longer able to work or when their minds have lost their acuity. This commandment also includes parental treatment of children. It is worth noting that this commandment places father and mother on the same footing. Given the patriarchal nature of Israelite society, this is significant. If the commandment reflects the fact that parents represent God to their children, then the female as God's representative is even more noteworthy.

6. "*You shall not kill*" (20:13). While the verb "honor" in the previous commandment usually concerns dependent relationships in biblical language, the remaining commandments all have to do with relationships among social equals. This is the first of the two word commandments in Hebrew, and partly because of its brevity, this has been one of the most misunderstood of the commandments. This is a categorical command, allowing for no extenuating circumstances. Like other negatively stated commandments, it is about limits in human society. But what is the precise nature of the limits implied here? Based on the translation "Thou shalt not kill " in the KJV and RSV, this commandment has been appealed to by those concerned about a wide range of social issues. These have included abortion, war, capital punishment, suicide, self-defense, euthanasia, and even vegetarianism. In the context of Exodus, however, the Israelites did not see this commandment as prohibiting the killing of one's enemies in combat. Neither did they see it as excluding capital punishment by public stoning, when it was decreed by recognized community authorities. Our only clue about what is intended here is the specific verb used, the verb *r-ts-ch,* translated in the NRSV as "murder." There are three Hebrew verbs in the Old Testament that are translated "to kill." The other two are *h-r-g* and *m-w-t. R-ts-ch* occurs 46 times, *h-r-g* 75 times, and *m-w-t* 210 times (Stamm and Andrew 1967: 98-9). *R-ts-ch,* in the Hebrew Bible can refer to unintentional killing (Deut 4:41–42) or to the execution of a convicted killer (Num 35:30). In 1 Kings 21:19 it seems to mean "murder." It is, however, *never* used in the Hebrew Bible concerning killing in war. Originally, it seems to have been used concerning violent deaths, accidental or intentional, which called for vengeance. By the eighth century B.C.E., however, it was limited to referring to death by malicious intent (cf. Isa 1:21; Hos 6:9; Job 24:14; Prov 22:13; Ps 94:6). It thus appears that given changing historical circumstances, the meaning of this verb changed in ancient Israel over the years.

But, has not this change gone on over the years? Does not the development of nuclear weapons, which constitute a threat to God's creation unknown in all human history, give new meaning to the word "kill"? Certainly, the commandment itself implies a broadly defined reverence for human life. Although the ancient Israelites, and we as well, may have difficulties with understanding the specific reference of this commandment, it provides a standard by which any act of killing must be called into question and judged by human society (Harrelson 1981: 115). Other laws in the Bible will deal with specific cases of killing and in what cases there can be such a thing as "justifiable manslaughter," to use a modern legal term.

7. "*You shall not commit adultery*" (20:14). Like the fifth commandment, this one concerns the stability of the family. "Adultery" here is a verb, not a noun. This commandment is addressed to the male and might, therefore, appear to be limited to an Israelite male having respect for the sanctity of his fellow

Israelite's marriage. The verb here, *n-'-f*, is used elsewhere in Israelite law with both men and women as the subject and concerns both those who are married and those who are betrothed (Lev 18:6–20; 20:10–21; Deut 22:23–29). There is, however, a double standard in the law's treatment of men and women. A woman who was either engaged or married was guilty of committing adultery if she had sexual relations with anyone other than her husband or the man to whom she was engaged. An Israelite man, however, was only guilty of adultery if he had sex with the wife or wife-to-be of another man. A man sins against his male neighbor when he has sexual intercourse with his neighbor's wife—the sin is not against the woman involved. It was not considered adultery for a man, even if he were married, to have sexual relations with a prostitute. Sexual intercourse with a young unmarried woman, however, was regarded as an act requiring special measures, even if it was not considered adultery. From these different situations we may infer that this commandment was designed to safeguard the institution of marriage, which was seen in ancient Israel to be threatened more by the free conduct of a wife than by her husband. Certainly any contemporary application of this commandment should include equitable treatment of men and women, if it would be faithful to the biblical practice of updating laws in view of changing perspectives and social circumstances.

8. "*You shall not steal*" (20:15). This commandment is a categorical prohibition of theft. Property in ancient Israel was an extension of the "self" of its owner, however, so that theft of the neighbor's property amounted to a violation of the neighbor's person. Given the environmental limitations on agriculture in Palestine, ancient Israel's economy often struggled and was sometimes marginal. Property, often in the form of the tools needed to work the land or of stored produce of the land, amounted to life itself and thus had to be respected and protected. The penalty for theft, except the theft of an individual—kidnapping—was a fine or restitution.

9. "*You shall not bear false witness against your neighbor*" (20:16). The positive complement of this commandment emphasizes the importance of truth-telling in any community. The specific language of the commandment refers to giving witness in a legal proceeding, probably a kind of people's court, which continued to exist in Israel's life even after judges were appointed by the kings in later Israelite history. The extension of the commandment to telling falsehoods was a later development of the commandment's basic intent. Again, the concern went beyond the protection of the individual, and aimed at the maintenance of the community.

10. "*You shall not covet*" (20:17). The last of the commandments is perhaps the most subtle. While most of the other commandments concern overt behavior that could be dealt with by a popular tribunal, this commandment seems, at least on first reading, to be concerned with attitudes. Perhaps this is why there are no exact parallels to this commandment elsewhere in Israel's legal corpus. This commandment is closely related to the commandments concerning theft and adultery because it concerns the proclivity to violate another person's rights. The external act of taking what belongs to someone else is normally preceded by the internal attitude of coveting. The basic interpretive problem here is figuring out just what "covet" entails. How is "to covet" different from "to steal"? Pixley suggests a reasonable answer (1987: 139): either (1) coveting refers to the internal initiation of an external act, and stealing is the external act itself, or (2) coveting is the act of a superior who has the power to take overtly what is another's and stealing connotes that one feels forced to take what is another's secretly because of a lack of such power. Following Pixley's second possibility, this last commandment can be directed especially against the powerful, who can use their privileged resources to take possession of what belongs to their weaker neighbors. Thus Yahweh is seen to be the protector of the weak.

Biblical Law: The Book of the Covenant and Other Collections of Laws in the Torah

The Torah includes several collections of laws. Sinai serves as the geographical focal point for many of these, although as we shall point out below, the laws themselves often reflect the changing circumstances of the lives of a people, rather than the wilderness environment of a newly liberated Israel. In the Torah, the legal materials set at Sinai are the following:

1. The Book of the Covenant (civil and religious law) (Ex 20:22-23:33)
2. The Ritual Decalogue (Ex 34:10-26)
3. Priestly legislation—Cultic instructions (Ex 25-31, with their enactment in Ex 35-40); Priestly laws (Lev 1-18, 27); The Holiness Code (Lev 19-26); Priestly supplements (Num 1-10)

Still other bodies of legal materials in the Torah, not set at Sinai are:

1. Priestly supplements (Num 28-31; 33-36)
2. Deuteronomic Code (presented as the repetition of the laws given at Sinai = Deut 12-26)
3. Laws sanctioned by a curse (Deut 27)

The Book of the Covenant (Ex 20:22–23:33)

Except for Islamic countries, the laws of modern nation states have a fundamentally secular outlook. They are not based on clearly stated religious principles and deal with religious matters only when they become the specific object of public or private law. In the ancient Near East however, law had a religious basis, whether it was dealing with specifically religious matters or not. This is reflected in the fact that it was perceived that the gods mediated the law to human beings, usually to a reigning sovereign. This is symbolized, for example, in the stele bearing the Code of Hammurabi in ancient Babylon (eighteenth century B.C.E.) On the top of the stele is a representation of the sun god Shamash, the Babylonian god of justice, handing over the symbols of authority to Hammurabi (see Figure 7.5).

In Israel, the emphasis on the religious character of law is obvious from the beginning of the Decalogue: "I am the LORD your God, who brought you out of

Figure 7.5   Hammurabi's Code

the land of Egypt, out of slavery" (Ex 20:1). Like other issues in biblical study, the question of the relationship between biblical and ancient Near Eastern law has been raised in modern times with the discovery and analysis of ancient Near Eastern law codes from Mesopotamia. There are eight major cuneiform documents that preserve laws from ancient Mesopotamia, as listed below:

Sumerian
  1. The Reform of Uru'inimgina (also known as Urukagina)
     —*ca.* 2350 B.C.E.
  2. Laws of Ur-Nammu—*ca.* 2050 B.C.E.
  3. Laws of Lipit-Ishtar—*ca.* 1875 B.C.E.

Old Babylonian
  4. Laws of Eshnunna—nineteenth century B.C.E.
  5. Code of Hammurabi—sponsored by Hammurabi
     (1792–1750 B.C.E.)
  6. Edict of Ammitsaduqa—sponsored by Ammitsaduqa
     (1646–1626 B.C.E.)

Middle Assyrian
   7. Middle Assyrian Laws—twelfth century B.C.E.

Old Hittite
   8. Hittite Laws—seventeenth century B.C.E.

Acknowledging the danger of oversimplification, the similarities and differences in biblical and Mesopotamian law are summarized in Table 7.2 (Walton 1989: 91).

The collection of civil and religious laws in Ex 20:22–23:33 for which the Decalogue serves as an introduction has been called "The Book of the Covenant" from the phrase that occurs in Ex 24:7. The laws are presented as if they were given directly to Moses, but closer examination reveals that they developed over time to serve the changing needs of the Israelite community. Unlike the Decalogue, this collection of laws lacks a coherent structure, but has a rather eclectic character. It has often been conjectured that the Book of the Covenant is a collection of laws that presupposes the formal establishment of legal administration in Israel. It seems more probable, however, that the Book of the Covenant is not a list of laws that were in force at any particular period in

TABLE 7.2 Comparative Summary of Biblical and Mesopotamian Law

SIMILARITIES	
CONTENT	
Both contain civil and criminal law	
Both cover similar topics using similar wording	
FORM	
Casuistic formulations	
FUNCTION	
Both serve "admonitory" function	
Both seek to demonstrate adherence to contractual obligations	

DIFFERENCES	
CONTENT	
Biblical	*Mesopotamian*
Less emphasis on civil law than religious law	No religious law
Penalties show different elements of concern, even when the problem's formulation is the same	Focus on civil law
FORM	
Apodictic basis for casuistic form	Very little apodictic form
FUNCTION	
Morality is goal	Justice is goal
More prescriptive	More descriptive
Adherence to covenant	Adherence to cosmic order
God reveals	Gods monitor

Israel's history. It does, however, presuppose an agriculturally-based community. This compilation of laws is probably the oldest one in the Bible, and reflects the popular justice of pre-state Israel. As a whole, its function is a religious one—to build on the principles of the Ten Commandments. In its present setting the Book of the Covenant is as much religion and ethics as law. It prescribes societal norms for the people of Yahweh. It is Yahweh who is the guarantor of the observance of the laws, so that the covenant relationship between God and people can be maintained.

The Book of the Covenant is bracketed by an introduction (20:18-26) and a conclusion (23:20-33). The introduction serves as a redactional note for inserting the Book of the Covenant at this point in the book of Exodus. Between the introduction and conclusion, the book is divided into two sections, based on the type of laws. The first section (21:1-22:20) contains casuistic laws. It specifies cases and describes penalties for infractions that threaten the basic order of society. The laws afford more generous treatment to men than women (21:1-11), and less severe punishment for a person who injures a slave than for a person who injures someone who is not a slave (21:12-14, 18-19). The laws in this section are not directly tied to the Yahwistic faith, but are conservative in their orientation, reflecting to a considerable extent the social milieu of the ancient Near East.

The second section (22:21-23:19) contains apodictic laws. In contrast to the conservative bent of the case laws, the material in this section is intimately connected with the Yahwistic faith. It thus helps us reconstruct a picture of how early Israel ordered its communal life as an extension of inferences drawn from the nature of the God who liberated them. This section goes beyond the maintenance of social order to set forth patterns of ethical behavior concerned with social justice. Behind these laws is a knowledge of Yahweh as one who acts in behalf of the socially marginalized—the poor, widows, orphans, and those "foreigners" who did not have citizenship in the community. The contents of the two sections can be summarized in the following list:

SECTION ONE (21:1–22:20)—CASE LAW

1. Laws dealing with the institution of slavery, specifically with the limitations on the power of a master over his Hebrew slaves, and the legal rights of slaves (21:2-11).

2. Laws dealing with the administration of capital punishment for four crimes: (1) first-degree murder (as distinct from accidental homicide); (2) assault on parents; (3) cursing parents; and (4) kidnapping (21:12-17).

3. Laws dealing with various kinds of physical injury inflicted by one person on another. Included in this subsection is the famous *lex talionis,* "eye for eye, tooth for tooth" [21:24] (21:18-27).

4. Laws dealing with various kinds of physical injury caused by or to domestic animals (21:28-36).

5. Laws dealing with the theft of domestic animals and burglary (22:1-3).

6. Laws dealing with compensation for damage to someone else's crops (22:4–5).

7. Laws dealing with restitution in the case of the loss of or damage to personal property entrusted to another for safekeeping or on loan (22:6–14).

8. Laws dealing with the liability of one who seduces a virgin not yet betrothed (22:15–16).

SECTION TWO (22:21–23:19)—APODICTIC LAW

1. Miscellaneous laws, many of which relate to the treatment of those who are socially marginalized: (1) the treatment of strangers, widows, and orphans (22:21–24); (2) the lending of money to the poor (22:25–27); and (3) a warning against oppressing the stranger (23:9).

2. Laws dealing with the sabbatical year, the sabbath, and the three major feasts (23:10–19).

It is instructive to compare this early corpus of Israelite law with other ancient Near Eastern law codes. Sometimes, the similarities are striking, especially in the area of civil law. Compare, for example the following laws as they are found in the Code of Hammurabi and in the Book of the Covenant:

Goring Ox

Hammurabi (Article 251): "If a member of the aristocracy is gored by the ox of an ordinary citizen, who neither tethered the animal, nor blunted its horns, even after the city council put the owner on notice that the animal was dangerous, then the owner's fine is eighteen ounces of silver" (Matthews and Benjamin 1991: 67).

Book of the Covenant: "When an ox gores a man or a woman to death, the ox shall be stoned, and its flesh shall not be eaten; but the owner of the ox shall not be liable. If the ox has been accustomed to gore in the past, and its owner has been warned but has not restrained it, and it kills a man or a woman, the ox shall be stoned, and its owner also shall be put to death" (Ex 21:28–29).

Damages

Hammurabi (Articles 196–197): "If a citizen blinds an eye of a member of the establishment, then the sentence is the blinding of an eye. If one citizen breaks a bone of another, then the sentence is the breaking of a bone" (Matthews and Benjamin 1991: 66).

Book of the Covenant: "When people who are fighting injure a pregnant woman so there is a miscarriage, and yet no further harm follows, the one responsible shall be fined what the woman's husband demands, paying as much as the judges determine. If any harm follows, then you shall give life for life, eye for eye, tooth for tooth, hand for hand, foot for foot, burn for burn, wound for wound, stripe for stripe" (Ex 21:22–25).

Lie Detection

Hammurabi (Article 107): "When a merchant entrusted (something) to a trader and the trader has returned to this merchant whatever the merchant gave him, if the merchant has then disputed with him whatever the trader gave him, that trader shall prove it against the merchant in the presence of god and witnesses and the merchant shall pay to the trader sixfold whatever he received because he had a dispute with his trader" (ANET 17).

Book of the Covenant: "If someone delivers to a neighbor money or goods for safekeeping, and they are stolen out from the neighbor's house, then the thief, if caught, shall pay double. If the thief is not caught, the owner of the house shall be brought before God [apparently some kind of ordeal experience], to determine whether or not the owner had laid hands on the neighbor's goods. In any case of disputed ownership involving ox, donkey, sheep, clothing, or for any other loss of which one says, 'This is mine,' the case of both parties shall come before God; the one whom God condemns shall pay double to the other" (Ex 22:7-9).

Restitution for Theft

Hammurabi (Article 8): "If a citizen steals an ox or a sheep from an official of the government or the temple, then the fine is thirty times the value of the stolen livestock; likewise, if one citizen steals an ox or a sheep from another, then the fine is ten times the value of the stolen livestock; however, if a thief fails to pay the fine imposed for stealing livestock, then the sentence is death" (Matthews and Benjamin 1991: 63).

Book of the Covenant: "When someone steals an ox or a sheep, and slaughters it or sells it, the thief shall pay five oxen for an ox and four sheep for a sheep. The thief shall make restitution, but if unable to do so, shall be sold for the theft. When the animal, whether ox or donkey or sheep, is found alive in the thief's possession, the thief shall pay double" (Ex 22:1,4).

Housebreaking

Hammurabi (Article 21): "If one citizen tunnels through the wall of another's house and robs it, then the sentence is death. The execution shall take place outside the tunnel, and the convict's body used to fill in the tunnel" (Matthews and Benjamin 1991: 63).

Book of the Covenant: "If a thief is found breaking in, and is beaten to death, no bloodguilt is incurred; but if it happens after sunrise, bloodguilt is incurred" (Ex 22:2-3).

Child Striking Parent

Hammurabi (Article 195): "If a citizen strikes his father, then the sentence is the amputation of a hand" (Matthews and Benjamin 1991: 66).

Book of the Covenant: "Whoever strikes father or mother shall be put to death" (Ex 21:15).

Cultic Legislation: Exodus 25–31 and The Book of Leviticus

Israel's ritual laws are found primarily in Ex 25 - 31 and in the book of Leviticus, which takes its name from the fact that the Levites were the designated, hereditary priests of Israel. These laws are concerned with the following issues.

IN EXODUS

1. The ark of the covenant and the tabernacle (25 - 27)
2. Priestly vestments (28)
3. Ordination of priests and related matters (29 - 31)

IN LEVITICUS

1. Laws dealing with sacrifices (1 - 7)
2. Consecration of the priesthood (8 - 10)
3. Distinction between things that are clean and those that are unclean (11 - 15)
4. The Day of Atonement (Yom Kippur) (16)
5. Laws concerning Israel's "holiness" (17 - 26)
6. Religious vows (27)

Exodus 25 begins the last section of the book, one in which priestly law accounts for the establishment of two cultic institutions—the ark of the covenant and the tabernacle—together with the setting apart of a hereditary Levitical priesthood as the custodian of these two institutions. The laws in this section of priestly law (which actually continues throughout Leviticus and into the tenth chapter of Numbers) are interspersed with narrative. The name "priestly" here is descriptive, and should not be equated with the Pentateuchal source of the same name. Authorship of these materials used to be credited to a hypothetical "Priestly Writer," but today scholars are more cautious on the subject.

THE TABERNACLE

Nearly one-third of the entire book of Exodus is given over to matters regarding the tabernacle, regarded here as Israel's sanctuary in the wilderness, a tentlike structure that Moses built to house the ark (see Figure 7.6). Ex 25 - 30 contains the directions for its building and the account of its actual construction is found in Ex 35 - 40. Graf, who with Wellhausen formulated the Documentary Hypothesis in its classical form, argued that the Tabernacle was a literary fiction. He thought that it was created out of whole cloth by someone living in the days of the second Jerusalem temple (built following the Exile, beginning in 520 B.C.E.). It was nothing more nor less than a literary transportation of the second temple back into the days of Moses. There is no doubt about the importance of the Tabernacle in the Bible, given the volume of material devoted to it. The picture sketched of the tabernacle, however, does raise questions about to what extent the tabernacle can be considered a historical reality during the wilderness period.

Figure 7.6 The tabernacle

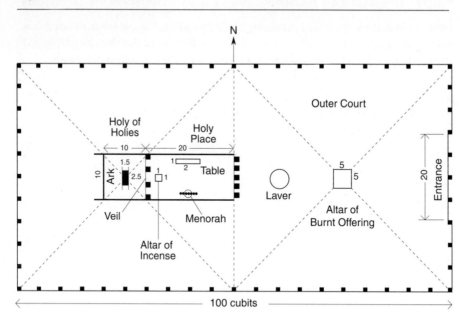

In the history of biblical interpretation, there have been several approaches to the study of the extensive block of material devoted to the Tabernacle. One of the most prevalent perspectives, for both Jews and Christians, is an allegorical or symbolic one. This approach says that "What you see is *not* what you get." Behind all the physical description and detail is a concealed spiritual meaning. Historical interpretations, on the other hand, see the text as an actual plan for a physical structure, either recreating the tent sanctuary or constructing a temple on its plan. Another approach is to study the tabernacle in terms of the development of ideas and institutions associated with God's earthly dwelling place. Those scholars using this approach conclude that the tabernacle is a literary creation of a later author, modeled on the second temple in Jerusalem. This approach prevailed in much biblical scholarship until recently; now the account is more often seen as more dependent upon an evolving tent tradition. This tradition was rooted in the ancient tent of meeting, the tent at Shiloh, and the tent that David built for the ark (and perhaps other tent shrines from the ancient world). "Rather than simply being an echo of the temple, in fact, this account may even be anti-temple in its understanding of God, who is not localized but on the move with Israel" (Fretheim 1991: 266).

Literary approaches to the Tabernacle materials have only recently begun to emerge. One of the more intriguing of these is that of Gabriel Josipovici (1988: 93-107). Josipovici begins his analysis with the observation that nowhere else in the Bible do we get repetition on such a grand scale as we do here. God first tells Moses exactly how the Tabernacle is to be built, how it is to be furnished, and what vestments the priests are to wear. Then, after the golden calf episode, we are told exactly how the Tabernacle was built, how it was furnished, and what vestments were made for the priests. Josipovici sees this repetition as the very point of the text. He suggests that if we think about what is happening to us as we read instead of what the text is saying, we may be able to understand the function of the descriptions. The text never allows us to stand back and contemplate the finished object. The emphasis is always on process—making, weaving, joining—not on the completed structure. And it is a process we readily accede to because for us too there has been a process: the process of reading. In neither case—the erecting of the tent or reading—do we have the finished object before us. We can only read, which means experience, it as an *unfolding.*

The other cultic institution in this section of Exodus, the ark of the covenant, is now a familiar object to many modern readers (if in somewhat fanciful form), thanks to the exploits of Indiana Jones. The ark (described in Ex 25) was nothing more than a rectangular wooden box with rings attached to its corners, through which passed the rods with which it was carried. The most important thing about the ark was that it was portable. It thus provided a fitting symbol for the presence of Yahweh moving with the people. It was regarded as a seat on which God sat, and thus, by extension, represented God. Moses, at one point (Num 10:35-36) addressed the ark as God.

The Holiness Code (Lev 17–26)

Another collection of priestly law, which has sometimes been identified as a separate law code (although its full extent is debated) is Lev 17-26, commonly called the Holiness Code. Called this because of the reiterated demand that Israel should be "holy" because God is holy (19:2 and elsewhere), this block of priestly law can best be understood in terms of its content and ideology. It deals with various kinds of ritual "pollution" caused by food (ch. 11), childbirth (ch. 12), disease (13-14), sex (15), blood (17), incest (18, 20), injustice (19), and death (21). Purification rituals are given, and priesthood and ceremonial are discussed in detail (16, 21-26).

When one compares these chapters in Leviticus to the Book of the Covenant, some marked dissimilarities appear. As we have observed, much of the Book of the Covenant deals with civil damages but does not mention priests. By contrast, the Holiness Code includes only six verses about damages (24:17-22) but concentrates on priests and their responsibilities. While there is limited similarity in content, there is a marked difference in perspective. The Holiness Code, as implied in the basic meaning of the word "holy" as "set apart," insists that the holiness of God requires a strict separation between priests and people, and between Israel and other peoples.

Because priests occupied the middle ground between the people and God, and functioned as links with God, special demands of ritual purity were imposed on them and their families. Lev 21:16-23 lays down these requirements for both priests and the high priest. Included are requirements regarding marriage, contact with corpses, and the sexual behavior of priests' daughters.

For ordinary people, the Holiness Code focuses on three things: sexual relations, religious life, and social relationships. Concerning sexual relations, chapters 18 and 20 prescribe degrees of relatedness within which sexual intercourse is prohibited and set boundaries regarding both marriage and incest. There is no way of knowing to what extent these regulations were enforced, or to what degree they could have been enforced. The prohibitions against homosexual acts (18:22; 20:13) and against intercourse with animals (18:23; 20:15-16) are probably to be seen in terms of preventing the violation of a perceived natural order in which men, women, and animals are "holy," that is, "set apart" for specific functions that should not be confused. When dealing with the people's religious life, the Holiness Code is much more detailed than the Book of the Covenant. Like the Book of the Covenant, the Holiness Code deals with the religious festivals (cf. Ex 23:14-17 and Lev 23:4-8, 15-22, 33-36). The Holiness Code is more concerned, however, with holiness on an everyday basis, the religious as it impinges on ordinary life.

The opening chapter of the Holiness Code (17) deals with the proper disposal of blood. Blood obviously has powerful religious and ceremonial symbolism from the priestly point of view. This symbolism carries over into New Testament explanations of the meaning of the death of Jesus on the cross. While we might think of blood as staining, the priestly point of view is just the opposite—blood cleanses that which has been stained by misdeeds. Given this strange, mystical power of blood, it must be handled carefully, even in the most mundane of circumstances.

Regulations concerning social relationships are included in two chapters in the Holiness Code, chapters 19 and 25. Whereas the basis of such regulations in the Book of the Covenant rested on the maintenance of social solidarity, here the emphasis is on mutual religious responsibility. This is especially evident in chapter 25, where laws prohibiting charging interest and release of servants are linked with the regulations about what is called the "jubilee year." The jubilee year, which is to occur every fiftieth year, had as its purpose the cancellation of all debts, the freeing of all Israelite slaves, and the reversion of real estate that had been sold to its original owner. It is doubtful whether such legislation was ever enforced, but it does embody a powerful ideal in which those societal acts that might serve to create a group of permanently poor persons could be undone and social equity restored.

The Holiness Code concludes in chapter 26 with God's promise that if these laws are kept, the land, the source of Israel's livelihood, would remain productive. If, on the other hand, these regulations were disregarded, Israel would lose the land. The very end of the Holiness Code (26:39-45) is addressed to "a people without a land and a land without a people"—an Israel who has lost its land and is sitting in Babylonian Exile:

> "And those of you who survive shall languish in the land of your enemies because of the iniquities; also they shall languish because of the iniquities

of their ancestors. But if they confess their iniquity and the iniquity of their ancestors, in that they committed treachery against me, and moreover that they continued hostile to me—so that I, in turn, continued hostile to them and brought them into the land of their enemies; if then their uncircumcised heart is humbled and they make amends for their iniquity; then I will remember my covenant with Jacob; I will remember also my covenant with Isaac and also my covenant with Abraham, and I will remember the land. For the land shall be deserted by them, and enjoy its sabbath years by lying desolate without them, while they shall make amends for their iniquity, because they dared to spurn my ordinances, and they abhorred my statues. Yet for all that, when they are in the land of their enemies, I will not spurn them, or abhor them so as to destroy them utterly and break my covenant with them, for I am the LORD their God; but I will remember in their favor the covenant with their ancestors whom I brought out of the land of Egypt in the sight of the nations, to be their God; I am the LORD". (Lev 26:39—45)

Laws in Deuteronomy (Deut 12–26)

The book of Deuteronomy stands as a conclusion to the Torah and as an introduction to the deuteronomistic history work. The name of the book in the Hebrew Bible is "These are the Words," taken from the words with which it begins. Early Jewish tradition called Deuteronomy *mishneh torah,* "a repetition of the Torah," based on Deut 17:18. The name Deuteronomy in English is derived from two Greek words, *deuteros* and *nomos,* which together mean "the second law." This name in turn comes from the fact that the book is cast as Moses' reiteration, in a sermon in Moab just before he died, of the narratives and laws found in Exodus-Numbers.

The author of Deuteronomy draws heavily on the Book of the Covenant, producing in effect a second edition of it, with modifications and new laws. In fact, the central chapters of the book of Deuteronomy (12-26) include laws that treat issues that are left untouched elsewhere in the Hebrew Bible. Some of the laws that are peculiar to Deuteronomy are: procedures for establishing courts and judges (16-17), regulations governing the conduct of war (20), and divorce (24). There is one regulation, however, that more than any other, is special to Deuteronomy—the law that mandates that sacrifices should be made to God *only* at one central sanctuary, chosen by God.

UNITY

Rogerson and Davies maintain that the basic idea that unites the regulations in Deuteronomy is the need for unity (1989: 246-247). There is one central sanctuary, and individuals or groups who worship elsewhere must be punished severely. False prophets who support other gods will be eliminated. Judges' decisions are to be accepted unconditionally. Rules about warfare imply the duty of all Israelites to serve in the army, though some exemptions are allowed. Along with the focus on the unity of the people and their absolute loyalty to God, Deuteronomy contains some of the most humane regulations anywhere in the Old Testament and is especially remarkable for its positive attitude toward women. Rogerson and Davies believe that when we bring the two themes of unity and humanitarianism together, we get the essence of Deuteronomy. The former guarantees the latter. Only a people that is fully united under God can be obedient to the calls for fair-dealing and compassion that characterize the book. Even the king himself is part of this unity, and is subject to its regulations.

COMPARED TO THE HOLINESS CODE

Rogerson and Davies also offer a perceptive comparison of the laws of Deuteronomy with the Holiness Code (1989: 249–250). If the Holiness Code sees purity in separateness, Deuteronomy understands purity more in ethical terms, and sees its expression as a matter of justice and compassion for the poor. Deuteronomy retains an emphasis on details of ritual as they affect purity, but priestly language and ideas are missing. In the Holiness Code the land will be restored to Israel when the number of ignored sabbatical years has been made good (and then out of consideration for the covenant with the ancestors). In Deuteronomy the land will be restored when Israel seeks God with all its heart and soul. The purpose of the Exodus in the Holiness Code was the creation of a people set apart from others by religious purity. For Deuteronomy its purpose was to create a people distinguished by their morality. While the religious element in Deuteronomy might appear to be dominant, it is in fact subordinate. The problem with the worship of other gods is simply the fact that they did not bring Israel out of slavery in Egypt. They cannot, therefore, command and inspire the type of society that truly reflects the nature of the God of Israel.

Excursus 3: Exodus as Liberation and is Exodus Enough?

We conclude this chapter by reflecting on the theme of liberation, which suffuses the first fifteen chapters of Exodus and echoes throughout the pages of the Hebrew scriptures. As Michael Walzer has reminded us (1985), many of the world's oppressed and excluded have drawn on the paradigm of Exodus to imagine their liberation. The book of Exodus has been the principal text of modern liberation movements, especially those in Latin America and South Africa. Zionism has long used it as a source of images and rhetoric supporting the national liberation of the Jewish people. These movements are associated with what has been called liberation theology. In Latin America, in the centuries following the Spanish and Portuguese conquests, the Roman Catholic Church was established throughout Central and South America. The Church, however, was unfortunately often allied with corrupt and brutal political regimes, as was so vividly portrayed in the movie *The Mission*. The Church was generally perceived as more concerned with the maintenance of the status quo than with the proclamation of the biblical message with its challenges to the established order. Similarly, following the Dutch colonial takeover of South Africa, the Dutch Reformed Church was the dominant church of the white leaders of South Africa. The Church not only did not oppose apartheid but until recently offered a theological rationale in support of apartheid.

For several reasons the liberation struggle in both areas has focused with particular strength on the Hebrew Bible, especially on the Exodus traditions. The perspective of J. Severino Croatto, a Latin American theologian, is shared by many in modern liberation movements:

> The Exodus is an event fraught with meaning, as indicated by the biblical account and the experience of Israel, and . . . it is still *unconcluded.* If our reading of the biblical kerygma [message or proclamation] means anything, the "memory" of the Exodus becomes a provocative Word, and announcement of liberation for us, the oppressed peoples of the Third World. We are enjoined to prolong the Exodus event because it was not an event solely for the Hebrews but rather the manifestations of a liberative plan from God for all peoples. . . . It is perfectly possible that we might understand ourselves *from* the perspective of the biblical Exodus and, above all, that we might understand the Exodus *from* the vantage point of our situation as peoples in economic, political, social or cultural "bondage." (Croatto 1981: 14–15)

The Exodus paradigm, as used in both Latin America and South Africa, includes the recognition that a class struggle is going on, that God is aware of the struggle, that God takes sides in the struggle, and that God calls people to join in the struggle. Most (North) Americans, when using the concept of class, use an approach in which classes are seen as strata, or layers. The classes are seen as stacked on top of one another, much as sedimentary rock strata are in geology. Classes are identified by ranking them from top to bottom. The most common indicator used for ranking the classes is wealth. In liberation theology, however, another approach is taken. Following a theoretical perspective developed by Karl Marx, a class is seen as a group of people who have a similar relationship to the process of production in a society. The process of production is one that manufactures all of the goods and services that people use in their daily lives. Each society has a particular class structure depending on the way in which such goods are produced and on the way in which the work force is organized. Peoples' interests are determined to a large degree by their relationship to the process of production. The major classes are seen as always being in a state of either potential or actual conflict because of their different interests.

Certainly the book of Exodus assumes class struggle. It is, as we have seen, a story of masters and slaves, kings and chattel, oppressors and oppressed, owners and workers. There are clearly two classes of people involved, and they are locked in struggle. Exodus, however, moves from a sociological account of a struggle in which the oppressed have come to believe that they are powerless to produce change, to the theological assertion that God is aware of the struggle; not only aware, but takes sides in the struggle. And, as is the pattern throughout the Bible, God sides with the powerless rather than the powerful. This God promises liberation from oppression *and* liberation to live as a new kind of society in a Promised Land. The people, trusting in the promises of Yahweh, are empowered to be the agents of their own liberation—God will not do it without their help. These, then, are the principal theological themes of liberation theology that are derived from Exodus.

Arthur Waskow has recently written a piece titled "Exodus is Not Enough" (1990). While he acknowledges that the Exodus paradigm remains crucial, he suggests that in our generation it is not enough—either for Jewish self-identity or for anyone's version of liberation and social transformation. He contrasts "the Genesis path" and "the Exodus revolution." As we saw in our journey through Genesis, the theme of conflict within and between families, beginning with Cain's murder of Abel, was replayed again and again. Waskow declares that the Torah suggests that after Cain slew Abel, God's will became clearer and more definite: justice and ultimately peace required that the younger, the lesser, the weaker, be redefined as the 'firstborn' and wield a wider authority. The rule of ordinary history, in which the rich get richer and the strong get stronger must be reversed. But the weaker must just not launch a "revolution" in which the revolving door of history makes them the new insiders. The goal is rather reconciliation, followed by the dissolution of the conflict itself. So Genesis teaches, according to Waskow.

He goes on to assert that the story of Exodus seems at first glance to be quite different. In the liberation of the People Israel from slavery in Egypt there is no reconciliation. The victory over Pharaoh opens the way to Israel's liberation. Only permanent departure from Egypt secures their freedom. The Exodus pattern serves as the model for modern revolutions and liberations, national and social, where the saving remnant hopes to wipe out oppression and corruption, depart physically or politically from their oppressors and corruptors, and remake their society. The Exodus pattern has been so powerful that we have paid little attention to the alternative that emerges from Genesis: the war between and then the peace of brothers, sisters.

Waskow concludes that in the world today, there is more and more reason to pursue the path of Genesis whenever we can. There is simply no way to "depart" from the powerful, seldom any way to smash them without breaking ourselves as well. Women cannot "depart" from men; African-Americans cannot depart from white America; Jews cannot really depart from Western or Arab civilization [and, we might add, black South Africans cannot depart from white South Africans]" (Waskow 1990: 518–519).

To the traditional Passover Seder, Waskow has added questions that incorporate into the ritual of the Passover Seder his reflections in "Exodus is Not Enough."

"Why is this Pesach [Passover] night different from every other Pesach night?"

Because on every Pesach night— tonight as well—
We call out to another people, "Let our people go!"

But tonight we also hear another people
Calling out to us: "Let *our* people go!"
Tonight the children of Hagar and Ishmael
and the children of Sarah and Isaac
call out to each other:
We too are children of Abraham!
We are cousins, you and we!
As Isaac and Ishmael once met
at the Well of the Living One Who Sees,
So it is time for us to meet—
Time for us to see each other, face to face.
Time for us to make peace with each other.
They met for the sake of their dead father, Abraham;
We must meet for the sake of our dead children—
Dead at each other's hands.
For the sake of our children's children,
So that they not learn to kill
And so tonight we must ask ourselves four more questions:

(1) Why does the Torah teach: 'When a stranger lives-as-a stranger with you in your land, you shall not oppress him. The stranger who lives-as-a-stranger . . . with you shall be one of your citizens; you shall love her as yourself.'

'For you were strangers in the Land of Egypt.'

(2) Why do we break the matzah in two?

Because the bread of affliction becomes the bread of freedom—when we share it. Because the Land that gives bread to two peoples must be divided in two, so that both peoples may eat of it. So long as one people grasps the whole land, it is a land of affliction. When each people eat from part of the Land, it will become a land of freedom.

(3) Why do we dip herbs twice, once in salt water and once in sweet charoset?

First for the tears of our two peoples, Israeli and Palestinian; then for the sweetness of two peoples, Palestinian and Israeli; for the future of both peoples, who must learn not to repeat the sorrows of the past but to create the joys of the future.

(4) Why is there an egg upon the Pesach plate?

It is the egg of birthing. When we went forth from Mitzrayim [Egypt], the Narrow Place, it was the birthtime of our people, the People of Israel; and today we are witnessing the birth of freedom for another people, the People of Palestine.
When the midwives Shifrah and Puah
Save the children that Pharaoh ordered them to kill,
That was the beginning of the birth-time;
When Pharaoh's daughter joined with Miriam
To give a second birth to Moses from the waters
She birthed herself anew into God's daughter, Bat-yah,
And our people turned to draw ourself toward life.
When God became our Midwife
And named us Her firstborn,

Though we were the smallest and youngest of the peoples,
The birthing began;
When the waters of the Red Sea broke,
We were delivered.
So tonight it is our task to help the Midwife
Who tonight is giving birth to a new people—
And so to give a new birth to ourselves." (Waskow 1990: 525–526)

STUDY QUESTIONS

1. Why do you think there is so little historical detail in the biblical story of the Exodus?
2. Find some symbols in the Exodus and covenant story besides those mentioned in this chapter and briefly discuss how they contribute to your understanding of the story.
3. Aaron, Miriam, and Jethro are important secondary characters in the Exodus and covenant story. Discuss the roles they play. What is the role of Aaron in Ex 6:2–77 compared to his place in the call of Moses in Ex 3–4? What is a possible explanation for the differences?
4. What connection between law and covenant does Exodus presuppose?
5. Read Ex 3–4. List four objections Moses made when God told him to return to Egypt and rescue the Hebrews. Next to each objection, write God's response.
6. The word *know* appears several times in Exodus 7–12. Go through these chapters and note every place the word occurs. What is it that God wants both the Egyptians and the Hebrews to know? Use chapter and verse citations for each point you make.
7. Can the plagues be both natural and miraculous at the same time? Explain your answer.
8. How is God depicted in the songs of Ex 15?

THE TEN COMMANDMENTS (EXODUS 20 AND DEUTERONOMY 5)

1. Read the two versions of the Ten Commandments (in Ex 20 and Deut 5) carefully. Which commandments differ in the two versions? Note some of the significant differences. How might you account for such differences?
2. How are "religious" and "social" commandments related in the Decalogue? Which commandments are "religious" in nature; which are "social"? Can you discern any significance in the order in which the commandments appear?
3. In what sense can the Ten Commandments be regarded as ethical guidelines for contemporary society? Are there some of the commandments that need to be altered for use today? Are there any that should be discarded as antiquated?

THE BOOK OF THE COVENANT (EXODUS 20:22–23:33)

1. Ex 23:20-33 has been considered to be a later addition to the Book of the Covenant. Can you give some evidence that would support such an assessment? How does this section fit in with the laws that precede it in 20:22-23:19? Is this latter section a legal text?

2. Compare and contrast the parallel laws in the Book of the Covenant and in Hammurabi's Code cited in the text. Pay particular attention to similarities and differences with respect to: harshness of penalty, distinctions between property and personal crimes, recognition of class differences, and the attention given to motivation for obeying the laws and sanctions for disobeying them.

3. Form criticism is concerned with the specific social context in which particular literary forms (genres) were used. Our lives are governed by numerous laws and regulations; some of these come from the local, state, or federal government, others come from the college or from family. Hearing just part of a law can sometimes indicate its social context: for example, contrast "Be sure you are in by midnight on week nights!" with "Possession or consumption of alcoholic beverages by minors is a violation punishable by. . . ." Assign each of the two literary forms of laws in the Book of the Covenant (apodictic and casuistic) to a specific social context. Do the activities associated with a particular category tend to be similar? What area of society is most concerned with such activities? Would one of these two groups of laws most likely be civil law enforced by the state? Or family law supervised by a family head? Or religious law governed by priests? and so on.

BIBLIOGRAPHY

Ahlström, G. W., and Edelman, Diana. 1985. "Merneptah's Israel." *Journal of Near Eastern Studies 44/1* (January): 59-61.

Coggins, R. J. 1990. *Introducing the Old Testament.* New York: Oxford University Press.

Croatto, J. Severino. 1981. *Exodus: A Hermeneutics of Freedom.* Maryknoll, N.Y.: Orbis.

Fokkelman, J. P. 1987. "Exodus." *The Literary Guide to the Bible,* Robert Alter and Frank Kermode, eds. Cambridge: Harvard University Press, 56-65.

Fretheim, Terence E. 1991. *Exodus.* Interpretation: A Bible Commentary for Teaching and Preaching. Louisville: John Knox.

Goldman, Solomon. 1958. *From Slavery to Freedom.* New York: Abelard Schuman.

Gottwald, Norman K. 1985. *The Hebrew Bible: A Socio-Literary Introduction.* Philadelphia: Fortress.

Har-El, M. 1973. *The Sinai Journeys: The Route of the Exodus in the Light of the Historical Geography of the Sinai Peninsula.* Tel-Aviv: Am Oved.

Harrelson, Walter. 1981. *The Ten Commandments and Human Rights.* Philadelphia: Fortress.

Josipovici, Gabriel. 1988. *The Book of God: A Response to the Bible.* New Haven: Yale University.

Lemche, N. P. 1988. *Ancient Israel: A New History of Israelite Society.* Sheffield, England: JSOT.

Matthews, Victor H., and Benjamin, Don C. 1991. *Old Testament Parallels: Laws and Stories from the Ancient Near East.* New York: Paulist.

Mendenhall, George E. 1955. *Law and Covenant in Israel and the Ancient Near East.* Pittsburgh: Biblical Colloquium.

Pixley, George V. 1987. *On Exodus: A Liberation Perspective.* Tr. Robert R. Barr. Maryknoll, N.Y.: Orbis.

Rogerson, John, and Davies, Philip. 1989. *The Old Testament World.* Englewood Cliffs, N.J.: Prentice Hall.

Shanks, Herschel. 1981. "The Exodus and the Crossing of the Red Sea, According to Hans Goedicke." *Biblical Archaeology Review 6/5* (September/October): 42-50.

Stamm, J. J., and Andrew, M. E. 1967. *The Ten Commandments in Recent Research.* London: SCMP.

Stiebing, William H. 1989. *Out of the Desert?: Archaeology and the Exodus/Conquest Narratives.* Buffalo, N.Y.: Prometheus.

Walton, John H. 1989. *Ancient Israelite Literature in its Cultural Context: A Survey of Parallels between Biblical and Ancient Near Eastern Texts.* Grand Rapids: Zondervan.

Walzer, Michael. 1985. *Exodus and Revolution.* New York: Basic Books.

Waskow, Arthur. 1990. "Exodus is Not Enough." *Cross Currents* (Winter, 1990): 516-25.

PART
III

THE FORMER AND
LATTER PROPHETS
IN THE
HEBREW CANON

Chapter 8

ISRAEL—A PEOPLE AND A LAND: JOSHUA AND JUDGES

Suggested Bible Reading
Joshua 1 - 24; Judges 1 - 21

*W*e have now reached a critical point in our journey—one where many who have traveled this way before us have come to a parting of the ways. *No questions in the study of biblical history and religion have been more intensely debated than those with which we deal in this chapter. The first set of questions concerns how Israel acquired her territory in the hill country of Canaan. The second set asks what kind of sociopolitical organization the early Israelites had in the years before the formation of the Israelite state. For many biblical scholars, this is the earliest part of Israel's story that can be recovered historically, the place where the distinctive socioreligious entity known as "Israel" first comes clearly into focus (cf. the first extrabiblical mention of Israel in the

Merneptah Stele—see Chapter 7), two centuries before the formation of the Israelite state under David.

While the historical reality underlying the biblical text has been the subject of spirited debate among biblical scholars in recent years, they agree that the Hebrew Bible makes the *theme* of the Promised Land a central component of God's covenant with Israel. This covenant began with the promise to the patriarchs and matriarchs and was reaffirmed in the narratives about the Exodus. The fulfillment of this promise comes in those narratives that follow an ill-defined group of slaves as they achieved deliverance from oppression in Egypt, through their victory at sea and wandering in the wilderness, into the Promised Land where they "miraculously" acquired land on which to settle and a clear identity as a people. The central proclamation of all the Hebrew Bible is the bold claim that God was uniquely revealed in the events of the Exodus from Egypt and the possession of the Promised Land. Everything else is commentary. The brief historical credo in Deut 6:20–25 summarizes this belief:

> "When your children ask you in time to come, 'What is the meaning of the decrees and statutes and the ordinances that the LORD our God has commanded you?' then you shall say to your children, 'We were Pharaoh's slaves in Egypt, but the LORD brought us out of Egypt with a mighty hand. The LORD displayed before our eyes great and awesome signs and wonders against Egypt, against Pharaoh and all his household. He brought us out from there in order to bring us in, to give us the land that he promised on oath to our ancestors. Then the LORD commanded us to observe all these statutes, to fear the LORD our God, for our lasting good, so as to keep us alive, as is now the case. If we diligently observe this entire commandment before the LORD our God, as he has commanded us, we will be in the right.'"

LITERARY GENRES IN JOSHUA AND JUDGES

The biblical text that deals with the last phases of the wandering in the wilderness through the conquest and settlement of Canaan is found in Numbers 13–31 and in the books of Joshua and Judges. Numbers 13 has the Israelite tribes in the wilderness at the oasis of Kadesh-barnea. It also describes the sending of spies into the land of Canaan; the unhappiness of the people with the leadership of Moses and Aaron; the initial entry into the land with victories over the Canaanites at Arad and Hormah; encounters with Amorites, Midianites, and Moabites, and later clashes in Ammon and Bashan in the Transjordan; a census in Moab preparatory to the crossing of the Jordan (thus the title of the book of Numbers); and ends with the ritual preparations for holy war in the camp opposite Jericho in the Jordan Valley. The narrative resumes in the last chapter of Deuteronomy, which tells of the death of Moses in Transjordan.

Figure 8.1   Part one of Joshua's campaigns according to the book of Joshua

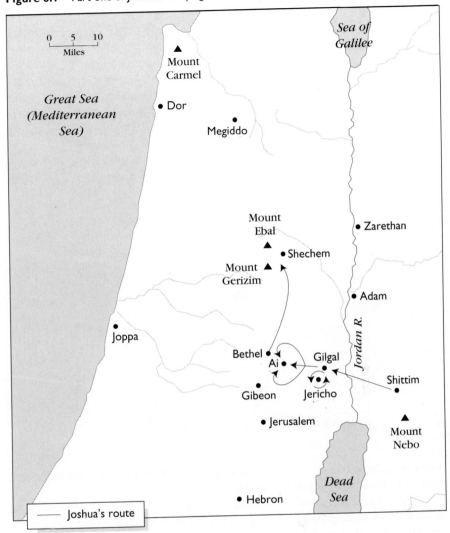

The book of Joshua takes its name from the figure of Joshua, the successor to Moses. Joshua leads the people across the Jordan near Jericho and penetrates into the highlands north of Jerusalem at Gibeon (Josh 2–9) (see Figure 8.1). From Gibeon a southward campaign secures the Judean highlands and foothills (Josh 10:28–39) (see Figure 8.2), while a northern one reduces the coast, Galilee, and the northern Jordan valley (Josh 11:1–11) (see Figure 8.3). In these campaigns, numerous cities and regions are said to have been occupied or to have been taken and destroyed. This conquered land (and that remaining

Figure 8.2   Part two of Joshua's campaigns according to the book of Joshua

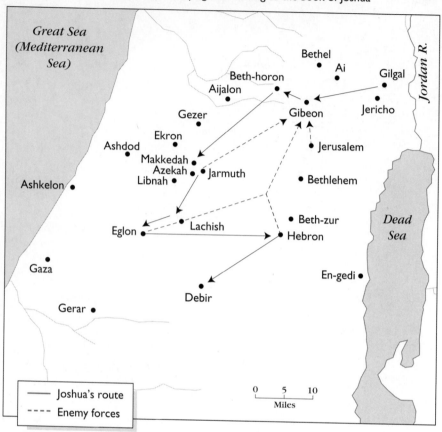

to be conquered) was then divided among the twelve tribes of Israel in the second half of the book of Joshua (see Figure 8.4).

The book of Judges takes its name from the charismatic tribal figures who emerged as leaders of Israel (variously called "deliverers" and "judges") in a series of crises. These crises were provoked by the fact that there were still Canaanites in the land who, from time to time, threatened to displace the Israelites. The book of Judges concludes with stories of tribal disunity and humiliation and with the editorial comment, written from a later perspective that saw the monarchy as the key to social order, "In those days there was no king in Israel; all the people did what was right in their own eyes" (Judg 21:25).

The books of Joshua and Judges contain a wide range of units of tradition that represent several literary types. Both books are part of a composite work that has been called the Deuteronomistic History, which begins with Deuteronomy and continues through 1 and 2 Samuel and 1 and 2 Kings. Joshua and

Figure 8.3   Part three of Joshua's campaigns according to the book of Joshua

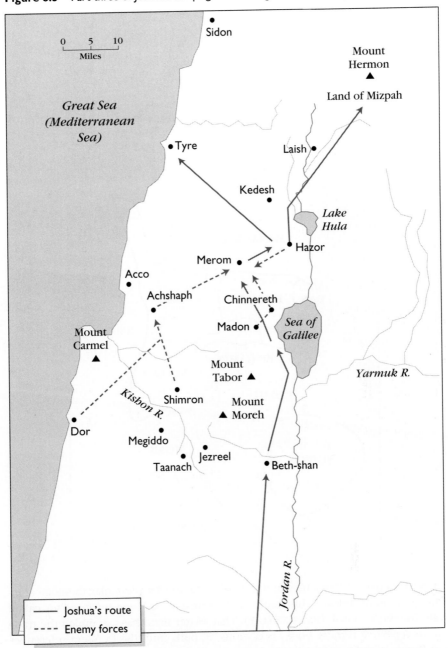

Figure 8.4 The tribal allotments according to the book of Joshua

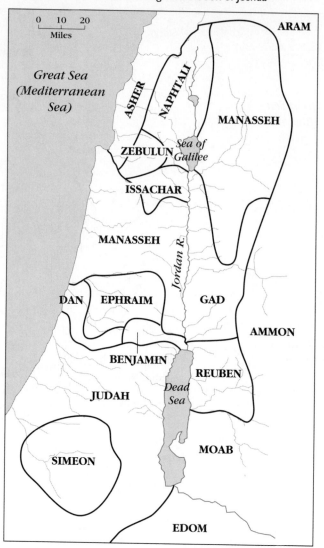

Judges, as part of this larger unit, bear the stamp of a particular theological interpretation of history. This stamp was impressed on them by an editor called the Deuteronomistic Historian (Dtr). That a later hand has assembled the traditions reported in these books is obvious, in part, from the frequent references to things in the future as if they existed during this early period. For example, iron is mentioned in describing chariots and implements (compare Judg 1:19; 4:3), although evidence shows iron did not replace bronze for such things for about another two centuries. Camels, which do not appear in the Near East as domesticated beasts of burden until the ninth century B.C.E., are mentioned often in Judges. In fact, the plot of the Gideon story in Judg 6-8 depends on camels (compare Judg 6:5; 7:12; 8:21, 26). Kings are mentioned ruling Moab (Judg 2:12-30; 11:25) and Ammon (Judg 11:13, 28), although these monarchies did not come into existence before the ninth century B.C.E. Similarly, the hand of an editor (Dtr) can be detected by the fact that conflicting traditions are not well integrated. Some cities are mentioned as having been taken twice in the record (for example, Bethel: Josh 12:16; Judg 1:23), others three times (for example, Hebron: Josh 10:36 ff; 15:13; Judg 1:10; Debir: Josh 10:38 ff.; 15:15-17; Judg 1:11; Hormah: Num 21:3; Josh 12:14; Judg 1:17). A careful reading of these books requires that the reader give balanced attention to both the content *and* the form of the separate tradition units. One should also be alert for the sometimes artificial and propagandistic editorial hand that has brought together what were originally discrete and diverse traditions.

The major divisions in Joshua and Judges and the literary types represented are as follows:

1. Joshua 1-12: Describes Israel's conquest of much of the Canaanite territory west of the Jordan River, led by Joshua in three major campaigns (Central, chs. 1-10; Southern, ch. 10; Northern, ch. 11). The dominant literary form here is a chain of *sagas* or legends. The term "legend" sometimes appears in English-language, form-critical study as a translation of the German *sage* or the Norse *saga*. Although the lines between them are fluid, it is possible to differentiate between legends or sagas, fairy tales, and myths. The sagas in these chapters of Joshua include etiological legends that explain the origins of place names (the tell of Ai in chs. 7-8) and natural phenomena (the stones of Makkedah in ch. 10).

2. Joshua 13-22: These chapters tell of the apportionment of land among the tribes of Israel. The primary literary form in this section consists of lists: boundary inventories, city inventories, and regional inventories. Interspersed among these lists are *annals* that tell of the activities of a single tribe.

3. Joshua 23-24: These two chapters include the farewell addresses of Joshua.

4. Judges 1: The first chapter of Judges is an account of the incomplete nature of the conquest, resulting in the inability of the Israelites to take effective possession of the land. The literary form used here is a string of *annals,* or tribal narratives that tell of the struggles (largely unsuccessful) of individual tribes to gain control of their allotted territory.

5. Judges 2: This chapter serves as a theological introduction to the stories about the "judges." This introduction consists of a theological *discourse* from the hand of the Deuteronomistic Historian.

6. Judges 3-16: The central part of Judges consists of narratives concerning the exploits of individual "judges/deliverers." This main section of Judges

contains several literary forms. The dominant form is the *saga.* Mixed with the sagas are two series of *annals* with annotations (10:1–5; 12:8–15). Judges 5, known as the Song of Deborah (to which we will return below) is a *hymn* or *song of victory.* Included in chapter 9 (vv. 7–15) is a *fable,* and the Samson story includes a *riddle* (14:14, 18). A fable is a story with "a moral" in which animals and other animate objects speak. A riddle is a "trick question" that sometimes involves a pun or play on words.

7. Judges 17–21: These chapters at the end of Judges include two stories about tribal disunity and pre-state social pathology. The book of Judges concludes with two lengthy *sagas.*

As part of the Deuteronomistic History, the books of Joshua and Judges bear the stamp of the Deuteronomistic Historian's distinctive theological view of the history of early Israel. For the Deuteronomistic Historian, the era of Joshua represented the completion of the program to take possession of the land, a program that had been frustrated by the sins of Moses and the people. Joshua and those under his leadership are pictured as faithful to Yahweh; those disloyal are singled out and punished so as not to "contaminate" the whole people and endanger their possession of the land. The land is shown as having been conquered and settled in Joshua's lifetime. Joshua promises the people that the unconquered parts of the land will be taken if the people remain faithful to Yahweh.

The imprint of the Deuteronomistic Historian's hand is seen also in Judges as a cyclical pattern, repeated again and again. The cycle is initiated by the unfaithfulness of Israel, which results in the Israelites' oppression by non-Israelite peoples. In response to the Israelites' cries of suffering, Yahweh raises charismatic leaders to deliver the people. When the delivery is accomplished, however, the people again forsake Yahweh, and the cycle begins again. In response to the people's continuing unfaithfulness, Yahweh is pictured as resolving not to eliminate all of Israel's enemies. Rather, they are left to be a "thorn in Israel's side" to help the Israelites learn the bitter lessons of warfare brought on by unfaithfulness.

MODELS FOR RECONSTRUCTING THE SETTLEMENT OF ISRAEL IN CANAAN

On first reading, the book of Joshua gives the impression of a straightforward historical account, describing Joshua and the Israelites as they enter the land by crossing the Jordan River from the east, miraculously capture Jericho, and then go on to take the rest of Canaan in three rapid, coordinated military campaigns. The passage concludes with a summary statement: "So Joshua defeated the whole land, the hill country and the Negeb and the lowland and the slopes, and all their kings; he left no one remaining, but utterly destroyed all that breathed, as the LORD God of Israel commanded" (Josh 10:40). The description in Joshua is so graphic and seemingly forthright, that many casual biblical readers have never questioned the picture presented there.

Without importing anything from outside the Bible, we find a strikingly different picture of "conquest" emerge as soon as we leave Joshua and read the first chapter of Judges. The account in Judges presumably knows of Joshua, because it locates itself temporally after the death of Joshua (1:1). The Judges account, however, seems to know nothing of the sweepingly successful military campaigns of Joshua and subsequent allotment of land among the tribes. Even the sequence of conquest followed by dividing up the land among the tribes is reversed in Judges; there, the land is first allotted and then conquered. Most of Judges 1 tells of scattered operations of individual tribes (sometimes working together with another tribe) rather than a coordinated effort by all Israel to take possession of the land. In contrast to the sweeping summary statement in Josh 10:40, sites *not* captured are listed (thirty in all), and formulaic phrases are given the form "X could not drive out Y" or "X did not drive out Y." The sites listed as not having been captured in Judges 1 are hardly peripheral ones. They are some of the most strategic and important ones in the later history of Israel: Jerusalem, Beth-shean, Ta'anach, Megiddo, Gezer, and Beth-Shemesh. This opening chapter of Judges, and indeed the rest of the book of Judges, pictures the possession of the land of Canaan by the Israelites as a "cultural conquest" that took many years. It was characterized by Israelites and Canaanites living side-by-side, with a gradual process of cultural change in which, in the end, Israel was the dominant cultural entity.

The reader is left with the distinct impression that Joshua and Judges are so at odds with one another as to preclude any harmonization. One cannot argue that one represents the "biblical" view over the other, because both are "biblical" views. Key to resolving this dilemma is in the recognition that *both* Joshua and Judges, as part of the Deuteronomistic History, were given their present form long after the settlement in Canaan took place. What we have in the books of Joshua and Judges represents the "official" view of later editors, who had access to traditions and sources that no longer exist. The editors had their own theological reasons for citing sources (unknown to us) such as the Book of Jashar (Josh 10:12-13). In attempting to understand the Israelite appearance and settlement in Canaan, while we have the disadvantage of not having access to such sources, we have the advantage of having three kinds of material at our disposal. First, we have the traditions preserved in parts of Numbers, Joshua, and Judges; second, we have extra-biblical textual evidence; and third, we have archaeological evidence. Our job as students of the Bible is to evaluate *all* of the evidence available to us—the biblical evidence, the extra-biblical textual data, and the archaeological evidence—and then to formulate a reconstruction that takes *all* of the evidence into account.

Three basic models of reconstruction of Israel's entry and settlement in the land have been proposed that can serve as guides for us in evaluating the evidence: (1) a conquest model; (2) an immigration model; and (3) a social revolution model.

The Conquest Model

The conquest model for understanding the Israelite settlement takes its cue from the conquest as related in the book of Joshua. This model guided the efforts of "biblical archaeology" in its formative years. In the excavation of tells, archaeologists concentrated on destruction layers that could be dated to the end of the Late Bronze Age and/or to the beginning of the Iron Age (*ca.* 1200 B.C.E.) and would provide evidence, so they believed, of the Israelite conquest. The Albright school accepted a fixed date of 1200 B.C.E. for the conquest based on extra-biblical textual data from Egypt. Especially important for this purpose were the Amarna Letters, the Merneptah Stele, and texts and pictures from the wall of an Egyptian temple at Medinet Habu.

THE AMARNA LETTERS, MERNEPTAH STELE, AND AN EGYPTIAN TEMPLE

The Amarna Letters, mentioned in the previous chapter, constitute some 350 tablets found at el-Amarna, the capital of Akhenaton in the fourteenth century B.C.E. These letters are the correspondence between Egypt and her vassal rulers in Syria-Palestine, which was at the time a part of the Asian empire of Egypt. These letters deal mostly with appeals from the vassal princes to the Pharaoh for military and economic assistance. The letters contain a wealth of information about the political, social, and economic conditions in Canaan at the time, and thus have been used to reconstruct the situation in Canaan immediately preceding the Israelite "conquest." Appearing in the Amarna Letters is a group of social bandits who make trouble for the Egyptian vassals. They are known as the *'Apiru,* a word etymologically related in East Semitic to the West Semitic term translated "Hebrew." The ethnic identification of *'Apiru* (or *Habiru*) with Hebrew, however, is not justified, though it has been used by some to support a fifteenth-century date for the Exodus, maintaining that the Amarna Letters represented evidence for the Hebrews already being in Canaan. However, the Albright school used the evidence from the Amarna Letters to support the weakening of Egyptian control over her Asiatic empire at the end of the Late Bronze Age, a weakening that paved the way for the Exodus and conquest. The evidence from the Amarna Letters about the *'Apiru* has been used in a different way by those favoring the social revolution model, as we shall see below. The Albright school based the correlation of late thirteenth-century destruction levels at some Palestinian sites with an Israelite conquest on evidence from the Merneptah Stele (see Chapter 7). For these scholars, this text showed beyond doubt that by 1210 B.C.E. a group of people known as Israel by the Egyptians was well enough established in Canaan that they posed a threat to Egyptian control there.

The third Egyptian text used to back up the historicity of an Israelite conquest at the Late Bronze-Iron Age horizon was found on the walls of an Egyptian temple at Medinet Habu. It tells of a clash in the eighth year of Rameses III (*ca.* 1175 B.C.E.) between the Egyptians and the "Sea Peoples," one subgroup of whom was the Philistines, who appear in the Bible as Israel's contemporaries and co-competitors for Canaanite land.

The cumulative evidence of these and other texts led the Albright school to fix the date of the Israelite conquest at *ca.* 1200 B.C.E., a date they then sought to confirm through archaeological evidence. That evidence was provided by what they saw as a major stratigraphic and cultural break in excavated sites that signaled the appearance of a new people occupying a site after its destruction.

JERICHO

What can be said today about the archaeological evidence that has been used to support a conquest model? How does it "match up" with the story told in the Bible? A test case in this regard is the city of Jericho. Jericho appears in the book of Joshua as the first Canaanite city to be conquered by the invading Israelites, with the well-known detail that "the wall fell down flat" (Josh 6:20). For any assessment of the agreement between archaeological evidence and the biblical text, Jericho thus becomes an important test site. The first excavations at Jericho were conducted by a German team from 1907 to 1909, when the science of archaeology was still in its infancy, with few reliable methods of dating finds. The report for this dig concluded that Canaanite Jericho had indeed been destroyed, but in 1600 B.C.E., a date that was too early even for the fifteenth-century date of the Exodus supported by many scholars at that time. The inescapable conclusion of this first excavation of Jericho was that there was no city there to be destroyed by Joshua.

In the 1930s, the English archaeologist John Garstang, whose work we referred to in Chapter 3, returned to Jericho to test the Germans' conclusions. Garstang presupposed a fifteenth-century B.C.E. date for the Exodus and the conquest in Joshua. He found a mudbrick city wall system that had fallen, together with evidence of destruction by fire. He dated these fallen walls to the fifteenth century B.C.E. and identified them with the walls of Jericho that had fallen before Joshua. Although Garstang's conclusions have been repudiated by later work on the site by Kathleen Kenyon, one still finds them referred to in many conservative biblical handbooks and commentaries (as if they were the last word, archaeologically speaking) as an example of archaeology proving the truth of the Bible.

The third archaeological expedition to Jericho was led by another British archaeologist, the late Dame Kathleen Kenyon. Kenyon worked at Jericho from 1952 to 1958. She used vastly improved techniques for controlling the site's stratigraphic excavation and thus for assigning dates to strata. Kenyon reconstructed Jericho's occupational history from its initial settlement in the Neolithic period (*ca.* 9000 B.C.E.) Kenyon established beyond any doubt that Garstang's collapsed mudbrick wall was in fact destroyed in the Early Bronze Age, *ca.* 2400 B.C.E., or about 900 years earlier than Garstang had claimed. She also found evidence of many wall collapses from the Early Bronze period (3200–2300 B.C.E.) which she attributed not to military campaigns but to the fact that Jericho is situated in a zone of frequent earthquakes. Even more striking than her refutation of Garstang's chronology was Kenyon's confirmation of the fact that there simply was *no* Late Bronze occupation at Jericho after 1350 B.C.E. Thus there was no occupation at all at the site in the time of Joshua, now reckoned in the thirteenth century (Kenyon 1957: 167-72, 256-63). Table 8.1, Archaeological Periods in Palestine, shows the dates for the different archaeological periods.

TABLE 8.1: Archaeological Periods in Palestine

ARCHAEOLOGICAL PERIODS	DATE
PALEOLITHIC	25,000–10,000 B.C.E.
MESOLITHIC	10,000–8000
NEOLITHIC	8000–5000
Pre-Pottery	8000–6000
Pottery	6000–5000
CHALCOLITHIC	5000–3400
Early	5000–3800
Late	3800–3400
EARLY BRONZE	3400–2000
Early Bronze I	3400–3100
Early Bronze II	3100–2650
Early Bronze III	2650–2350
Early Bronze IV	2350–2000
MIDDLE BRONZE	2000–1500
Middle Bronze I	2000–1800
Middle Bronze II	1800–1650
Middle Bronze III	1650–1500
LATE BRONZE	1500–1200
Late Bronze IA	1500–1450
Late Bronze IB	1450–1400
Late Bronze IIA	1400–1300
Late Bronze IIB	1300–1200
IRON AGE	1200–539
Iron Age IA	1200–1100
Iron Age IB	1100–1000
Iron Age IC	1000–900
Iron Age IIA	900–800
Iron Age IIB	800–722
Iron Age IIC	722–586
Iron Age III	586–539
PERSIAN	539–323
HELLENISTIC	323–37
ROMAN	37 B.C.E.–324 C.E.

AI

The next site to have been conquered by the Israelites according to the book of Joshua was Ai (Josh 7 – 8). The location of Ai is precisely noted: "near Beth-aven, east of Bethel" (Josh 7:2). The site of et-Tell, identified as the biblical Ai, also attracted excavators in the 1930s, when the French archaeologist Judith Marquet-Krause dug there. Her results were not unlike those of Kenyon at Jericho. Here again evidence showed the site's destruction in the Early Bronze Age *ca.* 2400 B.C.E., followed by its abandonment until Iron I, *ca.* 1200 B.C.E., when a village similar to other Israelite settlements in the central hills was established. This constitutes clear archaeological evidence for the lack of correlation between the story in Joshua 8, with all its topographic and tactical details, and historical reality. The archaeological evidence showed that there was no Canaanite city at Ai to be destroyed by the Israelites. A second expedition to Ai was led by the American archaeologist, Joseph Callaway, who worked there from 1964 to 1976. Callaway's results essentially confirmed those of Marquet-Krause. Callaway, however, attempted to resolve the inconsistency between the biblical account and the results of his archaeological work by suggesting that the city conquered by Joshua was the first phase of the small Iron Age I village on the site. Callaway's proposal is difficult to accept. The first phase of the Iron I village is basically the same as the second phase, and no major destruction layer separates them. In any case, the unwalled Iron I village at Ai cannot be construed as a fortified Canaanite city. It seems more likely that the story of the taking of Ai is an etiological one, explaining the existence of a tell at Ai. The Israelites who lived at Ai in the period of the judges knew that their village rested on the ruins of a fortified city (of the Early Bronze Age) and developed a story about its conquest, attributing it to Joshua.

GIBEON

A third site mentioned in the first ten chapters of Joshua is Gibeon, a site identified with el-Jîb, located about six miles north of Jerusalem. El-Jîb was excavated from 1956 to 1962 by James Pritchard. The biblical story about the fall of Gibeon is found in Joshua 9 – 10. Here again, the results of archaeology are at odds with the biblical account, as Pritchard found no evidence of a thirteenth-century B.C.E. occupation at the site, much less evidence for the site's destruction. Thus, in these three cases from the first ten chapters of Joshua, the archaeological results are uniformly negative and cannot be used to support the historicity of the biblical account of conquest.

LACHISH AND HAZOR

There is archaeological evidence that has been used in support of the conquest model at several sites. The site of Lachish, for example, which is mentioned in the account of Joshua's southern campaign (Josh 11:31 – 32) has been extensively excavated, and a massive destruction layer has been found there, dated to *ca.* 1230 B.C.E. and associated with the Israelite conquest by the excavators. Without inscriptions, however, the identity of the people who caused this destruction remains a matter of speculation.

In the story of Joshua's conquest of northern Palestine, the site of Hazor figures prominently (Josh 11:10-13). Hazor (Tell el-Qedah) was excavated by a team of Israeli archaeologists led by Yigael Yadin from 1955 to 1958. According to Yadin, a nearly 200-acre city at Hazor was destroyed at the end of the thirteenth century B.C.E., a destruction that he attributed to the Israelites. This destruction was followed by a qualitatively different kind of occupation, which Yadin associated with the Israelites. There has been considerable debate, however, about the identity of the people who caused this destruction. Disagreeing with Yadin, others have attributed Hazor's destruction at this time to the Sea Peoples or to the events of the Song of Deborah in Judges 5.

FOUR CATEGORIES OF THE RESULTS

Taken together, this type of archaeological evidence, when correlated with biblical references, yields four categories of results:

1. *Negative correlation* between sites mentioned as having been destroyed in the Bible, but which show no evidence of destruction archaeologically.
2. *Positive correlation* between sites mentioned as having been destroyed in the Bible that show material evidence of destruction.
3. Archaeological evidence of *sites destroyed ca.* 1200 B.C.E., *but not mentioned* in the Bible.
4. *A mixed record* with respect to biblical references and archaeological evidence concerning sites reportedly spared destruction by the Israelites.

Tables 8.2, 8.3, and 8.4 summarize the data (adapted from Dever 1990: 57-60). Dever summarizes the information contained in these three tables (1990:61):

> 1. Of sixteen sites said to have been destroyed in the Bible, only three have produced archaeological evidence for a destruction *ca.* 1200 B.C.E.: Bethel, Lachish, and Hazor.
> 2. Of the remaining thirteen sites, seven said to have been destroyed in the Bible either were not even occupied in the period, or show no trace of destruction.
> 3. For six of these thirteen sites, archaeology provides no evidence.
> 4. Of the twelve sites said not to have been destroyed in the Bible, five have been excavated and show no destruction *ca.* 1200 B.C.E. The others have produced no conclusive evidence.
> 5. There are at least twelve other LB-Iron I sites, either unidentified or not mentioned by name in the Bible, of which six were destroyed by the "Sea Peoples" or Egyptians and six were destroyed by unknown agents.

TABLE 8.2   Biblical References and Archaeological Evidence Concerning Canaanite Sites Claimed to Have Been Taken by the Israelites

SITE	REFERENCES	BIBLICAL REMARKS	ARCHAEOLOGICAL EVIDENCE
Zepath/Hormah	Num 21:1–3; Judg 1:17	Destroyed	No Late Bronze (LB) occupation (if site is identified with Tel Masos)
Jericho	Josh 6:1–21	Destroyed	No LB II occupation
Ai	Josh 8:24	Destroyed	No LB II occupation
Bethel	Josh 8:17; Judg 1:22–28	Destroyed	Destruction at end of LB
Jerusalem	Josh 10:1–27; Judg 1:8, 21	Contradictory	LB II occupation; no evidence of destruction
Libnah	Josh 10:29, 31	Destroyed	Identification uncertain
Lachish	Josh 10:31	Destroyed	Destroyed *ca.* 1150
Hebron	Josh 14:13–15; 15:13, 14; Judg 1:10	Implies it was taken but no destruction is described	No evidence
Debir	Josh 10:38, 39; 15:17; Judg 1:11–13	Destroyed	Identification uncertain. If Tell Beit Mirsim, then destruction; if Tell Rabud, no destruction
Makkedah	Josh 10:28	Destroyed	No LB occupation if identified as Khirbet el-Qom
Eglon	Josh 10:34, 35	Destroyed	No destruction if identified as Tell el-Hesi
Hazor	Josh 11:10–13	Destroyed	Destroyed *ca.* 1200
Dan	Judg 18:11–28	Destroyed	LB occupation; unclear evidence of destruction
Gaza	Judg 1:18	Taken	No evidence
Ashkelon	Judg 1:18	Taken	No evidence
Ekron	Judg 1:18	Taken	No evidence
Heshbon	Num 21:25–30	Destroyed	No LB occupation
Dibon	Num 21:30	Destruction implied	No LB occupation
Medeba	Num 21:30	Destruction implied	No evidence

TABLE 8.3   Biblical References and Archaeological Evidence Concerning Sites Reportedly Spared Destruction by the Israelites

SITE	REFERENCES	BIBLICAL REMARKS	ARCHAEOLOGICAL EVIDENCE
Gibeon	Josh 9:16; Judg 11:9	Absorbed into Israel by non-aggression	Scant LB II occupation; no destruction
Beth-shean	Judg 1:27	King killed; city not destroyed	LB Stratum VI not destroyed
Ta'anach	Judg 1:27; 12:21	Not destroyed	No LB II occupation; evidence of 12th century reoccupation
Dor	Judg 1:27; 12:23	King killed; city not destroyed	No evidence
Ibleam	Judg 1:27	Not destroyed	No evidence
Megiddo	Judg 1:27; 12:21	King killed; city not destroyed	LB II Stratum continues into Iron
Akko	Judg 1:31	Not destroyed	No evidence
Achziv	Judg 1:31	Not destroyed	No evidence
Rehob	Judg 1:31	Not destroyed	No evidence
Beth-shemesh	Judg 1:33	Not destroyed; inhabitants enslaved	LB Stratum destroyed
Gezer	Josh 10:33; 12:12	King killed; no mention of destruction	Stratum XIV destroyed by Philistines; became Israelite
Shechem	Josh 24; Judg 9	Entered Israel by treaty	LB continues into Iron without a break

TABLE 8.4   Sites Destroyed ca. 1200 B.C.E. but Not Mentioned in the Bible

SITE	ARCHAEOLOGICAL EVIDENCE
Tell Abu Hawam	Identification unknown; LB II Stratum VC destroyed, probably by "Sea Peoples"
Tell Qashish	Identification unknown; LB II destruction
Tel Yoqneam	Biblical Yoqneam; some LB II destruction
Tell Yin'am	Identification unknown; LB II occupation, some destruction
Tell el-Far'ah N.	Biblical Tirzah; possible destruction at end of LB II
Aphek	Biblical Aphek; LB II destruction, perhaps by "Sea Peoples"
Jaffa	Biblical Joppa; some LB II destruction
Ashdod	Biblical Ashdod; LB II Stratum XIV destroyed, undoubtedly by "Sea Peoples"
Tel Mor	Identification unknown; LB II ends in destruction
Tell es-Sharia	Possibly biblical Ziklag; Stratum IX destroyed ca. 1150, possibly by "Sea Peoples"
Tell el-Far'ah S.	Biblical Sharuhen?; some disturbance; Philistine tombs in early 12th century
Deir 'Alla	Identification unknown; LB II "sanctuary" destroyed; site reoccupied in 12th century

OTHER ARCHAEOLOGICAL EVIDENCE

There are other kinds of archaeological evidence cited by those advocating a conquest/invasion model of Israelite settlement. Besides evidence of destruction or lack of it, there is also, according to this line of thought, evidence for a cultural break. This cultural break suggests that the people who occupied these sites after their destruction (Israelites) were not the same people who occupied them before their destruction (Canaanites). This raises the question of how one can distinguish one ethnic group from another based on archaeological evidence. Clearly, destruction levels by themselves do not necessarily carry a distinctive ethnic signature. The destruction of Late Bronze/Iron Age Canaanite cities might have been carried out by Israelites as part of a coordinated campaign—or it might have resulted from infighting between cities, the Philistines, the Egyptians in a punitive raid, or another unidentified aggressor. But can one distinguish Israelite material culture from Canaanite material culture? If one could do so decisively, it would help in the identification of the post-destruction occupiers of sites, and by inference the sites' destroyers.

Three specific pieces of archaeological data have been cited as evidence of a new Israelite presence. They are:

- A particular pottery type known as a "collar-rim" storejar (see Figure 8.5)
- Plaster-lined water cisterns. The cisterns, which were carved into the limestone, were lined with a slaked-lime plaster to prevent the water from soaking into the limestone.
- A house plan known as a four-space pillared courtyard house (see Figure 8.6)

It has been suggested that the new "practical" Israelites, with their storejars, plaster cisterns, and house plan, moved into the sparsely populated Canaanite highlands and started a new village life. However, the certainty that these three items are reliable indicators of a distinctive new Israelite presence on the scene has faded with more recent archaeological finds. A consensus on the part of ceramic experts has been reached. Ceramically there is little "new" to distinguish the Iron I villagers/newcomers—"Israelites" or not—not even the highly touted "collar-rim" storejar. Similarly the cisterns and house plan are not necessarily Israelite innovations. It has been suggested that the invention of plastered cisterns to collect rainwater was one of the main factors enabling settlement in the hill country. This has been questioned, however, because such cisterns are now known to have been in use as early as the Middle Bronze Age. It has also become clear that they are abundant only at some Iron I village sites (for example, Ai), and are absent, and unnecessary, at others (Giloh, Shiloh) because some limestone had a self-sealing quality.

Two major questions have arisen concerning the three- or four-space pillared courtyard house. What was its origin? Was it a uniquely Israelite form of domestic architecture? The first question has been answered by the discovery of a similar Canaanite house form, which suggests that this type of house was a development from Canaanite architecture. As for the ethnic attribution of these houses, three- and four-space houses are common in Israelite domestic architecture of

Figure 8.5   A "collar-rim" storejar

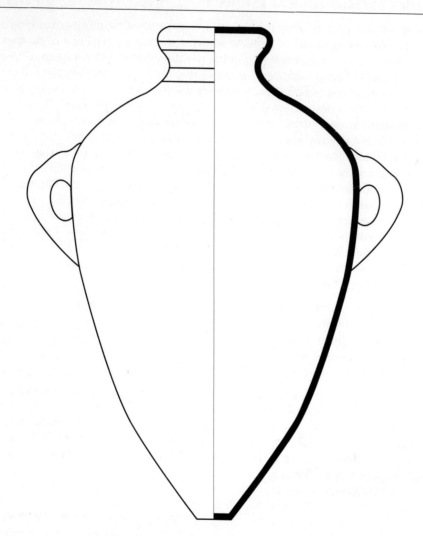

the period of the monarchy. In the Iron I period (especially in the eleventh century), however, they occur also in non-Israelite regions, such as Philistia, Phoenicia, and Transjordan. Pillared courtyard houses should not, therefore, be seen as an Israelite creation, but as a style of house that was popular throughout Palestine at this time.

The conclusion seems clear: Given the present state of our knowledge, archaeology does *not* offer clear confirmation of an Israelite "conquest" of the land. The "disappearance" of archaeological support has led some to doubt whether there ever was a "conquest" in any real sense. It has also led to the proposal of other models for understanding the process by which the Israelites established themselves in the land of Canaan.

Figure 8.6   A "four-space" house

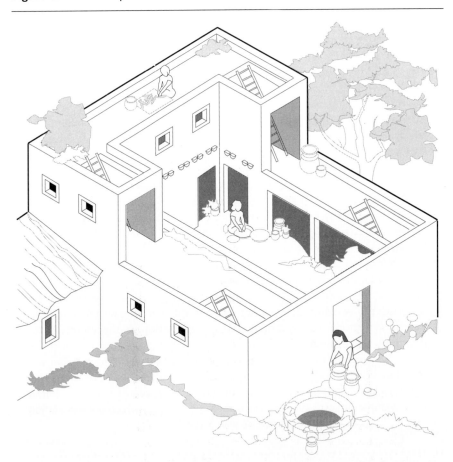

An Imaginative Portrait of Joshua

Moses was a hard act to follow. After the tired old man breathed his last on the slopes of Mt. Pisgah overlooking the Promised Land, which he never quite made it to, the job of leading the Israelites on in fell to Joshua. Since the Promised Land was inhabited by a group of native Canaanite tribes who weren't about to give it up without an argument, the result was years of war at its cruelest and most savage. And in the eyes of Joshua and his people, it wasn't just any old war. It was a holy war. It was Yahweh they were fighting for because the land they were out to get, come Hell or high water, was the land that centuries before, in Abraham's time, Yahweh had promised them so they could settle down in it and become a great nation and a blessing to all nations. Prisoners weren't supposed to be taken, and spoils weren't supposed to be divided, because Yahweh was the one they all belonged to. Ai, Jericho,

Continued

Gibeon—cities fell like clay pigeons at Joshua's feet, and everything that would burn was put to the torch, and everything that wouldn't, like men, women and children, was put to the sword. Holy wars are the worst kind.

The battle at Gibeon was one of the worst parts of it. Five Amorite kings were drawn up against the Israelites, and Joshua launched his attack just before dawn. His men leapt out of the mists with a terrible light in their eyes. There was a wild storm with hailstones as big as hand-grenades. The Amorites panicked. The slaughter was on. It was a long, bloody massacre, and in order to have enough daylight to finish it by, Joshua fixed the sun with his stern military gaze and gave it his orders.

"Sun, stand thou still at Gibeon!" he said (Joshua 10:12), and because he was in command of the operation and because Yahweh was in command of him, the sun snapped to attention and kept shining until the job was done. It was the longest day on record, and when it was finally over, the ground was strewn with the dead, and the mutilated bodies of the five kings were hanging from five trees, like meat in a butcher shop.

With one exception, there was nothing that Joshua hadn't been able to see in the prolonged and relentless light the sun had supplied him with. The one exception was that the God he was fighting for was the God of the Amorites too whether they realized it or not. But Yahweh saw it and brooded over it and more than a thousand years later, through the mouth of his Anointed, spoke about it.

"Blessed are those who mourn, for they shall be comforted," he said (Matthew 5:4), and then he also blessed the peacemakers so that even without any extra sunshine everybody would be able to see that peace is better than even the holiest wars, especially the kind of peace which not even a holy terror like Joshua can either give or take away.

Buechner (1979:81–82)

The Immigration Model

Biblical data about the indecisive nature of the "conquest" led some scholars to propose an immigration model. This model was developed in the 1920s, even before the heyday of "biblical archaeology," by a German scholar, Albrecht Alt. The model was expanded by his student Martin Noth. Alt began by applying what were at the time new analytical tools of form criticism and tradition history to the biblical texts. Form criticism underscored what was called in German the *Sitz im Leben,* or "setting in life" of particular literary forms. Alt was interested in the social context in which the stories about the conquest were remembered and handed down as part of oral tradition. The stories of the fall of Jericho and Ai were labeled etiological legends, stories told long after the fact to offer an imaginative explanation for a given situation. In the case of the conquest stories, they offered a theological explanation of the way in which Israel had come into possession of the land, emphasizing the miraculous agency of

God. Thus, the story of the conquest of Ai has no historical basis at all but was told to explain the presence of a well-known tell. This offers a ready-made answer to the seeming contradiction between the biblical narrative and the results of excavation at Ai. Archaeologists have found no evidence of an Israelite conquest of Ai because no such event ever occurred—it was simply the creation of the storyteller's theologically-fueled imagination.

In an essay titled "The Settlement of the Israelites in Palestine" Alt added his analysis of the Amarna Letters and other extra-biblical documents to the form-critical analysis of the biblical text. He proposed that the area settled by the Israelites in the central highlands was one that was sparsely settled and beyond the control of the Canaanite city-states. Instead of a violent conquest, Alt believed that the semi-nomadic Israelites gradually infiltrated into this vacuum. Military encounters, Alt believed, occurred at a later stage of Israelite settlement when the Israelites needed more space and began aggressive territorial expansion. This provided Alt with a way of accounting for the mixed archaeological evidence, as well as for the differences between Joshua and Judges.

The most recent statement of the model developed by Alt and Noth comes from Noth's student Manfred Weippert (1971: 5–6). Weippert believes that the settlement was carried out by individual clans or confederacies of clans of nomads with sheep and goats who, during the winter rainy season and the spring, lived with their herds in the territory between the desert and the cultivated land. In the summer, when the vegetation in that area was insufficient for their flocks, they penetrated further into the cultivated land. Clans that entered the country in this way during seasonal change of pasture, gradually settled in the relatively thinly populated wooded areas of the highlands. These were areas that were not directly exposed to the reach either of the Canaanite city-states or of Egyptian sovereignty. There, these clans began to practice agriculture once they had turned these wooded areas into arable land. This peaceful process of transition of nomads to a sedentary life was, according to Alt, the real process of settlement and it was, in the nature of things, a peaceful development.

Although the work of Alt and his successors can be accommodated to the biblical narratives of Joshua and Judges, the major weakness in Alt's position is its characterization of the Israelites as nomads, who like modern Bedouin, followed their flocks seasonally into the highlands and eventually became settled. More recent evidence shows that most of the new settlements in the highlands at the end of the thirteenth century B.C.E. were agricultural in nature from their foundation, with herding as a subsidiary form of livelihood. These villagers were not nomads or seminomads as Alt had supposed. They were primarily farmers and secondarily herders of sheep and goats who brought with them fixed cultural patterns of village life. We will return to a discussion of the nature of these villages below.

The Social Revolution Model

The inability of "biblical archaeology" to deliver what it had promised, coupled with a disavowal of a particular kind of theological approach to biblical history, resulted in a turning away from narrowly-conceived archaeological explanations in favor of socioeconomic models. One model for understanding the nature of the emergence of Israel in Canaan is built on the notion of social revolution, in particular, a peasants' revolt. This model proposes that Israel emerged not as the result of newcomers coming into the region, but as the result of an indigenous peasants' revolt against their overlords. This model was first formulated by the American scholar, George E. Mendenhall, in 1962. While the conquest model took its basic cue from a particular perspective on archaeology, and the immigration model developed out of a particular perspective on biblical literature, the social revolution model builds on sociological and anthropological models and methods. Mendenhall rejected the idea that the Israelites were nomads. The Hebrews were rather to be identified with the ʿApiru of the Amarna Letters, in the sense that both represented socially marginalized groups who had pulled away from the urban Canaanite culture of the Late Bronze Age. Mendenhall held that the Amarna materials and the biblical events represented the same process politically, which was the withdrawal, not physically but geographically and subjectively, of large population groups from their obligations to and protection by the Canaanite cities and their governments. Mendenhall asserts that there was no statistically important invasion of Palestine, there was no radical displacement of population, there was no genocide, and there was no large-scale driving out of indigenous population groups, but only of royal administrators (of necessity!). In summary, there was no real conquest of Palestine at all; what happened instead may be termed, from the point of view of the secular historian interested only in socio-political processes, a peasants' revolt against the network of interlocking Canaanite city states (Mendenhall 1962: 73).

For Mendenhall, the beginnings of Israel are to be found in an internal uprising in which the Hebrews who had experienced the Exodus played a catalytic role. They advocated commitment to, and covenant solidarity with Yahweh, the liberating God of the Exodus. Mendenhall, however, did not attempt to define Israelite ethnicity in terms of cultural artifacts that could be discerned in the archaeological record. Neither did he attempt to correlate the idea of a peasants' revolt with the stratigraphic evidence supplied by archaeology in the early 1960s.

The model proposed by Mendenhall was refined and developed into a detailed and far-reaching theory in the work of Norman Gottwald. The model is most fully developed in Gottwald's work published in 1979, *The Tribes of Yahweh: A Sociology of the Religion of Liberated Israel, 1250 – 1050 B.C.* Basic to the discussion for Gottwald are three theses:

- "Israel" did not originate as an ethnically distinct invasive element but was from the outset of the same stock as the Canaanites.
- The Israelites were not infiltrating, nomadic or seminomadic herders, but a sedentary, agricultural component of Canaanite society.
- The creation of the sociopolitical entity "Israel" resulted from a rejection of and withdrawal from the Canaanite city-state system, with its oppressive mechanism of taxation, military conscription and the corvée, or forced labor for the state.

Gottwald's work has blown across the overheated debates about the origins of Israel like a refreshing breeze after a *khamsin* (the hot, dusty wind from the desert) and has had the effect of exposing just how forced some interpretations of the biblical text and archaeological evidence have been. The work of Mendenhall, Gottwald, and others of this school of thought has also had the effect of adding a fourth kind of evidence to the discussion besides the three mentioned above (the Bible, extra-biblical texts, and archaeological data), that is, data and theories from the social sciences which can suggest illuminating controlled comparisons between Israel and other peoples. Increased attention to the social sciences, in turn, has led to a new role for archaeology in the debate, that of providing a material and sociocultural profile of Palestine in the thirteenth to eleventh centuries B.C.E. This can help set parameters for reading the biblical text and offer pointers to analogies from the social sciences. Gottwald's work in particular has cleared the way for a fresh understanding of the relationship of the newer Syro-Palestinian archaeology to biblical scholarship.

THE ARCHAEOLOGICAL EVIDENCE

As we have seen, the archaeological evidence today is overwhelmingly unsupportive of the classic conquest model of Israelite origins as envisioned in the book of Joshua and by some biblical scholars. With respect to the peaceful infiltration model, there is similarly virtually no archaeological support. The peasants' revolt model and the accounts of the book of Judges fare much better in the light of both recent archaeological work and literary analysis. What, then are the results of such work?

We can now say that the major change that occurred at the transition from the Late Bronze to the Iron Age was not the sudden, total destruction of Canaanite urban civilization by invaders. The real change took place not primarily in the cities, but in the pattern of settlement in the countryside. Toward the end of the Late Bronze Age no small unfortified settlements are known. However, with the beginning of the Iron Age they suddenly appear by the hundreds. The study of this phenomenon, the interpretation of the plans of the various sites, their spatial dispersion, their economic base, and their social structure, have become a focus of much recent Syro-Palestinian archaeology. This has replaced the fixation on the presence or absence of destruction layers in tells. Several villages of the twelfth and eleventh centuries B.C.E. have been excavated, extensive surface surveys have been conducted, and the results of these excavations help clarify the general picture. The small hilltop villages were unwalled and consisted of "four-space" pillared courtyard houses, each having one or more rock-hewn cisterns and stone-lined storage silos. The pottery repertoire at these sites derived from Late Bronze Age Canaanite types of the late thirteenth century B.C.E., including the distinctive "collar-rim" storejar. All these archaeological features are typical of the material culture of agrarian or peasant societies. The economy of these villages is based on small-scale terrace farming, with some herding and cottage industry. The social structure, unlike that of the Late Bronze

Age, was quite egalitarian. Most of these sites were abandoned by the end of the eleventh century B.C.E., with the growth of urban population under the Israelite Monarchy.

One of the most convincing applications of this kind of archaeological data to the understanding of the Israelite settlement is that of Lawrence Stager, a professor of Near-Eastern studies at Harvard and a field archaeologist who has done extensive work at Palestinian sites. In his analysis of early Israelite settlement, he utilizes recent excavations and surveys, together with the biblical texts and social scientific ideas concerning settlement patterns, house forms, demography, technology, economy, and ethnography (Stager 1985). Stager's analysis paints a clear picture of the emergence of a new kind of settlement at the beginning of the Iron Age characterized by small villages, an agrarian economy, and an egalitarian social structure. This is a picture than can favorably be compared with the biblical picture painted in Judges.

What can we conclude? Dever, from his perspective as a Syro-Palestinian archaeologist who is also well-informed concerning current trends in biblical scholarship, believes that archaeology has illuminated the settlement process brilliantly—but not in the way the earlier biblical archaeologists expected (1990: 83–84). Instead of simply confirming an Israelite military conquest of Canaan under Joshua, or documenting the sedentarization of incoming nomads from the desert, archaeology has presented us with a totally new way of looking at early Israel. The view of Israel as a "peasants' revolt" has been powerfully bolstered by the new interdisciplinary archaeology. Dever does not believe, however, that we must conclude that the Bible was wrong. He observes that the Deuteronomistic history was obviously a late construct, a theological one that deliberately overemphasized the themes of holy war and the covenant as extensions of the "Promised Land" motif. At the same time, the Deuteronomistic Historian also preserved earlier materials with alternative views, such as portions of Judges. What recent archaeological research has done is simply to retrieve one neglected strand of the biblical narratives concerning Israel's origins. For Dever, the real contribution of modern archaeology has been to provide for the first time a sociological setting accompanying the theological explanation that makes it possible to see the settlement process in a new light. The biblical writers were a part of the social setting, of course, but they were more concerned with viewing history as the *magnalia dei*, the "mighty acts of God." For people living at the end of the twentieth century, however, who have seen so many peasants' revolts in our time, the current sociological model may be more relevant. It can lead to a richer understanding of ancient Israel in all its diversity and vitality, as well as to a more profound appreciation of its dynamic relation to Canaanite religion and culture. Dever concludes:

> Finally, the new stress on the humanity of Israel need not depreciate the divine element—that is, faith. Ultimately, the Biblical writers faced the same problem we do: how to account for the unique reality of the people of Israel. They fell back on the only analogy they had, historical experience, which for them was their own firsthand knowledge of the power

of Yahweh over their pagan neighbors, and his ability to save and shape them as his people—despite their obscure origins, their lack of merit, and their disobedience. In the end, the Biblical writers concluded that Israel's election and survival were nothing less than a miracle. Who are we, their spiritual heirs, to disagree? (1990: 84)

RELIGION AND POLITICS IN ISRAEL BEFORE THE RISE OF THE MONARCHY

Canaanite and Israelite Religion

As we have already seen, early Israelite material culture cannot be distinguished easily from that of Canaan. Artifacts once thought to be unique diagnostic features associated with the appearance of Israel in Canaan are now more widely attested. Although archaeology may not now be able clearly to distinguish Israelite from Canaanite, archaeological features do not constitute the sole criteria for making historical decisions. Even if there is not one criterion for making a clear-cut distinction based on material culture, some early Israelites may have perceived themselves as radically different from the Canaanites. From the evidence available, one may conclude that although the Israelites were largely Canaanite according to currently available cultural data, Israelites expressed a distinct set of origins, worshiped a unique deity, and had a special geographical environment in the central highlands. But in religion, as in material culture, the Canaanite character of Israelite culture certainly shaped the ways in which ancient Israelites communicated their religious understanding of Yahweh.

Deities and their cults in Iron Age Israel represented aspects of the cultural continuity with the indigenous Late Bronze Age culture and the contemporary urban culture on the coast and in the valleys. Canaanite religion in all its manifestations was always polytheistic. Inscriptions from the Late Bronze Age and the Iron I period in Canaan indicate that the major deities of the land included El, Baal, Anat, Astarte, and Asherah.

Canaan, at the time of the judges, had a set of religious beliefs that loosely can be termed a "nature religion." The basic principle that gave shape to the religious system was a recognized connection of gods with natural phenomena. This religious system also was related closely to Palestinian geography and climate. The gods accorded the most attention were those who were seen to control the forces of nature that affected the climate and the annual cycle of rainy and dry seasons. Myths and rituals dealt with ways of bringing the gods/natural forces into their proper relationships so that fertility would result—fertility in the family, the flocks, and the field. A shortfall of crops or of domesticated animals could mean famine. Human birth rates had to remain high to offset the high rates of infant mortality and deaths of women at an early age, often in childbirth. The mortality rate for females in the childbearing years greatly exceeded that of males. In a population in which the life expectancy for males was about forty, women would have had a life expectancy closer to thirty. There was also the need for laborers in a very labor-intensive form of agriculture. Given the high infant mortality rate, coupled with endemic disease that caused many deaths among the pre-adult population, in normal times (that is, when no plagues caused an extraordinary number of deaths) families needed to produce nearly twice the number of children desired in order to achieve optimal family size (Meyers 1988: 112). Much of the myth and ritual involved human actions that would bring about fertility by human imitation of the gods' activities that bestowed fertility on the land and people.

THE GOD EL

The supreme Canaanite deity was El. El, the father of the gods, was the creator of the earth and of human beings. El was pictured in mythology as a beneficent, old, wise god with gray hair. In images of El, he is typically seated. His consort, or female companion, was the goddess Asherah. El is not, however, an active god in the Canaanite pantheon. He seems to have "retired" and handed over much of his authority to his son Baal. The seated El figures represent beneficent rule in the cosmos.

THE GOD BAAL

Baal is the most active Canaanite god. He brings the rain upon which the fertility of the soil depends. One of his titles in Canaanite mythology is "the Rider of the Clouds." In images of Baal he typically stands and carries a thunder club and a lightning spear, the accompaniments of the thunderstorm.

The stories of Baal and his consort Anat are preserved in a cycle of mythological texts discovered at Ugarit, a site in present-day Syria. These texts were written in the Ugaritic language (which, like Hebrew is a Semitic language) *ca.* 1400 B.C.E. The stories about Baal and Anat are divided into three main parts: (1) Baal's conflict as god of the storm with the god of the sea, Yamm; (2) the building of Baal's palace/temple on the rain clouds; and (3) a battle that pits Baal and his consort, Anat, against the god Mot, god of death. In this mythic cycle, Baal is killed but rises again, reflecting the cycle of the seasons. Baal's death is described in terms that reflect his association with the earth's fertility:

"I [Mot] will also devour the moisture of Baʿal,
Suck the rain drops of The Son of El down my throat. . . . of El's Beloved, The Hero,
    into my mouth. . . ."
Mot's lower lip stretches down to the earth,
His upper lip reaches to the sky,
He licks the stars with his tongue.
Baʿal's rain runs off into Mot's mouth.
and down into his throat.
The olives shrivel,
The earth's produce dies,

The fruit of the trees drops off.
Almighty Ba'al becomes frightened,
The Rider of the Clouds is terrified.
"Go! Tell Mot, the Son of El,
Deliver this message to El's Beloved, the Hero.
Hear the word of Ba'al the Almighty,
. . . the message of The Greatest Hero of All.
I salute you, O Mot, Son of El,
I will be your slave forever!" (Matthews and Benjamin 1991: 165)

Baal's death is mourned by the gods, who perform the proper mourning rituals. Anat then hunts down Mot to force him to release Baal. When Mot refuses her demand, Anat seizes him, chops him into pieces, and sows the pieces in a field. Anat returns to El and asks him to determine whether Baal is really dead. In a vision, El discovers that Baal is alive and that the crops will grow again. He instructs Anat to go to Shapshu, goddess of the sun, and ask her to search for Baal. Shapshu agrees to help Anat and pours wine into the dry furrows of the fields. In the end, Baal defeats both Yamm and Mot and regains his title as King of the Gods, restoring fertility to the earth.

THE GODDESS ANAT

Baal's chief consort is the goddess Anat. She is pictured as Baal's constant, devoted companion. She is also a very fierce warrior. As we have seen, after Baal's death, she dismembered Mot and scattered him like seed. She also defeated the chaos monster Leviathan. While there are allusions to the beauty and fertility of Anat, she is, oddly enough, never depicted as giving birth. She can be viewed as a fertility goddess, however, in her role of defeating Mot, thus enabling Baal to come back to life, bringing the rains that give fertility to the earth with him. While only rarely is there inscriptional evidence associated with figurines, comparative studies suggest that Anat was represented by the female figure, who typically appears on clay plaques and jewelry in a frontal nude pose.

THE GODDESS ASTARTE

Astarte, referred to in the Hebrew Bible as Ashtoreth (plural = Ashtaroth), was another of Baal's consorts in the Ugaritic myths, although a less prominent one than Anat. A common Ugaritic title of Astarte is "Astarte of the field." She has a Mesopotamian forerunner in Ishtar. The identity of Astarte with Ishtar, as well as later with Aphrodite, makes it virtually certain that she was equated with Venus.

THE GODDESS ASHERAH

The most complete source of information about the goddess Asherah also comes from the Ugaritic texts, where she is called Athirat ('trt). She is the mother of the gods and the consort of the supreme god, El. She plays an important role in the

Ugaritic cycle of myths involving Baal's desire for a palace/temple. Anat, Baal's consort, first demands a palace for him from El, but her demand is not met. When Athirat = Asherah intercedes with her husband, however, she is successful.

THE CANAANITE GODS AND GODDESSES IN THE BIBLE

In the Bible, traditions that these four principal Canaanite deities were known by the Israelites during the period of the judges are preserved in the book of Judges. The god of Shechem is, for example, identified as El-berith (Judg 9:46), which scholars have identified as a title of El. The Asherah, a symbol named for the goddess Asherah, which probably was a wooden pole, is explicitly described in Judg 6:25–26:

> That night the LORD said to him, "Take your father's bull, the second bull seven years old, and pull down the altar of Baal that belongs to your father, and cut down the sacred pole [Hebrew = 'Asherah] that is beside it; and build an altar to the LORD your God on the top of the stronghold here, in proper order; then take the second bull, and offer it as a burnt offering with the wood of the sacred pole that you cut down."

The word ba'al forms the theophoric (that is, divine) element in the name of Jerubaal (Judg 6:32; 8:35). There are only indirect and very limited traces of the goddess Anat in the Hebrew Bible. Three place names—Anathoth (Josh 21:18), Beth-anath (Josh 19:38; Judg 1:33), and Beth-anoth (Josh 15:59)—have usually been explained as preserving the goddess' name. The last two mean "House of Anath," suggesting that a temple of Anath was located there. The personal name Shamgar ben ("son of") Anat is also attested (Judg 5:6). The lack of either inscriptional or biblical evidence for Anat suggests that she did not have a cult dedicated to her in early Israel. Astarte appears in the Bible as Ashtoreth ("Astarte" in the NRSV) and Ashtaroth ("Astartes" in the NRSV). Ashtoreth, a singular noun, probably reflects a scribal distortion of 'astart, by supplying it with the vowels of the Hebrew word bosheth, "shame." The plural form of the name, Ashtaroth (or "Astartes" in the NRSV), is the one most common in the Bible. All the references to the Ashtaroth in the Bible are alongside references to the Baals (cf. Judg 2:13; 10:6) or simply "the foreign gods" (1 Sam 7:3), and are mentioned in connection with the unfaithfulness of the Israelites during the period of the judges. References to "the Baals and the Ashtaroth" ("the Baals and the Astartes" in the NRSV) may be a way of talking about Canaanite gods and goddesses in general. The pairing of Ashtaroth with the Baals is appropriate, since Astarte was a consort of Baal in the Ugaritic myths. While Anat plays a larger role at Ugarit than does Astarte, Astarte was apparently more prominent as Baal's consort in the world reflected in the Hebrew Bible.

Thus the principal deities in the territory of Israel during the period of the judges were Yahweh, El, Baal, Astarte, and Asherah. How were these gods, commonly regarded as "Canaanite" deities, related to Yahweh in belief and cult?

YAHWEH AND EL

El may well have been the original God of Israel. Note, for example, that Israel's name is Isra-el, not Isra-yah. The primacy of El is also supported by an argument from silence—there are no biblical attacks directed against El. The development of the name El (*'el*) into a generic term meaning "god" suggests that at an early point El was identified with Yahweh. According to Gen 33:20, Jacob built an altar at Shechem and called it "El-Elohe-Israel," that is "El the God of Israel." The author of Gen 33:20 assumes that Yahweh and El are identical. The temple at Shechem in Judg 9:26 is called "El-berith," or "El of the Covenant."

Just as there is no evidence of a cult devoted to Anat in Israelite religion, so there is no distinct cult attested for El, except in his identity as Yahweh. The characteristics and epithets of El were used to describe Yahweh. In both texts and graphic depictions, El is pictured as an elderly, enthroned bearded figure, presiding over a divine council; Yahweh is described as a deity enthroned amid an assembly of divine beings (1 Kings 22:19; Ps 29:1-2, and so forth.) The compassionate disposition of El and Yahweh toward humanity are similarly described. Both appear to humans in dreams.

YAHWEH AND BAAL

The biblical treatment of Baal is quite different from that of El. One gets the idea that Baal and Yahweh were in fierce competition with one another from a very early period. When did this rivalry begin? In Judges 6 the story of Gideon seems to be intended to convey the message that true Yahwists in the early phase of Israel's history eradicated devotion to Baal and Asherah (see esp. vv. 25-32). Jerubaal was the name given to Gideon after he destroyed his father's Baal altar. The name Jerubaal has been translated as "Baal makes (himself) great" or "Let Baal sue (his enemies)." The name is changed in 2 Sam 11:21, where the noun "shame" (*bosheth* in Hebrew) is substituted for Baal in the Hebrew text, giving the name Jerubbesheth in Hebrew and the RSV; Jerubaal in the NRSV. Like the accounts of the conquest, however, this story of the elimination of Canaanite religious practices seems to be in the vein of a "It's-too-bad-it-didn't-really-happen-like-this-since-look-what-happened-as-a-result" kind of story. That baalism was not eradicated once and for all is quite obvious from all the polemics that are poured out on it in the succeeding years of Israel's experience. Indeed, the stories in Judges point to the monarchy as the period of their redaction, although older traditions are also preserved there. It is probably safe to say that in the period of the judges, Baal was probably no more a threat than El. Later sources, however, treat Baal as a threat to Yahweh from the period of the judges on into the monarchy. The traumatic events of the ninth century under Ahab and his foreign queen, Jezebel, may have shaped the perspective of the redactors of the book of Judges and caused them to read back the threat into an earlier period.

YAHWEH AND ASHERAH

In the Hebrew Bible, the word Asherah is used to denote both the name of the Canaanite goddess and the wooden cult-object that was her symbol (the KJV translates Asherah with the word "grove"). Before the discovery of the Ugaritic texts, some biblical scholars wrongly equated Asherah with Astarte/Ashtoreth. Asherah is poorly attested as a goddess in the book of Judges. Arguments for Asherah as a goddess in this period rest on Judges 6 and other places where she is mentioned with Baal. In Judges 6, however, only "the asherah," the symbol that bears the name of the goddess, is criticized, not the goddess' name as such. Asherah never appears as a theophoric element in Hebrew proper names.

At Kuntillet 'Ajrud, a site in the northeastern Sinai, inscriptions have been found that refer to "Yahweh . . . and his Asherah" (Emerton 1982: 2). Scholars disagree on the meaning of "his Asherah." It has been suggested that it may refer to the goddess Asherah, her cult symbol, or a word meaning "chapel." The site Khirbet el-Qom, near Hebron, has also produced an inscription that includes the lines:

Blessed be Uriyahu by Yahweh.
For from his enemies by his (YHWH's) Asherah he (YHWH) has saved him. (Hadley 1987:5)

The meaning of these two inscriptions for our understanding of the religion of ancient Israel is still being debated. Asherah may have played a significant role in Israelite popular religion. Her lack of prominence in the biblical record may be due to suppression by male editors, for whom her cult was considered a threat to the "official" religion of Yahwism.

YAHWEH AND ANAT

Although the Hebrew Bible depicts Baal, and to a lesser extent Asherah, as distinct Canaanite gods, Anat is not pictured in this way. As we have observed, except in personal and place names, Anat does not appear in the Bible. Because Anat is not attested in the Bible, the lack of contact between her cult and that of Yahweh deters any theory of direct dependence. Parallels exist, nevertheless, between biblical descriptions of divine war and the battles of Anat in the Ugaritic myths. It has been suggested that Israelite religion inherited the martial language of Anat in a form that was combined with the storm language of Baal.

Polytheism, Monolatry, and Syncretism

Early Israelite religion in Canaan often has been discussed in terms of monotheism (the belief in one God) versus polytheism (the belief in many gods). General agreement exists among scholars today, however, that monotheism, in the strict sense of denying the existence of all deities except one, is not an accurate description of the religion of early Israel. The term monolatry is more descriptive because it emphasizes dominant allegiance to one deity without denying the existence of others. If one describes Yahwism from the perspective of Israel's sociopolitical identity, then one can simply say that Yahweh was the "national" god of Israel, just as Chemosh was the god of Moab (Num 21:29) and Milcom of the Ammonites (2 Kings 23:13).

The relation of Israel's religion to Canaan's religion had two dimensions. On the one hand, the Old Testament directs much criticism toward the fertility cult practices of the religion of Canaan. On the other hand, the Hebrew Bible appropriates elements from the religion of Canaan, transforming them into forms compatible with Israel's distinctive faith. In this way, the Canaanite religion exerted an influence on Israelite religion, in spite of the condemnation of Canaanite religion that characterizes so much of the Bible.

As a result of religious syncretism, the characteristics of Baal and Yahweh probably overlapped somewhat. The incorporation of Baal's attributes into descriptions of Yahweh highlights the centrality of Yahweh in Israel's earliest literature. J. Andrew Dearman has observed that the material culture of the early Iron I period (1200–1000 B.C.E.) in Palestine offers a constructive parallel for the consideration of polytheism and syncretism in early Israel (1992: 38–39). With the transition from the Late Bronze to the Iron I period, there was a sharp decline in the number of temples and a corresponding decline in the number and types of figurines that depicted deities. Dearman suggests that these two elements should be viewed together and are plausibly explained as reflecting an important feature of early Yahwism. Early Yahwism did not artificially separate socioeconomic concerns from theological ones. Both socioeconomic and theological concerns presupposed that the Canaanite ethos of early Israelite religion did not require (or want) any tangible representations of deities that were capable of political and religious manipulation and abuse. Temples and divine images were associated in early Israel with the oppressive practices of the Canaanite city-states. Because they were symbols of repressive control, many Israelite farmers and herders rejected them. Dearman suggests that it is better to think in terms of early Yahwistic *independence* from these two elements of the typical religious patterns in Canaan rather than a carefully thought out rejection of Canaanite religion and images of the divine. From a sociocultural viewpoint, Yahwism too was a Canaanite religion. How were religion and sociopolitical structures related in early Israel? We turn to this question now.

Sociopolitical Structures in Early Israel

The search for sociopolitical analogies to Israel in the period of the judges has explored several options. An early proposal relied on an analogy from Greece and Rome. In those societies there was an *amphictyony,* a confederation of tribes around a central sanctuary. From this analogy, it was proposed that the twelve tribes of Israel formed an amphictyony, in which each of the twelve tribes took its turn in caring for the central sanctuary. Whatever unity the tribes had was a result of their common worship of Yahweh at the central shrine. This proposal has, however, been rejected by most scholars, who believe that this model has been forced on premonarchic Israel. Certainly there is no evidence for a central sanctuary in Palestine of the period of the judges.

Another suggested model comes from what are known as "segmented societies." Segmented societies are ones that are *acephalous,* that is, not organized around a center. Their political organization is established by multi-graded groups of politically equal rank. The term "segmentary society" was coined by the British anthropologist E. E. Evans-Pritchard, who used it as an analytical device to denote the broader kinship system and territorial hierarchy of the Nuer in Africa (Frick 1985: 52–53). In segmented societies genealogies serve as indicators of social relationships, deities are protectors of clans and identified as the god(s) of the ancestors, and the tribes manage policies of judicial enforcement apart from hierarchical, centralized control (Dearman 1992: 27).

While not having an explicit theoretical basis in segmentary processes, Barnabas Lindars' study of the Israelite tribes in Judges, based upon an examination of the list of the "minor judges" (Judg 10:1–5; 12:7–15), the list in Judg 1, and the Song of Deborah (Judg 5) is instructive against the background of segmentary societies (Lindars 1980). We turn our attention now to the Song of Deborah, which appears to speak of Israel as a segmentary society at the end of the twelfth and beginning of the eleventh century.

THE SONG OF DEBORAH

In English translation, Judg 5:1–31, the Song of Deborah, is a poetic version of the prose account in Judg 4. There are, however, significant differences in the two chapters. The Song of Deborah is one of the oldest poems, if not *the* oldest, in the Hebrew Bible. As such it offers us direct access to the religion and political structure of Israel in the late twelfth to early eleventh centuries B.C.E. In the form of a song of victory, it celebrates the theophany of Yahweh who, like Baal, appears in a timely thunderstorm that enables the Israelites to defeat the chariot forces of the Canaanite commander, Sisera. In the midst of this victory song are vignettes of three women: Deborah, the leader of the Israelite forces; the mother of Sisera; and Jael, a Kenite woman who murders Sisera. Collectively, these pictures depict the women's response to war, their traditional and nontraditional roles in battle, and a theme of women assuming for themselves roles that were traditionally reserved for men. Deborah is the leader in the story, the "judge," who directs Barak, the active military commander. She plays the role of "mother" and prophet, ordering the course of the tribal call to arms—the tribal muster—but refraining from actual participation in combat. Contrasted with Deborah's active role is the passive one of Sisera's mother. In her traditional role of the nurturing mother, she spends her life caring for males but is powerless to alter their destiny. Jael occupies the middle ground between assertiveness and passivity. She responds to Sisera's request for hospitality as expected of a Kenite woman, whose people were allied to the Canaanites, and thus bound to follow the conventions of tribal hospitality toward those who seek sanctuary. She comforts and protects Sisera, then kills him as he sleeps by driving a tent stake through his temple.

The battle described in the Song of Deborah took place in an area that was a "breadbasket" of Palestine, the broad and fertile Esdraelon plain. Israel had control of the caravan routes through the highlands, but the Canaanites controlled the lowland of the plain, interdicting Israelite passage. The battle is thus for control of the Esdraelon.

At the very beginning of the poem, Deborah is described in the Hebrew in a way that calls the reader's attention to the fact that she is a woman, as described by Robert Alter. Alter quotes the very beginning of the story of Deborah (Judg. 4:4–5) in a very literal translation because he sees the Hebrew here as having "a certain purposeful awkwardness" that is smoothed over in English translations: "And Deborah, a prophet-woman ['ishshah nevi'ah], Lapidoth's woman, she was judging Israel at that time. And she would sit under the palm tree of Deborah. . . ." Alter observes that what is odd about these initial clauses in the Deborah story is the emphasis on feminine gender and on the term woman. Because all Hebrew nouns are either masculine or feminine, the moment you hear nevi'ah (feminine) and not navi' (masculine) you realize that you are dealing with a prophetess, not a prophet. This foregrounding of the feminine is then reinforced by the introduction of an easily dispensable pronoun: "Deborah, . . . she was judging Israel." Alter concludes that the "stylistic bumpiness" at the beginning of the story is intended to bump our sensibility as an audience. It is the rare exception to have a prophetess rather than a prophet, a female rather than a male judge. Thus, we have been alerted that a reversal of roles between female and male will be at the heart of the story, with Deborah's role as commander perfectly complemented by Jael's role at the end as assassin of the enemy general (Alter 1992: 41).

Deborah, as prophet and judge, calls the roll of the tribal muster. As a society without a political center, the Israelite polity lacked the ability to compel any tribe to come to the defense of another. The tribal muster as depicted in the Song of Deborah comes from a society that had to rely on moral persuasion grounded in a religious covenant uniting the tribes. In the Song of Deborah we see tribes both praised and denounced for responding to or disregarding Deborah's call (See the map of tribal territories in Figure 8.2). Six of the tribes are commended for "doing their duty" in responding to the muster: Ephraim, Benjamin, Machir (that part of Manasseh west of the Jordan?), Zebulun, Issachar, and Naphtali. Two tribes, Asher and Dan, are scolded for what sounds like subservience to the Sea Peoples. The poem thus seems to presuppose the earlier coastal location of Dan, rather than its later northern one (for traditions about Dan's migration to the north see Josh 19:47 and Judges 18:1–29). Two Transjordanian tribes, Reuben and Gilead (= the Transjordanian sector of Manasseh?) are castigated for their failure to respond. Two tribes that are commonly listed as belonging to Israel, Judah and Gad, are not mentioned at all. There is also no mention of Levi, suggesting that it was not a tribe that held territory at the time. The Song of Deborah is thus a strong witness to the absence of any strong sense of a tribal league that could *require* concerted action on the part of all its members. There is a varied response of the Israelite constituencies in rallying against a common threat. Here then is Israel as some kind of loosely-formed confederacy without a political center. Lindars' conclusion (in which we have interspersed our own comments in brackets) is helpful. He maintains that though Barak's [and Deborah's] success depended on cooperation, there is very little sign of it elsewhere. If the tribes do join together, it is usually for mopping up after the success of a local leader, when they hope to prevent further trouble from the enemy and cash in on the spoils (Judg 3:27; 7:23-25; 12:1-6). Nor do the individual tribes seem to have internal cohesion. They are rather groups of clans banded together temporarily for military purposes [on the basis of the principle of complementary opposition in segmentary societies as we noted in Chapter 2]. That is why the tribal names are mainly geographical rather then ethnic. The variation between geographical and ethnic names shows how haphazard the evolution of the tribes was. Some, like Ephraim and Gilead, answer well to the description of a group of clans banded together. Others, like Manasseh and Judah [not mentioned in the Song of Deborah], are individual clans which have established control over a wide region. Others, like Benjamin and Dan after its migration, are small clusters of clans which have retained their independence. The tribes in Judges are evolving unities of clans. The tribe is best regarded as a regional unit of clans, providing a wider circle for intermarriage. It is thus only to be expected that the growth of a national self-consciousness will be expressed in the formation of a genealogical system [that is, a segmentary lineage system], embracing all the tribes in one family (1980: 110–111).

Stories about "Judges" in the Book of Judges

As we have noted, Judges opens with a section that summarizes the "conquest" and settlement of Canaan (1:1-3:6). Judges presupposes the story line that began in Exodus and comes to a climax in Joshua. Between these two, Judges deals with a fundamental problem of biblical religion. Between oppression in Egypt and the establishment of a stable sociopolitical system in the land of the promise, there is the challenge of living a life of obedience to Yahweh. The judges are those charismatic leaders who arise to deliver Israel from the oppression brought on by their unfaithfulness to Yahweh.

The second part of Judges is made up of the stories of the judges proper (3:7-15:20). This section is subdivided into two subsections. The first of these deals with an initial phase of judges' activity, telling the stories of a total of ten judges. Also included within this subsection are mentions of two judges, Tola (10:1) and Jair (10:3-5), who are remembered but have no specific deeds associated with their names. The suggestion has been made that perhaps they were added to bring the total of judges named in the book to twelve. The other subsection deals with a subsequent set of judges, beginning in 10:6-16. This subsection goes on to tell about the activities of Jephthah, three "minor judges," and finally Samson (ending in ch. 16). Robert Boling has suggested that an appropriate label for the stories about the judges is "historical romance" (Boling 1992: 1113). The stories that comprise the body of Judges correspond to the "ideal" genre of historical romance. By this Boling means that they are stories of leaders whose varying Yahwistic effectiveness is evaluated in the telling.

The third part of Judges is a series of stories about Micah's shrine and Micah's Levite (chs. 17-18). The final story in Judges (19-21) also involves a Levite. By focusing on Levites in these closing chapters of the book of Judges, the narrator makes a telling comment on Israel's moral decline. The corruption that has infected both the judges and the people has also spread to the conservators of the Yahwistic tradition. The story of the Levite and his "concubine" is one of incredible sexual violence directed toward a woman who is never allowed to speak throughout the entire episode. After his wife is gang-raped all night long, the Levite seizes her (19:25) and cuts her body into twelve pieces, as if she were some sort of sacrificial animal. He then sends the pieces throughout the tribes of Israel in an attempt to call them together. The end of the story is a bloody civil war that nearly exterminates the tribe of Benjamin, in whose territory the rape and dismemberment had occurred. These stories at the end of Judges depict the growing threats, both internal and external, faced by tribal Israel. The horrific encounter between the tribe of Benjamin and the rest of the tribes provoked by the outrage at Gibeah is used in the narrative to point up the disastrous consequences that follow from the lack of central authority. The summarizing comment of the redactor of Judg 17-21 speaks directly to this (from an obviously promonarchical perspective):

> In those days there was no king in Israel; all the people did what was right in their own eyes (Judg 17:6; 21:25).

As the book of Judges has progressed, the motivations toward violence have become increasingly personal. Violence is transformed from a tool for the common good (in a "holy war" to secure the land) into the weapon for anarchy.

There is, however, included within Judges a tradition that is distinctly antimonarchical, reflecting tribal Israel's suspicion of monarchy with its excesses and strong arm. The antimonarchical fable of Jotham in Judg 9:7-21 makes strong use of irony to warn Israel against making "sticker-bush persons" into kings. These are persons who, like the bramble, offer no shade (that is, protection) for their people and are basically good for little else but starting fires (that is, causing problems).

Israel faced internal divisions from within and, as we shall see in the next chapter, increasing Philistine aggression on her borders. The last of Israel's judges, Samuel, presided over the transition to statehood. He is pictured as having such a strong influence outside his own tribe that when the time came to set a king over the people of Israel, Samuel would lead them in making the choice. With Samuel's story the book of Samuel begins its story about the formation of the state.

STUDY QUESTIONS

JOSHUA

1. Robert Alter (p. 117) has said that in the Bible:
   The matrix for allusion is often a sense of absolute historical continuity and recurrence, or an assumption that earlier events and
   figures are timeless ideological models by which all that follows
   can be measured.

   The beginning of Joshua takes us back in a variety of ways to the early
   chapters of Exodus. Illustrate this by comparing some of the literary motifs
   and details in Joshua 1-5 with those in Exodus 3-4; 14-15.
2. Write a brief evaluation of the archaeological evidence pertaining to the
   events narrated in the books of Joshua and Judges.
3. What are the three different models that have been proposed for explaining
   the Israelite conquest/settlement of Canaan? What are the strengths and
   weaknesses of each?
4. What are some of the most important characteristics of the "Deuteronomistic History"? Do you agree or disagree with the rewards/punishments
   schema used in the Deuteronomistic Historian's work? Why? Can you offer
   another model for understanding rewards and punishments?
5. How does the book of Joshua show that Yahweh is the main agent of the
   Conquest? How, for example, does the description of the battle of Jericho
   indicate the religious nature of the story?
6. Why do you think so much space is given over to the allotment of the land
   in the second half of Joshua?

JUDGES

1. Where, in addition to the Song of Deborah, do women play significant roles
   in Judges?
2. What meaning might Jotham's fable (Judg 9:7-15) have: (a) to Israelites
   living before the establishment of the monarchy; (b) Israelites living under
   the monarchy; (c) to Americans in a Presidential election year?
3. In the light of the story in Gen 22, how do you interpret the story of
   Jephthah's vow (Judg 11) that resulted in the killing of his daughter?

BIBLIOGRAPHY

Alter, Robert. 1992. *The World of Biblical Literature.* New York: Basic Books.
Boling, Robert G. 1992. "Judges, Book of." *The Anchor Bible Dictionary,* Vol. 3. New
York: Doubleday, 1107-17.
Buechner, Frederick. 1979. *Peculiar Treasures: A Biblical Who's Who.* San Francisco:
Harper & Row.

Dearman, J. Andrew. 1992. *Religion and Culture in Ancient Israel.* Peabody, MA: Hendrickson.

Dever, William D. 1990. *Recent Archaeological Discoveries and Biblical Research.* Seattle: University of Washington.

Emerton, J. A. 1982. "New Light on Israelite Religion: The Implications of the Inscription from Kuntillet 'Ajrud." *Zeitschrift für die alttestamentliche Wissenschaft,* 94:2-20.

Frick, Frank S. 1985. *The Formation of the State in Ancient Israel: A Survey of Methods and Theories.* Sheffield, England: JSOT.

Gottwald, Norman K. 1979. *The Tribes of Yahweh: A Sociology of the Religion of Liberated Israel, 1250-1050 B.C.* Maryknoll, NY: Orbis.

Hadley, J. M. 1987. "The Khirbet el-Qom Inscription." *Vetus Testamentum,* 37:50-62.

Kenyon, Kathleen M. 1957. *Digging Up Jericho.* London: Ernest Benn.

Lindars, Barnabas. 1980. "The Israelite Tribes in Judges." *Supplements to Vetus Testamentum,* XXX: 95-112.

Matthews, Victor H., and Benjamin, Don C. 1991. *Old Testament Parallels: Laws and Stories from the Ancient Near East.* New York: Paulist.

Mendenhall, George E. 1962. "The Hebrew Conquest of Palestine," *Biblical Archaeologist,* 25: 66-87.

Meyers, Carol. 1988. *Discovering Eve: Ancient Israelite Women in Context.* New York: Oxford University Press.

Pritchard, James B., ed. 1969. *Ancient Near Eastern Texts Related to the Old Testament.* 3rd ed. Princeton: Princeton University Press.

Smith, Mark S. 1990. *The Early History of God: Yahweh and the Other Deities in Ancient Israel.* San Francisco: Harper.

Stager, Lawrence E. 1985. "The Archaeology of the Family in Ancient Israel," *Bulletin of the American Schools of Oriental Research,* 260: 1-35.

Weippert, Manfred. 1971. *The Settlement of the Israelite Tribes in Palestine.* London: SCM.

Chapter 9

THE FORMATION OF THE STATE IN ANCIENT ISRAEL: 1 & 2 SAMUEL; 1 KINGS 1—11

Suggested Bible Reading
1 Sam 1 - 31; 2 Sam 1 - 24; 1 Kings 1 - 11;
1 Chr 9:35 - 22:19; 1 Chr 28:11 - 2 Chr 9:31

$\mathcal{T}$he narratives in the books of Samuel relate in a series of anecdotes how David rose to power as king and in the process united various factions. It is also clear that David's success was, to some degree, at the expense of Saul, a transitional figure. While David is pictured as a remarkable figure in Israel's history, he was plagued by problems in his family that, from the perspective of the Deuteronomistic Historian, had their effects on his son and successor, Solomon. In this chapter, we will examine the materials about Saul, David, and Solomon not as history-as-biography, but will focus our attention on the social and political dynamics of this period of transition in the sociopolitical life of ancient Israel. Because the biblical data concerning this period are sketchy, in this chapter we will show how data and theories from the social sciences, especially anthropology, can and do provide the student of the Bible with suggestive and illuminating controlled comparisons between many of the sociopolitical processes at work in early Israel and similar processes of state formation elsewhere.

When discussing the cultural and political evolution of societies, there is a special interest in how and why states were formed. Except for some contemporary multinational corporations, no more powerful sociopolitical entity exists than the state. States generally permit greater inequality among people than any other form of social association. We might ask under what circumstances then, have people given up, or why have they been forced to give up, so much local and individual autonomy to become part of, and subordinate to, the power of a state?

Because premonarchic Israel was a society which highly valued tribal autonomy and only temporarily surrendered to shifting tribal confederations, what set of circumstances could have moved the elders of Israel to appear before Samuel and ask him to "Appoint for us, then, a king to govern us, like other nations" (1 Sam 8:4)? A common answer to this question has been pressure caused by the Philistines. The Philistine menace, from this perspective, was the "prime mover" that forced statehood on Israel. Scholars have proposed that the Philistines were able to exert such pressure because: (1) they had a monopoly on the production of an inherently technologically superior metal in the form of iron and (2) they had a superior form of social (and military) organization. Here, however, an alternative viewpoint will be considered. The Philistine menace was, from our perspective, a *necessary* but not a *sufficient* cause leading to the formation of the Israelite state. The Philistines accelerated the emergence of the Israelite state as it evolved from a chiefdom, a societal form that already, as an adaptive strategy, necessarily had gone beyond any early tribal egalitarianism. Thus, internal changes were involved in the formation of the state, not just external pressure.

FROM TRIBAL LEAGUES TO CHIEFDOM TO MONARCHY—INTERNAL CHANGE AND EXTERNAL PRESSURE

Tribal Leagues

In anthropological terms, premonarchic Israel can be described as an agriculturally-based or agrarian, segmentary society. As we saw in the last chapter, a segmentary society does not organize itself around a political center of power. Instead, its political organization consists of "segments" of politically equal rank. In Israel's case segmentary organization was correlated with the lineage system, which we discussed in Chapter 2. In Israel, political organization was based on a particular way of genealogical reckoning and descent rules. The tribes of Israel encompassed lineages that were divided into maximal, major, minor, and minimal lines. There was at work in such a scheme a recurring pattern of the splitting apart and uniting of subunits within the tribal framework. How then is the idea of Israel as such a society relevant to the question of the formation of the state in ancient Israel, and how is it reflected in the biblical literature?

At one level, the state puts the brakes on the process of splitting apart of sociopolitical entities characteristic of segmentary societies. The individual tribes in early Israel were not fixed entities but were still in the process of formation. This process included both the phenomena of the splitting apart and merging of different tribal subunits. At the same time the tribes, as they were "successful" and invested their agricultural surplus in a growing population base, were also expanding territorially. As we have noted, the book of Judges gives no picture of an all-Israel tribal confederacy that had a fixed structure with a definite membership. As a segmentary society, early Israel's "segments" could (and certainly did in the social revolution model of settlement in the land) take in, and even incorporate, small groups, slaves, clients, and persons or groups related by marriage. Because there was no structural device, such as citizenship, for incorporating such groups, they had to be absorbed culturally and socially, which obviously would result in cultural exchange and leveling. The tribes that made up early Israel were faced with a good deal of pressure to incorporate other groups, since we can assume that all such groups were not exterminated in the "conquest." Since the sociopolitical form designated as a chiefdom is particularly consistent with increasing cultural diversity, it was the sociocultural adaptive device in early Israel that enabled this incorporation process.

Why Chiefdom Formation?

The term chiefdom is widely and loosely used to refer to hierarchically organized societies that lack the strong central governmental apparatus of states. Chiefdoms arise from: (1) the ranking of individuals within local communities and (2) regionally centralized organization of local communities. The second of these principles is an important development beyond segmentary societies and provides the key to understanding chiefdoms as distinct from segmentary societies. Early Israel can be seen as moving from a segmentary society in its "tribal" period (twelfth to early eleventh centuries B.C.E.), to a chiefdom in the days of Saul (1020–1000 B.C.E. and the early David (middle to late eleventh century B.C.E.), to statehood under the later David and Solomon (first half of the tenth century B.C.E.)—David ruled from 1000–961 B.C.E. and Solomon from 961–922 B.C.E.

As we have suggested, the movement from one form of sociopolitical organization to another was a result of *both* internal change and external pressure. The internal changes were adaptive strategies. As has been emphasized repeatedly, early Israel was an agrarian society, one that had an agricultural economic base. As such, constraints were imposed on it by the internal functioning of varying levels of agricultural intensification in the highland areas. In addition there were risks deriving from the climate of the region, as we described in Chapter 2. These constraints and risks provide the setting for understanding the mechanisms and processes of centralization as adaptive strategies.

It is now an established fact, no matter which model one may prefer—whether the conquest, settlement, or revolt model—that ancient Israel, before its development into a state, first became established as a recognizable sociopolitical entity principally in the central hill country of Palestine. The political movements that ultimately led to unification, the events that surrounded the formative stages of the chiefdom and then the state at the time of Samuel, Saul, and David, were all focused in the central highlands. Following "success" in the central highlands, Israel expanded into the lowlands, the plains of Jezreel and Esdraelon. Then they expanded into the Huleh basin north of the Sea of Galilee, onto the coastal plain of Philistia and the western Shephelah, the Transjordan, and finally into the Negev.

Most early Israelite territory in the central highlands is in what can be called a medium-risk agricultural environment. The lack of rainfall is not the only meteorological factor that must be considered in assessing agricultural risk. Other factors include the distribution of rainfall throughout the rainy season and of variability in temperature. These meteorological variables, when considered with the limited availability of water for agricultural purposes from other sources (springs and streams), added up to a considerable degree of agricultural risk. They required the development of technological means of water conservation and control, as well as the accompanying development of sociopolitical strategies that could deal with threats to subsistence.

Of all the technologies and techniques that enabled the development of a reliable agricultural subsistence under such conditions, the construction of agricultural terracing on the hillsides was one of the most important (see Figure 9.1). The construction of agricultural terraces in the highlands had three main functions: (1) they transformed the hillside slopes into a series of level surfaces suitable for farming; (2) they helped prevent runoff erosion while permitting the accumulation of soil and water; and (3) their construction removed stones from the soil. The retaining walls on the front edge of the terrace were made of unhewn stones that were taken from the soil. Not only did this "clean up" the soil, the construction of the terrace walls from unhewn stones facilitated drainage of the terrace, because terrace walls were constructed without the use of mortar. Thus, terrace construction made those soil types that were excessively rocky and that had poor drainage characteristics more arable.

Terracing was a complex operation that demanded a large investment of time and labor, both in the initial construction and in maintenance. Because of this time and investment and because one set of terraces could work well only in conjunction with ones adjacent to, above, or below it, terrace systems were not the result of the work of individual farmers. The construction and maintenance of terrace systems might well be an example of the kind of regular functions of the *mishpachah*, the societal unit between the *bet 'av* and tribe. The construction and maintenance of terraces are but two examples of interaction among society, the environment, and subsistence strategies that required sociopolitical structures that could help lessen the built-in fissioning tendencies of segmentary societies. This, in turn, resulted in movement toward more political centralization.

Figure 9.1   A terraced hillside

The development toward a centralized form of government can be seen, on the one hand, as the product of internal changes within a tribal society. These changes were caused by pressure on the available resources, due not only to a risky agricultural environment, but also to population growth that strained the ability of individual tribal territories to feed their populations. As far as population pressure is concerned, the Hebrew Bible is silent. But such a situation is not at all unthinkable, because the tribal territories were both of limited extent and finite fertility. It makes sense that the tribes bartered with one another to make up for shortfalls brought on by the widely differing set of environmental circumstances in the many micro-environments of ancient Israel. While there is limited information in the Bible on how such internal factors brought on change, considerable information describes external political and military pressure on the tribal societies in the mountainous regions of Palestine *ca.* 1000 B.C.E. This pressure came from a people known as the Philistines, whom we introduced in Chapter 2.

THE PHILISTINES—LAND AND POPULATION PRESSURE

While one may not remember them because they did not play crucial roles, we have encountered the Philistines in our journey long before we reached this point in 1 Samuel. There are references to the Philistines both in Genesis (21:32–34;

Figure 9.2   The Egyptians battling the "Sea Peoples"

26:1, 8, 14-15) and in Exodus (13:17; 15:14; 23:31). These references are clearly anachronistic, the product of a later author reading the Philistines into the past. Historically, the Philistines appeared in the region of the eastern Mediterranean at the beginning of the twelfth century B.C.E. Probably of Aegean origin, they were allied with other Sea Peoples who attempted to settle in Egypt. Inscriptions on the walls of Rameses III's mortuary temple in Medinet Habu record their names and much of what is known about the "peoples of the sea and of the north." The inscriptions are accompanied by detailed pictorial reliefs that show two battles—a land battle and a naval clash, *ca.* 1190 B.C.E. (see Figure 9.2) In the naval battle, the ships of the Sea Peoples have prows and sterns in the shape of birds' heads. A stylized bird is also a frequent motif on Philistine pottery (see Figure 9.3). The Sea Peoples' warriors wear a distinctive headdress. This headdress

Figure 9.3   Philistine pottery with stylized bird motif

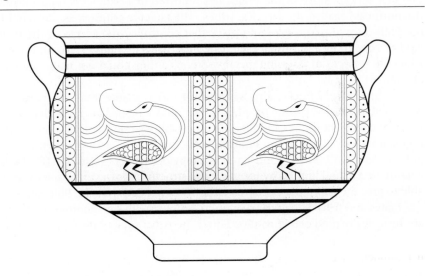

has a horizontal band with a geometric design. Above the design are vertical lines that represent feathers or strips of leather. In the portrayal of captured warriors, those wearing such a headdress are identified as Philistines, Denyen, and Tjekker, groups who made up the Sea Peoples. This same headdress is represented on clay coffins. Burial customs are sensitive indicators of culture. Philistine burial customs reflect the blending of their background in the Aegean (rock-cut chamber tombs) with Egyptian (anthropoid clay coffins, that is, ones having a human shape) influence. The anthropoid coffins are roughly in the outline of a body, with a lid that models the face and headdress (see Figures 9.4 and 9.5).

After defeating them, Rameses III permitted the Philistines to settle on the southern coastal plain of Palestine. They formed a *pentapolis* (a group of five cities—Gaza, Ashkelon, Ashdod, Ekron, and Gath)—in what became known as Philistia, a territory that is defined in Josh 13:2–3. Four of the cities of the Philistine Pentapolis have been positively identified—Gaza, Ashkelon, Ashdod, and Ekron. The location of Gath is still debated.

For well over a century, the Philistines occupied this region peaceably. Toward the end of the eleventh century however, they began to expand into areas occupied by the tribes of Dan and Judah. Dan was eventually forced out of the southern coastal plain and relocated in the far north, a story told in Judges (Judg 17–18). In the far north they took the city of Laish and renamed it Dan. Judah was also challenged by the Philistines. Judg 15:9–17 describes a Philistine attack on Judah in the region of the Shephelah, which was a buffer zone separating the Judean heartland from the Philistine territory. This was an area bound to be contested if one group wanted to expand at the expense of the other.

The initial clashes between the Philistines and Israelites mentioned in Judges take on a much more serious tone in 1 Samuel. While border skirmishes between Philistines and Judah are hinted at in Judges, the Bible tells us nothing about serious clashes between the two. However, 1 Samuel preserves several traditions about the Philistine advances into the hill country (1 Sam 4; 13–14). The first serious move of the Philistines reported in 1 Samuel is their move to the northeast against the Israelite tribes. The Israelite tribes were defeated by the Philistines in two battles at a place that controlled the access to the heartland of Israel. The Philistines established garrisons (1 Sam 13:16) and denied Israel the services of traveling metalworkers, so they could not make weapons (1 Sam 13:19–22).

In this crisis, Samuel emerges in 1 Sam 1–15 as a larger-than-life figure who is a combination of priest, prophet, judge, and king-maker. As a charismatic figure like those described in Judges, it is possible that he inspired some local or regional victories against the Philistines (1 Sam 7:2–17). He was trusted as a judge (1 Sam 7:17; 8:1–3) and acted as a religious leader (1 Sam 19:18–24). As a figure tied to and limited by Israel's tribal structure, however, Samuel was not able to give the tribes the decisive victory they needed over the Philistines.

States and tribal societies have often collided with one another, with what are historically predictable results. Either the tribal society disintegrates as the

Figure 9.4   A Philistine anthropoid clay coffin

Figure 9.5   A comparison of an anthropoid coffin lid from Beth-Shean and a protrait from Medinet Habu

result of political pressures with which it cannot cope, or it changes its character by centralizing its exercise of power. Confronted with the Philistine threat the Israelite tribes had two possibilities: they could submit to Philistine overlords, or they could change their internal structure. Had they followed the first course, they would have been integrated into the Philistine political entity, and within a few years they probably would have lost their cultural identity. Following the second course, which is the route they took, they felt they just might be able to resist the Philistine threat.

Recent studies of the rise of the monarchy in Israel (for example, Frick 1985; Flanagan 1981) have drawn attention to the cultural evolutionary aspects of this development. These studies are timely reminders that history is not created simply by the actions of "great" individuals, although much history is written this way. After all, Israel had faced and defeated enemies before without resorting to the establishment of a permanent, centralized governmental authority. So how was the Philistine threat unique, so different that it required making such a radical change? The difference was probably that the Philistine occupation of the land and their demand for agricultural surpluses led to a temporary breakdown of social organization among the Israelites. For example, 1 Sam 13:6–7 provides a vignette of Israel in a rather pitiful situation:

> When the Israelites saw that they were in distress (for the troops were hard pressed), the people hid themselves in caves and in holes and in rocks and in tombs and in cisterns. Some Hebrews crossed the Jordan to the land of Gad and Gilead.

In this grim situation, Saul emerged as the leader of the Israelite tribes.

Samuel and Saul—a Transitional Figure and a Tragic Hero

The books of 1 and 2 Samuel, and the first chapters of 1 Kings focus on three figures, each of whom is pictured as being in tension with one of the others. First, Samuel is in tension with Saul, then Saul against David, and finally David contends with the combined legacy of Samuel and Saul. Both 1 and 2 Samuel can be outlined based on these three main characters and their relationships as follows:

- 1 Sam 1-6   Samuel
- 1 Sam 7-15   Samuel and Saul
- 1 Sam 16-2 Sam 1   Saul and David
- 2 Sam 2-4   David in Hebron
- 2 Sam 5-20   David in Jerusalem
- 2 Sam 21-24   Appendices

Samuel

The first chapters of 1 Samuel introduce us to Samuel. Samuel serves as a transitional character who occupies the space between the demonstrated inadequacies of the tribal system in the face of the Philistine crisis and the appearance of the first king. Samuel's public style as a social critic—which is consistent throughout his career and, in at least one instance, even from beyond the grave (1 Sam 28:3-20)—is established from the beginning of his story. We are told almost nothing about Samuel's personal life. He is a public figure. He is portrayed as God's faithful representative to the people. Chapters 4-6 of 1 Samuel move the spotlight from Samuel onto the deepening Philistine crisis. In these chapters the Ark of the Covenant, rather than any person, is the focus. The Philistines defeat the Israelites at Ebenezer (1 Sam 4:1-10). The story of Israel's defeat at Ebenezer and the Philistines' capturing of the Ark of the Covenant has its comic touches but represents a tragic religious and political reality. The Israelites attempted to force God's hand against the Philistines by bringing the Ark, as a symbol of God's presence, to the battlefield to assure their victory. Not only did this *not* result in military victory, it resulted in the enemy capturing the Israelite God (or so they thought)! When the Ark was returned in 1 Sam 7, the Israelites, obviously shocked by the whole affair, "cleaned up their act," and we have, in 1 Sam 7:13-14 an idyllic description of how life *could* be without a king:

> So the Philistines were subdued and did not again enter the territory of Israel; the hand of the LORD was against the Philistines all the days of Samuel. The towns that the Philistines had taken from Israel were restored to Israel, from Ekron to Gath; and Israel recovered their territory from the hand of the Philistines.

But it was a very brief honeymoon indeed!

Saul

In the next five chapters (1 Sam 8–12), an aging Samuel begins a conflict-filled relationship with the young Saul in response to the people's demand for a king (8:5). Commentators have often noted that there are different perspectives and perhaps multiple sources represented in these chapters. In particular, some have seen here an early promonarchical, pro-Saul source and a later antimonarchical, pro-Samuel source. While there are clearly different views on the monarchy represented here, whether early and late sources are behind them is debatable. Brevard Childs, building on an earlier suggestion by Dennis McCarthy, has suggested that pro- and antimonarchical perspectives in this section of 1 Samuel are arranged symmetrically:

(anti)   *a*—8:1-22—Samuel warns *against* kingship.
(pro)   *b*—9:1-10:16—A basically positive portrait of Saul and his anointing by Samuel.
(anti)   *c*—10:17-27—Another warning from Samuel and the public choice of Saul as king, who is described derisively as "hiding in the baggage."
(pro)   *b'*—11:1-15—A positive portrait of Saul, who leads an inspired victory over the Ammonites.
(anti)   *a'*—12:1-25—Samuel's final admonition (in the classic style of the Deuteronomistic Historian). (1979: 277-278).

In these chapters there is not one, but three conflicting accounts of Saul's selection as Israel's first king. According to one account, Saul was secretly anointed by Samuel, as instructed by Yahweh (1 Sam 10:1). In another account, Saul, who had hidden himself, was chosen by lot and reluctantly anointed by Samuel (1 Sam 10:20-24). The third account presents Saul as plowing a field when he learned of an Ammonite threat to the Transjordanian town of Jabesh-Gilead. In the tradition of the judges, Saul won a victory over the Ammonites, and with the agreement of Samuel was proclaimed king at Gilgal (1 Sam 11:1-15).

The remainder of 1 Samuel focuses on Saul as he faces the intensified incursions of the Philistines. The movement toward permanent leadership is a gradual one. After the victory over the Ammonites in 1 Sam 11, Saul is pictured as leading the Israelites in successful campaigns against the Philistines (1 Sam 13-14) and the Amalekites (1 Sam 15). What began as charismatic leadership in the style of the judges, became permanent leadership under Philistine pressure.

1 Sam 13:1, with its characteristic Deuteronomistic formula regarding a king's accession, marks the formal beginning of the new period of the United Monarchy, which ends with the death of Solomon. There is, however, an obvious textual problem with 1 Sam 13:1 that is reflected in the NRSV translation: "Saul was . . . years old when he began to reign; and he reigned . . . and two years over Israel." The Hebrew text here reads "Saul was one year old when he began to reign, and he reigned two years over Israel." Numbers before the "one" and the "two" have been lost. Perhaps it should be read "Saul was *twenty*

one when he began to reign and he reigned *twelve* (10+2) years over Israel."
While we have no other indication of the length of Saul's rule, twelve years
would have been long enough for the Philistine pressure to bring about the social changes implied by permanent leadership. Four ways of understanding
Saul's role have been proposed. All of them use the same biblical and extrabiblical materials, but assess the materials differently. The four models are Saul as:
(1) permanent judge, (2) self-appointed protector, (3) chieftain, and (4) state-
builder.

PERMANENT JUDGE

The picture of Saul as *permanent judge* was developed by A. Alt in 1930, who
argued that Saul's leadership represented a transitional stage between premonarchic tribal league and nationhood (1967: 223–309). Responding to Philistine
pressure, the tribes united and "institutionalized" the charismatic office of judge,
making it a permanent rather than a temporary leadership position. Saul's leadership was, according to this model, limited to military affairs, and was not to be
handed down to his son. Saul was not really a king. This model, which is the oldest and most widely accepted picture of Saul's role, presupposes that the Bible at
this point is a reliable witness to the political situation and institutions of the premonarchic period.

SELF-APPOINTED PROTECTOR

The image of Saul as a *self-appointed protector* has been developed more recently as a challenge to the permanent judge model. According to this view, the
biblical witness to the premonarchic era is not entirely reliable historically.
In this period, Israel was not a unified tribal confederacy and was not led by a
single leader. Rather, Israel was a segmented society in which self-styled military
leaders could establish themselves as protectors over limited areas. Saul was
such a figure, able to extend his initial position of influence within his own
tribe of Benjamin to include adjoining areas. The title "king" can be applied to
Saul only if understood that he was not a dynastic monarch who administered a
full-blown state.

CHIEFTAIN

A recently-developed model for understanding Saul presents him as a *chief* in
the transitional, intermediate step between segmented society and statehood
(Flanagan 1981, Frick 1985). According to this model, Saul emerged as a chief
and based his authority on his skill as a military leader. Building on this base, he
solidified his support outside his tribe. As a "paramount chief," Saul occupied
an office that fell short of kingship. Beyond the hope that he might be able to
pass on his leadership gifts to his son, there was no guaranteed mechanism for

transfer of authority. In such a situation, the death of a chief usually set off a protracted struggle for power among potential successors both within and outside the chief's family. In Saul's case, this struggle began even before his death. Saul and David become competing paramount chiefs within Israel, on the eve of its movement to full-fledged statehood.

STATE-BUILDER

The fourth model, developed by Diana Edelman (1993), pictures Saul as the *monarchic founder of the Israelite state.* According to this model, Saul was a full-fledged king responsible for uniting tribal units to form the territorial state of Israel. He was indeed the founder of Israelite statehood and its first king.

Certainly, whichever model one prefers, Saul represented something new in Israel. The subunits that made up Israel came to the point where they could no longer effectively manage their affairs by using the services of a series of short-term leaders. It had been the case that when one leader died or became ineffective, everyone could return home until a new short-term crisis brought forth another such temporary leader. However, what was a more perilous threat called for a more permanent administrative apparatus. Therefore, Israelite society produced a permanent leadership group consisting of a king (although at first he might be called a paramount chieftain), one or more administrative officials who served at Saul's pleasure, and a small standing army of individuals who were responsible to Saul and loyal to him alone.

Once Israel had started down this path with Saul, there was no turning back. While Saul may have had a small court in comparison to other kings of the ancient Near East, the longer there was need for its services, the more extensive the bureaucracy became until it, like so many modern governments have done, made itself so indispensable that no realistic alternative to it can be envisaged. One expression of this can be seen in the fact that Saul's son, Ishbaal, was chosen king after him, not because of anything he did or did not do, but simply because he was Saul's son. The biblical narrative, in its first words concerning Ishbaal, says quite simply that Abner, the commander of Saul's army "made him king over Gilead, the Ashurites, Jezreel, Ephraim, Benjamin, and over all Israel. Ishbaal, Saul's son, was forty years old when he began to reign over Israel, and he reigned two years. But the house of Judah followed David" (2 Sam 2:9–10). Like any other dynastic monarch, Saul was succeeded by his son. Saul's dynasty, however, did not last. It was replaced by the dynasty of David.

Cheryl Exum and William Whedbee (1984) have demonstrated that the story of Saul in 1 Sam 9–31 displays the inverted U plot structure typical of tragedy. The story develops against the negative backdrop of Yahweh's misgivings about kingship in Chapter 8, and its movement to catastrophe is driven by the rejection stories of Chapters 13 and 15. Saul encounters a series of setbacks, from anxiety produced by his loss of prestige in the eyes of the people (18:7) to his inability to apprehend David; and his situation deteriorates until the narrative reaches its lowest point with the vision of Samuel conjured up from his grave by the medium at Endor (28:5 ff.) For sheer starkness and terror, few biblical narratives can rival the story of Saul and the medium at Endor. Notice the numerous references to Saul's anguished state in this story: he is "afraid" (v. 5), his "heart trembled greatly" (v. 5), he is "in great distress" (v. 15), he is "filled with fear" (v. 20), and he is "ter-rified" (v. 21). After this journey into the depths of abandonment by God, the story of his death that follows is almost anticlimactic. Tragic events pile up in 1 Sam 31: Israel is routed (v. 1); Saul's sons are killed (v. 2); Saul commits suicide, as does his armor bearer (vv. 3-6); the Israelites abandon their cities to the Philistines (v. 7); and the Philistines mutilate and desecrate Saul's body. The cruelest part of Saul's fate lies in his death in isolation from Yahweh. Typical of the tragic vision, there is no reconciliation, no restoration, no future for the house of Saul.

An Imaginative Portrait of Saul

Saul, the first king of Israel, has three things going against him almost from the beginning. One of them was the prophet Samuel, another was a young man named David, and the third and worst was himself.

Samuel never thought Israel should have a king in the first place and told them so at regular intervals. After Saul defeated the Amalekites, Samuel said the rules of the game were that he should take the whole pack of them plus their king and all their livestock and sacrifice them to Yahweh. When Saul decided to sacrifice only the sway-backs and runts of the litter, keeping the cream of the crop and the king for himself, Samuel said it was the last straw and that Yahweh was through with him for keeps. Samuel then snuck off and told a boy name David that he was to be the next king, and the sooner the better. In the meanwhile, however, they both kept the matter under their hats.

Saul was hit so hard by the news that Yahweh was through with him that his whole faith turned sour. The God he'd always loved became the God who seemed to have it in for him no matter what he did or failed to do, and he went into such a state of depression that he could hardly function. The only person who could bring him out of it was this same David. He was a good-looking young red-head with a nice voice and would come and play songs on his lyre till the king's case of the horrors was under at least temporary control. Saul lost his heart to him eventually, and when the boy knocked out the top Philistine heavy-weight, their relationship seemed permanently clinched.

It wasn't. David could charm the birds out of the trees, and soon all Israel was half in love with him, "Saul has slain his thousands and David his ten

Continued

thousands," the ladies would dither every time he rounded the bend in his fancy uniform (I Samuel 18:7), and Saul began to smoulder. It was one day when David was trying to chase his blues away with some new songs that he burst into flame. He heaved his spear at him and just missed by a quarter of an inch. When his own son and heir, Jonathan, fell under David's spell too, that did it. It was love-hate from then on.

He hated him because he needed him, and he needed him because he loved him, and when he wasn't out to kill him every chance he got, he was hating himself for his own evil disposition. One day he went into a cave to take a leak, not knowing that David was hiding out there, and while he was taking forty winks afterward, David snipped off a piece of his cloak. When David produced the snippet later to prove he could have tried to kill him in return but hadn't, Saul said, "Is this your voice, my son David?" and wept as if his heart would break (I Samuel 24). It was exactly what, in the end, his heart did.

He was told in advance that he was going to lose the battle of Gilboa and die in the process, but in spite of knowing that, or maybe because of it, he went ahead and fought it anyway.

There are two versions of what happened to him then. One is that after being badly wounded by arrows, he persuaded a young Amalekite to put him out of his misery. The other is that he took his own sword and fell on it. In either case, it is hard to hold it against him for tendering back to the God he had once loved a life that for years he had found unbearable.

Buechner (1979:154–155)

DAVID—FROM SHEPHERD TO OUTLAW TO KING

David, the Young Shepherd-Musician

Paralleling Saul's gradual decline in 1 Sam 16-31 is David's steady ascendancy. As David gained popularity, Saul became the victim of dark moods and fits of anger, directed mostly against David. David is introduced not once, but three times, each story having its own agenda. The first story (1 Sam 16:1-13) describes a secret mission of Samuel to the house of Jesse, David's father, in Bethlehem. The purpose of this trip was to find and anoint Israel's next king. As the sons of Jesse are brought before Samuel, he rejects them one by one, until the youngest appears, David. As David's brothers go before Samuel, God reminds him: "Do not look on his appearance or on the height of his stature . . . for the LORD does not see as mortals see; they look on the outward appearance, but the LORD looks on the heart" (1 Sam 16:7). This is a thinly veiled rejection of Saul, who was described as ". . . a handsome young man. There was not a man among the people of Israel more handsome than he; he stood head and shoulders above everyone else" (1 Sam 9:2). This introduction of David carries with it the message that Yahweh had definite plans for David, even when he was a child and his potential was not yet evident to anyone. The second story introducing David (1 Sam 16:14-23) makes the young David a member of Saul's court as a musician and armor-bearer, again pointing to future areas of David's success. David is hired as a kind of therapist for a mentally-disturbed Saul. The third, and best-known, of the stories introduces David as the Israelite champion facing the Philistine giant, Goliath (1 Sam 17:1-18:5). Although this story follows the other two, it reflects no knowledge of David's earlier introduction. The symbolism of this story is obvious. Goliath aptly represents the dimensions of the Philistine menace, which only David, not Saul, would succeed in conquering decisively. This story also provides a basis for the taunt song of the Israelite women:

> Saul has slain his thousands,
> and [or, *but*] David his ten thousands. (I Sam 18:7)

David, the Outlaw

Saul became increasingly paranoid regarding David and sought to eliminate this young man who threatened his power. David, in escaping from Saul, fled to the one area where the increasingly ineffectual Saul could not get at him—Philistia (see Figure 9.6). David as an outlaw began to build his political power base. He became a vassal of the Philistine king of Gath (1 Sam 27:1-7) and began to demonstrate his ability as a politician in a most interesting way. He raided the non-Israelite peoples living in the northern Negev but sold his boss on the idea that he was really raiding his own people, Judah. On the contrary, during this period David sent gifts to the people of Judah, accumulating political capital that he could cash in later (1 Sam 27:8-12; 30:26-31).

David as King of Judah

After Saul and his son Jonathan are killed, ironically enough, at the hands of the Philistines at Gilboa (1 Sam 31), the people of Judah, acting independently, can openly declare David their king at Hebron (2 Sam 2:4). The story of David as king in 2 Samuel has two parts. The first part, chapters 1-8, narrates his consolidation of power, picturing him both as a military and political genius. The second part, 2 Sam 9-20, shows us that David's considerable abilities as king are not matched in the area of parenting. David, who was able to conquer all Israel's enemies, has considerable trouble in dealing with problems in his own family.

In his consolidation of power, David is first anointed king by the people of Judah at Hebron (2 Sam 2:1-4a), where he reigns for seven-and-one-half years. He could not, however, extend his rule northward at this time because of the

Figure 9.6 David with the Philistines

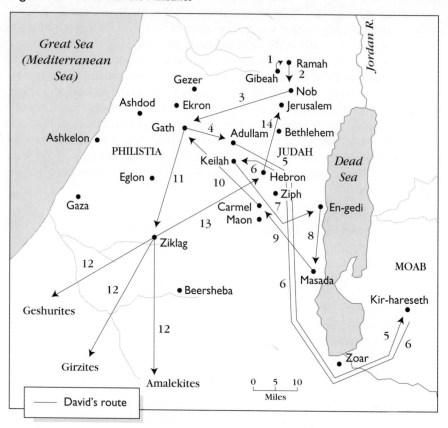

presence of Saul's surviving son, Ishbaal. The passage in 2 Sam 2–4 depicts the rivalry that existed between Judah and Israel, with Judah represented by the figure of David and Israel represented by Ishbaal. After Ishbaal is assassinated by members of his own court, nothing prevents David from assuming power over all Israel.

David as King of All Israel

Following the murder of Ishbaal, the northern tribes come to Hebron and anoint David as king, this time over the North, Israel (2 Sam 5:1–5). With the power of all Israel behind him, David initiates decisive action to resolve the Philistine threat. In two encounters (2 Sam 5:17–25), David's army forces the Philistines out of the middle of the country back into their old territory of Philistia. From this point on, the Philistines are reduced to the status of just another of Israel's neighbors, causing minor problems now and then, but never again constituting a major threat.

Having defeated Israel's only significant external opponent, David then set about conquering an internal enemy, the longstanding division between North and South. If David was to rule as king of all Israel, he could not do so effectively from Hebron, because of its clear identification with the tribe of Judah and the South. He needed a capital that had no traditional association with either South or North. Jerusalem was just such a "neutral" site. In addition, it was an old, well-fortified city, strategically located in the central hill country. David captures the city in an apparently bloodless takeover (2 Sam 5), and it acquires a new name, "The City of David." Here David established the center from which he would rule for the balance of his forty-five-year reign. The story of David's early rise to power concludes with a theological endorsement; he succeeded because God was with him: "And David became greater and greater, for the LORD, the God of hosts, was with him" (2 Sam 5:10).

David was faced, however, with the problem of making Jerusalem into a religious as well as a political capital. This city, with its Canaanite past and lack of Israelite traditions, had to be made into an Israelite city religiously, as well as politically (Jerusalem is *never* mentioned in all of the Pentateuch, with the possible exception of Salem, the city of Melchizedek in Gen 14). David's first step in the sanctification of Jerusalem as *the* city of Yahweh is the installation of the Ark of the Covenant, a symbol of Yahweh for *all* Israel, in a tent on the grounds of his palace (2 Sam 6:5, 12–19). The chapter that follows (2 Sam 7) details David's attempted second step in the sanctification of Jerusaleum. This chapter has been called "The theological highlight of the Books of Samuel . . . if not of the Deuteronomistic History as a whole" (Anderson: 112). This chapter involves an interesting play on words, based on two meanings of the expression "house." As part of his efforts to make Jerusalem into a Yahwistic center, David, in the pattern of other Near-Eastern kings, intends to build a "house" (a temple) for Yahweh in Jerusalem: "See now, I am living in a house of cedar, but the ark of God stays in a tent" (2 Sam 7:2). Yahweh, however, responds through the prophet Nathan, telling David that his son will build a house for God and promising David a sure "house" (that is, a dynasty), which would assure a Davidic descendant on the throne of Israel forever: "When your days are fulfilled and you lie down with your ancestors, I will raise up your offspring after you. . . . Your house and your kingdom shall be made sure forever before me; your throne shall be established forever" (2 Sam 7:12, 16). Following this theological peak, the following chapter (2 Sam 8) again moves us back to the lower ground of military history, offering a rather mundane catalog of David's military triumphs. But even this mundane list has a theological purpose—to show that David continued to have the blessing of Yahweh.

David's Decline

Following the list of David's victories in 2 Sam 8, the balance of the story of David is mostly a sad tale of decline. In it David no longer plays the active hero who makes things happen. Rather, he is on the receiving end of events set in motion by one huge blunder on his part.

The story of David's decline is told with remarkable candor in a single narrative that scholars have called "The Court History of David" or "The Succession Narrative," found in 2 Sam 9 – 20; 1 Kings 1 – 2. This narrative has been praised as a prose composition superior to anything else we know in biblical literature and as the oldest specimen of ancient Israelite history writing, the closest example in the Hebrew Bible of "objective" historiography, most likely written by a contemporary observer of the court. While the literary artistry of the Succession Narrative continues to be recognized, there is no longer a scholarly consensus concerning its nature as a historical source from the time of Solomon. The existence in it of numerous anachronisms, etiologies, and folkloristic elements date the storyteller to a later time. It is now recognized that the literary quality of this retrospective piece has nothing to do with how close in time the author was to the events. The Succession Narrative shows the same characteristics as the stories in 1 Samuel about David's early career under Saul, none of which mark it as historical of necessity or argue for contemporary composition. They are rather the hallmarks of hero tales and well-crafted stories the world over (Miller and Hayes 1986: 152 – 160). David Gunn has reviewed the various hypotheses on the genre of the Succession Narrative. He concludes that it should be labelled a traditional story written for purposes of serious entertainment, one that challenges one to self- or social-reassessment. Gunn also modifies the boundary of the story, including in it most of 2 Sam 5 and 6. He does not, however, relate it to the David stories that precede it in 1 Samuel (1978: 61 – 62; 1980: 11). By denying that the narrative's author intends to write history, the text is opened to multiple meanings, various readings, and numerous uses.

Certainly no attempt is made in the Succession Narrative to conceal David's faults or to gloss over the crises he faced. By contrast, the picture of David that emerges in the parallel narrative in the book of 1 Chronicles presents David as completely flawless and as very much concerned with religious matters. 1 Chronicles omits the entire story of David's rise to power, except for a passing glance at Saul (ch. 10), the list of his sons (1 Chr 3 : 1 – 4), his initial anointing at Hebron (1 Chr 11 : 1 – 3), and his capture of Jerusalem (1 Chr 11 : 4 – 9). 1 Chronicles includes most of the material related to David's consolidation of power, but omits almost all of the story of his decline (including the story of his affair with Bathsheba and the following cover-up).

The Succession Narrative also offers explanations for other strange twists of history, perceived at a distance. How did an outlaw from Bethlehem displace the dynasty of Saul, although he had married into Saul's line? How was it that David was succeeded by a younger son, Solomon, when he had older sons? The story in the Succession Narrative answers these questions and explains how the Davidic dynasty, as it was known to later generations, descended through the line of the "wise" Solomon. In short, besides rationalizing history, the Succession Narrative does what Gunn suggests—it provides a model to be avoided for those who would reform or reestablish the Davidic state.

THE BATHSHEBA AFFAIR

The "Bathsheba Affair," narrated as part of the "Court History" in 2 Samuel 11–12, was a pivotal event in David's life and narrated for the dual purposes of explanation and warning. Before his affair with Bathsheba, David seemed to move onward and upward from one triumph to another. After the Bathsheba incident the movement is all in the opposite direction. The story of David and Bathsheba is told with a minimum of explicit theological interpretation. There is, however, a real sense that even David the king could not escape the consequences of his actions, which played themselves out in his own family.

For some reason, David does not lead his army in the campaign against the Ammonites (2 Sam 11:1), but stays in Jerusalem, which provides the opportunity for his affair with Bathsheba (2 Sam 11:2–5). After the adulterous liaison, David is informed that Bathsheba was pregnant by him. He begins the coverup by calling her husband, Uriah, home from the battlefront to enjoy a furlough with his wife. Uriah, the dedicated soldier, frustrates David's scheme by refusing to sleep with his wife, depriving David of the possibility of claiming that Bathsheba had become pregnant when her husband was home on leave. Uriah, a Hittite, is the person with religious integrity here. He cites to David the tradition that sexual abstinence was required of soldiers consecrated for war (cf. 1 Sam 21:4–5). Uriah refuses to violate this taboo, even after David gets him drunk. Step two in the coverup takes a vicious turn, revealing a very dark side of David. Having failed in his first attempt at a solution to the problem of the paternity of Bathsheba's child, David now issues orders that result in Uriah's death in battle—a cruel abuse of royal power on David's part, motivated by base self-protection. David then takes the recently widowed Bathsheba as his wife.

David is forced to confront his actions by the court prophet, Nathan, who appears again here at a critical juncture in David's life. Nathan, who first appears with no introduction or pedigree in 2 Sam 7, has his greatest moment here as he confronts David after David's two great sins (2 Sam 12). He fearlessly accuses David by using a fictional legal case that appealed to David's sense of justice. When David became outraged at the injustice perpetrated by the rich man in the "fictional" story, Nathan boldly looked at David and said: "You are the man!" (2 Sam 12:7) David immediately repented, and Nathan pronounced forgiveness but announced that the child that had been conceived in the adulterous affair would die. After this incident (2 Sam 12:15b–23), David and Bathsheba, now "legally" married, have a second child, Solomon. Given the turns in the David-Bathsheba tale so far, one can hardly help but wonder whether there was a cloud hanging over Solomon's head from his birth.

ABSALOM

The next episodes in 2 Sam 13:1–18:33 reveal that David is still "under a curse" where the narrator carries on the theme of trouble in David's family. David's oldest son, Amnon, raped his half-sister, Tamar (2 Sam 13:1–22). In retaliation,

Tamar's full brother, Absalom, killed his half-brother and went into exile for three years (2 Sam 13:23-39). While all of this is going on, David is pictured as a relatively passive onlooker who reacts to events but does not act decisively.

Facing such violence within his family, David becomes entrapped again by a fictional story that moves him to compassion (2 Sam 14:1-24). This time the story is told by a wise woman from Tekoa employed by Joab, David's general and nephew. She plays the role of a mother in mourning. One of her two sons, so her fictional story went, was killed by his brother in a fight, and the surviving son's life was now threatened by a mob seeking revenge. Having trapped David with her story, she continues, telling him that Absalom's situation is the same as her surviving son's. David acknowledges her point and restores Absalom from exile (2 Sam 14:24-33). Shortly after that, however, Absalom plots rebellion against his father, the story of which is told in some detail in 2 Sam 15-19. During Absalom's rebellion, the situation for David grows so desperate that he is forced to leave Jerusalem and seek refuge east of the Jordan. While David thus secures his own safety, Joab, the commander of David's army, brutally kills Absalom (2 Sam 18:9-15). When word of his rebellious son's death is brought to David (2 Sam 18:9-32), David responds to Absalom's death with a moving lament (2 Sam 18:33): "The king was deeply moved, and went up to the chamber over the gate, and wept; and as we went, he said, 'O my son Absalom, my son, my son Absalom! Would I had died instead of you, O Absalom, my son, my son!'"

SOLOMON

The story of David's decline ends with the struggle for succession to his throne. This struggle pits Adonijah, his oldest surviving son (who, on the principle of primogeniture should have been the next king), against Solomon, Bathsheba's son (1 Kings 1:1-2:12), who is supported by both his mother and Nathan. David's last act is his instructions to his son and successor (1 Kings 2:1-4), in which the perspective of the Deuteronomistic editor (Dtr) shows through:

> When David's time to die drew near, he charged his son Solomon saying: "I am about to go the way of all the earth. Be strong, be courageous, and keep the charge of the LORD your God, walking in his ways and keeping his statutes, his commandments, his ordinances, and his testimonies, as it is written in the law of Moses, so that you may prosper in all that you do and wherever you turn. Then the LORD will establish his word that he spoke concerning me: 'If your heirs take heed to their way, to walk before me in faithfulness with all their heart and with all their soul, there shall not fail you a successor on the throne of Israel.'"

David's Wives

The proliferation of literary approaches to the Bible in recent years has taken many forms. Some of them have been characterized by a rather slavish application of one particular method or approach. In any literary criticism, however, one should take cues from the text itself. Different texts lend themselves to different types of criticism. Adopting such an approach, Adele Berlin has done a literary study of several narratives in the books of Samuel and Kings that have to do with David and the women who became his wives (1982). She is not so much concerned with clarification of individual texts as she is with the literary perspective that emerges from an overview of a number of related texts. Her primary focus is on the characterization of the women and an indirect view of the characterization of David in these texts. The stories examined are all about David, but David is not the main character in all of them. They all portray a relationship between David and a woman, but the characterization of each woman is quite different.

MICHAL

The first of David's wives was Michal, the daughter of Saul. Berlin compares the characterization of Michal with that of Jonathan, her brother (1982: 71-74). Their stories are juxtaposed in 1 Sam 18-20. Berlin sees an interesting inversion in the characterization of Michal and Jonathan: the characteristics normally associated with males are attached to Michal, and those usually perceived as feminine are linked with Jonathan. Michal, for example, is said to have loved David and made it known: "Now Saul's daughter Michal loved David. Saul was told, and the thing pleased him" (see also 1 Sam 18:28). Berlin notes that this is the only time in the Bible that a woman seems to have chosen a husband instead of the usual pattern of a husband choosing a wife. David, on his part, married Michal for political reasons, and his relationship to her is always colored by pragmatic considerations. The feelings of love and tenderness that David might have been expected to have for Michal are instead expressed for Jonathan. Jonathan, like his sister, made known his feelings for David, but in his case they were reciprocated. When they parted it is reported that "They kissed each other, and wept with each other; David wept the more" (1 Sam 20:41b). When David learns of Jonathan's death he says: " I am distressed for you, my brother Jonathan; greatly beloved were you to me; your love to me was wonderful, passing the love of women" (2 Sam 1:26).

The characterization of Michal reveals she is assertive and physical. Jonathan's deeds on David's behalf are certainly much less daring than Michal's. The last piece of information reported concerning Michal is the notice that she never had a child (2 Sam 6:23). Behind this notice is the suggestion that the husband who never loved her now stopped sleeping with her. Berlin goes on to suggest that it also suggests that Michal never fills a female role, or at least the role that the Bible usually views as the primary female role (72). Significant, too, may be the fact that Michal, unlike many women in biblical narrative, is never described as beautiful.

BATHSHEBA AND ABISHAG

The second of David's wives is Bathsheba, who enters David's story in 2 Sam 11-12 as a passive sex object. We have already reviewed the story of David and

Bathsheba; here we examine Berlin's description of Bathsheba's characterization in that story. Throughout the entire story, according to Berlin (73) the narrator has purposely subordinated the character of Bathsheba. Her feelings are ignored and her actions are only briefly noted. This is contrasted with a full description of David's emotions. Bathsheba is not really a minor character but simply part of the plot. For this reason, it is not said that she has committed adultery. She is not really characterized as an equal party to adultery, but she serves only as the means whereby it occurs. Berlin calls her an "agent" (73), an Aristotelian term that describes the performer of an action necessary to the plot.

Bathsheba as agent in 2 Sam 11 – 12 stands in marked contrast to Bathsheba as character in 1 Kings 1 – 2. Here she is an active person, a mother intent on securing the throne for her son, Solomon. A central character, she plays a significant role both in affairs of state and in family matters. She is contrasted in these chapters to Abishag, who is the agent here. Abishag appears in 1 Kings 1:4 with the notice that "The girl was very beautiful. She became the king's attendant and serves him, but the king did not know her sexually." This information about Abishag is repeated in 1 Kings 1:15. This repetition, according to Berlin, serves to contrast Abishag with Bathsheba. Bathsheba, who was once young and attractive like Abishag, is now aging and sees herself being replaced by Abishag, just as Bathsheba intends to see to it that Solomon replaces David.

ABIGAIL

The story of David's wife Abigail (1 Sam 25) precedes the story of David and Bathsheba chronologically and in some ways is a mirror image of it. Bathsheba's husband Uriah is described as a highly moral individual; Abigail's husband, Nabal, is described as "surly and mean" (1 Sam 25:3). Though Uriah was a good man, Bathsheba could not save him; Abigail attempted elaborate measures in order to save her offensive husband. The story of Bathsheba centers on illicit sex; no hint of sex exists in the Abigail story. Though David was obviously attracted to Abigail, there is not a hint of any sexual liaisons between them before they were married. Finally, in the Bathsheba story David commits murder because of a woman; in the Abigail story David is prevented from committing murder because of a woman. In 1 Sam 25 Abigail and Nabal are both exaggerated stereotypes. Nabal is the proverbial "fool" and Abigail epitomizes the "capable woman." She is an unrealistic character, and the plot of the story in which she appears is also unrealistic. As Berlin says: "It could be reduced to: 'fair maiden' Abigail is freed from the 'wicked ogre' and marries 'prince charming'" (1982: 77). The story of Abigail is not just another episode in the biography of David, but an allegory and a strong endorsement of David's destiny to reign as the chosen favorite of God. The point of the story is expressed in Abigail's comment:

> If anyone should rise up to pursue you and to seek your life, the life of my
> lord shall be bound in the bundle of the living under the care of the
> LORD your God; but the lives of your enemies he shall sling out as from
> the hollow of a sling. When the LORD has done to my lord according to

TABLE 9.1 **Correspondence of David's Public and Private Life with His Response to His Wives**

WIFE	DAVID'S PRIVATE LIFE	DAVID'S PUBLIC LIFE
Michal	emotionally cold, but uses her to political advantage	the cold, calculated gaining of power
Abigail	eager but gentlemanly response	self-assurance as a popular leader
Bathsheba	lust, grasping what is not his	desire to increase his holdings, expand his empire
Abishag	impotence	loss of control of the kingship

all the good that he has spoken concerning you, and has appointed you prince over Israel, my lord shall have no cause of grief . . . (1 Sam 25:29–31a).

Berlin concludes that none of these women are main characters in the stories in Samuel and Kings. All of the episodes focus on the king and kingship. David is the dominant character only in 2 Sam 11 – 12. Elsewhere he is presented indirectly, in a way in which various dimensions of his character emerge. Berlin offers Table 9.1 in which she demonstrates the correspondence between David's public and private life in terms of his response to his wives (79).

David's Significance

The story of David's rise and reign is told both as a political and historical affair and as a personal and domestic one. David's personal life is set in a larger context. The development of David's character must thus be understood on both a personal and a political plane. Some misconceptions of David have stemmed from the tendency to view the "Succession Narrative" as straightforward historical reportage. This view has been corrected by more recent literary study, which has shown that eyewitness reportage and narrative realism are not identical (Gunn 1978; Flanagan 1988: 38–40). But literary interpretations sometimes tend to overlook the degree to which an incisive political and historical judgment—one requiring considerable historical hindsight—is part of the *literary* delight the story fosters.

The stories of David's maturation and Israel's development as a new monarchy are one and the same story. Taken as a whole, the biblical picture of David is overwhelmingly positive, even apart from the highly idealized portrait of him in the book of 1 Chronicles. He was, according to the biblical record, a talented and divinely chosen figure who rose to power almost in spite of himself. He was a flawed but favored character. He was the recipient of an important divine promise that not only is highlighted in 2 Samuel 7, but is also celebrated and remembered throughout the rest of the Hebrew Bible. Indeed, it even carries into the New Testament, where Jesus is pictured as a descendant of David's line.

Figure 9.7   The State of Israel at the end of David's reign

David is important in the rest of the Bible not so much as a "historical" character, but as the model of the just king and as a symbol of the permanence of God's covenant with his people Israel.

The evaluation of the historical David obviously depends upon how one evaluates the historical reliability of the sources that provide us with information about him and his achievements. At the very least it can be said that there must have been an extraordinary individual behind so much historical and theological reflection. It is true that there were no major powers threatening Israel from the outside during David's time. It was still a remarkable accomplishment to move Israel from the status of a rather loosely organized people to that of a territorial state with expanded boundaries (see Figure 9.7).

SOLOMON—THE ABUSE OF POWER AND THE SEEDS OF PARTITION

When we move beyond the Succession Narrative and come to the block of material describing the reign of Solomon (1 Kings 3–11), we almost immediately sense a very different style of literature. The sensitivity to plot, detail, and characterization that we saw in the Succession Narrative cannot be found. It is replaced by the ordinariness of folktale, parable, and list.

THE REIGN OF SOLOMON

The account of Solomon's life is much longer than that of any other subsequent king. This might be due to his important historical role, but literarily the Solomon narrative is also thematically critical to the development of 1 and 2 Kings. On one level he represents the legitimate heir to David and the Davidic covenant. But he also represents the good king who "goes bad" because of idolatry, proving that God's promise is not unconditional, that the covenant cannot be disregarded without penalties being invoked.

Solomon is one of those biblical personalities who has achieved truly legendary status. The reign of Solomon is popularly thought of as one of unparalleled magnificence—a truly golden age. The Hebrew Bible, however, makes it clear that there was a sordid side to this grandeur. From the very beginning, Solomon sent out very clear signals that he would rule with an iron hand. He had his oldest brother, Adonijah, killed. He executed two of Adonijah's supporters and sent a third into exile. After this sordid beginning however, the Solomon who appears in the next eight chapters seems like a different person, pious and wise. The account of his sacrifice at Gibeon (1 Kings 3:4–15), God's appearance to him in a vision, and Solomon's request for wisdom in response to an "Anything-you-want, you-got-it" offer from God, set the tone for Solomon's legendary reputation. The language of the dream vision at Gibeon resembles Egyptian royal accounts in which the Pharaoh described himself as a little child who does not know how to go out or come in and asks for a hearing heart. Solomon consciously tried to model his rule after the Egyptian model, so such imagery is fitting (note that in 1 Kings 3:1 Solomon's first marriage [of *many*] is to the daughter of an unnamed Egyptian Pharaoh). The Gibeon experience is followed by a folktale about two harlots disputing who was the actual mother of a child (1 Kings 3:16–28). This tale is meant to establish, at the beginning of Solomon's story, that he was a person of superior practical wisdom. On the assumption that the child's actual mother would save the child and then surrender it rather than seeing it killed, Solomon made the test and then awarded the child to the woman who showed compassion. There are variants of this story in many cultures, which suggests that it was a common motif in the ancient world, used here to lionize Solomon.

By the end of Solomon's story in 1 Kings 11, a very different figure has emerged. Here we have a picture of a king who has a fatal attraction to foreign women, who brought with them their foreign cultures and religions (1 Kings 11:3–6):

> Among his wives were seven hundred princesses, and three hundred concubines; and his wives turned away his heart. For when Solomon was old his wives turned away his heart after other gods, and his heart was not true to the LORD his God, as was the heart of David his father. For Solomon followed Astarte the goddess of the Sidonians, and Milcom the abomination of the Ammonites. So Solomon did what was evil in the sight of the LORD, and did not completely follow the LORD, as his father David had done.

Solomon as Administrator

So what happened between such a glowing beginning and such a disappointing end? Solomon is a parade example of the adage of Henry Kissinger, "Power is the ultimate aphrodisiac" or of the saying of Bertrand Russell, "Power is a drug, the desire for which increases with the habit." Solomon was indeed a man of power, who used the limited resources of his people to surround himself with all the trappings of power. But these trappings were expensive, and therefore Solomon's greatest concern was getting money into the royal treasury. David had acquired wealth by conquering and annexing Israel's neighbors. This route was not open to Solomon, and he even lost territories that his father had added to Israel. Edom revolted against Solomon (1 Kings 11:14–22). Then Syria freed itself. A certain Rezon (1 Kings 11:23–25), who had escaped from David, raised the flag of revolt in Damascus. Solomon could not or did not do anything to stop any of these.

Solomon's major source of funding was taxation. Clearly Solomon did not invent taxation in ancient Israel, but he perfected it, making it include compulsory labor for the state (the *corvée*) as well as taxes in kind. Solomon divided the kingdom into twelve administrative districts and the land of Judah, each of which was governed under a district administrator (1 Kings 4:17–19) (see Figure 9.8). Because each district had to provide food for the king and his

Figure 9.8   Solomon's tax districts

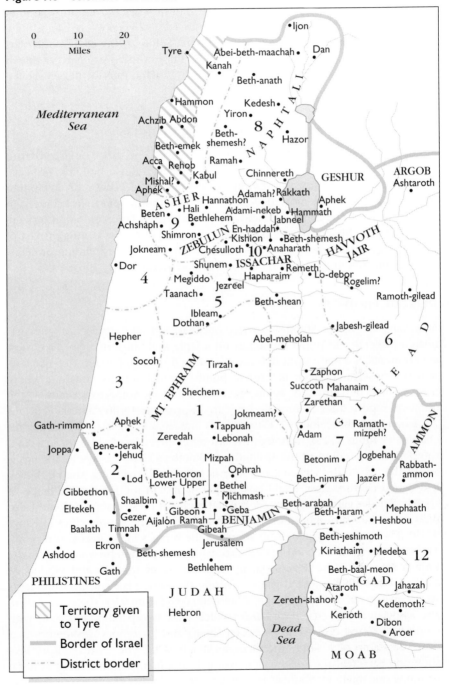

household for one month out of a year (1 Kings 4:7-27), the purpose of the system of the twelve districts must have been to improve the administration of tax collection. If the list of materials in 1 Kings 4:22-23 is not too exaggerated, such taxation was heavy indeed. Furthermore, Solomon's twelve tax districts are an early example of gerrymandering. The lines of the districts were drawn in a way that disregarded traditional tribal territories and thus further weakened any sense of tribal identity and independence.

Solomon's Building Projects

Besides assuring a luxurious lifestyle for himself and his court, a large part of the revenue that Solomon raised was spent on grandiose building projects. These projects were also the reason for instituting the corvée, an institution that was perhaps even more deeply resented by the people than taxation. In spite of the revenue generated, and even with unpaid labor, Solomon was unable to finance his construction projects, thus requiring the ceding of part of the territory he inherited from his father. What were these building projects, and why did Solomon put such high priority on them?

DEFENSE PROJECTS

According to 1 Kings, Solomon carried out two kinds of construction: defense-related projects and public buildings on a large scale in Jerusalem. Like most governments, Solomon's put defense spending first in its budget. Defense construction was undertaken at critical points throughout his kingdom where troops could be stationed. While we must allow for some exaggeration, the numbers reported for Solomon's army are impressive: 1,400 chariots (1 Kings 10:26), 12,000 horsemen (1 Kings 4:26) and 40,000 stalls of horses for his chariots (1 Kings 4:26). Although the last figure is reported as 4,000 stalls in 2 Chr 9:25, the account of the strength of Solomon's chariot corps in 1 Kings is reasonable, given the fact that the Assyrians reported that king Ahab of Israel, less than a century later, could put 2,000 chariots in the field at the battle of Qarqar. Besides garrison towns for the stationing of these troops, Solomon also built store-cities throughout his kingdom as arsenals and supply cities (1 Kings 9:19). The archaeological record supports the reports in 1 Kings at this point. There is evidence for a coordinated, defensive construction program during the time of Solomon at the sites of Hazor, Megiddo, Gezer, Lachish, and Ashdod. At all these sites six-chambered gates of nearly the same plan and measurements were constructed during the reign of Solomon (see Figure 9.9). These gates were also associated with *casemate walls* (which were two parallel thin walls with empty space and cross-walls between them) and governors' residences that bear the stamp of a single intent or master builder. The tenth century also shows archaeological evidence of expanded settlements and the kind of town planning one might attribute to a strong central authority.

Figure 9.9 Solomonic gates at Hazor, Megiddo, Gezer, Lachish, and Ashdod

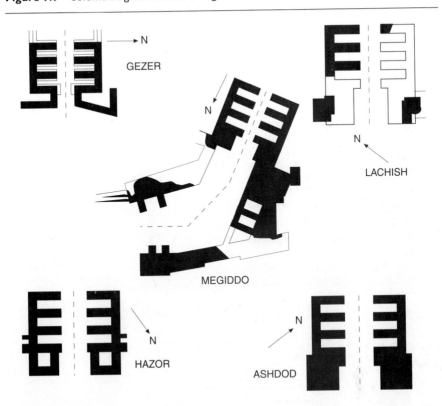

PUBLIC BUILDINGS

The building projects of Solomon to which the Deuteronomistic Historian devotes the most attention were those that were intended to make Jerusalem into a capital of which he and the Israelites could be proud. The centerpieces of the construction in Jerusalem were the royal palace and the temple. While the bulk of two chapters is given over to the details of the temple and its furnishings (1 Kings 6:2–38; 7:13–51), a scant twelve verses are devoted to the description of Solomon's palace. The careful reader will note that when one compares the size of the two buildings, the temple, whose ground plan measured 60×20 cubits (or about $90' \times 30'$, [1 Kings 6:2]), could have fit inside Solomon's palace (100×50 cubits (or about $150' \times 75'$, [1 Kings 7:2]) with room to spare. The temple seems to have been an attachment to the palace rather than vice versa (see Figure 9.10).

According to 1 Kings 9:10, the construction of these two buildings went on for twenty years (with thirteen years spent on the palace [1 Kings 7:1] and only seven on the temple [1 Kings 6:38]). There is ample detail about the construction of the temple and its furnishings, including its structural features, interior

Figure 9.10   Solomon's Temple

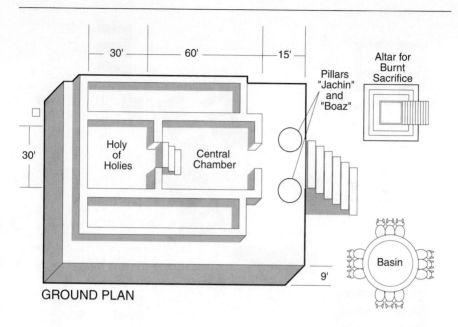

GROUND PLAN

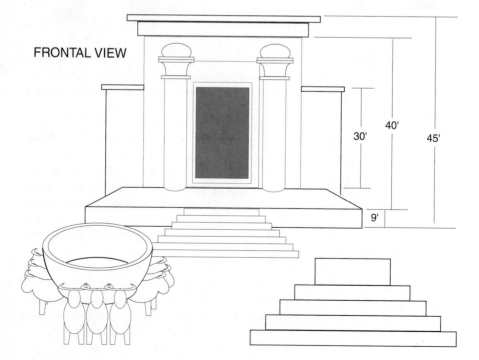

FRONTAL VIEW

furnishings and decorations, giving a sense of grandeur and completeness. Many details of the temple's architecture reflect Canaanite-Phoenician patterns. Indeed, a Phoenician craftsman, Hiram of Tyre, played an important role in its construction (1 Kings 7:13).

Because of its prominence in 1 Kings and the fact that architecturally it can be compared with other royal temples of the ancient Near East in this period, Solomon's Temple must have played an important role in the emergent national state. As a symbolic "house" for God, its religious significance goes without saying. To attempt to isolate its religious meaning from its part in the economic and political dynamics of the time would be to underestimate its religious meaning. It would also be to misunderstand the vital interaction between religion and the sociopolitical spheres in the ancient world.

We should be careful not to interpret the expression "God's house" in a superficial way. Clearly Israel did not conceive of God's presence as confined to a fixed spot. But the human need for the assurance of divine availability led the Israelites, like other peoples, to establish definite places where access to the transcendent could take place. The nearly universal human willingness to commit substantial resources to the construction of sacred buildings, the maintenance of expensive cultic practices, and the provision for extensive priestly personnel attests to the profound nature of humanity's insecurity about the nearness of divine power and protection.

The "visible" presence of God in Jerusalem was even more critical at the period of sociopolitical transition that marked the beginning of the monarchy. David's frustrated intention to construct a temple, followed by Solomon's doing so at the beginning of his reign, have little to do with their personal piety. The Jerusalem temple was an essential part of the formation of the Israelite state. A visible symbol of God's approval of the monarchs' actions was needed, and the temple supplied it. The legitimacy of the temple was intended to give legitimacy to the monarchy. These religiopolitical dynamics functioned on the economic level as well. The temple, with its treasures and treasury, was a kind of national bank. It was a secure structure in the most defensible part of Jerusalem. As a state institution, the temple thus represented the intersection point of religion and politics. It symbolized the transition from tribal organization to nation-state, with the clear inference that God approved of this transition because God "took up residence" in Jerusalem, next door to the king's palace. The fact that the temple and palace adjoined one another does not mean, as some scholars have suggested, that the temple was merely a private royal chapel for Solomon and his court. Both biblical and extrabiblical sources, as well as archaeological evidence, testify to the fact that a temple in a palace-complex like the Solomonic temple functioned as the royal sanctuary and as a temple of the kingdom.

Solomon in Decline

After the account of the dedication of the temple in 1 Kings 8, Solomon has a second vision at Gibeon (1 Kings 9). Unlike the one in 1 Kings 3, however, here the threat of the destruction of Solomon's life and of the temple itself emphasizes the conditional nature of the covenant. In a sudden shift, the temple no longer stands at the center of Solomon's world, and the projects described are clearly undertaken for Solomon's personal benefit. 1 Kings 9:26 begins a lengthy listing of Solomon's wealth. In spite of the praise heaped on Solomon by the Queen of Sheba, this whole section is cast in a negative light by the ominous warning in 1 Kings 9:6–9 and by the narrator's critical attitude toward Solomon's marriages in 1 Kings 11:1–9.

The rest of the Solomon narrative alternates between oracles telling of the division of the kingdom and descriptions of rebellions against Solomon's heavy-handed authority by both internal and external enemies. These challenges to Solomon's authority are seen by the narrator as punishments for his idolatry. For the first time since 1 Kings 2, Solomon is faced with a rival in Jeroboam (1 Kings 11:26–40), and like he did then, again he seeks to deal with him violently. The fact that he does not succeed in eliminating Jeroboam forbodes the rebellion to come, which will split the kingdom into two parts.

The Legendary Solomon

Solomon's legendary status is based, in no small part, on his wisdom. His administrative, or practical wisdom shows up in the story of the dream at Gibeon, followed by the narrative dealing with the two prostitutes (1 Kings 3:4–28). While the construction of the temple is regarded as Solomon's greatest innovation in 1 Kings 3–11, there is also a passage that praises Solomon's encyclopedic or gnomic wisdom (1 Kings 4:20–34). Solomon's wisdom in this sphere was international in its nature. Gnomic sayings in the classified lists of natural phenomena are found in Mesopotamia and Egypt. Solomon's legendary ability to answer riddles was also international in nature, as attested to in his answers to questions directed to him by the visiting Queen of Sheba (1 Kings 10:1–10, 13).

Outside of narratives about Solomon, Solomon's reputation for wisdom was such that Israel regarded him as the founder of their wisdom school. This school produced what has been called the Wisdom Literature in the Hebrew Bible and the apocryphal/deuterocanonical books (the Wisdom Literature includes five books: Proverbs, Job, and Ecclesiastes in the Hebrew canon and Ecclesiasticus and Wisdom of Solomon in the apocryphal/deuterocanonical books—see Chapter 14). Just as David became associated traditionally with the type of religious literature found in the book of Psalms, so Solomon, based on 1 Kings 4:29–34, was traditionally believed to have been the author of two of the "Wisdom" books—Proverbs and Ecclesiastes. There is another book in the English Bible that mentions Solomon in its title, the Song of Solomon, which is not a wisdom book. In the Hebrew Bible, the title of this book is Song of Songs. Even the very late book, the Wisdom of Solomon, which was written in Greek in the first century B.C.E., bears Solomon's name. A legend in the Babylonian Talmud says that Solomon wrote the Song of Songs in his sexually active youthful years, Proverbs in his mature middle age, and Ecclesiastes as a skeptical senior citizen!

The association of Solomon with wisdom literature is probably due more to his position as king than to his personal wisdom. As the monarchy became firmly established under Solomon, an extensive administrative structure became necessary, including many court officials. For Solomon's court these are listed in 1 Kings 4:1-6. Three of these are significant here: the "Reminder" (NRSV, "Recorder"), the "Scribes" (NRSV, "Secretaries"), and the "King's Friend." The first two of these positions, and maybe the third as well, must have had large numbers of assistants for record-keeping and correspondence. Together, these formed a corps of literate persons at the court (in a society that was still largely illiterate) for whose work, which included collecting sayings, songs, poems, and so forth, Solomon got the credit. There must have been extensive literary activity in this period, although it is mentioned only with respect to Solomon's proverbs and songs, as well as to annalistic records.

Solomon's Achievements

In spite of the problems we have outlined, Solomon accomplished some things on the domestic front that had been left undone by David (Ishida 1992: 112):

1. the consolidation of the kingship through a purge of political enemies;
2. the development of the administrative organization;
3. the building of the temple and the construction of the royal palace;
4. the crystallization of Zion theology around the doctrine of Yahweh's joint election of the House of David and of Jerusalem/Zion; and
5. the reinforcement of the defense system.

On the international front, Solomon abandoned David's policy of expansionism. Instead, he developed trade and diplomatic relations with other countries. His many wives were, at least in part, the result of political marriages.

POLITICAL POWER AND RELIGIOUS CHANGE UNDER THE EARLY MONARCHY

With considerable success, tribal Israel protected the individual interests of its members, while providing joint support to them in the form of temporary tribal alliances. There were, however, both internal and external stresses and strains on the tribal system that were aggravated by the appearance on the scene of a more tightly-organized enemy in the Philistines. The Israel of the period of the judges was a people who lived mainly in small, agriculturally-based villages. Under the United Monarchy of David and Solomon, however, there was increasing urbanization. The balance of power shifted to urban centers and their interests. Many urban-dwelling Canaanites were absorbed into Israel as a nation-state, people who did not share either traditional tribal loyalties or Yahwistic religious beliefs and practices. Many Israelites under the monarchy, however, retained much of their older tribal way of life, while simultaneously being swept along the path of state rule, a path that would bring Israel into the arena of international conflict in the ancient Near East. While some tribal patterns thus remained, four major enduring structural changes were effected by the monarchy (Gottwald 1985: 323–325):

1. **Political Centralization** Israel had become a state (and later would split into two states) with the power of taxation and conscription, backed up by the monopoly of force belonging to the state. To carry out state policies, standing armies and bureaucratic ranks were instituted and grew with their own inner dynamics. The power of the state reached into the fields of the Israelite villagers to take their crops and draft peasants for social purposes that were decided upon by a small minority in the royal court, rather than by tribal elders who sought to express the consensus of the people.

2. **Social Stratification** The monopoly of power in the state was the monopoly of an elite class. The state policy of transferring wealth from the peasant on the land to a dependent class of bureaucrats created not only a class of government officials, but also a group of merchants and landlords who, by means of government grants and monopolies, gained new wealth and status. These social divisions became even deeper with passing generations, putting severe strains upon the old tribally-based economic and legal structures.

3. **Shifts in Land Tenure** The original concept of land ownership in Israel maintained that land was held in perpetuity by extended families and could not be sold out of the family. By this means, no family could become landless and thus poor. As entrepreneurial wealth accumulated through taxation, plunder, and trade, the *nouveau riche* upper class looked for good investment opportunities. In time this acquisitive drive encroached upon tribal institutions and ways of life. Gradually loans at interest were extended to needy Israelite farmers who had been hit by crop failure, and their land was mortgaged. Many of these farmers, who had always worked their own land, now became tenant farmers, debt servants, or landless wage laborers. Tribal economic security and tribal religious identity were undermined, and the social unity and political trust of the people in their leaders was put in grave doubt.

4. **Domestic Repercussions of Foreign Trade, Diplomacy, and War** Under David and Solomon, Israel was amazingly successful in the political-military game of international trade, diplomacy, and war. For a minor power like Israel, with a relatively small population, limited economic resources, and situated in an area subject to frequent droughts, changes on the international scene could have serious effects. The effort required for a small state like Israel to secure favorable trade exchanges, to mount wars against neighbors, to absorb and turn back invasions, and to pay tributes to imperial powers were quickly felt in the impoverished and demoralized lives of the common people and in the factional struggles among leaders.

In this chapter we have examined books in which Israel is described as making the move from a tribal society to a state. In the next chapter we will look at that literature which describes how dynamics created by the state, with its centralization of power, led to a division within that state.

STUDY QUESTIONS

1 SAMUEL

1. Samuel is born to a couple who previously were unable to have children. Who else in the Old Testament was born to previously sterile parents, and what do you think is the intent of such a birth narrative?
2. What happened to the Ark of the Covenant after it was taken into battle against the Philistines? What lesson was God trying to teach the Israelites?—The Philistines?
3. Samuel anointed Saul, designating him to be king. Using a Bible dictionary (*Interpreter's Dictionary of the Bible, Harper's Bible Dictionary,* or the *Anchor Bible Dictionary*) determine what anointing is. Also define the terms "Messiah" and "Christ," and show how these three terms are related.
4. Who is Jonathan? Given the political dimensions of this section of 1 Samuel, what is significant about his friendship with David?

2 SAMUEL

1. David received news of the death of Saul and Jonathan and composed a lament over their death. He seemed to be deeply disturbed by their deaths, but at the same time, had the messenger who brought the news killed. Why do you think he did that? Was it an irrational act of a person in deep grief? Or might there have been a political rationale for his action?
2. The story in 2 Sam 2:8 (and elsewhere) gives the name of Saul's son as Ishbosheth. But 1 Chron 8:33; 9:39 (and references in this chapter) say that the name is Ishbaal. What do these two names mean? On the assumption that Ishbaal is the older form of the name, how might you explain the appearance of the name Ishbosheth?
3. In 2 Sam 7 is a reference to what becomes known as the Davidic Covenant. What kind of promise is made to David? What are the sociopolitical strengths and weaknesses of such a promise?
4. In everyday life in the ancient Near East, people recognized that their social world was a part of God's creation and therefore only a part of truth. While the social world seems real, it is also in the arena of the apparent, what lacks meaning, and even fraudulent. The people also realized that only God knows reality; human beings can know only appearances. God knows what *is*; human beings know *what appears to be*. Review the story in 2 Sam 16 (especially v. 7) about how Samuel found the new king that God had selected for Israel, and answer the following questions:

    (a)   What does God know?

    (b)   What does Samuel know?

5. How does Amnon's rape of Tamar begin to work out the punishment God intended for David because of David's affair with Bathsheba?

6. In 2 Sam 24:1–25 and 1 Chron 21:1–28 are parallel accounts of a census conducted by David. What are the significant differences in the two accounts? Assuming that Chronicles is later than 2 Samuel, how might you explain these differences? Do the accounts in Samuel and Chronicles have similar or different purposes?

1 KINGS

1. Solomon's long prayer is included in 1 Kings 8, in which he gives expression to a basic theological contradiction inherent in the very construction of the temple. What is that contradiction? Does the same contradiction exist in contemporary religious expression?

2. Because human beings know appearances, we spend a lot of time learning how to create a good appearance, how to make a good impression on others. We learn what kind of personality we would like others to perceive, and then strive to project that personality. Read 1 Kings 3; 4:29–34; 11:1–9 and then answer the following questions: (a) What does Solomon request of God? (b) How does Solomon demonstrate that he has this gift? (c) What kind of "impression" has Solomon managed to create? (d) How far does this impression extend? (e) What is the "reality of Solomon's life? and (f) In the case of Solomon, what was "revealed" or shown to his subjects, and what was "concealed" or hidden from them in this selection of readings?

3. Suppose that you were an Israelite living at the time of Solomon's death. What might be your political and religious alignments? Assuming that you are in a discussion with someone whose loyalties differ, offer some arguments supporting your views.

BIBLIOGRAPHY

Alt, Albrecht. 1967. *Essays on Old Testament History and Religion.* Tr. by R. A. Wilson. Garden City, NY: Doubleday.

Berlin, Adele. 1982. "Characterization in Biblical Narrative: David's Wives." *Journal for the Study of the Old Testament,* 23: 69–85.

Childs, Brevard. 1979. *Introduction to the Old Testament as Scripture.* Philadelphia: Westminster.

Edelman, Diana. 1993. *Saulide Israel: A Literary and Historical Investigation.* Winona Lake, IN: Eisenbraun's.

Exum, J. Cheryl, and Whedbee, J. William. 1984. "Isaac, Samson and Saul: Reflections on the Comic and Tragic Visions." *Semeia,* 32:5–40.

Flanagan, James W. 1981. "Chiefs in Israel." *Journal for the Study of the Old Testament,* 20:47–73.

——.1988. *David's Social Drama: A Hologram of Israel's Early Iron Age.* The Social World of Biblical Antiquity Series, 7. Sheffield: JSOT.

Frick, Frank S. 1985. *The Formation of the State in Ancient Israel.* The Social World of Biblical Antiquity Series, 4. Sheffield: JSOT.

Gottwald, Norman K. 1985. *The Hebrew Bible: A Socio-Literary Introduction.* Philadelphia: Fortress.

Gunn, David M. 1978. *The Story of King David: Genre and Interpretation.* JSOT Supplement Series, 6. Sheffield: JSOT.

——.1980. *The Fate of King Saul.* JSOT Supplement Series, 14. Sheffield: JSOT.

Ishida, Tomoo. 1992. "Solomon." *The Anchor Bible Dictionary.* Vol. 6. New York, Doubleday, 105 – 113.

Miller, J. Maxwell, and Hayes, John H. 1986. *A History of Ancient Israel and Judah.* Philadelphia: Westminster.

Chapter 10

TWO KINGDOMS AND
THE RISE OF PROPHECY

Suggested Bible Reading
1 Kings 12:1–22:51; 2 Kings 1:1–25:30

$\mathcal{A}$s we observed in Chapter 1, the Jewish Bible is divided into three

parts: the Law (*Torah*), the Prophets (*Nebi'îm*), and the Writings (*Ketubîm*). In

this threefold division, the second part, the Prophets, includes books that we

might not necessarily consider to be prophetic books, rather we regard them as

historical, because they are the products of the Deuteronomistic historian:

Joshua, Judges, 1 and 2 Samuel, and 1 and 2 Kings. The concept of prophecy,

however, is a central one for the Deuteronomistic historian, as the examination

of the Elijah story below will show. In fact, the entire Deuteronomistic History is arranged around a recurring pattern of prophecy and its fulfillment, some examples of which in 1 and 2 Kings are:

PROPHECY	FULFILLMENT
1 Kings 11:29-31	1 Kings 12:15
1 Kings 14:6-8	1 Kings 15:29
1 Kings 16:1-3	1 Kings 16:12
2 Kings 1:6	2 Kings 1:17
2 Kings 7:1-3	2 Kings 7:16-18
2 Kings 11:15-18	2 Kings 23:30

The second part of the Prophets section of the canon (the so-called Latter Prophets) includes those books that we more readily recognize as prophetic books: Isaiah, Jeremiah, and Ezekiel—which are called the *Major Prophets* because of their size, not their importance; and the smaller, not less important, books of the twelve *Minor Prophets*: Hosea, Joel, Amos, Obadiah, Jonah, Micah, Nahum, Habakkuk, Zephaniah, Haggai, Zechariah, and Malachi.

The terms "prophet" and "prophecy" are surrounded with a good deal of confusion and ambiguity in contemporary English usage. For many, a prophet is one who predicts the future. For others a prophet is pre-eminently a social critic. For still others, a prophet is a supernaturally authorized messenger, delivering messages from God to humanity. The English words "prophet" and "prophecy" derive from a Greek term, *prophetes*. The translators of the Septuagint did not translate the Hebrew word *nabi'*, the common Hebrew term for prophet, with the Greek word *mantis* (from which words like "necromancy," "divining the future through communication with the dead" are derived). Rather, they translated *nabi'* with the word *prophetes*, "one who could 'speak before,' " from which the English word "prophet" is derived. Sometimes, to "speak before" meant speaking in the presence of a divine being meaning interpreting his or her words. But it also meant "speaking before" in the temporal sense, that is, foretelling or predicting what would happen in the future. Prophecy means both proclamation ("forthtelling") and prediction ("foretelling"). "Prophets" thus include not only predictors who foresee events in the future, but proclaimers like Muhammad (who is called *'al Nabi*, "the prophet" by Muslims), St. Francis of Assisi, John Wesley, Martin Luther King, Jr., and others.

In the Hebrew Bible, however, prophets are primarily "forthtellers," rather than "foretellers." A basic definition of "prophecy" in the Hebrew Bible is the following: Prophecy is inspired speech initiated by a divine source, speech humanly understandable and commonly directed to a human audience in a normal, not an altered, state of consciousness. A prophet is thus one who delivers such a message.

The significance of the phenomenon of prophecy and the influence of "prophets" on the religion of Israel, and through Judaism, Christianity, and Islam, on the rest of the world, cannot be overstated. The immense significance of the phenomenon of Israelite prophecy, one of the most dynamic and creative movements in the history of religion, makes it imperative that our itinerary should include a significant investigation of it. Accordingly, we shall devote not just this chapter, but the following two chapters as well, to this important phenomenon.

FROM ONE KINGDOM TO TWO

While prophets appear in all parts of the Hebrew Bible, they begin to show up with more frequency with the division of the United Monarchy of David and Solomon into the two kingdoms of Judah in the South and Israel in the North. Before the establishment of the monarchy, the Hebrew word *nabi'* is used to refer to two quite different types of persons. Aaron, for example, was called Moses' *nabi',* that is, Moses' spokesperson or mouthpiece. A *nabi'* was also sometimes a member of a group that induced ecstatic or trancelike behavior. In such an altered state of consciousness they could "see" or "hear" that which was outside the range of ordinary human perception. In the former sense, *nabi'* conveys the idea of being a spokesperson; in the latter sense, the idea that the *nabi'* is one "possessed" by a spiritual force is most important. The two ideas later become associated, so that a prophet is one who, under the influence of God's spirit, becomes God's spokesperson.

Historians of ancient Israelite religion have said that kings and prophets needed each other, that it is hard to think of one group without the other. Certainly prophets, as spokespersons for God, come to the fore in the story of the division of the kingdom in the context of this critical political event in Israel's history. The division is not just a political event; it is one, according to the prophets, filled with religious significance.

As we said at the conclusion of the preceding chapter, the seeds of the division of the United Monarchy were planted during Solomon's forty-year reign. While Solomon may have assumed that the principle of a hereditary monarchy could be taken for granted, his son discovers otherwise. After Solomon's death, his son Rehoboam has to go to Shechem in the North to negotiate his accession to his father's throne with the leaders of the northern tribes. These tribes are led by Jeroboam, a former supervisor of Solomon's forced labor crews who revolted against Solomon, went into self-imposed exile in Egypt, and returned to live in the North. Faced with the two options of either backing off policies established by his father or affirming them, Rehoboam follows what turned out to be some bad political advice. Ignoring the counsel of "the older men who had attended his father," and taking the advice of the "young men who had grown up with him," Rehoboam chooses *not* to disown his father's policies (1 Kings 12:1-11). To show the people that he is no "wimp," but a power with whom they must deal, Rehoboam tells them, in a "You ain't seen nothin' yet!" speech, that instead of decreasing their heavy burden of taxation and labor for the state, he would add to it. In delivering this message, he uses the interesting metaphor "My little finger is thicker than my father's loins" (1 Kings 12:10). Having heard Rehoboam's "get tough" speech, the ten northern tribes (all the tribes except Judah and Benjamin) secede from the United Monarchy (1 Kings 12:16). Reho-

Figure 10.1   The two kingdoms of Israel and Judah

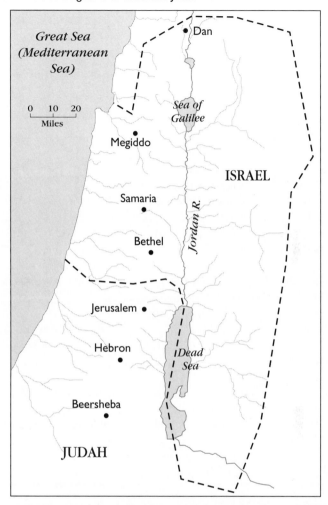

boam has to make a quick retreat to Jerusalem to save his life, whereupon the northern leaders installed Jeroboam as their king in a new state called Israel. This state existed for the next two hundred years adjacent to the southern state, which assumed the name of the tribe of Judah (see Figure 10.1). A chronology of the two kingdoms is presented in Table 10.1.

A prophet first enters the picture in the story of the revolt of Jeroboam and the northern tribes against Solomon. Ahijah (whose name means "Yah[weh] is my brother"), a prophet from Shiloh, anticipates that Jeroboam would be more loyal to Yahweh than Solomon had been, or Solomon's son might be. In the story of Ahijah's encounter with Jeroboam, we see a feature of prophetic communication that is often repeated—the use of dramatic, even somewhat bizarre visual aids to reinforce the spoken word. Jeroboam left Jerusalem wearing a

TABLE 10.1   Time chart of the two kingdoms in their **Near Eastern context**

ISRAEL	JUDAH	THE ANCIENT NEAR EAST
Jeroboam I (922–901)	Rehoboam (922–915)	Invasion by Shisak (918)
Nadab (901–900)	Abijah (915–913)	
Baasha (900–877)	Asa (913–873)	Ashurnasirpal II of Assyria (883–859)
Elah (877–876)		
Zimri (876)		
Omri (876–869)	Jehoshaphat (873–849)	
Ahab (869–850)		Shalmaneser III of Assyria (859–824)
Ahazaiah (850–849)		
Jehoram (849–842)	Jehoram (849–842)	
Jehu (842–815)	Ahaziah (842)	
Jehoahaz (815–801)	Athaliah ♀ (842–837)	
Jehoash (801–786)	Joash (837–800)	
Jeroboam II (786–746)	Amaziah (800–783)	
Zechariah (746–745)	Uzziah (783–742)	
Shallum (745)		Tiglath–Pileser III of Assyria (745–727)
Menahem (745–738)	Jotham (742–732)	Shalmaneser V of Assyria (727–722)
Pekah (744–732)		
Pekahiah (738–732)		
Hoshea (732–722)	Ahaz (732–715)	Sargon II of Assyria (722–705)
(Fall of Israel 722/1)	Hezekiah (715–686)	Sennacherib of Assyria (705–681)
Manasseh (686–642)		
	Amon (642–640)	
	Josiah (640–609)	
	Jehoahaz (609)	
	Jehoiakim (609–598)	Nebuchadrezzar of Babylon (605–562)
	Jehoiachin (597)	
	Zedekiah (597–586)	
	(Destruction of Jerusalem 587/6)	

new garment. When Ahijah meets him in the open country, the prophet rips off Jeroboam's garment and tears it into twelve pieces. He then invites Jeroboam to take ten pieces of the garment and delivers to him the following oracle: "Thus says the Lord, the God of Israel, 'See, I am about to tear the kingdom from the hand of Solomon, and will give you ten tribes'" (1 Kings 11:30-31). Using the schema of prophecy and fulfillment, the Deuteronomistic historian then reports Rehoboam's unwillingness to listen to the people with the words: "So the king did not listen to the people; because it was a turn of affairs brought about by the Lord that he might fulfil his word, which the Lord had spoken by Ahijah the Shilonite to Jeroboam son of Nebat" (1 Kings 12:15). In the Septuagint translation, a different prophet, Shemaiah, acts out this piece of symbolism, and at a different point in the story. In the Septuagint, Ahijah's action takes place *be-*

fore Jeroboam goes to Egypt; Shemaiah's action occurs *at* the meeting of the tribes in Shechem, following Solomon's death. Either way, however, the revolt is prophetically supported.

In addition to such lone prophets, we know from 1 Sam 10 and elsewhere, that groups of prophets were in the North who re-emerged in the ninth century during the reign of Ahab. We also know that Samuel, the leader of such a band, seems to have supported Saul at first and then opposed him. We can conclude that the prophetic groups in the North did not hesitate to do what they could to determine who should and who should not lead Israel. Their support of Jeroboam at the time of the schism was therefore one factor in the division of the kingdom.

Having received both the people's support and Yahweh's endorsement via prophetic oracle, Jeroboam set about to constitute a state with an identity of its own. Faced with the status of Jerusalem and its temple as a cultural center for the people, Jeroboam established two cultic centers as rivals to Jerusalem— one (Bethel) at the southern end and one (Dan) at the northern end of his kingdom. He set up a golden calf at each site so that Dan and Bethel would have a cultic symbol to compete with the Ark of the Covenant as a symbol of Yahweh (1 Kings 12: 28–30).

While Jeroboam's golden calf has not been found at Dan, archaeologists have excavated an extensive sacred area at Dan that sheds light on official cultic activities in the northern kingdom. A large rectangular platform, about 7 x 19 meters, made of carefully dressed limestone blocks, was built in the tenth century, the time of Jeroboam. Near this platform, large storerooms have been excavated that had in them numerous vessels, in particular two large store jars (with a capacity of about 300 liters each) decorated with a snake motif (see Figure 10.2). Also found in this area were a decorated incense stand, chalices, a bowl with a trident incised on its base, and the broken head of a male figurine, which formed part of an assemblage of a cultic nature (Biran 1992: 15). This sacred area was expanded to form a nineteen-meter square in the ninth century, and reached its zenith in the ninth and eighth centuries. It remained in use through the fourth century c.e.

The golden bull-calves set up by Jeroboam probably should not be interpreted as idolatrous representations of another god. Rather, they represented mounts for the invisible presence of Yahweh, just as the Ark of the Covenant represented Yahweh's seat. Such was not, however, the "spin" put on this act of Jeroboam by the Deuteronomistic historian (referred to below with the symbol Dtr), who consistently interpreted things from a pro-Jerusalem, pro-Davidic point of view. For Dtr, the secession of the northern tribes from the Davidic monarchy was an act of political *and* religious rebellion. This tendency of Dtr first surfaces in the editorial comment in 1 Kings 12:19: "So Israel has been in rebellion against the house of David to this day."

This wholesale condemnation of the North is given prophetic endorsement in a story in 1 Kings 13. This narrative, however, can be dated no earlier than the end of the seventh century by the fact that it refers to the northern

Figure 10.2   The author excavating a large store jar in the sacred area at Dan

kingdom as Samaria (1 Kings 13:32). The northern kingdom was not called Samaria until after the northern kingdom fell in 721 B.C.E. and Assyria named the province established there by that name. This narrative also knows Josiah (640–609 B.C.E.). In this story, the writer is looking back on and evaluating conditions that existed about three hundred years before his time. At the beginning of 1 Kings 13 an anonymous prophet or "man of God" from Judah issues an oracle and a "sign" against Jeroboam's altar at Bethel. Beginning in 13:11 there is the account of an "old prophet in Bethel" and his encounter with the "man of God," (another prophetic title) that ends with the old prophet endorsing the man of God's oracle: "For the saying that he proclaimed by the word of the LORD against the altar in Bethel, and against all the houses of the high places that are in the cities of Samaria, shall surely come to pass" (1 Kings 13:32).

Ahijah, the prophet who encouraged Jeroboam to revolt in the first place, returns in 1 Kings 14 when he is sought out by Jeroboam on the occasion of his son's illness. When Jeroboam sends his wife to Ahijah to ask about their son's fate, Ahijah is used by Dtr to deliver another oracle, this time one that idealizes David and expresses bitter disappointment in Jeroboam:

> Thus says the LORD, the God of Israel: "Because I exalted you from among the people, made you leader over my people Israel, and tore the kingdom away from the house of David to give it to you, yet you have not been like my servant David, who kept my commandments, and followed me with all his heart, doing only that which was right in my sight, but you have done evil above all that those who were before you and have gone and made for yourself other gods, and cast images, provoking me to anger, and have thrust me behind your back; therefore, I will bring evil upon the house of Jeroboam. I will cut off from Jeroboam every male, both bond and free in Israel, and will consume the house of Jeroboam, just as one burns up dung until it is all gone." (I Kings 14:7–10)

Here again, Dtr has written with the benefit of hindsight. Dtr knew that the house (dynasty) of Jeroboam had been short-lived (1 Kings 15:25–30), and that the northern kingdom had fallen to the Assyrians in 721 B.C.E. (1 Kings 14:15). He uses this story to offer an explanation of those events as having been caused by religious unfaithfulness. While Hosea 8:5–6 condemns the "calf of Samaria," none of the other eighth-century B.C.E. prophets who were active in the northern kingdom spoke out specifically against the shrines established by Jeroboam at Dan and Bethel as idolatrous. Only later did Dtr look back and make the connection between what Jeroboam did and the fate of the northern kingdom. It is also interesting that the northern kingdom produced more prophets than did the southern kingdom.

Following the breakup of the United Monarchy, neither of the two kingdoms enjoyed the luxury of shaping its own future, except for a few brief intervals. The border between Israel and Judah was only about ten miles north of Jerusalem, which after the split became the capital of the southern kingdom. Judah had a much smaller population, was more geographically isolated, and had more land unsuitable for agriculture than her sister kingdom to the north. Judah had the advantage of the stabilizing influence of the Davidic dynasty, as well as the temple in Jerusalem with its Ark of the Covenant—the two major symbols of Yahwism. Israel was the stronger of the two states, both in population and economic resources. It was, however, more exposed geographically, lacking buffers between its territory and that of the other nations to its north and east. Consequently, Israel became embroiled, willingly and unwillingly, in the international affairs of the ninth and eighth centuries. Both Judah and Israel were small states, which even together were smaller than Solomon's kingdom because the split resulted in the loss of most of the border territories conquered by David. An invasion by Pharaoh Shishak (Sheshonk I) of Egypt in Rehoboam's fifth year dealt a devastating blow to both kingdoms, as revealed in archaeological evidence and Shishak's inscriptions at Karnak in Upper Egypt (*ANET*, pp. 263–264).

The Northern Kingdom (922–721 B.C.E.)

For the northern kingdom, during the two hundred years of its life from 922 when Jeroboam was crowned until 721 when it fell to the imperialistic power of Assyria, war and international intrigue were the rule rather than the exception. There were border skirmishes with Judah, defensive campaigns against Assyria, struggles against revolting subject peoples such as the Moabites, and problems with the growing power of the new Aramean state to the immediate north. The northern kingdom, lacking the political stability afforded Judah by the Davidic dynasty, suffered from an internal political instability that reared its head early in its life. Jeroboam's son Nadab ruled for only two years before being assassinated by Baasha, about whom nothing is said before he is introduced in 1 Kings 15:16. According to 1 Kings 16:1–4, Baasha, like Jeroboam, received a prophetic oracle announcing that his dynasty would be short-lived. In Dtr's scheme of things, this prophecy too, was fulfilled. This time, however, the takeover was even messier. When the dust settled, a dynasty was established in Israel that gave the northern kingdom power and influence that it had not yet known, nor would it ever know again. Not coincidentally, this same period also gave rise to a strong prophetic movement.

Elah, the son of Baasha, had not yet ruled for a year when he, too, was assassinated by Zimri, "commander of half his chariots" (1 Kings 16:9–10). Zimri takes the questionable prize for having the briefest rule of any of Israel's kings—one week—at the end of which he committed suicide after being besieged in the capital by the commander-in-chief of the army, Omri (1 Kings 16: 15–20).

OMRI

Politically, Omri appears to have been one of the most able of Israel's kings. He not only brought an end to conflicts with Judah, but stabilized his northern border by marrying his son to Jezebel, the daughter of the ruler of Tyre and Sidon. He also regained the Transjordanian territories that had been lost. Most notably, he established a dynasty that would last for thirty-four years and include the reigns of four successive kings. In some respects, Omri was Israel's David. He began as ruler of a small, internally divided state and transformed it, in the space of only seven years, into a major power in the region, dominating Syria, Moab, and Judah.

Omri's accomplishments are testified to in the biblical text only implicitly, not explicitly. Explicitly, Omri's reign is allotted a meager six verses by Dtr, and in those verses he is described with the same kind of generic condemnation that Dtr metes out to all the kings of Israel (1 Kings 6:23–38). Implicitly, however, the biblical text testifies to Omri's political accomplishments by the fact that from 1 Kings 17 to 2 Kings 11, a total of thirty-three chapters, the text, although it was edited in Judah, is concerned principally with Israel. In these chapters Judah receives only incidental mention, an observation that is even more striking when one recalls the distinct pro-Jerusalem, anti-Israel bias of the editor.

Figure 10.3   The Stele of Mesha

Omri's power is also attested in the Stele of Mesha, an inscription on a stone plaque that measures about 24 x 46 inches (see Figure 10.3). The inscription on the Stele of Mesha, king of Moab, says of Omri:

> Omri, the King of Israel, controlled Moab for many years because Chemosh,
> our chief god, was angry at his people. (Matthews and Benjamin 1991:113)

Assyrian records continued to refer to Israel as "the land of the house of Omri" long after his dynasty had faded from the scene. Jehu, for example, is identified as "son of Omri" in Assyrian annals. In addition, archaeology attests to the fact that Omri (or his son Ahab) built new walls to replace those constructed by Solomon at Megiddo and Hazor. He, or his son, also built impressive water systems in these two important cities of the kingdom. Archaeology also supports

Figure 10.4   The hill of Samaria

the reference in 1 Kings 16:24 regarding Omri's establishing a new capital, Samaria, on a strategically secure site (see Figure 10.4). The selection and development of Samaria as the capital of the northern kingdom is comparable to David's action in establishing Jerusalem as the capital of his kingdom. Both represented the adoption of a symbolic new base of operations for the monarchy in a place without traditional associations. In each case, the move involved the building of a fortress and a palace and resulted in strengthening the king's rule and the stability of the dynasty. Jerusalem and Samaria differed from one another, however, in the fact that Jerusalem's history as a city went back centuries before David. Samaria had no urban history before Omri fortified it. Omri did such a good job of choosing the site of Samaria for his capital and fortifying it that the Assyrians, with all their military might, had to lay siege to it for more than two years before it finally fell (2 Kings 17:1–6).

If Dtr gives Omri scant mention in the biblical text, he overcompensates in the amount of attention that he directs to his son Ahab, who dominates the story from 1 Kings 16:29 to 22:53. Ahab appears to have consolidated the political accomplishments of his father. The attention given Ahab in the Bible however, has little to do with his abilities as king. The focus is on Ahab's infamous wife, Jezebel, "daughter of King Ethbaal of the Sidonians," and on his staunch prophetic critic, Elijah. With this fixation on Jezebel, the foreign Baalist, and on Ahab's relation to Elijah, the true prophet of Yahweh, Dtr leaves the most serious

Figure 10.5   Assyrian imperialism

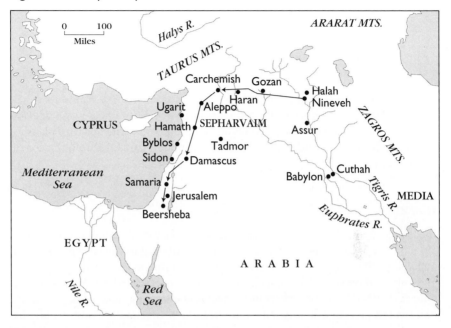

international crisis of the time unmentioned. Assyria, under King Ashurnasirpal II (883–859 B.C.E.) and his successor, Shalmaneser III (859–824 B.C.E.) initiated a policy of imperialistic expansion to the west (see Figure 10.5).

The first Israelite response to this policy of Assyrian aggression came when Ahab joined a coalition of states aimed at stopping Shalmaneser III at Qarqar on the Orontes River in Syria in 853 B.C.E. At the head of this alliance was the Aramean king of Damascus, Hadad-ezer. Ahab deployed the largest chariot force of all the allies. In his annals, Shalmaneser describes his first campaign into Syria-Palestine and the battle of Qarqar (Matthews and Benjamin 1991: 120–121):

> Qarqar was the next obstacle in this campaign. I laid siege to the city and burned it once it was captured. Irhuleni, who could muster only seven hundred chariots, seven hundred cavalry, and 10,000 soldiers, allied himself with twelve kings against me. They were:

Hadad-ezer of Aram:	1,200 chariots
	1,200 cavalry
	20,000 soldiers
Ahab the Israelite:	2,000 chariots
	10,000 soldiers
Queans:	500 soldiers
Musreans:	1,000 soldiers
Irqanateans:	10 chariots
	10,000 soldiers

Matiinuba'il the Arvadite:	200 soldiers
Usanateans:	200 soldiers
Adunu-ba'il the Shianean:	30 chariots
	xx soldiers
Gindibu the Arabian:	1,000 camels
Ba'sa, son of Ruhubi, the Ammonite:	xx soldiers

As is common in Assyrian royal inscriptions, according to Shalmaneser's annals the Assyrians won a great victory at Qarqar. It was more likely not a decisive win because Shalmaneser stopped his advance and apparently gave up plans for subduing the area. He did not follow up with another campaign into the area in succeeding years.

JEZEBEL

In dealing with Ahab, Dtr is mainly interested in Israel's internal crisis. From Dtr's point of view, this was a religious crisis centering in the struggle between Yahwism and Baalism for the hearts and minds of the people. In this encounter, Yahweh is represented by Elijah, and Baal is represented by Ahab's foreign Queen, Jezebel. As it is written in the Hebrew, the name Jezebel is probably a two-layered parody. The original name 'izebul ("Where is the Prince?") first became 'i-zebul ("No nobility"). Zebul, a title of Baal, was then distorted into zebel ("dung"; cf. 2 Kings 9:37), giving the form of the name as 'iyzebel. In the biblical narrative, Jezebel's passion for her Tyrian form of Baalism symbolizes everything that was wrong with the dynasty of Omri. The crisis was not however, solely a religious one, but had serious political implications as well. At issue behind the struggle between Yahweh and Baal was a Yahwistic understanding of the role of the king versus Jezebel's idea of kingship. Yahwism, especially the Yahwism of the north that did not recognize the Davidic covenant and its sanctioning of the Davidic dynasty, held on to the belief in the rights and responsibilities of all God's people under the guarantees of the Mosaic covenant. In sharp contrast, the Phoenician concept of kingship, represented by Jezebel, held that there were no checks on the power of the sovereign—basically a king could do anything he pleased, as long as he could get away with it. From a northern perspective, this was the problem of Solomon and his excesses all over again.

The excesses of monarchical power are sharply set against the rights of the people in the story of Naboth's vineyard in 1 Kings 21. Provisions in covenant law were meant to protect the Israelite small farmer against the very kind of abuses that Ahab, at Jezebel's urging, committed against Naboth. Ahab's act here symbolically represents the land-grabbing policies of the monarchy. These policies victimized those small farmers struggling to survive and created a growing class of landless poor—an issue that attracts intense prophetic interest in the eighth-century prophets, as we shall see in the next chapter.

The dynasty of Omri lasted through the second of Ahab's sons, Jehoram (849–842 B.C.E.). It ended when Jehoram was critically wounded in a battle at

Ramoth-Gilead against the Aramean king, Hazael, in his attempt to eject the Arameans from the northern Transjordan (2 Kings 8:25–29). Seizing the opportunity, Jehu, Jehoram's military commander, at the instigation of yet another prophet, Elisha, instigated a *coup d'état* that brought the dynasty of Omri to an end in a frenzy of violence in Jezreel. He killed both Jehoram and King Ahaziah of Judah (who was a descendant of Omri through his mother, Athaliah). He murdered Jezebel, forced the officials in Samaria to exterminate all of Ahab's descendants, and killed the relatives of Ahaziah and all the prophets of Ba'al (2 Kings 10:11–25). There remained of the house of Omri only Athaliah, Ahaziah's mother, who assumed power in Jerusalem upon the death of her son. Jehu's wholesale slaughter was intended to be a thorough housecleaning. Its extreme violence however, became a burden on the Israelite conscience in the years to come, as is indicated in Yahweh's instruction to the eight-century prophet Hosea about the naming of his son (Hos 1:4):

> And the LORD said to him, "Name him Jezreel; for in a little while I will punish the house of Jehu for the blood of Jezreel, and I will put an end to the kingdom of the house of Israel."

JEHU

Jehu's dynasty lasted for five generations and nearly one hundred years (842–745 B.C.E.), longer than any other dynasty in Israel. It was not, however, a peaceful century. Both Judah and Tyre were alienated by the tide of blood that swept Jehu into office, and Hazael, the Aramean king, took advantage of Jehu's isolation to occupy Israel's Transjordanian territory (2 Kings 10:32–33). Shalmaneser III, the Assyrian king, again advanced into the west in his fifth western campaign in 841 B.C.E. He set up a four-sided pillar of black limestone, six-and-one-half feet tall to celebrate this campaign. On this "Black Obelisk" Shalmaneser mentions extracting tribute from Jehu, and pictures Jehu, or his representative, bowing before him, with Israelite tribute bearers (Matthews and Benjamin 1991: 124):

My sixteenth campaign west of the Euphrates took place eighteen years after I became Great King.

Hazael, king of Aram [Syria], ran for his life leaving 1,121 chariots, 470 horses and a supply convoy on the battlefield.

Iaua [Jehu], king of Israel, ransomed his life with silver, gold [i.e., bowls, vases, cups, pitchers], lead and hard wood [i.e., scepter wood, spear wood].

During this period in the latter half of the ninth century (*ca.* 830–805) narratives such as those of 2 Kings 6, which describe Samaria's frequent sieges and consequent famine, are set. By the end of Jehu's reign, both Judah and Israel were weaker than at any time since the division of the United Monarchy, with both largely at the mercy of Syria.

At the beginning of the eighth century, circumstances began to shift in Israel's favor. King Jehoash (801–786 B.C.E.) succeeded in defeating Hazael's son Ben-hadad and in regaining some of the cities that had been lost to Aram (2 Kings 13:25; see also 1 Kings 20, which may belong to this period). This recovery continued under Jehoash's son, Jeroboam II (789–746 B.C.E.) Thanks to Assyrian pressure on the area from the east, Aram ceased to be a menace, and both Israel and Judah enjoyed about a half century of peace. This pacific period was, however, only the calm before the storm. From 745 B.C.E. on there was a sharp decline in Israel brought on by the aggressive Assyrian monarch Tiglath–Pileser III (744–727 B.C.E.), called Pul in 2 Kings 15:19; (see Figure 10.6). Tiglath-Pileser III inaugurated a new age of empires in the ancient Near East, which eventually subjugated all of Aram, Israel, Philistia, and Judah.

The events of Israel's final twenty-five years were tumultuous. There was a rapid turnover of kings, with six different monarchs in the twenty-five-year period 746–721 B.C.E. One *coup d'état* was followed by a counter *coup d'état.* Political factions squared off on the issue of whether it was wiser to "play along to get along" with the Assyrians, or openly to oppose them. In the end however, Tiglath-Pileser III in his campaigns of 734–732 B.C.E., conquered Aram, annexed the territory of Israel from the Jezreel valley northwards, and reduced Israel to a vassal state ruled by the Assyrian puppet, Hoshea (compare 2 Kings 15:29). Tiglath-Pileser III's campaigns are described in his annals:

I received subsidies from . . . Commagene, . . . Damascus, . . . Samaria, . . . Tyre, . . . Byblos, . . . Qu'e, . . . Carchemish, . . . Hamath, . . . Sam'al, . . . Tuna, . . . Tuhana, . . . Ishtunda, . . . Hubishna, . . . Arabia which included gold, silver, tin, iron, elephant-hide, ivory, linen garments embroidered with different colors, blue wool, purple wool, ebony, boxwood, luxury items [i.e., purple sheepskins, wild birds mounted with their wings extended and tinted blue], horses, mules, large cattle, small cattle and camels, some already bred. (Matthews and Benjamin 1991: 126)

In 725 B.C.E. Hoshea, who was to be Israel's last king, rebelled against Tiglath-Pileser's successor, Shalmaneser V, whereupon the Assyrians laid siege to Samaria. Following a siege of over two years, Samaria fell either to Shalmaneser or his successor, Sargon II in 721 B.C.E. Sargon II takes full credit for the fall of Samaria in his annals:

The governor of Samaria [Hoshea], in conspiracy with another king, defaulted on his taxes and declared Samaria's independence from Assyria. With the strength given me by the gods, I conquered them and took 27,280 prisoners of war along with their chariots. I conscripted enough prisoners to outfit two hundred groups of chariots. The rest were deported to Assyria. I rebuilt Samaria, bigger and better than before. I repopulated it with people from other countries I conquered. I appointed one of my officials over them, and made them Assyrian citizens.

. . .

I besieged and conquered Samaria, taking 27,290 prisoners of war. I conscripted enough from among them to outfit fifty groups of chariots. Subsequently, I rebuilt the city, repopulating it with people from other lands I conquered. I appointed a governor of my choosing, who reimposed the standard tribute payments. (Matthews and Benjamin 1991: 129)

Figure 10.6   Tiglath-Pileser III of Assyria in a bas-relief

So ended the history of the northern kingdom, which had been founded just over two hundred years earlier by Jeroboam's rebellion.

The Southern Kingdom Alone (721–586 B.C.E.)

Through most of the period of the two kingdoms, Israel was the dominant of the two. Under Omri's dynasty, the kings of Judah were subservient to Samaria. Judah did, however, have the stability provided by the Davidic dynasty. While Israel had nine different dynasties and nineteen kings in the two hundred years of its existence, during the same period Judah was ruled by only eleven monarchs, all of them (except Athaliah) in David's line. For another century-and-a-half after the northern kingdom ceased to exist, Judah, due in part to its political stability and buffered geographical position, was able to survive the crises brought on by Assyrian imperialism.

At the end of the eighth century, King Hezekiah of Judah was determined to get out from under Assyrian domination which had been imposed on Judah since Hezekiah's father, Ahaz, had appealed to Tiglath-Pileser III for aid against Aram and Israel. Rebelling against Assyrian strength was no easy task, as Hezekiah was to discover. He, with Philistia, Edom, and Moab, joined an unsuccessful revolt against Sargon II. When Sargon died in 705 B.C.E., Hezekiah decided to try his hand at revolt again. This time the effort was more carefully planned and included the beefing up of the fortifications of Jerusalem and other strategic points. A centerpiece of Hezekiah's efforts to secure Jerusalem was the construction of a water tunnel to insure the city's water supply in case of siege (2 Kings 20:20; 2 Chr 32:4–5, 30), described in the Siloam Inscription (Matthews and Benjamin 1991: 131):

> . . . The two teams working toward one another with picks. The workers began shouting to each other when they realized they were four and one-half feet apart. Then the teams turned toward one another following the sounds of their picks until they cut through the remaining rock and joined the tunnels. Thus, the water was able to flow through this tunnel one hundred fifty feet underground for some 1800 feet from the Gihon spring outside the city wall to the Siloam reservoir.

Hezekiah's engineers thus drove a tunnel from the spring of Gihon into the city. The tunnel, which can be seen and walked through in Jerusalem today, runs in an S-shape and is about 1,739 feet long, cut through the solid bedrock, a very impressive feat of engineering for the eighth century B.C.E. In 701 B.C.E. the inevitable happened—Sennacherib, Sargon's successor, invaded Judah to put down the revolt.

INVASION OF SENNACHERIB

Sennacherib's invasion demonstrated to Hezekiah just how unwise it was to challenge Assyrian dominion. Judah was occupied by the Assyrian army, and, according to both the Annals of Sennacherib and the Bible (2 Kings 18:13–19:36), Jerusalem was besieged. Sennacherib had his military exploits recorded on several hexagonal prisms, one of which, known as the Taylor Prism, describes, among other things, the events that took place in his campaign against Hezekiah. The city of Lachish, whose fortifications Hezekiah had strengthened in preparation for the anticipated Assyrian invasion, was forced to surrender, an event alluded to in the Lachish Letters (see Figure 10.7) and commemorated in Assyrian bas-reliefs.

Sennacherib extracted heavy tribute from Hezekiah as punishment for his rebellion (2 Kings 18:13–16), but Jerusalem itself was not conquered. According to 2 Kings 19:35, "The angel of the Lord set out and struck down one hundred eighty-five thousand in the camp of the Assyrians; when morning dawned, they were all dead bodies" (perhaps a reference to the outbreak of a plague among the Assyrians). This only strengthened the dangerous belief that Yahweh gave special protection to Jerusalem because of the presence of the Temple there (2 Kings 19:32–34).

Judah was now, more than ever, an Assyrian vassal state, a situation that would prevail throughout the rest of the reign of Hezekiah (715-686 B.C.E.) and that of his son, Manasseh (686–642 B.C.E.) Manasseh probably took effective power soon after his father's failed rebellion, and must have followed a policy of

Figure 10.7   One of the Lachish Letters

appeasing Assyria. While the accounts of all the kings are theologically colored, Dtr's account of Manasseh in 2 Kings 21:1–9 has an especially negative tone. He is said to have undone Hezekiah's religious reforms, to have permitted child sacrifice, and to have encouraged occult practices such as necromancy, communicating with the dead. The long reign of Manasseh was, however, something of a theological embarrassment. If, as Dtr believed, God rewarded good and punished evil based on an individual's moral balance sheet, how, if Manasseh were as evil as the account of his reign in 2 Kings suggests, could one explain his long reign? One answer is provided by a passage in 2 Chr 33:11-20, which suggests that at some point Manasseh rebelled against Assyria, was taken captive to Babylon [*sic*], "saw the light" and turned to God in desperation. Upon returning to Jerusalem, he carried out a Hezekiah-like reform:

> While he was in distress he entreated the favor of the LORD, his God and humbled himself greatly before the God of his ancestors. He prayed to him, and God received his entreaty, heard his plea, and restored him again to Jerusalem and to his kingdom. Then Manasseh knew that the LORD indeed was God. (2 Chr 33:12–13)

Assyrian power began to wane at the end of Manasseh's reign. His son Amon, who came to the throne in 642 B.C.E., ruled for only two years and was assassinated by members of the court (2 Kings 21:19-23). The "people of the land," a power elite, installed Amon's eight-year-old son, Josiah, on the throne (2 Kings 21:24; 2 Chr 33:25).

REIGN OF JOSIAH

Josiah's reign (640-609 B.C.E.), was probably the most important of any reign of a king of Israel or Judah for the development of the religion of ancient Israel. Josiah plays an important role in the Deuteronomistic History, where he, together with Hezekiah, are the only kings after David to escape condemnation (2 Kings 22:2). He is, on the contrary, pictured as giving his full attention to fulfilling the law of Moses. In 2 Kings 22:8-20 there is a story about the discovery of the "book of the law" during the refurbishing of the temple. This discovery prompted Josiah to carry out a thoroughgoing religious reform. Behind this reform is another prophet, this time a woman named Huldah, who appears to have been a court prophet, and is the only woman prophet mentioned in the books of Kings. Her oracle was one event that led to Josiah's reform. Huldah's oracle is in two parts. The first part is 2 Kings 22:16-17:

> Thus says the LORD, "I will indeed bring disaster on this place and on its inhabitants—all the words of the book that the king of Judah has read. Because they have abandoned me and have made offerings to other gods, so that they have provoked me to anger with all the work of their hands, therefore my wrath will be kindled against this place, and it will not be quenched."

The second part is in 22:18-20:

> But as to the king of Judah, who sent you to inquire of the LORD, thus shall you say to him, "Thus says the LORD, the God of Israel: 'Regarding the words that you have heard, because your heart was penitent, and you humbled yourself before the LORD, when you heard how I spoke against this place, and against its inhabitants, that they should become a desola-

tion and a curse, and because you have torn your clothes and wept before me, I also have heard you,' says the LORD. 'Therefore, I will gather you to your ancestors, and you shall be gathered to your grave in peace; your eyes shall not see all the disaster that I will bring on this place.'"

The first part of Huldah's oracle is a word of judgment against Judah; the second is a word of assurance to the king that he will die in peace before that judgment is carried out. The word of judgment is written in typically Deuteronomistic style and pictured as having been fulfilled in the remaining chapters of 2 Kings. The second part of Huldah's oracle, however, was not fulfilled. Though Josiah dies before Judah is destroyed, he does not die in peace, but violently in battle (2 Kings 23:29). Such unfulfilled prophecy is very uncharacteristic of Dtr and testifies to the authenticity of the second part of Huldah's oracle.

As long as Josiah was alive, he worked hard at carrying out religious reform. His reforms went on for some thirteen years. What was the "book of law" found in the Temple? At other places in the text, 2 Kings refers to it as "this book," "the book of the covenant," and "the law of Moses." A close comparison of the language used to describe the book in 2 Kings 22–23 with the contents of the Torah shows striking similarities with the central section of the book of Deuteronomy. This is especially true regarding the actions taken by Josiah to abolish pagan religious paraphernalia from the land. Table 10.2 correlates Josiah's reforms with similar provisions in Deuteronomy.

Meanwhile, new turmoil had arisen on the international scene, in response to which Josiah made a serious political miscalculation. The Babylonians had won victory after victory, and in 612 B.C.E. the combined armies of the Babylonians and the Medes destroyed Nineveh, the Assyrian capital. The remnant of the Assyrian army assembled at Haran for a last stand. The Egyptian Pharaoh, Neco, sent his forces to assist the Assyrians, and 2 Kings 23:28–29 reports that Josiah was killed when he went to encounter Neco.

While many biblical commentators have assumed that Josiah was trying to keep Neco from going to the aid of the Assyrians, the Hebrew of 2 Kings 23:39 says simply that Josiah was going to meet him, as is reflected in the NRSV:

TABLE 10.2   Josiah's Reforms and Their Correlation in Deuteronomy

JOSIAH'S REFORMS	2 KINGS	DEUTERONOMY
1. Elimination of the cult of Asherah	23:4, 6–7	7:15
2. Ends astrological cult	23:4–5	17:3
3. Ends worship of sun and moon	23:5, 11	17:3
4. Destroys cult prostitution	23:7	23:18
5. Defiles cult place of Molech	23:10	12:31
6. Tears down high places	23:13	7:15
7. Removes all foreign idols	23:13	12:1–32
8. Breaks the pillar idols	23:14	12:3
9. Renews the feast of Passover	23:21–22	16:1–8
10. Forbids the cult of the dead	23:24	18:11

> In his days Pharaoh Neco king of Egypt went up to the king of Assyria to
> the river Euphrates. King Josiah went to meet him; but when Pharaoh
> Neco met him at Megiddo, he killed him.

The parallel to this passage in 2 Chr 35:20–21, however, makes Neco's purpose quite explicit:

> After all this, when Josiah had set the temple in order, King Neco of Egypt
> went up to fight at Carchemish on the Euphrates, and Josiah went out
> against him. But Neco sent envoys to him, saying, "What have I to do
> with you, king of Judah? I am not coming against you today, but against the
> house with which I am at war; and God has commanded me to hurry.
> Cease opposing God, who is with me, so that he will not destroy you."

Robert Nelson has suggested that instead of going out against Neco, Josiah may
have gone out from Megiddo to welcome Neco as his ally, intending to open the
pass at Megiddo for the Egyptian army. Neco, however, wanted the strategically-
placed Megiddo, which controlled his communications with Egypt, for himself.
Unwilling to allow an ally who might change sides the opportunity of blocking
his retreat before a victorious army, Neco killed Josiah by treachery (Nelson
1983: 188).

Not only did Judah lose a promising young king in this encounter, but the
result was a brief period of subservience to Egypt (2 Kings 23:33). Although
Egypt failed in its attempt to rescue the Assyrians, the Egyptians did not leave
Palestine. They installed a garrison at Megiddo, hoping to use Judah as a buffer
against the Babylonians who were now the dominant power in the Near East. In
605 B.C.E. the Babylonians, under the leadership of Nebuchadrezzar (sometimes
spelled Nebuchadnezzar), defeated the Egyptians at the battle of Carchemish. A
year later, they moved into Syria and Israel. Jehoiakim, the king of Judah who
had been installed by Neco, shifted his allegiance to Nebuchadrezzar (2 Kings
24:1), but following a setback for Nebuchadrezzar in a battle against Egypt in
601 B.C.E., Jehoiakim changed loyalties again. In 597 B.C.E., Nebuchadrezzar
moved against Jerusalem, captured Jehoiakim's successor, Jehoiachin, and sent
him, with some members of his court, into exile in Babylon (2 Kings 24:8–17).
The last king to sit on the throne in Judah was the exiled Jehoiachin's uncle,
Zedekiah, who was a faithful vassal for ten years until he too decided to try his
hand at rebellion. This time the Babylonian response was decisive and final!
Jerusalem and its Temple were destroyed, and the monarchy that had been established by David came to an end.

EARLY PROPHETS IN ISRAEL AND JUDAH

What else can be said about the role of prophets in this troubled period of history in ancient Israel? In seeking an answer for this question, one can begin by
comparing the Israelite prophet to corresponding figures in other ancient Near

Eastern societies. From the several thousand texts now known from Mari on the Euphrates River, and dating to the first half of the eighteenth century, there are many references to prophets, using a variety of titles (Huffmon 1968; Matthews and Benjamin 1991: 109-110). These persons, both male and female, are typically associated with particular deities, though at times they communicate messages from other deities as well. Some of the descriptive titles used to refer to the figures at Mari are: "answerer" (implying that the person provides answers to inquiries); "cult functionary"; "ecstatic" (the most common title); and "diviner." These titles imply a range of functions, not all of which have direct parallels in Israelite prophets. Israelite prophets were regarded as having some kind of special power, but were differentiated from such figures as diviners, sorcerers, necromancers, and so forth (see Deut 18:10-11).

Recent application of methods and theories from the social sciences has contributed significantly to our understanding of the prophet's role and place in society, and to the difference between "true" and "false" prophets. It has been observed, for example, that a characteristic feature both of stories about prophets and of prophetic oracles is the fact that one prophet's message sometimes contradicts that of another prophet. This has raised the epistemological question of how one can know which prophet is the truth-teller. A particularly striking illustration of this phenomenon is provided in Jeremiah, where Hananiah and Jeremiah are both described as "the prophet"; both claim to be speaking in the name of "the LORD of Hosts, the God of Israel" (28:2, 14); and both employ symbolic devices as a means of authenticating their message (28:10-14). The message of the two, however, is totally contradictory (28:11, 15). Can one determine who is right and who is wrong? What test can be applied? In this story and in the story of a conflict between Micaiah ben Imlah and Ahab's prophets in 1 Kings 22, one can interpret the outcome of the course of events in a way that shows that one prophet was right and the other wrong. There must have been however, many occasions when there was no dramatic outcome that provided such a convincing authentication of "true" prophecy.

Assessments of the role played by prophets in society have provided another way of approaching confrontations such as these. Instead of making value judgments about truth and falsity, or sincerity and deception, perhaps a different assessment of the prophetic role in society can help. Such an assessment has been proposed in seeing the prophets as either "central" or "peripheral" (Wilson 1980; Petersen 1981). (Note that the term "peripheral" is used here in a descriptive sense, not in the sense that implies that something or someone is insignificant). These terms have been used frequently in the sociology of religion to describe two different kinds of roles played by religious figures such as prophets, corresponding to the role of religion in relation to society. Religion can be, and often has been, used by those in power as a prop, supporting and legitimating the existing norms and values of society, and expressing that support in terms of divine approval for the actions of a community. In other instances, religion critiques the status quo, challenging the moral and political bases of the society's structure. Religious authority is used to call into question the complacent assumptions of a community and its leaders that they are unquestionably doing "God's will." Individuals who function in the context of religion in the first sense may be spoken of as "central"; those operating in the second way can be called "peripheral." Prophets who operate with the support of the political or religious authorities are "central" prophets, while those prophets who are supported only by the less powerful and marginal persons in the society, are "peripheral."

This concept of "central" and "peripheral" prophets can be applied to the story of the confrontation between Jeremiah and Hananiah in Jer 28. Hananiah's assumption that God must be pleased with the worship of the community, and that any misfortune is only a minor "glitch," is characteristic of a "central" religious functionary. The role of such a functionary is to provide religious support for existing structures, assuring those in power that no substantive changes are needed—that "God is on their side." The bitter accusations of Jeremiah, by contrast, are those typically associated with a "peripheral" figure, one who is not a part of the "establishment." Here is one who is fundamentally opposed to the religious assumptions of the decision-makers in power.

Equally revealing is the picture in the court of Ahab in 1 Kings 22. Here the four hundred prophets (v. 6) are "central" figures, whose perception of the will of God (in *any* situation), could be counted on to produce an answer identical to that of the will of the king. Micaiah ben Imlah, on the other hand, is a classic "peripheral" figure. He already has a bad reputation with the king, because he could not be relied upon to deliver messages from God that were always supportive of the king (v. 8).

PROPHETS AND KINGS

As we have noted, prophecy throughout the ancient Near East was often associated with kings and rulers. In attempting to assess the role of prophets in ancient Israel, note that all of those whom we can plausibly identify as *nebi'im* were active during the monarchical period. While both Abraham (Gen 20:7) and Moses (Deut 18:15) are spoken of as prophets, this was probably a later reflection on their importance, and it would not be helpful to develop a picture of the prophetic role based on them. The earliest examples of Israelite prophecy for which we have any evidence belong to the period of the monarchy's beginnings. Samuel is part prophet, but also judge and priest. It is clear, in the form in which the text has come down to us, that Samuel is pictured both as the head of a group of *nebi'im* (1 Sam 19:20) and as one who played a crucial transitional role in the establishment of the monarchy. Beginning with the time of the institution of the monarchy, references to prophets become frequent. A good case can be made for saying that the period of activity of the *nebi'im* was, for all practical purposes, the time of the monarchy, especially the divided monarchy.

Having established that there is a link between prophecy and the monarchy, we can now go on to examine the functional role of the prophet as being in some kind of relationship to the royal court. Early on, prophets were attached to the royal court as paid professional advisers. Sometimes their number could be large. 1 Kings 22:6 speaks of four hundred prophets at the court of king Ahab of Israel in the ninth century, while the story of the conflict between Elijah and Ahab's wife Jezebel, alludes to "four hundred fifty prophets of Baal and the four hundred prophets of Asherah" who were in her service (1 Kings 18:19). Such numbers may well have been somewhat exaggerated in the interests of the Deuteronomistic historian. In each of these contexts it is one lone individual who remains loyal to Yahweh when all others have fallen away—Micaiah ben Imlah in 1 Kings 22 and Elijah in 1 Kings 18. More generally, the books of Samuel and Kings have numerous stories that show prophets to be royal servants in some sense. Occasionally they are pictured as obedient servants; more frequently we have scenes of conflict between prophet and king, since in Dtr's eyes most of the kings, beginning with Solomon, "did what was evil in the sight of Yahweh." When we come to the eighth-century prophets in the next chapter we will see strong examples of independent prophets who challenged the royal establishment, and were not officially connected to the court.

The Elijah Cycle (1 Kings 17–19; 21; 2 Kings 1–2)

The narratives concerning Elijah are more than accounts of an important ninth-century B.C.E. prophet from Israel. The Elijah Cycle, edited by Dtr, probably served as a model for Dtr's concept of prophecy. The three chapters with which the Elijah Cycle begins (1 Kings 17-19) form an independent literary unit, as can be demonstrated by the fact that it can be outlined in thirteen sections in chiastic form as follows:

A.   Elijah in Transjordan (17:2-7)
B.   Elijah outside Israel to the north (17:8-24)
C.   Yahweh's command and Elijah's return to Israel (18:1-2a)
D.   Ahab and Obadiah on the road to meet Elijah (18:2b-6)
E.   Elijah and Obadiah (18:7-15)
F.   Elijah and Ahab (18:16-20)
G.   Elijah on Mt. Carmel (18:21-40)
F'.   Elijah and Ahab (18:41-42)
E'.   Elijah and his servant (18:43-45a)
D'.   Elijah and Ahab on the road to Jezreel (18:45b-46)
C'.   Jezebel's threat and Elijah's flight from Israel (19:1-3a)
B'.   Elijah outside Israel to the south (19:3b-18)
A'.   Elijah in Transjordan (19:19-21)

These thirteen sections also show a division into Elijah in private (A, B, C and A', B', C') and sections in which Elijah is in a public confrontation with King Ahab (D, E, F, G, F', E', D').

The story of Elijah is so thoroughly infused with the ideals of Dtr that the historical Elijah is perhaps less accessible to us than any other major prophet.

Both within the Bible and in later Jewish, Christian, and Muslim tradition, Elijah is presented as the one who intervenes, unannounced, in times of crisis. In Jewish tradition, Elijah combats social ills by caring for the poor and punishing the unjust. He is identified with the "Wandering Jew" of medieval folklore, and a place is always set for him at the Passover Seder table. He is protector of the newborn, and the "Chair of Elijah" is present at circumcisions. In the New Testament Elijah is, after Moses, Abraham, and David, the most frequently mentioned Hebrew Bible character. In Jewish tradition, there are numerous stories of the ascended Elijah's intervention in human affairs on behalf of justice and righteousness. The Qur'an lists Elijah among the "righteous ones" (*sura* 8:85) and recalls his mission as a strong adversary of the cult of Baal (*sura* 37:123–130).

We have two stories of the private world of Elijah's communion with God. In the first section of the cycle, Elijah is miraculously fed by ravens. In section B' he is miraculously fed by an angel and confronted by God in a dramatic theophany. The confrontation between Elijah and God is represented successively in a great wind, an earthquake, a fire, and a "sound of sheer silence" (NRSV). The last of these phenomena is questionably translated in the RSV (following the KJV) as "the still small voice." This translation has led to the widely held view that this "still small voice" was the voice of God instructing Elijah to rely on quiet persuasion instead of the spectacular. This view is improbable for two reasons. First, there is a distinction between the series of natural phenomena referred to in 19:11–12 and the "voice" of God in 19:13. This suggests that the fourth phenomenon in the series was a mysterious sound rather than an intelligible voice: a "sound of sheer silence" (compare the Simon and Garfunkel song, "The Sounds of Silence") rather than the "still small voice" of popular tradition. The voice of God came later, after the prophet had responded to the enigmatic divine revelation by wrapping his face in a mantle and gone out to stand at the entrance of the cave (19:13).

The other argument against the usual view that the expression in v. 12 revealed the content of God's direction to Elijah is supported by what God actually said to Elijah:

> Go, return on your way to the wilderness of Damascus; when you arrive, you shall anoint Hazael as king over Aram. Also you shall anoint Jehu . . . as king over Israel; and you shall anoint Elisha . . . whoever escapes from the sword of Hazael, Jehu shall kill; and whoever escapes from the sword of Jehu, Elisha shall kill. (19:15–17)

This is hardly what one would call gentle persuasion! An extrabiblical piece of support for this interpretation of 1 Kings 19:12 comes from the famous medieval Jewish commentator, Rashi. Rashi said that the usual view in his day (twelfth-century France) was that the expression meant "the sound of private prayer," although he himself favored the view that it referred to the "ringing in the ears" (tinnitus) that you, but no one else, can hear. These are attempts to understand what the mysterious experience of communication with God really is. These two stories emphasize the spiritual strength of Elijah (as the model prophet for Dtr).

Elsewhere in the cycle of stories about him, Elijah himself miraculously appears, like an angel or a *deus ex machina,* to kings or widows or servants, wherever he is needed to bring help or justice to those in distress. This image of Elijah is highlighted in his first appearance on the scene (1 Kings 17:1) and in his departure from the scene in an ascension to the heavens in a "chariot of fire and horses of fire . . . [and] a whirlwind" (2 Kings 2:11–12).

At the turning point in the chiastic structure of 2 Kings 17–19 (2 Kings 18—G in the outline above), and thus at a point of particular significance, is the story of Elijah on Mount Carmel, a narrative that highlights his role as one who keeps the faith in a world that has sold out to idolatry. These chapters share with the Elijah Cycle as a whole the shaping of Elijah into the figure of a new Moses. Elijah is portrayed here as the prophetic champion for Yahwistic faith against its rivals, in this case Baalism. The story of the contest with Ba'al's prophets on Mount Carmel stands as a classic portrayal of the impotence of other gods when pitted against Yahweh. It serves as a fine example of the theological tone of the entire Elijah Cycle. From beginning to end, Yahweh, much more than the prophet, is the central subject of the action. As Gerhard von Rad has observed, "The world in which Elijah lived was chock-full of miracles, yet he himself never works a single one" (1965:18). Rather, the mighty works are Yahweh's alone. With Elijah, according to Dtr, we have reached that point in the development of prophecy where the potency of Yahweh's word bolsters what the prophet says and does in Yahweh's name.

• •

An Imaginative Portrait of Elijah

In the contest between Elijah and the prophets of Baal to see whose God was the real article, Elijah won the first round hands down. Starting out early in the morning on Mt. Carmel, the prophets of Baal pulled out all the stops to get their candidate to set fire to the sacrificial offering. They danced around the altar until their feet were sore. They made themselves hoarse shouting instructions and encouragement at the sky. They jabbed at themselves with knives thinking that the sight of blood would start things moving if anything would, but they might as well have saved themselves the trouble.

Although it was like beating a dead horse, Elijah couldn't resist getting in a few digs. "Maybe Baal's flown to Bermuda for the weekend," he said. "Maybe he's taking a nap." The prophets whipped themselves into greater and greater frenzies under his goading, but by mid-afternoon the sacrificial offering had begun to get a little high, and there was still no sign of fire from above. Then it was Elijah's turn to show what Yahweh could do.

He was like a magician getting ready to pull a rabbit out of a hat. First he had dug a trench around the altar and filled it with water. Then he got a bucket brigade going to give the offering a good dowsing too. Then as soon as they'd finished a third go-round, the whole place was awash, and Elijah looked

Continued

as if he'd just finished swimming the channel. He then gave Yahweh the word to show his stuff and jumped back just in time.

Lightning flashed. The water in the trench fizzled like a spit on a hot stove. Nothing was left of the offering but a pile of ashes and a smell like the Fourth of July. The onlookers were beside themselves with enthusiasm and at a signal from Elijah demolished the losing team down to the last prophet. Nobody could say whose victory had been greater, Yahweh's or Elijah's.

But the sequel to the event seems to have made this clear. Queen Jezebel was determined to get even with Elijah for what he had done to her spiritual advisers, and to save his skin he went and hid out on Mt. Horeb. Again he gave Yahweh the word, not because he wanted anything set on fire this time but just to keep his hand in.

Again the lightning flashed, and after that a wind came up that almost blew Elijah off his feet, and after that the earth gave such a shake that it almost knocked him silly. But there wasn't so much as a peep out of Yahweh, and Elijah stood there like a ringmaster when the lion won't jump through the hoop.

Only when the fireworks were finished and a terrible hush fell over the mountain did Elijah hear something, and what he heard was so much like silence that it was only through the ear of faith that he knew it was Yahweh. Nonetheless, the message came through loud and clear: that there was no longer any question who had been the star at Mt. Carmel and that not even Elijah could make the Lord God of Hosts jump through a hoop like a lion or pop out like a rabbit from a hat.

Buechner (1979:28–30)

●●●

The Elisha Cycle (2 Kings 1–10)

Elisha was a follower of and the designated successor of Elijah. He appears to have been active during the reigns of Ahab, Ahaziah, and Jehoram, *ca.* 850–800 B.C.E. The stories recorded about Elisha, from the very outset, give the impression that Elisha was trying to outdo Elijah's achievements by performing miracle upon miracle. The Elisha tales have the distinct flavor of folk tradition, presenting what appears to be an unordered assortment of miracles and wonders that the narrator did not attempt to diminish. Richard Moulton has written an interesting assessment of the role of miracles in the stories about Elisha in which he suggests that with Elisha we seem to see a change affecting prophecy. Prophetic action naturally includes miracles, but in the Elisha tales we begin to find the miraculous becoming an interest in itself. The "sign of the prophet" is at first the symbolic act—tearing of robe or rending of altar—which serves merely as a preface to the prophetic message. But in the Elisha stories, according to Moulton, it comes to be the wonder-working act which draws attention for its own sake: the cycle of Elisha stories reads for the most part as a succession of mystic wonders, much like the cycle of Samson with its feats of physical strength: wonders of axe heads swimming (2 Kings 6:5-7), a jar of oil multiplying (2 Kings 4:1-7), children cursed and destroyed by bears (2 Kings 2:23-24), leprosy healed or returning at the prophet's word (2 Kings 5:1-27). Moulton concludes that there appears a decadence, not in prophecy itself, but in the public perception of prophecy; the wonder of the sign has become to the onlooking people more than the moral truth which that sign is to convey (Moulton 1907: 1380).

Elisha's dramatic feats of power appear to operate in the biblical narrative as *the* means of establishing his authority as a prophet. After his commissioning by Elijah, his authority is confirmed by his ability to part the waters of the Jordan (2 Kings 2:13-14), to clear the spring at Jericho of impurities (2 Kings 2:19-22), and to fatally curse children who taunted him (2 Kings 2:23-25). Such prophetic acts of power are repeated throughout the cycle. The Deuteronomistic setting of these legendary stories is important, since Elijah provided a model of the prophet in the image of Moses. The transfer of authority from Elijah to Elisha is modeled on the transfer of power from Moses to Joshua (see Num 27:18-23; Deut 34:9). The miracle stories, which seem to provide little evidence of prophetic activity, are basically concerned with authenticating the role of Elisha as a model Mosaic prophet who plays a central role in the overthrow of Omri's dynasty.

The prophecy and fulfillment scheme of Dtr that we have observed before, is evident again in Elijah's prophecies of the overthrow of the Omri's dynasty and in Elisha's active role in the rebellion of Jehu (1 Kings 19:15; compare 2 Kings 8:7-15; 1 Kings 21:23-29; cf. 2 Kings 9:1-10).

Elisha is pictured as constantly in conflict with the house of Omri. As an Israelite, it is he who is responsible for Hazael's accession as king of Aram (2 Kings 8:7-15). His opposition to the Omri dynasty peaks in the central role attributed to him in legitimizing the rebellion of Jehu (2 Kings 9:1-10). Wilson maintains that Elisha's social role changed after Jehu's assumption of power from that of "peripheral" to "central" prophet (1980: 205-206). After Jehu was in power, Elisha became more closely associated with the royal court, particularly in the military arena (2 Kings 6:8-7:20; 13:14-19).

In all of this, Elisha clearly stands in Elijah's shadow. As his solo career began, Elisha imitated Elijah (compare 2 Kings 2:8) by parting the water—using *Elijah's* mantle, and did so in the name of "the Lord, *the God of Elijah*" (2 Kings 2:14). But there is a method in Dtr's madness—he uses the traditions about Elisha carefully, limiting Elisha's contribution in subtle ways in order to strengthen the prophetic profile of Elijah. Elisha is pictured as being intimidated or "ashamed" by a band of prophets (2 Kings 2:17). Although he can use his miraculous powers to good ends (2 Kings 2:19-22), he can also use them pointlessly to curse boys who tease him about his lack of hair (2 Kings 2:23-25). His miracles seem to be without divine authority and lack even a consistent divine reference. To top it off, there are even crucial things that God hides from him.

There seems to have been a large stock of stories about Elisha, and perhaps collections of them were available to the Deuteronomistic historian, from which the stories included in 2 Kings were selected. Most of the references to the "sons of the prophets" or prophetic "guilds" ("company of prophets" in the NRSV) in the Hebrew Bible occur here (2 Kings 2:3, 5, 7, 15; 4:1, 38; 5:22; 6:1; 9:1), perhaps pointing to the group responsible for preserving and collecting the stories about Elisha. They clearly believed that God had given great power to people such as Elisha, their "father," and used the legends to explain their own existence and origins. Whatever the truth about the Elisha of history, his wonders and miracles enhance his standing and exalt his memory.

Elijah and Elisha represent early prophets in Israel. The prophetic role would come to maturity, however, in the eighth century prophets, whom we shall meet in the next chapter of our journey through the Hebrew scriptures.

STUDY QUESTIONS

THE DIVISION OF THE UNITED MONARCHY

1. Explain why two kingdoms developed out of the United Monarchy. Briefly describe some characteristics of each of the kingdoms.
2. What happened to the Davidic covenant and its promise when the kingdom was divided?
3. What image from Israel's past do you think the Deuteronomist wished to bring to his readers' mind with the "golden calves" of Jeroboam's shrines at Dan and Bethel? Is this the only, or even the most likely meaning of the golden calves?
4. How did the period of the divided monarchy provide the Deuteronomist with an ideal illustration of his view of history?

PROPHETS AND KINGS

1. What is the origin of the English word "prophet"? How does this derivation relate to the basic meaning of *nabi'* in Hebrew and the role of a prophet in ancient Israel?
2. How does the interaction of Ahijah and Jeroboam draw the battle lines between prophecy and kingship?
3. Compare Jezebel's view of kingship, as illustrated in the story of Naboth's vineyard, with that found in Israel's view of a king's power as understood in the Sinaitic and Davidic covenants.

THE ELIJAH AND ELISHA CYCLES

1. As is evident from the chiastic structure of 1 Kings 17–19, the central scene is Elijah's confrontation on Mt. Carmel. Not only does 1 Kings 18:21–40

demonstrate the historical conflict between Baalism and Yahwism, it also illustrates an important function of the Israelite prophet. This scene can be organized around the different parties whom Elijah addresses. Indicate the groups/persons with whom Elijah speaks (the *addressees*) and then describe that group's/person's *response* to Elijah.

2. With which addressee is Elijah most concerned? How would you describe the nature of Elijah's concerns regarding that addressee?

3. This scene is also concerned with the literary motif of "answering." The true god is the one who can *answer* (18:24); and so there is a sharp contrast between silence and response. Where does the word "answer" occur in this scene (1 Kings 18:21–40)?

4. The shifting loyalty of the Israelites plays an important role in ch. 18. How does the initial stance of the people resemble that of the frenzied Baal prophets (vv. 26–29)? What is the author suggesting by this correspondence? How else does the author indicate the people's primary allegiance?

5. The rebuilding of the altar of YHWH (1 Kings 18:31 ff.) recalls the ceremony of Gen 35. List some of the correspondences between these two passages and suggest the significance.

6. Where in ch. 18 is Elijah first called a "prophet"? Putting together all of the information that you have garnered, what does this chapter suggest about the role of an Israelite prophet?

7. Review the miracles Elijah performed. How did the people who witnessed these miracles respond to them? What was the relationship between Elijah's deeds (his miracles) and Elijah's words (his prayers and proclamations)?

8. Compare and contrast Elijah and Elisha. How are they alike and how are they different? Pay particular attention to the role of miracles in the stories about Elijah and Elisha.

BIBLIOGRAPHY

Biran, Avraham. 1992. "Dan (Place)." *The Anchor Bible Dictionary.* Vol. 2. New York: Doubleday, 12-17.

Buechner, Frederick. 1979. *Peculiar Treasures: A Biblical Who's Who.* New York: Harper & Row.

Huffmon, Herbert B. 1968. "Prophecy in the Mari Letters," *Biblical Archaeologist, XXXI,* 101-124.

Matthews, Victor H., and Benjamin, Don C. 1991. *Old Testament Parallels: Laws and Stories from the Ancient Near East.* Mahwah, NJ: Paulist.

Moulton, Richard G. 1907. *The Modern Reader's Bible.* New York: Macmillan.

Nelson, Robert D. 1983. *"Realpolitik* in Judah (687–609 B.C.E.)." *Scripture in Context II,* W. W. Hallo, J. C. Moyer, and L. C. Perdue, eds., 177–189. Winona Lake, IN: Eisenbraun's.

Rad, Gerhard von. 1965. *The Theology of Israel's Prophetic Traditions,* Tr. by D. M. G. Stalker, New York: Harper & Row.

Petersen, David L. 1981. *The Role of Israel's Prophets. JSOTSup* 17. Sheffield: University of Sheffield.

Wilson, Robert R. 1980. *Prophecy and Society in Ancient Israel.* Philadelphia: Fortress.

Chapter 11

LITERATURE, CULTURE, AND PROPHETIC CRITIQUE: AMOS, HOSEA, MICAH, AND ISAIAH

Suggested Bible Reading
Amos 1 - 9; Hosea 1 - 14; Micah 1 - 7; Isaiah 1 - 23; 28 - 39

EIGHTH-CENTURY PROPHETS

Having arrived at this point in our journey through the Hebrew Bible, we now have the opportunity to look at four classical or writing prophets, two of whom were active in Israel and two of whom worked in Judah. The books of the writing prophets frequently have been regarded by interpreters as *the* most distinctive element in the Hebrew Bible. Before we look at these individual prophets in detail, we need to talk about a shift that takes place in prophets when we reach Amos. In our itinerary, we have already encountered several prophets—Samuel, Nathan, Ahijah, Micah, Elijah, and Elisha. We have read stories about what these prophets did, with their prophetic speeches inserted only occasionally. We have seen little of the content of what they said. Starting with

Amos, the situation changes. From Amos on we will see mostly the words attributed to prophets, with occasional narrative as the framework for the words. We will read very little about the prophets' lives and activities. Instead the focus will be on the what they said. What caused this change?

All the eighth-century prophets worked under the shadow of Assyrian expansionism, which we discussed in the previous chapter. Assyria initiated this expansionist program in the ninth century B.C.E. By the end of that century, Assyrian armies had taken territory in present-day Syria and southern Turkey. They also had placed enough pressure on the neighboring states to bring an end to conflict between Israel and Damascus. With the eighth century, however, came a decisive shift in Assyrian policy. The change had to do with the way the Assyrians made treaties. Prior to the eighth century, treaties were usually in the form of agreements between rulers, with the individual rulers held responsible for keeping the treaty's stipulations. Accordingly, the work of those prophets we encountered in the last chapter was directed primarily at the rulers of Israel. In the eighth century, however, the Assyrians began making treaties and covenants with peoples, not just with their rulers. The people *as a whole* were responsible for keeping the stipulations in the treaty. This shrewd political move on the part of the Assyrians put people on notice that they, not just their rulers, would be subject to reprisals for treaty-breaking. At about this time, Assyria also began using the fear-inspiring tactics of collective punishment, of massacres and mass deportations. If a people broke a treaty with the Assyrians, large-scale massacres and deportations could follow. This change in Assyrian policy contributed to a corresponding change in Israelite prophecy.

From Amos on, the prophets addressed the people, not just their rulers. The threat was no longer just to a rebellious ruler. The threat now was to the people. This also meant that the prophets' message was a public one, addressed to the threat of the extermination of a people—a threat that became reality for the northern kingdom of Israel in 722 B.C.E., after which we can speak of the "ten lost tribes of Israel," meaning that they were lost to history as definite sociopolitical units. As public figures, the prophets delivered their messages in a variety of contexts and institutions.

Books of the Eighth-Century Prophets

Given this statement on the beginnings of the "writing" prophets, it is important to say a word about the books that bear the names of Amos, Hosea, Micah, and Isaiah. These books, in the form in which we have them, are probably not the direct products of the prophets, but of scribes who compiled the books under the names of the individual prophets. Commonly found in commentaries and introductions to the Hebrew Bible are attempts to discern how much of each book goes back to the prophet for whom it is named and to what degree the historical circumstances of his time are reflected in the book. If the eighth-century prophets are seen as important primarily as witnesses to the social and economic conditions of eighth-century Israel and Judah, then it would be crucial to bracket out anything in their books that comes from a later period. But to approach the books named for the eighth-century prophets in this way is to misconceive what these books are. Anticipating what we will see in the book of Amos, two examples illustrate this point.

In the first part of Amos (1:3-2:16) a series of oracles (see p. 360 for the definition of oracle) of indictment is directed against Israel's neighbors, ending with an oracle of judgment against Israel herself. Details from these oracles, both those said and those omitted, have often been cited as illustrative of the political and economic situations in the mid-eighth century B.C.E. Many scholars have maintained that the oracle against Judah (2:4-5) that is included in this series of oracles is actually a later addition to the book of Amos. The form of this oracle lacks some of the formal features of the other oracles in the series and it is less specific in its denunciations. It says simply:

> Thus says the LORD:
> "For three transgressions of Judah,
>   and for four, I will not revoke the punishment;
> because they have rejected the law of the LORD,
>   and have not kept his statutes,
> but they have been led astray by the same lies
>   after which their ancestors walked.
> So I will send a fire on Judah,
>   and it shall devour the strongholds of Jerusalem." (2:4–5)

From this kind of generally-worded oracle, one cannot infer any particular historical setting. It is, however, important to observe that this oracle directed against Judah was included in a book that reached its present form in Judah. If our interest in studying Amos were limited to learning about the sociopolitical conditions in Syria-Palestine in the mid-eighth century B.C.E., we would come away from such a study disappointed. To study Amos, and the other eighth-century prophets as well, as part of the text of a continuing religious community brings far more rewards. It is critical that we recognize that Amos' words, originally directed to the northern kingdom in the mid-eighth century B.C.E., lived on after that state ceased to exist. Some Israelites believed that the meanings of Amos' message were not bound by time and space and held significance for those living outside Israel after the eighth century B.C.E. These people recognized that God's words, through Amos, were still important, albeit in completely different circumstances. This readiness to update the prophetic words showed that those words were not regarded as tied to only one historical situation. They had a continuing effectiveness in quite different conditions.

Another example from Amos illustrates in a different way how a purely historical approach, with a concern only for what is original to the prophet himself, is inadequate for the study of the eighth-century prophets. Most of the book of Amos has a negative tone, consisting of oracles of judgment. Thus, the heady optimism of the last half of the last chapter of the book (9:11-15) is startling. While some scholars support the originality of these verses, most commentators conclude that, because their tone differs so markedly from what precedes them, they are a later addition to the book of Amos. On the historical level, however, a few clues surface in Amos 9:11–15 about the setting of these verses. A purely historical approach concludes that they are the over-optimistic imaginings of a later editor. Again, a more constructive approach to this passage sees it as part of a larger whole, a link that helps incorporate the book of Amos into the Book of the Twelve, or the Minor Prophets. Just as the beginning of Amos is connected with the end of Joel (compare Joel 3:19–21 with Amos 1–2), so the conclusion of Amos provides a link with the book of Obadiah that follows it. Amos says that eventually God will rebuild the booth of David "as in the days of old" (Amos 9:11),

> in order that they may possess the remnant of Edom
> and all the nations who are called by my name. (9:12)

The book of Obadiah begins with an oracle directed against Edom (vv. 1–14), followed by one aimed at "all the nations" (vv. 15–21). This extension of themes makes sense only when Amos and Obadiah are looked at together as part of a larger body of literature. A purely historical approach, however, that dates Amos to the eighth century and Obadiah to the sixth, makes such a linkage impossible.

PROPHETIC ORACLES

In our examination of the books of the individual prophets, we will view those books as literary products. The primary literary unit of these books is the prophetic *oracle.* The Hebrew term translated "oracle" in modern English versions is *massa,* which has a literal meaning of "burden." Oracle has been used as a technical term for various kinds of utterances delivered by a prophet in response to a worshipper's question. Both senses of the term, together with an ironic twist, are reflected in Jer 23:33: "When this people . . . asks you, 'What is the burden of the LORD?' you shall say to them, 'You are the burden, and I will cast you off, says the LORD.' " Oracles include everything from short utterances addressed to a specific situation to lengthy speeches and whole books (for example Nahum, Habakkuk, and Malachi). Many oracles probably originated in the prophet's experience and were in the form of a single striking word or phrase in poetic form.

MESSENGER FORMULA

A second literary type presents the prophet as a messenger bringing the word of God to the people to whom it is addressed. This is the most common form in which prophecy is recorded. The message itself begins with phrases like "Hear this . . ." or "Listen . . ." Then a description of the current situation follows, accompanied by the main component of the prophecy, the announcement of what will happen. At this point the typical "messenger formula," "Thus says the LORD" or "It is the LORD who speaks" appears. The political analogy to an oracle is the message delivered by a royal messenger, who begins his proclamation with the words "Thus says the king." The prophetic pronouncement is thus cast as a message from Yahweh (the king), delivered by the prophet (his messenger). The words do not come from the prophet but from God. Finally there may be a concluding sentence of the same form to end an oracle.

Amos 7 is an instructive example of a prophetic messenger speech, delivered to the priest at Bethel:

A. *Instruction:* Amos is given an instruction to prophesy to the people: "The LORD took me from following the flock, and the LORD said to me, 'Go, prophesy to my people Israel'" (7:15).

B. *Summons:* The message itself is introduced: "Now therefore hear the word of the LORD" (7:16a).

C. *The Situation:* The accused's offense is identified. This can take the form of a question, a statement, or a quotation of the accused's own words: "You say, 'Do not prophesy against Israel, and do not preach against the house of Isaac'" (7:16b).

D. *The Announcement Proper:* The actual announcement of the divine judgment in the form of words addressed directly to the accused: "Therefore thus says the LORD: 'Your wife shall become a prostitute in the city, and your sons and your daughters shall fall by the sword, and your land shall be parceled out by line; you yourself shall die in an unclean land, and Israel shall surely go into exile away from its land'" (7:17).

While many prophetic utterances take the form of announcements of judgment, oracles of salvation also are composed in the same form as the announcement of judgment and are thus all the more effective. Isaiah 37 presents an example of an oracle of salvation:

A & B. *Instruction and Summons:* "Then Isaiah son of Amoz sent to Hezekiah, saying: 'Thus says the LORD, the God of Israel'" (37:21a).

C. *The Situation:* "Because you have prayed to me concerning King Sennacherib of Assyria, this is the word that the LORD has spoken concerning him" (37:21b–22a).

D. *The Announcement Proper:* "Therefore thus says the LORD concerning the king of Assyria: He shall not come into this city, shoot an arrow there, come before it with a shield, or cast up a siege ramp against it" (37:33).

The books of the prophets often add prose materials to these poetic oracles — discourses, brief biographical notices, or historical narratives. The contribution of any particular individual prophet to the book ascribed to him will be seen to vary considerably.

In addition to giving attention to the literary features of the prophetic books in our study, we also will be concerned with recent sociological and anthropological approaches to Israelite religion that have examined the place of prophets in their society. One result of these approaches is the recognition that the prophets were not the kind of individualists that many commentators have assumed them to be. The prophets were not "loners." Whether they were "central" or "peripheral," prophets had their supportive communities who valued their work and consequently preserved their words for subsequent generations. From this sociological perspective, as well as from a literary one, behind every prophetic book stands not only the lone prophet, but those who concurred with the prophet's assessment of society, even if that agreement sometimes came some time after the prophet's declarations.

Thus, while we recognize that the individual prophets originally addressed specific sociohistorical contexts, they also address the people of God across the years. This does not mean that the prophetic books are nothing but the products of later scribes. The compilers of the books added to and adapted the prophets' messages so that the prophets might continue to instruct subsequent generations.

TWO PROPHETS IN ISRAEL: AMOS AND HOSEA

Amos

When they brought together the collection of "The Twelve Prophets," the compilers of the Hebrew Bible apparently intended a roughly chronological arrangement of the books. The book of Amos appears third among the twelve in the Hebrew Bible (after Hosea and Joel) and second in the Septuagint. Chronologically however, most scholars consider the book of Amos to be the earliest of the prophetic books.

The book of Amos presents us with a good example of the way in which the books of the prophets developed. Redaction studies have discerned several stages in the formation of the book of Amos. Robert Coote, who makes more use of sociological criteria in investigating the redactional process than others, sees three stages in Amos: Amos A, Amos B, and Amos C (1981):

1. *First stage:* Amos' words of judgment directed at Israel's ruling class in the mid-eighth century B.C.E. (= Coote's "Amos A": 2:6-8, 13-16; 3:9-12; 4:1-3; 5:2, 11-12, 16-18; 6:1-7, 8a, 11; 8:4-10; 9:1-4—excluding passages listed below that were added in "Amos B" and "Amos C").

2. *Second stage:* The reinterpretation and expansion of Amos' words. This redactional stage adapted Amos' words, urging repentance on Judah and the remnants of Israel in the context of the positive reforms of Josiah in the last third of the seventh century B.C.E. (= Coote's "Amos B": 1:1-2; 1:3-3:8; 3:9-6:14; 7:1-9:6—excluding those passages listed above in "Amos A").

3. *Third stage:* Another reinterpretation and expansion of Amos. This time it was directed at Judahite exiles or recent returnees to Palestine after both Israel and Judah had fallen (= Coote's "Amos C": 1:11; 2:4; 9:7-15).

Coote differentiates between those social conditions that Amos himself condemned, those that Josiah sought to address in his reforms, and those that the exilic/postexilic redactor hoped to revive. What was the socioeconomic situation that "Amos A" addressed? The author of the superscription of the book of Amos (1:1) provides information for dating Amos:

> The words of Amos, who was among the shepherds of Tekoa, which he saw concerning Israel in the days of King Uzziah of Judah and in the days of King Jeroboam son of Joash of Israel, two years before the earthquake.

We know that Uzziah reigned over Judah from 783-742 B.C.E. and that Jeroboam II was king of Israel from 786-746 B.C.E. Phillip King (1988: 21, 38) has suggested that "the earthquake" referred to here (which is mentioned again in Zech 14:4-5) was a severe one, archaeological evidence of which appears in the remains of Stratum VI at Hazor. Josephus, a first-century C.E. Jewish historian, described this earthquake and connected it with insolence on Uzziah's part:

> In the meantime, a great earthquake shook the ground, and a rent was made in the temple, and the bright rays of the sun shone through it, and fell upon the king's face [that is, Uzziah], insomuch that the leprosy seized upon him immediately; and before the city, at a place called Eroge, half the mountain broke off from the rest on the west, and rolled itself four furlongs, and stood still at the east mountain, till the roads, as well as the king's gardens, were spoiled by the obstruction. (*Antiquities* 9:225)

From the Deuteronomistic History we know very little about Jeroboam II (2 Kings 14:23-29). He receives the usual negative theological assessment afforded to the northern kings. The Deuteronomistic historian does say however, that he "restored the border of Israel" from the Sea of the Arabah (the Dead Sea) in the south to Lebo-Hamath, forty miles north of Damascus (2 Kings 14:25). Most commentators believe that Amos 6:13-14 refers to this territorial expansion of Jeroboam:

> You who rejoice in Lo-debar,
>   who say, "Have we not by our own strength
>   taken Karnaim for ourselves?"
> Indeed, I am raising up against you a nation,
>   O house of Israel, says the LORD, the God of hosts,
> and they shall oppress you from Lebo-hamath
>   to the Wadi Arabah.

Although the textual information is meager, most commentators picture the reign of Jeroboam as a period of peace and prosperity for the northern kingdom. The threat from Assyrian imperialism, for the time being, was minimized, because the Assyrians were preoccupied with internal disputes. Archaeological data from the mid-eighth century supports the assessment that in this period "the rich got richer, and the poor got poorer." The excavations of Samaria, the capital of the northern kingdom, have produced imported luxury items such as carved ivories (see Figure 11.1). At Samaria, over 500 ivory fragments were found (see Amos 3:15). Archaeology has also uncovered well-constructed houses built of carefully-worked ashlar masonry from this period, an expensive building material (compare Amos 5:11) (see Figure 11.2).

Figure 11.1   An eighth-century carved ivory plaque from Samaria

The monopolized wealth of the elite class, as it was associated with the crushing of the poor, creates a central theme in the book of Amos. During the "prosperous" and "peaceful" years of Jeroboam II's reign in Israel, probably no more than five percent of the population enjoyed this "prosperity" and "peace." How did such an economic stratification come about?

An earlier generation of biblical scholars raised few questions about the picture of a very small wealthy elite and a large poverty-stricken peasantry implied in Amos. For biblical Israel, as well as for their own society, they simply took wealth and poverty for granted, as something that was built into the structure of society, "the way things are." The most that could be done, from this perspective, was to inspire the generosity of the rich so that they could "sweeten" their wealth and soften the harshness of poverty somewhat through their acts of charity. For these commentators, the role of the prophet (then and now) is to provide such inspiration.

A different view of economic stratification in ancient Israelite society has been taken by scholars in recent decades. This view is commonly found in many introductions to the Old Testament/Hebrew Bible. According to this view,

Figure 11.2   Ashlar masonry in the excavations at Tel Dan

the gap between rich and poor is a characteristic of the urban culture of ancient Palestine. Poverty was a curse of city life. In this view, the prophets represented anti-urban sentiments that arose from the nomadic ideal that they embraced (Frick 1977: 209–231). The prophets launched their protests as representatives of this supposed nomadic ideal of community solidarity that knew nothing of social classes.

However, neither of these perspectives regarding the prophetic approach to wealth and poverty explain *how* an exploitative system developed in ancient Israel. An explanation, based on agriculturally-based preindustrial societies as studied by social anthropology, has been developed by Bernhard Lang (1983: 114–127). Lang cites three traits of a peasant or agrarian society:

1. A peasant is not just a farmer or an agricultural entrepreneur, but the manager of a household. Instead of earning a profit in the marketplace, his goal is to provide for his family, which is the basic economic unit. Normally any "profits" he makes are invested in the family.

2. Peasants are only half of a society. The other half is the propertied elite who control public affairs.

3. The ruling class makes permanent changes that affect the agricultural production of the peasantry. Taxation may cause the peasant to become indebted to an urban lender or merchant, or the peasant may be forced to cultivate land owned by others as a tenant farmer.

In the Near East, the third relationship between the peasantry and the elite has found expression in what has been called *rent capitalism*. The urban propertied class skimmed off the largest possible portion of agricultural produce as rent or taxes. We have seen that the Palestinian farmer worked in a medium- to high-risk environment. When crop failures occurred, the peasant was forced to take out a loan. Taking a loan almost inevitably led to long-term or even permanent dependence, a kind of serfdom. With this system in operation, the urban propertied class was able to accumulate land into large estates, or *latifundia*. Any idea of covenant responsibilities for their fellow Israelites was forgotten. Instead of offering low or no-interest loans to help a family through hard times, the urban landowners exacted high interest rates. When the peasant could not pay, they seized the land. The peasant, without ownership of land, became permanently poor. Coupled with this expropriation of land by the ruling class was the attempt to use religious ritual as a means for covering their actions, as if right ritual could compensate for wrong behavior.

Huffmon (1983: 111-112) suggests that when the social pathology referred to in Amos is placed in the socioeconomic context of the book, four basic points in the message of Amos emerge:

1. The socioeconomic lifestyle of the Israelites opposes traditional Yahwistic values.

2. Socioeconomic reorganization without compassion is unacceptable.

3. The resulting oppression of the poor cannot be tolerated.

4. Participation in the cultus gives a false sense of confidence.

STRUCTURE AND THEMES IN THE BOOK OF AMOS

Scholars have divided the book of Amos in several ways. Limburg (1987) has proposed a three-part structure:

1. **Chapters 1–2** This part has a brief introduction, followed by oracles against Israel's immediate "foreign" neighbors (1:3-2:3), an oracle against Judah (2:4-5), and one against Israel (2:6-16).

2. **Chapters 3–6** The second part of Amos contains oracles against Israel and predictions of its imminent doom. Most scholars believe that this section stems from Amos himself.

3. **Chapters 7–9** The last part of Amos includes five visions of Amos, interrupted by a biographical narrative (7:10-17). The visions are followed by two oracles that conclude the book.

Part One: Chapters 1–2.   Several things about the oracles against Israel's neighbors in the first two chapters of the book of Amos merit comment. First, they follow an interesting geographical pattern (see Figure 11.3). Starting with Israel's neighbor to the northeast, the second oracle is the neighbor to the

Figure 11.3   The pattern of Amos' oracles in chapters 1–2

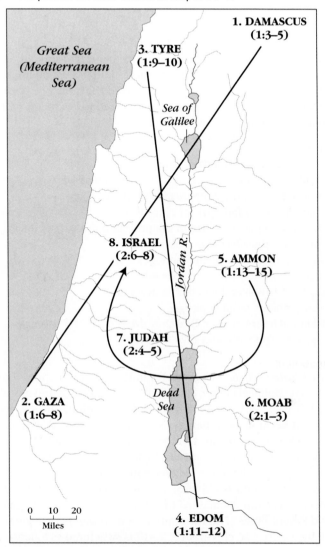

southwest. Oracle three is in the northwest and oracle four crosses back to the southeast. When one draws a line connecting the locations of oracles one and two and another joining oracles three and four, the result is a crosshair, whose center, the target, is in Israel. Similarly, when one moves from oracle five to oracle six to oracle seven, the resulting trail is an arc, whose end points at the heart of Israel. Israel is thus the bull's-eye of this series of oracles.

This initial series of oracles in Amos may have been patterned after a liturgy represented in the Egyptian Execration texts, in which curses were spoken against foreign enemies and domestic sinners. If such a liturgy was recited in Israel's cultic life, the book of Amos may have been drawing on its presuppositions and language to structure this series of oracles. In these oracles, Israel's foreign neighbors are indicted for what can be called crimes against humanity. These were crimes so heinous that they violated international law and the most basic sense of morality. Israelites, hearing these "barbarians" condemned, would no doubt have cheered Amos on. Having swayed the audience to his side with this rhetorical technique, the series of oracles then concluded with the most damning one of all, directed against Israel (2:6-8):

> Thus says the LORD:
> "For three transgressions of Israel,
>   and for four, I will not revoke the punishment;
> because they sell the righteous for silver,
>   and the needy for a pair of sandals—
> they who trample the head of the poor into the dust of the earth,
>   and push the afflicted out of the way.
> Father and son go in to the same girl.
>   so that my holy name is profaned;
> they lay themselves down beside every altar
>   on garments taken in pledge;
> and in the house of their God they drink
>   wine bought with fines they imposed."

Part Two: Chapters 3–6.   The oracles in this second section of Amos focus on Israel. Both its political center, Samaria (3:9-12; 4:1-3) and its cultic center, Bethel (3:13-15; 4:4-5), are the targets of denunciation. Amos 4, starting with verse 6 says that because Israel has ignored the LORD's repeated signals in nature and history, they must: "prepare to meet your God, O Israel!" (4:12), with the obvious sense that the meeting will not be a pleasant one. Amos 4 ends with a doxology (4:13), and chapter 5 begins with a lament (5:1-2). This lament opens a section structured as a chiasm, a pattern that we have seen several times earlier. Older scholarship maintained that 5:1-17 consisted of fragments of material from different times. The recognition of a chiasm here suggests a literary unit (de Waard 1977). The chiasm in 5:1-17 is structured as follows.

A   Lament (vv. 1-3)
B   "Seek me and live" (vv. 4-6)
C   Complaint (v. 7)
D   Doxology (vv. 8-9)
C'   Complaint (vv. 10-13)
B'   "seek good and not evil" (vv. 14-15)
A'   Lament (vv. 16-17)

A series of woes (5:18-6:14) brings this second part of Amos to an end.

Part Three: Chapters 7–9.   The last part of Amos includes five "visions." These visions are not necessarily the products of an altered state of consciousness. Rather they can be ordinary scenes interpreted symbolically. The first pair of visions—locusts (7:1-3) and fire (7:4-6)—depict natural catastrophes capable of destroying the land. In both cases, Amos intercedes, and the judgments are revoked. The third vision (7:7-9) sees a plumb line against a wall. The vision implies that Israel is a wall so out of vertical alignment that any additions to the top of the wall will result in its collapse. The wall *and* Israel are doomed.

The series of five visions is interrupted at this point by a biographical narrative concerning a confrontation between Amos and Amaziah, the priest at the national sanctuary in Bethel (7:10-17). This biographical narrative may have been inserted at this point because of the "catchword principle," a word used that causes one to say "Oh, that reminds me. . . ." Jeroboam is mentioned at the end of the vision of the plumb line (7:9) and at the beginning of the biographical insert (7:10). This passage makes up the only incident from Amos' life recorded in the book of Amos or anywhere else in the Hebrew scriptures.

Amos 7:10-17 is an important passage, but some details in it present difficulties. One of these difficulties is how to understand Amos' response to Amaziah in v. 14. Speaking as a loyal supporter of state and king, Amaziah confronted Amos with the charge that his message was unwelcome and treasonous. He called Amos a "seer" and advised him to go home to Judah to make his living by prophesying there (v. 12). Amos responded:

> I *am* no prophet, nor a prophet's son; but I *am* a *herdsman,* and a *dresser of sycamore trees,* and the LORD took me from following the flock, and the LORD said to me, "Go prophesy to my people Israel." (7:14, emphasis mine)

If one supplies the linking verb "am" in Amos's response, as English translators do (there is no verb at all in the Hebrew), Amos may have been responding to Amaziah's having called him a "seer" by denying that he is a "professional" prophet or member of a prophetic "union." He is not a "central" prophet in the employ of the state. One can also read Amos' statement as saying "I *was* no prophet . . . I *was* a herdsman," which places the emphasis on the fact that Amos was a "herdsman and a dresser of sycamore trees" *until* Yahweh called him to be a prophet. He did not choose to be a prophet, the role was thrust upon him. What does the phrase "herdsman and a dresser of sycamore trees" tell us about Amos' life before he was called to be a prophet?

Early scholarship made Amos out to be a poor shepherd who, in the off season, pricked fruit on the trees so that it would ripen properly. This interpretation of Amos' occupation was based on the presupposition that because he criticized the rich and championed the poor, he must himself have been poor. The word translated as "herdsman" here, *noqed,* occurs only one other time in all of the Hebrew Bible. This is in 2 Kings 3:4, where it is used in reference to king Mesha of Moab (see his stele in the previous chapter, Figure 10.3), "who used to deliver to the king of Israel one hundred thousand lambs, and the wool of one hundred thousand rams," hardly what one would expect from a "poor shepherd." The Septuagint and the KJV translate *noqed* in 2 Kings 3:4 as "sheep-master." The NRSV translates it as "sheep breeder." Mesha was obviously not a poor shepherd, but a breeder and owner of huge flocks of sheep. By analogy, because *noqed* is used here to describe Amos, instead of the more common term for shepherd, we can conclude that Amos was rich enough to own large herds. This understanding of *noqed* could also help explain the reference to Amos' being a "dresser of sycamore trees." While the poor did eat sycamore figs, this fruit was used mostly as food for animals. The reference to Amos as a "dresser of sycamore trees" may mean that he also owned orchards whose produce could be as food for his flocks.

Amos was thus probably not a poor shepherd, who identified with the poor out of a spirit of class solidarity. He was more likely a member of the landed class, who was called by Yahweh to be a prophet to the northern kingdom. After the events of 7:10-17, we don't know what Amos did. Perhaps he returned to his home in Judah.

This biographical narrative is followed by the last two visions. The fourth vision is of a basket of summer fruit (8:1-3), probably overripe fruit on the verge of spoiling. This vision includes an interesting play on words in Hebrew. The word for summer fruit in Hebrew here is *qayits* and the word for end is *qets,* both of which would have been pronounced as *qets* (rhymes with "gates") in the Hebrew of the northern kingdom. The last vision in 9:1-4 follows an indictment of Israel in 8:4-14. It is the most severe vision of all. Not only will Yahweh destroy the land and its inhabitants he will demolish the ritual centers. No one will escape.

The visions are followed by two oracles that conclude the book. The first of these (9:7-10) continues the theme of Israel's destruction. The second (9:11-15) is a prophecy of the restoration of the Davidic dynasty and of prosperity and security in the future. As we indicated earlier, this final oracle is generally considered a later addition to the book of Amos, perhaps after Jewish hopes of restoration were encouraged by the decree of Cyrus in 538 B.C.E. (see "Second Isaiah" in our chapter 12). This oracle, however, expands on elements in part two of the book of Amos (Chapters 3-6).

Hosea

Like Amos, the book of Hosea opens with a superscription that dates it:

> The word of the LORD that came to Hosea, son of Beeri, in the days of Uzziah, Jotham, Ahaz, and Hezekiah of Judah, and in the days of King Jeroboam son of Joash of Israel.

The kings of Judah mentioned here ruled from 783-686 B.C.E. Jeroboam, who was on the throne of Israel from 786-746, is the only king of Israel mentioned. This focus on kings of Judah in a book that scholars agree is about a northern prophet who worked in the north probably betrays the hand of a later editor from Judah, who added the superscription to the book. Other references to Judah in the book (1:7, 11; 4:15; 5:5, 10, 12, 13, 14; 6:4, 11; 8:14; 10:11; 11:12; 12:2) are mostly secondary applications of the words of Hosea redirected at the southern kingdom. Also puzzling, none of the kings of Israel who reigned after Jeroboam are mentioned, although many scholars believe that Hosea's prophetic career began during the closing years of the reigns of Jeroboam and Uzziah and continued through the troubled decades following the death of Jeroboam. He probably continued to work at least until the fall of the northern kingdom in 721. Thus, Hosea, who was active from about 750–721, was a younger contemporary of Amos.

There is little agreement among scholars about how successful attempts to reconstruct the historical background of the book have been. Few references in the book of Hosea point to specific historical situations. Those scholars who believe it is possible to reconstruct the historical background of the book observe that while the political context of Amos was the stability provided by Jeroboam's long and prosperous reign, Hosea worked in the context of considerable political instability. In the period from the death of Uzziah until the fall of Samaria, a period of twenty-three years, Israel had six kings, one of whom ruled only six months. Of these six, four were assassinated. The climate of the day was the politics of desperation. Just three years after the death of Jeroboam, Tiglath-Pileser III set off on his western campaign. In the face of the advance of the Assyrians, the rulers of those states that stood in the path of their advance had to decide whether to submit or resist. The response of Israel's last six kings had no consistency. Jeroboam's successor, Menahem (745–738), elected to pay the tribute demanded by Assyria (2 Kings 15:19–20). When Tiglath-Pileser died in 727, Hoshea (732–722) withheld tribute from the Assyrians (2 Kings 17:4). Shalmaneser V, Tiglath-Pileser's successor, came against Israel in a punitive expedition in 725. The withholding of tribute payments from Assyria was accompanied by frantic attempts to form alliances with other nations to delay the inevitable. For Israel the end came in 721 with the destruction of Samaria by the Assyrians. While there are several allusions in Hosea to the final days of Samaria (9:1–9; 10:3–10; 11:5–7), there is no explicit mention of the fall of Samaria.

The socioeconomic background of Hosea is closely related to the political situation behind the book. The payment of tribute to Assyria was an extremely heavy economic burden for tiny Israel to bear. As much as possible, the elite passed this burden to the peasants, many of whom by now had been forced to work as tenant-farmers on land owned by the wealthy landowners. Certainly nothing had happened to reverse the situation we described as the socioeconomic background for the book of Amos. If anything, the rich had gotten richer, seizing more land from the peasantry. In the face of the Assyrian advance, the wealthy had "hunkered down" and were determined to protect their own interests, at the expense of everyone else. Religion for them was meant to undergird the status quo.

STRUCTURE AND THEMES IN THE BOOK OF HOSEA

The book of Hosea divides into three parts:

1. **Chapters 1–3: Marriage and Children**   These chapters form an introduction to the entire book. This section opens with a narrative about God's command for Hosea to marry, followed by Hosea's marriage to Gomer, and the birth of their three children (1:2-11). This is narrated in the third-person. Chapter 2 is a poem that uses the imagery of faithful husband-unfaithful wife as a metaphor for the relation between Yahweh and Israel. This chapter is written in the first-person. Chapter 3, also in first-person, has Hosea buying back his unfaithful wife.

2. **Chapters 4–13: Oracles of Judgment and Hope**   These chapters reflect the structure of the first three chapters, juxtaposing oracles that condemn Israel for her cultic and political sins with those that hold forth the promise of renewal following a period of purging. As in the first three chapters, so in these oracles, the metaphor of God as a faithful husband and Israel as the unfaithful spouse is continued. Symbolism drawn from the family is also behind the image of Yahweh as the patient parent who loves and disciplines Israel, the rebellious child (11:1-7).

3. **Chapter 14: Restoration after Judgment**   This concluding chapter is a call to return and a promise of restoration following judgment.

While this three-part structure seems straightforward, many questions remain about the actual literary composition of the book of Hosea. One reconstruction of the process of its composition (Wolff 1974: xxix-xxxii) proposes a combination of three collections that were developed at about the same time. The first of these collections (chapters 1-3) was assembled around Hosea's own words in 2:2-15; 3:1-5. A disciple of Hosea's supplemented these words with later sayings attributed to the prophet and with the account of Hosea's marriage and the birth of three children to Gomer and him. The second collection (4:1-11:1), which opens and closes with formulae ("Hear the word of the LORD, O people of Israel," 4:1; "says the LORD," 11:11), consists of transcripts of Hosea's speeches and of private communications to his disciples. The third collection (11:12-14:9) is another assortment of public and private communications.

Another difficulty scholars face in studying Hosea is the poor state of the Hebrew text of the book. Many scholars have concluded that the text of Hosea is the most corrupt and poorly preserved of any book in the Hebrew Bible. The NRSV includes many textual footnotes that indicate where problems occur with the Hebrew text of Hosea. Because of these textual problems, one will discover many differences in English translations of Hosea, depending on which Hebrew textual variant the translators chose to use for their translation.

The Marriage of Hosea.   The marriage metaphor in chapters 1-3 is not an easy one to understand, given the form in which it appears. There is not one but two accounts of Hosea's marriage, one written in the third-person form and the other in first-person. According to the first account, God said to Hosea: "Go, take for yourself a wife of whoredom and have children of whoredom, for the land commits great whoredom by forsaking the LORD (1:2)." In response to God's command, an obedient Hosea married Gomer. Some have suggested that Gomer was a cult prostitute. Others say that she was unfaithful to Hosea but not a professional prostitute. Questions have also been raised about whether this was a real or fictional marriage. Andersen and Freedman, in their commentary on Hosea, offer an extensive discussion of the possible connections between the marriage metaphor, both as a literary form and conceptually, and its rootage, real or imagined, in the prophet's family life (1980: 115 – 309). Our focus here, however, will be limited to the birth of the three children and the symbolic names given to them. The first child was a son who was named Jezreel (1:4 – 5). Jehu's bloody coup d'etat at Jezreel (2 Kings 9 – 10) is remembered and condemned in this name. One should remember that Jeroboam II belonged to the dynasty of Jehu. The child is named Jezreel as a sign of imminent doom for Israel, specifically for the dynasty of Jehu. There is no reference, implicit or explicit, to Hosea's wife's unfaithfulness in this name. The second child born to Gomer was a daughter who received the name Lo-ruhamah, which means "Not pitied" (1:6). The third child's name, Lo-ammi, "Not my people" (1:8 – 9), in addition to being a statement about Israel, may also suggest that Hosea knew of his wife's unfaithfulness and was thus unsure of the boy's paternity. The implication to be drawn from the names of the last two children is that Gomer/Israel, in her/their actions was/were no longer faithful to Hosea/Yahweh.

In Hosea 3, the prophet is commanded: "Go love a woman who has a lover and is an adulteress, just as the LORD loves the people of Israel, though they turn to other gods and love raisin cakes" (3:1; see Figure 11.4). Is this woman Gomer or is she someone else? If this is another woman, the metaphor would imply that God might abandon Israel and adopt another people. If the woman in chapter 3 is Gomer, the metaphor suggests that God will restore an unfaithful Israel, just as Hosea restores an unfaithful Gomer. If Gomer is the woman of chapter 3, then she was without a family. She had been offered for sale in the slave market, where Hosea found her and bought her (3:1 – 3). Hosea's actions toward Gomer thus parallel God's actions toward Israel. "Just as the LORD loves the people of Israel, though they turn to other gods" (3:1b) is a theme for the book of Hosea. God's love for Israel means that just as Hosea disciplined Gomer after he had bought her back, God would bring punishment on Israel for a period and then redeem her. The second chapter of Hosea focuses on the relationship between God and Israel in an allegorical interpretation of the marriage.

The theme that unites the entire book of Hosea is religious infidelity. Hosea is especially concerned with cultic offenses and the problem of religious syncretism. In spite of Jehu's campaign against Baalism a century earlier, Baalism was alive and well in Hosea's day. It was not that the people had consciously chosen Baal in place of Yahweh. The problem was that because of the thoroughgoing syncretism, in which aspects of Baalism were incorporated into

Figure 11.4   A female figurine, probably a goddess, holding a "raisin cake" – from a mold found at Ta'Anach

Yahwism, the people no longer knew the difference between Yahweh and Baal. The problem was mass ignorance. The people no more "knew" Yahweh:

> There is no faithfulness or loyalty,
>> and no knowledge of God in the land.
> Swearing, lying, and murder, and stealing and adultery break out;
>> bloodshed follows bloodshed. (4:1b–2)

Hosea 4 uses the same terminology of harlotry to describe Israel's religious life that was used to describe Gomer's activity. In a fertility religion, public rituals integrated the rhythm of the agricultural cycle with the particular circumstances of a given culture. As Dearman has suggested (1992: 179–180), ritual sex acts, sacred marriage ceremonies enacted by priestly classes and royalty, and other sacramental efforts very likely were made to ensure the vitality of the agricultural cycle and thus the maintenance of community wholeness. The fertility of family, flocks, and crops was always a powerful inducement for ritual activity on the part of the cult officials and worshippers alike. Hosea's criticism of Israelite culture and public worship is aimed at syncretism and the related divinization of sex, not at the concept of fertility religion as such. Dearman maintains to portray Hosea and the fertility religion of Canaan simply as opposing forces would be wrong. The relationship between them was much more complicated than that. Given that Israel was Yahweh's chosen people in Canaan, and given that Yahweh's sovereignty included those activities that were necessary for a thriving community, the natural rhythms associated with the agricultural cycle were compatible with the affirmation of Yahweh's unique acts in the historical process. Or so Hosea assumes. The criticism of fertility religion in Hosea is a criticism of its excesses, which reflect polytheism, magic, superstition, and eroticism (180).

Hosea was the first Israelite prophet to use the analogy of a husband-wife relationship to describe the covenant relationship between Yahweh and Israel. The marriage and family metaphors in Hosea reveal, however, the patriarchal nature of Israelite society, where gender relationships were asymmetrical. On the positive side, the use of these metaphors provided powerful images for describing God's relationship with Israel. On the negative side, the metaphors, with their implied theme of the subordination of women, have all too often become an end in themselves, used by some to justify a theology of continuing male dominance on "biblical grounds." This kind of patriarchal theology interprets the divine as male and the sinful as female. Using this imagery, the book of Hosea described God's legitimate punishment as physical violence against the wife by her husband. As Gale Yee has said (1992: 195): "The problem arises when the metaphorical character of the biblical image is forgotten and a husband's physical abuse of his wife becomes as justified as is God's retribution against Israel."

The divine isolation of Israel from other lovers/gods serves as a model for Hosea's isolation of Gomer in 3:3–4. But, the behavior of Israelite husbands with respect to their wives represents God's actions in what precedes this in

Hosea 2, not the behavior of wives in relation to their husbands. The husband inflicts a series of physical and psychological punishments on his wife:

1. He takes food and clothing away from her (2:9).
2. He humiliates her by exposing her genitalia before her lovers (2:10).
3. He puts an end "to all her mirth, her festivals" (2:11).
4. He destroys her vineyards and her fig trees (2:12).
5. Having subjected her to these punishments, he will "allure her, and bring her into the wilderness, and speak tenderly to her" (2:14).

Commenting on this series of actions in Hosea 2, Gale Yee has commented that as beautiful and profound as these religious images are, the human level on which they are based is very problematic for women. Studies have shown that many wives remain in abusive relationships because periods of mistreatment are often followed by intervals of kindness and generosity. Hosea's metaphor of the marriage between Yahweh and Israel gives an entrée into the divine-human relationship. It engages the reader in a compelling story about a God who is loving, forgiving, and compassionate, in spite of Israel's sinfulness. Yee concludes, however, that this metaphor makes its theological point at the expense of real women and children who were and still are victims of sexual violence (200).

An Imaginative Portrait of Hosea and Gomer

She was always good company—a little heavy with the lipstick maybe, a little less than choosy about men and booze, a little loud, but great at a party and always a good laugh. Then the prophet Hosea came along wearing a sandwich board that read "The End Is at Hand" on one side and "Watch Out" on the other.

The first time he asked her to marry him, she thought he was kidding. The second time she knew he was serious but thought he was crazy. The third time she said yes. He wasn't exactly a swinger, but he had a kind face, and he was generous, and he wasn't all that crazier than everybody else. Besides, any fool could see that he loved her.

Give or take a little, she even loved him back for a while, and they had three children whom Hosea named with queer names like Not-pitied-for-God-will-no-longer-pity-Israel-now-that-it's-gone-to-the-dogs so that every time the roll was called at school, Hosea would be scoring a prophetic bulls-eye in absentia. But everybody could see the marriage wasn't going to last, and it didn't.

While Hosea was off hitting the sawdust trail, Gomer took to hitting as many night spots as she could squeeze into a night, and any resemblance between her next batch of children and Hosea was purely coincidental. It almost killed him, of course. Every time he raised a hand to her, he burst into tears. Every time she raised one to him, he was the one who ended up apologizing.

Continued

He tried locking her out of the house a few times when she wasn't in by five in the morning, but he always opened the door when she finally showed up and helped her get to bed if she couldn't see straight enough to get there herself. Then one day she didn't show up at all.

He swore that this time he was through with her for keeps, but of course he wasn't. When he finally found her, she was lying passed out in a highly specialized establishment located above an adult bookstore, and he had to pay the management plenty to let her out of her contract. She'd lost her front teeth and picked up some scars you had to see to believe, but Hosea had her back again and that seemed to be all that mattered.

He changed his sandwich board to read "God is love" on one side and "There's no end to it" on the other, and when he stood on the street corner belting out

How can I give you up, O Ephraim!
How can I hand you over, O Israel!
For I am God and not man.
The Holy One in your midst.
    (Hosea 11:8–9)

Nobody can say how many converts he made, but one thing that's for sure is that, including Gomer's, there was seldom a dry eye in the house.

Buechner (1979: 43–44)

Two Prophets in Judah: Micah and Isaiah

Micah

Like Amos and Hosea, the book of Micah has a superscription supplied by an anonymous editor that places the book: "In the days of Kings Jotham, Ahaz, and Hezekiah of Judah." These kings ruled from 742–686 B.C.E., but Micah is not usually regarded as having been active throughout the reigns of these three kings. Although the book of Micah is difficult to date, Micah is usually seen as a younger contemporary of Isaiah. Micah, a southern prophet from the small town of Moresheth in southwestern Judah, was probably active from around the time of the fall of Samaria (721 B.C.E.) until the Assyrian invasion under Sennacherib in 701 B.C.E. Nothing in the book suggests that Micah was active as a prophet as early as the reign of Jotham (742–732 B.C.E.).

Like Amos and Hosea, Micah is also one of the Book of the Twelve or Minor Prophets. In the Jewish and Christian canons, Micah is sixth in order in the Minor Prophets. It follows Amos and Hosea in the Septuagint. The characteristics of the period during which Micah spoke were similar to those we have seen as the background to the books of Amos and Hosea as well as those that we will see underlying the book of Isaiah.

Commonly, scholars describe Micah as a rural prophet: "Unlike the city-bred Isaiah, Micah was a country prophet who spoke for the poor farmers who were suffering at the hands of the powerful landlords" (Anderson 1986: 337). By itself, however, such a social location of Micah is not very helpful for our understanding of the book of Micah. Itumeleng Mosala, a South African scholar, has developed a way of looking at the social location of Micah by examining the class nature and commitments of those involved at the various stages of the literary composition of the book of Micah. Mosala's analysis is based on the approach suggested by Coote in his study of the redactional processes at work in Amos (1981). Mosala describes the book's composition in terms of three main stages: Micah A, Micah B, and Micah C, with an intermediary stage between A and B (1989: 126–153). Mosala assigns the material in the book of Micah to the three stages as follows:

MICAH A	MICAH A/B	MICAH B	MICAH C
1:10–16	1:8–9	1:5b–7	1:1–5a
2:1–5, 8–9		2:6–7, 10–11	2:12–13
3:8–12		3:1–7	
	4:3–4		4:1–2, 5–13
5:9–14		5:1, 4–6	5:2–3, 7–8
6:9–15		6:1–8, 16	
		7:1–7	7:8–20

In his analysis, Mosala is not so much interested in the dating of the three stages as he is in discerning "the class and ideological conditions of production and existence of the text" (153).

The A-stage oracles in Micah are specific about the class of people they address. This class is made up of those in power: rulers, the nobility, landlords, and judicial authorities. The A-stage oracles are unambiguous in specifying the crimes of the ruling class. They are economic exploiters who accumulate wealth by underhanded means (2:2, 9):

> They covet fields, and seize them;
>   houses, and take them away;
> they oppress householder and house,
>   people and their inheritance. . . .
> The women of my people you drive out
>   from their pleasant houses;
> from their young children you take away my glory forever.

The Micah-A oracles are not sympathetic with the interests of the class under attack. On the contrary, they prophesy the destruction of this class and its political and ideological structures.

The B-stage material in Micah is addressed to a general audience. The basic message of these oracles is: "Perform justice or else." The materials in this stage are characterized by a preference for abstract rather than concrete description. Their identity derives from what they do not say: they are silent on the struggles of the exploited peasants. In these B-stage texts, Mosala says that both oppression and justice have been "thingified," appearing as vaguely good and evil. The original message of Micah, directed at the ruling classes of Judah during the eighth century B.C.E., has now been stolen from its concrete situation, where it concerned the condition of the poor and exploited, and is now applied to the Judean ruling class in their relationships to their foreign oppressors. The more basic contradiction between the exploited and the exploiters in Judah has now been replaced by the secondary contradiction between Babylon and Judah or other nations and Israel (143).

For Mosala, the C-stage texts provide the dominant ideology of Micah. The God of the C-stage material is the God of restoration (2:12-13). This God reconstructs the citadel of power of the former ruling classes of Judah and transforms it into an international meeting place (4:1-2). At this stage, generalities have replaced specifics in describing evil. The theology of this stage is more suited to the interests of a formerly powerful class than to a previously oppressed class. Thus, Mosala sees the redactional history of Micah as one in which the original message of Micah was transformed over the years to serve the interests of the ruling class.

STRUCTURE AND THEMES IN THE BOOK OF MICAH

The book of Micah in its present form has two parts unequal in length. Part one is the longer part, consisting of chapters 1-5. Part two is shorter, consisting of chapters 6-7. Part one opens with oracles of judgment (1-3) and concludes with oracles of salvation (4-5). Part two also begins with oracles of judgment (6:1-7:7) and ends with oracles of promise (7:8-20). This gives the book an A-B-A-B pattern, with alternating oracles of judgment and salvation. After the judgment oracles in chapters 1-3, some of the materials in the book seem to have been grouped together on a catchword principle. This principle does not make for smooth transitions between one unit and the next. The powerful oracle of judgement in 3:9-12 (= Mosala's Micah A), concludes with the phrase "the mountain of the house" (4:12). This phrase acted as a catchword for linking that oracle with 4:1-2 (= Mosala'a Micah C), which begins with the phrase "the mountain of the LORD's house." Micah 4:1-4, the familiar "swords into plowshares" oracle, is essentially the same as Isaiah 2:2-4. There is no satisfactory explanation for this duplication. Some proposals suggest that either the oracle belonged to Isaiah and was copied into Micah, or that the reverse is the case, or that the oracle originally belonged to neither Isaiah nor Micah, but was drawn by the redactors of Isaiah and Micah from another source.

Near the beginning of the second part of Micah is perhaps the best known verse from the book (6:8):

> He has told you, O mortal, what is good;
>   and what does the LORD require of you
> but to do justice, and to love kindness,
>   and to walk humbly with your God?

This verse has been called "the celebrated epitome of prophetic religion" (Gottwald 1985: 376). It comes at the end of a passage (6:1-8) that uses the language of a trial in a court of law, in a form that has been called a "covenant lawsuit" or *rîb*, from the Hebrew verb that means "to plead a case" (6:1). This form has four parts, corresponding to the proceedings in a court of law:

1. **Call to order (6:1–2)** God, acting (through the prophet) as both presiding judge and prosecuting attorney, calls the mountains and the foundations of the earth to serve as witnesses in the case to be brought against Israel.

2. **The plaintiff states his complaint (6:3–5)** The case is not based on the violation of specific laws by Israel, but on Israel's violation of the covenant relationship with Yahweh. This is especially serious given all that God had done for Israel, beginning with the Exodus from Egypt:

> For I brought you up from the land of Egypt,
>   and redeemed you from the house of slavery;
> and I sent before you Moses, Aaron, and Miriam. (6:4)

3. **The defendant's response (6:6–7)** Israel's answer to the indictment is basically an admission of guilt. Israel has attempted to replace the covenant requirements of social justice and loyalty to Yahweh with an elaborate sacrificial program.

4. **The indictment (6:8)** The climax is a statement about what Yahweh requires from the covenant people, which combines in one sentence "Amos' demand for justice, Hosea's appeal for the faithfulness that binds people in covenant with God and with one another, and Isaiah's plea for the quiet faith of the 'humble walk' with God" (Anderson 340).

Isaiah

Before we begin to talk about Isaiah as the eighth-century prophet whose name the book bears, we need to look at the book of Isaiah itself. With sixty-six chapters, it is the second longest book in the Bible (Psalms is the longest). However, not all of the book that bears Isaiah's name is associated with Isaiah of Jerusalem, the eighth-century prophet, or even with those who were his disciples and interpreters to a later audience. Most scholars agree that chapters 40–66 have nothing to do with Isaiah of Jerusalem. The name Isaiah, for example, never appears in 40–66. The prophetic author of these chapters remains anonymous. These chapters do, however, mention Cyrus of Persia (44:28; 45:21), which presupposes a historical situation two centuries after Isaiah of Jerusalem (Cyrus was king from 550–530 B.C.E.). There are references in 44:28 and 52:9 to Jerusalem's being in ruins. Life in Babylon is talked about in 46:1–24; 47:1 ff.; and 48:20. Assyria has no role at all in these later chapters of Isaiah. Accordingly, Isaiah of Jerusalem is sometimes called "First Isaiah" and the anonymous author of chapters 40–66 is labeled "Deutero" or "Second Isaiah." Some scholars also talk of the author of chapters 56–66 as "Trito" or "Third Isaiah."

The idea that the book of Isaiah was not a unity was first raised in the twelfth century by Abraham ibn Ezra, and possibly even earlier by Moses ibn Gikatilla. The idea was again given prominence in the late-eighteenth century by German scholars. That an anonymous sixth-century author wrote chapters 40–55, and another author or authors, also anonymous, wrote chapters 56–66, is now accepted by most scholars. The speeches of these sixth-century prophets had been added to the material associated with Isaiah of Jerusalem by the third or second century B.C.E., when the Septuagint was translated, because it included all sixty-six chapters in the book of Isaiah. The historical, as opposed to the literary relationship between "First," "Second," and "Third" Isaiah is a puzzle. No satisfactory explanation has been offered for why chapters 40–55 and 56–66 were appended to the material attributed to Isaiah of Jerusalem. One possibility is that these later chapters were the work of followers of Isaiah, who saw them as complementing the work of the eighth-century Isaiah. The book of Isaiah, in striking fashion, presents us with an example of the kind of relationship between a named prophet and a book that we see in all of the classical eighth-century prophets. Isaiah of Jerusalem is presented as a known historical figure at the beginning; at the end of the book, we have an anonymous and only approximately datable collection of materials.

While the historical relationship between the different parts of the book of Isaiah is a puzzle, there is, in spite of this, a remarkable literary and theological continuity between them. Passages from the later chapters quote from earlier ones (for example, 65:24 quotes 11:6–9). Major themes such as the action of God in history appear both early and late in the book (see 7:17; 29:1–4; and 45:1 ff.). The concept of an individual savior figure is present in both "First" and "Second Isaiah" (9:2–7; 11:1–5; 32:1; 42:1–4; 52:13–53:12). The central role of Jerusalem/Zion is pervasive throughout the book. The distinctive title of God as "the Holy One of Israel" appears thirty-one times in the Hebrew Bible. Of these occurrences, twenty-four appear in Isaiah, with eleven in "First Isaiah," ten in "Second Isaiah," and three in "Third Isaiah." From the very start Isa 40 shows continuity with the earlier chapters of the book. The voice heard in 40:1 echoes Isaiah's vision in chapter 6. In both cases the prophet interrupts to ask "What shall I cry?" and is given his commission. The "Suffering Servant" songs (see p. 413) pick up on the theme of the diseased body of Israel from 1:5–6. Whatever the case for separate authorship and date of the different parts of the book of Isaiah, "Second" and "Third Isaiah" are integral parts of Isaianic tradition.

As we have seen in the other eighth-century prophets, the book of Isaiah, in the form in which we have it, is the product of later redactors. These redactors passed on the work of the prophet Isaiah, his message to eighth-century Jerusalem and Judah, and the implications of that message for those living up to and in the Babylonian exile that followed the destruction of Jerusalem in 587 B.C.E. The book of Isaiah, like the books of the other eighth-century prophets, has a superscription that positions the prophet relative to reigning monarchs: "The vision of Isaiah son of Amoz, which he saw concerning Judah and Jerusalem in the days of Uzziah, Jotham, Ahaz, and Hezekiah, kings of Judah" (1:1). Nothing is known about the early life of Isaiah, but his "call vision" in 6:1–13 begins with the phrase "In the year that king Uzziah died." Uzziah died in 742 B.C.E. and Hezekiah ruled from 715–686 B.C.E. Isaiah thus began his ministry around 742 and worked until around 700. This active career of about forty years is matched only by Jeremiah.

As the superscription suggests, Isaiah's message was directed primarily at Judah and Jerusalem. In addition to the superscription, suggestions that Isaiah had access to the royal court and affairs in the capital appear in two other narrative sections, 6:1–8:23 and 36:1–39:8. Isaiah's access to the king has led some to suggest that he was from a well-to-do Jerusalem family. The fact that his commissioning as a prophet came in the Jerusalem temple (6:1–13) has led some to suggest that he was born into a priestly family. There is, however, no "hard" evidence for his often-assumed connections with court and temple. Isaiah was married to a woman called a "prophetess" (8:3) and they had children, at least two of whom are mentioned in the book. Like Hosea, Isaiah and his wife gave their children symbolic names. One son was named "Shear-jashub" (7:3), which means "A remnant shall return." His birth was a "sign" in the context of the Syro-Ephraimite War (Ephraim = Israel) that, even assuming the worst possible outcome, God's promise to David (2 Sam 7:8–16) would not be broken, but would be continued with a remnant of the people. The second son has a long and difficult name, "Maher-shalal-hash-baz (8:1, 3). This child was also born during the Syro-Ephraimite crisis, and his name is also meant to be a sign to the people. The name means "The spoil speeds, the prey hastens."

Throughout the second half of the eighth century B.C.E., the period of Isaiah's activity, Assyria dominated the ancient Near East. Isaiah's work, as well as sections of the book of Isaiah, can be set against the backdrop of four crises that were the product of Assyrian imperialist policies:

1. The Syro-Ephraimite War (734–733 B.C.E.). The historical background of this war is found in 2 Kings 16:1–20. This was the first major crisis during the reign of Ahaz. This crisis underlies Isaiah 2–9.

2. The Fall of Samaria (721 B.C.E.) This event also provides the historical context for Isaiah 2–9.

3. The Revolt against Assyria (713–711 B.C.E.) This revolt was led by Ashdod, and was joined by Edom and Moab. Hezekiah at first joined the revolt, but dropped out early. This revolt is the historical context for Isaiah 18–20.

4. The Siege of Jerusalem (701 B.C.E.). Following open rebellion on the part of Hezekiah, Sennacherib, king of Assyria, came into Judah on a punitive expedition, during which he laid siege to Jerusalem. The siege of Jerusalem provides the backdrop for Isaiah 28–32.

In our analysis of Isaiah we will focus on those materials in Isaiah that are associated with the first and last of these crises, the Syro-Ephraimite War and the Siege of Jerusalem. Isaiah holds up these two moments in history as especially illustrative of God's work with Judah and Jerusalem.

STRUCTURE AND THEMES IN THE BOOK OF ISAIAH

In addition to material that presupposes different historical crises, other kinds of material also appear in Isaiah 1–39. Chapters 24–27, which seem to be unrelated to their context, are sometimes called "The Little Apocalypse" or "The Isaiah

Apocalypse" (for a discussion of apocalyptic literature, see our Chapter 16). These chapters in Isaiah probably reflect a later stage in the Isaiah tradition. Chapters 34-35 also are apocalyptic in nature and generally are assigned to a later period. With some small differences, the last four chapters, 36-39, are essentially duplicated from 2 Kings 18:13-20:21. This is material that reports events related to the attack of Sennacherib in 701 B.C.E. In formal terms, chapters 36-37 resemble chapters 7-8. Both focus on a meeting between Isaiah and the king (Ahaz in 7-8 and Hezekiah in 36-37).

As we have observed, only chapters 1-39 can be associated historically with Isaiah of Jerusalem, and even they include later materials. While the dating of prophetic oracles is always problematic, one way of understanding the ordering of material in Isaiah 1-39 is the following:

- **Chapters 1–12** This section includes Isaiah's memoirs and oracles against Judah, probably from his early years. The materials in this section group around the centrally positioned segment in 6:1-8:18, which has been called "Isaiah's Memoirs," "The Book of Signs," or "The Book of Immanuel." As we have suggested, the historical context for these chapters is the Syro-Ephraimite crisis of 735 B.C.E. Chapters 11-12, which conclude this section, are oracles of salvation.

- **Chapters 13–23** This section includes oracles against foreign and domestic enemies, probably from Isaiah's middle years. Oracles from the eighth century against Assyria (14:24-27), Philistia (14:28-31), Syro-Ephraim (17:1-14), Egypt (18-19), and Judah (22) are included. These oracles have an eighth-century historical setting, but have been augmented with oracles concerning Babylon (13:1-16; 14:3-23; 21), Persia (13:17-22), Moab (15-16), and Tyre (23) that are more appropriate in the sixth century.

- **Chapters 24–27** The "Isaiah Apocalypse." These chapters offer a picture of Yahweh's cosmic judgment, followed by complete restoration. As indicated above, these chapters are probably not from the eighth-century Isaiah.

- **Chapters 28–33** This section includes oracles generally concerned with Judah's dealings with Egypt in the context of the advance of Sennacherib (705-701 B.C.E.). These oracles are from Isaiah's later ministry. This section ends with chapter 33, which is a prophetic liturgy that looks ahead to God's victory over the Assyrians and a restored Jerusalem.

- **Chapters 34–35** These chapters describe a future world judgment in apocalyptic fashion. As Christopher Seitz suggests, these two chapters amplify and extend the message of the preceding chapters (32-33) regarding the future judgment and the ensuing reign of peace and forgiveness. At the same time, they remind the reader of chapters 36-39 that the deliverance of Jerusalem in 701 B.C.E. is temporary and the cleansing judgment of God will continue past Hezekiah's time. "In so doing, they ease the transition (temporal and literary) between the former and the latter things—or between the judgments of the Assyrian period and of the Babylonian period and the dawn of a new day in God's dealings with Israel, such as this takes form in Isaiah 40-66" (Seitz 1992: 485).

■ **Chapters 36–39** These chapters are a historical appendix that essentially is replicated from 2 Kings 18–20.

In the face of the relentless advance of the Assyrians westward in their annual campaigns, the smaller city-states and kingdoms in their path joined together to form alliances in a doomed attempt to stop the Assyrian onslaught. Pekah, who was king of Israel from 744–732, formed an alliance with Rezin of the kingdom of Aram. These two kings then tried to force Judah, under king Ahaz, to join their alliance. Pekah and Rezin threatened to invade Judah to force Ahaz to join their alliance or, if he refused, to oust him in favor of someone who would cooperate with them. In this context Isaiah confronted Ahaz in chapters 7–8. These two chapters follow immediately after Isaiah's vision in chapter 6. Chapter 6, sometimes referred to as Isaiah's "call vision," was probably not Isaiah's inaugural call, but a commission for a specific task. In the first five chapters of the book, Isaiah preached a message of warning before the death of Uzziah. In 6:1–13 Isaiah is given a new commission by the heavenly council to preach repentance:

> Until cities lie waste
>   without inhabitant,
> and houses without people,
>   and the land is utterly desolate;
> until the LORD sends everyone fall away,
>   and vast is the emptiness in the midst of the land. (6:11b–12)

Following this commission in chapter 6, in chapter 7 Isaiah counsels Ahaz to "be quiet, do not fear, and do not let your heart be faint because of the two smoldering stumps of firebrands" (7:4b). Isaiah's oracle advises Ahaz that if he will stand fast and trust in Yahweh, Pekah and Rezin's threat will pass. In a play on words in Hebrew, Ahaz must "stand firm in faith" (*te'amînu*) or he and Judah will "not stand at all" (*te'amenu*) (7:9b). Together with the word of God, Ahaz is confronted with three children, who represent visible confirmation that God would save him if he would stand fast. The first child, Isaiah's son Shear-jashub ("A remnant shall return") had already been born (7:3). Isaiah announces that Yahweh will give Ahaz a second sign in the birth of another child in the very near future (7:14–16):

> Therefore the LORD himself will give you a sign: Look, the young woman is with child and shall bear a son, and you shall name him Immanuel. He shall eat curds and honey by the time he knows how to refuse the evil and choose the good. For before the child knows how to refuse the evil and choose the good, the land before whose two kings you are in dread will be deserted.

The sign of Immanuel, which means "God with us," is perhaps more familiar in its translation in the KJV: "Behold, a virgin shall conceive, and bear a son, and shall call his name Immanuel." Christian tradition has seen this verse as a prediction of the virgin birth of Jesus. It should be noted, however, that the NRSV accurately translates the Hebrew in v. 14 that indicates that the mother *is* pregnant and that the child *will be born* in the very near future. Even before the child reaches the age of discretion, the Syro-Israelite alliance will have disappeared. It is impossible to tell who the mother-to-be was. She may have been Ahaz's wife or Isaiah's wife, whom Isaiah would know was pregnant. At any rate, the sign is the birth of the child and the timing of the birth, not the identity of the mother or unusual circumstances of the birth. There is no reason to translate the Hebrew noun *'almah* here as "virgin." The same noun appears elsewhere in the Hebrew Bible (Gen 24:43; Ex 2:8; Ps 68:25, Prov 30:19, and so forth) without any specific reference to a young woman's sexual status. The usual Hebrew term for virgin is *bethulah*, which is used throughout the Hebrew Bible (Gen 24:16; Ex 22:16; Lev 21:3, 14; Deut 22:19; and so forth). In this passage the Septuagint translators rendered the Hebrew *'almah* with the Greek *parthenos*, "virgin," even though elsewhere they translated it as "young woman." While this is not the place to enter into a discussion of the doctrine of the virgin birth of Jesus, it can be said that understanding this passage as a prophecy of the virgin birth of Jesus is a secondary application of Isaiah's words. The primary intent of his words was directed at Ahaz and the immediate crisis. The message was that better times were coming soon, no matter how desperate the present situation may have looked to a faithless Ahaz.

The third sign-child is Maher-shalal-hash-baz, "The spoil speeds, the prey hastens":

> And I went to the prophetess, and she conceived and bore a son. Then the LORD said to me, "Name him Maher-shalal-hash-baz; for before the child knows how to call 'My father' or 'My mother,' the wealth of Damascus and the spoil of Samaria will be carried away by the king of Assyria." (8:3–4)

Because of Ahaz' unbelief, the positive child-signs turn negative. The "spoil speeds," first against the Syro-Ephraimite alliance (8:4), but eventually against Judah itself (8:6–7). Positive signs are turned into judgments directed at the lack of faith of the king and pointing to a new day.

In spite of the Isaiah's words and the child-signs, Ahaz did not respond in faith, but instead followed a strategy of *Realpolitik*. Rather than joining the Syro-Ephraimite coalition, he chose to side with Assyria. Ahaz lived to see Assyria conquer the northern kingdom and make Judah into a vassal state. After his death in 715 B.C.E., Hezekiah became king, an event that may have been the occasion for the messianic poem in 9:2–7, which describes a just and faithful king. Hezekiah at first initiated a gradual reversal of the pro-Assyrian policy of his father. He instituted cultic reforms that removed or downplayed the Assyrian cultic objects that his father had brought into the temple. When Sargon II of Assyria died in 705 B.C.E. Hezekiah saw an opportunity to throw off the Assyrian yoke, and engineered a revolt against Assyria. This revolt brought on the invasion of Sennacherib and the crisis of 705–701 B.C.E. It also brought Isaiah "out of retirement," because he had withdrawn from public life shortly after the accession of Hezekiah.

Many of the oracles of chapters 28–32 are associated with the Sennacherib crisis. The Assyrian annals of Sennacherib confirm Hezekiah's revolt (Matthews and Benjamin: 139):

As for Hezekiah of Judah, he did not submit to my yoke, and I laid siege to forty-six of his strong cities, walled forts, and to the countless small villages in their vicinity, and conquered them using earth ramps and battering rams. These siege engines were aided by the use of foot soldiers who undermined the walls. I drove out of these places 200,150 people — young and old, male and female, horses, mules, donkeys, camels, large and small cattle beyond counting and considered them as booty. I made Hezekiah a prisoner in Jerusalem, like a bird in a cage. I erected siege works to prevent anyone escaping through the city gates. The towns in his territory which I captured I gave to Mitinti, King of Ashdod, Padi, King of Ekron, and Sillibel, King of Gaza. Thus I reduced his territory in this campaign, and I also increased Hezekiah's annual tribute payments.

Sennacherib, however, did not take Jerusalem. Why Assyrian forces withdrew and broke off the siege is unclear. Whatever the reason, the account in Isaiah and 2 Kings sees the ultimate cause as divine intervention.

As Gottwald has observed, two strands of thought in the book of Isaiah occur in relation to Hezekiah's actions and Sennacherib's response (1985: 380–381). One strand shows Isaiah relentlessly pronouncing doom throughout Hezekiah's revolt and the decimation of Judah until only Jerusalem was left and Hezekiah was forced to surrender. This strand is represented in 22:1–4; 29:1–4; 30:1–5; 31:1–3. Another strand pictures Isaiah announcing a reprieve and imminent deliverance of Jerusalem, coupled with the destruction of Assyria. This strand shows up in the historical narratives in 36–39 and in 29:5–8; 31:5, 8–9. One explanation for these two strands puts forth that Isaiah changed his mind as the siege of Jerusalem wore on, turning from a message of doom to one of salvation. Because the book of Isaiah is a compilation and redaction of material over a long tradition history, it is also possible to attribute the second strand to postdeliverance Isaiah traditionists who were impressed by the historical fact that Jerusalem escaped destruction at the hands of the Assyrians in 701 B.C.E. and who later inserted this "miracle" into the prophecies of Isaiah. In light of how the Assyrians treated the rest of Judah and neighboring countries, Sennacherib's failure to take Jerusalem was a matter of no small theological significance.

Like other eighth-century prophets, Isaiah speaks out against oppression and the lack of social justice (3:15). There are similar denunciations of idolatry and unfaithfulness to Yahweh (1:4). Like the others, Isaiah condemns worship that tries to cover for unethical behavior (1:13). He also shares with Hosea Yahweh's desire for Israel to "come home." This desire is powerfully portrayed in allegorical form in Isaiah's "Song of the Vineyard" in 5:1–7. This unique poem borrows the form of a song of celebration at the time of the grape harvest:

My beloved had a vineyard
    on a very fertile hill.
He dug it and cleared it of stones,
    and planted it with choice vines;
he built a watchtower in the midst of it,
    and hewed out a wine vat in it;
he expected it to yield grapes,
    why did it yield wild grapes. (5:1–4)

So far, this allegory is rather transparent, and one can easily understand who the beloved represents, what the vineyard is, and so forth, which is all made explicit in 5:7. In 5:5 Isaiah then turned from talking about what Yahweh had done for Israel and the disappointing results to the demand for justice and what Yahweh will do:

And now I will tell you
    what I will do to my vineyard.
I will remove its hedge,
    and it shall be devoured;
I will break down its wall,
    and it shall be trampled down.
I will make it a waste;
    it shall not be pruned or hoed,
    and it shall be overgrown with
        briers and thorns;
I will also command the clouds
    that they rain no rain upon it.
For the vineyard of the LORD of hosts
    is the house of Israel,
and the people of Judah
    are his pleasant planting;
he expected justice [mishpat],
    but saw bloodshed [mishpach];
righteousness [tsedeqah],
    but heard a cry [tse'aqah]. (5:5–8)

This poem pulls together many of the themes we have seen in the eighth-century prophets:

1. A covenant God of love who has been active for good in the history of Israel;

2. one God who is *both* lord of history *and* lord of nature; and

3. a God who is both a God of love and a God of justice.

Note the double play on words in the last four lines of the poem, which contrast what God expected the special covenant relationship with Israel to produce (justice and righteousness) with what were the actual results (bloodshed and cries).

Beyond themes that Isaiah shares with the other eighth-century prophets, two are uniquely his own. These are the royal/Davidic tradition and the Jerusalem/Zion tradition. These two traditions reinforce one another and point to the failings of God's people. Isaiah makes use of these traditions throughout his oracles, at the expense of ideas related to the Mosaic covenant. The theme of the centrality and permanence of Mt. Zion/Jerusalem is expanded in Isaiah to present Jerusalem/Zion as a potential model and "cornucopia" for other nations (2:2-5). Linked with this vision of Jerusalem is the vision of an ideal ruler, who will "come out from the stump of Jesse," that is, the line of David (11:1-5), whose rule would result in a utopian society (11:6-9). In Isaiah these two themes are ironically set against the backdrop of the social pathology and historical turmoil of the late eighth century.

In the history of traditions, these themes in Isaiah were picked up and used in different contexts. The Jewish community, while it languished in exile and when it set about rebuilding a Jewish society after the Exile, saw both a hope and an ideal for which to strive in these themes in Isaiah. The Christian community has seen these traditions in Isaiah as references to Jesus as the messiah from the line of David and the hope that he offers for the transformation of society.

THE EIGHTH-CENTURY PROPHETS: A SUMMARY

Having remained at this point in our itinerary for all too brief a time, what can be said to summarize what we have seen in the eighth-century prophets? We, at this point, will rely on the thoughts of Abraham Heschel, whose two-volume work on the prophets is a classic, both in terms of content and style. In a chapter on justice in the prophets, he puts forth that for a long time the importance of the prophets was seen to lie in the fact that they transformed the religion of ritual to a religion of morality. Their contribution to humanity's spiritual growth was what was called "ethical monotheism." The religion introduced by the prophets was a sort of proto-protestantism directed against all sorts of paganism and ritualism, with the main emphasis placed on faith. The popular image of the prophets was that of preachers of morals and spiritual religion as opposed to ceremonialism and ritual. According to Heschel, this view has now been questioned, and "ethical monotheism" must no longer be regarded as the original contribution of the classical prophets, because "ethical monotheism" was known in Israel long before the time of Amos. Nor is the concern with morality the chief characteristic of prophetic thought. Rather, the chief characteristic of prophetic thought is God's involvement in history. Given this focus on history, the prophets were moved by a sense of responsibility for society, by a sensitivity to what the moment demanded.

Because, from Heschel's perspective, the prophets do not speak primarily in the name of the moral law, it is inaccurate to describe them as proclaimers of justice, or *mishpat*. It is more accurate to see them as proclaimers of:

God's pathos, speaking not for the idea of justice, but for the God of justice, for God's concern for justice. Divine concern remembered in sympathy is the stuff of which prophecy is made. To the biblical mind the implication of goodness is mercy. Pathos, concern for the world, is the very ethos of God. The ethical sensitivity of God—not the ethical in and for itself—is reflected in the prophets' declarations. Prophetic morality rests upon both a divine command and a divine concern. Its ultimate appeal is not to the reasonableness of the moral law, but to the fact that God has demanded it and its fulfillment is a realization of His concern. (Heschel 1962: 218–219).

STUDY QUESTIONS

AMOS

1. What are the different levels in the book of Amos and how do these different levels illustrate the fact that prophetic books were the texts of a continuing religious community?
2. What is the basic literary unit in the book of Amos? What are some of the characteristics of this form and what are its origins?
3. What eighth-century social situation is addressed by Amos? How did such a situation develop in Israel?
4. With respect to literary structure, Amos can be divided into three main parts. What are these parts and how are they related to one another?
5. What can be said about Amos' prophetic vocation and his possible relation to prophetic guilds on the basis of the biographical section in Amos 7:10–17?

HOSEA

1. Briefly describe the historical context of the book of Hosea. How does it differ from that of the earliest level of the book of Amos? How is it related to the international political scene?
2. Compare and contrast the primary themes in Hosea with those in Amos.
3. Hosea was the first Israelite prophet to use the analogy of a husband-wife relationship to describe the covenant relationship between Yahweh and Israel. How is this analogy used in the first three chapters of Hosea? How are gender relationships in ancient Israel illustrated in the use of this analogy?

MICAH

1. How are class interests reflected in the different stages of the book of Micah?
2. What are the major characteristics and elements in Micah's prophecy? What is his central message?

ISAIAH

1. Why do many scholars believe that the book of Isaiah is not a unity, but represents the work of several prophets from different historical periods? What are the main divisions proposed and to what periods do they belong?
2. What do the materials in Isa 6:1-8:18 tell us about Isaiah and his use of symbolism to convey his message?
3. Explain the images in Isaiah's vision in 6:1-13. Do you think this is Isaiah's initial "call vision"? If not, where would you place it in his career?
4. What was the Syro-Ephraimite crisis and what did Isaiah advise King Ahaz to do in response to it? Was Isaiah's advice "good" advice? Why or why not? Did Ahaz follow Isaiah's counsel?
5. Two strands of thought appear in the book of Isaiah in relation to Sennacherib's invasion of Judah at the end of the eighth century B.C.E. and Hezekiah's response. What are they? What is the theological significance of the fact that Sennacherib could not or did not take Jerusalem?
6. How are the dominant themes of the royal/Davidic tradition and the Jerusalem/Zion tradition related to one another in Isaiah? How were these themes in Isaiah used by later communities?

BIBLIOGRAPHY

Andersen, Francis I., and Freedman, David Noel. 1980. *Hosea.* Anchor Bible 24. New York: Doubleday.

Anderson, Bernhard W. 1986. *Understanding the Old Testament,* 4th ed., Englewood Cliffs, NJ: Prentice-Hall.

Buechner, Frederick. 1979. *Peculiar Treasures: A Biblical Who's Who.* San Francisco: Harper & Row.

Coote, Robert B. 1981. *Amos Among the Prophets: Composition and Theology.* Philadelphia: Fortress.

Dearman, J. Andrew. 1992. *Religion and Culture in Ancient Israel.* Peabody, MA: Hendrickson.

Frick, Frank S. 1977. *The City in Ancient Israel.* SBL Dissertation Series, 36. Missoula, MT: Scholars.

Gottwald, Norman K. 1985. *The Hebrew Bible: A Socio-Literary Introduction.* Philadelphia: Fortress.

Heschel, Abraham J. 1962. *The Prophets: An Introduction.* Vol. 1. New York: Harper & Row.

Huffmon, Herbert B. 1983. "The Social Role of Amos' Message." *The Quest for the Kingdom of God: Studies in Honor of George E. Mendenhall.* H. B. Huffmon, F. A. Spina, and A. R. W. Green, eds. Winona Lake, IN: Eisenbraun's, 109-116.

King, Phillip J. 1988. *Amos, Hosea, Micah—An Archaeological Commentary.* Philadelphia: Fortress.

Lang, Bernhard. 1983. *Monotheism and the Prophetic Minority: An Essay in Biblical History and Sociology.* The Social World of Biblical Antiquity Series, 1. Sheffield, England: Almond.

Limburg, J. 1987. "Sevenfold Structures in the Book of Amos." *Journal of Biblical Literature, 106,* 217–222.

Matthews, Victor H., and Benjamin, Don C. 1991. *Old Testament Parallels: Laws and Stories from the Ancient Near East.* New York: Paulist.

Mosala, Itumeleng J. 1989. *Biblical Hermeneutics and Black Theology in South Africa.* Grand Rapids: Eerdmans.

Seitz, Christopher R. 1992. "Isaiah, Book of (First Isaiah)." *The Anchor Bible Dictionary, III,* 472–488. New York: Doubleday.

Waard, J. de. 1977. "The Chiastic Structure of Amos V, 1–17," *Vetus Testamentum 27,* 170–77.

Wolff, Hans Walter. 1974. *Hosea,* Hermeneia. Philadelphia: Fortress.

Yee, Gale A. 1992. "Hosea." *The Women's Bible Commentary,* Carol A. Newsom and Sharon H. Ringe, eds. Louisville: Westminster/John Knox, 195–202.

Chapter 12

PROPHETS, THE FALL OF JUDAH, AND SHIFTING POWERS ON THE INTERNATIONAL HORIZON

Suggested Bible Reading
Jeremiah 1-52; Isaiah 40-55

THE DESTRUCTION OF JERUSALEM AND THE DEVASTATION OF JUDAH— PROPHETIC EXPLANATIONS OF DISASTER AND VISIONS OF RECONSTRUCTION

There are points in every journey when something forces one to pause and reflect upon what one has seen. The destruction of Jerusalem by Nebuchadrezzar's armies is a dramatic pivotal event in the history of ancient Israel and one of those points. A state that had existed for over four hundred years, ruled by David and his descendants, came to an end. Given what had happened to their northern neighbors in Israel, the Judahites must have wondered if the collapse of their state would also mean their historical oblivion. Would their identity as a people fade with the loss of their state? Or, could they survive this disaster and anticipate a future when Jerusalem would be restored as the capital of an autonomous, Jewish nation?

The prophets whom we have already seen provided a large part of the answer to these questions. When viewed through the perspective of hindsight, the prophets' oracles of judgment provided a means of understanding why the disaster had happened. From the viewpoint of the prophets, the fall of Jerusalem was not some kind of absurd, tragic historical accident. Neither did it mean that Yahweh had been defeated by the superior gods of the Babylonians. Rather, as the prophets had said, it had come as the predictable response of a faithful covenant God. The faithfulness of Yahweh, who had not abandoned the people of Israel had not been met with corresponding loyalty from the covenant people. Therefore, so the prophets maintained, Yahweh had used the Babylonians, as he had used the Assyrians before them, as instruments for disciplining the people for their infidelity, hoping to bring about a renewal of the covenant relationship. Thus, the prophets had provided an explanation in advance for the calamity.

Included with the prophetic explanation for the disaster was the prescription for renewal. Survival as a people and renewal in the future would take place only when and if the people recaptured and recommitted themselves to the standards for a just society that were demanded by their covenant relationship with Yahweh. The prophets' interpretation was that God was present, not absent, in the tragic events of Israel's history, so what was demanded was the people's repentance for their infidelity and an openness to learn from the lessons of their history with Yahweh.

The assassination of the Assyrian king Sennacherib, who had presided over the siege of Jerusalem at the end of the eighth century, was an omen foreshadowing troublesome times ahead for the Assyrian empire. The Assyrians had not been able to consolidate the extensive territories they had brought under their control. As a result, revolts were a persistent threat. In the mid-seventh century, Egypt came under Assyrian rule, making Assyria the largest empire in the history of the world to that time. This expansion came when Assyria was already "over the hill" and was sliding toward its end (see Figure 12.1).

The Assyrian domination of Egypt was short-lived. The Pharaoh Psammetichus I (663–609 B.C.E.) expelled the Assyrian forces of occupation and began a period of Egyptian renewal. Assyria also experienced difficulties on the eastern end of its empire. Ashur fell to the onslaughts of the Medes and the Babylonians in 614 B.C.E. In 612 B.C.E., Nineveh fell. After this, the Assyrians, even with the support of the Egyptians, who feared the Babylonians even more than their former masters, could offer little resistance to the growing power of the Babylonians. Retreating westward to Haran, what was left of the Assyrian army was defeated there in 609 B.C.E., a date that formally marks the end of the Assyrian empire.

Having disposed of the Assyrian threat, the Babylonians turned their attention elsewhere. In 605 B.C.E., under the leadership of Nebuchadrezzar, they defeated the Egyptians at the Battle of Carchemish. A year later they moved into Syria and Palestine. In 604 B.C.E., Nebuchadrezzar conquered the Philistine city of Ashkelon. Jeremiah, like his prophetic predecessors, saw God at work in this move, and he declared the impending downfall of Judah in an oracle that is dated to "the fourth year of King Jehoiakim son of Josiah of Judah (that was the

Figure 12.1   Rival empires in the Ancient Near East in the time of Jeremiah

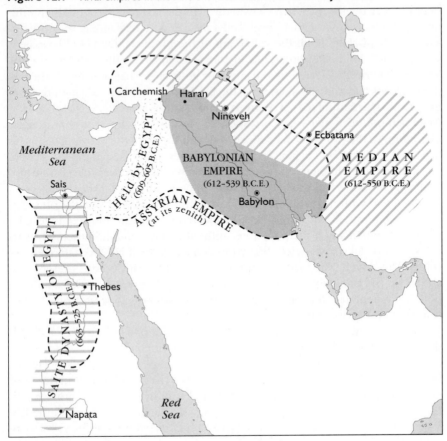

first year of King Nebuchadrezzar of Babylon)," after Nebuchadrezzar's victory over Neco of Egypt (Jer 25 : 1 - 14). The king of Judah, Jehoiakim, who had been put on the throne by Neco in 609 B.C.E., first transferred his allegiance to the Babylonians and then shortly after that, in 597 B.C.E., he rebelled against them. Nebuchadrezzar responded to Jehoiakim's defiance in a rather lenient way. After the surrender of Jerusalem, Jehoiakim's successor, Jehoiachin, was deported to Babylon with a group of his officials (2 Kings 24 : 8 - 17). The Babylonian Chronicles tell of this event:

> Year 7 [598 - 597 B.C.E.], Month Kislimu [= Kislev = December 18, 598 - January 15, 597 B.C.E.]: The king of Akkad [a title used by Nebuchadrezzar to tie his rule back into antiquity] moved his army into Hatti land, laid siege to the city of Judah [= Jerusalem] and the king took the city on the second day of the month of Addaru [= Adar = March 15 or 16, 597 B.C.E.]. He appointed a new king to his liking and carried away great amounts of booty from the city to Babylon. (Matthews and Benjamin (1991: 143)

The "new king to his liking" mentioned in this Babylonian document was Zedekiah, an uncle of Jehoiachin, who was probably subjected to a suzerainty treaty and made to swear an oath of loyalty to the Babylonians. The Babylonians did not, at this time, dismantle the Judahite monarchy and state. Judahite nationalists used this opportunity to foment rebellion again. Sometime early in the 580s, Judah rebelled, a move symbolized by Zedekiah's refusal to submit the annual tribute payment (2 Kings 24:20b). This time, the Babylonians made a no-nonsense response. They destroyed Jerusalem, burning the Temple, the palace, and "all the houses of Jerusalem" (1 Kings 25:9). The city walls were also pulled down. Some residents of Jerusalem were forced to flee, others were led into exile (2 Kings 25:11), and still others were executed (2 Kings 25:18-21). 2 Kings 25:12 tells us, however, that "The captain of the guard left some of the poorest people of the land to be vinedressers and tillers of the soil."

The impact on Jerusalem and Judah of the Babylonian action is clear. Archaeology testifies to the destruction of many of the fortified centers in Judah around the time of the fall of Jerusalem. The destruction of major cities seriously damaged the economy of the area. The primary economy of the country reverted to subsistence agriculture in the many villages that remained intact. The peasants in these villages could now reclaim the land that had been taken from them by the upper classes, who had been exiled to Babylon. With no superstructure to inhibit it, peasant life in the villages could reassert itself. Unfortunately, the Hebrew Bible, largely the product of a literate elite, tells us little about the life of these peasants, choosing instead to follow the story of the exiles.

Nebuchadrezzar's deportations to Babylon and the flight of other Judahites to Egypt meant that the center of the community had become dispersed. Scholars commonly refer to the period from 587-539 B.C.E. as the Babylonian Exile. This label is somewhat misleading, in that it suggests that most, if not all, of the surviving population of Judah was moved to Babylon. More accurately, one should regard the deportations to Babylon as part of a process of the dispersion of the community, a breakup that had begun with the policy of the Assyrians in dealing with the population of the northern kingdom in the eighth century. While some lost their identity as members of a distinctive covenant community, others did not. The Jewish community in Babylon, for example, became a thriving center of Jewish culture, which endured until modern times. This community produced the Babylonian Talmud *ca.* 500 C.E., a compendium of postbiblical Jewish life and thought. Two factors helped Jews in Babylon maintain their identity: (1) they were permitted to live in their own communities and (2) the presence of the former king provided a symbol of their identity as a people, as well as hope for renewed political autonomy in the future.

While Babylon was an important center of the Jewish diaspora, another community of Jews outside Palestine developed in Egypt. We know about this community from the book of Jeremiah (43-44; 46) and from the community's archives, which were found on the island of Elephantine, near the First Cataract of the Nile River in Upper Egypt. Documents of the Jews in Elephantine, who were originally Persian mercenaries, and thus from a later period, inform us about Jewish life in the Egyptian diaspora. We lack any other direct evidence about Jewish life in Egypt. Groups of Jews who fled to the delta region of Egypt in Jeremiah's time, taking Jeremiah with them (Jer 43:1-7), were probably the beginnings of those Jewish communities that would become major centers of the Jewish world during the Hellenistic period.

JEREMIAH—BEFORE AND AFTER "THE FALL": CRISIS AND COVENANT

Jeremiah lived during the twilight of the seventh and the dawn of the sixth centuries, when Babylon replaced Assyria as the major power in the ancient Near East. This means that he also lived in a "before and after" period in the life of Judah—before and after the fall of Jerusalem, also before and after the reform program of the young king Josiah (640-609 B.C.E.). We are told more about the life of Jeremiah than we are about any of the other "writing" prophets. This information is in the form of narratives about Jeremiah and in the first-person "Confessions" of Jeremiah. Jeremiah's book, like the other prophetic books we have examined, opens with a lengthy superscription supplied by one of the book's redactors (Jer 1:1-3):

> The words of Jeremiah son of Hilkiah, of the priests who were in Anathoth in the land of Benjamin, to whom the word of the LORD came in the days of King Josiah son of Amon of Judah, in the thirteenth year of his reign. It came also in the days of King Jehoiakim son of Josiah of Judah, and until the end of the eleventh year of King Zedekiah son of Josiah of Judah, until the captivity of Jerusalem in the fifth month.

According to this superscription, Jeremiah was born into a priestly family in Anathoth, a village about five miles north of Jerusalem. Based upon the information in this superscription, he would have been active from 626 (the thirteenth year of Josiah's reign) until 586 B.C.E. (the eleventh year of Zedekiah). This term of activity would have covered four distinct periods: (1) The early period, during the reign of Josiah; (2) The second period, during the reign of Jehoiakim; (3) The third period, during the reign of Zedekiah; (4) The fourth period, during the immediate aftermath of Jerusalem's fall.

The book of Jeremiah makes up the longest of the three "major prophets" in the Hebrew Bible. The book survives in two ancient versions: the Hebrew text, from which English translations are made, and the Greek Septuagint. There is more difference between the Hebrew text of Jeremiah and the Septuagint than for any other book in the Hebrew Bible. The Septuagint text of Jeremiah is about an eighth shorter than the Hebrew and arranges the materials in a different order after 25:13a. Even without this difference between the sequence of materials in the Septuagint and in the Hebrew Text, there is considerable confusion about the order of materials in the Hebrew text itself. It has often been remarked that the book of Jeremiah is in great disarray. Materials appear to be out of order chronologically, and the logic of their organization is unclear. We need to remember, however, that like the other prophetic books, the book of Jeremiah as we have it, is the product of a long development. This means that our analysis of the book must confront issues that would not exist had the book been composed at one point in time by a single author.

Despite the seeming disarray of the book, Jack Lundbom has noted that one can see several principles of organization at work in Jeremiah (1992: 711). He observes that the book as we have it does have a certain chronological order. Jeremiah's call to be a prophet comes in the first chapter. His last recorded activities in Egypt are near the end of the book, chapter 44 in the Hebrew Text, or at the very end, chapter 51 in the Septuagint. Chapter 2 contains Jeremiah's earliest oracles. All of chapters 1–20, with only a few exceptions, are earlier than the narratives of 24–29 and 34–44. The account of Jeremiah's final suffering in 37–44 follows a chronological sequence with a few exceptions. While attention is paid to chronology, Lundbom observes that there are other principles of organization at work as well.

Literary forms and themes are also organizational principles in the book of Jeremiah. Sometimes materials are brought together because of a common literary form, for example, the "Confessions" in chapters 11–20. Literary form, combined with theme, provides the basis for groupings such as chapters 2–3, which are speeches focusing on the nation's religious harlotry. The group of speeches that goes from 4:5 through 10:25 constitutes a "foe cycle," because they deal with the foe from the north. The theme of hope controls the speeches in the so-called "Book of Comfort" in 30–33. In some cases, material is grouped on the basis of the audience to which it is addressed. In chapters 21–23 one set of utterances is directed at kings (21:1–23:8) and another at prophets and priests (23:9–40). The audience forms the controlling organizational center in the oracles to foreign nations in 46–51. Association techniques, such as the catchwords we have seen before, also provide organizational links.

Lundbom (712) also sees rhetorical structures at work in the composition of Jeremiah. Chapter 1, for example is a chiasm:

A.   Articulation of the call vision (1:4–10)
B.   Vision of the call (1:11–12)
B'.   Vision of the foe (1:13–14)
A'. Articulation of the foe vision (1:15–19).

Near the end of the foe cycle, four originally separate utterances have been combined using a chiasm:

A.   Jeremiah *weeping* for the slain of Judah (8:22–9:2)
B.   Jeremiah warning about evil *tongues* (9:3–5)
B'.   Jeremiah warning about evil *tongues* (9:7–9)
A'. Jeremiah *weeping* for all creation (9:10–11)

Liturgical requirements may have provided a structure for some materials, for example 14:1–15:4.

By relying on the distinction between poetic oracles, prose sermon, and prose history, Joel Rosenberg has discerned a chiastic structure for the *entire* book of Jeremiah in the form it has in the Hebrew text (1987: 190-191):

A.   **Historical** headnote (1:1-3)
B.   **Prophet's** Commission (1:4)
C.   **"Prophet to the nations"** theme introduced (1:5-10)
D.   **Doom** for Israel; **poetic oracles** predominate (chaps. 1-10)
E.   Prophet cut off from **Anathoth;** focus on prophet's trials and conflicts; **prose** predominates (11:1-28:17)
F.   Optimistic prophecies; renewal of Israel; prose brackets **poetic center** (chaps. 29-31)
E'.   Prophet returns to **Anathoth;** focus on prophet's trials and conflicts; **prose** predominates (32:1-45:5)
D'.   **Doom** for the nations; **poetic oracles** predominate (chaps. 46-51)
C'.   **"Prophet to the nations"** theme culminates (chaps. 50-51)
B'.   **Prophet's** concluding message (51:59-64)
A'.   **Historical** appendix (chap. 52)

The Book of Jeremiah and Jeremiah's Early Career (622–605 B.C.E.)

When surveying materials in the book of Jeremiah that might be associated with Jeremiah's early career, the central issue is usually the religious reform of King Josiah and Jeremiah's response to it. On the one hand, some scholars have suggested that Jeremiah was encouraged to take up a career as a prophet in response to Josiah's reforms, with which he later became disillusioned. On the other hand, some scholars argue for a shorter ministry of Jeremiah. They base this on the fact that the book of Jeremiah is virtually silent regarding Josiah's reforms. If Jeremiah were active at this time, so they argue, it is difficult to imagine his not having taken a public stance for or against these religious reforms. At the most, a few references in Jeremiah *may* echo Josiah's reforms and Jeremiah's early support of them. These references, however, do not include any explicit references to Josiah's reforms. In Jer 11:1-13, for example, we are told that Jeremiah walked through the streets of Jerusalem encouraging people to "heed the words of this covenant" (11:3). Those who maintain that Jeremiah began his career in the time of Josiah suggest that the phrase "this covenant" is a reference to the Deuteronomic Covenant of Josiah's reform, which was a renewal of the Sinai Covenant. Another reference used to support the idea that Jeremiah was publicly active in the time of Josiah and initially supported the reforms is Jer 15:16:

> Your words were found, and I ate them,
>   for your words became to me a joy
>   and the delight of my heart;
> for I am called by your name,
>   O Lord, God of Hosts.

For those inclined to support an early ministry of Jeremiah, the phrase "your words were found" are understood as a reference to the scroll of the law that was found in the Temple in 622 B.C.E. (2 Kings 22:8). This scroll provided the stimulus for the launching of Josiah's reforms.

In places Jeremiah issues a warning about an "enemy from the north" (1:13-15; 4:5-8; 6:1, 22, and so forth). This "foe from the north" is, however, never named. Those who support an early ministry for Jeremiah assume that the enemy in these references was the Scythians, tribes who inhabited the area north and east of the Black Sea beginning in the seventh century B.C.E. Those who support a beginning for Jeremiah's ministry in the reign of Jehoiakim claim that the reference to the "thirteenth year of Josiah's reign" in 1:2 alludes to the birthdate of Jeremiah, not the beginning of his ministry. The enemy from the north would be the Babylonians, not Scythians. Some televangelists and other fundamentalists, before the breakup of the Soviet Union, often warned that the "enemy from the north" in Jeremiah was a prediction about the menace represented by the Soviet Union.

Those arguing for Jeremiah's having been active during the reign of Josiah argue that the persecution Jeremiah experienced early in his career from "the people of Anathoth" (11:21) was the response of members of Jeremiah's extended priestly family. They were priests, so the argument goes, who became unemployed with the centralization of worship in Jerusalem, a centerpiece of Josiah's reforms that was supported by Jeremiah. Jeremiah's father may have been a priest, but that does not mean that all the residents of Anathoth were priests, nor is the reason for opposition of "the people of Anathoth" to Jeremiah ever specified. The origin of the grievance against Jeremiah might have been his identification of some of his fellow citizens of Anathoth with the false prophets and priests who opposed him (23:9-40). Nothing in this passage dates it to the time of Josiah.

While there is some possibility that Jeremiah began his public career in the time of Josiah and the Deuteronomic reform (622-609 B.C.E.), little in the book of Jeremiah suggests that he became a significant figure until after the death of Josiah and the failure of the Deuteronomic reform movement. As mentioned above, the superscription of the book can be interpreted as referring to the date of Jeremiah's birth, not the beginning of his ministry. This makes good sense given Jeremiah's idea that he was predestined to be a prophet even before he was born, and thus, in one sense, his ministry began with his birth (1:4).

Jeremiah's work presupposes the collapse of Josiah's reforms and the shift of power from Assyria to Babylonia. The prominent place of nations other than Judah in Jeremiah's oracles reflects the influence wielded by Babylon and Egypt at the time. This becomes important in Jeremiah's thought since political vassalage was inextricably linked to religion. Recognition of the political superiority of another country also included bowing to their gods as symbols of their culture. Josiah's religious reforms thus had serious political implications, coming as they did at the time of Assyria's precipitous decline. The years from 609-605 were difficult ones, as the earliest clearly datable material in Jeremiah makes clear. The installation of Josiah's successor, Jehoiakim, by the Egyptian

Pharaoh Neco signaled a change in the political climate. It also signaled an end of the Josianic reforms. Jehoiakim, who at first pledged loyalty to the Egyptians and then shifted to the Babylonians, lacked the freedom and/or the will to sustain those reforms. The only legacy of the reforms, a negative one, was a false reliance on the protection thought to be afforded by the presence of the Temple. This is decried in Jeremiah's temple sermon (Jer 7:1–8:3), which was delivered in Jehoiakim's accession year, according to Jer 26:1–6.

The Book of Jeremiah and Jeremiah's Later Career (604–586 B.C.E.)

Jeremiah 36 relates that "in the fourth year of Jehoiakim" (604/603 B.C.E.) Jeremiah dictated his oracles to Baruch, who committed them to writing. Probably because of the highly critical nature of his temple sermon, Jeremiah had been barred from the temple. In "the fifth year of Jehoiakim" (Jer 36:9) Baruch read Jeremiah's words to a public assembly in the temple precincts. This was reported to Jehoiakim's officials who ordered Baruch to read the same scroll to them. Having heard the words of Jeremiah, they took the scroll from Baruch and one of them read it to Jehoiakim (36: 21b–24):

> Jehudi read it to the king and all the officials who stood beside the king. Now the king was sitting in his winter apartment (it was the ninth month), and there was a fire burning in the brazier before him. As Jehudi read three or four columns, the king would cut them off with a penknife and throw them into the fire in the brazier, until the entire scroll was consumed in the fire that was in the brazier. Yet neither the king, nor any of his servants who heard all these words, was alarmed, nor did they tear their garments.

After the destruction of this first scroll, Jeremiah again dictated to Baruch (36:32):

> Then Jeremiah took another scroll and gave it to the secretary Baruch son of Neriah, who wrote on it at Jeremiah's dictation all the words of the scroll that King Jehoiakim had burned in the fire; and many similar words were added to them.

Jeremiah and Baruch disappeared from public view after this. It is unlikely that Jeremiah had any public ministry in Jehoiakim's remaining years (604–598 B.C.E.) When the city surrendered to Nebuchadrezzar in 597, Jeremiah was again active. Nebuchadrezzar installed Zedekiah on the throne. Zedekiah was powerless in the face of a chaotic political situation. Materials in the book of Jeremiah suggest that Jeremiah was active during the first four years of Zedekiah's reign (597–594/3 B.C.E.), and again when Jerusalem was under siege prior to its fall in 587. Materials in the book of Jeremiah cannot clearly be linked, however, with the middle years of Zedekiah.

A good deal of information appears in the book of Jeremiah regarding Jeremiah's activities in the context of the fall of Jerusalem. When the city was under siege, Jeremiah attempted to leave the city to attend to some business in Anathoth, but was arrested and accused of deserting to the Babylonians (ch. 37). Jeremiah was thrown into prison, but was released and put under house arrest, where he remained until the city fell (37:21). After the fall of the city a group of people left to settle at Tahpanhes in Egypt, taking Jeremiah and Baruch with them. Jeremiah was about fifty-five years old when he arrived in Egypt in 586 B.C.E. We hear nothing else about Jeremiah after this. Later sources contain conflicting reports. Some of these tell of Jeremiah's martyrdom, while others say he died a natural death in Egypt.

Structure and Themes in the Book of Jeremiah

While we have attempted to offer a brief sketch of the career of Jeremiah, the way in which biographical information about Jeremiah is wedded to the conception of Jeremiah as prophet makes it extremely difficult to distinguish between historical fact and literary fiction. Of how much of the profile we have sketched of Jeremiah can we be certain? Rogerson and Davies offer a reasonable assessment. They maintain that little information comes from material most plausibly ascribed to Jeremiah. Although some scholars feel confident in reconstructing his life and the words that belong to each period in it, there are also good reasons for viewing Jeremiah as a shadowy figure, a creation of later groups who, among them, brought the present collection of materials constituting the book of Jeremiah together. Of all the prophets, Jeremiah, as an individual human being who suffers from his call, has attracted the most interest, although his so-called "confessions" may not be authentic. Like Isaiah and Micah, the book contains material that relates to the Jerusalem community of the Persian period (1989: 290–291).

For a long time, theories about the structure and composition of Jeremiah were based on the observation that three kinds of literary materials appear in the book—shorter poetic oracles, longer prose biographical narratives, and prose sermons. This observation was combined with the assumptions that these three kinds of materials originated independently and were then combined in stages to form the book as we have it. The shorter pieces of poetry were thought to be Jeremiah's original oracles, mostly in chapters 1–25 and 46–51. Later, these poetic oracles were elaborated and developed in the exilic and postexilic communities, perhaps by members of the Deuteronomic school, which explains the source of the longer prose sermons that are found scattered through chapters 1–25, but also later in the book. An example of the two kinds of material is the temple sermon, which appears in two versions—a short, "early" poetic one in chapter 7 and a longer prose one in chapter 26 (see below for a comparison of the two). Finally, the third kind of material, the memoirs or biographical narratives, were assembled to provide a sense of the response to Jeremiah's work. These narratives were considered the work of someone other than Jeremiah, but they are not completely orderly, so may well have come from several different sources. This material is mostly in chapters 26–45.

TRADITION COMPLEXES

This kind of analysis of the materials in Jeremiah was succeeded by those scholars who argued that all three kinds of material developed simultaneously in "tradition complexes." These "tradition complexes" in Jeremiah can be identified as follows:

- Jeremiah's words of judgment against Judah and Jerusalem, in the form of brief poetic oracles in the first person. These occur mainly in chapters 1 – 25.
- Third-person prose narratives about the response to Jeremiah's words. This includes a relatively cohesive extended narrative about Jeremiah and the last years of Judah. These narratives are in 19:1 – 20:6; 26 – 29; and 37 – 45.
- First-person sermons in prose with headings in the first person. The sermons occur in 1:4 – 10; 7; 11; 18; 21; 25; 32; and 34.
- Jeremiah's oracles against foreign nations. These oracles are in poetry found in chapters 46 – 51.
- The final chapter in the book (52) consists of a prose historical appendix describing the fall of Jerusalem that replicates the account found in 2 Kings 24:18 – 25:30. (Gottwald 1985: 398; Crenshaw 1986: 195)

Even within these "tradition complexes," however, the materials are not always of the same kind. The complex process by which these materials were organized into their present form has been the subject of extensive scholarly discussion. The present book of Jeremiah was probably preceded by earlier compilations. Recent studies of rhetoric and composition suggest that these compilations were written documents, not oral traditions, from the very beginning. Lundbom has identified six early collections (1992: 712 – 716):

1. **The Scroll of 605** This is the scroll described in Jer 36. There has been much speculation about the contents of this scroll. Most scholars think that its contents are found in 1:4 – 25:13a, though not all the material in those chapters should be included. These scholars assume that the phrase in 25:13a, "everything written in this book," signaled the end of this scroll.

2. **The First Edition of the Book of Jeremiah** Lundbom sees this "first edition" in chapters 1 – 20, which are bracketed by an *inclusion,* a literary device that uses the same or similar elements to mark the beginning and end of a unit (in italics in the passages that follow):

    > Before I formed you in *the womb* I knew you,
    > and before you were born I consecrated you.
    > I appointed you a prophet to the nations. (1:5)
    > Why did I come forth from *the womb*
    >   to see toil and sorrow,
    >   and spend my days in shame? (20:18)

3. **The Appendix on Kings and Prophets** Following the "First Edition," an appendix in chapters 21 - 23 focuses on the royal house of Judah and the religious establishment in Jerusalem.

4. **The Baruch Prose Collection** Within chapters 24 - 45 are passages said by many to have come from the hand of Jeremiah's scribe, Baruch, in the years following 605 B.C.E.

5. **The Book of Comfort** This includes all of chapters 30 - 33; the controlling theme is hope for national restoration. Within this collection, catchwords link some passages.

6. **The Foreign Nation Oracles** In the Septuagint this collection follows 25 : 13a, but in the Hebrew text it comprises chapters 46 - 51. The inclusion of material in this collection is based on its audience, as in collection 3 above.

Each of these collections has its own complex history, which may include an oral prehistory. The scope of our work here does not allow us to examine these complex histories. In what remains of our investigation of the book of Jeremiah, we will turn to some themes that appear in the "tradition complexes" mentioned above.

CHAPTERS 1–25

Associated with Jeremiah's call are two "visions" that set the theme of much of the book's first twenty-five chapters. In the first of these "visions" (1 : 11 - 12) Yahweh shows Jeremiah an almond tree and asks him what he sees. Jeremiah responds "I see a branch of an almond tree." The word for almond in Hebrew is *shaqed.* Yahweh then answers: "You have seen well, for I am watching (*shoqed* in Hebrew) over my word to perform it." The almond tree is one of the first plants to bloom in the spring in Palestine. Curiously enough, the only other place in the Hebrew Bible where the blooming of the almond tree is mentioned is in Eccl 12 : 5, where a normally hopeful sign is transformed into a sign of terror as part of the pathology of old age, a reminder that another year has passed and death is that much closer: "When one is afraid of heights, and terrors are in the road; the almond tree blossoms, the grasshopper drags itself along and desire fails; because all must go to their eternal home, and the mourners will go about the streets." Here in Jeremiah the blooming of the almond tree is definitely a sign of terror—terror that stems from the fact that God will see that his word accomplishes its purpose, that it will bring judgment upon the people of God. Jeremiah's task is to warn the people of the imminent judgment. In the second "vision" (1 : 13 - 16) Jeremiah saw a boiling pot in the north, tipped to the south with its contents about to spill out. The message of this vision, like the almond tree, was that disaster was soon to come upon Judah. Because of the geography of the region, with the desert to the east of Palestine, invaders often came from the north, following the line of the fertile crescent. Everyday images, in the form of "visions" and parables to illustrate the message, occur frequently in the first twenty-five chapters of Jeremiah. Other examples are:

OBJECT	REFERENCE	TYPE
The loin cloth	13:1-7	vision
Jeremiah's unmarried status	16:1-4	parable
The potter's workshop	18:1-12	parable
The broken pot	19:1-20:6	parable
The basket of figs	24:1-10	vision
The wine drinkers	25:15-38	vision

In the oracles of chapters 2-6, the infidelity of God's people is described in imagery resembling that in Hosea. Judah is described as Yahweh's bride, comparing the Sinai covenant with the marriage vow. Yahweh as a loving, faithful husband has defended his wife against all attempts of others (the Amalekites, Canaanites, Philistines, and so forth) to violate her. God pleads with Judah to return. Combining images from Hosea and Isaiah, unfaithful Israel is likened to a rebellious wife who turns to promiscuity (2:20-22):

> "For long ago you broke your yoke
>   and burst your bonds,
>   and you said, 'I will not serve!'
> On every high hill
>   and under every green tree
>   you sprawled and played the whore.
> Yet I planted you as a choice vine,
>   from the purest stock.
> How then did you degenerate
>   and become a wild vine?
> Though you wash yourself with lye
>   and use much soap,
>   the stain of your guilt is still before me,"
>   says the LORD God.

The use of such sexual imagery in Jeremiah is somewhat ironic, because Jeremiah himself remained unmarried (16:1-4) as a symbol of the impending catastrophe upon Judah; having children would be a horror instead of a joy. In chapters 5-6 the utter corruption of God's people is lamented and the imminence and horror of invasion is described. At the beginning of chapter 5, in a scene reminiscent of Abraham's bargaining with God over the fate of Sodom and Gomorrah (Gen 18:23-33), Jeremiah is instructed to search Jerusalem for "one person who acts justly and seeks truth" (5:1b). If one such person could be found, God would pardon Jerusalem. Jeremiah looks among both the poor (5:4) and the rich (5:5) with no success. Judah must be punished.

In chapters 5 and 6 Jeremiah indicts both Judah's religious leadership and the people who have followed them:

> The prophets prophesy falsely,
>> and the priests rule as the prophets direct;
> my people love to have it so,
>> but what will you do when the end comes? (5:31)
> Of what use to me is frankincense that comes from Sheba,
>> or sweet cane from a distant land?
> Your burnt offerings are not acceptable,
>> nor are your sacrifices pleasing to me. (6:20)

This condemnation of the people's attempt to substitute religious ritual for covenant faithfulness peaks in Jeremiah's long and bitter Temple Sermon in chapter 7. Since Jerusalem's deliverance from Sennacherib's siege of Jerusalem in 701 B.C.E., the belief in the inviolability of Jerusalem had become an article of faith for many. This belief rested on God's promise of perpetuity for the Davidic dynasty, coupled with God's permanent presence in the Jerusalem temple. Jeremiah attacks this idea in the temple sermon in 7:1-15 (cf. 26: 1-6). His attack begins with an appeal to the people of Judah to change their behavior. *If* they stop oppressing the needy and worshiping other gods, they will be able to continue to live in the land (vv. 3-7). But apart from this introduction, Jeremiah's sermon offers no hope to the people (7:8-8:3). The people's crimes are bluntly listed, first of all in words taken from the Ten Commandments (v. 9). The people participate in the worship of the Queen of Heaven (v.18), a rite referred to again in chapter 44. Ritual has replaced covenant faithfulness (vv. 21-26). Not only that, but their rituals are abominable, including child sacrifice (v. 31). This recitation of the people's offenses is topped off by Jeremiah's assertion that with their hands soiled by all these things, they dare to enter the temple expecting to be purified. Far from being sanctified by some magical holiness that attaches to the temple, Jeremiah maintains that the temple is desecrated by their behavior. All that remains for them is exile (7:14; 8:3) or death (7:32-33; 8:1-2). Their land will be desolate (7:34), and those few who survive the catastrophe will wish they were dead (8:3). The text tells us almost nothing about the context of Jeremiah's sermon. No date is given and nothing is said about the audience's response. Instead the content of the sermon is presented in six carefully constructed paragraphs, with each unit in the form of a prophecy of judgment, first describing the present situation, then announcing future judgment using the formula "Therefore thus says the LORD . . ." or "Therefore the days are coming." In a parallel temple sermon of Jeremiah in chapter 26, just the opposite is the case. It is dated to "the beginning of the reign of Jehoiakim" (609 B.C.E.). Only five verses are devoted to what Jeremiah said (vv. 2-6). The rest of the chapter contains a detailed description of the response to the sermon. While the two accounts supplement one another, with chapter 26 offering a context for the isolated sermon in chapter 7, there are substantial differences in the two. These differences suggest that chapter 26 contains some account of what happened and little of what was said, while chapter 7 is an elaborate rewriting of the sermon in the light of the actual destruction of the temple and the Babylonian Exile, written in unmistakable Deuteronomistic style.

The oracles in 11 – 20 include some of the best-known passages of the book of Jeremiah. These passages are often called the "Confessions" of Jeremiah. There are five of these "Confessions":

1. 11:18 – 12:6   "Like a gentle lamb led to the slaughter"

2. 15:10 – 21   "Woe is me, my mother, that you ever bore me"

3. 17:14 – 18   "Heal me, O Lord, and I shall be healed"

4. 18:18 – 23   "Come, let us make plots against Jeremiah"

5. 20:7 – 18   "I have become a laughingstock all day long"

The deeply personal quality of these "Confessions" has led many scholars to conclude that they represent autobiographical accounts of Jeremiah's wrestling with God. This understanding of the so-called "Confessions" has recently been challenged, based on the strong resemblance between the language used in them and the language of laments in the book of Psalms (see Ps 22; 44; 89), for which a cultic setting is taken for granted. In the "Confessions," Jeremiah may have been voicing a lament for a worshiping community, and thus what is said provides no historical evidence about Jeremiah. If the laments in the book of Psalms expressed the individual and collective yearnings for God to overcome various enemies, personal or otherwise, then Jeremiah could have chosen to express his own inner struggles in such familiar language (Crenshaw 1986: 201). The first two "Confessions" are in the form of a dialogue between God and the prophet. The last three are in the form of increasingly bitter monologues, with the prophet receiving no answer from God. The climactic "Confession" in the series (20:7 – 18) is the strongest of all, bordering on blasphemy and ending with a curse. This "Confession" is in two parts, separated by a short hymn of praise (v. 13). It begins with Jeremiah accusing God of having seduced him: "O Lord, you have enticed me, and I was enticed; you have overpowered me, and you have prevailed. I have become a laughingstock all day long; everyone mocks me" (20:7). The Hebrew word translated "enticed" by the NRSV is an interesting one. It commonly occurs in contexts where an intimate, often private, relationship is involved (compare its use in Ex 22:11 – 12 and in Gen 3:13). In a passage with obvious similarities to Jeremiah, a lying spirit is sent by God, through the agency of a prophet, to "entice" Ahab into a battle in which he will be killed (1 Kings 22:20 – 22).

Even those who understand the "Confessions" as communal expressions, acknowledge that the prophetic calling of Jeremiah brought him considerable personal grief. Certainly the people suffered too, and the "Confessions" of Jeremiah undoubtedly could symbolize their plight. They, too, were beaten, imprisoned, and taken from their land. They, too, cried out to God in anger and despair in their exile.

CHAPTERS 26–35

These chapters are primarily narrative materials concerning Jeremiah's activity after the exile in 597 B.C.E. This "tradition complex" contains several expressions of hope concerning the future of Yahweh's people on the other side of the destruction of their state. The theme of hope is seen in Jer 29, which speaks of "The letter that the prophet Jeremiah sent from Jerusalem to the remaining elders among the exiles, and to the priests, the prophets, and all the people, whom Nebuchadnezzar had taken into exile from Jerusalem to Babylon" (29:1). The exiles in Babylon were being misled by overly optimistic, unjustified assurances of a speedy return to Palestine. To counter these misleading promises, Jeremiah sent a letter that counseled the exiles to establish homes in Babylonia and to "Seek the welfare of the city where I have sent you into exile, and pray to the LORD on its behalf, for in its welfare you will find your welfare" (29:7). God would be with the exiles and would restore them to their land. Such advice presupposes a long exile. Here and in 25:10–11 appear references to a seventy-year period of Babylonian rule before release could come. While Ezekiel speaks of a forty-year exile (4:6; 29:11), the seventy-year exile in Jeremiah may be the result of calculating Babylonian rule as having begun with their defeat of the Assyrians at Haran in 609 B.C.E. Cyrus of Persia overthrew Babylonian rule in 539 B.C.E., seventy years after Haran. The seventy years may have carried overtones of a fixed world period as implied in a text of the Assyrian king Esarhaddon, who said that his predecessor Sennacherib's destruction of Babylon was to last seventy years according to a decree of the god Marduk (Gottwald 1985: 400).

This "tradition complex" reports a symbolic act of Jeremiah; he is said to have purchased land in Anathoth in chapter 32. Chronologically, this chapter should follow chapter 37. Its placement here emphasizes the validity of the preceding oracles about the restoration of Judah. When Jerusalem was under siege in 587 B.C.E., in order to prevent the loss of family property, Jeremiah purchased a field from his cousin Hanamel. This is one of the most detailed accounts of a business transaction in the Hebrew Bible. By the logic of cost-benefit analysis Jeremiah's action here seems to be all wrong. Why buy property that would soon be lost? In this symbolic act, however, Jeremiah declared his faith in the future renewal of Judah: "For thus says the LORD of hosts, the God of Israel: Houses and fields and vineyards shall again be bought in this land" (32:15). Although the end of this chapter in Jeremiah includes references to the return of the exiles, the point of Jeremiah's act was to assure a future for those who remained on the land in Judah.

A third passage in this "tradition complex" that speaks of hope for the future makes up one of the best-known passages in the book of Jeremiah. This passage forms a part of what has been called the "Book of Consolation" or the "Little Book of Comfort." Whether these promises of hope come from Jeremiah or his disciples is disputed. The best-known passage in this complex is one about the "new covenant" in 31:31-34. Using the old expression for covenant-making, "to cut a covenant," and opposing a limited interpretation of the Sinai covenant, Jeremiah says that God will "cut a new covenant with the house of Israel and the house of Judah" (31:31). This new covenant will be unbreakable, written on the hearts of people, not on tablets of stone. Like the "old covenant" the "new covenant" will be communal in nature. Jeremiah's image of an old and new covenant was used by the Jewish community at Qumran, the community who produced the Dead Sea Scrolls. Christian interpretations of this passage as an anticipation of the new covenant in Jesus Christ (see Luke 22:20; 1 Cor 11:25; Heb 8:8-13; 10:16) have sometimes distorted it into a highly individualized and spiritualized expectation (Gottwald 1985: 401).

•••

An Imaginative Portrait of Jeremiah

The word *jeremiad* means a doleful and thunderous denunciation, and its derivation is not a mystery. There was nothing in need of denunciation that Jeremiah didn't denounce. He denounced the king and the clergy. He denounced recreational sex and extramarital jamborees. He denounced the rich for exploiting the poor, and he denounced the poor for deserving no better. He denounced the way every new god that came sniffing around had them all after him like so many bitches in heat; and right at the very gates of the Temple he told them that if they thought God was impressed by all the mumbo-jumbo that went on in there, they ought to have their heads examined.

When some of them took to indulging in a little human sacrifice on the side, he appeared with a clay pot which he smashed into smithereens to show them what God planned to do to them as soon as he got around to it. He even denounced God himself for saddling him with the job of trying to reform such a pack of hyenas, degenerates, ninnies. "You have deceived me," he said, shaking his fist. You are "like a deceitful brook, like waters that fail" (*Jeremiah 15:18*), and God took it.

But the people didn't. When he told them that the Babylonians were going to come in and rip them to shreds as they richly deserved, they worked him over and threw him into jail. When the Babylonians did come in and not only ripped them to shreds but tore down their precious Temple and ran off with all the expensive hardware, he told them that since it was God's judgment upon them, they better submit to it or else; whereupon they threw him into an open cistern that happened to be handy. Luckily the cistern had no water in it, but Jeremiah sank into the muck up to his armpits and stayed there till an Ethiopian eunuch pulled him out with a rope.

He told them that if they were so crazy about circumcision, then they ought to get their minds above their navels for once and try circumcising "the foreskins of their hearts" (*Jeremiah 4:4*); and the only hope he saw for them

Continued

was that someday God would put the law in their hearts instead of in books, but that was a long way off.

At his lowest ebb he cursed the day he was born like Job, and you can hardly blame him. He had spent his life telling them to shape up with the result that they were in just about as miserable shape as they'd have been if he'd never bothered, and urging them to submit to Babylon as the judgment of God when all their patriotic instincts made that sound like the worst kind of defeatism and treachery.

He also told them that, Babylonian occupation or no Babylonian occupation, they should stick around so that someday they could rise up and be a new nation again; and then the first chance they got, a bunch of them beat it over the border into Egypt. What's even worse, they dragged old Jeremiah, kicking and screaming, along with them, which seems the final irony: that he, who had fought so long and hard against all forms of idolatry—the Nation as idol, the Temple as idol, the King as idol—should at last have been tucked into their baggage like a kind of rabbit's foot or charm against the evil eye or idol himself.

What became of him in Egypt afterwards is not known, but the tradition is that his own people finally got so exasperated with him there that they stoned him to death. If that is true, nothing could be less surprising.

Buechner (1979: 59-61).

"SECOND ISAIAH," THE REDEMPTIVE VALUE OF SUFFERING, AND HOPE FOR THE FUTURE

After the destruction of Jerusalem and the Temple, the Jewish population was divided into three groups. There were those who were left behind on the land. There were those who fled into Egypt and founded communities that would become important in the Persian and Greek periods. Then, there were those inhabitants of Judah and Jerusalem who were deported to Babylon by Nebuchadrezzar, where they settled on the banks of the Chebar canal. At this point in our journey we travel east with this group.

The Chebar canal, which flowed eastward out of Babylon toward the shrine of Nippur, was a fertile region that was well situated for commerce. As we observed above, Jeremiah had advised the exiles in Babylon to settle down there and go about their business. While they were doing so, the wheels of state on an international level took another turn, causing yet another shift in power arrangements in the ancient Near East. The Babylonian Empire had reached its zenith under Nebuchadrezzar. In the reigns of his three successors, the empire would fall into a rapid downward spiral. To the north and east of Babylon, Cyrus the Persian appeared *ca.* 550 B.C.E. as the ruler of a small kingdom within the empire of the Medes and as a rival to the Babylonians (see

Figure 12.1). Cyrus was able to gain control of the Median Empire and positioned himself to pick up the pieces of the disintegrating Babylonian Empire. In this situation, from the rise of Cyrus to his triumphal entry into Babylon in 539 B.C.E., "Second Isaiah," who was actually an anonymous prophet, addressed the exiled Jewish community with words of comfort and hope.

Because "Second Isaiah" is appended to the end of the book associated with Isaiah of Jerusalem and is not a freestanding book, it does not have a superscription like the other books of the classical prophets. Nevertheless, clearly the historical context of "Second Isaiah" (referred to from here on simply as Second Isaiah) differs from the eighth-century Isaiah of Jerusalem. Assyria as the great imperial power of the ancient Near East is no more. The people are in Babylon, not Jerusalem. The tone of judgment has been replaced by one of comfort. Cyrus of Persia is mentioned by name in 45:1, where he is called God's "anointed" (*meshiach* in Hebrew, "Messiah" in English). Careful readers in all eras have noted the differences between Isaiah of Jerusalem and Second Isaiah. Why then did the unity of the book of Isaiah go unchallenged for so long, and why do some scholars still maintain it? Richard Clifford has suggested that the answer to this question lies in the belief in the verbal inspiration of the Bible (490). According to this belief, the biblical authors wrote as scribes, recording what was dictated to them by God under the inspiration of the Holy Spirit. This belief discounts the differences between Isaiah 1–39 and 40–55 by maintaining that the events and persons (including Cyrus) mentioned in chapters 40–55 were revealed to Isaiah of Jerusalem. As we mentioned in our discussion of Isaiah, however, most scholars regard Isaiah 40–55 as having a unity and coherence of its own. Besides presupposing a different historical situation, some 150 years later than that of Isaiah of Jerusalem, these chapters have a literary style and vocabulary of their own. The final ten chapters of the book of Isaiah, 56–66, are thought to be even later. We will focus here on Second Isaiah, chapters 40–55.

The anonymity of the prophet in 40–55 makes it difficult to extract any biographical information from these chapters. There are no explicit narratives dealing with the prophet's life, only speeches. The prophet's call is implied in the scene described in 40:1–11 where the prophet witnesses a meeting of God's council in heaven. Prophetic attendance at the divine assembly is also reported in 1 Kings 22:19–23 (of Micaiah ben Imlah) and in Isaiah 6. The prophet hears that the time of punishment of God's people is at an end. The time has come for a message of comfort and hope:

> "Comfort, O comfort my people," says your God.
> "Speak tenderly to Jerusalem,
>   and cry to her
> that she has served her term,
>   that her penalty is paid,
> that she has received from the LORD's hand
>   double for all her sins." (40:1–2)

Other references to the prophet may be found in the "Servant Songs" (42:1-4; 49:1-6; 50:4-6; 52:13-53:12; see p. 413). The position of Second Isaiah after Isaiah 1-39 and the anonymity of the author, argue that whoever placed chapters 40-55 where they are understood the message to be continuous with what preceded it. Perhaps the absence of biographical detail was deliberate, to show that the speeches actualize traditions of Isaiah for the exiles.

Second Isaiah has been intensely studied, but as Gottwald writes, the focus of such study has often been guided by concerns that do not help its distinctive character to come through (1985: 496). He maintains that in spite of the enormous amount of study invested in these chapters, the focus has been limited, revolving around questions that miss the distinguishing qualities of the work. Some of these questions have been: Does Second Isaiah give the first explicit biblical statement of monotheism? Does the prophet look forward to the conversion of the nations to the Jewish faith? Was he influenced by Zoroastrianism or by the Babylonian New Year Festival? Can we connect historical references within the poems to phases in the career of Cyrus? Who is the servant of Yahweh? While Gottwald does not think that these questions are necessarily unimportant, he does think that they are unproductive when they are pursued in relative isolation from one another and out of the context of "Second Isaiah's" place within Israelite tradition history. When pursued in this way they can be given quite forced answers that do not throw much light on the work as literature or as a statement about how Jews should respond to their forthcoming freedom. In the discussion of "Second Isaiah" that follows, we hope to take at least a small step beyond such restrictive questions.

Structure and Themes in Second Isaiah

The poems in Second Isaiah (there is very little prose) build on the theme that is stated in 40:1-11: Yahweh is coming with compassion in the near future to restore his people. While the same thing could have been said earlier and often, it is especially the case with Second Isaiah. In Second Isaiah we encounter powerful poetry that resonates with themes and literary forms that we have encountered earlier in our journey through the Hebrew Bible. One should remember that by the time of Second Isaiah, the prophetic literary tradition had two centuries of history behind it. The most that can be done here is to call attention to some major aspects of the work that can help guide its reading.

A structural analysis of Second Isaiah's oracles shows the prophet's use of fundamental opposition. Richard Clifford has said that these oppositions or polarities are so pervasive that they are "at once the substance of much of the oratory and the chief mode of development. They bear on both form and content" (1992: 498-499). Five oppositions in Second Isaiah are:

1. First and Last Things,
2. Babylon and Zion,

3.   Yahweh and the Gods,

4.   Israel and the Nations,

5.   The Servant and Israel.

We will comment on the first two and the last two of these oppositions in what follows.

FIRST AND LAST THINGS

The opposition of first and last things is used in several ways in Second Isaiah. One use is to symbolize eternity:

> I, the LORD, am first,
>   and will be the last. (41:4b)

Opposition is also used to predict the deeds of Yahweh in the future, symbolized by "the last," based on what he has done in the past, "the first" (41:22-23; 42:9; 43:9-13; 44:6-8; 45:21; 48). A third use of this opposition is in signifying the first and the second Exodus: Conquest. The clearest statement of this is in 43:16-21. Just as Yahweh made a way through the sea for the Israelites fleeing from the Pharaoh (43:16), so he will clear a path through the desert for the return of Israel to Palestine in a second and greater Exodus (43:19, reading "paths" instead of the NRSV's "rivers," following the Hebrew text of one of the scrolls of Isaiah found among the Dead Sea Scrolls). The analogy between the event that brought Israel into being in the past and the event that will reconstitute them in the future is a central theme in Second Isaiah.

BABYLON AND ZION

Related to the opposition between first and last is the contrast between Babylon and Zion. Just as Jerusalem is the focus and personification of the whole people of God, so the Babylonian capital represents the entire enemy nation. Isaiah 45:14-25 talks about the *rebuilding* of Zion in contrast to the *ruins* of Babylon in chapter 47. In chapter 46 the gods have to *be carried* away from a doomed Babylon, but God *carries* Israel to safety. Zion *receives back* her husband Yahweh and her children in 49:14-26 and in 50:1-3. Babylon, by contrast, *loses* both in chapter 47. The message is clear: Israel will vacate a doomed Babylon and return to a renewed Jerusalem.

ISRAEL AND THE NATIONS

The practice of other nations' use of images to represent their deities is employed by Second Isaiah to draw a sharp contrast between Israel and the other nations. As we saw in our discussion of the Ten Commandments in Chapter 7, the prohibition against making images of God was a basic feature of Israelite law. Second Isaiah presupposes this prohibition:

> I am the LORD, that is my name;
>> my glory I give to no other,
>> nor my praise to idols. (42:8)

In trial scenes (41:1-20 = 41:21-42:9) the nations bring mute images that represent their gods into the courtroom to testify in their behalf. In a passage full of sarcasm, Second Isaiah describes the process by which these images of gods are made (44:12-17):

> The ironsmith fashions it and works it over the coals . . . he becomes hungry and his strength fails, he drinks no water and is faint. The carpenter stretches a line, marks it out with a stylus, fashions it with planes, and marks it with a compass; he makes it in human form, with human beauty, to be set up in a shrine. . . . He plants a cedar and the rain nourishes it. Then it can be used as fuel. Part of it he takes and warms himself; he kindles a fire and bakes bread. Then he makes a god and worships it, makes it a carved image and bows down before it. Half of it he burns in the fire; over this half he roasts meat, eats it and is satisfied. He also warms himself and says, "Ah, I am warm, I can feel the fire!" The rest of it he makes into a god, an idol, bows down to it and worships it; he prays to it and says, "Save me, for you are my god!"

In contrast to the idols, which can do nothing and say nothing, Yahweh's power is emphasized again and again.

THE SERVANT AND ISRAEL

In developing this opposition, Second Isaiah uses another familiar theme in the Hebrew Bible. The servants chosen by Yahweh often exemplified God's intent for all the people. The servants represent what all Israel was supposed to be. The word "servant" occurs twenty times in Second Isaiah. In thirteen of these occurrences, Israel is identified as the servant. The other seven make up what are called the "Servant Songs" and verses connected with them. Four of these Servant Songs have been identified. They are the best known and most intensely studied parts of Second Isaiah. The four Servant Songs are as follows:

1. 42:1-4,
2. 49:1-6,
3. 50:4-9,
4. 52:13-53:12.

Some scholars maintain that the Servant Songs are probably from an author other than Second Isaiah and "were inserted awkwardly in their present context" (Clifford 499). The view that these passages tell a story separate from the rest of Isaiah 40-55 goes back to a commentary on the book of Isaiah published in 1892 by Bernard Duhm. If one subscribes to the idea that the Servant Songs are intrusive, then the servant of the songs and the servant of the rest of Second

Isaiah (the term "my servant" occurs frequently outside the Servant Songs—
41:8; 42:19; 43:10; 44:1; 45:4) must have had two different identities that a
redactor has tried unsuccessfully to harmonize. Gottwald maintains that the claim
that the Second Isaiah reads more smoothly and continuously without the Servant Songs is a dubious one (497). The position supported here is that the
Servant Songs ought to be read as an integral part of Second Isaiah. It is better
to treat each song as one comes to it, in its own context, and try to understand
what it is about. The Servant Songs contribute information about the servant
central to the message of Second Isaiah. What kind of information about the servant is included in the Servant Songs? Here is a summary of what the four songs
say about the servant.

Servant Song 1: 42:1–4. In this song, the speaker is Yahweh, who says the following about the servant:

- The servant is chosen by Yahweh (42:1b),
- He has Yahweh's spirit on him (42:1c),
- He will bring forth truth and justice (42:1d),
- He will accomplish his mission nonviolently (42:3),
- His strength will not fail until he has established justice in the earth (42:4).

Servant Song 2: 49:1–6. In this song, the servant himself speaks, describing
his call:

- He was called by Yahweh before he was born [like Jeremiah] (49:1b),
- His mouth was to be a weapon for God (49:2),
- God would be glorified through what the servant does (49:3),
- The servant expresses disappointment in the results of his work (49:4),
- The servant's job is initially to restore Israel to God (49:5),
- The servant's expanded mission is to be a "light to the nations," to make
  God's salvation available to all the earth (49:6).

Servant Song 3: 50:4–11. Here again, the servant speaks in a song of trust
in God:

- The servant speaks faithfully to sustain the weary (50:4),
- The servant is the target of the people's abuse (50:6),
- Using lawcourt terminology, the servant expresses unshakable confidence
  that he will be vindicated by God (50:7-9),
- God leads his servant safely through the faithless people's rejection (50:
  10-11).

Servant Song 4: 52:13–53:12. This is the longest and most complex of the
Servant Songs, which can be divided into three parts:

A. In this first part of the fourth song, 52:13-15, the speaker is Yahweh:

God affirms that his servant shall prosper (52:13),
Before he prospers, however, the servant will be disfigured so that he will
no longer resemble a human being (52:14),
The servant's words will astonish the world's leaders (52:15).

B. In the second part of the fourth song, 53:1-10, the speaker is Israel or
a congregation:

The servant has an undistinguished background and does not have a commanding physical presence (53:1-2),
The servant was despised and rejected by the people (53:3),
The people, who thought the servant's punishment was fitting retribution
for his deeds, discovered that he was suffering for them (53:4-6),
The servant suffered quietly and innocently, was unjustly executed, and
shamefully buried (53:7-9).

C. In the last part of the fourth song, 53:11-12, the speaker is again
Yahweh:

The servant through his actions will make many righteous vicariously
(53:11),
The servant will be rewarded for his work in bearing the sins of many and
interceding for the transgressors (53:12 a, b).

In all of the songs, the servant acts as the prophetic mediator for the world.
The songs do not speak of the servant in the past, but talk of the coming of the
servant in the future. While the identity of the servant in the Servant Songs has
been the subject of much discussion, the most promising question to ask about
the servant is probably not, "*Who* is the servant?" As Gottwald suggests (1985:
497), more helpful questions to ask are,

- "*What* does the servant do in relation to all that is to occur in the deliverance
of Israel?" or
- "*How* does the servant function in relation to the other imaginatively developed figures?" or even
- "*Which* future tasks of God, Israel, and the nations will be done by the servant?"

When we approach the problem of the servant in this manner, we see that the
servant figure provides a way of speaking about Israel; here, Israel's self-conscious
aspects are represented by figures from the past, and in the present someone will
again act as servant, probably the prophet himself.

The servant figure, especially as represented in the fourth song, found its
way into the New Testament because of the early Christians' identification of
the servant with Jesus of Nazareth (for example Acts 8:32-35). The history of
Christian interpretation of the Bible has continued what was begun in the New
Testament, reading the Servant Songs as directly predictive of Jesus, his death,
and resurrection. As we saw in our discussion of the interpretation of the sign

to Ahaz in Isaiah 7, a problem with this interpretive approach develops: This approach does not help one see what meaning these texts could have had in their historical context, here the experiences of the community of Jews in Babylonian exile. Respecting the integrity of the Hebrew Bible, it is preferable to see the Servant Songs as providing the early Christian community with a way of explaining how they perceived Jesus and his mission.

CREATION

Apart from the structure of oppositions, creation is a significant theme in Second Isaiah. Second Isaiah speaks of God as Redeemer in his plans for a new Exodus and a revitalized Jerusalem in connection with God as Creator. God as Redeemer and God as Creator are closely linked in Second Isaiah's message. The connection between Creation and the story of God's acts in behalf of Israel does not originate with Second Isaiah, but he does more with the connection than anyone else. Creation and redemption language are both used to describe the same event. Creation accounts in the ancient Near East, such as the Enuma Elish, which we looked at in Chapter 5, were intended to present, in mythic form, accounts of how the structures in human society mirrored those in the world of the gods. In Second Isaiah, creation metaphors show that the new redemption of Israel is really a re-creation. The mythological understanding of creation as arising out of chaos and conflict is applied by Second Isaiah to God's struggle to rescue oppressed Israel. The mix of creation and redemption language in a passage that also reflects the conflict motif of creation myths shows up most clearly in 51:9-10 (see also Isa 27:1; 30:7):

> Awake, awake, put on strength,
>   O arm of the LORD!
> Awake, as in days of old,
>   the generations of long ago!
> Was it not you who cut Rahab in pieces,
>   who pierced the dragon?
> Was it not you who dried up the sea,
>   the waters of the great deep;
> who made the depths of the sea a way
>   for the redeemed to cross over?

On the assumption that God alone is Creator, Second Isaiah regards Yahweh as the Lord of the whole world. Scholars have long commented that no book in the Hebrew Bible puts greater stress on the idea of monotheism than Second Isaiah. It has been suggested that Second Isaiah contains the earliest explicit statement of theoretical or philosophical monotheism—that is, the belief that there is only one God, Yahweh, for all nations. The other gods simply do not exist. Yahweh in Second Isaiah is not a national god. Yahweh is the sole creator of all the earth (40:12-31), and the gods of the other nations are nothing but inventions of human beings (41:21-24; 44:9-20; 46:1-13). Because of the belief in God as the sole Creator of the world, Second Isaiah can anticipate the time in the future when all nations will recognize Yahweh as God. This conviction is the source of universalism in Second Isaiah's message.

Second Isaiah and the Cyrus Cylinder

The assumption that Yahweh is the Lord of history who has a plan for all creation, while not without its antecedents in the Hebrew Bible, is asserted in striking ways by Second Isaiah. One example of this is the application of the title *meshiach,* Messiah, which was previously reserved for the kings of Israel and Judah, to the Persian ruler Cyrus (41:2–4, 25–29; 44:28; 45:1–13; 46:8–11). The reason for this is that Cyrus acts as the agent of God for Israel's redemption by overthrowing Babylon in 539 B.C.E. and issuing an edict allowing the exiles to return home. The Cyrus Cylinder, dated to 528 B.C.E. instituted the Persian government policy of re-establishing subject peoples in their homelands and promoting the cults of their gods. The language of the Cyrus Cylinder resembles the language used by Second Isaiah regarding Cyrus as liberator and respecter of native religions. In the fall of 539 B.C.E., the last of the Babylonian kings, Nabonidus, fled Babylon, and Cyrus' army entered the capital city without a battle (see Figure 12.2).

Figure 12.2   The Cyrus Cylinder

The first part of the Cyrus Cylinder lists charges against Nabonidus, focusing on his improper prayers and sacrifices and his institution of the hated corvée (Matthews and Benjamin 148):

The worship of Marduk, The King of the Gods in Babylon, Nabonidus made into an abomination. . . . He tormented Babylon's people with the yoke of forced labor, never giving them any relief. Because of the complaints of the people, Marduk, the Lord of the Gods, became angry, departing the region along with The Gods whose statues had been moved to Babylon. Marduk . . . searched through all the countries for a righteous ruler willing to lead him in the annual procession. He spoke the name of Cyrus, King of Anshan, declaring him Ruler of All the World. . . . Marduk, the Great Lord and Protector of his People, looked with pleasure at Cyrus' good deeds and upright heart. Thus, Marduk ordered Cyrus to march against his city of Babylon. He marched with Cyrus as a friend while the army strolled along without fear of attack. Marduk allowed Cyrus to enter Babylon without a battle . . . and delivered Nabonidus, the king who did not worship him, into Cyrus' hands.

In the second part of the cylinder, Cyrus reflects on his victory and its consequences, describing how he became the worshiper and servant of all of the gods (Matthews and Benjamin 149–150):

When I entered Babylon as a friend and established my seat of government there in the palace of the king, Marduk caused the people to love me and I worshipped him daily. My troops kept order in the streets of Babylon and throughout the land of Sumer and Akkad. In Babylon I ended the practice of forced labor and helped rebuild their ruined houses.

All the kings of the entire world, from the Upper to the Lower Sea, those seated in throne rooms, or other types of dwellings as well as the tent dwellers from the land in The West, brought me tribute and kissed my feet in Babylon.

To all the regions, as far as Ashur and Susa, Agade, Eshnunna, the towns of Zamban, Me-Turnu, Der and the region of the Gutians, I returned the images of their gods to their sanctuaries which had been in ruins for a long period of time. I now established for them permanent sanctuaries. I also gathered all the former inhabitants of these places and returned them to their homes.

Furthermore, upon the command of Marduk, I resettled all The Gods of Sumer and Akkad, which Nabonidus had moved to Babylon, unharmed in their former places to make them happy . . . and I endeavored to repair their dwelling places. (See the image of Marduk in Figure 12.3.)

In 538 B.C.E. Cyrus issued a decree that allowed the Jerusalem temple to be rebuilt with Persian funds. Cyrus also organized the return to their homelands of a number of people who had been held in Babylonia by the Babylonian kings. The document authorizing the rebuilding of the Jerusalem Temple is cited in the postexilic historical book of Ezra (6:3–5). The subsequent return of the Jews to Palestine (Ezra 2) was also a manifestation of the policies of Cyrus.

Figure 12.3   An image of the god Marduk

There is little information about how many Babylonian Jews, who had apparently become well established in their adopted land, chose to return to Palestine. We know that some did, however, and the last eleven chapters of Isaiah, 56–66, were addressed to those returnees who struggled to rebuild the temple and reconstitute their community in at least partial fulfillment of Second Isaiah's grandiose visions of a New Exodus, a New Zion, and a New Creation.

STUDY QUESTIONS

JEREMIAH

1. Briefly describe the different time periods in which Jeremiah worked.
2. The apparent disorderly nature of the book of Jeremiah has often been commented upon. However, some principles of organization can be observed in the book. What are some of them?

3. What was Jeremiah's relationship to the Deuteronomic reform movement? What reasons might a prophet like Jeremiah have given in support of or against external political reforms such as the program of Josiah? Might similar reasons be given in support of or in opposition to such political reforms today?

4. What shifts taking place on the international scene are mirrored in Jeremiah's oracles? How, in the case of Jeremiah, were international politics and religion related?

5. Analyze two of Jeremiah's symbolic dramatizations not discussed in the chapter.

6. Of all the prophets, Jeremiah as an individual human being suffered from his call. Why does Jeremiah suffer as the result of his prophetic call? How is this related to the English word "Jeremiad"? Are Jeremiah's "Confessions" necessarily autobiographical?

7. Compare the two versions of Jeremiah's "temple sermon" in chapters 7 and 26. What is the basic theme of the "temple sermon"?

SECOND ISAIAH

1. What is the historical context of Second Isaiah? What is its relationship to the rest of the book of Isaiah?

2. What role does the theme of the Exodus play in Second Isaiah? How is this theme "reworked" by Second Isaiah?

3. What are some of the oppositions used by Second Isaiah? What is the function of these oppositions?

4. What is the role of the "Servant of Yahweh" in the four "Servant Songs" in Second Isaiah? Describe one possible historical scenario that would provide a context and background for the Servant and his experience.

5. How is the idea of creation used in Second Isaiah?

6. How is the God of Second Isaiah maternal?

BIBLIOGRAPHY

Clifford, Richard J. 1992. "Isaiah, Book of (Second Isaiah)." *The Anchor Bible Dictionary, Vol. III*, 490–501. New York: Doubleday. .

Crenshaw, James L. 1986. *Old Testament Story and Faith: A Literary and Theological Introduction.* Peabody, MA: Hendrickson.

Gottwald, Norman K. 1985. *The Hebrew Bible: A Socio-Literary Introduction.* Philadelphia: Fortress.

Lundbom, Jack R. 1992. "Jeremiah, Book of." *The Anchor Bible Dictionary, Vol. III*, 706–721. New York: Doubleday.

Matthews, Victor H. and Benjamin, Don C. 1991. *Old Testament Parallels: Laws and Stories from the Ancient Near East.* New York: Paulist.

Rogerson, John W., and Davies, Philip R. 1989. *The Old Testament World.* Englewood Cliffs, NJ: Prentice-Hall.

Rosenberg, Joel. 1987. "Jeremiah and Ezekiel," *The Literary Guide to the Bible.* Robert Alter and Frank Kermode, eds. Cambridge, MA: Harvard University Press, 185–206.

THE "WRITINGS"
IN THE JEWISH
CANON AND BEYOND

SONGS—SACRED AND SECULAR

Suggested Bible Reading
Psalms 2; 6; 8; 17; 19; 22; 23; 29; 32; 33; 41; 45; 51;
74; 80; 89; 90; 100; 104; 109; 116; 130; 132; Song of Solomon 1–8

HEBREW POETRY

*W*ith the book of Psalms, we have arrived at the beginning of the third division of the Jewish canon, the Writings. Having come this far in our journey, we have already encountered many examples of Hebrew poetry. Indeed, poetry comprises about one third of the Hebrew Bible. Because so much of the Hebrew Bible is written in poetry, the student must have some understanding of and appreciation for the characteristics of Hebrew poetry. While it is printed on the page in lines like English poetry in modern English translations, Hebrew poetry does not share other features that poetry in English sometimes has, such as rhyme. At this point we need to pause to examine Hebrew poetry more closely, in an attempt to discover "how it works." We shall do so by looking at two books in the Hebrew Bible that are composed entirely of poetry—the book of Psalms, which includes examples of ancient Israel's sacred songs, and a book of Israel's love songs, the Song of Solomon, also known by its Hebrew title, the Song of Songs, and its title in the Latin Vulgate, the Canticle (of Canticles). These two books, together with Proverbs, which we will discuss in Chapter 15, are distinguished from all other books in the Hebrew Bible by the fact that they are anthologies.

Parallelism and Other Features of Hebrew Poetry

In 1753, a "discovery" by Robert Lowth was published in Latin in a volume titled *De sacra poesi Hebraeorum (Lectures on the Sacred Poetry of the Hebrews).* Lowth's "discovery" was that something that he called *parallelismus membrorum,* "parallelism of members," was the predominant feature of poetry in the Hebrew Bible. From Lowth's "discovery" until the 1980s, parallelism, as defined by Lowth and elaborated by other scholars, ruled the discussion of Hebrew poetry. In the 1980s, the work of two American biblical scholars, James Kugel and Robert Alter, caused scholars to reconsider the phenomenon of parallelism, which is very important for biblical interpretation and translation. In 1981 James Kugel published his book *The Idea of Biblical Poetry,* and in 1985 Robert Alter published *The Art of Biblical Poetry.*

PARALLELISM AND THE HISTORY OF IDEAS

Actually, Lowth did not discover parallelism. His was an example of a timely idea expressed by a prominent person. Lowth was the son of an Anglican priest. He attended New College, Oxford, where he was elected fellow in 1734 and awarded the M.A. degree in 1737. He then went on to become professor in the Oxford chair of poetry from 1741–1751. It was during this time that he delivered his lectures on Hebrew poetry that were published in Latin in 1753. In 1751 he gave up his professorship at Oxford and became the Bishop of Limerick in Ireland. Later he was to become the Bishop of St. David (1766), Oxford (1766), and London (1771), a post he held until his death in 1787.

Lowth was an amateur poet who published his first poem at the age of nineteen. He achieved distinction in Latin verse and Latin translation of Hebrew poetry. Lowth's parallelism is another of those ideas in biblical scholarship, like the documentary hypothesis, which is best understood as arising out of a particular "pregnant" moment in the history of ideas. Lowth lived and worked during the so-called neoclassical era. As the name of this period suggests, the Greek and Latin classics played an important role, but with something new added. The new dimension was supplied by the new natural philosophy, represented in England by Thomas Hobbes (1588–1679) and John Locke (1632–1704), who applied it to literary criticism. However, not until the eighteenth century was an extensive theory of literary criticism based on natural philosophy formulated.

In the eighteenth century the Bible was becoming discredited in some circles because of the critical and rationalistic approach to it. It was a time when a new approach to the Bible might revive interest in it. A literary reading of the Bible was one possible way of retrieving the Bible's diminished authority, and Lowth was in a position to pave the way for a systematic reading of the Bible as literature. As a child of his time, Lowth bridged classical ideas with new ones. He began his *Lectures on the Sacred Poetry of the Hebrews* by integrating the Hebrew scriptures into the literary critical theory of the neoclassical era, the standards of which were set by the Greek and Roman classics. In accordance with the special sensitivity of literary critics of his day to the social environment in which writers produced their work, Lowth judged biblical style by its own standards and not by those imposed upon it by the rhetoric of the classics. His starting point was that Israel was an oriental people, who differed totally from the Greeks and the Romans. This opened a new approach to literary criticism. By making use of the Bible itself as much as possible in his work, Lowth opened up the Bible as a sourcebook of the literary criticism of his day and subsequent generations.

PARALLELISM AND THE DISTINCTIVENESS OF HEBREW POETRY

Lowth, according to Kugel, delineated the following differences between classical and Hebrew poetry (Kugel 1981: 274–282):

- **Hebrew poetry is "sententious,"** that is, it displays a brief proverb-like quality. This terseness was highly suitable for what Lowth saw to be the educational function of Hebrew poetry, which was used for moral instruction.
- **Hebrew poetry is metrical because of parallelism.** Lowth observed "a certain conformation of sentences," which meant that "they express the same thing in different words, or different things in a similar form of words; when equals refer to equals, and opposites to opposites . . ."
- **Hebrew poetry is figurative or parabolic.** Lowth distinguished a "mystical" class of allegory (and typology) that is different from classical allegory because, as he saw it, it was used only by the Holy Spirit.
- **Hebrew poetry is sublime.** In speaking of sublimity, Lowth says: "The language of passions is totally different [from that of reason]: the conceptions burst out in a turbid stream, expressive in a manner of the internal conflict. . . . In a word, reason speaks literally, the passions practically." Unusual syntax, ellipses, and shifts in grammatical person or tense are some characteristics of Lowth's "sublime style."

PARALLELISM BEFORE LOWTH

Of these distinctive features, the second was Lowth's great "discovery." One might ask why it took so long for someone to articulate the principle of parallelism. This interesting story is told in detail by Kugel (1981). Here we can offer only a few highlights of the story. Although there are several reasons why the rabbis did not see or hear parallel lines in Hebrew poetry (or at least did not articulate that they saw them), what really screened them from the phenomenon was their method of interpretation. They extracted meaning from every detail of the text. Describing the rabbinic method of interpretation, Kugel says that the rabbis believed that every detail of the text was put there to teach something new and important and was capable of being discovered by careful analysis (1981: 104). Therefore, the rabbis did not interpret the complementary lines in Hebrew poetry as a reiteration or reassertion of ideas, but, on the contrary, they interpreted them by juxtaposition, missing the point of this important stylistic feature of Hebrew poetry.

Similarly, the church had failed to discover parallelism. The church recognized that the Bible could be read on several levels. It could be read on the surface level, but could also be approached metrically and rhetorically. The Church recognized that the Hebrew Bible, like Greek or Latin literature, was written in both poetry and prose, and that its poetry was characterized by meters that could be compared to those known from classical models (Kugel 1981: 170). To the early church, however, parallelism was a rhetorical figure used as embellishment to beautify speech, not a significant literary phenomenon.

Despite the fact that they did not clearly articulate the phenomenon of parallelism, however, there were those whose work prepared the way for Lowth. One, the Renaissance Jewish scholar Azariah dei Rossi (*ca.* 1511–1578), noticed that Hebrew lines divide into roughly equal halves. Azariah, whose work was known by Lowth, wrote (as quoted by Kugel 1981: 200–201):

> There exist without doubt poetic measures and structures to the Biblical songs,. . . but they are not dependent on the number of complete or incomplete syllabic feet . . . but their structure and measures are in the number of ideas and their parts . . . in every sentence or clause that is written. You must not count the syllables nor yet the words themselves, but the ideas.

Another who prepared the way for Lowth was Christian Schoettgen, who published his ideas in an essay titled "*Der exergasia sacra*" just twenty years before Lowth's *Lectures*. He defined *exergasia* as "the joining together of whole *sententiae* of the same significance" (Kugel 1981: 267). Schoettgen's basic rules for *exergasia* anticipated Lowth's categories. His "Rule I" is an example of the similarity between his work and that of Lowth: "*Exergasia* is perfect when individual members of the two clauses correspond to each other in such a way that there is nothing extra." Compare this to Lowth's explanation of the parallelism of members (1824: xiv):

> The correspondence of one verse, or line, with another, I call parallelism. When a proposition is delivered, and a second is sub-joined to it, or drawn under it, equivalent, or contrasted with it in sense; or similar to it in the form of grammatical construction; these I call parallel lines; and the words and phrases, answering one to another in the corresponding lines, parallel terms.

UNITS IN HEBREW POETRY

Hebrew poetry is made up of lines that divide into at least two, often three, clauses, which together are called a *colon* (plural = *cola*). A *colon* is thus a single line of poetry. A unit that is composed of two *cola* is called a *bicolon;* a three-*cola* unit is called a *tricolon.* An example of a *bicolon* can be seen in Ps 46:1:

> God is our refuge and strength,   *colon* ⌉
>   ⌉ *bicolon*
> a very present help in trouble.   *colon* ⌋

Ps 24:7 is a *tricolon*:

> Lift up your heads, O gates!   *colon* ⌉
> and be lifted up, O ancient doors!   *colon* ⌉ *tricolon*
> that the King of glory may come in.   *colon* ⌋

Some scholars, in speaking of a *colon,* prefer the term *stich* (pronounced "stick," from the Greek word *stichos*). The *bicolon* is called a *distich* (sometimes spelled *dystich*) and the *tricolon* a *tristich.*

The division of the lines of Hebrew poetry into "members" or clauses can be represented schematically in the following manner, where / represents a brief pause and // represents a full stop (Gottwald 1985: 522):

$$A \underline{\qquad\qquad} / + B \underline{\qquad\qquad} //$$

or, sometimes

$$A \underline{\qquad\qquad} / + B \underline{\qquad\qquad} / + C \underline{\qquad\qquad} //.$$

KINDS OF PARALLELISM

Synonymous Parallelism.   Having noted that the units in Hebrew poetry are usually divided into two, sometimes three lines that are in a parallel relationship with one another, Lowth described three kinds of parallelism: synonymous, antithetic, and synthetic. In synonymous parallelism the second *colon* of the *bicolon* echoes or repeats the idea of the first *colon* in equivalent but different terms. The synonymous parallelism in Psalm 24:1–3, seen schematically looks like (with the parallel elements in the three *bicola* numbered with superscripts and put in italics):

> v. 1 A   The *earth*[1] is the Lord's and *all that is in it*[2] /
>   B   the *world*[1] and *those who live in it*[2]; //
> v. 2 A   for he has *founded*[1] it on the *seas*,[2] /
>   B   and *established*[1] it on the *rivers*[2]. //
> v. 3 A   Who shall *ascend*[1] the *hill of the LORD*?[2] /
>   B   And who shall *stand*[1] in *his holy place*?[2] //

According to C. F. Burney, synonymous parallelism is best exemplified in those instances where the subject, verb, and object of the first line are paralleled in the second (1925: 17). Ps 19:1 is an example of such "perfect" synonymous parallelism (with the parallel elements numbered with superscripts and put in italics):

> The *heavens*[1] are *telling*[2] the *glory*[3] of *God*[4];
> and the *firmament*[1] *proclaims*[2] his[4] *handiwork*[5].

Antithetic Parallelism.   In antithetic parallelism, Lowth saw two *cola* related to one another by opposition. The first *colon* of the *bicola* expresses a thought, and the second *colon* is stated as a contrast to the first. The second *colon* could be thought of as introduced with the conjunction "but" or "however." The antithesis can be precise or general. This form is especially frequent in the Wisdom literature, which we shall examine in Chapter 15, but is also represented often in the Psalms. Ps 20:8 contains a *bicolon* that is an example of antithetic parallelism:

A   *They*[1] *will collapse and fall*[2], /
B   but *we*[1] *shall rise and stand upright*[2]. //

Synthetic Parallelism.   In many cases the precise relationship between the two (or three) *cola* is not easily discerned. The parallelism involved is not so much of ideas, but of form. There often seems to be a grammatical break between the *cola,* but the relationship between them is neither synonymous nor antithetic. Lowth called this third form of parallelism "synthetic," although often there is no really clear parallelism. In some cases, the second (and sometimes third) *cola* expands on the first by supplementing or completing its thought (Burney 21). The first *cola* states a thought, the second adds another, and the third (if present) completes the statement. This is the most inexact of Lowth's categories and has received the most criticism. Some have seen it as a kind of catchall category, while others do not see it as a legitimate form of parallelism at all. Ps 40:1–3 is an example of synthetic parallelism:

> I waited patiently for the LORD;
> he inclined to me and heard my cry.
> He drew me up from the desolate pit,
> out of the miry bog,
> and set my feet upon a rock,
> making my steps secure.
> He put a new song in my mouth,
> a song of praise to our God.
> Many will see and fear,
> and put their trust in the LORD.

PARALLELISM IN RECENT SCHOLARSHIP

Parallelism is *the* characteristic feature of biblical Hebrew poetry. This was the premise that resulted from Lowth's work. But can this statement still be made with conviction, given developments in contemporary linguistic and literary theory as they have been applied to Hebrew poetry since the 1980s? Although many scholars have finely tuned Lowth's three types and added others to them, Kugel's book, *The Idea of Biblical Poetry* (1981), was the first original comprehensive discussion of parallelism that took contemporary literary and linguistic theory into account. Under the title: "The parallelistic line: A is so, and what's more, B" he states his hypothesis:

> The basic feature of Biblical songs—and, for that matter, of most of the sayings, proverbs, laws, laments, blessings, curses, prayers, and speeches found in the Bible—is the recurrent use of a relatively short sentence-form that consists of two brief clauses.
>
> . . . The clauses are regularly separated by a slight pause—slight because the second is . . . a continuation of the first and not a wholly new beginning. By contrast, the second ends in a full pause. (1981: 51)

Kugel discusses various kinds of parallelism and then asks and provides an answer to the crucial question (1981: 51):

> What is the essence of biblical parallelism? What this means is simply: B, by being connected to A—carrying it further, echoing it, defining it, restating it, contrasting it with, *it does not matter which*—has an emphatic 'seconding' character, and it is this, more than any aesthetic of symmetry or paralleling, which is at the heart of biblical parallelism.

Kugel sees the nature of biblical poetry essentially as follows (1981: 57):

- the way in which B contributes to the satisfying closure of the parallelistic line;
- the function of parallelism is to "establish the connection between parallelistic lines and not-so-very-parallelistic lines, encountered both in books like the Psalter and in the Pentateuch and Prophets;" and that
- parallelism characterizes the vast majority of lines in the Psalter and other poetic books of the Bible.

For Kugel absolute symmetry does not need to be demonstrated, nor is it even practically attainable, but just the existence of a pattern needs to be shown. In a similar vein, Robert Alter has spoken of the "consequentiality" of parallel lines (1985). Like Kugel's, Alter's work emphasizes that in synonymous parallelism the two lines are not simply repeating the same thing. The second line of the parallelism leads in some way beyond the first.

OTHER FEATURES OF HEBREW POETRY

While the key feature of Hebrew poetry in the Bible is parallelism, biblical poetry also has other characteristics, many of which are lost in translation. For example, only occasionally does rhyme or near-rhyme appear in Hebrew. Instead, other techniques that are based on the sound of words are used. These include assonance, words that have similar vowel sounds; paronomosia, or plays on words; and onomatopoeia, where words sound like what they describe.

Meter.   In a 1984 addendum to his 1981 book on biblical poetry, James Kugel outlined four areas of research that need more attention with regard to biblical style. One of these was the role of meter in the definition of Hebrew poetry (1984). It is important to distinguish between meter and rhythm. Meter is the almost mathematical pattern in terms of which an accented syllable is grouped with one or more unaccented syllables. Rhythm is a regular pattern of accented syllables. In order to determine the meter of a poem, we need to be able to distinguish the accented syllables in a word or word group from unaccented parts. Because we really do not know how ancient Hebrew was spoken—the vowels of the Hebrew text date back no earlier than the early Middle Ages, the exact reading of the original consonantal text is sometimes a matter of conjecture—meter is difficult to determine with certainty. Several systems have been proposed for determining meter, none of which seem to work consistently for all Hebrew poetry. According to Douglas Stuart (1976), four main schools of thought exist concerning meter in Hebrew poetry:

1. **The traditional school** This school is represented by Julius Ley, who in 1866 first asserted that the word forms the chief unit upon which Hebrew meter is based. This school argued that Hebrew meter is determined by counting the number of accented syllables.

2. **The semantic parallelism school** This school, represented by Lowth, suggested that the determining factor in Hebrew meter is found in the parallelism of semantic units rather than in phonetic phenomena. A counter argument to this school is that semantic parallelism is an element of style, not meter.

3. **The alternating meter school** Represented by the Scandanavian scholar, Sigmund Mowinckel, as well as others, this school sees Hebrew poetry as characterized by a regular alternation of accented and unaccented syllables. In most cases, this school relied on the vowels supplied by the Masoretic text.

4. **The syllabic school** P. Haupt, a German scholar whose work was published in the first decade of the twentieth century, and W. F. Albright, the American biblical scholar and archaeologist, are representatives of this approach, which is closely related to the traditional school. The syllabic school bases its approach on a syllabic scansion of the text and does not rely on the Masoretic text. Scansion is a technical term meaning "to determine the poetic rhythm of." This method identifies *cola* according to precise numbers of syllables.

For practical reasons based on limitations of space, we shall illustrate here the traditional method of metrical analysis that counts the number of accented syllables a line contains.

Because parallelism and meter are closely linked, a common metric pattern (4 + 4) involves four accented syllables in each line. An example of this can be seen in Ps 46:2. We have transcribed the two lines of this verse from the Hebrew, indicating in boldface letters where the four accents fall in each line:

> 'elo**him** la**nu** maga**se** wa**oz** (4 accented syllables)
> '**ezra** betsa**rot** nim**tsa** me**od** (4 accented syllables)

Another common meter is 3 + 3, and an early 2 + 2 meter is evident in the Song of Miriam (Ex 15:21). An irregular, "limping" meter of 3 + 2, called the *qinah* meter (*qinah* is a Hebrew word meaning "lament") indicates sadness, such as in the book of Lamentations. The imbalance in the two lines of the *qinah* captures the tension of extreme emotion, usually grief, but sometimes joy (see Ps 65). While the meter usually is lost in translation, Lamentations 2:11a is a good example of it (we have approximated the Hebrew accents in English translation):

> My eyés are spént with weéping;
> my stómach chúrns.

When there are three lines in the poetic unit, a 3+3+3 meter is common (see Ps 111:9-10). Since metrical irregularities are acceptable in the rhythmic patterns of Hebrew poetry, it is not unusual to see several different meters in one poem.

Strophes. Larger verse units of Hebrew poetry group themselves into units called *strophes* (from the Greek word for "turning.") Ordinarily, they are not of equal length in a poem. Though the strophic structure of many poems in the Hebrew Bible is elusive—Hebrew poetry is characterized by parallelism of thought, not by rhyme or metrical regularity—there are features that have been used to indicate strophes. A few include: the use of a recurring refrain (Ps 42-43), changes of grammatical person, the use of key words, and recourse to an acrostic pattern in which each strophe begins with a successive letter of the alphabet (Ps 119).

SACRED AND SOCIAL ASPECTS OF THE PSALMS: FORM CRITICISM

The Beginnings of Form Criticism

Probably no single aspect of the study of the book of Psalms has received more attention from scholars in recent years than the issue of genre. The pioneer studies in this area were done in the early twentieth century by the German pioneer of form criticism, Hermann Gunkel (1967). Gunkel's academic career spanned the years from 1888 to 1927. He observed five predominant literary forms in the book of Psalms and a variety of mixed types. Gunkel said that about one hundred psalms (out of one hundred fifty) fit one of the five major classifications. He placed the rest of the psalms into one of five minor classes. Gunkel's successors refined the categories. In particular, Sigmund Mowinckel built on Gunkel's work in his major work on the Psalms published in 1951. Mowinckel maintained that not only did the genres in the Psalms have their *Sitz im Leben* ("setting in life") in Israel's liturgical activity, but that most of the psalms were originally composed for and used in such a setting. In no other area of biblical literature is genre so pronounced. The five predominant types identified by Gunkel were:

1. Hymns or Songs of Praise,
2. Individual Laments or Songs of Supplication,
3. Individual Thanksgiving Songs,
4. Communal Laments,
5. Royal Psalms.

Recent Refinements of Form Criticism

While Gunkel's work has stood the test of time better than that of his contemporary, Wellhausen, recent literary criticism of the Psalms has pointed out some ways in which the form critics misconceived the phenomenon of genre in psalms (Alter 1987: 246–247). Gunkel, who was concerned with the issues of dating and development, assumed that one could plot the evolution from simple early versions of a particular genre in psalms to later, complex versions. Such evolutionist notions have been generally rejected by subsequent scholarship. Gunkel's determination to reveal the *Sitz im Leben* of particular psalms has, however, proved to be of continuing interest.

It is obvious, from even a casual reading, that some of the psalms were intended for very specific liturgical or cultic occasions. But, speaking of some form critics' work, Alter (1987: 247) has suggested that there is a good deal of misplaced concreteness in the energy expended by scholars to discover in psalm after psalm the libretto to some unknown cultic music-drama. In fact it is hardly self-evident that all the psalms were used liturgically.

The most pervasive form-critical misconception about genre in the study of psalms is the notion that genre is a fixed entity. Evidence from literary history suggests that writers juggle and transform genres. Again Alter observes that we are more likely to perceive the poetic richness of psalms if we realize that a good deal of such transformation of genres exists in the collection, even when the recurrence of certain formulas suggest that a particular generic background is involved (Alter 1987: 247).

Sociological Criticism and the Psalms

Because we cannot assume that all of the psalms were either written for or had their setting in life in public worship, what more can be said about their social setting? One of the five genres of Gunkel is the Individual Lament, a genre that comprises almost a third of the psalms, according to Gottwald's analysis (1985: 528). Various causes of distress appear in psalms of this genre: physical illness, psychological torment, and/or socioeconomic oppression. Why do we have so many examples of this genre in the Psalter?

In our survey of the eighth-century prophets in Chapter 11 we discovered that the monarchy, in collusion with the upper classes had caused widespread systemic poverty among the peasant farmers. The prophets' message, however, rested on egalitarian ideals. These ideals, expressed in Israel's covenant and laws, espoused guaranteed access to resources and means of production. Land was to stay within lineages and permanent slavery was prohibited. All of this became increasingly threatened under the monarchy. The state extracted much of the farmer's produce in taxation. Ancestral property was lost by failure to pay debts or government confiscation. Land use patterns changed, with more and more land in large estates given over to the production of wine and olive oil for export instead of subsistence agriculture for the support of the local population. While the prophets voiced the concerns of the poor and dispossessed, this social situation may also provide the background for the voices heard in the Individual Laments in the Psalter, most of which are later than the eighth century B.C.E. Some interpretations of this genre of psalms have individualized them, pointing out the psychological aspects of the suffering that surfaced in them. These interpretations often have failed to point out the larger socioeconomic context that was so often the source of the suffering. They have focused on the symptoms rather than the illness. Attention to the social setting of these psalms provides an important perspective for our understanding of them. The work of the Nicaraguan poet Ernesto Cardenal applies such a perspective to the psalms by paraphrasing them and using situations from contemporary Central America. One of Cardenal's paraphrases is of Psalm 22, an individual lament (1971: 35 – 36):

My God my God why have you abandoned me?
I am only a mockery of a man
   a disgrace to the people
They ridicule me in all their newspapers
Armored tanks surround me
I am at machine gun point
encircled by barbed wire
   by electrified barbed wire
All day long they call my name from the rolls
They tattooed a number on me
They have photographed me among the barbed wire
all of my bones can be counted as in an X-ray
They have stripped me of all identity
They have brought me naked to the gas chamber
and divided among them my clothes and my shoes
I cry out begging for morphine and no one hears
I cry out in the straightjacket
I cry out all night in the asylum of mad men
in the ward of terminal patients
in the quarantine of the contagiously sick
in the halls of the old people's home
I squirm in my own sweat in the psychiatric clinic
I suffocate in the oxygen tent
I weep in the police station
in the army stockade
   in the torture chamber
     in the orphanage
I am contaminated with radioactivity
   and fearing infection no one comes near me
Yet will I speak of you to my brothers
I will praise you in the meetings of our people
My hymns will resound in the midst of this great people
The poor will sit down to banquet
Our people will celebrate a great feast
This new generation soon to be born."

PSALM TYPES

Hymns or Songs of Praise

The title of the book of Psalms in Hebrew is *Tehillim,* "Praises." This noun comes from a verb that occurs often in the book of Psalms, *hallel,* "to praise," which we know best in the expression "Hallelujah!" ("Praise Yah[weh]"). The title given to the book of Psalms is fitting in that it includes many examples of the genre that Gunkel called "Hymns" or "Songs of Praise." Gottwald (1985: 529) includes the following psalms in this genre: 8; 19:1-6; 29; 33; 95:1-7c; 100; 103; 104; 111; 113; 114; 117; 135; 145; 146-149; 150.

Many of these songs begin and end with a call for the people to praise God. Following this invitation are the reasons for praising God, which may include God's deeds in the history of Israel (78; 105; 106) and/or as Creator of the natural world (8; 19:1-6; 104; 148). The basic structure of the Hymn or Song of Praise shows clearly in Ps 117, the shortest psalm in the Psalter:

A.   v. 1   **Introduction: Call to Worship**
Praise the LORD, all you nations!
Extol him, all you peoples!

B.   v. 2   **Body: Reasons for Worshiping**
For great is his steadfast love toward us,
and the faithfulness of the LORD endures forever.

C.   v. 3   **Conclusion: Call to Worship Repeated**
Praise the LORD!

In some Songs of Praise in the Psalter one will observe many of the major themes that we have seen in our journey through the Hebrew Bible repeated as the basis for Israel's praise: the Exodus, the deliverance at the Sea of Reeds, the wilderness wandering, and the settlement in the promised land. These are made a separate category and called Psalms of (Salvation) History by Kraus (1960) and include Ps 78; 106; and 136. In other psalms of this type, however, the motivation for praising God the Creator does not derive from events in Israel's history, but they praise God because he is the Creator of an ordered and dependable created order. Psalm 8, for example, begins with the exclamation: "O LORD, our Sovereign, how majestic is your name in all the earth!" In the body of the psalm God is praised as the Creator of the heavens and human beings, who were given dominion over the rest of creation. This psalm ends with the same phrase with which it began: "O LORD, our Sovereign, how majestic is your name in all the earth!"

Another important example of a Song of Praise that celebrates Yahweh as Creator is Psalm 104. This psalm has a close parallel in the Egyptian "Hymn to Aton," which also has elements resembling those found in other psalms praising God in nature. This Egyptian poem was found inscribed on the wall of the tomb Pharaoh Akhenaton (1365-1348 B.C.E.) built for Queen Nefertiti's father at Tell el-Amarna. The "Hymn to Aton" celebrates Aton, the god represented by the

Figure 13.1 Bas-relief of Akhenaton worshiping Aton

sun disc. Akhenaton in his religious reform emphasized the exclusive worship of Aton (see Figure 13.1).

In reading the "Hymn to Aton" notice the female imagery (which we have put in italics) applied to Aton, who is likened to a caring midwife (Matthews and Benjamin 1991: 154–156):

As you rise over the horizon, O Aton, First Among the Gods
  Your beauty is made manifest, O Giver of Life.
You rise in the east
  You fill every land with beauty.
Your glory shines high above every land,
  Your rays enrich all the lands you created.
O Ra [another of the sun gods in Egypt], you reach to the ends of the earth,
  You bestow them on Akhenaton, your beloved son.

Although you are far away,
    Your rays touch the earth.
Although you shine on every face,
    No one sees you go.
When you set upon the western horizon,
    The earth lies in darkness and death.
Sleepers lie beneath their covers,
    Seeing no one around them.
Their pillows could vanish,
    They would not even notice.
The lion leaves his cave,
    The serpent strikes,
    The darkness blankets the land [compare Ps 104:20–21].
The lands lie silent,
    He who made them rests on the horizon.
At daybreak, you rise again over the horizon,
    You shine as The Aton bringing day.
Your rays chase away the darkness,
    The Two Lands of Egypt [Upper and Lower] rejoice [compare Ps 104:22–23]!
Awake and erect,
    You raise them up.
Bathed and dressed,
    They raise their hands in praise.
The whole land goes to work . . . ,
Cattle graze contented,
    Trees and plants turn green.
Birds fly to their nests [see Ps 104:11–14],
    They spread their wings to praise your Ka [something like one's 'vital energy'].
All things come to life,
    When you have risen.
Ships and barges sail up and down,
    Canals open at your rising,
Fish swim the river. (compare Ps 104:25–26)
    Your rays penetrate even dark waters.
O Lord, our Lord, how majestic is your name (see Ps 8:1),
    You join a woman and a man,
You form the fetus in its mother's womb (compare Ps 139:13),
    You soothe the crying child unborn,
You nurse the hungry infant in the womb,
    You breathe into its nostrils the breath of life (see Gen 2:7).
You open the newborn's mouth on the day of its birth
    You meet every human need. . . .

In Khor [Syria-Palestine], Kush and Egypt,
    You assign each a place.

You allot to each both needs and food,
    You count out to each the days of life [see Ps 104:27]. . . .

You made the heavens in which to rise,
    That you might observe all things.
You alone are The Aton [compare Ps 104:24],
    Yet you alone rise—The Source of Life.
You alone are so far away,
    . . . and yet so near.
Your manifestations are numberless
    You are The Aton, The Source of Life.
Every town, harbor, field, road and river sees your light,
    . . . feels your warmth.
You are The Aton,
    You are The Daylight of The Earth.
. . . You are my desire,
    No one knows you except Akhenaton, your son.
You have revealed yourself to me,
    You have shown me your plans and your power.
Your hand made The Earth,
    You created it.
When you rise,
    The Earth lives.
When you set,
    The Earth dies [see Ps 104:29–30].
You are Life itself,
    All live through you.
Every eye sees clearly until you set,
    All work must wait until you rise again.
At your rising, every arm works for The Pharaoh,
    At your creation, every foot sets off to work.
You rise up the people for the son of your body,
    . . . for The Pharaoh of Upper and Lower Egypt,
Who rules with the spirit of Maat, The God of Truth,
    . . . Akhenaton and her royal highness, Nefertiti.

Individual Laments or Songs of Supplication

As we have noted, this psalm type outnumbers all other types in the Psalter. Included in this type are the following psalms: 3; 5-7; 13; 17; 22; 25-28; 35; 38-39; 41-43; 51; 54-57; 59; 61; 63-64; 69-71; 86; 88; 102; 109; 120; 130; 140-143 (Kraus). As mentioned above, these psalms deal with problems faced by individuals. They have a characteristic structure, but with some variations (Westermann 1965: 52-81):

A. **Invocation:** a brief cry to God or an expression of praise,

B. **Complaint:** the reasons for the individual's appeal to God,

C. **Confession:** an articulation of the individual's trust in God,

D. **Petition:** the appeal for God's remedial intervention,

E. **Vow:** confident of God's response, the individual promises to testify to God's saving work before the community.

Some of these song types (for example, Ps 51) have superscriptions that relate them to particular crises in the life of David, although the association with David is uncertain. The superscription to Psalm 51 reads: "*A Psalm of David, when the prophet Nathan came to him, after he had gone in to Bathsheba.*" Usually, however, the complaint is couched in more general terms, making the identification of any particular individual difficult. Psalm 22, Cardenal's paraphrase of which was quoted above, is a particularly interesting example of this psalm type due to its association with one of the traditional "seven last words" of Jesus from the cross. Both Matthew (27:46) and Mark (15:34) have Jesus quoting the first part of the first verse of this Psalm, "My God, my God, why have you forsaken me?," which is misunderstood by the bystanders and subsequent interpreters. Matthew reports Jesus' words (in Aramaic) as: "Eli, Eli, lema sabachthani?" The word *'elî* in Aramaic means "my God." It could also sound like the nickname for Elijah (*'elîyahu* = "My God is Yah[weh]"). Interpreters, isolating the first line of the psalm from the rest of the psalm and ignoring the significance of the psalm type, have often understood Jesus' cry from the cross as a cry of dereliction, one lamenting the fact that God had deserted him. This psalm type, however, only begins with such a cry of desperation. In Psalm 22 the anonymous individual goes on to recall God's intercession for those in need (22:3-5) and God's help in former times (22:9-11). The psalm includes a vivid account of the individual's plight, including the detail, "They divide my clothes among themselves, and for my clothing they cast lots" (22:18), which is reproduced in the story of Jesus on the cross. Psalm 22 concludes with the individual making a vow. He pledges that once delivered, he will offer a formal thanksgiving "in the midst of the congregation at the temple" (22:22). The last verses (23-31) are the hymn of praise that the individual will sing after his recovery.

Individual Thanksgiving Songs

According to Gottwald (1985: 530), there are nine Individual Thanksgiving Songs in the Psalter (30; 32; 34; 41; 52; 66; 92; 116; 138) that provide a counterpart to the Individual Laments. Like the Individual Lament, the Individual Thanksgiving Song has its own structure that is subject to variation. This simple structure can be seen in Ps 116, which is a thanksgiving for healing:

Ps 116:1-2   A. **Introduction:** the individual addresses the congregation, citing the reason for his thanksgiving.

Ps 116:3-9   B. **Body:** the experience of the individual, here a serious illness.

Ps 116:10-19   C.   **Conclusion:** the individual expresses trust in God and makes a vow to offer public testimony and to make a libation offering, that is, an offering of something that is poured out.

The verb *yadah* occurs often in these psalms and is translated in several ways in the NRSV: 30:4, "give thanks"; 30:9, "praise"; 32:5, "confess." Westermann has argued that the verb *yadah* should be translated "praise" rather than "thank," and on that basis classifies these psalms as "narrative praise of the individual" (1981: 25-30). Although these songs are labeled *Individual* Thanksgiving Songs, this does not mean that they were necessarily recited in isolation. There are indications that individuals recited these songs before a group of relatives and/or friends in a shrine or the Jerusalem temple. There is a song of this type inserted into the book of Jonah (2:1-9). There it serves to express Jonah's thanks for his being saved through the agency of the fish that swallowed him after he had been thrown overboard and later deposited him on dry ground.

Communal Laments

Communal Laments reflect times of national crisis. They include the following psalms: 60; 74; 79-80; 83; 85; 89-90; 137 (Kraus). The structure of this genre closely resembles that of the Individual Lament. This genre is sometimes, however, more specific about the problem that provides the occasion for the lament. Anderson has suggested that "lament" may not be the best description of this literary form if it is equated with a lamentation (1986: 552). There is a difference between a lamentation and a lament, according to form critics. A lamentation or dirge is suitable in a situation that cannot be changed (the death of someone or the destruction of a city). A lament presupposes that a situation of distress can be changed if and when Yahweh intervenes. As Anderson (552) observes: "The surprising thing is that psalms of this type display so little whining self-pity or vindictive bitterness and that the praise of Yahweh reverberates through human sorrows."

Royal Psalms

Gunkel's fifth major type in the Psalter was the Royal Psalm. Strictly speaking, this category does not constitute a special genre. Instead it is a topical category, bringing together those psalms that are associated with an event in the life of the king. Included in this type are the following psalms: 2; 18; 20-21; 45; 72; 89; 101; 110; 132; and 144:1-11 (Limburg 1992: 533). Psalm 2 was intended for a king's coronation, a time when Israel's subject peoples might plot a rebellion against the new king (2:1-3). Psalm 18, which is also found with minor variations in 2 Sam 22, is an Individual Thanksgiving Song intended to be recited by the king in gratitude for victory in battle. Psalm 20 is a prayer for the king's victory in battle, which may have been intended to accompany a sacrifice offered before the battle (20:3). Like Psalm 18, Psalm 21 is an Individual

Thanksgiving Song sung after the king's victory in battle. It is intentionally paired with Psalm 20. Psalm 45 is a marriage song for a royal wedding. Psalm 72 is a prayer for God's blessing on the king, at the time of his coronation or at its annual commemoration. Psalm 89 is a prayer for the king's deliverance from his enemies. In Psalm 101 a king pledges to rule justly, perhaps in the context of a coronation ceremony. Psalm 110 again fits a coronation setting. Psalm 132 is a liturgy commemorating God's choice of Jerusalem and of the Davidic line. In Psalm 144:1-11 a king prays for deliverance from his enemies. Obviously, because they do not really form a single literary genre but a topical category, the Royal Psalms include many structural variations.

Other Types of Psalms

Besides Gunkel's five basic categories there are several minor categories in the Psalter, and mixed types. Gunkel himself had five subclasses:

1. Songs of Pilgrimage (for example, Ps 84; 122),
2. Community Songs of Thanksgiving (for example, Ps 67; 124),
3. Wisdom Poetry (for example, Ps 1; 8; 37; 73; 127),
4. Two Types of Liturgies: Torah (Ps 15; 24; 121; 134) and Prophetic (Ps 12; 53; 75; 91; 95),
5. Mixed (Ps 9; 10; 36; 94).

SACRIFICES AND SONGS: RITUAL AND CELEBRATION IN THE PSALMS

Increasingly, scholars in the twentieth century have come to see the religion of the book of Psalms as "cultic"—that is, the origin and purpose of the psalms are to be found in the context of the communal worship of ancient Israel. This theory has replaced an earlier "historicizing" tendency to search for the rootage of individual psalms in specific historical events, a tendency reflected in the superscriptions attached to some psalms.

Organization of the Book of Psalms

At the beginning of this chapter we said that the book of Psalms is an anthology of 150 poems. This collection of songs achieved its present form sometime in the postexilic period, so it can be called "the hymnal of the second Temple." The collection developed over time around a fivefold division, echoing the five books of the Torah. The five divisions or "books," each of which ends with a doxology, are as follows:

Book 1:   Psalms 1-41: A collection in which the divine name Yahweh is preferred and which is assigned to David. (Concluding doxology = Ps 41:13)

Book 2:   Psalms 42-72: A collection that includes Psalms 42-49, which are associated with the "Sons of Korah" (a musical guild). This "book" has been called the "Elohistic Psalter," since it uses Elohim as the divine name. (Concluding doxology = Ps 72:18-19)

Book 3:   Psalms 73-89: A short collection that includes most of the Community Laments. In their titles, Psalms 73-83 are associated with Asaph, a musician from the tribe of Levi, who was appointed by David to provide music when he brought the Ark of the Covenant up to Jerusalem (compare 1 Chr 6:39; 15:17-19; 16:4-6). Asaph's family remained active in music in the time of Josiah (2 Chr 35:15) and even into the postexilic period (Neh 12:35; Ezra 3:10). (Concluding doxology = Ps 89:52)

Book 4:   Psalms 90-106: Another short collection that includes six of the seven Psalms extolling Yahweh's kingship. (Concluding doxology = Ps 106:48)

Book 5:   Psalms 107-150: The largest of the collections. It has Psalms attributed to David at its beginning (108-110) and toward its end (138-145). Also included in this section is a subcollection of "Songs of Ascent" or "Pilgrimage Psalms" (120-134) and a series of Individual Laments (140-143). (Concluding doxology = Ps 150, also a concluding doxology for the entire book of Psalms)

BOOK 1: "DAVIDIC" PSALMS

That there are several stages behind this collection of five "books" is evident from the note that follows the doxology concluding book 1: "The prayers of David son of Jesse are ended." This suggests that at one stage these "Davidic" psalms formed a separate collection. Most of the psalms in book 1 have the Hebrew word *leDavid* prefixed to them. This word can mean "for David," "to David," or "belonging to David." This label does not necessarily mean that the psalms bearing that label were written by David. By the first century C.E., it was believed that David was the composer of some psalms, as is evident, for example, in the quotation of Ps 110:1 in the New Testament (Mark 12:36; see also Matt 22:44; Acts 2:34):

> David himself, by the Holy Spirit, declared,
> "The LORD said to my LORD,
> 'Sit at my right hand,
> until I put your enemies under your feet.'"

Psalms were associated with David at an early stage. This may mean that David had some role in collecting them as a royal patron or that they were seen as part of a "royal collection." Other smaller collections that preceded the larger ones and were subsequently incorporated into them are suggested by subgroups in the five "books," such as those associated with the "Sons of Korah" (42–49), Asaph (73–83), and the "Songs of Ascent" (120–134).

THE RELATIONSHIP OF BOOK 1 TO BOOK 2

Another piece of evidence that points to the existence of earlier, smaller collections is the repetition of psalms across the lines of the "books." There are two examples that cut across the lines of books 1 and 2. Psalm 14 (from book 1) is almost identical with Ps 53 (from book 2). Psalm 40:13–17 (book 1) corresponds to Psalm 70 (book 2). The only significant difference is that Psalm 14 and Psalm 40:13–17 use Yahweh as the divine name while Psalms 53 and 70 use Elohim. As in the Pentateuch, this may reflect regional collections, with book 1 being a southern collection and book 2 being a northern one.

SUBCOLLECTIONS OF PSALMS AND INDIVIDUAL PSALMS USED IN WORSHIP

While one can discern clues of earlier collections behind the present book of Psalms, it is also important to look into the origins and use of individual psalms included in the collections. Why were these particular songs remembered and saved? As implied above, the answer to this question lies, in large part, in their use in the worship life of ancient Israel, the details of which are beyond recovery. There are, however, clues here and there. We know, for example, from later Jewish liturgical tradition that the psalms in the so-called "Egyptian Hallel," Ps 113–118, were used in connection with the celebration of the Passover festival. Ps 113–114 were sung before the meal and 115–118 were sung afterwards (see Mt 26:30, which reflects first-century C.E. practice). Some interesting notes here and there in the book of Psalms point to the use of psalms in public worship. In the superscription to Ps 4, 6, 54, 55, 61, 67, and 76, there is the note "To the leader: with stringed instruments." Similarly, Ps 8, 81, and 84 have prefixed to them the note "To the leader: according to the Gittith," which is probably the name of a tune. Because the Psalter is not a manual providing directions for worship leaders but a collection of songs for the people's use, the settings for individual psalms in worship and/or elsewhere must be inferred from the psalms themselves (Limburg 1992: 524–525).

The Hymns or Songs of Praise imply congregational worship involving vocal and instrumental music. This worship could include singing and shouting (33:3), dancing (149:3; 150:4), and the use of a variety of musical instruments (33:1–3; 149:3; 150). Some psalms were used as liturgies, with actions accompanying the words of the psalm. Psalms 48 and 132 were associated with processions; the latter would fit a re-enactment of David's bringing the Ark of the Covenant into Jerusalem (2 Sam 6). Psalms 15 and 24 appear to be entrance liturgies that were sung at the gate of the temple by antiphonal choirs. In Ps 15 the question is: Who can be admitted to the temple for worship? The answer is:

Only those who have the requisite moral qualities. The question would be sung by those outside the gates, and would be answered by those on the inside. Then the gates could be opened and the worshipers admitted. Many attempts have been made to reconstruct liturgies and even entire festivals in some detail, but such reconstructions are only hypothetical.

Zion Psalms.   Psalm 48, mentioned in the previous paragraph as a processional liturgy, and Ps 46 are hymns celebrating the Jerusalem temple. These psalms form part of a complex of traditions in the Psalter (and elsewhere) called the Zion tradition. Although they are not all found in every Hymn of Zion, the following elements are part of the Zion tradition:

- Mount Zion in Jerusalem is regarded as the mountain on which God dwells. Yahweh, who originally was associated with Mount Sinai "moved" to Mount Zion with the construction of the temple. In this connection, note that Yahweh is described as "moving out" of Jerusalem after its destruction in Ezek 10:1-22; 11:22-25. Zion is sometimes symbolically identified with Mount Zaphon, present-day Mount Casius on the border between Syria and Turkey, which was the home of Baal. This identification is made in Ps 48:2-3, translated by Mitchell Dahood (1966: 288) as follows:

> Great is Yahweh,
> and much to be praised.
> In the city of our God
> in his holy mountain;
> The most beautiful peak,
> the joy of all the earth.
> Mount Zion is the heart of Zaphon,
> the city of the Great King.

Although the word *zaphon* in Hebrew can also mean "north," there are three other poetic passages where its ancient Canaanite sense as the name of a specific mountain is preserved: Ps 89:13; Isa 14:13; and Job 26:7.
- Like Zaphon, Mount Zion was viewed as the source of a mythological sacred river that flowed from the temple, freshened the brackish waters of the Dead Sea, and watered the Wilderness of Judah, turning it into a new paradise (Ezek 47:1-2; see also Joel 3:18 and Zech 14:8). The mythological nature of this river, also known in Canaanite and Mesopotamian sources, is evident in that there were no rivers near the Jerusalem temple, only the Spring Gihon in the Kidron Valley.
- The mythological nature of Zion in the Zion Tradition is further reinforced when it is seen as the site at which Yahweh defeated all the powers of the watery chaos, often depicted as sea monsters (Ps 74:14):

> You crushed the heads of Leviathan;
> you gave him as food for the creatures of the wilderness.

■ Because of Yahweh's special presence there, Zion was believed to be inviolable to any earthly enemy. This myth was no doubt reinforced with the "miraculous" delivery of Jerusalem from the siege of Sennacherib in 701 B.C.E. In the mythology of the Zion Tradition, Mount Zion/Jerusalem was to become a world center to which, in the future, all of the nations of the world would come bearing their tribute to Yahweh (Ps 102:12–22).

Pilgrimage Psalms.   The "Songs of Ascent" or "Pilgrimage Psalms" found in book 5 (120–134) probably belonged to a collection of songs used on the occasion of the three major Jerusalem pilgrimage festivals in ancient Israel: Passover, Pentecost, and Booths (Lev 23). These songs are associated with different moments in the pilgrimage. Ps 121 could be sung when the pilgrims set out for Jerusalem, Ps 133 when they arrived, and Ps 134 at a concluding evening worship.

Community Laments.   The Community Laments probably functioned as part of community services of prayer and fasting at times of crisis. While these psalms originated in times of specific community need, their continued use indicates that they were appropriated and adapted for other situations. Gerstenberger (1988) has observed that some psalms were used for gatherings of family and friends on special occasions. These occasions would include not only the rites of passage at birth, marriage, and death, but other events as well. He suggests that the community laments were used for "group therapy" in moments of crisis, under the direction of a ritual expert. Gerstenberger's work forms a fitting conclusion to our observations about the place of psalms in Israel's worship life. The use of psalms did not belong solely to communal worship in a sanctuary. People's lives were also lived out with family and friends, and the psalms reflect those life settings as well.

Psalm 151

English Bibles include one hundred fifty Psalms, reflecting the fact that some manuscripts of the Hebrew Bible number the psalms in the Psalter from 1 to 150. However, the oldest extant complete Hebrew manuscript of the Bible, Codex Leningradensis (1008 C.E.), on which all current scholarly translations into modern languages are based, includes only one hundred forty-nine psalms, combining Ps 115 and 114. The three oldest Greek manuscripts of the Hebrew Bible, dating to the fourth and fifth centuries C.E., all include Psalm 151. Psalm 151 did not appear in any Hebrew manuscripts of the psalter until the discovery in 1956 of a Psalter manuscript among the Dead Sea Scrolls. The three early Greek manuscripts of the Psalter all include a superscription that says that Psalm 151 is "outside the number . . . ," supposedly of the one hundred fifty psalms of the Hebrew Bible. In Codex Sinaiticus, one of the oldest, best, and most complete manuscripts of the Septuagint, dating to the fourth century C.E., Psalm 151 is included as an integral part of the Psalter, for which there is a subscript that reads "The 151 Psalms of David." The subject of Psalm 151 is David's celebration of his victory over Goliath.

THE SONG OF SONGS AS SECULAR SONG AND SCRIPTURE

As we stated at the beginning of this chapter, the Song of Songs, like Psalms, is an anthology of poems. Unlike Psalms, which consists of sacred songs, Song of Songs is a collection of secular poems "to be read rather than a song to be sung, despite the title (1:1) which gives it the unity of *one* song" (Murphy 1992: 151). But what is the difference between sacred and secular? To the ancient rabbis, the answer was quite simple. A sacred piece of literature, if touched, caused ritual pollution.

In the Mishnah, the oldest postbiblical collection of Jewish laws from *ca.* 200 C.E., it is said that "All the Holy Scriptures render the hands unclean" (Danby 1933: 781, *Yadaim 3, 5*) Why so? As explanation for this rule, the rabbis cited the former custom of storing the heave-offerings (offerings that were set apart from a larger mass and taken up or "heaved," initially for Yahweh and then for the priesthood) with the scrolls. Mice among the heave-offerings sometimes destroyed the scrolls. Therefore it was ruled that the scrolls suffered "second-degree uncleanness." Similarly, any hands that touched the scrolls were considered to suffer the same "second-grade uncleanness" (Danby 1933: 626). The rabbinic debate about which books "defiled the hands" arose concerning another book attributed to Solomon, Ecclesiastes/Qoheleth (which we shall explore in Chapter 15). In the same passage in the Mishnah cited above, Rabbi Judah opened the debate by saying "The Song of Songs renders the hands unclean, but about Ecclesiastes there is dissension." Rabbi Jose disagreed and said "Ecclesiastes does not render the hands unclean." It is worth noting that these comments did not occur in the context of a debate about the canon of scripture, but in a discussion about what does and does not pollute.

The Canonicity of the Song of Songs

The matter of the Song of Songs' place in the Bible has been and continues to be the subject of considerable debate and speculation. Its poetry is not only secular, but uses explicit sexual language and imagery. This unrestrained talk of sex in the Bible, which usually regards sexuality, especially female sexuality, as requiring careful regulation, is quite surprising. Another distinct feature sets this book apart from its biblical context: like Esther, Song of Songs never makes any direct reference to God. A third characteristic of Song of Songs makes it unique among the books of the Hebrew Bible. The protagonist is the only unmediated female voice in scripture, and Song of Songs is the only biblical book probably spoken more by women than by men. According to the indication of speakers in the poems themselves, 53 percent of the text is spoken by females, as opposed to 34 percent uttered by males (Brenner 1985: 47–49). In the remaining 13 percent there is no indication of gender. Renita Weems says that the voice and thoughts of the anonymous woman are conveyed to the reader not through a narrator's voice, as is the case in Esther and Ruth, but through monologues, soliloquies, and love songs. Nowhere else in scripture do the thought, imaginations, yearnings, and words of a woman predominate in a book as in the Song of Songs (1992: 156).

So how did a book that differs in all these ways from other biblical works find its way into the canon of scripture? We should first admit that it is not possible to discern the precise reasons for its inclusion in the canon or when the decision was finally made to include it (Murphy 1992: 150). It is commonly suggested that there were two principal reasons for its canonization: the tradition of Solomonic authorship and the practice of allegorical interpretation of the book. These reasons are not conclusive, however, and apart from them, the evidence for the early acceptance of the Song into the canon, by Jews and Christians alike, is as well attested as any other book in the Bible. As one of the five festival scrolls, books of the Bible that were used on the occasion of the major religious festivals, the Song was read by Jews at the festival of Passover as an allegorical reflection on Yahweh's love for and relation with Israel since the Exodus. Rabbi Aqiba, in the Mishnaic debate referred to above, said in somewhat hyperbolic language: "No man of Israel ever disputed about the Song of Songs, that it did not defile the hands. The whole world is not worth the day on which the Song of Songs was given to Israel, for all the Scriptures are holy, but the Song of Songs is the Holy of Holies."

The Song of Songs: The History of Interpretation

The medieval Jewish commentator, Saadia, in the introduction to his commentary on the Song of Songs said: "Know, my brother, that you will find great differences in interpretation of the Song of Songs. In truth they differ because the Song of Songs resembles locks to which the keys have been lost" (as quoted by Pope 1977: 89). In part because of its explicit sexual imagery, the Song of Songs has had a varied history of interpretation which continues to this day. It is interesting, for example, that some contemporary introductions to the Old Testament that are otherwise comprehensive in their coverage, omit the Song of Songs. Marvin Pope has written: "In proportion to its size, no book of the Bible has . . . had so many divergent interpretations imposed upon its every word" (1977: 89). There are, however, discernible patterns in the history of the interpretation of the Song. Murphy sees its interpretation as having taken two basic directions: allegorical and literal (1992: 154). The modern view, especially since the seventeenth century, sees the Song literally dealing with human sexual love. Before this, however, the common way of understanding the Song grew out of allegorical interpretation, in which it was seen as describing a divine-human spiritual love. In the following, we offer a brief sketch of six ways of approaching the Song.

1. Allegorical or Traditional Early on, the literal meaning of the erotic lyrics was skirted by a Jewish allegorical approach, which maintained that the Song's sexually explicit language was a way of expressing God's mystical love for

Israel. Israel as a people was God's bride. In a similar way, Christian commentators interpreted the Song as celebrating the love between Christ (the bridegroom) and the Church (the bride). Though the Song was probably not written as an allegory, the allegorical method of interpretation, so popular in the Hellenistic period and later, has been prevalent in its interpretation. A turning point away from the traditional view occurred in Judaism with Moses Mendelssohn's translation of the Song in 1788, where a literal sense began to appear (Ginsburg 1970: 58–59).

2. Dramatic Because the poems in the Song are dialogical, two major Greek manuscripts of the book included character headings that indicate different speakers, namely, the bride, the bridegroom, and their companions. Beginning with a simple two-character exchange, some scholars expanded this into an intricate dramatic production involving a beautiful maiden, her shepherd lover to whom she remains faithful, and King Solomon.

3. Cultic In this century there has developed what might be called a cultic or liturgical interpretation of the Song, which sees it as originating in the sacred marriage rite of fertility cults. The lyrics of the song are thought to have originally fulfilled a fertility cult function in the Babylonian Tammuz festival or the Baal cycles of Canaanite mythology. This approach views the bride as a goddess seeking her lost lover, who has descended to the underworld, as Anat looked for Baal. Once re-united, their sexual union restored fertility to the natural world.

4. Wedding Week Since the seventeenth century several scholars have observed the parallels between the language of the Song and Arab wedding songs from modern Syria. Syrian weddings include a week-long celebration. They feature a dance with a sword by the bride on the day before her wedding, during which she recites a poem describing her beauty (compare Song 1:5; 2:1). During the wedding week the couple is enthroned as king and queen, and celebrating includes much feasting and more recitation of poems praising the wife's beauty (see Song 4:1–15; 5:10–16). In the Song, however, only 3:6–11 undeniably depicts a wedding celebration.

5. Literary In the last half of the twentieth century, there has been a trend toward the interpretation of the Song as a collection of beautifully composed love songs. They are not restricted to the love of married persons, for the lovers enjoy one another outside the marriage relationship as well. The poems are independent of one another, but have been brought together based on refrains, themes, and catchwords. For example, the same refrain appears at three points in the book—Song 2:7; 3:5: 8:4:

> I adjure you, O daughters of Jerusalem,
> by the gazelles or the wild does:
> Do not stir up or awaken love until it is ready.

The literary approach also recognizes parallels between poems in the Song of Songs and Egyptian love songs from the eighteenth through the twentieth dynasties (1570–1197 B.C.E.). The following excerpts are taken from an Egyptian anthology dated to 1314 B.C.E. that consisted of seventeen love songs. The

Figure 13.2   "Lovers" by Glynis Sweeny

translation and the notations of specific parallels to the Song of Songs are from
Matthews and Benjamin (1991: 227-231):

Her song:

. . . I am still here with you,
But you are no longer here with me.
  Why have you stopped holding me?
Has my deed come back upon me?
  . . . the amusement.
If you seek to caress my thighs . . . .
Would you leave me to get something to eat?
  Are you that much a slave to your belly?
Would you leave me to look for something to wear?
  And leave me holding the sheet?
If you are thinking about something to eat,
  Then feast on my breasts, make my milk flow for you.

Better a day in the embrace of my lover . . .
  Than thousands of days elsewhere . . . .

  Her song:

Mix your body with mine,
  Like . . .
  Like honey mixes with water,
  Like mandrake mixes with gum,
  Like dough mixes . . .
Come to your lover,
  Like a horse charging onto the field of battle,
  Like a falcon swooping toward the marsh . . . .

  His song:

My lover is a marsh lush with growth . . .
Her mouth is a lotus bud,
  Her breasts are mandrake blossoms (Song 7:13–14),
Her arms are vines,
  Her eyes are shaded like berries,
Her head is a trap built from branches . . .
  . . . and I am the goose!
Her hair is the bait in the trap . . .
  . . . to ensnare me. 453

(Song 7:5)

  Her song:

My cup is still not full from making love with you,
  —my little wolf, you intoxicate me (Song 4:10).
I will not stop drinking your love (Song 5:1),
  Even if they batter me with sticks into the marsh,
Even if they beat me into Syria,
  Even if they flog me with palm branches into Nubia,
Even if they scourge me with switches into the hills,
  Even if they whip me with rushes into the plains
I will not take their advice,
  I will not abandon the one I desire!

  His song:

I am sailing north with the current,
  Pulling the oar to the captain's command.
My bed is ready for a lover,
  I am headed for a holiday at Memphis.

I will pray to Ptah, the Lord of Truth,
    That a lover will sleep with me tonight!
The Nile makes me drunk with love (Song 2:10–13),
    I see Ptah in the reeds,
Sekhmet in the lotus leaves,
    Yadit in the lotus buds,
Nefertem in the lotus blossoms . . .
Just thinking of a woman lightens my load,
Memphis is a jar of sweet mandrake,
    Set before Ptah the gracious. (Song 7:13)

    His song:

I will lie down inside my house,
    I will pretend to be sick (Song 5:8),
Then my neighbors will come in to see,
    And my lover will come with them.
She will put the doctors to shame,
    She knows how to cure my illness. (Song 2:5)

    His song:

My lover is the lady of a great house,
    Whose entrance is right in the middle!
Both doors are left wide open,
    The bolt is unfastened (Song 5:2–6).
And my lover is furious!
If she hired me as her doorman,
    At least when I made her angry,
I would get to hear her voice,
    Even as I tremble like a child.

    Her song:

I am sailing north,
    On the Canal of Pharaoh.
I turn into the Canal of Pre,
    I will pitch my tent overlooking the canal.
I have raced without rest,
    Since I first thought of the Canal of Pre.
I can already see my lover . . .
    He is heading for the Houses of . . .
I will stand with you at the entrance to the Ity canal,
    You will lead me to Heliopolis.
As we walk away,
    . . . into the trees of the Houses of . . .
I gather branches,
    And weave them into a fan.

We will see if it works,
    And sends me on my way to the Garden of Love.
My breasts are smothered with fruit,
    My hair glistens with balm.
When I am with you . . .
I am a noble woman filled with pleasure,
    I am the Queen of Egypt!

We do not know what role the love songs played in Egyptian society (Fox 1992: 294). They do not seem to be wedding songs, for they never speak of the couple as married or about to be. They show no signs of a religious-cultic function, such as a Sacred Marriage liturgy. They show no interest in fertility. Their function and that of the Song were probably similar—they are love songs that were sung or recited to describe the joys of sexual love.

The literary approach has the distinct advantage of grasping the poetry on its own terms and to appreciate it as a product of high literary merit. Typical of assessments of the Song stemming from such an approach is that of B. Davie Napier (1962: 356):

It has on occasion been carelessly said that the Song has no religious-theological value. I must take emphatic personal exception. If it informs and nourishes and enriches the category of joyful, rapturous, sexual love; and if it has power to restore something of tenderness and fresh-ness to the marriage relationship, then surely . . . the Song of Solomon has even theological justification. As one who continues to delight in the poems, I cheer the ingenuity and inspiration of the allegorical inter-pretation which preserved the Song of Solomon. The Song properly be-longs in a canon of sacred literature from a people who were able to look at *all* the gifts of a rich creation with gratitude to the Giver and joy in the gift.

6.   Feminist/Womanist   A recently-developed approach to the interpre-tation of the Song of Songs is the feminist or womanist (Trible 1978; Falk 1990; Weems 1992). The term "womanist" is a term preferred by African-American biblical scholars, to distinguish their approach from a feminist one. The wo-manist approach is represented here by the work of Renita Weems. Proponents of this approach believe that to interpret the Song simply as a tribute to human sexuality and love is not only to modernize the book but to fail to see its unique social significance with respect to female sexuality. From this perspective, the Song makes very specific assertions about female sexuality. For example, as Weems maintains, the female protagonist in the Song stands out as a woman who is not just the recipient of male-initiated sexual activity, but one who in-sists on her right to initiate love and to explore the power of her sexuality (1992: 158). The subtle defensive tone of the book hints that the poet under-stood that some aspects of the lovers' relationship went against prevailing so-cial norms. Weems asserts that it is not simply the beauty of love and the wholesomeness of human sexuality in the abstract that the lovers value. It is the beauty of *their* love for each other and *their* irresistible attraction to each other that they emphasize. They are two lovers whom society, for inscrutable reasons sought to keep apart, perhaps because they were from different classes, different backgrounds, or of a different color.

The Song of Songs: *"Amor Vincet Omnia*—Love Conquers All"

Many commentators recognize that the setting of love and passion in opposition to the power of death in 8:6-7 serves as the climax of the Song and the distillation of its message. That message is that love is the *only* thing known by humans that can conquer death. This message provides a fitting conclusion to our exploration of the Song of Songs:

> Set me as a seal upon your heart,
> as a seal upon your arm;
> for love is strong as death,
> passion fierce as the grave.
> Its flashes are flashes of fire,
> a raging flame.
> Many waters cannot quench love,
> neither can floods drown it.
> If one offered for love
> all the wealth of his house,
> it would be utterly scorned. (Song 8:6–7)

STUDY QUESTIONS

PSALMS

1. What are some of the differences between Greco-Roman classical poetry and Hebrew poetry?
2. Describe and discuss the use of parallelism in Hebrew poetry. Include in your discussion definitions of: line, colon, bicolon, tricolon. What are the different kinds of parallelism?
3. Some of the ideas that are characteristic of wisdom literature in the Hebrew Bible (which we will examine in Chapter 14) also appear in the Psalms. Read Psalms 44 and 89 and comment on how they question the conception of history that underlies the work of the Deuteronomistic historian (Joshua-Kings).
4. About a fourth of the psalms can be classified as hymns or songs of praise that typically include three literary elements: (1) a call to praise God;

(2) reasons for praising God (which may cite [a] God's action in history and/or [b] God's creative activity); and (3) the call to praise repeated. Read the following hymns in the book of Psalms: 100, 113, 135, and 146. Mark the literary elements in these hymns with brackets and number the brackets using the numbers 1, 2a, 2b, and 3.

5. About a third of the psalms in the book of Psalms can be classified as laments, either individual or communal. The characteristic structure of this type of psalm includes five literary elements: (1) invocation; (2) complaint; (3) confession; (4) petition; and (5) vow. Read the following laments in the book of Psalms: 13, 22, 80, and 123. Identify each psalm as either individual or communal. Mark the literary elements in these laments with brackets and number the brackets using the numbers 1, 2, 3, 4, 5.

6. How can you relate the wider socioeconomic context of Israel (both northern and southern kingdoms) during the period of the monarchy to the fact that the largest single type of psalm in the book of Psalms is the individual lament?

7. Nine of the Psalms can be classified as individual thanksgiving songs that have three literary elements: (1) introduction; (2) body; and (3) conclusion. Read Psalms 30, 52, and 138 and mark the literary elements in them with brackets numbered 1, 2, and 3.

8. Give an example of a psalm that seems to have been composed for cultic purposes. Point out some of the elements in this psalm that point to its use in public worship.

THE SONG OF SONGS

1. What are some of the distinctive features of the Song of Songs and how do these features relate to the purpose of the book and its place in the canon of the Hebrew Bible?

2. The Song of Songs is one of the five festival scrolls (*Megillot*) that were read on the major festival days in the Hebrew calendar: Pentecost (*Shavu'ot*); Passover (*Pesach*); Tabernacles (*Sukkot*); The Ninth of Av; and Purim. The Song of Songs was read at the feast of Passover. What about this book might have led it to be associated with Passover?

3. How are the issues of canonization and interpretation related with respect to the Song of Songs?

BIBLIOGRAPHY

Alter, Robert. 1985. *The Art of Biblical Poetry.* New York: Basic Books.

___. 1987. "Psalms." *The Literary Guide to the Bible.* Frank Kermode and Robert Alter, eds., pp. 244–62. Cambridge, MA: Belknap Press of Harvard University Press.

Anderson, Bernhard W. 1986. *Understanding the Old Testament.* 4th ed. Englewood Cliffs, NJ: Prentice-Hall.

Brenner, A. 1985. *The Israelite Woman: Social Role and Literary Type in Biblical Narrative.* Sheffield: JSOT.

Burney, C. F. 1925. *The Poetry of Our Lord.* Oxford, Eng.: Clarendon.

Dahood, Mitchell. 1966. *Psalms I: 1-50.* Anchor Bible, 16. Garden City, NY: Doubleday.

Cardenal, Ernesto. 1971. *Songs of Struggle and Liberation.* New York: Herder and Herder.

Danby, Herbert, ed. 1933. *The Mishnah.* Clarendon: Oxford University Press.

Falk, Marcia. 1990. *Love Lyrics from the Bible, The Song of Songs: A New Translation and Interpretation.* San Francisco: Harper-Collins.

Fox, Michael V. 1992. "Egyptian Literature (Love Songs)." *The Anchor Bible Dictionary, II,* 393-395. New York: Doubleday.

Gerstenberger, E. S. 1988. *Psalms: Part I with an Introduction to Cultic Poetry.* Grand Rapids: Eerdmans.

____. 1971. *Psalms of Struggle and Liberation.* New York: Herder and Herder.

Gottwald, Norman K. 1985. *The Hebrew Bible: A Socio-Literary Introduction.* Philadelphia: Fortress.

Ginsburg, C. D. 1857. *The Song of Songs.* Edinburgh: T & T Clark. Repr. 1970.

____. 1985. *The Hebrew Bible: A Socio-Literary Introduction.* Philadelphia: Fortress.

Gunkel, Hermann. 1967. *The Psalms: A Form-Critical Introduction,* Tr. by Thomas M. Horner. Philadelphia: Westminster.

Kraus, Hans Joachim. 1960. *Psalmen, vols. I-II.* Neukirchen: Neukirchener Verlag.

Kugel, James. 1981. *The Idea of Biblical Poetry, Parallelism and Its History.* New Haven: Yale University Press.

____. 1984. "Some Thoughts on Future Research into Biblical Style: Addenda to 'The Idea of Biblical Poetry.'" *Journal for the Study of the Old Testament 28,* 108-117.

Limburg, James. 1992. "Psalms, Book of." *The Anchor Bible Dictionary, V:* 522-536. New York: Doubleday.

Lowth, Robert. 1787. *Lectures on the Sacred Poetry of the Hebrews,* Tr. by G. Gregory. London: Johnson.

____. 1824. *Isaiah: A New Translation with a Preliminary Dissertation and Notes,* Vol. 1. London: Robinson & Evans.

Matthews, Victor H., and Benjamin, Don C. 1991. *Old Testament Parallels: Laws and Stories from the Ancient Near East.* New York: Paulist.

Murphy, Roland E. 1992. "Song of Songs, Book of." *The Anchor Bible Dictionary, VI:* 150-155. New York: Doubleday

Napier, B. Davie. 1962. *Song of the Vineyard: A Theological Introduction to the Old Testament.* New York: Harper & Brothers.

Pope, Marvin H. 1977. *Song of Songs.* Anchor Bible, 7C. Garden City, NY: Doubleday.

Stuart, Douglas K. 1976. *Studies in Early Hebrew Meter.* Missoula, MT: Scholars.

Trible, Phyllis. 1978. "Love's Lyrics Redeemed." *God and Rhetoric of Sexuality,* pp. 144-165. Philadelphia: Fortress.

Weems, Renita J. 1992. "Song of Songs." *The Women's Bible Commentary,* Carol A. Newsom and Sharon H. Ringe, eds. Louisville: Westminster/John Knox.

Westermann, Claus. 1965. *The Praise of God in the Psalms,* Tr. by Keith R. Crim. Richmond: John Knox.

____. 1981. *Praise and Lament in the Psalms,* Tr. by Keith R. Crim and Richard Soulen. Atlanta: John Knox.

Chapter 14

THREE SHORT STORIES— WOMEN AS DELIVERERS: RUTH, ESTHER AND JUDITH

Suggested Bible Reading
Ruth 1 - 4; Esther 1 - 10; Judith 1 - 16

GENDER CONSTRUCTS IN ANCIENT ISRAEL AND IN CONTEMPORARY SOCIETY— WOMEN AS LEADERS

Having traveled this far in our journey through the Hebrew Scriptures, students should know that Biblical literature was neither produced in, nor can it be read and understood in a social vacuum. Every one of us who reads the Bible does so in a particular context, which includes our own distinctive social location. Social location includes such things as one's nationality, socioeconomic stratum, ethnicity, and gender. As readers, we are affected, consciously or unconsciously, by issues related to the ways in which the society of which we are a part understands gender roles and relationships. Serious reflection on current gender relationships, especially on the status and role of women in our society, has also stimulated renewed consideration both of the status and role of women in biblical societies, and on how one's gender affects the way in which she or he reads and understands biblical literature.

There can be no question that ancient Israel was a patriarchal society, a society in which males played dominant roles. It is just as obvious that patriarchal arrangements are reflected in biblical literature. Clearly, many biblical texts presuppose a form of social organization that is hierarchical with respect to gender relationships. Carol Meyers, citing the work of anthropologist S. C. Rogers, lists and comments on six characteristics of societies in which the male dominance myth is active (1988: 43 – 45):

1. Women are primarily associated with domestic matters.

2. The society is domestic-oriented; life centers on the home, and what happens in the home has implications for life beyond the home.

3. Formal rights may disadvantage females; but the day-to-day informal interactions in which females can exert power in a small community are at least as important a force as authorized rights.

4. A corollary and prior condition of item 3 is that males have greater access to judicial, political, and other formal aspects of community structure.

5. Men are occupied with activities that are culturally valued.

6. Males and females experience mutual interdependence in important ways, for example, politically, economically, and/or socially; males may appear autonomous, but in fact can no more act or survive on their own than can females.

The last point is particularly critical. It means that both men and women tend to perpetuate the system of social balance that offsets male authority with female power. Commenting on this list with respect to the issue of patriarchy in the Hebrew Bible, Meyers thinks that items 3, 4, and 5 are obvious and need no investigation. The patriarchal stance of the Bible establishes the male-centered nature of ancient Israel with respect to legal rights, formal positions in society, and prominent activities in the community. Item 1 can also be assumed without question, in that females are all but invisible in the Bible, with its predominantly public, rather than domestic, orientation. Items 2 and 6 on the list remain. Meyers asks whether the combined resources of archaeology, the biblical text, and comparative sociology and social anthropology can provide us with sufficient evidence for an evaluation of domestic orientation and mutual interdependence. She concludes that an analysis of female and male interaction as a function of these two points is possible, and she goes on to show that there was a lack of functional hierarchy in Israelite gender relations.

Gender issues present us, as readers of the Hebrew scriptures, with two tasks. First, we must consider gender constructs as they existed within the social structure of ancient Israel. Then we must consider how gender constructs in our society influence the ways in which we read and understand the Bible.

Gender Constructs in Ancient Israel

What do we know about gender constructs in ancient Israel? While a great deal of explicit information appears throughout the Hebrew scriptures regarding the status and roles of males in Israelite society, the same cannot be said about the status and roles of women, about whom information is both spotty and less explicit. The Bible as a whole is male-centered in its subject matter, its authorship, and its perspectives. Meyers has pointed out one example of how the Hebrew Bible focuses far more on men than on women. This is in the simple matter of personal names (Meyers 1992: 245). The Hebrew Bible mentions a total of 1,426 names, of which 1,315 are those of men. Thus, only 111 women's names appear, about nine percent of the total number of names. Obviously, women constituted more than nine percent of ancient Israelite society.

Legal texts in the Hebrew Bible set forth legislation that would appear severely to restrict women's roles in ancient Israel (see, for example, laws in Lev 15; Num 5; and Deut 22). As important as biblical law is, however, its character and function are not always clear. It is possible to view legal materials that seem unfavorable to women as not concerned with women as such but with trying to promote family and territorial stability in a patrilineal context. It is risky to assume that a society's ethical values and actual social arrangements can be inferred from a reading of a society's laws, or part of them. In reading legislation in the Hebrew Bible concerning women, one should ask to what degree the sanctions stipulated by such laws were actually brought into play, the extent to which they were applied in the actual life of people. The formal canons of codified patriarchal law are generally more restrictive than the actual interaction and relationship of women and men and the social realities that they govern. For example, in rabbinic Judaism women are grouped with children and slaves for legal religious purposes. Biblical stories about women however, tell of women who clearly were not perceived as minors or slaves in everyday life. Biblical women such as Hannah (in 1 Samuel), Ruth, or Esther are characterized with "typical" female roles and behavior, but they are not minors, nor mentally deficient. Thus, the actual status of women should be determined by their economic autonomy and social roles rather than by ideological or prescriptive legal statements. As a rule, prescriptive injunctions for "appropriate feminine" behavior and submission tend to increase whenever women's actual socioreligious status and power within patriarchy increase.

Narrative literature in the Hebrew Bible provides a different kind of evidence for understanding the ways in which gender constructs were understood in ancient Israel. McKeating (1979: 65), in reflecting on ethics in the Hebrew Bible, observes that narrative literature portrays certain aspects of human behavior, and then often proceeds to reflect on the acceptable or unacceptable nature of that behavior in the ways that characters in the story react and in the comments supplied by the narrator. But, just as caution must be exercised in assuming that laws were rigidly applied, one also must be careful to avoid the error of overgeneralizing about gender roles based on such stories. Stories that are narrated in the

Hebrew Bible do not usually have ordinary people as their subjects, and thus cannot uncritically be regarded as representing what was typical in Israelite society.

Current Gender Constructs

Concerning our second task, that of considering the ways in which the gender constructs of our own society affect our interpretation of biblical literature, obviously our own preconceptions about relationships between men and women often influence (sometimes unconsciously and in subtle ways) our understanding of gender arrangements as they appear in the Bible. Recognizing this, we should avoid two extremes. On the one hand, some feminist biblical interpreters, operating out of the context of the contemporary women's movement whose goal is to liberate women from male domination, may, because of their political agenda, exaggerate the subordination of women in the Hebrew Bible. They may read such subordination *into* the text, and overlook or play down any elements of judgment against such subordination that also may be in the text. At the other extreme are those interpreters (usually men) who would, in an apologetic attempt to defend the Bible from what they perceive as feminist attacks, minimize the unequivocal evidence of inequality between the sexes reflected in both legal and narrative texts in the Hebrew Bible. An example of such an apologetic approach to gender issues can be seen in J. H. Otwell's book, *And Sarah Laughed: The Status of Women in the Old Testament.* Otwell asserts that outside the home, women seem to have had access to nearly every activity we normally associate with men. The fact that fewer women than men ruled is most easily explained, by Otwell, by the more dangerous and demanding role of woman within the family than by any hypothesis of the repression of woman in ancient Israel (1977: 151).

Our knowledge of the status and role of women in ancient Israel has increased significantly in recent years. Methods and insights from the fields of sociology, anthropology, psychology, history, literary criticism, folklore studies, and women's studies have been applied to the study of gender-nuanced questions in ancient Israel (see, for example, Day, 1989). Methodological strategies have been developed for filling in the gaps regarding such questions in the biblical text and fleshing out the cultural profile of women in ancient Israel. Recent studies of gender in ancient Israel do not allow the gender biases present in the text of the Hebrew Scriptures to delimit and define the range of gender-nuanced questions that one can address to the biblical text. Instead, scholars interested in gender recognize the obvious fact that Israelite women existed within a patriarchal Israelite culture, and these scholars take that fact as their point of departure, rather than granting the text the unquestioned authority to speak for women. With this point of departure, contemporary studies of gender try to determine the realities of women's everyday lives in ancient Israel, beyond what the text appears to say, or not to say, about women's existence.

It can certainly be affirmed that women in ancient Israel, through their positions in the community, played decisive roles in Israel's story. A few women are singled out in such roles in the Hebrew scriptures, and their stories are told. Taking for granted the important role of women in the domestic sphere, what can be said about the role of women in the community, especially in relation to the important political and religious institutions of monarchy, prophecy, and wisdom? While the specific evidence in the text considering women in leadership roles is hardly abundant, one cannot, relying on an argument from silence, simplistically assume that *only* those few women (or men, for that matter) whose stories are preserved in the Bible played roles as leaders in ancient Israel.

With respect to the political institution of the monarchy, it is interesting that the title "queen" is *never* applied to any Israelite or Judahite woman in the entire Hebrew Bible, not even Athaliah, who is clearly described as a reigning monarch. Athaliah assumed power after the death of her son, King Ahaziah (2 Kings 11:1–6 and 2 Chr 22:10–23:15). The only title conferred on Athaliah is one that defines her in relation to a male, "the mother of Ahaziah." This hesitation to apply the title of "queen" to a reigning Israelite monarch suggests that the idea of women as rulers was seen as an anomaly in Israelite political life. The title "queen" is applied to foreign women (the Queen of Sheba in 1 Kings 10:1; Queen Tahpenes of Egypt in 1 Kings 11:19; the queen of Persia in Neh 2:6; and so forth). The only "official" title applied to a woman in the setting of the ancient Israelite monarchy, and that in only a few instances, is the Hebrew term *gebîrah*. The NRSV translates this term "queen mother," while the KJV misleadingly translates it "queen" (1 Kings 15:13 = 2 Chr 15:16; 2 Kings 10:13; Jer 13:18). The precise significance of this title, as well as the kind of power it signifies is unclear. It may have been a title conferred when a break occurred in the normal succession from king to his son, in which case a woman, the *gebîrah,* wife of the king who had given birth to the next king, acted as a temporary regent (Brenner 1985: 9).

The situation with respect to women and the institution of prophecy is not much better. Only five women in all the Hebrew Bible are called prophets (or "prophetesses"), and one of them, Noadiah, is only mentioned in passing as a "prophetess," grouped with "the rest of the prophets who wanted to make me afraid," which may mean that she was regarded as a "false" prophet by Nehemiah (Neh 6:14). Isaiah's wife is called a "prophetess" in Isa 8:3. The three named "true" women prophets are Miriam (Ex 15; Num 12), Deborah (Judg 4; 5), and Huldah (2 Kings 22). While women as prophets are not widely attested in the Hebrew scriptures, it also can be said that there was no prejudice against women in prophetic roles. Women were not, as they were with respect to the monarchy, considered stopgaps in the absence of male prophets. No evidence suggests that females were at a disadvantage in the exercise of prophetic gifts, though being a female may have had a bearing on the extent to which a woman's prophetic oracles were preserved and passed on in the tradition (Emmerson 1989: 376). Furthermore, one can reasonably assume that the few women prophets mentioned by name represent others not named because the Hebrew Bible must always be viewed as only a partial record of social and religious realities in ancient Israel.

Women were also a part of the wisdom school in the Hebrew Bible, which we will discuss in Chapter 15. The adjective "wise" with the noun "woman" occurs only twice in the Hebrew Bible. In both cases the "wise woman" is anonymous. In 2 Sam 14:2 the reference is to the "wise woman" from Tekoa who was employed by Joab to cause the return of Absalom. In 2 Sam 20:16 the term refers to an anonymous "wise woman . . . from the city." According to Claudia Camp (1981) this designation indicates a recognized role in the community in the time of the judges and in the early monarchy. Camp suggests that this role of "wise woman" derives from a mother's role in educating her children. By extension, it was applied to the "wise woman" of a village, who was concerned with the political affairs of the village. Camp concludes that while female images, either as significant "historical" persons or symbolic figures, are relatively rare in the Hebrew scriptures, the emphasis on female imagery associated with wisdom reveals a latent tendency in Israel's theological reflection that was underdeveloped because of the male-dominated priesthood and generally patriarchal milieu. Female imagery was not, however, insignificant in Israel's understanding of the relationships between persons in community and between the community and Yahweh (1981: 29). Note as well that the wisdom literature also contains some very negative images of women, as we shall see in our next chapter.

BIBLICAL SHORT STORIES— THE NATURE OF THE GENRE

Women appear in important roles in three short stories that are named for the women who are the center of attention in them—Ruth, Esther, and Judith. Ruth and Esther appear in the Jewish canon, while Judith is included among the apocryphal/deuterocanonical books. While only later editions of Judith now exist, the basis of the later Greek versions was almost certainly Hebrew. In the Jewish canon, both Ruth and Esther belong to the five *Megilloth*, the five festal scrolls that are associated with five sacred seasons in the Jewish calendar. The story of Ruth is the festal scroll for the feast of Shavuoth (= Weeks or Pentecost), originally associated in the agricultural calendar with the wheat harvest, probably because of the references in the story to the agricultural activities of harvest and threshing. The story of Esther is the festal scroll for the holiday of Purim, a Jewish festival celebrated on the 14th and 15th of the month of Adar (that is, the twelfth month of the Babylonian calendar, corresponding to our March–April). The book of Esther tells the story of the origins of the holiday in the account of the casting of lots (*purim*) in the plot to destroy the Jews.

The three short stories concerning Ruth, Esther, and Judith that exist as freestanding books are not, however, the only examples of biblical short stories. Other examples of the short story genre appear as parts of other books throughout the

Hebrew canon and the apocryphal/deuterocanonical books. What are the literary characteristics of this genre?

The Hebrew short story, while bearing some resemblance to its counterpart in English literature, has its own distinguishing characteristics. Campbell (1975: 5-6) lists four such characteristics:

1. The Hebrew short story has a distinctive literary style that employs an artistic and elevated prose containing rhythmic elements that are poetic. These elements no doubt served as an aid to memory in the oral transmission of the short story.

2. A second characteristic of Hebrew short stories has to do with their content. Generally speaking, they combine an interest in typical (if important people) with an interest in ordinary events, even when these events are seen to be of significance on a broader scale.

3. These stories have multiple purposes—some entertaining, some instructive. They have a distinctive theological purpose as well in that they wish their reader to see the seemingly ordinary events they narrate as the scene of God's subtly providential activity.

4. The reader or hearer (ancient and modern) of the Hebrew short story delights in the capacity of the creators of these stories to do what they do extremely well—the stories "work," involving the reader or hearer in what is narrated.

Typically the Hebrew short story combines fairy tale, legendary, heroic, or mythic elements with an orientation that has the appearance of being historical. Historical vagueness and irregularities in the temporal settings of the stories, symmetries and extremities of plot, and stark reversals of fortune for the characters attest that the genre should *not* be confused with objective, documentary history. Rather, the genre should be seen as extremely believable fiction with sociocultural lifelikeness, what earlier commentators called "verisimilitude" (Gottwald 1985: 551-552).

Besides its distinctive literary characteristics, the Hebrew short story appears to have been a literary form that came into use early in Israel's life as an effective vehicle for conveying basic truths of Yahwism. In speaking of this aspect of the short story form, Campbell says that the short story was designed to portray the radical effect of a new and great commitment to Yahweh upon the part of a new people, the Israelites, who were once not a people. The purpose of these stories was not simple entertainment, but instruction in the meaning and implications of the new faith-commitment to Yahweh. Thus, the literary form was new, the people were new, and the purpose was new (1975: 8-9).

While we may be able to discern distinctive literary characteristics and purposes of these stories, their historical settings and the ways in which they seem to report historical events are more problematic. For example, the story of Ruth begins with the statement "In the days when the judges ruled . . ." (Ruth 1:1), which implies a historical setting in the early days of Israel, before the rise of the monarchy. Ruth's placement in Christian Bibles suggests this historical setting, as Ruth appears immediately following the book of Judges (where the Greek translators of the Hebrew Scriptures placed it). In the Jewish Bible, however, a later date for Ruth may be suggested by the fact that it falls within the third division of the canon, the Writings, the last part of the Bible to achieve canonical status, rather than among the historical books of the Former Prophets. The story of Esther clearly presupposes the Persian period. Not only does it have a setting in the Persian empire, but it was probably composed in the eastern Jewish Diaspora in the Persian empire. Other than its Persian setting, the book of Esther gives no clear indication of date, and therefore a range of dates from the fourth to the second century B.C.E. has been proposed. Judith includes a puzzling mix of names and events from the Persian, Babylonian, and Assyrian eras. Although Judith appears to be a historical account, it abounds in puzzling statements concerning both history and geography, especially in its first two chapters. Because of the mixed signals in these three books, scholars differ widely in the dates they assign to them in their finished form. While the historical character and date of composition of these short stories may be uncertain, one should remember that the short story genre does not depend upon either the story's being historical nor on its having a definite historical setting.

Some interpretations of these stories, however, have presumed a definite historical setting. For example, some interpretations of Ruth insist upon a post-exilic date for the story, around 400 B.C.E. In these readings, Ruth is seen as a piece of protest literature, written to oppose the narrowly nationalistic programs and theological perspectives of Ezra, who saw liaisons with foreigners as a serious threat to Jewish identity. Ruth was thus viewed as both a model of Yahwistic faith *and* a foreign woman married to an Israelite, attacking the post-exilic idea that foreign women were threats to true faith. This line of interpretation also observes that Ruth, a foreigner, was the great-grandmother of David, according to the genealogy at the end of the book of Ruth (4:17). Other scholars, whose interpretation of Ruth does not depend upon this historical setting, date the composition of Ruth to the tenth–eighth centuries B.C.E., relying mostly on linguistic analysis. This historical setting would explain the emphasis on the genealogy at the end of the book and the book's special interest in Bethlehem, which was David's home town.

The historical hodgepodge of Judith, with its strange mix of names and events from the Assyrian, Babylonian, and Persian periods is most likely not the product of the author's ignorance. It was probably a deliberate device used by the author to suggest to the reader that the work should be read as a fictional short story, not as a historical essay. The story may have been written in the Maccabean era and may reflect the defeat of the Seleucid general Nicanor by Judah the Maccabee (161 B.C.E.—see Chapter 16).

Before we go on with our investigation of the individual stories, one final common characteristic of all three should be noted. Although it may already be obvious, due to the title of this chapter and the context in which we have chosen to discuss them, these stories all concern women in dominant roles as deliverers. In these three books women are thrust into the role of deliverers *precisely because* men have failed the community. These books thus provide us with important perspectives on gender constructs in ancient Israel. In them we see the typical Israelite male virtues of military prowess (Judith), political clout (Esther), and socioeconomic status (Ruth). In each case, however, these virtues are not sufficient to save the day, and in all three of the stories the main weapon of the hero is her female sexuality. All three women are doubly disadvantaged. Besides their gender that put them in a subordinate position in society, they also are pictured as belonging to groups that were socially marginalized in Israelite society—Judith is a widow, Esther is an orphan, and Ruth is a foreigner. Nevertheless, these socially marginalized women save not only themselves, but their people (an *adopted* people in the case of Ruth) as well. As we examine these three books in turn, remember the subtitle of this chapter—"Women as Deliverers." As you read these three books, ask yourself what concept of deliverance is suggested. Because deliverance implies freedom *from* something, from what type of oppression did Ruth, Esther, and Judith free themselves *and* their people?

RUTH THE FOREIGNER—WOMEN AND THE PATRIARCHY

Ruth and Relationships

While there are scholarly differences of opinion concerning several issues in the book of Ruth, there is widespread agreement that here we have a charming and beautifully-crafted short story in the finest traditions of Israel's faith. The story line is relatively simple. It tells the story of two women, Naomi, a Judahite from Bethlehem, and Ruth, a woman from Moab. Their lives become interrelated when Ruth marries Naomi's son after her family traveled from Bethlehem into Moab, to escape a famine. The story becomes focused on the two women after both their husbands die, leaving a widow and her daughter-in-law to work out their survival and welfare as women. They also have the job of securing the perpetuation of the family line (traced through the male in a patrilineal society) for the dead husband of Naomi through the institution of levirate marriage. The actions of these two women bring them into contact with two relatives of Naomi's deceased husband, Elimelech. These relatives are Boaz and another unnamed man. In the end, Boaz marries Ruth and their offspring constitute the family line of none other than King David (Ruth 4:17-21). While the story line of Ruth may be simple, the story itself needs to be read as we would read any novel or short story, with an eye for plot development, for the fleshing out of characters and their relationships, and for the artistic use of language that makes the story interesting and helps us understand several levels of meaning in it.

STRUCTURALISM APPLIED TO RUTH

One of the newer literary critical perspectives that has been successfully applied to Ruth is structuralism, which can help us understand why the story "works" so well. Structuralism is a text-centered theory of interpretation based on the idea that meaning depends on the *structures* of a cultural system. Source, form, and redaction criticism, which were introduced in Chapter 1, try, in one way or another, to seek out the world behind or beneath the text—the traditions or sources behind the text, the early communities that shaped the text, or the intentions of the author. With structuralism, this changes. Issues such as the identity of the author and his/her purpose, the original audience to which the text was directed, and the sociopolitical conditions that produced the text are all bracketed out as areas of concern. Structuralism is not concerned with *what* a text might have meant to its original author or audience, but with *how* a text has meaning for the contemporary reader. Meaning in the human world, unlike the animal world that is more dependent upon instinct, is created and sustained by culture. Culture structures our relationships with one another in particular ways. Human relationships reflect an underlying, largely unconscious, system of conventions that govern the way humans order their existence into meaningful structures. Culture, for example, attaches meanings to simple physical gestures such as handshakes. These meanings have little or nothing to do with the physical act itself. Meaning in culture is determined by implicitly agreed upon conventions. What, for example, is the difference between a weed and a flower in common understanding other than the fact that we agree to call one a weed and the other a flower? Similarly, words or sentences in a language do not have a fixed meaning, but such meanings as we give them are functions of the system or structure of which they are a part. Words have meanings that derive from the sentence of which they form a part. Sentences in a story have meanings that are a function of the story of which they form a part.

Structuralists apply the idea that myths and stories are attempts to deal with "binary oppositions" that are inherent in human existence. Some of these "binary oppositions" are male/female, love/hate, life/death, youth/old age, sin/righteousness, and fullness/emptiness. Myths and stories attempt to develop reconciliation out of these oppositions. Structuralists seek to uncover the structures that work out such reconciliation, and in doing so they discover the fundamental system of convictions (not explicitly specified) upon which the author operated.

Examining Ruth from a structuralist perspective has led to the observation that the book can be divided into six scenes. Of these six, the first two are characterized by "emptiness" and are balanced by the last two that deal with the opposite of "emptiness," which is "fullness." Between these two poles are two scenes that describe the reconciliation of these opposites, ways in which the pole of emptiness is transformed into its polar opposite, fullness (Gottwald 1985: 555). This structural progression of scenes can be charted as follows:

EMPTINESS	TRANSFORMATION	FULLNESS
Scene 1	**Scene 3**	**Scene 5**
Famine and Flight	Fields and Food (2)	At the City Gate
(1:1-5)		(4:1-12)
Scene 2	**Scene 4**	**Scene 6**
The Women Return	On the Threshing	A Child Is Born
(1:6-22)	Floor (3)	(4:13-21)

Symbols of Emptiness		**Symbols of Fullness**
Famine, Isolation,		Food, Community,
Childlessness, Old Age,		Fertility, The Aged
Despair		with Youth, Hope

Within this structure, a rich interplay of characters centers on the paradoxically assertive deeds of the two women, Naomi and Ruth. The story has an ironic twist about "fullness" and "emptiness" at its beginning. Bethlehem, which means "house of bread" in Hebrew, is here caught in the grips of one of Palestine's recurrent famines, brought on by the lack of rainfall. This famine requires the shift of locales to Moab, to which Elimelech and his family travel in search of food. Why, one might ask, did the author of Ruth choose Moab as the destination? Why did Elimelech, like his ancestor Jacob, not go down into Egypt in search of food? The answer to these questions must lie in the connotations that Moab held for the Israelite author and reader/hearer of the story. What might some of those connotations have been? A deep-seated animosity existed toward Moab and the Moabites throughout Israel's history. This enmity toward Moab and Moabites appears throughout the Hebrew scriptures as well. Balak, king of Moab, opposed Israel's movement into the promised land (Josh 24:9). Eglon, king of Moab, oppressed Israel during the period of the Judges (Judg 3:12). Moabites are pictured as enemies of Saul. Moabite religion is one of the foreign religions that caused problems in Solomon's time (1 Kings 11:17). Moab rebelled after the death of Ahab (2 Kings 3:5 and the Mesha Inscription). Several prophets direct oracles against Moab (Jer 48:9; Ezek 25:8-11; Amos 2:1-2; Zeph 2:9). In the Psalms, Moab is described as God's "washbasin" (60:8; 108:9). Israel's dislike of Moab is portrayed most vividly, however, in the story of Moab's origins, contained within the story of Lot and his daughters in Genesis 19. That story, when read through an ethnic lens, tells how Lot's daughters, after the destruction of their home town and the death of their mother, live in a cave with their father and proceed to get him intoxicated so that he would have sexual intercourse with them. The children resulting from this incestuous union are none other than Moab, "the ancestor of the Moabites" (Gen 19:37) and Ben-Ammi, "the ancestor of the Ammonites" (Gen 19:38). While the Israelites saw themselves as the children of the promise to Abraham, the "miraculous" births, and saving events that kept their line going, by contrast, the Moabites' origins are traced to deception, not divine promise; incest, not saving intervention from God.

RUTH AND NAOMI

So the story of Ruth begins on two unfavorable notes—famine and flight to Moab. It can only get better from this point—or can it? Once in Moab the story takes still another turn toward emptiness. Elimelech dies, and Naomi is left as a widow with two unmarried sons. These two young men, Mahlon and Chilion, have names that may have signaled to the Hebrew reader or hearer that more misery is yet to come in the story. Mahlon, in Hebrew, means something like "sickly" or "diseased," while Chilion means "consumption." These are hardly names one would give to characters expected to play a significant role in the story. Mahlon and Chilion do however, live long enough to marry Moabite women, Orpah and Ruth, respectively. The name Orpah is also a symbolic one. It comes from a Hebrew word meaning "stiff-necked" or "stubborn," which can be contrasted with Ruth, which means "companion." After ten years Naomi's sons die so that "the woman was left without her two sons and her husband" (1:5).

Hearing that the famine in Judah had ended and sensing that she has no future in a foreign country without any relatives or social support structure, Naomi decides to return home. Ruth and Orpah start out to accompany their mother-in-law back to her country. Naomi, however, urges them to remain in their own homeland and to seek their future there with Moabite husbands (1:8-13). Naomi, whose name means "my pleasantness" begins to show genuine bitterness in her speech as she attempts to persuade Ruth and Orpah to stay in Moab. While *they* might have a future, she does not believe that she does. While she asks that God might deal faithfully with them, she complains that God has not done so with her. She ends her speech by saying: "It has been far more bitter for me than for you, because the hand of the LORD has turned against me" (1:13). Naomi claims that her emptiness and bitterness are God's doing. Orpah, after initial resistance, acquiesces to Naomi's request that she remain in Moab. Ruth refuses to do so, and the words of her refusal are both familiar and moving:

> Do not press me to leave you
> or to turn back from following you!
> Where you go, I will go;
> where you lodge, I will lodge;
> your people shall be my people,
> and your God my God.
> Where you die, I will die—
> there will I be buried.
> May the LORD do thus and so to me,
> and more as well,
> if even death parts me from you! (1:16–17)

While we as readers may be moved by Ruth's touching assertion of loyalty to Naomi, Naomi was not. As Trible suggests, "Ruth's commitment to Naomi is Naomi's withdrawal from Ruth" (1978: 172-173). This withdrawal of Naomi is obvious when she arrives back in Bethlehem. When she is greeted by the women of the village, she refuses to be called by her old name and says that in view of her bitter misfortune she should now be called Mara, which means "bitter one" in Hebrew (1:20–21). Here then we see the full extent of the emptiness suggested by a structural view of the book of Ruth. This point is as empty as the story gets. The tale of the transformation of this emptiness into fullness begins in the second chapter of the book.

At the time of harvest, the Israelite custom reserved the right to glean to the socially marginalized resident aliens, orphans, and widows. Out of desperation and relying on that custom, Ruth proposes that she go into the fields to glean after the harvesters. Naomi does not offer her any advice or warning about the hazards that might await a young, unaccompanied woman there, but simply says, "Go, my daughter" (2:2). By happy coincidence, Ruth finds her way to a field belonging to a relative of her dead father-in-law, a man named Boaz, whose name means "strength" or "quickness." When Boaz learns of Ruth's identity, he warns her of the risk of sexual assault (2:8). He then gives the men working for him instructions to give Ruth especially liberal gleaning privileges in his fields. He also orders them not to sexually harass her (2:15). When Ruth returns to Naomi after her first very successful day of gleaning, Naomi picks up on the potential threat of sexual molestation (2:22).

RUTH AND BOAZ

The transition from emptiness to fullness, begun in chapter 2, continues in chapter 3, where Naomi turns the threat of sexual molestation into a strategy based on the sexual potential of the situation. Naomi instructs Ruth to bathe, put on perfume and her best clothes, and then go down to Boaz's threshing floor in the middle of the night. Here is real risk—going to a threshing floor at night, where the men sleep to guard the day's harvest, probably after having had a drink or two (see Figure 14.1)!

Both Naomi's coaching and Ruth's response are filled with *double entendres:* Naomi's instructions:

> . . . go down to the threshing floor; but do not *make yourself known* [for a man and a woman "to know" each other in the Hebrew Bible, can mean for them to have sexual intercourse; compare Gen 4:1, 17, 25; I Sam 1:19; I Kings 1:4] to the man [that is, Boaz] until he has finished eating and drinking. When he *lies down,* observe the place where he lies; then, go and *uncover his feet* ["feet" is sometimes used as a euphemism for the male genitalia; see Ex 4:25; Isa 6:2; 7:20] and *lie down;* and he will *tell you what to do.* (3:3–4)

Ruth's actions:

> When Boaz had eaten and drunk, and *he was in a contented mood, he went to lie down* . . . . Then she came *stealthily, and uncovered his feet, and lay down.* At midnight the man was startled, and turned over, and there, *lying*

Figure 14.1 A threshing floor

at his feet was a woman! He said, "Who are you?" And she answered, "I am Ruth, your servant; *spread your cloak over your servant,* for you are next-of-kin." (3:7–9, emphasis mine)

Commenting on these *double entendres,* Campbell (1975: 131) believes that it is simply incomprehensible that a Hebrew storyteller would use the words "uncover," "cloak," and a noun for "legs" ["feet" in the NRSV] that is a standard euphemism for the penis, and not mean to suggest to his audience that a provocative set of circumstances confronts them.

One might also add, that the Hebrew reader, especially because of the fact that Ruth is from Moab, might also be reminded of the strategy of Lot's daughters, who got their father drunk so that he would have sex with them! Why did Naomi feel that she needed to resort to sexual entrapment? Fewell and Gunn offer a compelling answer sensitive to the social arrangements in ancient Israel (1990: 79). They suggest that the fact that Ruth is a Moabite woman stands as a formidable barrier to the possible marriage of Ruth and Boaz. They point out that the text repeatedly refers to Ruth using the phrase "Moabite woman." With this in mind, Naomi understood that social conventions would not allow a pillar of the community like Boaz to pursue an interest in marrying a Moabite woman, *unless* he were to do so under some kind of cloak or compulsion. Hence, Naomi elects to go for a strategy of compulsion.

As the sexual overtones of the night are exposed to the light of day, Boaz had to face social reality. Both his standing in the community, as well as Ruth's reputation, would be endangered if Ruth were to be seen leaving the threshing floor (3:14). So, before the light of day could leave the two of them exposed, Boaz responded to what was an ambiguous situation. Had he and Ruth had sexual intercourse? If so, might she be pregnant? Perhaps by sending her away before the light permitted recognition, Boaz wished to guard her reputation as well as his own. Perhaps he did not want their relationship to be known to the other relative of Elimelech, so that his motives concerning Ruth would appear to be totally aboveboard. Boaz reminded Ruth of something she already knew, that he was a relative of her dead father-in-law. He also told her that he was prepared to accept the responsibility of acting as redeemer. Boaz admitted, however, that there was something, or rather someone, standing in the way of his taking on the role of redeemer—there exists a man who is on a branch nearer than he to Elimelech on the family tree! Ruth addressed Boaz as "the one with the right to redeem" or "next of kin" (3:9). Just what Ruth implied by the term is, however, uncertain. Perhaps the storyteller wants the reader to think that she knew about the Israelite institution of redemption of property, by which a relative could prevent property from passing out of the line of a man who died without a male heir (Lev 25 and 27). Maybe Ruth also knew about the law of levirate marriage (Deut 25:5–10), which stipulated that the brother of a man who died without an heir was supposed to marry his dead brother's widow. The children of this union would be the heirs of the dead brother. But Ruth's recognition of Boaz as "next of kin" does not necessarily carry with it the knowledge of these two legal institutions, which themselves are not necessarily linked. Boaz's response, in fact, makes sense *only* if there is no implied connection between the respective obligations of redeemer and levirate marriage.

In chapter 4 of the book of Ruth, we finally see emptiness transformed into fullness. This chapter begins with Boaz's convening a kind of "municipal court" in the open space at the city gate, a group of ten men (perhaps a "quorum") who could serve as witnesses to a legal transaction (see Figure 14.2).

Boaz then proceeds to confront the other, unnamed relative of Elimelech. After informing him that Naomi intended to sell a piece of land that belonged to Elimelech, and that he (the unnamed relative) had the right to redeem it, Boaz asked him if he wished to act as redeemer. The unnamed relative answers without hesitation: "I will redeem it" (4:4). What Boaz said next (4:5) depends on how one reads the Hebrew text. The NRSV, with other English translations and ancient versions (the Septuagint and the Vulgate) translates a change of the Hebrew text proposed by scribes that makes Boaz's response read:

> The day you acquire the field from the hand of Naomi, *you* are also acquiring Ruth the Moabite, the widow of the dead man, to maintain the dead man's name on his inheritance. (emphasis mine)

This would mean that Ruth and the land are a "package deal" for the unnamed relative. Fewell and Gunn point out that the Hebrew text, however, permits another, equally valid and more helpful translation. They read 4:5 as follows:

> Then Boaz said: "The day you acquire the field from the hand of Naomi, *I* am also acquiring Ruth the Moabitess, the widow of the dead, in order

Figure 14.2   Model of the open space in the city gate at Dan

to establish the name of the dead over his inheritance." (Fewell and Gunn 1990: 90)

The reading adopted by Fewell and Gunn maintains the important distinction between the laws of redemption and levirate marriage. It also provides a logical requirement that contributes to the plot of the story. Some surprise is needed to get the other relative to back off from what looked like a good deal—a piece of land, perhaps at a bargain price, and a wife! That surprise is Boaz's announcement that *he* (not the unnamed relative) would "acquire" or marry Ruth. The relative knew that if Boaz married Ruth and they had a son, that son would be the legal inheritor of the land that he, the relative, was about to buy. To spend good money for a piece of real estate that could revert to someone else made no sense. This turn in the plot only works *if* there is no expected connection between the two legal institutions of redemption and levirate marriage (Fewell and Gunn: 91). Boaz's solution was carefully couched in socially acceptable terms, in terms that the *men* at the gate could understand and appreciate—establishing the name of the deceased *man* over his inheritance, rather than in terms of helping a poor widow. Boaz's reputation in the community was not stained by what he proposed. Here was a man, who generously acted in behalf of the name of another man, agreeing to marry a *Moabite* woman!

Having eliminated any threat to the masculine concerns of social standing and inheritance of property, the narrator again turns our attention back to Ruth and Naomi. It is reported that Yahweh gave Ruth conception and that she bore a son (4:13), an event described by the women of the city in this way: "Your daughter-in-law who loves you, who is more to you than seven sons" (4:15) has borne a child whose birth is described with the words "A son has been born to Naomi" (4:17). The emptiness of Naomi at the end of chapter 1 is now transformed into fullness as she becomes the nurse of Ruth's child, one who promises to be "a restorer of life and a nourisher of . . . old age" (4:15). While Naomi's restoration is clearly described in terms of a patriarchal society, the reader knows that she owes her transformation from emptiness to fullness to Ruth, a woman whose loyalty to another woman challenged the male-centered values that permeate both the story and Naomi's world view. In commenting on Naomi, Fewell and Gunn have said:

> Calamity from the god of the patriarchy she has been quick to proclaim. Generosity from a wealthy man she is quick to praise. Grace from a foreign woman is perhaps beyond her comprehension. Little wonder that to the message, "your daughter-in-law who loves you is better than seven sons," her response is silence. (82)

Boaz, the unnamed male relative, and Naomi are all "saved." What about Ruth? Ruth, a foreign woman whose own religious convictions are only hinted at ("Your God will be my God," 1:16), is the agent of Yahweh, whose only direct appearance in the story is in 4:13: "When they came together, the LORD made her conceive, and she bore a son." At the conclusion of the story, Ruth, the agent through whom the faithfulness of a hidden God is realized for others, is assimilated into a genealogy, an instrument of a patrilineal society. She does have a noble male descendant—no less than King David! She is also remembered in the New Testament in Matthew's version of the genealogy of Jesus (Matt 1:3-6). But apart from these genealogical notices, she fades into biblical obscurity, being mentioned nowhere else in all the Hebrew Scriptures, the apocryphal/deuterocanonical books, or the New Testament. Apart from her lack of recognition outside the book that bears her name, we can hope that perhaps some ancient readers (and hopefully more modern readers) saw in Ruth a woman of great strength and determination, a redeemer and liberator in her own right, part of the "underside," often untold Israelite story, where the female half of humanity performed its part in the drama of the divine-human encounter.

ESTHER—WOMEN AND THE STRUCTURES OF POLITICAL POWER

The Place of the Book in the Bible

The book of Esther did not find its way into the canon of the Hebrew Bible either easily or early. The core of the book was written sometime during the period of Persian dominance in the ancient Near East (539-332 B.C.E.), but its status in the Jewish community was still being questioned centuries later. No evidence suggests that the book of Esther was recognized as scripture by the Council of Jamnia in 90 C.E. The extensive library of biblical and non-biblical works belonging to the Jewish community at Qumran, that dates from the end of the third century B.C.E. to the latter part of the first century C.E., known to us as the Dead Sea Scrolls, did not include Esther. As late as the third century C.E., some rabbis still refused to regard Esther as sacred scripture. They did not regard it as one that "defiled the hands" (that is, canonical), for we read in the Babylonian Talmud (*Meg.* 7a):

> Rav Judah said in the name of Samuel: [the scroll of] Esther does not make the hands unclean. Are we to infer from that, that Samuel was of the opinion that Esther was not composed under the inspiration of the holy spirit? How can this be, seeing that Samuel has said that Esther was composed under the inspiration of the holy spirit?—It was composed to be recited [by heart], but not to be written.

Why were questions raised about the book of Esther? Certainly one reason may have stemmed from the religious perspective of the book, or lack thereof. God is nowhere mentioned in the book of Esther. The book contains no mention of the Torah or covenant. Neither is there any mention of such basic themes as election, prayer, the temple, Jerusalem, or sacrifice. Also missing are Jewish virtues such as kindness, mercy, and forgiveness. Many readers of Esther have been unconvinced by scholarly attempts to explain away such events as Esther's unwillingness to spare Haman's life when he begged her (6:7), her requests both for another day so that she can exterminate more of her enemies in Susa (9:13), and her request that the ten sons of Haman be hanged (9:13-14). The most difficult passage in the book in this regard is 8:11:

> The king allowed the Jews who were in every city to assemble and defend their lives, to destroy, to kill, and to annihilate any armed force of any people or province that might attack them, with their children and women, and to plunder their goods.

Esther is a Jewish woman, married to a Gentile, and living in a pagan environment. That these characteristics of Esther were problematic for some in the Jewish community is attested to by the writing of a book in the second century B.C.E. called the Greek Additions to Esther, found in the apocryphal/deuterocanonical books. In this book, prayers that clarify Esther's identity as a Jew in a Gentile environment, and which, from the perspective of this later author, were omitted from the book of Esther, are supplied. The Greek Additions to Esther make clear that Esther detested being married to a Gentile and assert that although she lived in a pagan environment, she scrupulously kept the Jewish dietary laws.

The Jewish festival of Purim traces its origins to the book of Esther. The probable reason for Esther's inclusion in the canon is its connection with this festival, an extremely popular one first celebrated by Jews in the Diaspora. Purim is a festival of exuberant rejoicing. For example, during the celebration of Purim, it is recommended that people should drink until they can no longer tell the difference between "Blessed be Mordecai!" and "Cursed be Haman!" The inclusion of the book of Esther in the canon was probably the result of popular pressure in connection with this holiday.

The book of Esther tells the story of the Persian king Ahasuerus, also known as Xerxes, who deposed his queen Vashti because she refused to be trotted out as a sex object. An attractive young Jewish woman named Esther then attracted the king's attention and she became his new queen. Her adopted father (and cousin) Mordecai got involved in a quarrel with the king's vizier, Haman. Out of revenge against Mordecai, Haman hatched a plot that would have slaughtered all of the Jews in the empire. His plot, however, was discovered and backfired on him, thanks to Esther. Haman ended up being hanged on the very gallows he had constructed for the Jews, and the other enemies of the Jews were destroyed as well. Mordecai was then appointed as the new vizier and instituted the festival of Purim to celebrate this great victory.

While the book may not always have been a popular one, the book of Esther does seek to inform Jews that their festival of national liberation originated in a historical event. It explains to them why such a festival bears a non-Hebrew name, Purim, meaning "lots," referring to the fact that Haman intended to destroy all Jews in the kingdom on a day chosen by the drawing of lots. It also presents to Jews living in the Diaspora an inspirational story about the accomplishments of their ancestors, who also lived in the Diaspora and faced some formidable foes.

The Plot of the Story of Esther

As a short story, the book of Esther is designed to be heard or read in a single sitting. Indeed, the entire scroll of Esther is read on Purim. When read, noisemakers are used by the listeners to drown out Haman's name when it appears in the story. The plot of the story unfolds rapidly, with much less dialogue than we find in other narratives in Hebrew scripture. The four main characters—Ahasuerus the king, Mordecai, Haman, and Esther—carry the story. Ahasuerus is pictured as an ineffectual king who seems ready to accept any advice offered. The plot of the story exploits this fatal character flaw. Mordecai is the wise and virtuous courtier who battles with his colleagues at the court. He represents the Jew who will not be bowed by circumstances, who will seize opportunity when it is nearby. Haman is an insecure bootlicker who is so obsessed with destroying Mordecai that he abandons his master plan so that he can, hopefully, kill Mordecai a bit sooner. His vanity turns him into a buffoon, so his fall is not a tragic one, and does not elicit the reader's sympathy. Esther enters the story as a woman regarded as a sex object, but increases in stature throughout the tale. A Jewish orphan raised by her cousin Mordecai, she is attractive and charming, but also has the political savvy to respond to what others expect of her. She becomes queen because she lets others make decisions crucial to her future, yet she is a woman who comes into her own because men create crises for themselves that they cannot resolve. Esther rises to the occasion, and even after Mordecai has been appointed vizier, she finds the means by which to save her people:

> On that day King Ahasuerus gave to Queen Esther the house of Haman, the enemy of the Jews; and Mordecai came before the king, for Esther had told what he was to her. Then the king took off his signet ring, which he had taken from Haman, and gave it to Mordecai. So Esther set Mordecai

over the house of Haman. Then Esther spoke again to the king; she fell at his feet, weeping and pleading with him to avert the evil design of Haman the Agagite and the plot that he had devised against the Jews. The king held out the golden scepter to Esther, and Esther rose and stood before the king. She said, "If it pleases the king, and if I have won his favor, and if the thing seems right before the king and I have his approval, let an order be written to revoke the letters devised by Haman son of Hammedatha the Agagite, which he wrote giving orders to destroy the Jews who are in all the provinces of the king. For how can I bear to see the calamity that is coming on my people? Or how can I bear to see the destruction of my kindred?" Then King Ahasuerus said to Queen Esther and to the Jew Mordecai, "See, I have given Esther the house of Haman, and they have hanged him on the gallows, because he plotted to lay hands on the Jews. You may write as you please with regard to the Jews, in the name of the king, and seal it with the king's ring; for an edict written in the name of the king and sealed with the king's ring cannot be revoked." (8:1–8)

The fact that Esther is returned to Mordecai's control after her moment of triumph, however, indicates much about the status and role of women in antiquity.

Assessments of Esther

Androcentrism characterizes many commentaries on Esther, and most commentators have focused on the character of Mordecai as the paradigm for Jewish life in the Diaspora. Carey Moore, for example, says: "Between Mordecai and Esther the greater hero is Mordecai, who supplied the brains while Esther simply followed his directions" (1971: lii). Or, compare the assessment of Esther in an older, standard commentary:

Esther, for the chance of winning wealth and power, takes her place in the herd of maidens who became concubines of the king. She wins her victories not by skill or by character, but by her beauty. She conceals her origin, is relentless toward a fallen enemy, secures not merely that the Jews escape from danger, but that they fall upon their enemies, slay their wives and children, and plunder their property. (Paton: 96)

Sidnie Ann White, however, has sketched out a very different characterization of Esther, one that sees her as the true hero of the tale (1989). The traits in her character and the actions that make her successful are those that a Jew must emulate if he or she is to be successful in the precarious world of the Diaspora. Mordecai, while certainly a sympathetic character, is not successful because he stubbornly refuses to fit into the situation in which he finds himself. Esther unravels the plot of Haman and strengthens her position, while affirming, in the end, her ethnic identity as a Jew (White: 166). White uses some recent studies on the psychology of women to show that women function differently in the world than men, and that therefore their actions must be judged according to their own standards. Societies characteristically include those who are dominant and those who are subordinate. The Jews in the Diaspora were clearly in a subordinate position under the dominant Persian authorities. The Jews had to adjust to their lack of immediate political and economic power and learn to work within the system to gain whatever power they could. In the book of Esther, Esther is presented as a role model for this adjustment. "Not only is she a woman, a member of a perpetually subordinate population, but she is an orphan, a powerless member of Jewish society" (White: 167). With no inherent power of her own, owing to her sex or her position in society, Esther had to learn to make her way among the powerful and to cooperate with the powers that be to secure a place for herself and her people.

THE ACTIVE ESTHER

From the point in the book where she is introduced (in 2:7), Esther is not a passive character, but one who takes steps, within the situation in which she finds herself, to position herself as best she can. At first Esther does not reveal that she is Jewish because Mordecai has instructed her not to do so (2:10). Some commentators have used this fact to affirm Mordecai's dominance over Esther. A more sympathetic reading would reveal that she sensibly follows the advice of the more experienced politician Mordecai, who after all, "sits in the king's gate." The story then goes on (2:15-18) to explain how Esther won the king's favor and ascended to the position of queen. Again, her actions show her taking advantage of existing opportunities to improve her position. White, in commenting on this part of the narrative, says that it is necessary to reflect on some of the presuppositions of the story and our own prejudices. She observes that to our ears, becoming a member of a harem and attempting to win the favor of a man by sexual means sounds degrading, and to do so would be degrading in our society. However, if we think in terms of Esther's historical period and the acceptable means of winning power, her actions become less problematic. Her behavior is no more reprehensible than the "boot-licking" responses of Xerxes' counselors and the ruthless behavior of Haman in trying to obtain power. Esther's actions simply include a sexual element, and there is no note of censure in the Hebrew text for this; in fact, Esther's behavior is applauded (1989: 168).

ESTHER AS DELIVERER

Esther's next appearance in the book is at a pivotal point, in chapter 4. As the chapter opens, Mordecai is staggered by the news of the king's plan to annihilate all Jews. He "tore his clothes and put on sackcloth and ashes, and went through the city, wailing with a loud and bitter cry" (4:1). When Mordecai's demonstration is brought to Esther's attention, she first responds in a nurturing way—she sends him some clothes. At this point in the story, Esther begins to leave behind any subordination to Mordecai. She starts to actively take on the role of their people's deliverer. At first (4:11) Esther states that she cannot go before the king, for her status simply does not allow for such an uncalled-for audience. Mordecai, however, reminds Esther of her relationship to her family and the Jewish community as a whole (4:13-14). From this point on, Esther shows that she is willing to take the lead. She orders a fast and prepares to go to Ahasuerus. The last verse of chapter 4 communicates the impact of her actions: "Mordecai then went away and did everything as Esther had ordered him" (4:17). In her decision to confront the king, Esther pursues the same course she has taken up to this point. She does not foolishly risk everything without having assessed the prospects of success. She realizes that the best chance of success for her as a woman is appealing to the king's emotions, not to his logical powers. Her strategy meets with success and Ahasuerus offers to give her whatever she wants, "Even to the half of my kingdom" (5:6). Rather than asking him to dismantle the plan to annihilate the Jews at this point, Esther proceeds on a different tack. White observes that this might seem like the right time to ask the king to save the Jews. That would not neutralize Haman however, as Esther realized. So, rather than making such a request and leaving the results to the discretion of a capricious king very easily swayed, she sets out to lull Haman into a false sense of complacency. This will place the king in a position where a strong emotional response from him is guaranteed. She invites the king and Haman to a [second] private dinner party. This puts the king in *her* territory, the women's quarters, where she can more easily control the situation (1989: 171).

At the second banquet (chapter 7) Esther makes her request to the king: "If I have won your favor, O king, and if it pleases the king, let my life be given me—that is my petition—and the lives of my people—that is my request. For we have been sold, I and my people, to be destroyed, to be killed, and to be annihilated" (7:3–4). She then exposes Haman's plot.

ESTHER'S VICTORY

Chapter 8 wraps up the story of Esther and Mordecai. Esther is given Haman's property by Ahasuerus, and on her recommendation, Mordecai is made vizier in place of Haman. Esther now controls wealth, court appointments, and access to the king. But the edict for the destruction of the Jews still has be dealt with. Esther again petitions the king in an emotion-laden scene. As Clines has pointed out, her speech in 8:5–6 is a masterpiece of courtier's rhetoric (1984: 101). She prefaces it with four conditional clauses: "*If* it pleases the king, and *if* I have won his favor, and *if* the thing seems right before the king, and *if* I have his approval. . . ." The first two are familiar from earlier speeches of Esther (5:4, 8 and 7:3); the third and fourth are new here. In the third and fourth clauses she shifts the responsibility for overturning Haman's decree to the king and appeals to her relationship with him. As a result, the king grants her *carte blanche:* "You may write as you please with regard to the Jews, in the name of the king, and seal it with the king's ring" (8:8).

White's assessment of Esther is fitting as a conclusion for our study of Esther: Her conduct throughout the story has been a masterpiece of feminine skill. From beginning to end, she does not make a misstep. . . . She is a model for the successful conduct of life in the often uncertain world of the Diaspora: the once-powerful Jewish nation has become a subordinate minority within a foreign empire, just as Esther, as a woman, is subject to the dominant male. However, by accepting the reality of a subordinate position and learning to gain power by working within the structure rather than against it, the Jew can build a successful and fulfilling life in the Diaspora, as Esther does in the court of Ahasuerus. (1989: 173)

JUDITH—A GENERAL'S NEMESIS AND A PEOPLE'S SAVIOR

The Nature of the Book

Like Ruth and Esther, the book of Judith is a short story in which a woman plays a dominant role. Like the book of Esther, this story is characterized by nationalism and includes the motif of feminine beauty facilitating deliverance. In contrast to Esther and Ruth, in this book no figure of an uncle or a newly discovered male relative guides the action or provides rescue by marriage. Judith alone plays the hero. Unlike Esther, the story of Judith has deeply religious elements. Also, unlike the stories of Ruth and Esther, the book of Judith is not a part of the canon of the Hebrew Bible. For Catholics it is a deuterocanonical book, while, for Protestants, it is included in the Apocrypha. The Hebrew original of Judith has been lost. It was, however, one of only two apocryphal books with sufficient popularity in the Western church (the other was Tobit) to convince Jerome to include it in his translation of the Bible, the Latin Vulgate. The story of Judith has been a popular subject for Western artists as well. Especially during the Renaissance, when artists were freed from earlier restrictions, this biblical story featuring two universally appealing themes, sex and death, became one that attracted the attention of a number of artists.

While the stories of Ruth and Esther have the ring of historicality about them, Judith is a curious mix of historical inaccuracies and anachronisms, combined with fantastic geography. These historical errors and geographical blunders are so glaring as to make one entertain the idea that they are not accidental or a result of the author's ignorance. Rather, they may have been deliberate literary devices used by the author to alert the reader to the fact that he or she is reading a piece of "historical fiction" that should not be taken literally. The author seems intentionally to have defied history so as to distract the reader's attention from the historical content and focus it instead on the religious conflict and outcome. A short list of historical errors in Judith is instructive at this point:

- Nebuchadrezzar II, who ruled Babylonia from 605 to 562 B.C.E. appears at the beginning of Judith (1:1) as reigning over the Assyrians in Nineveh, which in fact had been destroyed by his father Nabopolassar.
- The Assyrian campaign against Persia is set at a time after Nineveh had already fallen (612 B.C.E.).
- The author compresses time, placing the return of the Jews from the Exile (538 B.C.E.), the rebuilding of the temple (515 B.C.E.), and even perhaps the

purification of the temple after its profanation by Antiochus IV (165 B.C.E.), all in the lifetime of Nebuchadnezzar (4:1; 5:19).

- The characters Holofernes and Bagoas may represent two generals by these names (Orophernes and Bagoas) who served under the Persian ruler Artaxerxes III Ochus and waged a campaign against Phoenicia and Egypt in about 350 B.C.E.
- The route of march of Holofernes' army (2:21-28) is a geographical impossibility, as is the fact that his army completed a march of 300 miles in three days.
- Bethulia (which means "virgin" in Hebrew), Judith's village, is not only otherwise unknown, but is placed in the geographically and historically improbable position of being a Judean site in the Valley of Esdraelon in the period immediately following the Exile (4:1-7).

If, as some scholars have suggested, this book was written in Palestine toward the middle of the second century B.C.E. in an atmosphere of nationalistic and religious fervor generated by the Maccabean Revolt, then some of its themes and its historical confusion might be better appreciated. Like apocalyptic literature such as Daniel, which attacks the contemporary tyrant Antiochus Epiphanes IV (see our Chapter 16), not by mentioning him by name but by speaking of him as a figure from the past, so, for the author of Judith, Antiochus may appear as Holofernes. Holofernes' demand that the people worship Nebuchadnezzar may point to Antiochus as well. Just as the apocryphal/deuterocanonical book of 1 Maccabees tells the story of the overthrow of Antiochus, the rededication of the temple, and of the origins of the festival of Hanukkah, so the book of Judith has long been popular among Jews at the time of Hanukkah.

The Story's Plot

While the historical and geographical errors have sometimes provided ammunition for the book's detractors, on the plus side is the artistry in the telling of the story, especially after chapter 8, where Judith is finally introduced. The plot of the story is deceptively simple. The tiny postexilic Jewish nation faces the overwhelmingly superior forces of the army of Nebuchadrezzar, under the leadership of his general Holofernes. Holofernes is not only bent on military conquest, but also intends to destroy all religions other than the one of his "deified" commander-in-chief.

As the story develops, Holofernes' army has besieged the Jews in the town of Bethulia. The most serious threat to a besieged city has appeared—the water supply has failed, leaving the Jews at the point of surrender. With the stage being set, Judith appears on the scene, an attractive, young, wealthy widow, who, as the plot develops, is also seen to be intelligent, religiously dedicated, and resolute of will. She faces and conquers, in turn, two enemies: first, the cowardice of the male leadership of her own people, and then, the might of the Assyrian army. Her very first words in the story, after having been informed of the gravity of the situation, are ones of reproach to the leading men of the city for their lack of faith in God as shown in their willingness to surrender Bethulia to the Assyrians (8:11-13):

> Listen to me, rulers of the people of Bethulia! What you have said to the people today is not right; you have even sworn and pronounced this oath between God and you, promising to surrender the town to our enemies unless the Lord turns and helps us within so many days. Who are you to put God to the test today, and to set yourselves up in the place of God in human affairs? You are putting the Lord Almighty to the test, but you will never learn anything!

She then turns to prayer (9:1-14), after which she takes off her widow's clothing, adorns herself, and sets out from Bethulia for the Assyrian camp (10:1-10). Passing herself off as a defector who can provide Holofernes with valuable military intelligence, she is led into the general's presence, where she proceeds to dazzle him with her beauty and deceive him with her carefully chosen words (11:5-19). After three days has passed, she is invited to a banquet/drinking party (12:1-20). After everyone else has retired, Judith is left alone with Holofernes, who has passed out on his bed in a drunken stupor. Taking down his own sword, she beheads him, bags his head, and sets off for Bethulia with her grisly trophy (13:1-14). When the Assyrians discover that their leader had been decapitated, they panic and run for the hills, whereon the Jews plunder their camp for thirty days (15). Judith then leads a triumphal procession up to Jerusalem, where the people feast for three months. When the festival is over, Judith returns to Bethulia, where, although she is wooed by many suitors, she remains a widow and lives to the age of 105.

For the reader familiar with narratives of the Hebrew Bible, the story of Judith is rich with allusions. The resemblances to the story of Esther are obvious. Judith's returning home with the head of an enemy is reminiscent of the story in 2 Sam 20:14-22, where a woman has the head of Sheba, an adversary of David, delivered to Joab. Echoes appear, too, of Jael's killing Sisera in her tent (Judg 5), the exploits of Ehud in Judg 3:12-30, and of the story of David and Goliath (1 Sam 17). These echoes of past heroism, just under the surface in the story of Judith, could have provided much-needed encouragement for the Jewish community in time of crisis, whether in the time of Antiochus IV or at another time.

The Book's Structure

The literary structure of the book has attracted the attention of many commentators. Moore has observed that in the eyes of many, Judith consists of two very unequal parts: chapters 1-7 and chapters 8-16. The two parts are unequal not so much with respect to their length as to their respective importance, interest, and literary quality (1985:56).

Recently, however, as scholars have begun to assess Judith as a short story rather than as a historical novel, a greater appreciation of the structure of the book's first seven chapters has emerged. These chapters structurally serve, at several levels, as a foil to the book's second half. Structurally speaking, the story's first half is dominated by men, and the theme is fear or its denial; the second half is dominated by a woman, and the theme is beauty. A convincing schematization of the two parts of Judith has been developed by Toni Craven (1977). Her study shows a threefold chiastic structure in both halves of the book. Craven's schema for the book looks like this:

CHAPTERS 1-7

1. Introduction to Nebuchadrezzar and his campaigns against Arphaxad (1:1-16)
2. Nebuchadrezzar commissions Holofernes to take vengeance on the disobedient nations (2:1-13)
3. Development
    A. The campaign against the disobedient nations; the people surrender (2:14-3:10)
    B. Israel hears and is "greatly terrified"; Joakim orders war preparations (4:1-15)
    C. Holofernes talks with Achior. Achior is expelled from the Assyrian camp (5:1-6:11)
    C'. Achior is received into Bethulia; he talks with the people of Israel (6:12-21)
    B'. Holofernes orders war preparations; Israel sees and is "greatly terrified" (7:1-5)
    A'. The campaign against Bethulia; the people want to surrender (7:6-32)

CHAPTERS 8-16

    A. Introduction of Judith (8:1-8)
    B. Judith plans to save Israel (8:9-10:8)
    C. Judith and her maid leave Bethulia (10:9-10)
    D. Judith overcomes Holofernes (10:11-13:10a)
    C'. Judith and her maid return to Bethulia (13:10b-11)
    B'. Judith plans the destruction of Israel's enemy (13:12-16:20)
    A'. Conclusion about Judith (16:21-25)

Literary Artistry in Judith

Within its chiastic structure, the tale of Judith is told with consummate artistry. Moore has observed that an important key to understanding the artistry of Judith is the use of irony: "A number of biblical books . . . make effective use of irony, but few, if any, are as quintessentially ironic as Judith" (1985: 78). While several species of literary devices could be classified as irony, at the root of irony is the fact that a writer often means precisely the opposite of what he or she says, or describes something contrary to what actually was or was expected. The book of Judith is ironic in its very nature, from its first verse until its last. The principal characters themselves are ironic. Judith is a childless widow who gives birth to new life for her people. She is a wealthy woman whose lifestyle is quite simple. While very "feminine"—in the sexist sense of the term—she refuses to play sexually stereotypical roles. She is scrupulously moral in keeping Jewish dietary laws but does not hesitate to prevaricate with abandon. The character of Holofernes is also an ironic one. An indomitable general, he cannot bring about the submission of a small town of Jews. Hoping to abuse a defenseless widow, he is subdued by her. He even falls by his own sword. While thus several forms of irony abound in the narrative of Judith, all of the following passages are ironic in some way: 6:2, 5, 7-8; 8:34; 11:1, 3b-4a, 5, 6, 7, 16, 22-23; 12:4, 14, 18; 13:7-8; 16:9.

The Book's Purpose and Value

Assessments of Judith are telling illustrations of the social location of commentators, for they say as much about how the commentator regards social arrangements in his or her day as they say about Judith. Moore sets forth some of these assessments (1985: 64-66). In the first century, in a period in which Christians were threatened with persecution by pagans, Judith was seen as a brave and godly woman by the likes of Clement of Rome. When religious persecution was not so much a threat to the Church Fathers as was sexual temptation, in the second to fourth centuries, Judith was praised more for her self-imposed celibacy than for her courage in facing and defeating Holofernes. Commentators living in Victorian England of the nineteenth century, with their tightly defined paradigms of womanly behavior, regarded Judith's use of deception and her compromising herself by even being in Holofernes' bedroom as constituting moral turpitude. Contemporary feminists, who contend with socially restrictive gender roles, have seen in Judith "the archetypal androgyne," that is, man-woman. "In her marvelous androgyny, Judith embodies yet somehow transcends the male/female dichotomy. To this extent, she is a heroine who rises above the sexism of her author's culture" (Montley 1978: 40).

Judith is a character of passionate piety. She prays regularly, not just in times of crisis. She remains faithful to God in a singular manner. Therefore, the incredible risk that she took is even more set into relief. Her faith is an active one. She does not just pray, but she acts in the name of a God who acts for those who are marginalized by their own society or by the power brokers of the world. Her prayer recalls her ancestors' extreme action in avenging the rape of Dinah in Genesis 34 (9:2) and praises a God who defends the defenseless:

> For your strength does not depend upon numbers, nor your might on the powerful. But you are the God of the lowly, helper of the oppressed, upholder of the weak, protector of the forsaken, savior of those without hope. Please, please God of my father, God of the heritage of Israel, Lord of heaven and earth, Creator of the waters, King of all your creation, hear my prayer! (9:11-12)

Eileen Schuller's remarks regarding Judith provide an appropriate conclusion for our journey through Judith's book and those of her sisters in the faith,

Ruth and Esther. Schuller thinks that Judith provides an example of a female who challenges and overcomes both the male enemy and the male establishment within her own community. She is presented as a model of faith and wisdom, combining prayer and piety with human initiative and unconventional action. In parallel situations of oppression, as in Latin America today, the story of Judith is remembered and retold by women as a model for women's involvement in the struggle to liberate their people. Schuller ends by observing that in much of North-American culture, women are more attuned to other aspects of the story, such as Judith's independent control of her estate and the role of her maid "who is in charge of all she possessed" (8:10) (1992: 243).

Still some aspects of the narrative raise questions from a feminist perspective. At the most basic level, this book serves as a caution against the simplistic assumption that every woman portrayed, or even praised, in the Bible necessarily provides a model for women to emulate. The lesson here is not that women should be liars, murderers, and *femmes fatales!* Neither would many women today want simply to emulate Judith either in the withdrawal from sexual activity during her long period of widowhood or in her exploitation of her sexuality to seduce and ensnare Holofernes. Though the principal character and hero of the book of Judith is a woman, it has rarely even been suggested that the author of the book might have been a woman. In some ways, this is still very much a man's story!

STUDY QUESTIONS

RUTH

1. Look at the following transition verses and comment on how they mark the transition from one scene to the next: 1:5, 1:22, 2:23, 3:18, 4:12.
2. How are the specific symbols of emptiness in the first two scenes transformed into symbols of fullness in the last two scenes?
3. List and comment on examples of similarity and difference between scene three (Ruth 2) and scene four (Ruth 3).
4. What does the scene on the threshing floor (Ruth 3) suggest about views on sex and marriage in the Hebrew Bible?
5. Some have suggested that parallels can be drawn between Ruth and Abraham in the book of Genesis (especially Gen 12). Why might Ruth be compared to Abraham?
6. Develop your own *thesis* for the Book of Ruth. What, in your opinion, is a *central* idea of the book, an idea that is as valid today as it was in ancient Israel?

ESTHER

1. The plot of the book of Esther is replete with dramatic reversals. What are some of these reversals?

2. Look at the organization of Esther. How do banquets/drinking parties provide the main literary structure for the book?
3. Where is the turning point in the story of Esther? Why?
4. Research on the book of Esther reflects two main theological concerns: (1) Esther has too little reference to God and religion for a biblical work; (2) Esther has too much violence and vengeance for a religious work. With these concerns in mind, make a case for the inclusion of Esther in the canon of scripture.

JUDITH

1. As noted, the book of Judith can be divided into two parts. When any book is so sharply split into two distinct parts, what messages does such a division convey?
2. A motif that is found in both halves of the book is the motif of fear. Trace the motif of fear in part one (chapters 1 - 7) and part two (chapters 8 - 16). Who inspires or causes fear in the respective parts?
3. List those passages in Judith that speak of what "the hand" does. The "hand of Yahweh" is spoken of often in the narrative of the Exodus (Exod 3 : 19, 20; 6 : 1; 7 : 5; 13 : 9). Likewise Exodus refers to the hand of Moses as the agent of God's plan to liberate his people. What role does this phrase play in the book of Judith? How might it remind the reader of the Exodus theme?
4. We have observed that the book of Judith is full of irony. Why do you think that this literary device is appropriate for the kind of religious situations that are addressed by the postexilic books of Esther and Judith?
5. How does the book of Judith contrast masculine strength in the first part of the book with feminine strength in the book's second half?

BIBLIOGRAPHY

Brenner, A. 1985. *The Israelite Woman: Social Role and Literary Type in Biblical Narrative.* Sheffield, England: JSOT.

Camp, Claudia. 1981. "The Wise Women of 2 Samuel: A Role Model for Women in Early Israel." *Catholic Biblical Quarterly 43,* 14 - 29.

Campbell, E. F., Jr. 1975. *Ruth: A New Translation with Introduction and Commentary. The Anchor Bible,* 7. Garden City, NY: Doubleday.

Clines, D. J. A. 1984. *The Esther Scroll.* JSOTSup 30. Sheffield, England: JSOT.

Craven, Toni. 1977. "Artistry and Faith in the Book of Judith." *Semeia 8,* 75 - 101.

Day, Peggy L., ed. 1989. *Gender and Difference in Ancient Israel.* Minneapolis: Fortress.

Emmerson, G.I. 1989. "Women in Ancient Israel," in R. E. Clements, ed. *The World of Ancient Israel: Sociological, Anthropological and Political Perspectives.* pp. 371 - 394. Cambridge, England: Cambridge University Press.

Fewell, Danna, and Gunn, D. M. 1990. *Compromising Redemption: Relating Characters in the Book of Ruth.* Louisville: Westminster/John Knox.

Gottwald, Norman K. 1985. *The Hebrew Bible—A Socio-Literary Introduction*. Philadelphia: Fortress.

McKeating, H. 1979. "Sanctions against Adultery in Ancient Israelite Society, with some reflections on Methodology in the Study of Old Testament Ethics." *Journal for the Study of the Old Testament 11*, 57-72.

Meyers, Carol L. 1988. *Discovering Eve: Ancient Israelite Women in Context*. New York: Oxford University.

———. 1992. "Everyday Life: Women in the Period of the Hebrew Bible," in *The Women's Bible Commentary*, Carol A. Newsom and Sharon H. Ringe, eds., 244-251. Louisville: Westminster/John Knox.

Montley, Patricia. 1978. "Judith in the Fine Arts: The Appeal of the Archetypal Androgyne," *Anima 4*, 37-42.

Moore, Carey A. 1971. *Esther: Introduction, Translation, and Notes*. The Anchor Bible, 7B. Garden City, NY: Doubleday.

———. 1985. *Judith: A New Translation with Introduction and Commentary*. The Anchor Bible, 40B. Garden City, NY: Doubleday.

Otwell, J. H. 1977. *And Sarah Laughed. The Status of Women in the Old Testament*. Philadelphia: Westminster.

Paton, Lewis Bayles. 1908. *A Critical and Exegetical Commentary on the Book of Esther*, ICC. New York: Scribner.

Schuller, Eileen M. 1992. "The Apocrypha." *The Women's Bible Commentary*, Carol A. Newsom and Sharon H. Ringe, eds., 235-243. Louisville: Westminster/John Knox.

Trible, Phyllis. 1973. "Depatriarchalizing in Biblical Interpretation." *Journal of the American Academy of Religion 41*, 30-48.

———. 1978. *God and the Rhetoric of Sexuality*. Philadelphia: Fortress.

White, Sidney Ann. 1989. "Esther: A Feminine Model for Jewish Diaspora," Peggy L. Day, ed., 161-177. *Gender and Difference in Ancient Israel*. Minneapolis: Fortress.

Chapter 15

SAGES—THE WISDOM
MOVEMENT IN ANCIENT ISRAEL

Suggested Bible Reading
Job 1:1–2:13; 4:1–14:22; 28:1–42:17;
Proverbs 1:1–9:18; 22:17–24:22; 25:1–29:27;
Ecclesiastes 1:1–12:13; Sirach 1:11–30; 24:1–34; 42:15–50:24;
Wisdom 1:1–6:21; 11:1–19:22

WHAT IS "WISDOM" AND WHO
WERE THE "SAGES"?: THE SOCIOHISTORIC
HORIZONS OF THE WISDOM MOVEMENT

In the course of our journey through the Hebrew Bible we have had several *déjà vu* experiences. Here, in the next-to-the-last stop on our itinerary, an image we have seen before reemerges and undergoes a striking transformation. In the story of the Garden of Eden in Gen 2–3 the tree of life was in the center of the garden. Because of the first couple's disobedience, they were expelled from the garden before they could eat from the tree of life and live forever. We also observed that in the history of biblical interpretation, many interpreters have placed the primary responsibility for the expulsion from the garden on the woman. As we begin our examination of biblical wisdom literature, the image of the tree of life reappears:

> She [wisdom] is a tree of life to those who lay hold of her; those who
> hold her fast are called happy. (Prov 3:18)

Here, wisdom as a woman is the tree of life. "Woman Wisdom" is not the source of humanity's problems. On the contrary, whoever finds this woman "finds life" (Prov 8:35) and all who hate her "love death" (Prov 8:36).

The "Wisdom" Books and Their International Character

What is "wisdom" in the Hebrew Bible? In terms of books, three have been called "wisdom" books in the Hebrew Bible and two in the apocryphal/deuterocanonical books. The three in the Hebrew Bible are Proverbs, Job, and Ecclesiastes (called Qoheleth in Hebrew). The two in the Apocrypha are Ben Sirach (also known as Ecclesiasticus or Sirach) and the Wisdom of Solomon. What characteristics do these five books share that set them apart as "wisdom literature"?

On one level, we can observe what these books do *not* include, or at least do not emphasize. Missing from this literature are the usual themes that permeate the rest of the literature of ancient Israel. There is no mention of the promises to the patriarchs, the Exodus and Moses, the covenant and Sinai, the promise to David, and so forth. The exceptions to this statement appear in the very late apocryphal/deuterocanonical books (Sir 44–50 and Wis 11–19) and only prove the rule (Murphy 1990: 1). On the positive side, these five books share an interest in observing life as experienced by the individual and then drawing conclusions about the meaning of life from those observations. On one level, "wisdom" simply refers to the ability to discern meaning from the immediate experience of life.

The books classified as wisdom literature also share certain literary forms, such as the proverb, the parable, the admonition, and a certain kind of discourse and vocabulary. Wisdom literature is also international in scope. Proverbs, Job, and Ecclesiastes all have parallels in theme, literary genre, or historical connection with Egypt and Mesopotamia. These parallels derive in part from the fact that wisdom literature does not draw its images from ethnically-specific Israelite history but from more universal human observations. From Egypt there are pieces called "teachings" or "instructions." Two important examples of such "instructions" are "The Teachings of Ptah-Hotep" and "The Teachings of Amen-em-ope." "The Teachings of Ptah-Hotep" has many parallels in Proverbs, Ecclesiastes, and Sirach. Many explicit similarities exist between "The Teachings of Amen-em-ope" and Prov 22:17–24:22. Both follow the same format—an introduction followed by thirty "chapters" of similar admonitions. Other Egyptian works have sometimes been compared with biblical wisdom literature, but no evidence provides an explicit "Egyptian connection."

Like those examples from Egypt, a type of literature from Mesopotamia has often been discussed in relation to Job and Ecclesiastes. Prominent among this Mesopotamian literature are "Man and His God," a Sumerian text, and "I Will Praise the Lord of Wisdom," "Dialogue of Pessimism," and "The Dialogue about Human Misery" (or "The Babylonian Theodicy"), all of which come from Babylonia. "The Dialogue about Human Misery," "Man and His God," and "I Will

Praise the Lord of Wisdom" are often cited in connection with Job. "The Dialogue of Pessimism" is compared with Ecclesiastes.

The Sages

Who were the "sages" who gave us the wisdom literature? A verse in Jeremiah offers a clue: "Instruction shall not perish from the priest, nor counsel from the wise, nor the word from the prophet" (18:18b). This verse refers indirectly to three types of religious leaders in ancient Israel—the priest, the wise, the prophet. Here the sage, or "the wise," is one who offers "counsel," complementing the "instruction" of the priest and the "word" of the prophet. So what is "counsel"? For one thing, because the counsel of the sage is grouped with the Torah (instruction) for which the priest was responsible, and the oracular utterances of the prophet, the "counsel" of the sage did not differ qualitatively in authority from what came from the priest and prophet. In the apocryphal/ deuterocanonical book of Sirach, wisdom as the counsel of the sage is identified explicitly as in no way inferior to the Torah. As part of a poem praising Woman Wisdom, Sirach identifies Wisdom with the Torah:

> All this is the book of the covenant of the Most High God, the law that Moses commanded us as an inheritance for the congregations of Jacob. (24:23)

What the sage said, deriving from the observation of the experience of individuals, was regarded, like the priestly Torah and the prophetic word, as coming from God. The clearly religious quality of wisdom teaching at its foundations is voiced in the introduction to the book of Proverbs: The fear of the LORD is the beginning of knowledge" (1:7; see also Prov 9:10; Job 28:28; Sir 1:14). This verse voices the belief that the prerequisite to the giving of counsel based on one's observations is an attitude of awe and reverence toward God. Wisdom teaching is *not* at its roots secular knowledge. As Gerhard von Rad has written: "Israel knew nothing of the *aporia* [doubt] which we read into these proverbs. It was perhaps her greatness that she did not keep faith and knowledge apart. The experiences of the world were for her always divine experiences as well, and the experiences of God were for her experiences of the world." (1972:62)

One should not, however, confine the sages to a class of religious specialists. At the most basic level, the sages in ancient Israel were one's parents. Because one's parents were one's elders and had accumulated years of experience in observing life, they were to be listened to as "sages." The importance of the family, which we observed in Chapter 2, appears again here. Children come into a world already shaped by their parents, their parents' parents, and so on. Parents first interpret the world to their children. This primary process of education and socialization within the family enabled individuals to find their place in society. While parents may not be described as "official sages," their teaching clearly forms the foundational level of wisdom's program. They serve as the source of the "common sense" adages of oral tradition that capture and distill life's important lessons. Written collections such as the book of Proverbs however, do not have their setting in popular culture. "The *written* transmission of *collections* of proverbs presupposes a cultural milieu different from that of the oral transmission of isolated proverbs used occasionally in everyday life. . . ." (Lemaire 1984: 272).

SAGES AND THE ROYAL COURT

Many scholars have argued that wisdom literature, as written collections, has its origins in the life and needs of the royal court. The final literary products of Proverbs, Job, and Ecclesiastes, which more formally embody wisdom, are seen as the products of a rather narrow and specialized class among the elite in ancient Israel, that of the scribes, which developed thanks to royal patronage. As primary states were formed at both ends of the Fertile Crescent in the ancient Near East, and later a secondary state in Israel in imitation of them, the centralized bureaucracy required skilled record keepers. Out of this bureaucratic need developed state scribal schools, which taught not only the basics of "reading, writing, and arithmetic," but also courses in "how to succeed in elite circles" to the "yuppies" of the ancient world.

The royal setting of wisdom literature in Israel implies that this literature is a product of the ruling elite. The values and interests of the wisdom writers were the same as those of the urban elite whom they served. Success in the circles of the elite, then as now, depended upon learning how to act appropriately in the presence of others, both those above and below one on the social ladder. The ethics of the scribal schools were distinctly pragmatic—if it "works" it must be good. The "Teachings of Ptah-Hotep" is a good example of the output of such state-sponsored scribal schools, including as it does practical, opportunistic advice on how to succeed in specific careers and professions (Matthews and Benjamin: 1991: 185–186):

If you *work for someone* else,
    Take what your master offers.
Do not look about with envy,
    Do not always hope for more.
Stand humbly until your master speaks to you,
    Speak only when spoken to.
Laugh when your master laughs,
    Try to please your master in everything.
But remember this—
    No one knows what is in another's heart. (Prov 23:1–3)
When masters are at the table,
    They may seem to dispense favors as they see fit,
    —to favor those who are useful,
    —to favor those who think as they do.
But Ka, The Human Soul, is guided by The Gods,
    Therefore do not complain about their choices.
If you become *a messenger* for the mighty,
    Be completely reliable on every assignment.

Carry out your orders to the letter.
  Withhold nothing.
  Forget nothing,
  Forge nothing,
  Repeat nothing,
  Embellish nothing.
Do not make harsh language worse,
  Vulgarity turns the mighty into enemies. (Prov 25:13)
If you *work for the newly rich,*
  Ignore their former lack of wealth and distinction.
Do not be prejudiced against them,
  Do not detest them for once being lower class.
Respect them for their accomplishments,
  Acknowledge them for their acquisition of property.
Property does not come of itself,
  Property must be earned.
It is their law for those who wish it.
  As for those who overstep, they are feared.
It is the gods who determine the quality of people.
  God defends them even when they sleep. . . .

According to biblical tradition, state scribalism originated with Solomon (1 Kings 4:29–34) and continued throughout the monarchy. Besides keeping state records, serving as counselors to kings, and training future bureaucrats, these scribal schools also "produced" literature. As an educated elite, they had both the necessary skills and time to compose and copy literary works. Parts of the book of Proverbs may be the only actual wisdom texts that have come down to us from these royal scribal schools. As members of the royal establishment, many of these scribes would have been taken into exile in Babylonia. Suggesting a royal court source for wisdom literature does not, however, tell us the whole story, if only because Proverbs, Job, and Ecclesiastes came to completion *after* the fall of the states of Israel and Judah and *before* a new kind of scribalism developed (Gottwald 1985: 569–570).

The third institutional matrix in which wisdom literature was propagated was the *religious* scribalism that developed during and after the exile. Before the Deuteronomic Reformation in the time of Josiah, legal texts were interpreted and applied by tribal elders and state-appointed judges. The Deuteronomistic circles in the late monarchy and afterward, which were responsible for the Deuteronomistic History, probably included state-trained scribes. After the Exile, these Deuteronomistic circles with their state-trained scribes linked up with the scribes who were a part of the Priestly circles who produced the Pentateuch. The Deuteronomistic wing of this coalition that redacted the finished Pentateuch was "sympathetic to wisdom and probably was a factor in encouraging the shift toward equating wisdom with Torah which eventually transferred most of the wisdom activities from the political scribal context to the religious scribal-legal context" (Gottwald 1985: 570). The apocryphal/deuterocanonical wisdom book of Sirach, which dates to *ca.* 180 B.C.E., with its identification of the Torah and wisdom, is the culmination of this process of the merging of two kinds of scribalism. A direct line of development exists from this new kind of scribalism to the rabbinic Pharisaism that came to rule Jewish life and thought in New Testament times and continues to the present day among Orthodox Jews.

THE WORLDVIEW OF THE SAGES

Because they were members of the elite, the sages' worldview betrays a class consciousness. Those who produced the wisdom literature had little in common with the poorer peasants clinging desperately to their holdings or with the petty tradesmen and the artisans in the cities. . . ." (Gordis 1971: 162). If this view is correct, then the wisdom teaching on poverty should bear the marks of values and attitudes adhered to by the educated elite (Pleins 1987). One way of testing this view is to examine the perspective on poverty and the poor in wisdom teaching.

Various strands of biblical literature discuss the plight of the poor, offering different analyses of their situation. As David Pleins has observed (1992: 402–403), legal texts seek to regulate the treatment of the poor. Prophetic texts concern themselves with the poor who are economically exploited by the large landowners and ruling members of ancient Israelite society. In the wisdom tradition, Proverbs, in a somewhat condescending and possibly censorious tone, promotes the traditional idea that poverty is the undesirable, but inevitable consequence of laziness. Job and Ecclesiastes (to a lesser extent) understand poverty to be the result of political and economic exploitation. In the book of Psalms it is difficult to determine to what extent the language concerning poverty has moved away from concrete cases of poverty to a more spiritualized level. Outside these blocks of literature, the topic of poverty is treated only occasionally. It receives the least attention of all in the narrative literature of the Pentateuch and in the Deuteronomistic History (Frick, forthcoming). Five principal Hebrew words for "poor"/"poverty" cumulatively appear a total of 224 times in the Hebrew Bible. The term *'anî* is the most common term for "poor" in the Hebrew Bible, occurring a total of eighty times, sixteen in the wisdom literature. The use of this term in Proverbs lacks the comprehensive and concrete social justice vision for the *'anî* that we find in the legal and prophetic materials. Unlike the prophetic materials, Proverbs does not link the term *'anî* to the socioeconomic oppression of the poor by the ruling elite.

The next most frequently occurring term for "poor" in the Hebrew Bible is *'ebyôn,* which occurs fifty-nine times in the Hebrew Bible, of which ten are in wisdom texts. The term *'ebyôn* occurs more times in Job than in Proverbs, and while it is difficult to know precisely what significance to give such a small sample, the slightly larger number of occurrences in Job seems to fit a curious distribution pattern for the words for "poor" in the Hebrew Bible. The terms for "poor" in Job are those also found in the prophetic writings, while the most distinctive wisdom words for "poor" are conspicuously absent from Job. This gives the book of Job a "prophetic" character in its defense of the poor and its concrete understanding of their situation (Pleins 1992: 404).

In contrast to the rest of the Hebrew Bible, the wisdom literature has a special vocabulary for discussing poverty. The three most distinctive wisdom words for "poor" in wisdom literature are *rash, machsor,* and *misken.* The way in which these three terms are used shows no awareness that the poor as a group are poor because they have been wronged by the ruling elite, as the prophets proclaimed. Pleins concludes that the wise merely *observe* that taking from the poor is as pointless as giving to the rich. In the end one ends up with nothing. The prophetic view, by contrast, contends that much material gain is made by those who take from the poor! For the wise, however, poverty, like wealth, was accepted as one of the givens of existence with which the student must learn to cope (1987: 67–68).

TYPES OF WISDOM LITERATURE

There are many genres in the wisdom writings, and each of the wisdom books has its own particular mix of them. The principle genres in wisdom literature, their definitions, and examples of where they are found, are indicated in Table 15.1 (adapted from Gottwald 1985: 565).

THE BOOK OF PROVERBS AND COMMON SENSE

From this list of literary forms in biblical wisdom literature, the most common genre is the proverb, *mashal* in Hebrew. The Hebrew title for the book of Proverbs is *mishlê shelomoh,* "The Proverbs of Solomon." The basic meaning of *mashal* in Hebrew is a "comparison." The Hebrew *mashal* includes a wider range of forms than does the ordinary English proverb, which is usually a "one-liner" like: "A stitch in time saves nine," "You can't teach an old dog new tricks," or "Birds of a feather flock together." The literary proverb, found in the book of Proverbs and in the two apocryphal/deuterocanonical wisdom books, Sirach and the Wisdom of Solomon, follows the structure of Hebrew poetry that we discussed in Chapter 13. Commonly the *mashal* is in the form of a bicolon and sometimes a tricolon. The form of the bicolon is well-suited for the *mashal* as a comparison, in which the image in the first line is compared or contrasted with another image in the second:

> The sated appetite spurns honey,
> but to a ravenous appetite even the bitter is sweet. (Prov 27:7)
> Like a gold ring in a pig's snout
> is a beautiful woman without good sense. (Prov 11:22)

Not every *mashal,* however, compares two things. Some extend beyond a single bicolon, multiplying the number of similarities or dissimilarities.

TABLE 15.1   Genres in Wisdom Literature

GENRE	DEFINITION	EXAMPLES
SAYING OR PROVERB	A pithy expression distilling human experience into a clever and memorable form	Prov 10:7; 11:24; 14:31;15:33; 17:27–28; 18:16
ADMONITION	Generally structured in verse form, either appearing in isolation among proverbs or grouped as an instruction delivered by an authoritative teacher to a learner	Prov 1–9; 22:17–24:22
RIDDLE	A "tricky" question whose answer or solution is ambiguous	Judg 4:10–18 is the only complete biblical example; riddles referred to in Prov 1:6
ALLEGORY	An extended metaphor	Prov 5:15–23; Eccl 12:1–6
HYMN	A praise of personified wisdom	Job 28; Prov 1:20–33; 8; Sir 24:1–22; Wis 6:12–20; 7:22–8:21
EXAMPLE STORY	Concrete illustration of a point made by sage	Prov 7:6–23; 24:30–34; Eccl 4:13–16
CONFESSION, AUTOBIOGRAPHICAL NARRATIVE, OR REFLECTION	A sage shares his rich experience with pupils or readers	Prov 4:3–9; Eccl 1:12–2:26; Sir 33:16–18
NAME LIST OR ONOMASTICON	Catalogs of geographical, cosmological, meteorological phenomena	Job 28; 36:27–37; 38:4–39: 30; 40:15–41:34; Sir 43; Wis 7:17–20, 22–23; 14:25–26
CONTROVERSY SPEECH OR DISPUTATION	Characteristic of the dialogue of Job with his friends, mixed with lament and lawsuit genres	Job 4–31

Structure of the Book of Proverbs

The book of proverbs is an anthology of sayings. Superscriptions (quoted below as they appear in the NRSV) suggest the structure of the book of Proverbs, designating seven distinct collections:

1. **1:1–9:18**   "The proverbs of Solomon son of David, king of Israel"
2. **10:1–22:16**   "The proverbs of Solomon"
3. **22:17–24:22**   "The words of the wise"
4. **24:23–34**   "These also are sayings of the wise"
5. **25:1–29:27**   "These are other proverbs of Solomon that the officials of King Hezekiah of Judah copied"
6. **30:1–33**   "The words of Agur son of Jakeh. An oracle"
7. **31:1–9**   "The words of King Lemuel. An oracle that his mother taught him"

THE FIRST COLLECTION

In the first collection (1:1–9:18) the concern is persuading the reader to follow the path of wisdom. The principal literary device used is parental advice, a father speaking to a child (or a teacher to a student), warning of the traps that society sets for the undiscerning. While the mother's voice is never heard in this section, perhaps it surfaces in "Woman Wisdom" who is introduced in 1:20–33 and speaks in 8:4–36. For some, "Woman Wisdom" reflects international wisdom's association with "sponsoring" goddesses. For others, "Woman Wisdom" represents a blend of the highly valued roles of wife, mother, wise woman, and princess-counselor. Still others see "Woman Wisdom" simply as a literary personification, but this does not account for the striking amount of power that is attributed here to a female figure in a male-dominated society (Fontaine 1992: 147). The sayings in this section also warn against "Woman Wisdom's" antithesis, "Woman Stranger" (5:1–23).

The speech of "Woman Wisdom" in 8:4–36 includes some items about which there have been spirited debates. There is, for example, considerable disagreement about how to translate 8:22a, where "Woman Wisdom" describes her divine origin as the very first act of God's creation. The KJV, reflecting the Vulgate, reads: "The Lord possessed me. . . ." The RSV and NRSV, on the other hand, read: "The Lord created me. . . ." The Hebrew verb used here, *qanah*, translated as "possessed" or "created" is more commonly understood as "acquire," or "get." (This is the same verb with which the name Cain is associated in Gen 4:1.) An equally valid reading of 8:22a, one supported by literalistic ancient translations would be "Yahweh acquired me as the beginning of his way." The problem for monotheistic editors and translators, both in antiquity and in modern times, has been how to avoid the notion that "Woman Wisdom" is either a sexually-conceived child of God or a pre-existent being whom Yahweh acquires in order to begin creation (Fontaine 1992: 148). The dilemma about how to translate the verb in 8:22a is reflected in problems with a noun in 8:30, which is variously translated as "master worker" (NRSV), "little child" (NRSV footnote), or "one brought up with him" (KJV). Given "Woman Wisdom's" statement that she was rejoicing in the created order and delighting in humanity, the reading favored is one resembling the reading in the NRSV footnote, "darling child" (Fontaine 1992: 148).

Because this first collection in Proverbs differs so much from those that follow, several ideas have developed about the setting and date of these chapters. One perspective sees the influence of Egyptian wisdom literature dominating this collection. Prov 1–9 can be seen as consisting of ten wisdom speeches that apparently were practice texts for students who were in training to become court officials. This Egyptian influence matches an early dating of these chapters, as early as the time of Solomon (Murphy 1990: 19). Another perspective sees this collection as having been formed over a longer period, with the final shape having been arrived at only in the postexilic period.

THE THIRD COLLECTION

The international character of wisdom literature shows up in the book of Proverbs where collections 3, 6, and 7 above are seen as deriving from non-Israelite sources (Crenshaw 1992: 513). As mentioned above, the striking feature of the third collection (22:17–24:22) is its resemblance in both structure and content to the earlier Egyptian text, "The Teachings of Amen-em-ope." The correspondence between the two is represented in Table 15.2 (adapted from Crenshaw 1992: 516).

The marked similarity between these two pieces suggests that either the author of Proverbs drew on the Egyptian text, or that the authors of both Proverbs and "The Teachings of Amen-em-ope" were dependent upon an unknown common source.

THE FIFTH COLLECTION

The proverb, that is, the *mashal,* appears often in the fifth collection in the book of Proverbs, chapters 25–29. Many sayings in this section achieve their comparison by using the preposition "like," in the formula "X is like Y" (25:11, 12, 13, 14,18, 19, 20, 25, 26, 28; 26:1, 2, 4, 7, 8, 9, 10, 11, 17, 18, 22, 23; 27:8, 15). Other sayings indicate correspondence by setting two images over against one another: "Perfume and incense make the heart glad, but the soul is torn by trouble" (27:9).

TABLE 15.2   **Proverbs and the Teachings of Amen-em-ope**

PROVERBS	AMEN-EM-OPE	CONTENT
22:17–18	3:9–11, 16	Appeal to listen
22:19	1:7	Purpose of instruction
22:20	27:7–8	Thirty sayings
22:21	1:5–6	Learning a worthy response
22:22	4:4–5	Do not rob the poor
22:24	11:13–14	Avoid friendship with violent people
22:25	13:8–9	Lest you become trapped
22:28	7:12–13	Do not remove landmarks
22:29	27:16–17	Skilled scribes will get jobs in the royal court
23:1–3	23:13–18	Observe good manners when eating with a ruler
23:4–5	9:14–10:5	Wealth is fleeting
23:6–7	14:5–10	Do not eat a stingy person's food
23:8	14:17–18	Lest you vomit
23:9	22:11–12	Don't talk in the presence of fools
23:10–11	7:12–15; 8:9–10	Do not encroach on the fields of orphans
24:11	11:6–7	Rescue those condemned to death

THE SIXTH COLLECTION

The superscription of the sixth collection in Proverbs, 30:1–33 is "The words of Agur son of Jakeh. An oracle." This is another collection that has a non-Israelite origin. We know nothing about who Agur was. The word translated "oracle" in the NRSV is understood by some scholars as "from Massa," making the title of this section "The words of Agur, son of Jakeh, the Massaite," a non-Israelite. This section displays remarkable rhetorical skill. It utilizes double meanings and clashing symbols. "Promising prophetic revelation ("an oracle"), it offers human words that are either Delphic gibberish or astonishing confession of . . . atheism" (Crenshaw 1992: 517). This section includes several sayings that are in the form of numerical proverbs, characteristic of nature wisdom. These numerical proverbs take the form "two things" (30:7), "two . . . three . . . four things" (30:15–16), "three things . . . four things" (30:18–19, 21–23, 29–31), "four things" (30:24). In vv. 15–16 a numerical saying compares *four* things that can never be satisfied with the *two* daughters of the leech who are always crying "Give, give!" Another numerical saying in this section brings together four similar things (30:18–19). The four things are: "the way of an eagle in the sky, the way of a snake on a rock, the way of a ship on the high seas, and the way of a man with a girl." The probable point of comparison rests in the fact that in every case the means of passage from point "A" to point "B" is mysterious—flying, moving without legs, sailing, and the road of romance.

THE BOOK OF JOB AND THE PROBLEM OF THEODICY

The popular phrase "the patience of Job" does not come from the Hebrew Bible, but from the KJV translation of a verse in the New Testament (James 5:11): "Behold, we count them happy which endure. Ye have heard of the patience of Job, and have seen the end of the Lord, that the Lord is very pitiful, and of tender mercy." The figure of Job, as presented in the book bearing his name, however, is better understood as steadfast in the face of adversity rather than patient. While the Job of the prose prologue of the book of Job (1:1–2:13) might be thought of as "patient," once the poetic dialogue begins in 3:14, patience is lacking in Job.

The Prose Prologue of Job

In the prologue of the book of Job, Job is introduced as a non-Israelite. He is described as a wealthy man from "the land of Uz" (1:1), which may be a reference to northwest Arabia. The structure of the prologue presents Job in a series of scenes alternately located on earth and in the heavens. The first scene (1:1–5) is on earth. In it Job is described as a "blameless and upright" individual who has seven sons, three daughters, large numbers of domesticated animals, and "very many servants." In addition, he is characterized as being meticulous about keeping a regimen of sacrifice. The second scene (1:6-12) shifts to the heavens, where a meeting of God's council is in session. Among the members of God's court is one called *ha-satan* in Hebrew, "the Accuser" (to whom we shall return below). As a result of an agreement struck between God and *ha-satan,* Job's family meets with a series of disasters in the third scene (1:13-22), where the locale is again on the earth. In the tragedies that befall Job's family there is an alternation between human agencies (Sabeans in 1:15, Chaldeans in 1:17) and natural ones (fire in 1:16, wind in 1:19). The fourth scene in the prologue (2:1-6) is again in God's heavenly assembly. The fifth and final scene is back on the earth (2:7-13).

The figure of Job as a righteous individual is also mentioned in the book of Ezekiel, where he is associated with Noah and Daniel:

> "Mortal, when a land sins against me by acting faithlessly, and I stretch out my hand against it, and break its staff of bread and send famine upon it, and cut off from it human beings and animals, even if Noah, Daniel, and Job, these three, were in it, they would save only their own lives by their righteousness," says the Lord God. (Ezek 14:13–14)

From the context clearly the three individuals are named because of their indisputable righteousness. Noah, as we have seen, is known from the flood narratives in Genesis, but is not a historical character. The Daniel mentioned here is not the later figure of Daniel of the book of Daniel in the Hebrew Bible (see the discussion in our next chapter) but the Dan'el (or Dan'il) of Canaanite mythology (Ezekiel, in fact, spells it that way). In Canaanite mythology, in the Ugaritic Story of Aqhat, Dan'el is pictured as a righteous judge and king. Thus neither Noah nor Dan'el were historical persons. What about Job? Certainly the style of narrative in Job 1-2 does not provide any concrete historical setting with explicit references to clearly identifiable places or events. It seems likely that there were cycles of tales associated with these three righteous figures of legendary antiquity, and that the author of the prologue of Job chose one of them as the hero of his work.

HA-SATAN

The other figure in the prologue that needs some explanation is that of "the Accuser," *ha-satan* in Hebrew, misleadingly translated in the NRSV with the proper name Satan. In Hebrew, *ha-satan* is one word, consisting of the definite article *ha* (= "the") prefixed to the beginning of a verbal root that means "to accuse." While this is not the place to discuss in detail the development of the figure of Satan in the Bible, it is important for our understanding of the book of Job to observe that "the Accuser" in the prologue is not yet the independent demonic

personification of evil that appears in later Judaism and Christianity. In the prologue of Job *ha-satan* is one of the "heavenly beings" (which translates a phrase
meaning "sons of God" in Hebrew) who make up God's heavenly council. The
"heavenly beings" are God's courtiers who perform certain limited tasks for God
and serve as divine counselors, a kind of heavenly cabinet (see Isa 6:8). They
have no independent power of their own, but carry out assignments given to
them by God. Accordingly, *ha-satan* is a kind of "prosecuting attorney" who
roams the earth searching out evil, which he then reports to God in the divine
assembly. In 1:8, God maintains that Job is a righteous individual. "The Accuser"
doubts this, but is unable to present any evidence to the contrary. Instead he
raises the question of Job's motivation for being an upright individual. Behind
ha-satan's question is the belief that stands at the center of the Deuteronomistic thinking we have encountered at several places in the course of our journey. That fundamental theological belief is that doing good results in divine
rewards, while doing bad leads to punishment from God. Following this line of
thought, because Job was prosperous and healthy, he must have been so because he had been rewarded by God for being a righteous individual. *Ha-satan,*
however, goes on to suggest to God that there is a cause-and-effect loop working
here—Job prospers *because* he is righteous, and he continues to be righteous
because he believes that it guarantees continuing prosperity. If this cause-and-
effect loop could be interrupted, so *ha-satan* contends, as soon as Job discovered that it did not "pay" to be good, he would abandon his righteousness. So
ha-satan says:

> Does Job fear God for nothing? Have you [Yahweh] not put a fence
> around him and his house and all that he has, on every side? You have
> blessed the works of his hands and his possessions have increased in the
> land. But stretch out your hand now, and touch all that he has, and he
> will curse you face to face. (1:9–11)

This leads God to agree to let *ha-satan* test Job. The first test (scene three
in the prologue) brings calamity on Job's property and family. Job's person,
however, remains untouched, according to restrictions that God imposed on
ha-satan's test. At the conclusion of this test the narrator reports: "In all this
Job did not sin or charge God with wrongdoing" (1:22). When the scene shifts
back to the divine assembly (scene four, 2:1–6), God scolds *ha-satan* for having brought suffering on Job for no reason. *Ha-satan* maintains, however, that
he was unsuccessful in his testing of Job only because of God's restrictions on
the test. He maintains that if God would grant him more unrestricted power to
afflict Job's actual person, Job would indeed "throw in the towel." God again
agrees to a testing of Job with the sole condition, "only spare his life" (2:6). Job
is then afflicted with a loathsome skin disease that drives others away from him.
But again Job's steadfast response to personal illness and even to his wife's urging that he shorten his suffering by cursing God and dying is a profession of
faith in the form of a question: "Shall we receive the good at the hand of God,

and not receive the bad?," to which the narrator adds, "In all this Job did not sin with his lips" (2:10).

Because we are privy to what has been going on in the prologue, we as readers know something that was hidden from Job as well as from his wife and his three friends, whom we meet at the conclusion of the prologue. We know the reason for his suffering. We know that he suffered because of God's agreement to let *ha-satan* test him in order to prove that selfless worship of God, worship not motivated by the desire for personal gain, is possible. Job, on the other hand, never knows why he suffers. Even when God answers him out of the whirlwind at the end of the poetic section of the book, the question of why Job had to suffer, as a particular individual, is left unanswered. In the prose epilogue of the book (42:7-17) *ha-satan* does not appear, nor is there any allusion to the arrangement made in the prologue between God and *ha-satan*. As one who attributed all that happened to God, good and evil, Job had to accept his suffering as a mystery because he had no other explanation. There is no suggestion that he suffered because of the existence of some demonic power that stood over against God.

At the conclusion of the prose prologue (2:11-13), three friends of Job come on the scene to console and comfort him. Like Job, his friends are non-Israelites. They go through the traditional gestures of mourning (2:12) in Job's presence for seven days and seven nights, but never speak to him. Their silence is broken only in the book's poetic central section.

The Central Poetic Section

The poetic central section of Job, which constitutes the bulk of the book (3:1-42:6), differs from the prose prologue in viewpoint, in vocabulary, and in form. While the Job of the prologue is a silent sufferer who is a model of forbearance, in the poetic section of the book he becomes a bold questioner who fearlessly challenges God, as well as his overbearing friends. In the prose envelope, which consists of the prologue and epilogue, God's name is Yahweh. In the poetic middle section of the book, Job's friends refer to God as El, Eloah, or Shaddai. In this section of the book, God is called Yahweh once by Job (12:9), once in a hymn on the inaccessibility of wisdom (28:28) that is secondary to its context, and several times by the narrator in the closing chapters of the poetic section (38:1; 40:1, 3, 6; 42:1).

The long central poetic section consists of three parts:

1. A debate between Job and his three friends, Eliphaz, Bildad, and Zophar (3-31).

2. A monologue attacking Job and his friends from a person named Elihu (32-37).

3. Two divine speeches with brief responses from Job (38:1-42:6).

THE DEBATE BETWEEN JOB AND HIS FRIENDS (CHS. 3–31)

The debate between Job and his three friends goes through three rounds as follows:

ROUND ONE
a   First speech of Eliphaz (4:1–5:27)
a′   Job's response to Eliphaz's first speech (6:1–7:21)
b   First speech of Bildad (8:1–22)
b′   Job's response to Bildad's first speech (9:1–10:22)
c   First speech of Zophar (11:1–20)
c′   Job's response to Zophar's first speech (12:1–14:22)
ROUND TWO
a   Second speech of Eliphaz (15:1–35)
a′   Job's response to Eliphaz's second speech (16:1–17:16)
b   Bildad's second speech (18:1–21)
b′   Job's response to Bildad's second speech (19:1–29)
c   Second speech of Zophar (20:1–29)
c′   Job's response to Zophar's second speech (21:1–34)
ROUND THREE
a   Third speech of Eliphaz (22:1–30)
a′   Job's response to Eliphaz's third speech (23:1–24:17)
b   Third speech of Bildad (25:1–6)
b′   Job's response to Bildad's third speech (26:1–14)
c   Third speech of Zophar (Zophar's third speech is miss-
                     ing. If there ever was a third speech for Zophar it disap-
                     peared very early. The present form of the text is
                     supported by the scroll of the Targum of Job (11QtgJob),
                     which was discovered among the Dead Sea Scrolls and
                     dated to the first century C.E.)
c′   Job's response to Zophar's third speech (27:1–23)

There have been numerous attempts by scholars, none totally convincing, to reconstruct Zophar's missing third speech by rearranging chapters 24–27. Because Zophar's third speech is missing, the whole third cycle of speeches is in doubt and the outcome of the debate between Job and his friends is uncertain. Within the course of the debate, the friends of Job speak from the orthodox perspective that understands Job's predicament to be the direct consequence of his sinfulness. All of their speeches rest on that premise. They lecture Job directly, never addressing God. As the debate proceeds, its tone becomes more harsh. Eliphaz's first speech (4:1–5:27) is courteous and sympathetic. In his last speech (22:1–13) he accuses Job of great wickedness, naming specific misdeeds. The neat outline of three rounds of three speeches and three responses is somewhat misleading, however. The course of the dialogue between Job and each of this three friends is actually quite uneven. While dialogue usually implies that a person listens to what another has to say and bases his or her response on what is heard, this does not characterize the debate in Job. It has often been remarked that the disputants in Job seem to be talking past each other. Job's friends almost appear programmed to say certain things in their speeches, no matter what Job says. They have points to make. Job, on the other hand, sometimes grows weary in his attempts to be heard by his friends. He then turns from them to address God directly, venting his feelings of frustration, and insisting on arguing his case before God. In a well-known passage in 19:25-27, which includes textual problems that make its translation difficult, Job expresses certainty in his vindication. This certainty, not the notion of resurrection that has often been associated with these lines, is the point of the passage:

> For I know that my redeemer (NRSV = Redeemer) lives,
> and at last he will stand upon the earth;
> and after my skin has been destroyed,
> then in my flesh I shall see God
> whom I shall see on my side,
> and my eyes shall behold, and not another.
> My heart faints within me! (19:25–27)

While neither Job's arguments nor those of his friends seem to move to a satisfying denouement, the dialogue really concludes with Job's speech in chapters 29-31. Here he stops addressing his friends, and instead finishes his defense by presenting an assessment of his past and present circumstances. To underscore the fact that he has not misrepresented the truth, he takes a number of oaths in the form "If . . . , then . . ." (31:5-40), inviting God to strike him down if he has acted wickedly. Chapter 31 concludes: "The words of Job are ended."

ELIHU'S SPEECHES

Inserted at this point in the book of Job (chapters 32-37) are a series of speeches by an individual named Elihu, introduced in 32:2-5:

> Then Elihu son of Barachel the Buzite, of the family of Ram, became angry. He was angry at Job because he justified himself rather than God; he was angry also at Job's three friends because they had found no answer, though they had declared Job to be in the wrong. Now Elihu had waited to speak to Job, because they were older than he. But when Elihu saw that there was no answer in the mouths of these three men, he became angry.

In the balance of chapter 32, Elihu rebukes Job's friends. In chapter 33 he challenges Job for contending with God and invites Job to respond to him, to Elihu. In his concluding speech in chs. 34-37 Elihu proclaims God's justice, goodness and majesty, in a speech that anticipates God's response to Job that begins in 38:1, immediately following Elihu's speeches. For this reason and others, many scholars hold that Elihu's speeches are a later insertion into the book of Job.

Elihu appears out of nowhere in chapter 32, and disappears without a trace after chapter 37. His speeches are monologues, and we have no record of any responses to him. He is truly an enigmatic figure.

GOD'S SPEECHES AND THEOPHANY

There are two remarkable speeches of Yahweh and two responses from Job at the end of the central poetic section of the book. Given the indecisive nature of the three-round debate and adding Elihu's contribution, the reader might anticipate that the theophany in chapter 38 would wrap things up neatly, settle the debate, and provide answers that would prove Job right and his friends wrong. Yahweh's speeches, however, raise new questions rather than provide answers.

The first speech of Yahweh in 38:1–40:2 begins with a theophany in a whirlwind (compare Nah 1:3; Zech 9:14; Ps 18:7–15; 50:3; Ezek 1:4; Hab 3). God answered Job out of the whirlwind by asking Job questions about Job's knowledge of the mysteries of God's creation. These questions do not address the issues that Job had set forth in the debate with his friends. Instead, they shift the discussion into a larger arena, the whole of creation. The issue is not whether God is just in his dealings with human beings. At issue is God's power as master of the whole created order. Job is forced to recognize that he knows very little about the secrets of God's creation, of which his personal situation is only an infinitesimal part. The first series of God's questions to Job climaxes with a biting piece of sarcasm: "Surely you know, for you were born then, and the number of your days is great" (38:21). God's first speech closes with a challenge to Job to reply (40:1–2).

Job's response to Yahweh's first speech is a brief one, found in 40:3–5. Job is neither defiant nor repentant. God then "answered Job out of the whirlwind" (40:6) a second time, and the issue of Job's complaints in the dialogue section is finally joined in God's questions to him in 40:8: "Will you even put me in the wrong? Will you condemn me that you may be justified?" Curiously enough, the second of Yahweh's speeches focuses on descriptions of two special animals, Behemoth (40:15–24) and Leviathan (41:1–34). While Behemoth may seem to be an ordinary hippopotamus and Leviathan a crocodile (see the NRSV footnote b for 41:1), here these creatures are probably meant to represent the mythological chaos monsters of ancient Near-Eastern creation myths, who have been domesticated here to become playthings for God's amusement.

Job's response to Yahweh's second speech differs from his earlier response. In 42:2–4 Job admits that his earlier knowledge of God was secondhand, based on hearsay. Now that he knows God on a firsthand basis, he can acknowledge the divine purpose. While he has received no direct responses to his questions, Job is satisfied with the fact that the God in whom he trusted is no longer hidden from him:

> I know that you can do all things,
> and that no purpose of yours can be thwarted.
> "Who is this that hides counsel without knowledge?"

Therefore I have uttered what I did not understand,
things too wonderful for me, which I did not know.
"Hear, and I will speak;
I will question you, and you declare to me."
I had heard of you by the hearing of the ear,
but now my eye sees you;
therefore I despise myself,
and repent in dust and ashes. (42:2–6)

The Prose Epilogue

The book of Job ends with a prose epilogue (42:7-17) whose style, language, and situation relates it to the prologue. God declares in favor of Job and against his friends because they "have not spoken of me what is right, as my servant Job has" (42:7). Job, in a gesture of reconciliation, intercedes with God on his friends' behalf and God hears Job's prayer. Job's restoration follows upon this intercession. For some readers, the "happy ending" of 42:10-17 seems to undermine the integrity and force of Job's arguments in the poetic section that seem to say God does not guarantee "happy endings." It is perhaps misleading to consider the restoration the point of the story.

THE INTERNATIONAL CHARACTER OF JOB

Like Proverbs and other examples of wisdom literature in the Hebrew Bible, Job has an international dimension. The international wisdom movement assumed that the universe operated on a rational basis that could be understood by human beings. This conviction, of necessity, carried with it the idea that the deities who governed the universe played by a set of rules in their relationships with human beings, including principles of reward and retribution. This conservative notion was sorely tested, however, when it did not appear to be confirmed by the experience of individuals. Evil individuals did seem to be rewarded and righteous individuals appeared to receive unwarranted punishment. Nor could political revolutions be understood using the model of an orderly creation. The international wisdom movement, noting these inconsistencies, produced a kind of speculative literature that raised questions about the order of the universe. Job can be considered an example of this kind of literature.

Mesopotamian Parallels

The oldest example of this type of literature is the Sumerian text "Man and his God," which has sometimes been called the "Sumerian Job." This text describes the suffering of an individual and defends the deity by asserting that humans are sinful from birth. The later text, "I Will Praise the Lord of Wisdom," also comes from Mesopotamia. In this document, a Job-like figure suffers misfortunes but accepts the inscrutability of the gods and the necessity for humans to perform the proper cultic acts. A third piece of wisdom literature out of Mesopotamia that bears a resemblance to Job is "The Babylonian Theodicy." Like Job, a sufferer in this text engages in a debate with a friend. A poem of twenty-seven stanzas with eleven lines each, this debate has the orthodox friend admitting that sometimes the gods do permit minor bad things to happen to good people. The sufferer however, maintains that the gods are at fault and that morality does not profit. A fourth Mesopotamian text, "The Dialogue Between a Master and his Slave," resembles Ecclesiastes more than the book of Job, but some of its features echo the conditions underlying Job's distress (Crenshaw 1992: 865).

Egyptian Parallels

Three Egyptian texts resemble Job in some ways. A section of "The Admonitions of Ipuwer" laments the wickedness that the gods permit. "The Dispute Between a Man and His Ba" is a dispute over suicide. This text, which comes from a time of social upheaval in Egypt, takes the form of a lawsuit in which the sufferer is the attorney for death, and Ba, the soul, is the attorney for life. The sufferer proposes committing suicide:

Hear me out, my Soul.
My life now is more than I can bear,
Even you, my own Soul, cannot understand me.
My life now is more terrible than anyone can imagine.
I am alone.
So, come with me, my Soul, to the grave!
Be my companion in death. . . .
If you cannot take away the misery of living,
Do not withhold the mercy of dying from me. (Matthews and Benjamin 1991: 207)

The third Egyptian text that is often mentioned in discussions of Job is "The Eloquent Peasant." This text includes the protests of a farmer who argues for his rights in the courts of Egypt. Narrative sections of prose introduce nine exchanges, which are composed in poetry, between the farmer and various judges.

THE READERS' RESPONSE TO JOB

As Roland Murphy has said, "Few books in the Old Testament call for a response from the reader as urgently as the Book of Job does" (1990: 45). In a volume that contains several contemporary perspectives on Job, the editors have said that by its seeming refusal to offer simplistic prescriptions, the book of Job has elicited extraordinarily different readings. The history of interpretation of Job is the history of a long discussion, in which shifting points of tension in the history of culture have refocused the point of the text. Different readers in different contexts have reread and retold the story of Job in ways that have given it multiple and sometimes directly conflicting meanings. In the histories of Judaism and Christianity, there is not one Job but many (Perdue and Gilpin 1992: 11 – 12).

Because the reader's response to a piece of literature is influenced by his or her social location, no wonder one of the most striking modern attempts to come to terms with Job comes from the South American liberation theologian Gustavo Gutiérrez in his *On Job: God-Talk and the Suffering of the Innocent* (1987). The title of Gutiérrez's book in Spanish is *Hablar de Dios desde el sufimiento del inocente,* "Speaking of God from the Perspective of the Suffering of the Innocent." In his reading of Job, Gutiérrez focuses on what it means to talk of God in the context of contemporary Latin America, and more concretely in the context of the suffering of the poor—which is to say, the vast majority of the population:

> How are human beings to speak of God in the midst of poverty and suffering? This is the question the Book of Job raises for us. . . . We ask the same question today in the lands of want and hope that are Latin America. Here the masses of the poor suffer an inhuman situation that is evidently undeserved. Nothing can justify a situation in which human beings lack the basic necessities for a life of dignity and in which their most elementary rights are not respected. The suffering and destructive effect on individuals go far beyond what is seen in a first contact with the world of the poor. . . . It is important that we be clear from the outset that the theme of the Book of Job is not precisely suffering—that impenetrable human mystery—but rather how to speak of God in the midst of suffering. (1987: 12 – 13)

THE BOOK OF ECCLESIASTES/QOHELETH— HOW DID A BOOK LIKE THIS GET INTO A BIBLE LIKE THIS?

Ecclesiastes is the name in Greek and Latin of the book called Qoheleth in the Hebrew Bible. The name Qoheleth derives from the Hebrew verbal root *qhl,* which means "to assemble." The participle Qoheleth is thus usually taken as referring to the leader of an assembly, "One Who Assembles."

The inclusion of Ecclesiastes in the canon of the Hebrew Bible has puzzled many. How did a book that adopts such a radical viewpoint gain acceptance into the Bible? Rabbinical sources indicate that its value as scripture was a matter of serious debate among competing rabbinic schools. As we indicated in Chapter 13 in our discussion of the Song of Songs, Qoheleth was mentioned in a rabbinical discussion about books that "defile the hands" because of their sacred character. One answer to the question of how Qoheleth became canonical has been its traditional attribution to Solomon. This answer is inadequate, however, in view of the fact that a similar device did not work for the Wisdom of Solomon and the Odes of Solomon. A better answer is that the book has an epilogue added in 12:9 – 14, which softens the hopeless skepticism of the bulk of the book and commends keeping God's commandments.

Language, Style, and Genre in Qoheleth

A striking feature of Qoheleth is repetition. Within the 2,643 words in 1:4-12:8, about twenty-five Hebrew roots (appearing as nouns, verbs, and so forth) occur at least five times, some of them thirty and fifty times. These words account for about 21 percent of the words used (Murphy 1990: 50).

The Hebrew of Qoheleth has been called an Aramaizing Hebrew because it contains a high percentage of terms that stem from Aramaic rather than Hebrew. Persian loan words such as *pardes,* "park" and *medina,* "province" appear as well. There is also evidence for Hellenistic coloring behind some of the book's vocabulary.

To what literary genre or genres does Qoheleth belong? Murphy suggests that Qoheleth is *sui generis,* unique, and lies somewhere between a treatise and a collection of sayings and thoughts (1990:50). The sayings are predominantly reflections based on personal observation. Qoheleth also uses such literary forms as autobiographical narrative, example story, anecdote, parable, antithesis, and proverb (Crenshaw 1992b: 275).

Structure, Themes, and Interpretation of Qoheleth

STRUCTURE

There has been little agreement about the structure of Qoheleth. Most scholars recognize a prologue (1:1-11) and an epilogue (12:9-14). A helpful outline of the book is presented by Schoors (1982):

1:1	Title
1:2	General theme of the book
1:3-2:26	Solomon's confession
3:1-22	Human beings under the law of time
4:1-16	Life in society
4:17-5:8	The advantage of silence over unreflected speech
5:9-6:9	On wealth
6:10-12	Transitional unit
7:1-9:10	The experience of life and death
9:11-10:20	Wisdom and folly
11:1-6	The necessity of taking risks
11:7-12:7	The necessity of enjoying life
12:8	Inclusion: the general theme of the book
12:9-14	Epilogue

The questions of structure and themes are closely interrelated. One can form an idea about the theme(s) in the book and then try to show how the structure of the work communicates the intuited meaning. Or, alternatively, one can put the search for structure first, without predetermining the theme(s). Starting with the structure, we can observe that there are two poems that serve to support the heart of the book like a pair of bookends. Thematically, they also present the book's principal themes. At one end is the poem in 1:3-11:

> What do people gain from all the toil
> at which they toil under the sun?
> A generation goes, and a generation comes,
> but the earth remains forever.
> The sun rises and the sun goes down,
> and hurries to the place where it rises.
> The wind blows to the south,
> and goes round to the north;
> round and round goes the wind,
> and on its circuits the wind returns.
> All streams run to the sea,
> but the sea is not full;
> to the place where the streams flow,
> there they continue to flow.
> All things are wearisome;
> more than one can express;
> the eye is not satisfied with seeing,
> or the ear filled with hearing.
> What has been is what will be,
> and what has been done is what will be done;
> there is nothing new under the sun.
> Is there a thing of which it is said,
> "See, this is new"?
> It has already been,
> in the ages before us.
> The people of long ago are not remembered,
> nor will there be any remembrance
> of people yet to come by those who come after them.

On the other end is 11:7-12:7. The first poem begins by emphasizing the futility of human work; the second recommends enjoying one's youth, adding the reminder that even the joys of youth are temporary and will soon be followed by old age and death: "Remember your creator in the days of your youth, before the days of trouble come, and the years draw near when you will say, 'I have no pleasure in them'" (12:1). This pattern—negative evaluation, followed by an admonition to enjoy, with an added qualification to the limits of enjoyment—is carried into the body of the work.

THEMES

One can discern three themes that run all through Qoheleth:

1. **Wisdom has its limits.** Proverbs assumes that practical wisdom, "common sense," can enable one to figure out a formula for success and to follow that path in life. Qoheleth, by contrast, recognizes the futility of striving for success because he sees such efforts frustrated over and over again. The kind of practical wisdom assumed by Proverbs either does not always prove to be true (8:16-17) or cannot be achieved (7:23-24). "Vanity of vanities! All is vanity" (1:2).

2. **Because wisdom is neither certain nor accessible, one should accept and enjoy life.** Given the uncertainty of wisdom, instead of speculating about ultimate reality or the nature of God, one should accept and enjoy life—"Don't worry, be happy!" (9:7-10; cf. 2:24-26; 3:22; 5:18-20).

3. **Death is a certain reality and a great leveler.** The finality of death has a fundamental place in the thought of Qoheleth. Death cancels all human achievements. It is a great leveler, erasing all distinctions between the wise and the foolish: "For there is no enduring remembrance of the wise or of fools, seeing that in the days to come all will have been long forgotten. How can the wise die just like fools?" (2:16).

INTERPRETATION

Roland Murphy offers the following advice for readers of Qoheleth as they approach the task of its interpretation. The reader should be ready to keep the tensions within the book in careful balance. One must do this without eliminating certain phrases or verses as being insertions of a later hand. There is another danger to which Murphy alerts us. Precisely because Qoheleth's viewpoints are so sharp and extreme, some may attempt to relativize them. The radical features of his thought can be tamed by the way in which the book is read in a larger context, even a biblical or religious context. No matter what the context however, the cutting edge of the book has to be retained. It should not be tamed (1990: 53).

WISDOM LITERATURE IN THE APOCRYPHAL/DEUTEROCANONICAL BOOKS: BEN SIRACH AND THE WISDOM OF SOLOMON

With the books of Ben Sirach and the Wisdom of Solomon our journey takes us beyond the bounds of the Jewish canon while remaining within the realm of wisdom literature. Ben Sirach is one of the earliest and certainly the longest of the deuterocanonical/apocryphal books, dating from the early second century B.C.E. While the Wisdom of Solomon is not so easily dated, a date in the first century B.C.E. is generally agreed upon, with most scholars favoring a date in the second half of that century. These two books present us with some ideas about continuing developments in the wisdom school that produced the wisdom books in the Jewish canon.

Sirach

The author of Ben Sirach is commonly referred to as either Ben Sira or Sirach (the Greek spelling of Sira). The book is also known as Ecclesiasticus, a term taken directly from many manuscripts of the Latin Vulgate. The full title of the book in the NRSV is "Ecclesiasticus, or the Wisdom of Jesus Son of Sirach." Unlike other books in the Hebrew Bible that are anonymous, the author of this book gives us his name in 50:27: "Jesus, (the Greek form of the Hebrew name Yeshua) son of Eleazar son of Sirach of Jerusalem." The author's grandson translated the book into Greek, as he says in the foreword:

> My grandfather Jesus, who had devoted himself especially to the reading of the Law and the Prophets and the other books of our ancestors, and had acquired considerable proficiency in them, was himself also led to write something pertaining to instruction and wisdom. . . . You are invited therefore to read it with goodwill and attention, and to be indulgent in cases where, despite our diligent labor in translating, we may seem to have rendered some phrases imperfectly. For what was originally expressed in Hebrew does not have exactly the same sense when translated into another language. . . . When I came to Egypt in the thirty-eighth year of the reign of Euergetes . . . I found opportunity for no little instruction. . . . During that time I have applied my skill day and night to complete and publish the book.

Here we have the identification of the author of the book, the book's purpose, and a clear indication of the date of the translation, which was during the reign of Ptolemy VII Physkon Euergetes II, whose accession date was 170 B.C.E. The thirty-eighth year of his reign would be 132 B.C.E.

TEXT

Until the end of the nineteenth century C.E., Sirach existed only in Greek, Latin, Syriac, and other translations. Between 1896 and 1900, fragments of the Hebrew text of Sirach were found in the geniza (a repository for old scrolls) of a synagogue in Cairo. Since then, other Hebrew manuscript fragments have been found among the Dead Sea Scrolls at Qumran, and at Masada, which is south of Qumran on the Dead Sea. All of the Hebrew manuscript fragments now known to us amount to about two-thirds of the book of Sirach. Apparently the Hebrew text of Sirach began to disappear after the book was excluded from the canon. The RSV translation of Sirach is from a Greek text, with occasional footnotes about readings in Hebrew manuscripts. The NRSV translation, however, is based on a critically established text, using the Hebrew, Greek, and other ancient versions.

STRUCTURE

Sirach's structure is not easily discerned. In this respect it resembles Proverbs. It appears to be a compilation of lecture notes on moral behavior that Ben Sirach used with his young Jewish male students (Di Lella 1992: 936). The book contains several literary forms. Unlike Proverbs 10 and following, individual proverbs are not set apart from one another in Sirach, but incorporated into longer poems. Sirach 1:11-30, for example, is a poem of twenty-two lines, corresponding to the number of letters in the Hebrew alphabet. Within this poem there are sayings (vv. 11-14) and commands (vv. 28-30). Other literary forms found in the book are hymns of praise (1:1-10; 18:1-7; 39:12-35; 42:15-43:33; 50:22-24; 51:1-12), prayers of petition (22:27-23:6; 36:1-22), autobiographical narrative (33:16-18), lists (39:16-35; 42:15-43:33), and instructional narrative (44:1-50:24). Sirach 51:13-30, an appendix to the book, concerns Sirach's love for Wisdom in the form of an acrostic poem, in which each successive line begins with a successive letter of the Hebrew alphabet.

THEMES

While it is impossible to summarize the contents of Sirach because it treats such a variety of topics, Roland Murphy suggests that three central topics can be highlighted: (1) retribution, (2) the relation of wisdom and Israel's sacred traditions, and (3) the fear of the Lord (1990: 74-170). We would add a fourth important topic in Sirach—his attitude toward women.

Retribution in Sirach.   If we view Sirach as an extension of wisdom thinking, it is striking to note that with respect to its perspective on retribution, the continuity is with Proverbs rather than with Job or Qoheleth. The only hint that Sirach at least knew of a figure named Job, whether or not the Job of the book of Job, is a passing reference in 49:9: "For God also mentioned Job who held fast to all the ways of justice." Along with Proverbs, Sirach believes that prudent behavior *will* lead to success and the good life. There is no recognition of the fact that sometimes the righteous do *not* prosper. He asserts that what happens to humans is the consequence of God's actions, all of which are for good:

> All the works of the Lord are very good,
> and whatever he commands will be done at the appointed time. (39:16)
> To the faithful his ways are straight,
> but full of pitfalls for the wicked. (39:24)

Wisdom and Israel's Sacred Traditions.   In one of the most important passages in Sirach, he identifies Wisdom with the Torah. Traditionally, as we have noted, wisdom literature does not make appeals to Israel's sacred history. In 24:23, however, in the midst of his praise of Woman Wisdom, Sirach makes an arresting identification:

> All this [that is, Wisdom] is the book of the covenant of the Most High God, the law that Moses commanded us as an inheritance for the congregations of Jacob.

Wisdom, like the Torah before it, is an authentic expression of Israel's self-understanding, a vehicle for God's revelation. The link with the Torah and Israel's sacred traditions is also made in Sirach 44–50 in a section that bears the title "Hymn in Honor of Our Ancestors" in the Greek and Latin manuscripts of the book. In this section, which like chapter 24 stands in contrast to the rest of the book, Sirach celebrates the covenant with the patriarchs and Israel by praising figures out of Israel's past. The list begins with Enoch (compare Gen 4:17) and offers a compact, unified list that has no parallel anywhere else in the Bible. There are no women included, however.

Fear of the Lord in Sirach.   Sirach's primary theme is wisdom *as* fear of the Lord, and his fundamental thesis is this: Wisdom, identified with the Law, can be acquired only by one who fears God and keeps the commandments. The expression "fear of God," or its equivalent, occurs fifty-five to sixty times in Ben Sirach. In the rest of the Hebrew Bible, only Psalms, where the expression is found seventy-nine times, has a larger number of occurrences (Di Lella 1992: 940).

> The whole of wisdom is fear of the Lord,
> and in all wisdom there is the fulfillment of the law. (19:20)

Sirach's Attitude Toward Women.   Over one hundred verses in Sirach deal with women (for example, 3:2–6; 7:19, 24–26; 9:1–9; 19:2–4; 22:3–5; 23:22–26; 25:1, 8, 13–26:18; 28:15; 33:20; 36:26–31; 40:19, 23; 42:6, 9–14). As we have seen is the case in much of the Hebrew Bible, Sirach treats women in terms of their relationship with men. The women in Sirach are wives, mothers, daughters, adulteresses, or prostitutes. Sirach's perspective is that of an upper-class male. Sirach was probably not, however, motivated by a personal dislike of women. Rather, in his attitudes toward women, he is a representative of his culture. This is not to excuse Sirach, however, for including such blatantly sexist passages as 25:13–26, which relishes in the special wickedness of women. There is *nothing* else in the Bible that can rival the sheer sexism of Sirach 42:14:

> Better is the wickedness of a man than a woman who does good;
> it is woman who brings shame and disgrace.

As we noted in our discussion of the role of women in Israelite society in Chapter 14, it is difficult to figure out to what degree texts reflect realities in society. Here one might ask how what Sirach has to say about women reflects the specific reality of women's lives in Jerusalem in the second century B.C.E. It may be that his warnings to men regarding women derive in part from the changing Hellenistic environment that brought increased freedom and public access for women, bringing young men into uncharted territory in their relationships with women. Such a situation might provide the background for the following admonitions of Sirach:

> Never dine with another man's wife, or revel with her at wine. (9:9)
> There is wrath and impudence and great disgrace
> when a wife supports her husband. (25:22)

Di Lella maintains that Ben Sira wrote his book only for the instruction of young men in a male-dominated society. For this reason, his vocabulary and grammar are masculine-oriented. Like the other biblical wisdom writers before him, he simply had no intention of instructing young women. When we take such factors into account, we may understand why Ben Sira wrote about women the way he did. But that does not make his distressing, often cynical, even caustic, comments about women any more acceptable to us today (1992: 944).

The Wisdom of Solomon

With the Wisdom of Solomon we come to the last of the five wisdom books. Although this book belongs to the wisdom tradition, it also belongs at the end, bearing more resemblance than other wisdom books to the Hellenistic thought that came to the eastern Mediterranean with the conquests of Alexander the Great. Not only is this the latest book in the stream of wisdom literature, it is also the wisdom book about which there are very widely divergent opinions with respect to authorship, original language, and integrity. No consensus has emerged regarding the date of Wisdom, but the linguistic evidence suggests a date in the late first century B.C.E.

HELLENISTIC TRADITION

In Greek the title of this book is The Wisdom of Solomon. In Latin it is known simply as The Book of Wisdom. Solomon is never mentioned by name in the book. At one time it was thought that the first part of the book was a translation from a Hebrew original because of some Hebrew "flavor" such as poetic parallelism. It is now generally agreed that it was composed in Greek. The Wisdom of Solomon is an important book for an understanding of Judaism in the Hellenistic period, as the influence of Hellenism on The Wisdom of Solomon is striking. The book contains a vocabulary of 1,734 different words, of which 1,303 appear only once, and 355 (about 20 percent) are not found in any other book of the Jewish Bible (Murphy 1990: 85). This richness of vocabulary is very "unhebraic." The author of the Wisdom of Solomon uses Hellenistic literary forms to elaborate his vision of the Jewish faith. The precise genre of the book is the *logos protreptikos* or protreptic, a form of instructional or morally motivating discourse. This genre was a combination of philosophy and rhetoric used by the Sophists and condemned by Plato. Within the protreptic other genres are included, such as the diatribe, which simulates direct address by creating an imaginary figure with whom the author debates.

STRUCTURE AND THEMES

The Wisdom of Solomon can be divided into three parts:

1. 1:1-6:21   Immortality as the reward of wisdom
2. 6:22-10:21   Solomon and wisdom
3. 11:1-19:22   Wisdom and the Exodus

It has been suggested that Wisdom is a mosaic, to which no fewer than seventy-nine wise men contributed (Winston 1992: 121). In the mid-nineteenth century, however, the uniformity of language and style that characterize the book led to the suggestion that it was the work of a single author, which is the consensus today. The traditional attribution of authorship to Solomon is a conventional way of recognizing Solomon as a patron of wisdom.

In spite of its hostility to Egyptians in particular and to Hellenistic culture in general, Wisdom borrows many ideas, as well as literary forms, from its Hellenistic environment. One example of this is the central place given to the doctrine of immortality in the first part of Wisdom of Solomon, which is a new emphasis in Jewish tradition. Here, and in Daniel 12 (which we will discuss in our final chapter), exists a perception of immortality unknown elsewhere in the Hebrew Bible. In contrast to the traditional Hebrew idea, reflected in Genesis 2, that human beings consist of a material body (originally molded from the soil) animated by the life-giving breath of God that leaves a person when he or she "expires," here the background is the distinctive Platonic dualism of a mortal body and an immortal soul. The soul is imprisoned in a body, which makes possible the belief that long life is not necessarily a reward for righteous living and that the balancing of the scales of God's justice for an individual can take place after death.

In the second section of Wisdom, which forms the core of the book, the author identifies himself with Solomon (without naming him) and describes his quest for wisdom, identified as Woman Wisdom. The author tells us that he loved Wisdom and desired her more than anything else (7: 8-10). Some of the language used here to describe Wisdom resembles that seen in the Song of Songs. In 7:22b-23 Wisdom is given twenty-one (3 × 7) attributes, borrowed largely from Greek philosophy. Wisdom teaches the four cardinal virtues (according to Plato and the Stoics) of temperance, justice, prudence, and fortitude that were central to Greek moral instruction, but which appear only here in the Bible (8:7). Wisdom comes to the author in answer to a three-part prayer that is found in 9:1-6, 7-12, and 13-18. The second section ends with a listing of seven historical events in which the saving power of Wisdom has been demonstrated from Adam to the Exodus from Egypt.

The mention of the Exodus from Egypt at the end of the second section of Wisdom leads into the third section of the book, which is a historical meditation contrasting Israel and Egypt. The form used here is a series of five contrasts (11:6-19:22). The principle behind the contrasts is the idea that Israel benefited from the same things by which the Egyptians were punished (11:5). The book ends abruptly with a doxology in 19:22, which gives the lesson of the historical survey:

> For in everything, O Lord, you have exalted and glorified your people, and you have not neglected to help them at all times and in all places.

WISDOM IN THE BIBLE: A CONCLUSION

Roland Murphy offers a fitting conclusion for our examination of wisdom literature in the Bible:

> The wisdom movement within Israel is not without surprises. The security preached by Proverbs is jarred by the experience of Job and buffeted by the hard-nosed insistence upon vanity by Qoheleth. Unruffled, Sirach seems to put it all together again with his emphasis on traditional wisdom and Law. Perhaps the most surprising twist is the appearance in the Diaspora of the Wisdom of Solomon. Here Greek language and culture make a significant entree into the Bible, but under the aegis of Solomon, no less. Wisdom and salvation history come together; both are recognized as integral to the experience of the people. (1990: 94)

STUDY QUESTIONS

WISDOM LITERATURE

1. What are the institutions in the ancient Near East from which the wisdom movement arose, and how did they contribute to the production of formal wisdom literature?
2. How is the class consciousness of the author(s) of Proverbs evident in his/their worldview. In particular, comment on how the following topics are treated: laziness (Prov 6:6–11); proper speech (Prov 11:12); reputation (Prov 22:1); poverty and wealth (Prov 30:7–9).
3. With few exceptions, women are not depicted favorably in wisdom literature. What are some of those exceptions and what is their significance?
4. What is the most characteristic literary genre in biblical wisdom literature? What are its basic characteristics? Name some of the other genres.

PROVERBS

1. Suppose you overheard a doctor giving the following advice to a patient: "Limit the amount of fat in your diet, eat more fresh fruits and vegetables, and take a brisk, thirty-minute walk at least three times a week." Hearing this, you could infer that the question for which this prescription was being given was "How can I reduce my weight and limit the risk of a heart attack?" In the first nine chapters of Proverbs, a solution is being offered to a

problem. What is the *unwritten* question that lies behind the prescription in these chapters? Why should the reader heed the advice offered in these chapters?

2. Note the places in Prov 1 – 11 where "life" is referred to. What do you think is the understanding of "life" that is implied? What are some of its characteristics?

3. What are some of the important issues of interpretation in Prov 8? Why are they significant?

4. What might you add to or subtract from the description in Prov 22:17 – 24:22 of a wise person's outlook?

JOB

1. How does the figure of Job in the prologue and epilogue compare with the Job in the poetic section of the book? To what characters does Job related in: (a) the prologue; (b) the central poetic section; and (c) the epilogue?

2. How does the figure of *ha-satan* in the prologue differ from the figure of Satan in later Jewish and Christian theology?

3. From a monotheistic perspective, the book of Job questions traditional views of God's responsibility for human suffering. For example, it rejects the idea of sin inherited from Adam and Eve, a demonic rebellion against God, or the existence of an afterlife in which imbalances in reward will be redressed. In maintaining his integrity, if not his complete innocence, why does Job refuse to "cave in" to the theological demands of his "friends"? How is Job addressed by God in the speech from the whirlwind?

4. Do you consider the epilogue to be an appropriate conclusion to your reading of the book of Job? Why or why not? What changes might you make in an epilogue you might write for the book of Job?

5. Do the speeches of Elihu add or detract to the literary development of the central poetic section in the book of Job? How do you see their function in the book as it is structured?

6. Do you think that the book of Job could help people cope with the violence and injustice that millions of people in the so-called "third world" endure every day? How might a survivor of the Holocaust, in which six million Jews died as a result of the genocidal policy of the Nazis, read the book of Job?

ECCLESIASTES/QOHELETH

1. How is the traditional identification of King Solomon as the author of Qoheleth ironic?

2. What ideas does the author of Qoheleth use to support the central thesis: "Vanity of vanities! All is vanity"?

3. The author of Qoheleth uses the word "vanity" so often that it has become a defining characteristic of the book. What does this word mean in the context of this book? Elsewhere in the Hebrew Bible, for example, this word

has been translated as "fog." Mark all the occurrences of the term "vanity" in Qoheleth and then suggest a synonym or synonyms for it.

4. Construct an imaginary dialogue between Job and Qoheleth on the issue of God's responsibility for supposedly unwarranted human suffering.

5. It has often been suggested that 12:9–13 is a later addition to the text of Qoheleth. Do these verses stand *inside* or *outside* the overall structure of the book? (Remember that authors in the Hebrew Bible often use the device called inclusion, beginning and ending a literary unit using the same word, phrase, or sentence). What about 12:8? Where else does this phrase appear in Qoheleth? What about the content of 12:9–14? Would Qoheleth agree with 12:13? What does Qoheleth say, elsewhere in the book, about God's judgment? Would he agree with the statement in 12:14?

SIRACH AND THE WISDOM OF SOLOMON

1. What are some of the principal continuing developments in the wisdom school that are evidenced in Sirach and the Wisdom of Solomon?

2. How would you characterize Sirach's attitude toward women? Why might he have felt this way about women?

3. What are some of the characteristics of the Wisdom of Solomon that make it unique among the wisdom books?

BIBLIOGRAPHY

Crenshaw, James L. 1992a. "Proverbs, Book of." *Anchor Bible Dictionary, V,* 513–520.

———. 1992b. "Ecclesiastes, Book of." *Anchor Bible Dictionary, II,* 271–280.

Di Lella, Alexander A. 1992. "Wisdom of Ben-Sira." *Anchor Bible Dictionary, VI,* 931–945.

Fontaine, Carole R. 1992. "Proverbs." *The Women's Bible Commentary,* Carol A. Newsom and Sharon H. Ringe, eds. Louisville: Westminster/John Knox.

Frick, Frank S. (Forthcoming). Cui Bono?—*History in the Service of Political Nationalism: The Deuteronomistic History as Political Propaganda.*

Gordis, Robert. 1971. *Poets, Prophets, and Sages: Essays in Biblical Interpretation.* Bloomington: Indiana University Press.

Gottwald, Norman K. 1985. *The Hebrew Bible—A Socio-Literary Introduction.* Philadelphia: Fortress.

Gutiérrez, Gustavo. 1987. *On Job: God-Talk and the Suffering of the Innocent.* Tr. by Matthew J. O'Connell. Maryknoll, NY: Orbis.

Lemaire, A. 1984. "Sagesse et Ecoles." *Vetus Testamentum* 34, 270–281.

McCreesh, T. 1985. "Wisdom as Wife: Proverbs 31:10–31." *Revue Biblique* 92, 25–46.

Matthews, Victor H., and Benjamin, Don C. 1991. *Old Testament Parallels: Laws and Stories from the Ancient Near East.* New York: Paulist.

Murphy, Roland E. 1990. *The Tree of Life: An Exploration of Biblical Wisdom Literature.* The Anchor Bible Reference Library. New York: Doubleday.

———. 1992. "Wisdom in the OT." *Anchor Bible Dictionary, VI,* 920–931.

Perdue, Leo G., and Gilpin, W. Clark, eds. 1992. *The Voice from the Whirlwind: Interpreting the Book of Job.* Nashville: Abingdon.

Pleins, J. David. 1992. "Poor, Poverty (Old Testament)." *Anchor Bible Dictionary, V,* 402–413.

Rad, Gerhard von. 1972. *Wisdom in Israel.* Nashville: Abingdon.

Schoors, A. 1982. "La structure littéraire de Qoheleth." *Orientalia Lovaniensia Analecta, 13,* 91–116.

Van Leeuwen, R. 1986. "Proverbs 30:21–23 and the Biblical World Upside Down." *Journal of Biblical Literature, 105,* 599–610.

Winston, David. 1992. "Solomon, Wisdom of." *Anchor Bible Dictionary, VI,* 120–127.

APOCALYPTIC LITERATURE, VISIONS OF THE END, AND PATHS TO THE FUTURE

Suggested Bible Reading
Daniel 1 - 12; Isa 24 - 27; Zech 9 - 14

THE MEANING AND SCOPE OF APOCALYPTIC

*A*s we arrive at the last stop on our journey through the Hebrew Bible, we appropriately conclude with a type of literature concerned with endings—*and* beginnings. The term "apocalyptic" in contemporary English usage is not commonly used when speaking of ordinary endings, but rather when referring to some kind of cataclysmic conclusion. Apocalyptic visions speak of imminent disaster and total or universal loss and destruction. One of the darkest movies about the Vietnam War is titled "Apocalypse Now." What is the connection between this contemporary connotation of the term apocalyptic and its use to describe a genre of biblical literature?

The noun apocalypse and the adjective apocalyptic, used in discussing a genre of biblical literature, come from a Greek noun *apokalypsis,* which means "revelation," "disclosure," or "unveiling." This term came into our English vocabulary by way of the New Testament book of Revelation (1:1), where the author refers to his work as "The revelation of Jesus Christ. . . ."

The revelation to which apocalyptic literature refers is one typically disclosed through a vision or by means of an otherworldly mediator, often an angel. The revelation is often said to have been communicated to a renowned person from the past, such as Enoch (in the case of 1 Enoch, an apocalyptic text composed between the fourth century B.C.E. and the turn of the era, fragments of which were found among the Dead Sea Scrolls), Abraham (in the case of the Apocalypse of Abraham, an apocalypse written after 70 C.E.), or Daniel (see the discussion below). While we are acquainted with Abraham, Enoch as one to whom revelations are given is not so familiar. Enoch is mentioned in Gen 4:17 as the son of Cain and his wife. In Gen 5:24 it is said of Enoch that he "Walked with God; then he was no more, because God took him." This rather cryptic reference was interpreted to mean that Enoch did not die, but was taken directly into the presence of God. This interpretation is reflected in the New Testament: "By faith Enoch was taken so that he did not experience death; and 'he was not found, because God had taken him.' For it was attested before he was taken away that 'he had pleased God'" (Hebrews 11:5). The book of 1 Enoch presents a series of revelations that Enoch received and transmitted to his son, Methuselah, for the benefit of the faithful who would live in the troubled end times. The primary myth of 1 Enoch centers on Enoch's journeys to the heavenly throne room and through the cosmos, where he was given the revelations.

The term apocalyptic, in addition to being used to designate a literary genre, has also been employed in connection with an apocalyptic perspective, apocalyptic movements, and apocalypticism. "Apocalyptic perspective" usually refers to a particular viewpoint from which one experiences one's environment. "Apocalyptic movement" refers to a social grouping. The terms "Apocalyptic" or "apocalypticism" have commonly been used to allude to a crisis phenomenon that arises when the values and cultural structures of a society become meaningless for a minority group within that society. As commonly understood, this minority group becomes alienated, marginalized, and comes into conflict with the majority group's culture. The majority group seeks to bolster the status quo, but the minority group constructs a new symbolic meaning system that reinterprets the past and present in light of the future envisioned in its symbolic meaning system.

That the term apocalypse or apocalyptic derives from a Greek term testifies to the fact that apocalypticism, an apocalyptic perspective, and apocalyptic literature came to maturity only near the end of the period represented in the Hebrew Bible, in the years following Alexander the Great's conquest of the eastern Mediterranean region and the spread of Hellenism in the last third of the fourth century B.C.E. Apocalyptic movements emerged clearly in the third century B.C.E., and continued into the third century C.E. Apocalypticism finds expression in apocalyptic literature in a few places in the Hebrew Bible, continued into "intertestamental" times, and was a popular genre in early Christian communities.

"Proto-Apocalyptic" Literature

In the Hebrew Bible, one of the most significant sections of apocalyptic literature is in the book of Daniel (chs. 7–12), which is usually dated to the second century B.C.E.. Daniel does have, however, some antecedents in the Hebrew Bible. One such forerunner is the book of Ezekiel, which is structured around five visions and opens with the line: "In the thirtieth year, in the fourth month, on the fifth day of the month, as I was among the exiles by the river Chebar, the heavens were opened, and I saw visions of God" (Ezek 1:1). The visions of Ezekiel are far from ordinary and differ greatly from those of Amos, who saw ordinary things in an extraordinary way. Ezekiel's visions are of extraordinary things seen in an extraordinary manner. Some of the most striking and "apocalyptic" visions of Ezekiel are found in chapters 38 and 39.

Another example of "proto-apocalyptic" literature in the Hebrew Bible is Isa 24–27. Before the destruction of the Temple by the Babylonians, the Zadokite priesthood (believed to be descendants of Zadok, a priest in the time of David— 2 Sam 8:15–17) had dominated the Temple and the cult at Jerusalem. Because they belonged to the upper levels of the society, however, they were taken away into exile. While in exile, they made plans for the restoration of the temple cult and priesthood, some of which are reflected in the book of Ezekiel. In the absence of the Zadokites, the Levites, with others who remained in Judah, exercised control of the cult and developed their own plans concerning the restoration of the Temple cult and priesthood. When the Zadokites returned to Jerusalem, conflict arose between them and the Levites. The Levites gradually lost ground in this struggle and had to endure much suffering. In the struggle with the Zadokites, the Levites were excluded from the principal religious and social institutions of the postexlic community, becoming a marginalized group. Isaiah 24–27, together with Zech 9–14, probably originated within the context of this struggle.

Later Jewish Apocalypses

Late Jewish writings in the "intertestamental" period and Jewish-Christian works that are generally classified as apocalypses include: 1 Enoch, 2 Enoch, 2 Baruch, 4 Ezra, the Assumption of Moses, and the Apocalypse of Abraham, which was one of the most significant works of the Jewish world in the first century C.E. In the New Testament, apocalyptic literature is represented by the book of Revelation, which closes the New Testament and dates to the end of the first century C.E. It is also present in the Christian tradition of the later second and third century in writings that were not included in the New Testament canon.

The Function of Apocalyptic Literature

Apocalyptic literature has as its basic function "the transmission of esoteric knowledge acquired (as it is claimed) not by human observation of reason but by revelation" (Davies 1989: 254). This functional definition of the apocalyptic genre implies the belief in the existence and accessibility to humans of heavenly secrets that once perceived, allow human beings to understand earthly events in a qualitatively different way, and even to predict their occurrence. This preliminary definition provides us with a combination of the essentials of form and content that we can now apply in our analysis of the subject matter and literary genres of apocalyptic. At the same time, this definition leaves open the question of the social setting of apocalyptic movements or schools of thought, to which we shall return below.

THE SUBJECT MATTER AND SOCIAL CONTEXT OF APOCALYPTIC WRITINGS

Subject Matter

Because the term apocalypse means revelation, what is revealed in an apocalypse and in what form? As we have observed, the first known use of the term apocalypse concerning a literary work is in the New Testament book of Revelation. While no book in the Hebrew Bible or in the apocryphal/deuterocanonical books uses the term apocalypse as part of its title, form critics have identified several characteristics of the apocalyptic genre in the Hebrew Bible. These characteristics, according to Gottwald, have to do both with the form of the revelation and its typical subject matter:

- The revelation may be delivered by sight (*vision*) or by a spoken statement (*audition*), or by both together.
- The vision may be expanded into an *otherworldly journey.* Always, an *otherworldly mediator,* usually pictured as an angelic being, either serves as a guide or delivers and/or explains the revelation.
- The human recipient of the revelation is usually identified as a well-known figure out of the past. In Jewish apocalypses bearing *pseudonyms,* the names are typically drawn from the early period of the Hebrew Bible (for example, Enoch and Abraham) and especially from the era of exile and early restoration (for example, Daniel, Ezra, Baruch). (Gottwald 1985: 583)

With respect to the subject matter of revelation, Gottwald observes that the revelation can concern either a temporal or a spatial perspective (Gottwald 1985: 583–584). The revelation on the temporal level is usually concerned with an approaching time of persecution and/or other sociopolitical disturbances. These conditions are seen as leading in the very near future to the end of the present world order, with accompanying judgment and the dawning of a new age. This end may involve a transformation of the world, but always leads to salvation for the faithful believer in some form of afterlife, often bodily resurrection. To set the stage for the end time, there is often a "revelation" about history in the form of prophecy-after-the-event related by the ancient recipient. Daniel, for example, is depicted as a figure from the time of the Babylonian exile who is shown the course of events in the second century B.C.E.

The spatial dimension of the revelation may take the human recipient on a guided journey through otherworldly regions, the heavens or the netherworld, where he or she meets supernatural creatures, angels and demons, and finally approaches the throne of God. In these otherworldly regions the future course of world history is determined, as suggested in Dan 11:36: "The king shall act as he pleases. He shall exalt himself and consider himself greater than any god, and shall speak horrendous things against the God of gods. He shall prosper until the period of wrath is completed, for *what is determined shall be done*" (emphasis mine). The apocalypse usually concludes with reassurance to the faithful that God is the Lord of history. Though prospects may look bleak now, God will bring about a new age in which the faithful will find salvation.

A working group of biblical scholars, headed by J. J. Collins, has analyzed all of the texts that can be classified as apocalypses from the period 250 B.C.E. – 250 C.E. and offered the following definition of apocalyptic as a literary genre, which summarizes the discussion above:

> Apocalypse is a genre of revelatory literature with a narrative framework, in which a revelation is mediated by an otherworldly being to a human recipient, disclosing a transcendental reality which is both temporal, insofar as it envisages eschatological salvation, and spatial, insofar as it involves another, supernatural world. (Collins 1979: 9)

Social Location

The efforts of scholars in the past fifty years in the search for the social setting within which apocalyptic literature arose have been surveyed recently by P. R. Davies (1989: 255–270). Davies begins with the work of H. H. Rowley. Many assumptions still prevalent in discussions of the social world of apocalyptic can be traced to an influential work of Rowley's, *The Relevance of Apocalyptic*, which was first published in 1944. At every level, Rowley explains the phenomenon of apocalyptic in simple terms. He assumes that apocalyptic is a child of prophecy. He reasons that just as the prophets addressed their contemporaries in times of historical crisis, so the apocalypticists did the same, the crisis for them and their people taking the form of persecution. Thus, for the apocalypticists, the emphasis was on the announcement of an end to the persecution and imminent salvation for the faithful. Rowley, however, never asked the important question: What accounts for the use or appearance of *this* particular literary form on *this* (or any) occasion? As Davies comments: "To say that apocalypticists are heirs of prophets is to explain neither apocalyptic literature nor prophecy; it is merely playing with theological picture-cards" (1989: 256).

Davies then turns to a discussion of Paul Hanson's *The Dawn of Apocalyptic,* published in 1975. Hanson's work sought to fill some gaps in Rowley's work. Hanson is more careful to define his use of "apocalyptic" than was Rowley. Acknowledging the differences between "apocalypse" as a literary genre, "apocalypticism" as a movement or school of thought, and "apocalyptic eschatology" as thought dealing with the end-time, Hanson seeks to explain the origin and development of the last of these terms. What emerges from Hanson's work is that apocalyptic ideas arose from the counter-establishment, from those whose aspirations saw no realistic hope of fulfillment, those who had been socially marginalized and were on the fringes of political and religious power. Davies, however, disagrees with this idea of Hanson's, observing that it is difficult to find very many pieces of apocalyptic literature that clearly point to authors who lived in such a context. Rather, in fact those in power *also* appealed to such things as esoteric knowledge and heavenly revelation to justify *their* status and to undergird *their* exercise of ideological control over people. Both the book of Daniel and the sectarian documents among the Dead Sea Scrolls combine a reverence for the "established" priesthood and cult with a strong belief in an imminent end-time. Both Daniel and the Dead Sea Scrolls probably arose from inner-establishment disputes, not from disputes between those on the "outside" with those on the "inside."

A third influential work in the development of ideas about the social world of apocalyptic surveyed by Davies is M. Hengel's *Judaism and Hellenism,* published in 1974. Hengel minimized the link between prophecy and apocalyptic and instead emphasized the multiplicity of influences at work in apocalyptic. He accepted the influence of Israelite prophecy but also saw Persian and Babylonian mythology, as well as Greek Orphic ideas incorporated into Jewish apocalyptic writings. (Orphism, a religious movement that appeared in Greece in the sixth century B.C.E., takes its name from the legendary figure Orpheus. Orpheus was represented as a musician and enchanter, who had the special ability to charm animals. A story in Orphic literature tells about his descent into the underworld.) In particular, Hengel observed the stress on revealed wisdom and instruction in the earliest Jewish apocalyptic literature, and pointed out that in this literature the wise acquired prophetic features and the prophets became inspired wisdom figures.

Davies' concludes regarding the work of these three scholars of apocalyptic that they "took us a long way, but up the wrong road" (1989: 260). Having assessed what he believes to have been flawed approaches, Davies then proceeds to discuss some more productive contemporary approaches to the social world of apocalyptic writings that have focused on a phenomenon known as "manticism."

MAUTICISM

One form of wisdom tradition represented in the Hebrew Bible that is widely attested in the ancient Near East generally, but especially in Mesopotamian wisdom literature, is concerned with esoteric knowledge derived from omens deciphered by specialists sometimes called diviners. A common source of omens for diviners

Figure 16.1   A model liver of clay from the first dynasty of Babylon, 1820–1530 B.C.E.

was the examination of animal organs. In an article written in 1971, H. P. Müller gave the name "mantic wisdom" to this art/science of interpretation. A clay model liver that was used by diviners is divided into some fifty sections that are inscribed with omens and magical formulae (shown in Figure 16.1). This model is from the First Dynasty of Babylon (*ca.* 1830–1530 B.C.E.).

Although we have no formal account of the theory on which Mesopotamian manticism rests, it seems to have included the two following elements:

1. The conviction that all human experience is interlocking. Because of this, any and all patterns of association between or among observable phenomena are significant and potentially predictive as omens. By cataloging these associations, the recurrence of the omen could be interpreted as predictive of a subsequent event.

2. Not only is all human experience connected, manticism also held that natural and otherworldly realities are interrelated. Natural events can be understood as the result of decisions made by otherworldly beings.

When these two elements are combined, it can be concluded that because, at least in principle, *any* natural occurrence has revelatory potential and could be an omen, the accumulation of natural scientific knowledge is necessary for understanding all reality, including its otherworldly dimension. Some current approaches suggest that apocalyptic literature developed from the study of mantic lore, understood this way.

While considerable evidence suggests that manticism was widely practiced in Mesopotamia, was there manticism or divination in ancient Israel? On the theory that one only condemns actions that actually exist and are perceived as a real threat, then yes, divination did occur in ancient Israel, as divination is soundly denounced several times in the Hebrew Bible. Deut 18:10-11 provides the most inclusive list of mantic phenomena in the Hebrew Bible, together with a denunciation of them:

> No one shall be found among you who makes a son or daughter pass through fire, or who practices divination, or is a soothsayer, or an augur, or a sorcerer, or one who casts spells, or who consults ghosts or spirits, or who seeks oracles from the dead.

One of the characteristics of false prophets in Jeremiah is the fact that they were diviners:

> And the LORD said to me: The prophets are prophesying lies in my name; I did not send them, nor did I command them or speak to them. They are prophesying to you a lying vision, worthless divination, and the deceit of their own minds." (Jer 14:14)

Second Isaiah spoke in an ironic way to a Jewish community in exile in Babylonia that apparently was well acquainted with manticism:

> Both these things shall come upon you in a moment, in one day: the loss of children and widowhood shall come upon you in full measure, in spite of your many sorceries and the great power of your enchantments. You felt secure in your wickedness; you said, "No one sees me." Your wisdom and your knowledge led you astray, and you said in your heart, "I am, and there is no one besides me." But evil shall come upon you, which you cannot charm away; disaster shall fall upon you, which you will not be able to ward off; and ruin shall come on you suddenly, of which you know nothing. Stand fast in your enchantments and your many sorceries, with which you have labored from your youth; perhaps you may be able to succeed, perhaps you may inspire terror. You are wearied with your many consultations; let those who study the heavens stand up and save you, those who gaze at the stars, and at each new moon predict what shall befall you. See, they are like stubble, the fire consumes them; they cannot deliver themselves from the power of the flame. No coal for warming oneself is this, no fire to sit before! Such to you are those with whom you have labored, who have trafficked with you from your youth; they all wander about in their own paths; there is no one to save you." (Isa 47:9-15)

It thus seems reasonable to conclude with Davies that "Manticism is the mother of Jewish 'apocalyptic'; what determines the production of apocalyptic literature is not a millenarian posture [the idea that end times are imminent], not a predicament of persecution, though these may be contributory factors" (Davies 1989: 263). What does generate the creation of apocalyptic literature is scribal convention reflecting a worldview determined by the premises and devices of manticism. To consider the social context of actual examples of apocalyptic literature more carefully, one needs to examine them individually. We thus turn our attention to the book of Daniel as the book containing the major example of apocalyptic literature in the Hebrew Bible.

DANIEL 7–12 AND APOCALYPTIC LITERATURE

Daniel the Hero

The book of Daniel is a composite collection, not all of which represents apocalyptic literature. It is divided into two major parts, chapters 1-6 and chapters 7-12. It can be described as a series of apocalypses (chapters 7-12) appended to a cycle of court-tales (chapters 1-6) that celebrates the virtues of Daniel, a Jewish wise man initiated as a young man into Babylonian manticism. A person named Daniel, who may be the person after whom the hero of the court-tales in Dan 1-6 is modelled, is mentioned, together with Noah and Job, as a model of righteousness in Ezekiel 14:14: "Even if Noah, Daniel, and Job, these three, were in it, they would save only their own lives by their righteousness, says the Lord God" (cf. Ezek 14:20; 28:3). In the early chapters of the book that bears his name, Daniel is depicted as an interpreter of dreams and mysterious writing. He pursued a career as a courtier, working first for the Babylonians and then the Persians. According to the author of chapters 1-6, Daniel's special abilities were the result of his faithfulness to the Torah, even in difficult situations. Daniel, the exilic figure, is mentioned in a list of heroes in the apocryphal/deuterocanonical book of 1 Maccabees (2:60) as having been rescued from a den of lions. The familiar story of God's rescue of Daniel from the lion's den appears at the end of the first section of Daniel (6:7).

Additions to the Book of Daniel

In the Greek Septuagint the book of Daniel is considerably longer than in the Hebrew. The additions to the book of Daniel, which later entered the Latin text, include three separate works: (1) the Prayer of Azariah (the Hebrew name of Daniel's companion, Abednego; Dan 1:7; 2:9; and so forth); (2) Susanna; and (3) Bel and the Dragon. The story of Susanna concerns a faithful Jewish woman who resisted seduction and preferred death to dishonor. She is rescued by a young Daniel. The two short stories included in Bel and the Dragon depict Daniel as one whose mantic powers take on a kind of Sherlock Holmes quality as he becomes a detective in the service of true religion. In the first story,

Daniel proves to Cyrus the king that the idol Bel does not consume offerings. Daniel does this by secretly scattering ashes on the floor of the temple containing the idol and then locking the doors. The priests of Bel enter at night via a secret entrance, eat the offerings left for Bel, but are betrayed by their footprints in the ashes. The story ends with Daniel destroying the temple. In the other story, Daniel feeds a great dragon made of a mixture of pitch, fat, and hair, causing it to explode. The people are angered by this and demand that the king surrender Daniel to them. Daniel, as in chapter 6 in the book of Daniel, is thrown into a lion's den. In the end, Daniel is released from the lion's den unharmed and his accusers are thrown into it and perish.

Structure of the Book of Daniel

The book of Daniel has a curious feature: it forms a Hebrew-Aramaic-Hebrew "sandwich." The book begins in Hebrew (1:1–2:4a), switches to Aramaic (2:4b–7:28), and ends in Hebrew (8:1–12:13). This change in language does not correspond to the form-critical division between the narratives of chapters 1–6 and the vision reports of chapters 7–12. While there is no completely satisfactory explanation for the bilingual form of the book, some interesting suggestions have emerged. Chapters 2–7, which are in Aramaic, have a chiastic structure as follows:

Chapter 2	"Four kingdom" prophecy
Chapter 3	Tale of miraculous deliverance
Chapter 4	Divine judgment of a king
Chapter 5	Divine judgment of a king
Chapter 6	Tale of miraculous deliverance
Chapter 7	"Four kingdom" prophecy

The tone and idiom of chapter 7, however, are quite different from those of chapters 2–6. Collins has suggested that the two languages in the book reflect the history of its composition (Collins 1992: 31). Chapters 2–6 (and probably chapter 1) were composed in Aramaic and chapter 7 was added in the time of Antiochus Epiphanes. Then either the same author or others in the same circle composed chapters 8–12 in Hebrew (possibly because of nationalistic fervor). Chapter 1 was translated from Aramaic into Hebrew or it was written in Hebrew to form a Hebrew *inclusio* or "sandwich" around the Aramaic chapters. The fact that chapter 1 is now in Hebrew and chapter 7 is in Aramaic provides an overlap that connects the two halves of the book, forming an editorial unity. The parallelism in content of chapters 2 and 7 also serves this purpose.

Apocalypses in Daniel 7–12

The apocalypses in the second part of Daniel, chapters 7–12, draw most of their inspiration either from the tales about Daniel and his companions or from mantic-scribal conventions and interests. They give an apocalyptic review of the history of the postexilic period. Chapter 7 deals with the "plot" of this history in a sequence of world-kingdoms, which is continued in chapter 8. Chapter 9 is concerned with the hidden meaning of ancient books. Chapters 10–12 tell of pseudo-predictions of political events and ancient mythical motifs.

The ostensible historical setting of the book of Daniel is during the Babylonian Exile at the courts of the Babylonian, Median, and Persian kings. Daniel thus represents those Jews for whom the Exile opened up the opportunity of service in the administrations of foreign rulers and who were able to work in such an environment without compromising their faith. While the tales in chapters 1–6 are outwardly set in the period of the Exile, several striking inaccuracies appear in the historical information about that period in these chapters. For example, the opening verse of the book states: "In the third year of the reign of King Jehoiakim of Judah, King Nebuchadnezzar of Babylon came to Jerusalem and besieged it" (Dan 1:1). The third year of Jehoiakim would be 606 B.C.E. We know, however, that Nebuchadnezzar's siege of Jerusalem actually occurred in 597 B.C.E. In Daniel 5, Belshazzar, the king, is called the son of Nebuchadnezzar. Actually, Belshazzar was the son of Nabonidus, and he was never king of Babylonia. Darius is designated a Mede in 9:1; he was actually a Persian. These and other historical inaccuracies in the early chapters of Daniel have led scholars to question a date for the book in the Babylonian or Persian period. Scholarly consensus now dates Daniel to the second century B.C.E., specifically to the time of Antiochus IV Epiphanes and the Maccabean Revolt, 168–164 B.C.E. While descriptions of earlier events are often inaccurate, the closer one gets to the second century B.C.E., the more detailed and accurate the descriptions in Daniel become. The existence of historical errors in Daniel has also led scholars to believe that Daniel, like other examples of apocalyptic writing, was written pseudonymously (that is, by an author using a name other than his own) employing the technique of prophecy after-the-event.

ANTIOCHUS EPIPHANES

While the court-tales in the early chapters are set in the Babylonian exile, the setting of the apocalyptic visions in chapters 7–12 is quite different. The setting of the visions is the persecution of the Palestinian Jewish community under Antiochus IV Epiphanes (175–164 B.C.E.), a successor of Alexander the Great. Alexander the Great overthrew the Persian Empire in the late fourth century B.C.E., but died without naming a successor. His empire was divided among his generals, with Palestine coming under the control of Seleucus and his successors, who came to be known as the Seleucids. The last Seleucid ruler of Palestine was Antiochus IV Epiphanes. To consolidate his empire, Antiochus IV Epiphanes ordered the forced Hellenization (the imposition of Greek culture) of all the different ethnic groups under his control so that there would be unity. To finance military campaigns against his rivals, he twice stripped the Jerusalem Temple. He ordered Jews not to practice circumcision, not to abstain from pork, not to observe the Sabbath, and not to offer sacrifices at the Temple. He violated the sanctity of the Jerusalem

Temple by building an altar to Zeus in it. In 167 B.C.E. a revolt against Antiochus erupted, a revolt described in the apocryphal/deuterocanonical book of 1 Maccabees. This revolt, called the Maccabean War, ended on Chislev 25 (= 14 December), 164 B.C.E., when the Temple was reconsecrated.

The restrictions on the practice of Judaism that Antiochus attempted to enforce are reflected in the visions of Daniel:

> He shall speak words against the Most High, shall wear out the holy ones of the Most High, and shall attempt to change the sacred seasons and the law; and they shall be given into his power for a time, two times, and half a time. [Dan 7:25. Note that the reference to "a time, two times, and a half a time" is a "prediction" that the persecution would last three-and-one-half years, 167–164 B.C.E.] He shall return to his land with great wealth, but his heart shall be set against the holy covenant. He shall work his will, and return to his own land. For ships of Kittim [= Cyprus] shall come against him, and he shall lose heart and withdraw. He shall be enraged and take action against the holy covenant. He shall turn back and pay heed to those who forsake the holy covenant. (Dan 11:28,30)

Daniel's visions also reflect the desecration of the Temple by Antiochus:

> Forces sent by him shall occupy and profane the Temple and fortress. They shall abolish the regular burnt offering and set up the abomination that makes desolate. . . . From the time that the regular burnt offering is taken away and the abomination that desolates is set up, there shall be one thousand two hundred ninety days. (Dan 11:31; 12:11)

Here, the length of the persecution is 3.6 years, instead of the 3.5 years of Dan 7:25. Still another figure, 1150 days = 3.2 years, is given in Dan 8:14. The different periods of time given for the duration of the persecution under Antiochus (3.5 years, 3.6 years, 3.2 years) probably reflect attempts to adjust the prediction to adapt to the actual course of events.

The visions also speak of the deaths of many righteous Jews in the revolt that is described in 1 Maccabees:

> The wise among the people shall give understanding to many; for some days, however, they shall fall by sword and flame, and suffer captivity and plunder. When they fall victim, they shall receive a little help, and many shall join them insincerely. Some of the wise shall fall, so that they may be refined, purified, and cleansed, until the time of the end, for there is still an interval until the time appointed. (Dan 11:33–35)

DANIEL 7

The first apocalypse in the second part of Daniel—chapter 7—has two parts: the first contains the description of the vision (7:1-14), the second its interpretation (7:15-27). In this vision Daniel sees four incredible beasts arising from the sea. This vision rests on the notion that the history of the world can be divided into periods. The four creatures in the vision symbolize four periods of history, four successive empires in the ancient Near East:

1. The first beast to arise is a lion with eagle's wings (7:4), which represents the Babylonian Empire.

2. The second beast is a bear that "was raised up on one side, had three tusks in its mouth among its teeth" (7:5), which represents the Median Empire.

3. The third creature is a leopard with four wings and four heads (7:6), representing the Persian Empire.

4. The last beast to arise from the sea is a ferocious dragon-like beast with iron teeth and ten horns (7:7). This creature represents the empire of Alexander the Great, with the ten horns symbolizing his ten successors. This beast is represented in particular by one horn, the "little" horn (compare Dan 8:9) with eyes and a mouth, who is Antiochus IV. This horn oppresses the holy ones of the Most High and seeks to change the religion mandated by God: "He shall speak words against the Most High, shall wear out the holy ones of the Most High, and shall attempt to change the sacred seasons and the law." This horn is described as a fourth king who subdues three previous rulers, pointing to the fact that Epiphanes gained his throne by eliminating his competition.

Antiochus' period of persecution comes to an end when "the Ancient One" (God) appears and executes judgment against the little horn. God's everlasting kingdom is then inaugurated on earth. Chapter 7 is a crucial chapter for the interpretation of the book of Daniel as a whole because it uses many themes from the court narratives, especially the theme of world empires that appears in Dan 2. It also sets a pattern for the other visions that follow.

DANIEL 8

The second vision, in Dan 8, dated two years after the one in Dan 7, elaborates on the theme of the animal empires. It pictures a struggle between two animals, a ram with two horns, representing the Medes and Persians, and a male goat from the west, representing Alexander who overthrew the Persian Empire. The goat has one large horn which, when broken off produces four more, representing the four most important successors of Alexander (Cassander in Macedonia, Lysimachus in Asia Minor, Ptolemy in Egypt, and Seleucus in Syria and Palestine). Out of the last of these horns arises a "little horn," Antiochus IV Epiphanes, pictured as struggling with the heavenly host and stopping the daily Temple offerings:

> Out of one of them came another horn, a little one, which grew exceedingly great toward the south, toward the east, and toward the beautiful land. It grew as high as the host of heaven. It threw down to the earth some of the host and some of the stars, and trampled on them. Even against the prince of the host it acted arrogantly; it took the regular burnt offering away from him and overthrew the place of his sanctuary. Because

of wickedness, the host was given over to it together with the regular burnt offering; it cast truth to the ground, and kept prospering in what it did. (Dan 8:9–12)

This vision also contains the prediction that the little horn will eventually be broken (8:13-14).

DANIEL 9

The third vision, in Daniel 9, begins with a reference (9:2) to a prophecy from the book of Jeremiah (29:10): "For thus says the LORD: Only when Babylon's seventy years are completed will I visit you, and I will fulfill to you my promise and bring you back to this place." The angel Gabriel appears to Daniel (9:21) and tells him that it is actually seventy *weeks* (of years) (9:24), or 490 years (70 × 7), before the kingdom of God will come, thereby opening up the four-century time span between the Babylonian exile and the Maccabean war. In other words, Daniel is told that God's kingdom and the downfall of "the prince who is to come" (9:26) is imminent!

DANIEL 10:1–12:4

The last vision of Daniel, 10:1-12:4, represents the longest. It emphasizes both Antiochus' persecution and the expectation that God will bring an end to it. It presents a thinly-veiled account of the history of the Hellenistic era, set in the context of a heavenly battle between angelic "princes." The death of Antiochus initiates the final events of world history, when God sends the archangel Michael, the patron angel of the Jews, who rescues God's people:

> At that time Michael, the great prince, the protector of your people, shall arise. There shall be a time of anguish, such as has never occurred since nations first came into existence. But at that time your people shall be delivered, everyone who is found written in the book. Many of those who sleep in the dust of the earth shall awake, some to everlasting life, and some to shame and everlasting contempt. Those who are wise shall shine like the brightness of the sky, and those who lead many to righteousness, like the stars forever and ever. (Dan 12:1–3)

This reference in Daniel is the first explicit mention of the resurrection of the dead in the Hebrew Bible. The ancient Israelites seemed to have had no concept of individual life after death, but only one of an indistinct, shadowy existence in sheol, the place of the dead. While Daniel 12:2-3 contains a reference to the resurrection of the dead, even here resurrection is only partial: "Many . . . shall awake. . . ."

THE MESSAGE OF THE VISIONS

The overall message of the four visions in Daniel declares that God's control of history cannot be compromised. Although tyrants like Antiochus IV Epiphanes may prevail for a brief period, God will overthrow them and reaffirm his dominion. We have set forth only a very general overview of the visions in Daniel. The visions of Daniel are actually very complex and, like much of apocalyptic literature, they are only partially understood. Also like other apocalyptic literature, Daniel has been misused. Crenshaw has observed that perhaps more than any other book (in the Hebrew Bible), Daniel has been trivialized by religious enthusiasts who want to identify contemporary political figures destined to play a role in the final battle just before the end of history. The book does not deserve such treatment, for it is a powerful testimony to faithful conduct in the midst of an almost unbearable persecution. If the message that the author sought to leave with his fellow Jews appears to be a flight from reality, it is because the times were so difficult. But, as Crenshaw concludes, that message was also one of courage and resolute conduct in serving God. The imagery in Daniel may be bizarre, the stories may be unrealistic, but both arise from a vital faith in the Lord of history. To be sure, the author was mistaken in viewing the confrontation with Antiochus IV as the final battle that would bring in God's kingdom, but more importantly, the writer recognized the responsibility to serve God faithfully, regardless of one's circumstances. This message is the real legacy left by the author of the Book of Daniel, not some mistaken timetable about the last days (Crenshaw 1992: 372–373).

BEYOND THE HEBREW BIBLE: MOVEMENTS WITHIN JUDAISM AND THE EMERGENCE OF CHRISTIANITY

With the book of Daniel, assuming its authorship in the 160s B.C.E., the period of the Hebrew Bible comes to a close, if we consider only those books that were included in the canon of the Jewish Bible. While in the Septuagint and in Christian Bibles, Daniel appears among the prophetic writings, in the Jewish Bible it forms part of the "Writings," coming just before the works of the Chronicler (Ezra, Nehemiah, 1–2 Chronicles), which conclude the Hebrew Bible. While the Hebrew Bible ends with an apocalyptic vision in which the end of oppressive tyranny is envisaged, accompanied by the imminent dawning of a new age characterized by the rule of God, in fact history produced no such positive outcome. Instead of the inauguration of God's rule as envisioned in Daniel, historical reality replaced Greek overlords with Roman ones. The Maccabean revolt did produce a temporary respite from foreign domination, but the Jewish leaders who succeeded the Maccabees were certainly not models of religious fidelity, but figures who played the game of political intrigue as well as any of their non-Jewish counterparts. They in fact paved the way, after about a century of Jewish independence, for the entry into Palestine of a foreign power that had not been perceived in Daniel's visions, the Romans. Roman rule in Palestine began when Pompey marched into Jerusalem in 63 B.C.E. and continued throughout all the New Testament period.

Sectarian Judaism

By the end of the second century B.C.E. all of those books to be included in the canon of the Jewish Bible had been written. By the second century C.E. two distinct religions had developed, Christianity and "Rabbinic" Judaism, which began to develop after the destruction of the temple by the Romans in 70 C.E. In the transitional period between the Maccabean revolt and the emergence of Christianity as an offshoot from Judaism in the first century C.E., Judaism was a religion involved in considerable struggle. This struggle, which had both internal and external dimensions, produced many subgroups and trends within Judaism. A popular way of describing the Judaism of this period derives from the description of Jewish "parties" given by Flavius Josephus, a Jewish historian who lived during the first century C.E. Josephus listed four parties: Sadducees, Pharisees, Essenes, and a "fourth philosophy," which some scholars identify as the revolutionary party of the Zealots, but which is actually much older because the Zealots did not arise until the middle of the first century C.E. Josephus does not deal with the origins of these groups nor with their relationships with one another. Nor does he say anything about those Jews who did not belong to one of these parties. While Josephus describes a part of the Judaism of this period, it is too simplistic to divide the whole Jewish community neatly into these four segments. These four parties do, however, represent important variations in the view of Jews as a "holy" or distinct religious community separated from other nations and obedient to the Torah. In what follows, we present brief sketches of these four parties.

SADDUCEES

The Sadducees' viewpoint of the nature of Israel as a religious community and on obedience to the Torah was so strongly influenced by their economic and social interests that in some ways it is stretching a definition to call them a "religious" party. The Sadducees were composed mainly of wealthy priestly and aristocratic families of considerable prestige and political influence. They claimed to be loyal to the Torah alone—the Torah as written, not in its oral enlargement. In fact, they collaborated with Rome to protect their class interests. The preservation of the lucrative temple cult, in which they had vested interests, and a good business climate with the Romans were high on their list of priorities. Holiness was defined by them in narrow cultic terms. Religion for them centered on the proper conduct of ritual. Holiness for them depended on being separate. Separation was class separation. Priests should keep separate from non-priests and wealthy Jews should keep apart from poor Jews. Separation for them, however, did not mean separation from the Romans who had the resources to help them maintain their position of privilege. Because they were so closely linked to the temple and its cult, they disappeared as a force in Judaism after the destruction of the temple in 70 C.E.

PHARISEES

The Pharisees were associated with those whose adherence to the Torah brought them into conflict with Hellenistic culture and with their fellow Jews who compromised or collaborated with that culture. Like Daniel and his companions, the Pharisees practiced a commitment to the Torah that strictly separated Jews from gentiles in such things as dietary laws, circumcision, fasting, and prayer. They accepted the oral expansion of the written Torah and accepted belief in traditions not spelled out in the written Torah, such as the doctrine of resurrection. This oral law, which interpreted the written Torah and was called "the tradition of the elders," was itself committed to writing *ca.* 200 c.e. in the Mishnah. The Mishnah in turn provided the basis for a continuing tradition of interpretation of the written Torah, represented in definitive form in the Babylonian Talmud. The Pharisees' emphasis on separation from anything that would compromise their obedience to the Torah translated into a withdrawal from the arena of worldly politics. They did not represent any particular social or economic interests because their membership cut across class boundaries, including persons from many different classes. After the fall of Jerusalem in 70 c.e., they remained the dominant force in Judaism, which after that date can fairly be called Pharisaic Judaism.

ESSENES

A third group within Judaism in this period was the Essenes. While the New Testament speaks of the Sadducees and Pharisees, it never mentions the Essenes. In addition to Josephus' description of the Essenes, they are also discussed by another first century c.e. Jewish writer, Philo, and by the first century Roman, Pliny the Elder. Interest in the Essenes has received a tremendous boost in the past fifty years, owing to a spectacular archaeological discovery in 1947 at Qumran on the northwest shore of the Dead Sea. Due to the intense publicity and controversy surrounding this discovery, many people know that a library called the Dead Sea Scrolls was first discovered in a cave near the mouth of the Wadi Qumran by an Arab shepherd. That library belonged to a nearby community that was one of the strictest of the Essene groups. Since 1947, scrolls have been found in eleven caves and the nearby community at Khirbet Qumran has been excavated. (Figure 16.2 depicts one of the caves in which scrolls have been found.)

Scholarly consensus, as represented by James Charlesworth (1992), now recognizes that the ruins at Khirbet Qumran are the remains of a center for Jewish priests forced to live in the Judean desert because they were exiled from Jerusalem and the temple. These priests, and other Jews who later joined the community, worked at Qumran, often living in nearby caves, from about the second half of the second century b.c.e. to 68 c.e., the year that marked the third year of the first Jewish revolt against Rome (66–70 c.e.). The settlement at Qumran was destroyed by the Tenth Roman Legion during the first revolt (Charlesworth 1992: 2).

Figure 16.2   Qumran cave number four

Besides scrolls or fragments of scrolls of biblical books, the library of the Essene community at Qumran included a document called *The Rule of the Community.* Considerable agreement exists between material in *The Rule of the Community* and the description of the Essenes in Josephus. The Essenes as represented at Qumran were clearly a group of Jews who removed themselves from the rest of their fellow Jews to practice a strict observance of the Jewish law. They believed that God had revealed to their founder, the "teacher of righteousness," the true law that was now lost to the rest of the Jewish community. Their separation from the rest of Judaism is evident at Qumran not only with respect to its physical location in the Judean desert, but also in their admission procedures. Following a multi-year process of admission, during which the candidate surrendered private property to the community, an individual was accepted as a member of the community. To emphasize their separation, the Essenes at Qumran even rejected the lunar Jewish calendar. They did not marry, and they abandoned the temple cult, believing that they were participants in the worship of a "heavenly temple." Commenting on the community at Qumran, Rogerson and Davies hold that the clues all point to a group formed in anticipation of the "end of days," the last times. When the hopes of such a group are not realized, their ideology becomes unstable and erratic. This is reflected in their writings which contain, for example, description of a war between the forces of light and darkness, and in their elaborate efforts to prove from Scripture that their experiences were really foretold. It would not be surprising to find that they participated in the war against Rome, which may have occurred. They obviously regarded themselves as the only true Israel, and, like other Essenes, regarded the rest of Israel as doomed (1989: 342).

THE "FOURTH PHILOSOPHY"

As mentioned above, besides these three sectarian Jewish groups, Josephus writes about a fourth, unnamed group that he calls the "fourth philosophy." This group, according to Josephus, was founded by Judas of Gamala and Zadok the Pharisee in 6 C.E. In the year 37 B.C.E., Herod the Great was appointed by the Romans as king of Judea. As an Idumean he was disliked by the Judeans. Perhaps the most prevalent opinion toward Herod is represented in the *Psalms of Solomon,* a collection of poems written during his reign. One of these poems (number 17) calls for a king from David's line who would reprove the gentiles and reign justly. The animosity toward Herod was one of the factors stimulating the growth of a movement after his death, of which Josephus' "fourth philosophy" was a part. Josephus tells us that this group was extremely nationalistic, calling upon Jews to resist the Romans, rebelling against Roman "slavery." Although it is unclear whether resistance to the Romans included armed revolt or just the withholding of tax payments, Josephus reports that Judas and his followers were willing to suffer torture and death for their beliefs. During the 50s C.E. a group called the Sicarii came into being. This group, which may have been a descendant of the "fourth philosophy" took its name from the *sica,* a curved dagger that its members carried, anticipating the opportunity of knifing Jews who collaborated with the Romans. This group was active in the revolt against Rome. Another group, known as the Zealots, was also active in the revolt. They have sometimes been mistakenly identified with the Sicarii or the "fourth philosophy." They were, however, one of several revolutionary movements that believed that Judaism was incompatible with Roman domination.

SAMARITANS

In addition to the four parties mentioned by Josephus, another group was present at the turn of the era, the Samaritans. The term Samaritan is first a geographic term, referring to anyone who lived in Samaria, the region of Palestine around the city of Samaria established under that name by the Assyrians after the fall of the northern kingdom. Were Samaritans Jews? Soon after Palestine was conquered by Alexander the Great, the Jewish inhabitants of the city of Samaria rebelled. As punishment they were replaced by Macedonians and moved to Shechem, where, according to Josephus, they built a temple on nearby Mount Gerizim. The erection of this temple brought the Samaritans into conflict with Judean Jews. The Samaritans produced their own version of the Pentateuch, edited so as to provide justification for their temple. They accepted as scripture only their Samaritan Pentateuch. The conflict between the Samaritans and Judean Jews climaxed in the destruction of the Samaritan temple in 129 B.C.E. by John Hyrcanus. The Samaritans themselves would have rejected identification as Jews, seeing themselves as Israelites who had retained the ancient form of the faith. It seems best, however, to view them as another one of the "Judaisms" of this period.

OTHER JEWS

Most Jews of this period would not have identified themselves as belonging to any of the groups mentioned above. As we have seen, various expressions of Judaism developed during the Hellenistic and Roman period, each of which saw itself as representing the "true" Judaism. The groups we have described included only a minority of the Jews of Palestine. Many Jews belonged to a group referred to by the Pharisees as the "people of the land," a group about whose religious practices we are ignorant. Diaspora Judaism, the culture of those Jews living outside Palestine, is simply too complex a phenomenon to be discussed here.

BRIDGES TO THE FUTURE

From the rich variety of options that developed during Hellenistic and Roman times, Judaism eventually chose the course of Rabbinic Judaism, a Judaism that accepted both a written and an oral Torah. Jewish Christianity chose the path of a "new covenant," identifying Jesus of Nazareth with the promised Davidic Messiah. At the close of the period of the Hebrew Bible, the faith that had produced this great body of literature was far from dead, although it was restricted by foreign domination. The hope, envisioned in Daniel, that God would bring an end to oppression and replace unjust human rule with a new order characterized by peace and righteousness was still waiting to be realized.

On one level, the Hebrew Bible is rooted in the past. It looks back to defining moments in history such as the Exodus from Egypt. In answer to the question of the nature of God, the prophets and others pointed to what they believed were God's actions in the history of God's people, Israel. On another level, however, the Hebrew Bible never relegates God to the past, as if history were a record of the declining activity of a God who has become more and more withdrawn. On the contrary, on page after page of the Hebrew Bible appears the testimony that this God can be known by ordinary people in the everyday events of their ordinary lives. The prophets and the writers of the later apocalyptic literature simply carried this conviction a step further. If God had made himself known in the past and could be known in the events of the present, then God is not temporally bound, but leads the way into the future. The Hebrew Bible is a book of ever increasing anticipation. John Drane has extracted three fundamental strands in this anticipation (Drane 1987: 339–342):

1. A New Covenant Most notable is the expectation of a "new covenant" that would take up and fulfill the Sinai covenant that had been abandoned by many of the Jewish people. This hope emerged during the time of the Exile, when the prophets interpreted the failure of the original covenant as due to the people's unfaithfulness. In order for the relationship between God and God's people to be restored, God would forgive them for their lack of fidelity in the past and empower them to keep the covenant, a belief that is shared by Jeremiah and Ezekiel:

> But this is the covenant that I will make with the house of Israel after those days, says the LORD: I will put my law within them, and I will write it on their hearts; and I will be their God, and they shall be my people. (Jer 31:33)
> I will give them one heart, and put a new spirit within them; I will remove the heart of stone from their flesh and give them a heart of flesh, so that they may follow my statutes and keep my ordinances and obey them. Then they shall be my people, and I will be their God. (Ezek 11:19–20)

2. A Messiah The Hebrew term *mashiach,* together with its Greek translation *Christos,* means one who has been "anointed." Anointing was an act that set one apart for a particular vocation. The Davidic monarch was called "God's anointed." The king was to be God's regent on earth. That was the theological theory; the sociopolitical reality was something altogether different. Israel's kings were no better, and sometimes far worse, than other human rulers, representing not God's standards for a just society but base human aspirations based on greed and personal ambition. There was always the hope that the next king would be better, but from the time of Isaiah on, the prophets became increasingly disillusioned with the Davidic line of kings. Out of this frustration the messianic hope was born. Messianic expectation was more a political reflex than a religious doctrine. There was no "messianic Judaism," and no "messianic doctrine," but by the end of the period of the Hebrew Bible, the notion of a "messiah" became widespread. Psalm 72, a prayer for God's blessing on the king, reveals the aura that surrounded the person of the king and informed messianic imagery:

> Give the king your justice, O God,
>   and your righteousness to a king's son.
> May he judge your people with righteousness,
>   and your poor with justice.
> May the mountains yield prosperity for the people,
>   and the hills, in righteousness.

May he defend the cause of the poor of the people,
>give deliverance to the needy, and crush the oppressor.
May he live while the sun endures,
>and as long as the moon, throughout all generations.
May he be like rain that falls on the mown grass,
>like showers that water the earth.
In his days may righteousness flourish
>and peace abound, until the moon is no more.
May he have dominion from sea to sea,
>and from the River to the ends of the earth.
May his foes bow down before him,
>and his enemies lick the dust.
May the kings of Tarshish and of the isles render him tribute,
>may the kings of Sheba and Seba bring gifts.
May all kings fall down before him,
>all nations give him service.
For he delivers the needy when they call,
>the poor and those who have no helper.
He has pity on the weak and the needy,
>and saves the lives of the needy.
From oppression and violence he redeems their life;
>and precious is their blood in his sight.
Long may he live!
>May gold of Sheba be given to him.
May prayer be made for him continually,
>and blessings invoked for him all day long.
May there be abundance of grain in the land;
>may it wave on the tops of the mountains;
may its fruit be like Lebanon;
>and may people blossom in the cities like the grass of the field.
May his name endure forever,
>his fame continue as long as the sun.
May all nations be blessed in him;
>may they pronounce him happy.
Blessed be the LORD, the God of Israel,
>who alone does wondrous things.
Blessed be his glorious name forever;
>may his glory fill the whole earth. Amen and Amen.

3. A New World The Hebrew Bible anticipates a physical renewal of the natural world. Beginning with the consequences of human actions in the Garden of Eden, biblical narrative often links the infidelity of God's people with corruption in the world of nature. Included in apocalyptic imagery are disturbing signs in the natural world that are seen as forerunners of the end times. Biblical ideas about renewal on the personal and social levels include visions of a revitalized natural world. Many passages in the Hebrew Bible picture the natural world sharing in the rejuvenation of the human world. Isa 11:6–9 and Amos 9:13–15 are two examples of this:

> The wolf shall live with the lamb, the leopard shall lie down with the kid, the calf and the lion and the fatling together, and a little child shall lead them. The cow and the bear shall graze, their young shall lie down together; and the lion shall eat straw like the ox. The nursing child shall play over the hole of the asp, and the weaned child shall put its hand on the adder's den. They will not hurt or destroy on all my holy mountain; for the earth will be full of the knowledge of the LORD as the waters cover the sea. (Isa 11:6–9)

> The time is surely coming, says the LORD, when the one who plows shall overtake the one who reaps, and the treader of grapes the one who sows the seed; the mountains shall drip sweet wine, and all the hills shall flow with it. I will restore the fortunes of my people Israel, and they shall rebuild the ruined cities and inhabit them; they shall plant vineyards and drink their wine, and they shall make gardens and eat their fruit. I will plant them upon their land, and they shall never again be plucked up out of the land that I have given them, says the LORD your God. (Amos 9:13–15)

At its heart the Hebrew Bible is a story about people in search of community under God. The Israelites' unity and sense of purpose did not derive from a sense of ethnic identity, but from their belief, beginning with the Exodus and even before, that their God Yahweh was present and involved in their struggle to be a free people in the face of all the political and social forces that would enslave them. In the Hebrew Bible we have seen many stories of the experience of oppression and subsequent liberation. There is however, no liberation as a once-and-for-all experience. The process must be repeated again and again in human history. If we would understand the struggles of the Israelite people about which we have read in the narratives of the Hebrew Bible, we must also read with one eye looking forward into our own times to see the oppressive situations in our world where the same kinds of struggles are going on. The Hebrew Bible is the product, the record, the site, and the weapon of class, cultural, gender, and racial struggles. Itumeleng J. Mosala, a South African biblical scholar has written:

> There is a trajectory of struggle that runs through all biblical texts, and a recognition of this fact means that it is no longer accurate to speak of the . . . Word of God unproblematically and in absolute terms. . . . What one can do is take sides in a struggle that is not confirmed by the whole of the Bible, . . . but is rather encoded in the text as a struggle representing different positions and groups in the society behind the text. (Mosala 1989: 27)

The last word in this journey through the Hebrew scriptures is an invitation and a challenge that has echoed through the pages of the Bible. The invitation is for those readers who may have seen themselves as removed from contemporary struggles to view their encounter with the struggles recorded in the Hebrew Bible as a challenge to examine the ways in which they can become involved in the ongoing struggle:

- for more just and fair arrangements in our world's economic order,
- for women's full access to and participation in decision-making and power-brokering processes, and
- for an end to discrimination against any human being based on gender, race, class, religious or political beliefs, age, or mental, physical, or emotional/psychological disadvantages.

STUDY QUESTIONS

APOCALYPTIC

1. Discuss the sources and some characteristics of the apocalyptic movement, worldview, and literature. How, in particular, did "manticism" contribute to apocalyptic?
2. How are form and content related to one another in apocalyptic literature?
3. How are the two parts of the Book of Daniel—chapters 1-6 and chapters 7-12—related to one another in form, content, and purpose?
4. Why does the author of Daniel place the hero in the sixth century B.C.E. when he is writing for a second century B.C.E. audience?
5. "In the transitional period between the Maccabean revolt and the emergence of Christianity as an offshoot from Judaism, Judaism was a religion involved in considerable struggle. This struggle, which had both internal and external dimensions, produced many subgroups and trends within Judaism." How does this statement help to explain the emergence of the Christian movement? In what ways were the early Christians like other sectarian Jewish groups of the time and in what ways were they different?

BIBLIOGRAPHY

Charlesworth, James H., ed. 1992. "The Dead Sea Scrolls and the Historical Jesus." *Jesus and the Dead Sea Scrolls*, pp. 1-74. The Anchor Bible Reference Library. New York: Doubleday.

Collins, J. J. 1979. ed. *Apocalypse: The Morphology of a Genre. Semeia* 14.

_____. 1992. "Daniel, Book of." *The Anchor Bible Dictionary,* II, 29-37. New York: Doubleday.

Crenshaw, James L. 1992. *Old Testament Story and Faith: A Literary and Theological Introduction.* Peabody, MA: Hendrickson.

Davies, Philip R. 1989. "The Social World of Apocalyptic Writings," R. E. Clements, ed. *The World of Ancient Israel. Sociological, Anthropological and Political Perspectives,* 251-271. Cambridge: Cambridge University Press.

Dearman, J. Andrew. 1992. *Religion and Culture in Ancient Israel.* Peabody, MA: Hendrickson.

Drane, John. 1987. *Introducing the Old Testament.* San Francisco: Harper & Row.

Gottwald, Norman K. 1985. *The Hebrew Bible: A Socio-Literary Introduction.* Philadelphia: Fortress.

Rogerson, John, and Philip Davies. 1989. *The Old Testament World.* Englewood Cliffs, NJ: Prentice-Hall.

GLOSSARY

A

Amarna Letters. An archive found near the modern Egyptian village of el-Amarna, the site of the Egyptian capital in the fifteenth century B.C.E., which contains letters from Egyptian vassals in Palestine to the Pharaohs Amenhotep III and Amenhotep IV (who, as part of a program of religious reform, changed his name to Akhenaton). This correspondence testifies to a very unstable situation in Palestine, with infighting among the Egyptian agents there, and considerable unrest generated by a group called the Habiru.

Amorites. The word Amorite is used in the Hebrew Bible as a synonym for Canaanite. The use of one term rather than the other is due to the preference of an author or the tradition on which the author depends. Source criticism of the Pentateuch generally assumes that Amorite was preferred by the Elohist tradition (E), while Canaanite was preferred by the Yahwist tradition (J). All Hebrew Bible references to the Amorites have one characteristic in common—the reference is always to a people living in the past.

Amphictyony. A form of social organization in which each of twelve tribes took their turn in caring for the central sanctuary for one month in a year.

Anat. Baal's chief consort in Canaanite myths. She is pictured as Baal's constant, devoted companion. She is also a very fierce warrior.

Androcentrism. A male-centered perspective on things.

Antithetic parallelism. In antithetic parallelism, Lowth saw two *cola* related to one another by opposition. The first *colon* of the *bicola* expresses a thought and the second *colon* is stated as a contrast to the first.

Apocalypse, apocalyptic. The noun apocalypse and the adjective apocalyptic, which are used in discussing a genre of biblical literature, come from a Greek noun *apokalypsis*, which means "revelation," "disclosure," or "unveiling." Apocalypse is a genre of revelatory literature with a narrative framework. Within this framework a revelation is mediated by an otherworldly being to a human recipient, disclosing a transcendental reality which is both temporal, insofar as it envisages eschatological salvation, and spatial, insofar as it involves another, supernatural world.

Apocrypha. From a Greek term meaning "hidden things or writings," Apocrypha refers to books written between *ca.* 200 B.C.E. and 100 C.E. Although used by Greek-speaking Jews living outside Palestine, these books did not become a part of the accepted Jewish canon. They became part of the canon of Catholic Christianity and Eastern Orthodoxy, where they are called "deuterocanonical" (that is, the "second" set of canonical Old Testament books) in the face of objections to them from Protestant Christians.

Apodictic Law. A form of law stated absolutely, without any conditions. Apodictic law is characteristically Israelite, and is not common in other ancient Near Eastern law codes.

Aramaic. A Semitic language, closely related to Hebrew. Aramaic was the successor to Hebrew as a spoken language in Palestine and was the language spoken by Jesus in the first century C.E.

Arameans.   The Bible notes a kinship of Arameans with the Hebrew patriarchs. It also records a checkered history of relationships between the two peoples in later times. The Aramaic language is used in parts of the biblical books of Ezra and Daniel and remained in everyday use among Jews for over a thousand years. By *ca.* 1100 B.C.E. Arameans were present not only in Syria, but in the northern Transjordan (the area east of the Jordan River). The kingdom of Aram, which was centered in Damascus, became the foremost Aramean state in Syria in the ninth–eighth centuries B.C.E. This state is sometimes simply referred to in the Bible as Damascus.

Ark of the Covenant.   One of the most important symbols of Yahwism. The Bible describes its origins during Israel's time in the Sinai wilderness. It represented the presence of God with God's people in the form of a throne on which the invisible God sat. David brought it to Jerusalem, and Solomon installed it in the Jerusalem Temple.

Asherah.   The mother of the gods and the consort of the supreme god, El, in Canaanite myth. She played an important role in the Ugaritic cycle of myths involving Baal's desire for a palace/temple. In the Hebrew Bible, the word Asherah is used to denote both the name of the Canaanite goddess and the wooden cult-object that was her symbol (the KJV translates Asherah with the word "grove").

Assyria.   The name of a powerful Mesopotamian-based power that began expanding westward in the late tenth century B.C.E. The threat of Assyrian expansion affected all states of Syria and Palestine. The Assyrians conquered Israel near the end of the eighth century B.C.E.

Astarte.   Referred to in the Hebrew Bible as Ashtoreth (plural = Ashtaroth), Astarte was another of Baal's consorts in the Ugaritic myths, although a less prominent one than Anat.

Atrahasis Myth.   A Babylonian text, dating to the seventeenth century B.C.E., which tells of the beginnings of humanity, problems arising after creation, the near-destruction of humanity by a flood, and its re-creation after the flood. Atrahasis plays a role corresponding to that of Noah in the biblical flood story.

B

B.C.E.   "Before the Common Era." An abbreviation for dates referred to in the Christian calendar as B.C., "Before Christ."

Baal.   The most active Canaanite god. He brought the rain, upon which the fertility of the soil depended. One of his titles in Canaanite mythology is "the Rider of the Clouds." In images of Baal he typically stands and carries a thunder club and a lightning spear, the accompaniments of the thunderstorm. Baal's consort was Anat.

Babylonia.   Babylonia is a flat, alluvial plain between the Tigris and Euphrates Rivers, about 300 miles long. The Babylonians, a Semitic people, have a long history and produced a great deal of literature important to the study of the Hebrew Bible. They replaced the Assyrians as the dominant imperial power in the ancient Near East. The Babylonian ruler, Nebuchadnezzar II (also spelled Nebuchadrezzar), conquered Jerusalem in 597 B.C.E.

Babylonian Exile.   Scholars commonly refer to the period from 587–539 B.C.E. as the Babylonian Exile. This term is somewhat misleading, in that it suggests that most, if not all, of the surviving population of Judah was moved to Babylon. It was the upper strata of Israelite society that was departed.

Bêt 'āv.   "Father's house." The primary kinship group in Israelite social organization. The closest counterpart of this term in English is the nuclear family.

Bicolon.   A unit of Hebrew poetry composed of two *cola* is called a *bicolon* (sometimes called a *distich*).

Book of the Covenant.   The collection of civil and religious laws in Ex 20:22–23:33 to which the Decalogue serves as an introduction. It is called "The Book of the Covenant" from the phrase that occurs in Ex 24:7. The laws are presented as if they were given directly to Moses, but closer examination reveals that they developed over time to serve the changing needs of the Israelite community. Unlike the Decalogue, this collection of laws lacks a coherent structure and has a rather eclectic character.

C

C.E.   "Common Era." An abbreviation for dates referred to in the Christian calendar as A.D. ("Anno dominii"), "In the Year of Our Lord."

Canaan.   One of the earliest names of the region that later became known as Palestine. The name Canaan is derived from the name of the area's principal inhabitants, the Canaanites, who were a people made up of several subgroups.

Canon.   A term designating those books that make up the Jewish Bible, or the Old Testament as it is called by Christians (who believe that it forms part of a Bible that also includes the New Testament). The English term canon comes from the Greek word *kanon,* which was used to refer to a straight reed that was used as a standard or measure for straightness. When we speak of the Jewish canon or the Hebrew Scriptures, we are referring to a specific collection of writings that came to be viewed as a written source of authority, or scriptures, for a religious community.

Casuistic Law.   A form of law found throughout the ancient Near East. This type of law is typically stated in the form: if *x* occurs, then *y* will be the legal consequence. This type of law is found in the Hebrew Bible in the first part of the "Book of the Covenant" and in Deut 12–26.

Chiasm.   Also called a palistrophe. A literary structure that builds to a climax element-by-element and then unfolds those elements in reverse order. In a chiasm the first item matches the last item, the second item matches the next-to-the-last item, and so on. The second half is thus a mirror image of the first.

Colon.   Hebrew poetry is made up of lines that divide into at least two, often three, clauses, which together are called a *colon* (plural = *cola*). A *colon* is thus a single line of poetry. Some scholars prefer the term *stich*.

Communal Lament.   A genre of psalm that reflects a time of national crisis. The structure of this genre closely resembles that of the Individual Lament.

Corvée.   Compulsory labor demanded by the state.

Cosmology.   An orderly description of the structure of the created order. Ancient Near Eastern cosmologies conceived of a three-tiered universe, with a flat, circular earth occupying the middle tier, water above the earth as the upper tier, and water beneath the earth as the lower tier.

Cyrus Cylinder.   This document, dated to 528 B.C.E., issued by the Persian ruler Cyrus, instituted the Persian policy of re-establishing subject peoples in their homelands and promoting the cults of their gods.

D

D.   A symbol that represents one of the four sources or traditions in the Pentateuch. The Deuteronomist is the name given the tradition or school that produced the Deuteronomic Code (the central section of the book of Deuteronomy, chapters

12–26). The book of Deuteronomy, to which this source is almost, if not exclusively limited was appended to the JE epic sometime after the seventh century B.C.E.

Dendrochronology.   Dendrochronology or tree-ring dating has two distinct archaeological uses: (1) for calibrating radiocarbon dates; and (2) as an independent method of absolute dating. Dendrochronology is based on the fact that most trees produce a ring of new growth every year.

Deuteronomistic Historian.   See *Dtr.*

Dittography.   An unintentional error in copying of a text by hand in which something is written twice that should have been written only once.

Dtr.   The symbol for the Deuteronomistic Historian, whose work is found in Joshua, Judges, 1 and 2 Samuel, and 1 and 2 Kings.

E

E.   Used as a symbol representing one of the four sources or traditions in the Pentateuch. The Elohistic tradition, like J, takes its designation from the word it uses when referring to God, here, the Hebrew word *'elohim,* translated into English as "gods" or "God."

Edom/Edomites.   The territory of Edom is in Transjordan to the south of Moab and is barely mentioned in the Hebrew Bible. In Genesis, Esau is regarded as the patriarch of the Edomites.

El.   The supreme Canaanite deity, the father of the gods and the creator of the earth and of human beings. El was pictured in mythology as a beneficent, old, wise god with gray hair. In images of El, he is typically seated. His consort, or female companion, was the goddess Asherah.

Enki.   Enki was one of the four great cosmic gods in Mesopotamian culture. He is the god of wisdom, incantation, and of fresh waters on the earth and under the earth.

Enlil.   Enlil was one of the principal Mesopotamian deities. He was god of the atmosphere and the earth. As the most powerful of the gods he was the possessor of the "tablets of destiny," by means of which the fates of humans and gods were decreed.

Enuma Elish.   The best-known extrabiblical ancient Near Eastern myth of creation. This Babylonian myth was recited annually as part of the great Babylonian New Year festival. It tells of the birth of the gods and of the creation of humankind in a well-ordered universe. It was written *ca.* 1100 B.C.E.

Essenes.   A group within Judaism in the first century C.E. While the New Testament speaks of the Sadducees and Pharisees, it never mentions the Essenes. In addition to Josephus' description of the Essenes, they are also discussed by another first century C.E. Jewish writer, Philo, and by the first century Roman, Pliny the Elder. They separated themselves from the rest of their fellow Jews to practice a strict observance to the Jewish law.

Etiological.   A "just so" story that concentrates on origins as a way of explaining how something got to be the way it is.

Exegesis.   The process by which one reads in order to draw meaning or meanings *from* a text.

F

Fertile Crescent.   An area consisting of the agriculturally fertile areas of Palestine, with Mesopotamia and Egypt. This name for the area was first used by James H. Breasted, a renowned Egyptologist.

Form criticism.   A subdiscipline of biblical studies that focuses on the smaller units that make up larger texts, especially in the oral or preliterary stage of a text.

G

Galilee.   The northern end of the central hill country of Palestine.

Ger.   A Hebrew term, sometimes translated "sojourner." A resident alien in ancient Israel.

Gilgamesh Epic.   The *Epic of Gilgamesh* is perhaps the best-known myth of the ancient Near East. It is the world's oldest epic poem. It was written on clay tablets in the Akkadian language (an eastern Semitic language) *ca.* 1750 B.C.E. Copies of at least part of the epic have been found all over the Near East, from ancient Sumer (the southern part of modern Iraq) to the Hittite capital (in what is modern Turkey), to the Israelite city of Megiddo. It has striking parallels with the Genesis creation and flood narratives.

Graf-Wellhausen Hypothesis.   The classic statement of what has been called the documentary hypothesis of the Pentateuch, which has also been referred to as the Newer Documentary Hypothesis.

H

Haplography.   An unintentional error in copying a text by hand in which a syllable, word, or line is omitted because a repeated sequence of a letter, word, or phrase was copied only once when it should have been written twice.

Hendiadys.   A literary phenomenon consisting of a figure in which one compound idea is expressed by two words linked by a conjunction.

Holiness Code.   A collection of priestly law found in Lev 17 - 26. It is called this because of the reiterated demand that Israel should be "holy" because God is holy.

Homoioteleuton.   A copying error whose name comes from a Greek word meaning "having similar endings." This error involves the omission of material that appears between two words that are the same or have similar endings.

Hyksos.   A group of Asiatics, mostly Semites, who ruled over Egypt during the Second Intermediate Period, *ca.* 1665 - 1560 B.C.E. They were expelled from Egypt by Ahmose in 1560.

Hymns (or **Psalms of Praise**).   One of the predominant types of psalms in the book of Psalms. Hymns consist of three basic parts: (1) introduction; (2) body; (3) conclusion.

I

Individual Thanksgiving Song.   A type of psalm which, like the Individual Lament, has its own structure that is subject to variation. This simple structure consists of an introduction, body, and conclusion.

Individual Laments (or **Songs of Supplication**).   This psalm type outnumbers all other types in the Psalter. These psalms deal with problems faced by individuals. They have a characteristic structure: (1) Invocation; (2) Complaint; (3) Confession; (4) Petition; and (5) Vow.

Isaiah Apocalypse.   This title has been given to the apocalyptic material in chapters 24 - 27 of Isaiah. This section of Isaiah has also been called the Isaiah Apocalypse.

J

J.   Used as a symbol for one of the four sources or traditions in the Pentateuch. "J" stands for the "Yahwist" (or Yahweh, *Jahweh* in German). The Yahwistic tradition (J) takes its name from the fact that the divine name "Yahweh" is predominant in this stratum as God's personal name. J is also appropriate as a symbol for this source, because Judah, the southern kingdom, is prominent in it.

Jebusites.   A subgroup of the Canaanites who held Jerusalem (Jebus) until the time of David.

Jezreel, Valley of.   Also called the Esdraelon Valley. This valley is a large triangular plane about 20 ¥ 50 miles in size. It is the only major clear passageway from the coastal plain to the Jordan valley.

Judah.   The name of the southern part of Palestine (Judah is also the name of one of Jacob/Israel's sons and of the largest tribe in the south). The name of the southern kingdom in the period of the divided monarchy was also Judah.

Judea.   A geographical name that is initially attested in the books of Ezra, Nehemiah, and Maccabees (in the Apocrypha), denoting the postexilic Jewish state.

K

Ketuvim.   "Writings." The last section of the Hebrew Bible, consisting of the books of Psalms through Chronicles in the Jewish canon.

L

Levirate marriage.   The term "levirate" comes from the Latin word *levir,* meaning a husband's brother. According to the ancient widespread custom of levirate marriage (which is still practiced in some African societies), the legal details of which are spelled out in Deut 25:5–10, it was a brother's obligation to marry the widow of his childless deceased brother.

M

Manticism.   A form of wisdom tradition represented in the Hebrew Bible that is widely attested in the ancient Near East generally, but especially in Mesopotamian wisdom literature. It is concerned with esoteric knowledge that is derived from omens deciphered by specialists sometimes called diviners. A common source of omens for diviners was the examination of animal organs. The name "mantic wisdom" was given to this art/science of interpretation.

Marduk.   Babylon's chief male deity.

Mashal or (Proverb).   A genre of wisdom literature—a pithy expression distilling human experience into a clever and memorable form. Proverb, or *Mashal* in Hebrew, has the basic meaning of "comparison."

Masoretes.   Families of Jewish scholars who collected and catalogued errors found in the text of the Hebrew Bible and added vowels and accents to the consonantal text in the seventh to ninth centuries C.E. The Masoretes produced the "received" or standard form of the Hebrew text known as the Masoretic tradition (MT).

Merneptah Stele.   This Egyptian inscription includes the first mention of Israel outside the Bible. It comes from the fifth year of the reign of Pharaoh Merneptah, *ca.* 1207 B.C.E. It is a victory inscription, celebrating Merneptah's victories over peoples living in Libya and Palestine.

Mesopotamia. A term from the Greek meaning "between the rivers." It designates the fertile area between the Tigris and Euphrates rivers, the area inhabited by the Babylonians and Assyrians.

Meter. Meter is the almost mathematical pattern in Hebrew poetry in terms of which an accented syllable is grouped with one or more unaccented syllables.

Millennium. A period of 1,000 years.

Mishnah. The oldest postbiblical collection of Jewish laws from *ca.* 200 C.E.

Mišpāchâ. A term usually translated "clan" in modern English Bibles. This translation is somewhat misleading, however, because in anthropological literature the term "clan" has a multiplicity of meanings. On the basis of Josh 7 : 16 - 17, the *mišpāchâ* was the intermediate level between the *bêt 'a⁻ v* and "tribe" in Israelite social structure.

Moab/Moabites. Israel's neighbors whose territory was south and east of the Dead Sea. One of the best known Moabites in the Hebrew Bible is Ruth.

Myth. A specialized kind of metaphor, a story about the past that embodies and expresses truths about a people's traditional culture.

N

Negev. The high plateau region at the southern end of the central hill country of Palestine.

Nevi'im. "Prophets." The central part of the Hebrew Bible, consisting of the books of Joshua through the Book of the Twelve (= the "Minor Prophets"). This large section is divided into the Former Prophets and the Latter Prophets in the Jewish Bible.

O

Oracle. The primary literary unit of the prophetic books is the oracle. The Hebrew term translated "oracle" in modern English versions is *massa,* which has a literal meaning of "burden." Oracle has been used as a technical term for various kinds of utterances delivered by a prophet in response to a worshipper's question. Oracles include everything from short utterances addressed to a specific situation to lengthy speeches and whole books (for example, Nahum, Habakkuk, Malachi).

P

P. The symbol that represents the Priestly document or tradition in the Pentateuch. This tradition, as its name suggests, is marked by the unmistakable interests of the priesthood and ceremonial sanctity, and by the kind of precise attention to detail associated with a priestly way of thinking and acting. A concern with ritual origins and laws, as well as with the chronological details of Israel's past is evident. Because the priesthood was a hereditary office in Israel, there is also an interest in genealogies.

Parallelism. Parallelism is the most distinctive feature of biblical Hebrew poetry. It concerns the relationship of lines of poetry to one another. As originally described by Lowth, there are three main kinds of parallelism: (1) synonymous; (2) antithetic; (3) synthetic.

Patrilineal. A descent system that traces lineage through one's male ancestors only.

Pesach. The Hebrew word for Passover, which has been connected with a Hebrew verb meaning "protect" (Isa 31 : 5). *Pesach* is celebrated during the first month of spring (Nisan) in the Jewish calendar.

Peshitta. A translation of the Hebrew Bible into Syriac, the dialectical form of Aramaic that was common among Christians in Syria and Mesopotamia during the Byzantine and later eras.

Pharisees. One of the four principal groups among Jews in the first century C.E., as described by Josephus. The Pharisees were associated with those whose adherence to the Torah brought them into conflict both with Hellenistic gentile culture and with their fellow Jews who compromised or collaborated with that culture. They practiced a commitment to the Torah that strictly separated Jews from gentiles in such things as dietary laws, circumcision, fasting, and prayer. They accepted the oral expansion of the written Torah and accepted belief in things that were not spelled out in the written Torah, such as the doctrine of resurrection.

Philistines. One of the "Sea Peoples" who migrated to the southwest coastal plain of Palestine from their home in Crete or Asia Minor after failing in their attempt to settle in Egypt. This migration occurred *ca.* 1200 B.C.E., at about the same time the Israelites were establishing themselves in the country. The Philistines were centered in five major cities: Ashkelon, Ashdod, Ekron, Gath, and Gaza.

Phoenicians. The Phoenicians were Israel's neighbors to the north. They were a part of the Canaanites culturally and ethnically.

Prophet, prophecy. The English words "prophet" and "prophecy" derive from a Greek term, *prophetes*. The translators of the Septuagint translated the Hebrew word *nabi'*, the common Hebrew term for prophet, with the Greek word *prophetes,* "one who could 'speak before,'" from which the English word "prophet" is derived.

Q

Qinah. An irregular, "limping" meter of 3+2, called the *qinah* meter (*qinah* is a Hebrew word meaning "lament") is a meter that indicated sadness, such as in the book of Lamentation. It is thought that the imbalance in the lines captures the tension of extreme emotion, usually grief, but sometimes joy (compare Ps 65).

Qoheleth. Ecclesiastes is the name in Greek and Latin of the book that is called Qoheleth in the Hebrew Bible. The name Qoheleth derives from the Hebrew verbal root *qhl,* which means "to assemble." The participle Qoheleth is thus usually taken as referring to the leader of an assembly, "One Who Assembles."

R

Radiocarbon dating. One of the best-known and most useful methods of dating organic artifacts employed by archaeologists. It is based on the measurement of the radioactive isotope of carbon in a sample.

Redaction criticism. That part of biblical study that continues the processes begun by source and form criticism. Redaction criticism focuses on the final stage in the formation of a biblical unit or book, and is concerned with the theological perspectives and intentions of the redactor/editor as perceived in the way in which that redactor/editor arranged, edited, and expanded upon the sources.

Redactor. This term refers to individuals who joined together literary material from different sources and providedg connecting links in the form of editorial comments.

Rîb. A literary form in the Hebrew Bible that has been called a "covenant lawsuit." The term comes from the Hebrew verb that means "to plead a case." The form has four parts, corresponding to the proceedings in a court of law: (1) call to order; (2) statement of complaint; (3) defendant's response; and (4) the indictment.

Rites de passage.   "Rites of passage"—a French expression that is used to denote those critical points in the life of an individual or community at which a fundamental change of status takes place.

S

Sadducees.   One of the four principal groups in the Judaism of the first century c.e., as described by Josephus. Their viewpoint on the nature of Israel as a religious community and on obedience to the Torah was strongly influenced by their economic and social interests. They were composed mainly of wealthy priestly and aristocratic families of considerable prestige and political influence. They claimed to be loyal to the Torah alone—the Torah as written, not in its oral enlargement.

Sagas (or legends).   The term legend sometimes appears in English-language form-critical study as a translation of the German *sage* or the Norse *saga*. Although the lines between them are fluid, it is possible to differentiate between legends or sagas, fairy tales, and myths.

Samaritans.   In addition to the principal Jewish parties mentioned by Josephus, another group was present at the turn of the era, the Samaritans. The term Samaritan is first a geographic term, referring to anyone who lived in Samaria, the region of Palestine around the city of Samaria that was established under that name by the Assyrians after the fall of the northern kingdom.

Second Isaiah.   The name sometimes given to the anonymous sixth-century b.c.e. author of chapters 40–55 of the book of Isaiah. This part of Isaiah is also called Deutero-Isaiah. Some scholars also refer to Isaiah 56–66 as Trito- or Third Isaiah.

Segmented societies.   A society that is acephalous, that is, not organized around a center. Their political organization is established by multi-graded groups politically of equal rank.

Septuagint.   Sometimes abbreviated with LXX (the Roman number for 70). The first translation of the Hebrew Scriptures into another language, Greek. This translation of the Hebrew scriptures took its name from the tradition that seventy (or seventy-two in another version of the tradition) Jewish scholars, one from every known nation, were brought to Alexandria at the order of Ptolemy II (*ca.* 285–247 b.c.e.) to work on a translation of the Torah. The Septuagint became the favored translation of the Old Testament among early Christians.

Servant Songs.   These poems are the best known and most intensely studied parts of Second Isaiah. The four Servant Songs have been identified as follows: 1) 42:1–4; 2) 49:1–6; 3) 50:4–9; 4) 52:13–53:12.

Šēvet.   The outermost circle of Israelite social groupings. The word *šēvet* is usually translated as "tribe."

Shephelah.   A term referring to the foothills leading up to the central hill country of Palestine.

Sociological criticism.   A recent extension of historical biblical criticism that seeks to place texts (and sometimes readers as well) in their appropriate social context. It uses methods and theories from the social sciences to help bridge the gap between our society and the social world of ancient Israel.

Source criticism.   A tool used by biblical scholars that attempts to discover the written sources behind the text in the form in which it now exists and to suggest how these sources became part of larger units.

Strophe.   Larger verse units of Hebrew poetry group themselves into units called strophes (from the Greek word for "turning").

Synonymous parallelism. In synonymous parallelism the second *colon* of a *bicolon* echoes or repeats the idea of the first *colon* in equivalent but different terms.

Synthetic parallelism. In many cases the precise relationship between the two (or three) *cola* is not easily discerned. The parallelism involved is not so much of ideas, but of form. Lowth called this third form of parallelism "synthetic," although often there is no really clear parallelism.

T

Tabernacle. Israel's sanctuary in the Sinai wilderness. Nearly one-third of the entire book of Exodus is given over to matters regarding the tabernacle, a tentlike structure that Moses built to house the ark. Ex 25 – 30 contains the directions for its building and the account of its actual construction is found in Ex 35 – 40.

Tanak. An acronym representing *Torah, Nevi'im,* and *Ketuvim,* the three major sections of the Hebrew Bible.

Targums. Translations of the Hebrew Bible into Aramaic. The use of Aramaic increased as Hebrew waned as the spoken language of Palestinian Jewry, and oral paraphrases in Aramaic were needed to follow the reading of the scriptures in Hebrew in the synagogues. These oral paraphrases were then committed to writing in the Targums. The two most important Targums are the *Targum of Onkelos,* for the Torah, and the *Targum of Jonathan,* for the Prophets.

Tell. A word in Hebrew and Arabic that refers to an uninhabited mound whose formation is the result of repeated human occupation in the past.

Textual criticism. The branch of biblical scholarship that has as its intent the restoration, as nearly as possible, of the original form of the biblical text. Textual critics seek to uncover "textual corruptions" or places where errors have crept into the original text, intentionally or accidentally, during its transmission.

Theophany. An encounter between a deity and a human being in which the deity becomes temporarily visible in some way.

Thermoluminescence dating. A recently developed method for dating ceramics. It has a distinct advantage over radiocarbon dating (whose use is limited to organic materials) in that it can be used to confirm dates of pottery, the most abundant inorganic material on most Palestinian archaeological sites.

Torah. Sometimes translated as "Law." The first five books of the Hebrew Bible.

Tradition criticism. This branch of biblical studies looks at the entire process of change and adaptation of a tradition from its earliest oral stage, through the compilation of written sources, to the final redaction into books as we now have them, and even further through its later use and readaptation by subsequent generations.

Type scene. The stylized treatment of a conventional situation, for example, a typical episode in the life of an ancestor that is made up of stock elements that a narrator varies and elaborates upon.

U

Ugarit. An ancient city near the Mediterranean coast in present-day Syria where an important collection of Canaanite myths was found.

V

Vulgate. From the Latin word meaning "common" or "popular." The translation of the Hebrew Bible into Latin done by Jerome. It was completed in 405 c.e.

W

Wisdom literature. Three books in the Hebrew Bible have been called wisdom literature: Proverbs, Job, and Ecclesiastes (called Qoheleth in Hebrew). Also two examples of wisdom literature appear in the apocryphal/deuterocanonical books: Ben Sirach (also known as Ecclesiasticus or simply Sirach) and the Wisdom of Solomon.

Y

Yam suf. "Sea of Reeds" in Hebrew. *Yam suf* was translated "Red Sea" in the Septuagint, and that translation was retained by the KJV and many subsequent English translations.

YHWH. The consonants of Yahweh, the Israelite personal name for God. Out of reverence, and as a way of assuring that they will not take God's name "in vain," Orthodox Jews never pronounce God's name. The NRSV translates Yahweh as "LORD."

Z

Ziggurat. Ziggurats were temple-towers found in ancient Mesopotamia, a flat plain between the Tigris and Euphrates. Ziggurats were terraced towers that represented an artificial mountain, with a stairway leading to a temple at the top of the tower.

ANCIENT NAME INDEX

CONTEMPORARY NAME INDEX

INDEX OF BIBLICAL REFERENCES[1]

---

[1] Does Not Include Study Questions, Tables, and Text Boxes

7:1 *52*
10:5 *224*
10:8 *91*
11:11 *47*
11:14 *47*
11:4 *91*
11:8-12 *38*
12:32 *7*
12-26 *100, 108, 223, 225, 231, 241*
16-17 *241*
17:18 *241*
18:10-11 *347, 525*
18:15 *348*
20 *241*
22 *458*
22:19 *385*
22:23-29 *230*
23:3 *53*
24 *241*
26:5 *54*
27 *231*
27:2-3 *224*
27-28 *224*
28:1 *101*
28:15 *101*
28:57 *213*
29:4 *91*
31:10-11 *224*
33:28 *48*
34:6 *91*
34:9 *353*

JOSHUA
1-10 *257*
1-12 *257*
2-9 *253*
3:10 *52*
5:1 *52*
6:20 *261*
7:2 *263*
7:16-17 *61*
7-8 *257, 263*
9-10 *263*
10 *257*
10:12-13 *259*
10:28-39 *253*
10:36 *257*
10:38 *257*
10:40 *258, 259*
11 *257*
11:1-11 *253*
11:10-13 *264*
11:13 *66*
11:31-32 *263*

12:14 *257*
12:16 *257*
13-22 *257*
15:13 *257*
15:15-17 *257*
15:59 *278*
19:38 *278*
19:47 *283*
21:18 *278*
23-24 *257*
24:2a *223*
24:2b-13 *223*
24:9 *466*
24:14 *223*
24:22 *224*
24:27 *224*

JUDGES
1 *257, 282*
1:1 *259*
1:1-3:6 *284*
1:10 *257*
1:11 *257*
1:17 *257*
1:19 *256*
1:23 *257*
1:33 *278*
2 *257*
2:12-30 *257*
2:13 *278*
3:7-15:20 *284*
3:11 *155*
3:12 *466*
3:12-30 *480*
3:27 *284*
3-16 *257*
4 *282, 460*
4:3 *256*
4:4-5 *283*
5 *258, 264, 282, 460, 480*
5:6 *278*
5:31 *155*
6 *280*
6:5 *257*
6:11-24 *211*
6:25-26 *278*
6:25-32 *279*
6:32 *278*
6:38 *48*
6-8 *257*
7:12 *257*
7:23-25 *284*
8:21 *257*
8:26 *257*

PROVERBS

LITERARY CREDITS

Selection in Chapter 6 from page 48 of *The Art of Biblical Narrative* by Robert Alter. Copyright © 1981 by Robert Alter. Reprinted by permission of BasicBooks, a division of HarperCollins Publishers, Inc.

"Comments on Song of Deborah" in Chapter 8 from page 41 of *The World of Biblical Literature* by Robert Alter. Copyright © 1992 by Robert Alter. Reprinted by permission of BasicBooks, a division of HarperCollins, Inc.

Selected excerpts in chapters 6, 7, 9, and 12 from *Peculiar Treasures: A Biblical Who's Who* by Frederick Buechner. Copyright ©1979 by Federick Buechner. Illustration copyright © 1979 by Katherine A. Buechner. Reprinted by permission of HarperCollins Publishers, Inc.

Excerpt in Chapter 6 reprinted from *Encounter With the Text,* edited by Martin J. Buss, copyright © 1979 Society of Biblical Literature. Used by permission of Augsburg Fortress.

Tables 8.1, 8.2, 8.3 from *Recent Archaeological Discoveries and Biblical Research* by William D. Dever. Used by permission of University of Washington Press.

Excerpt in Chapter 15 from *The Anchor Bible Dictionary* by Noel Freedman, ed. Copyright © 1992 by Doubleday, a division of Bantam Doubleday Dell Publishing Group, Inc. Used by permission of Doubleday, a division of Bantam Doubleday Dell Publishing Group, Inc.

Excerpt in Chapter 14 from *The Hebrew Bible* by Norman K. Gottwald, copyright © 1985 Fortress Press. Used by permission of Augsburg Fortress.

Selection in Chapter 11 from pages 218–219 of *The Prophets* by Abraham Heschel. Copyright © 1962 by Abraham Heschel. Copyright renewed. Reprinted by permission of HarperCollins Publishers, Inc.

Excerpt in Chapter 5 from *Before Abraham Was* © 1985 by Isaac Kikawada and Arthur Quinn. Used by permission of the authors.

Excerpts in chapters 7, 8, 10, 11, 12, and 13 reprinted from *Old Testament Parallels* by Victor H. Matthews and Don C. Benjamin. ©1991 by Victor H. Matthews and Don C. Benjamin. Used by permission of Paulist Press.

Figure 6.3 from "Patrilineal Genealogy of Genesis 12-50" from *Hagar The Egyptian: The Lost Tradition of The Matriarchs* by Savina J. Teubal.

PHOTO CREDITS